THE INDIAN LEGAL PROFESSION IN THE AGE OF GLOBALIZATION

This book provides the first comprehensive analysis of the impact of globalization on the Indian legal profession. Employing a range of original data from twenty empirical studies, the book details the emergence of a new "corporate legal sector" in India including large and sophisticated law firms and in-house legal departments, as well as "legal process outsourcing" companies. As the book's authors document, this new corporate legal sector is reshaping other parts of the Indian legal profession, including legal education, the development of pro bono and corporate social responsibility, the regulation of legal services, and gender, communal, and professional hierarchies with the bar. Taken as a whole, the book will be of interest to academicians, lawyers, and policymakers interested in the critical role that a rapidly globalizing legal profession is playing in the legal, political, and economic development of important emerging economies like India, and how these countries are integrating into the institutions of global governance and the overall global market for legal services.

David B. Wilkins is the Lester Kissel Professor of Law, Vice Dean for Global Initiatives on the Legal Profession, and Faculty Director of the Center on the Legal Profession at Harvard Law School. He is also a Senior Research Fellow of the American Bar Foundation and a Fellow of the Harvard University Edmond J. Safra Foundation Center for Ethics.

Vikramaditya S. Khanna is the William W. Cook Professor of Law, faculty director of the Directors' College for Global Business and Law, and co-director of the Joint Centre for Global Corporate and Financial Law & Policy.

David M. Trubek is Voss-Bascom Professor of Law and Dean of International Studies Emeritus at the University of Wisconsin – Madison and a Senior Research Fellow at the Center on the Legal Profession, Harvard Law School.

The Indian Legal Profession in the Age of Globalization

THE RISE OF THE CORPORATE LEGAL SECTOR AND ITS IMPACT ON LAWYERS AND SOCIETY

Edited by

DAVID B. WILKINS

Harvard Law School

VIKRAMADITYA S. KHANNA

University of Michigan Law School

DAVID M. TRUBEK

University of Wisconsin-Madison

CAMBRIDGE
UNIVERSITY PRESS

CAMBRIDGE
UNIVERSITY PRESS

University Printing House, Cambridge CB2 8BS, United Kingdom

One Liberty Plaza, 20th Floor, New York, NY 10006, USA

477 Williamstown Road, Port Melbourne, VIC 3207, Australia

4843/24, 2nd Floor, Ansari Road, Daryaganj, Delhi - 110002, India

79 Anson Road, #06-04/06, Singapore 079906

Cambridge University Press is part of the University of Cambridge.

It furthers the University's mission by disseminating knowledge in the pursuit of education, learning and research at the highest international levels of excellence.

www.cambridge.org
Information on this title: www.cambridge.org/9781107151840

First published 2017

Printed in the United Kingdom by Clays, St Ives plc

A catalogue record for this publication is available from the British Library

ISBN 978-1-107-15184-0 Hardback

To the countless lawyers leading India into the future

Contents

Contributors

Amrita Bahri is director, Global Legal Skills and Common Law System at ITAM University in Mexico.

Swethaa Ballakrishnen is a postdoctoral fellow at New York University – Abu Dhabi.

Shamnad Basheer is founder of IDIA – Increasing Diversity by Increasing Access to Legal Education.

John Flood is professor of law and director of Law Futures Centre at Griffith University, Australia

Bryon Fong is assistant research director of the Harvard Law School Center on the Legal Profession.

Marc Galanter is Professor of Law Emeritus at the University of Wisconsin – Madison.

Jonathan Gingerich is a PhD candidate at the University of California, Los Angeles.

Arpita Gupta is an SJD candidate at the University of Wisconsin – Madison.

Vikramaditya S. Khanna is William W. Cook Professor of Law and the faculty director of the Directors' College for Global Business and Law at the University of Michigan Law School.

Jayanth Krishnan is professor of law, Charles L. Whistler Faculty Fellow, and director of the Center on the Global Legal Profession at the Indiana University Maurer School of Law.

K. V. Krishnaprasad is a DPhil candidate in law at Exeter College, Oxford.

C. Raj Kumar is founding vice-chancellor of O. P. Jindal Global University and the Dean of the Jindal Global Law School.

Pavan Mamidi is Co-director, CESS Nuffield-FLAME University.

Sree Mitra is a trainee solicitor at Allen & Overy and worked as the director of the Research and Policy Wing, IDIA.

Prajna Mohapatra is an M&A lawyer with Cipla Limited, Mumbai and previously was the director of the Research and Policy Wing, IDIA

Ashish Nanda is director of the Indian Institute of Management – Ahmedabad.

James Nedumpara is associate professor, Assistant Dean for Projects and Institutional Development, and executive director of the Centre for International Trade and Economics Laws at Jindal Global Law School.

Mihaela Papa is Lecturer in Sustainable Development and Global Governance at Tufts University and an overseas member at the Center for BRICS Studies at Fudan University, Shanghai.

Nick Robinson is visiting lecturer in law and Robina Foundation Visiting Human Rights Fellow at Yale Law School.

Aditya Sarkar is a lawyer and a master's candidate at the Fletcher School of Law and Diplomacy.

Gregory Shaffer is Chancellor's Professor of Law and director of the Center on Globalization, Law, and Society at the University of Irvine School of Law.

Aditya Singh is an associate at White & Case LLP's New York City office.

Rahul Singh is assistant professor of law and director, Institute of Competition Law and Economics at the National Law School of India University, Bangalore

Aseema Sinha is Wagener Chair of South Asian Politics and George R. Roberts Fellow at Claremont McKenna College.

Patrick W. Thomas is professor of practice and director of the tax clinic at Notre Dame Law School.

David M. Trubek is Voss-Bascom Professor of Law and dean of International Studies Emeritus at the University of Wisconsin–Madison and a senior research fellow at the Harvard Law School Center on the Legal Profession.

Umakanth Varottil is Associate Professor, Faculty of Law at the National University of Singapore.

David B. Wilkins is Lester Kissel Professor of Law, faculty director of the Center on the Legal Profession, and Vice Dean for Global Initiatives on the Legal Profession at Harvard Law School.

Mark Wu is assistant professor of law at Harvard Law School.

Bhargavi Zaveri is a legal consultant and a researcher at the National Institute of Public Finance and Policy, New Delhi.

Acknowledgments

The editors would like to thank all the contributors to this volume, without whom none of this work would have been possible. They would also like to thank the support provided by the Harvard Law School Center on the Legal Profession, which serves as the institutional home of the Globalization, Lawyers, and Emerging Economies (GLEE) project, and has provided essential support of every kind. This book would not have been possible without the generous support – in time, advice, and funding – of the Center's world-class Advisory Board. Indeed, the initial impetus for the GLEE project came at the 2010 spring annual meeting of the Advisory Board in New York City where Cyril Shroff suggested that we begin a project on the impact globalization was having on the legal profession in the world's most important emerging economies. We would also like to thank the other sources of support the GLEE India project has received, including from the Narotam Sekhsaria Foundation, the Centre for Policy Research, the Indian School of Business – Hyderabad, and Khaitan & Co. Finally, the editors thank the hundreds of Indian lawyers who generously devoted their time, insights, and talents through countless interviews and surveys. Without their contributions this book would never have been possible. We are eternally grateful.

SECTION I

SETTING THE STAGE

1

An Introduction to Globalization, Lawyers, and Emerging Economies: The Case of India

David B. Wilkins, Vikramaditya S. Khanna, and David M. Trubek

This book is the first in a series by the Project on Globalization Lawyers and Emerging Economies (GLEE). GLEE examines how globalization is reshaping the market for legal services in important emerging economies such as India, Brazil, and China and how these developments are in turn contributing to the transformation of the political economy in these countries and the reshaping of the global legal services market. In this first book of the GLEE project, we present original empirical research documenting how India's legal profession is being transformed by the "global shift" that the world's largest democracy embarked on in 1991 when it began the process of moving from an essentially closed state-controlled economy to one that is still state-led, but also increasingly open to foreign investment and influence.

As the book's 20 empirical studies demonstrate, this shift in India's economy has produced a new "corporate legal hemisphere" that is playing an increasingly important role in the Indian legal profession, the development of the Indian economy, the elaboration of its administrative state, and in India's capacity to exert its influence in the new global order. Together with the GLEE project's current work in Brazil and China, and the forthcoming expansion of the project to the Middle East, Africa, and the CIS states of the former Soviet Union, this book begins an important and largely unexplored debate about how the creation of a "corporate legal hemisphere" in emerging economies is contributing to the broader processes of globalization.

This introduction proceeds in five parts. Part I sets out an overview of the GLEE project and locates its historical, theoretical, and methodological commitments in relation to three literatures: the sociology of the legal profession, globalization studies, and law and development. Part II then briefly discusses why we have chosen to focus on India, and the relationship between our project and the other literature on this increasingly important country. Part III describes the organization of the book and summarizes its chapters. Part IV steps back from the specifics of each study to identify important themes that appear throughout the book that we believe are key to understanding the current state of India's rapidly expanding corporate legal sector and the implications of this growth for the broader theoretical and empirical questions GLEE investigates. Part V briefly concludes by discussing how the pending liberalization of the Indian corporate legal market might shape the future trajectory of India's corporate legal sector.

I. THE GLEE PROJECT

It is by now common knowledge that globalization is transforming virtually every sector of the world's economy and that this transformation has important implications for the rapidly globalizing market for legal services. Moreover, it is also clear that countries such as Brazil, Russia, India, China, and South Africa (the BRICS) and other emerging powers are playing an increasingly important role in this transformation. In documenting this shift in economic and political power from the traditional centers in the Global North to the emerging Global South, scholars from a variety of disciplines have long debated the role of law and lawyers in facilitating – or undermining – the processes of development in these rising powers. Yet, while there is substantial literature on each of these topics, there has been relatively little attention to the intersection among them – particularly from the perspective of the emerging economies themselves. As a result, the analytical field is ripe for theoretical expansion driven by inquiry into how globalization is changing the broader architecture and dynamics of the legal professions in important emerging economies and how these changes in turn are helping to reshape the global legal services market and the broader economic, political, social, and cultural aspects of globalization in which lawyers play an increasingly important role.

A. *The Global Shift*

The GLEE project charts the transformation in the legal services market we seek to study from a signal change in how India and other emerging economies relate to the global economy that began in the 1990s. During this period, India, Brazil, and China each made a decision to move from a "closed" economic model to one that is increasingly "open" to both foreign investment and private enterprise, including the privatization of many state-owned assets. This "global shift" has had a major impact on the legal system in each country, fueling a growing demand for new laws, regulations, and administrative apparatus to facilitate this new economic activity and to interface with the broader global economic and political environment. This, in turn, has created the need for lawyers capable of practicing law within this new legal and regulatory environment, particularly in corporate law fields such as mergers and acquisitions, project finance, securities, and initial public offerings that are increasingly being demanded by the growing number of foreign and domestic companies operating in these jurisdictions. Although each of these countries has, to a greater or lesser extent, called on the international law firms that are eager to serve these new markets to provide this necessary expertise – a subject we return to below – each has also developed an important domestic corporate legal sector as well.

Today, this new corporate legal elite, by which we mean lawyers who work in law firms that serve a clientele composed primarily of foreign and domestic corporations, and lawyers who work in the internal legal departments of the growing number of corporations based in or serving these new markets, has significantly increased in size and importance in many emerging powers in the Global South. Each of the three countries we are currently studying, for example, can now boast several law firms comprised of hundreds – and in the case of China, thousands – of lawyers, as well as corporate legal departments, such as the 500-lawyer general counsel office of India's Tata Group, that are almost as large.

GLEE maps the terrain of this developing "corporate hemisphere" of the bar in emerging economies, including the new forms of corporate legal practice that are being developed in these jurisdictions, and examines how this sector is influencing – and being influenced by – other parts of the legal, economic, political, and social order in these countries. To do so, the project borrows from existing literature on lawyers, globalization, and development to build grounded theory based on original research on a wide array of topics relevant to the current status and likely future trajectory of emerging economy legal professions in the age of globalization.

B. *Socio-Legal Studies: The Ecology of the Corporate Hemisphere*

Our theoretical model begins with the "hemispheres thesis" first developed by Heinz and Laumann to describe the social structure of the Chicago bar (Heinz and Laumann 1982). As these scholars, and their co-authors in subsequent work, meticulously document in studies conducted in 1975 and 1995, "The" legal profession is actually comprised of two distinct sectors of the bar, one focused primarily on individuals and small businesses and the other catering to large companies and other similar organizations (Heinz and Laumann 1982; Heinz et al. 2005). At the core of the GLEE project is an examination of whether emerging economies such as India, Brazil, and China are also developing a separate corporate legal hemisphere and, if so, to what extent its characteristics are similar to, or different from, the corporate sector in the United States.

As indicated above, there are good reasons to believe that aspects of what one of us has previously called "The American Mode of the Production of Law" are diffusing to India and other emerging economies, just as aspects of the model spread to more developed legal markets in Europe and Asia in the 1980s (Trubek et al. 1994). This mode of legal production first emerged in New York City at the turn of the twentieth century when a group of law firms established a set of guiding principles that scholars have come to refer to as the "Cravath Model," after the law firm Cravath Swain & Moore. Three features of this model are particularly relevant to our inquiry (Swaine 1946). First, the *work* of Cravath Model firms consisted of providing a full range of services to corporate clients. Second, the *lawyers* in these firms were hired exclusively from top law schools, as opposed to laterally from other law firms, and after a six- to ten-year apprenticeship were either promoted to partnership or asked to leave the firm. Third, Cravath Model firms were *governed* as true partnerships, in which all partners shared equally in the firm's profits and losses through a "lock-step" compensation system, and were entitled to equal participation in firm decision-making.

Socio-legal scholars have tracked the evolution of this model through three distinct periods: the "golden age" circa 1900–1980, in which Cravath Model law firms rose to become the unquestioned market leaders, representing the most important companies, hiring the best law school graduates, and occupying the most lucrative and prestigious position in the American legal profession. The rise of "neo-Cravathism" circa 1980–2008, marked by an exponential growth in the large law firm sector, but also by many – although not all – firms abandoning key elements of the original Cravath structure, particularly around lateral hiring, lockstep compensation for partners, and democratic governance, in favor of more bureaucratic, managerial, and entrepreneurial structures and practices; and an evolving "age of disruption" circa 2008–present following the Global Financial Crisis, characterized by unprecedented instability in the corporate law firm market (including several law firm failures), leading commentators to predict everything from "The Death of Big Law," to "The End of Lawyers," to the triumph of traditional Cravathist principles over the apostasy of neo-Cravathist commercialism (Galanter and Palay 1991; Galanter and Henderson 2008; Susskind 2008; Ribstein 2012).

Although there is considerable debate among socio-legal scholars about what has caused these changes in the Cravath Model – and about how radically this model is likely to change in the coming years – there is widespread consensus that a key element that has and will continue to drive this change has been the growth in the size and sophistication of in-house counsel in large US companies. In the last two decades the lawyers heading corporate legal departments have gone from a position of marginality and subservience – "house counsel" – to being the "General Counsel" (GC) or "Chief Legal Officer" (CLO) overseeing all of the company's internal and external legal needs. Indeed, many US GCs also oversee a number of other related functions such as human resources, public relations, government affairs, and compliance. And virtually all GCs in major US companies now play a key role in the company's strategic decision making on par with the chief financial officer (CFO) and other senior corporate officers (Coates et al. 2011; Wilkins 2012).

This "in-house counsel movement," as the American legal scholar Robert Eli Rosen aptly labeled this transformation to signal the key role that internal lawyers themselves were playing in furthering their growing economic power and professional standing, has been fueled by three interlocking claims:

1. An *economic* argument that taking work inside saves costs;
2. A *substantive* justification that, because of their proximity to the business, the advice inside lawyers give corporate managers is likely to be better than the advice given by outside counsel; and
3. A *professional* argument that because they are the guardians of the company's long-term interests and reputation, GCs are better able to fulfill the gatekeeping role of insuring that companies comply with both the letter and the spirit of the law than their counterparts in large law firms, who (so the argument goes) have largely abandoned this role in the pursuit of short-term profits per partner.

These arguments, in turn, have helped to spur six important changes in the organization of internal counsel offices in the United States – and the relationship between these offices and other key constituents both inside and outside the organization – that are consistent with the basic tenets of the inside counsel movement (Wilkins 2012). We summarize these six changes below:

1. *Size*. Since the 1980s, GC offices have grown rapidly, with many now rivaling the size of major law firms (Baker and Parkin 2006; Coates et al. 2011).
2. *Credentials and identity*. Internal law departments are now a premier employment destination for top associates and partners from large law firms, especially among women (Dinovitzer et al. 2009).

3. *Control over the legal function.* Inside lawyers now act as the primary diagnostician of the company's legal problems and the chief purchasing agent for outside legal services (Gilson 1988; Coates et al. 2011).
4. *Expanded responsibility and membership in senior leadership.* Most GCs report directly to the CEO, overseeing functions adjacent to the legal department (e.g., public relations, government affairs, human relations, compliance) and serving on senior leadership teams with jurisdiction over strategy and other major corporate decisions (Morrison 2006; Coates et al. 2011).
5. *Professional status.* GCs are increasingly viewed as equal – and in many respects dominant – members of the legal profession who exercise significant authority over the profession's norms and practices (Wilkins 2012).
6. *Influence over public policy.* GCs in the United States exercise important influence, both individually and through collective action by the Association of Corporate Counsel and other similar organizations, over important public policy issues, both domestically and globally (Rostain 2008; Coates et al. 2011).

It is against this background that we investigate the development of the corporate legal hemisphere in India and other emerging economies. Experiences in other countries that have developed a distinct corporate legal sector indicate that the Cravath Model and other US innovations are likely to be influential. Prior to the 1980s, there were virtually no large law firms outside of the United States. Today, such firms are found throughout the developed economies of Europe and Asia (Wilkins and Papa 2013). Moreover, in all of these developed legal markets, one can now find in-house legal departments of increasing size, scope, and sophistication (Wilkins 2012). And just as their US counterparts have done, these sophisticated and price-conscious clients are unbundling and repackaging the legal services they consume and arranging them across an increasingly global supply chain of providers, many of which are not traditional law firms.

The fact that the "American Mode of the Production of Law" has spread throughout the developed world, however, does not mean that this is a simple story of diffusion and mimesis (Trubek et al. 1994). Although corporate lawyers in Europe and Asia have clearly looked to US precedents, there has also been considerable resistance to the importation of the Cravath Model and other innovations linked to American-style legal practice, as well as considerable adaptation of these forms to fit local regulatory and cultural conditions (Trubek et al. 1994; Quack 2012; Dezalay and Garth 2013). Even in the United Kingdom, where the evolution of the corporate legal hemisphere most resembles the US model, there are important variations – variations that have become more apparent as the Cravath Model upon which the large English solicitor firms were originally based has been transformed in the second and third phases of the development of the Cravath Model (Flood 2013).

GLEE's original empirical research investigates whether there is similar complexity in the diffusion of Anglo-American models of corporate practice in newly emerging powers such as India, Brazil, and China. Not surprisingly, when a more sharply defined corporate sector began to emerge in these countries following the global shift in the 1990s, the initial response of the lawyers who created the first generation of large law firms in these jurisdictions was to look to Anglo-American models to meet the growing demand for corporate legal services (Krishnan 2007; Liu 2013). Thus, there was a conscious effort to assimilate global lawyering styles and organization modes. Firms that looked like the Cravathist or neo-Cravathist Model firm began to grow in all three countries. Great emphasis was put on overseas legal education and local lawyers flocked to LLM programs in the United States and Europe. To one degree or another, local systems of legal education, both those based in the academy and otherwise, were upgraded along global lines. In China and Brazil, foreign lawyers were allowed to practice albeit with clear limitations. In India, they were formally banned but, as we will see, have managed to maintain a role in the Indian market.

While processes of diffusion and mimesis have therefore been very important in the growth of the corporate legal hemisphere in India and other emerging economies, lawyers in these jurisdictions found that simple copying was neither feasible nor desirable. It was not feasible because the models they might copy – even the neo-Cravathist model of the 1980s and 1990s – were themselves undergoing rapid change by the time emerging economy law firms and corporate legal departments began to grow rapidly in the early 2000s. As a result, corporate lawyers in emerging economies have found themselves chasing a moving target whose final resting place is increasingly uncertain. Moreover, even if diffusion and mimesis had been feasible, many in the new corporate legal elite in these countries have recognized that it might not be desirable to do so given that conditions in the Global South differ significantly from those in the core countries from which the models emerged.

Moreover, as the chapters in this volume demonstrate, the corporate sector that has emerged in these jurisdictions forms an interrelated "system" or "ecology" where actions taken in one sector interact in complex ways with those taken in another. Thus, the scope of action by external firms will depend on the role played by in-house legal departments, the availability of specialized firms, and the potential for outsourcing in a particular field or transaction (Liu 2016. Similarly, the role of in-house offices in the ecology will be affected by the nature and capabilities of outside providers. Finally, the more alternatives to traditional law firms are available, the easier it becomes for in-house legal departments to unbundle parts of complex legal transactions, thus bringing about more change within the system.

The chapters in this volume explore this complex interaction. In so doing, we also offer a fresh perspective on the processes of globalization.

C. *Globalization Studies: Diffusion, Hybridization, and Glocalization*

GLEE builds on and extends theoretical frameworks from globalization studies. Specifically, we follow the work of scholars who theorize globalization as a multidimensional set of social processes, rather than as a single process focused solely on a narrow set of actors or purely on economic activity (Scholte 2000; Steger 2003). Within this framework, we examine three social processes commonly identified by globalization scholars which help to explain the changes currently taking place in the market for legal services in countries such as India, Brazil, and China: economic globalization, globalization of knowledge, and globalization of governance. GLEE investigates how each of these three forms of globalization is helping to frame the ecology of the corporate legal hemisphere and how the newly emerging corporate elite is in turn promoting or impeding globalization in each domain.

Economic globalization refers to the increasing interdependence of national economies across the world and their progressive integration into the global economy through trade, investment, and capital flows. At the heart of economic globalization is the case for free trade, which rests on claims about the efficiency of the market-determined allocation of resources, and on the belief that opening markets will in turn produce economic opportunity that is widely shared throughout society (Bhagwati 2004). GLEE engages this broader debate on two levels.

First, we investigate the conflict over the opening of the legal services markets in emerging economies around the world – one of the final frontiers of globalization. This conflict is currently playing out in India, China, and Brazil amidst concerns over how best to protect and develop the domestic legal services sector, and broader criticisms of the effect of neoliberal global capitalism, unregulated corporate political power, and unrestricted profit maximization on economic development and social justice (Cavanagh and Mander 2004).

Second, GLEE examines what role the rising corporate elite in emerging economies is playing in economic globalization generally. As indicated above, the emergence of this elite is expressly tied to the creation of a new corporate sector in these countries and the greater integration of their markets into the world economy. Given this connection, will these new actors simply become agents of corporate globalization, contributing to the growing corporatization of the legal profession itself and the privatization of governance? Or will they instead act as a mitigating force on corporate power, championing the profession's traditional socially minded ideals through pro bono, corporate social responsibility, or other similar practices? GLEE contributes to an understanding of these broader impacts by examining whether organizational structures and professional norms created in the Global North to promote law as an independent and public regarding profession are present – whether as a result of diffusion, local traditions, or hybridization – in the various parts of the corporate ecosystem in the Global South, and if so how they are being experienced by lawyers in these jurisdictions.

In turn, this inquiry has implications for – and is affected by – the globalization of knowledge. As globalization increases the flow of people and information across borders, it inevitably leads to the interchange of knowledge traditions (Held and McGraw 2003, 2007). This is particularly relevant to law since as economies adapt to globalization, law can no longer be constrained within national boundaries. Legal systems influence each other, boundaries blur, and international law extends its coverage to more subjects. GLEE contributes to the understanding of this complex process by focusing attention on the role that lawyers – particularly corporate lawyers – are playing in the globalization of knowledge about Anglo-American norms of legal practice, and, just as importantly, in promoting resistance to these norms. GLEE therefore examines how the growing importance of a new corporate elite is influencing key debates about the formal structure of legal education in emerging economies and the value placed on foreign educational credentials and experience. GLEE also investigates how the corporate hemisphere is contributing to the tacit diffusion of new ideas about the appropriate norms and practices of lawyers, and the adaptation of these global norms to local conditions. Finally, since lawyers have long used bar associations and other similar organizations to present their views on public policy issues and to promote their collective interests, GLEE investigates the role that local and transnational networks of lawyers are playing in shaping express and tacit understandings of what it means to be a lawyer in countries such as India, China, and Brazil.

This last point underscores the importance of a third framework developed by globalization scholars: the globalization of governance. This framework focuses on the transformation of the state's regulatory power when international and transnational regulation increasingly governs many policy arenas, and non-state actors become more engaged in policy decisions (Karns and Mingst 2004; Drezner 2007). Given the global shift that has led countries such as India,

Brazil, and China to move from a closed state-controlled economy to one that is increasingly integrated into the global economy, it is predictable that these countries find themselves drawn into the complexity of the globalization of governance.

As with the other two processes of globalization, GLEE contributes to our understanding of these critical issues by investigating how the governance of the legal profession itself is becoming more globalized, and how emerging economies are investing in developing the corporate hemisphere of the bar in order to build capacity in domestic regulatory institutions and to participate in the institutions of global governance (Wilkins and Papa 2012). With respect to the legal profession's own governance models, GLEE examines how local regulation is increasingly challenged by global actors such as the World Trade Organization (WTO) which seek to diminish or eliminate restrictions on trade in legal services. At the same time, India, Brazil, and China's ambitions in other areas of global governance have increased, creating a demand for legal capacity building, both to upgrade domestic institutions and to develop viable strategies for participating in, and perhaps even redesigning, global institutions to better fit the needs of these rising powers. Given that there is no single "global law," let alone a unitary global legal culture, what we have – and are likely to have for the foreseeable future – is a complex "glocal" system that blurs the boundary between the global and the local (Silver, Phelan, and Rabinowitz 2009). By highlighting this complex boundary blurring in an area that has traditionally been among the "most local" in terms of its own governance and its relationship to global governance, GLEE therefore extends our understanding of the processes of globalization and challenges many of our fundamental ideas about the role that corporate lawyers play in the processes of global governance.

To understand how this complex dynamic operates in emerging economies, the GLEE project builds on the work of scholars in the field of law and development.

D. *Law and Development: The New Developmental State*

For more than half a century, a growing body of scholarship has documented the complex relationship between law and legal institutions and economic, social, and political development in the Global South. GLEE builds on this rich tradition, particularly on the pioneering work of Yves Dezalay and Bryant Garth in their series of books on law and globalization, beginning in 2002 with *The Internationalization of Palace Wars: Lawyers, Economists and the Contest to Transform Latin American States* (Dezalay and Grath 2002).

The original Dezalay–Garth theory is based on a model of institutional diffusion under conditions of core–periphery hierarchy, with economic and legal developments determined by the interaction of intra-elite struggles within the legal profession and policy conflicts at the state level – which the authors refer to as "palace wars." This in turn takes place in a global context in which strong interests in the core work to engage actors in the periphery in policy changes that will benefit global capital. At the same time, local elites are able to resist some pressures from the core leading to hybrid solutions. The overall picture that emerges from this analysis is one in which "double agents" in the North and South work together in ways that preserve and enhance international hegemony. By constructing a market for new legal forms and economic ideas while adapting them to local conditions and the interests of local elites, these double agents shore up both international hegemony and domestic systems of dominance.

GLEE builds on these insights to investigate the intersection of two issues not fully covered by the prior literature. The first is the role of the new generation of corporate lawyers in the process of development. As indicated above, traditional law and development scholarship concentrates primarily on public law and the elaboration of law through the institutions of state power, such as legislatures and courts. While Dezalay and Garth discuss the role of private corporate lawyers, their analysis took place at a time when the development of the new corporate elite in countries such as India, Brazil, and China was far less advanced than it is today. Similarly, GLEE operates in a world in which traditional ideas about the "core" and the "periphery" and the dominance of the Washington consensus are far less clear than they were even a decade ago. Since theories of law and globalization first developed and the new corporate law sector began to grow and adopt new lawyering styles, there have been major changes in the global economy, conditions for capital accumulation, global governance, and national economic policy. Taken together, this global shift in the world political economy creates a fundamentally new context for legal professions in emerging economies and, along with diversification of the new lawyering field, is reshaping the scope of action for the corporate law sector.

Given these new developments, the GLEE project is able to investigate questions posed by law and development scholars along a much richer continuum. For example, is the new corporate elite committed to particular policies and developmental models? Dezalay and Garth suggest that these lawyers hold neo-liberal views on free markets and limited government and primarily serve as agents or "compadors" for global capital. But given the power of the new developmental state, there are reasons to question this narrative, and to suggest that in countries such as India, China, and Brazil corporate lawyers are just as likely to support the kind of state capitalism and heterodox development policy favored by the regimes in those countries. By examining what values these new legal actors have adopted and promoted, and what policies they have pushed for, the GLEE project provides a badly needed empirical foundation for these debates.

Similarly, GLEE research helps determine whether the rising corporate elite in the BRICs and other emerging economies is simply little more than traditional elites in new clothing or whether the creation of this new hemisphere of the bar is opening pathways for new entrants. Dezalay and Garth come down firmly in favor of the former interpretation. Once again, there are reasons to question this conclusion and to ask whether the corporate hemisphere we see developing is being driven by "new" men and women who have used this opportunity for professional and social advancement. GLEE's research will help determine the identity of the lawyers who occupy this new corporate sector and how these lawyers achieved their new positions.

Finally, what role is the new corporate elite playing in the development of the rule of law, both within emerging economies and generally. For some, the rise of the corporate law sector will strengthen these countries' commitment to the rule of law. In this view, the sector gains intellectual capital if the law is actually enforced: Otherwise, why is there a need for legally trained and expensive professionals? But skeptics suggest that the sector thrives when there is a façade of legalism but in fact the system allows great room for manipulation and corruption that lawyers can exploit for their clients. Once again, by investigating the actions of the new generation of corporate lawyers in relation to their role in promoting or impeding economic development, providing access to justice and facilitating greater equality, protecting individual rights and promoting political accountability, and helping to build capacity for emerging economies to participate in the institutions of global governance, the GLEE project provides an invaluable foundation for beginning to answer these and other similar questions about the connection between the rise of the corporate elite in the emerging economies and the rule of law.

As the chapters in this volume underscore, the GLEE project is committed to investigating these and the other questions we have identified at the intersection of the sociology of the legal profession, globalization studies, and law and development by conducting original empirical research.

E. *Theory from the Ground Up*

Although there has been significant discussion about the rise of the emerging corporate legal sector in countries such as India, China, and Brazil, there is very little systematic empirical research about this development or its implications. What research there is has often been conducted by bar associations, government organizations, or other partisans seeking to press a particular point of view. The GLEE project seeks to address this gap by conducting original quantitative and qualitative research on a broad range of issues surrounding the emergence of a new corporate legal profession in these jurisdictions.

To do so, GLEE has assembled a multinational, multidisciplinary, and multi-institutional team of researchers. In India, this team consists of more than 30 scholars from leading institutions in India, the United States, and Europe incorporating theoretical and methodological insights from a variety of disciplines including law, sociology, political science, international relations, psychology, organizational behavior, and economics. In conducting this research, we do not begin with a predefined theoretical model that we seek to apply across the countries we study. Instead, building on what we regard as the best of the law and society tradition, GLEE is committed to allowing our theoretical insights to emerge from a detailed examination of the facts on the ground in each country. As the chapters in this volume underscore, this approach is particularly suited for studying jurisdictions such as India where we are attempting to understand a set of phenomenon that are changing rapidly as the participants in the new corporate hemisphere seek to keep pace with, and respond to, developments in both the domestic and international arenas.

II. INDIA AS A SITE OF – AND CATALYST FOR – GLOBALIZATION

There are several reasons why we chose to begin our study of how globalization is reshaping the market for legal services in India. First, in 1991, India, like other important emerging economies, experienced the "global shift" described above when a balance of payments crisis led the government to abandon the closed, state dominated, model of "Indian Socialism" that had governed its economy since the country's independence in 1947 and embarked on a path toward liberalization of its domestic markets and increasing integration into global markets. Second, India continues to be one of the world's most important countries, constituting over one-sixth of humanity and, along with the United States and China, producing 80 percent of Global GDP growth in 2014. Third, India's population is incredibly diverse along almost every dimension – ethnicity, religion, language, class – thereby providing an important laboratory for how other heterogeneous countries, and indeed the rest of the world (which, of course, is even more heterogeneous) may respond to the challenges of globalization. Finally, India is a democracy, which unlike many other emerging economies has remained largely free of military dictatorship. It therefore provides an important test of how the legal profession responds to the pressures of globalization in an environment in which the state and its institutions remain largely open to democratic control.

In addition to these general features, as the chapters in this volume underscore, four aspects of India's historical and cultural context make it an ideal place to study the interplay among lawyers, globalization, and state development:

1. An embedded social structure based on caste, clan, and kinship networks that operates alongside formal mechanisms of governance and exchange;
2. A legacy of colonization that produces complex and conflicting responses to "foreign" influence;
3. Deep-seated stratification and divisions within the legal profession that produce continuing conflict about the profession's proper role in society; and
4. A legal and regulatory structure that seeks both to produce and to harness change.

While these factors are specific to India's unique heritage, they are also representative of similar developments in other emerging economies like Brazil and China.

Notwithstanding these features that make India an ideal site for studying the effects of globalization on the market for legal services, there has been remarkably little scholarly writing on the Indian legal profession, particularly following the country's global shift in 1991. Within India there has been virtually no empirical tradition of studying lawyers. Outside of India, the seminal work on the development of the Indian Legal Profession in the years following independence was published in 1968 in a special issue of *Law & Society Review* edited by Marc Galanter. This issue, which focuses broadly on lawyers in developing societies with a special emphasis on India, contains 15 articles ranging from the history of Indian lawyers to examining what were then contemporary practices of the Indian bar (Galanter et al. 1968). Since 1968, a few foreign scholars have turned their attention to India's legal profession, but only very selectively. For example, Charles Epp in *The Rights Revolution: Lawyers, Activists and Supreme Courts in Comparative Perspective* discusses the development of public cause lawyering in India, the United States, the United Kingdom, and Canada (Epps 1998). Mitra Sharafi has recently published a book on legal history in South Asia: *Law and Identity in Colonial South Asia: Parsi Legal Culture, 1772–1947* (Sharafi 2014). In 1988, J.S. Gandhi wrote a chapter entitled "Past and Present: A Sociological Portrait of the Indian Legal Profession," in which he examines the historical roots of the legal profession in India and, in particular, the role British rule has had on its development (Gandhi 1988). The chapter is part of a pioneering comparative volume edited by Richard Able and Phillip Lewis on lawyers from across the common law world (Able and Lewis 1988). In a short 2006 article in the *Journal of South Asian Studies*, Oliver Mendelsohn analyzes how globalization has led to new types of cases for Indian litigators and briefly reports on the development of a corporate bar (Mendelsohn 2006). Finally, in 2010 Jayanth Krishnan, who like Galanter also has a contribution that appears in this volume, published "Globe Trotting Law Firms" in the *Georgetown Journal of Legal Ethics* documenting the conflict in India over the proposed entry of foreign law firms (Krishnan 2010). All of these works are foundational for the present volume, but none purports to match its breadth or contemporary resonance.

The same is true of Dezalay and Garth's research on India. In *Asian Legal Revivals* (2010), the authors explore the increasing importance of lawyers in Asian societies through the prism of their colonial experiences. The authors use India as a case study for their thesis. As the title – "The British Empire and the Indian Raj: A Legal Elite from Colonial Co-optation to State Independence" – implies, the chapter concentrates primarily on the Indian legal elite's performance during the colonial period and the years leading up to independence, and on the continuing importance of this history in the profession's contemporary role. Once again, this important book is foundational to GLEE, but as we explained in Part II, our analysis incorporates an array of theoretical perspectives, and covers a variety of topics, beyond those Dezalay and Garth employ or examine.

It is against this background that we decided to begin our research on the GLEE project in India. We launched the project in 2010 by recruiting a team of senior and junior scholars in India, the United States, and the United Kingdom to investigate a broad range of topics relating to the development of a distinct corporate legal sector in India in the years following the country's global shift in 1991, and how that sector is in turn affecting other sectors of the Indian legal profession and the development of the Indian state. The following sections briefly provide an overview of the specific research undertaken, and the major conclusions reached.

III. THE ORGANIZATION OF THE VOLUME

This volume is divided into seven parts: **Section I Setting the Stage**, which in addition to this Introduction, contains an Overview entitled *India Rising and the Rise of the Modern Indian Legal Profession* that summarizes key elements in the development of India and the Indian legal profession that form the common foundation for the book's substantive chapters. This introductory section is followed by six substantive sections: **The Growth of the Corporate Legal Core; New Actors and Functions within the Corporate Core; Regulation and Foreign Competition; Old Lawyers, New Layers, and Transforming Roles; Legal Education; and Capacity Building.**

The following provides a brief summary of each of these substantive sections.

Section II *The Growth of the Corporate Legal Core*

The chapters in this section address the question at the heart of the GLEE project: Has India's global shift since 1991 produced a distinct corporate hemisphere of the Indian bar, and if so what are its central attributes? The section answers this question by presenting original quantitative and qualitative data on the central actors in the corporate arena – large law firms (Chapter 3 by Ashish Nanda, David B. Wilkins, and Bryon Fong entitled *Mapping India's Corporate Law Firm Sector*) and in-house counsel (Chapter 4 by David B. Wilkins and Vikramaditya S. Khanna on *Globalization and the Rise of the In-House Counsel Movement in India*). The section also contains a chapter on one of the primary new activities generated by India's engagement with economic globalization, cross-border mergers and acquisitions (Chapter 5 by Umakanth Varottil entitled *The Impact of Globalization and Cross-Border Mergers and Acquisitions on the India Legal Profession*).

Section III – *New Actors and Functions within the Corporate Core*

The chapters in this section explore how the development of India's new corporate legal hemisphere is in turn spawning the development of new actors and functions within these emerging institutions, and how these changes are shaping the process of mimesis and differentiation within these organizations. Specifically, the section explores the career trajectories and motivations of two groups of relative newcomers who are helping to redefine India's corporate sector: A new generation of Indian corporate lawyers who have chosen to "peel-off" from the "Big 5" law firms that have come to dominate the Indian corporate legal market since 1991 (Chapter 6 by Jayanth K Krishnan and Patrick W. Thomas entitled *Being Your Own Boss: The Career Trajectories and Motivations of India's Newest Corporate Lawyers*); and a growing number of women lawyers who have found a surprisingly receptive home in India's new corporate hemisphere (Chapter 7 by Swethaa Ballakrishnen on *Women in India's "Global" Law Firms: Comparative Gender Frames and Advantages of New Organizations*). The section also explores two relatively new activities for India's corporate elite: the rise of a new "pro bono" culture in India's corporate law firms (Chapter 8 by Arpita Gupta entitled *Pro Bono and the Corporate Legal Sector in India*), and an expansion in the role that corporate lawyers are playing in the development of Indian public policy (Chapter 9 by Bhargavi Zaveri, on *How India's Corporate Law Firms Influence Legal, Policy, and Regulatory Frameworks*).

Section IV – *Regulation and Foreign Competition*

The chapters in this section explore how economic globalization has put pressure on India's regulatory system, particularly around the entry of foreign lawyers, and how this pressure is in turn challenging other forms of regulation in both India and in the countries seeking to serve the Indian legal market. The section begins by exploring how the UK "Magic Circle" law firms have attempted to serve the Indian legal market as a part of their own transformation to becoming "global" entities (Chapter 10 by John Flood entitled *Theories of Law Firm Globalization in the Shadow of Colonialism: A Cultural and Institutional Analysis of English and Indian Corporate Law Firms in the Twentieth and Twenty-First Centuries*). It then addresses how India has addressed the potential entry of foreign law firms (Chapter 11 by Aditya Singh on *Globalization of the Legal Profession and Regulation of Law Practice in India: The "Foreign Entry" Debate*). Finally, the section addresses how this debate has in turn affected the overall regulation of the legal profession in India (Chapter 12 by Rahul Singh entitled *Festina Lente or Disguised Protectionism: Monopoly and Competition in the Indian Legal Profession*).

Section V – *Old Lawyers, New Lawyers, and Transforming Roles*

The chapters in this section explore how the same process of economic globalization that has spawned India's new corporate law firms and in-house legal departments is also creating new players in the global corporate hemisphere, while also reshaping other traditional sectors of the Indian bar who now must cooperate and/or compete with those in the core corporate sector. The new competitors include India's burgeoning legal process outsourcing (LPO) sector (Chapter 13 by Vikramaditya S. Khanna on *The Evolving Global Supply Chain for Legal Services: India's Role as a Critical Link*), while the country's "Grand Advocates," who traditionally occupied the top of the Indian legal profession's prestige and financial hierarchy (Chapter 14 by Marc Galanter and Nick Robinson entitled *Grand Advocates: The Traditional Elite Lawyers*, and the countries "small town lawyers," who traditionally have occupied the lower rungs in the profession's hierarchy (Chapter 15 by Pavan Mamidi on *Aggregation of Land for a Growing and Globalizing Economy: The Role of*

Small-Town Lawyers in India) have had to adapt to the potentially disruptive presence of India's new corporate bar.

Section VI – *Legal Education*

The chapters in this section focus on the impact of India's rising corporate hemisphere on the globalization of knowledge and the transformation of the country's legal education sector. The chapters explore the impact of globalization on the project of creating "elite" legal education by pushing India's National Law Schools to respond to the pressures of globalization, both in their curriculum (Chapter 16 by Jonathan Gingerich and Nick Robinson entitled *Responding to the Market: The Impact of the Rise of Corporate Law Firms on Elite Legal Education in India*), and in how these schools interface with the new corporate employment market for law school graduates (Chapter 17 by Jonathan Gingerich, Vikramaditya S. Khanna, and Aditya Singh on *The Anatomy of Legal Recruitment in India: Tracing the Tracks of Globalization*). Another chapter examines how globalization and the rise of the corporate legal sector are effecting the goal of using the legal profession as a vehicle for social mobility for India's disadvantaged minorities (Chapter 18 by Shamnad Basheer, K. V. Krishnaprasad, Sree Mitra, and Prajna Mohapatra on *The Making of Legal Elites and the IDIA of Justice*). Finally, the section concludes by exploring India's first attempt at creating an expressly "global" law school (Chapter 19 by C. Raj Kumar on *Experiments in Legal Education in India: Jindal Global Law School and Private Nonprofit Legal Education*).

Section VII – *Capacity Building*

The chapters in this final section examine the impact of India's rising corporate sector on the globalization of governance in trade (Chapter 20 by Gregory Shaffer, James Nedumpara, Aseema Sinha, and Amrita Bahri on *Equalizing Access to the WTO: How Indian Trade Lawyers Build State Capacity*), the elaboration of the Indian administrative state (Chapter 21 by Mark Wu on *Indian Corporations, The Administrative State, and the Rise of Indian Trade Remedies*), and investment arbitration (Chapter 22 by Mihaela Papa and Aditya Sarkar entitled *Rising India in Investment Arbitration: Shifts in the Legal Field and Regime Participation*).

IV. KEY FINDINGS

Taken as a whole, the rich empirical data presented in the chapters in this book provide important insights into how India has responded to the global shift of the 1990s, and how these changes impact broader issues regarding lawyers, globalization, and development that the GLEE project studies. In this section, we provide a summary of these key findings with respect to four questions at the heart of the GLEE project:

1. To what extent has the Anglo-American model of corporate legal practice shaped the ecology of India's emerging corporate hemisphere?
2. What processes have contributed to this diffusion?
3. How has India's political, economic, and cultural contexts nevertheless reshaped these global transplants to produce uniquely Indian institutions and practices within this increasingly globalized environment? and
4. What are the implications of this hybridized and conflicted reality for India's political economy, social structure, and economic development?

A. *Diffusion of the Anglo-American Model*

The empirical studies in this book provide ample evidence that the core elements of the Anglo-American model have been diffusing to India since the country liberalized its economy in 1991. As Nanda, Wilkins, and Fong (Chapter 3) document, India's Big 5 law firms self-consciously emulated many of the Cravathist and neo-Cravathist policies of US and UK large law firms – practices that allowed the Big 5 to supplant, if not fully replace, the older and more prestigious "British Raj" firms whose failure to respond to these "disruptive innovations" left them unable to take full advantage of the opportunities presented by India's expanding corporate legal market. Similarly, Wilkins and Khanna (Chapter 4) demonstrate that both private- and state-owned Indian companies are beginning to emulate the foreign multinationals operating in India by developing in-house legal departments that resemble in aspiration, if not always in fact, the kind of sophisticated internal counsel that have become a standard feature of the corporate legal hemisphere in the United States and many European countries.

Nor has this diffusion been limited to the structural features of the Anglo-American models of the large law firm and in-house legal department. Key elements of the practices of these institutions are also increasingly becoming a part of the Indian corporate legal ecosystem. Thus, Varottil (Chapter 5) describes how Indian law firms are increasingly trying to build capacity to engage in cross-border mergers and acquisitions (M&A) by emulating Western models. Similarly, Gupta (Chapter 8) documents how India's top law firms are beginning to import Anglo-American approaches to pro bono to India, in part to establish their bona fides as world-class firms on the global stage.

Even in areas where Indian law and culture would seem to make diffusion difficult, important mimesis is nevertheless taking place. Consider, for example, the practice of seeking to shape or influence the legislative process. Such "lobbying" has traditionally been considered unethical in India, even when not accompanied by any illicit payment or quid pro quo. Yet, as Zaveri (Chapter 9) demonstrates, the Western model of an influential lawyer in a corporate law firm commenting on proposed or pending legislation is becoming increasingly common among Indian law firms. Wilkins and Khanna (Chapter 4) confirm that a growing number of general counsels in Indian companies are also increasingly playing this role, emulating a practice that is now de rigueur in the Anglo-American context.

As we indicate below, the empirical research presented in this volume – including all of the studies cited above – underscore that India's new corporate hemisphere is not simply the product of the diffusion and mimesis of Anglo-American models. But before exploring these differences, it is first important to examine the complex ways in which Western practices have spread to the Indian corporate legal market. As we will see, these diverse modes of transmission have played a key role in the creation of India's hybridized corporate legal ecosystem.

B. *The Processes of Globalization*

As we indicated at the outset of this Introduction, it is not surprising that India's emerging corporate legal sector has adopted many of the attributes of the Anglo-American model. The global shift that India embarked on when it liberalized its economy in 1991 opened the country to the three forces of globalization – economic globalization, the globalization of knowledge, and the globalization of governance – through which dominant global models such as the Anglo-American mode of the production of law typically travel. Thus, when India opened its markets to foreign investment, the Western companies that arrived brought with them a demand for outside legal representation, and eventually internal legal counsel, that resembled the Anglo-American models that they were used to in their home jurisdictions (Nanda, Wilkins, and Fong Chapter 3; Wilkins and Khanna Chapter 4).

This demand, encouraged Indian law firms to develop structures and practices – e.g., a promotion-to-partnership tournament, functional division of work along corporate legal specialties such as M&A, project finance, initial public offerings, etc. – that at least appeared to resemble those found in US and UK large law firms. And to the extent that India's new corporate legal elite paid insufficient attention to the demand by their clients for Western models, the US and UK global firms that continue to serve the Indian market notwithstanding India's regulatory ban on foreign law firms practicing in the country, have been there to continue to put the pressure on their Indian counterparts by their ability to "fly in and fly out" to serve both multinational and Indian corporates, or to reach the market through "joint ventures" and other thinly veiled cooperative associations with local Indian law firms (Flood Chapter 10; A. Singh Chapter 11; Nanda, Wilkins, and Fong Chapter 3). Indeed, the forces of economic globalization, including the growing presence and influence of transnational actors such as NGOs, Western and international bar organizations, and various trade organizations have pushed India's large law firms and in-house legal departments to go beyond structural mimesis to adopt normative policies such as gender equality (Ballakrishnen, Chapter 7) and pro bono (Gupta, Chapter 8) that helped to make their Western clients feel at home.

These developments have been reinforced by both the globalization of knowledge and the globalization of governance. With respect to the former, notwithstanding considerable resistance – a subject to which we will return below – India's elite National Law Schools have slowly begun to adapt their curricula to respond to the growing demand by both law firms and law students for courses that will prepare the next generation of Indian lawyers to work in the new corporate hemisphere (Gingerich and Robinson, Chapter 16). Similarly, Shaffer, Nedumpara, Sinha, and Bahri (Chapter 20) describe how the Indian government established a chair in WTO law at the prestigious National Law School of India University in Bangalore to encourage the dissemination of knowledge about the best practices in this field for lawyers going into both the public and private sectors. Indian students who want even more exposure to Western models can now attend one of a growing number of private law schools – including schools like the Jindal Global Law School, where global models and partnerships are expressly encouraged – or join the increasing number of Indians pursing an LLM from a US or UK university (Gingerich and Robinson, Chapter 16; Kumar, Chapter 19). The fact that corporate employers increasingly value these global credentials and connections has only hastened the diffusion of knowledge about Anglo-American practices and standards (Nanda, Wilkins, and Fong, Chapter 3; Wilkins and Khanna, Chapter 4)

Similarly, India's growing engagement with global governance regimes such as the WTO, trade remedies, and bilateral investment treaties has also predictably served to accelerate the diffusion of Western models and practices. As Shaffer, Nedumpara, Sinha, and Bahri (Chapter 20) document, the Indian government has put significant pressure on India's corporate law firms to develop the legal and structural capacity to represent the country's interests in the WTO. These efforts, as the authors make clear, were fueled by India's desire to become a leading voice in the new BRICs movement, which was seen by the government as a way to reset the balance of the global governance regime so that it better protected the interests of India and other emerging powers. Both Wu (Chapter 21) and Papa and Sarkar (Chapter 22) tell a similar story with respect to antidumping proceedings and bilateral investment litigation. Indeed, as Rahul Singh (Chapter 12) and Aditya Singh (Chapter 11) note in their respective contributions, even India's notoriously restrictive regulatory limits on the ability of foreign lawyers to practice law in India are being challenged through the mechanisms of global governance – which are in turn putting pressure on domestic regulation that restricts the ability of India's new corporate law firms to adopt Anglo-American practices such as large multicity partnerships, limited liability, and sophisticated websites and other forms of advertising.

Although these studies highlight how the globalization of governance has helped to diffuse the Anglo-American mode of the production of law in India, they also underscore that the mechanisms that produced this diffusion have also helped to shape the Indian corporate ecosystem in ways that differ from standard Anglo-American models. Thus, Wu (Chapter 21) notes that the principal "norm entrepreneurs" responsible for building India's capacity in antidumping and other trade remedies were not the standard transnational actors seeking to "transplant" Western practices to the Indian context that a straightforward diffusion story might imply. Instead, the policymakers who crafted India's policy in this area were primarily mid-level government officials, often with relatively little international experience. Although these actors borrowed from Western models, they also incorporated many distinctly Indian elements into how the policy was created, implemented, and sold to Indian companies. These local features, Wu argues, have helped to shape how the Indian corporate law firms that represent both Indian corporates and the government operate, and have helped India to become one of the leading countries in the world in the area of trade remedies. Both Shaffer, Nedumpara, Sinha, and Bahri (Chapter 20) and Papa and Sarkar (Chapter 22) document similar hybridized outcomes in the areas of WTO law and bilateral investment.

Nor is the trade area unique in this respect. Although important elements of Anglo-American practice have diffused into virtually every part of India's emerging corporate ecosystem, the studies presented in this volume underscore the continuing importance of uniquely Indian norms, structures, and practices in virtually all areas. It is to these critical local elements, and the resulting "glocal" synthesis, that we now turn.

C. *Local Resistance and Glocal Synthesis*

In Part I B of this Introduction, we hypothesized that the new corporate law sector in emerging countries such as India would find the straightforward transplantation of Anglo-American models neither possible nor desirable. The empirical studies in this volume support this conclusion. Thus, notwithstanding many superficial similarities to their US and UK counterparts, Nanda, Wilkins, and Fong (Chapter 3) demonstrate that India's five largest and most influential law firms nevertheless retain important elements that are deeply connected to India's history, culture, and values. To a greater or lesser extent, family and communal ties remain critically important in each of these major Indian corporate firms – ties that have both contributed to their success by cementing connections to important clients, but which have also made even the largest and most prestigious of these organizations vulnerable to defection or even dissolution when communal relationships are broken, or are seen as too much of an impediment to those outside of these traditional structures. Indeed, Krishnan and Thomas (Chapter 6) argue that the continuing importance of communal ties has contributed to the fracturing of India's corporate ecosystem through the creation of a growing number of "peel off" firms, many of which purport to embrace traditional Cravathist policies of meritocracy and egalitarianism to a greater degree than their more established Big 5 competitors, while eschewing cultural practices such as "ragging" that the authors argue are entrenched in the social fabric of many Indian institutions. Yet even these second-generation Indian corporate firms have had a difficult time emulating the Western models they purport to adopt since, as Flood (Chapter 10) argues in his contribution to this volume, those models are themselves shifting from the traditional "production of producers and production by producers" that was at the heart of the traditional Cravathist model, to the much more entrepreneurial and competitive policies of neo-Cravathism, to the bureaucratization and uncertainty of the "new institutionalism" of the post-global financial crisis era.

At the same time, elements of India's history, culture, and traditions have helped to shape the Indian corporate ecosystem in ways that paradoxically have ended up promoting values central to the Anglo-American model better than are accomplished in the typical US or UK law firm. Three chapters exemplify this paradox. The first, by Ballakrishnen (Chapter 7), documents how India's new corporate law firms have a better record at retaining and promoting women lawyers than either the traditional Indian litigating bar or similar law firms in the West. Ballakrishnen argues that the fact that these corporate structures provide a "new frame" that has not yet been gendered, while at the same time arising in the existing framework of India's traditional social structure in which most women lawyers have access to relatively inexpensive child care and other domestic help through extended families or low-wage workers, has produced an environment in which female lawyers do not feel the same kinds of pressures as their Western counterparts in similar law firms and are therefore more able to succeed.

Gupta's portrait (Chapter 8) of the growth of pro bono in Indian law firms provides a second example of how global norms can intersect with local conditions to produce impressive results. As Gupta explains, Indian law firms have not followed the traditional Western model of creating pro bono programs that revolve around litigation on behalf of individual clients who otherwise could not afford a lawyer. Given the massive delays in India's court system and India's existing tradition of "social action litigation" through which judges can directly address systemic issues through the courts on their own initiatives, the traditional Western model was neither practical nor particularly useful. Instead, Indian law firms have created a model of pro bono that builds on norms of "corporate social responsibility" that highlights providing assistance to social entrepreneurs and business, with the goal of direct poverty alleviation – an approach that many advocates, including many in the West, believe is more likely to produce meaningful change than the traditional litigation-centered model typically followed by Anglo-American firms.

Khanna's analysis (Chapter 13) of India's burgeoning LPO industry provides a third example. For more than a century, Anglo-American law firms patterned on the Cravath model have been held up as the gold standard for providing the best legal services to clients. But, as Khanna documents, in addition to producing law firms that have attempted to copy this Anglo-American model, India has pioneered a new mode of the production of law that is rapidly displacing Anglo-American law firms and other traditional legal service providers, particularly when it comes to basic legal work. This new "disruptive innovation" not only has the potential to continue to move up the value chain by combining low-cost labor with technology and process management to produce work that is of higher quality than what is typically produced by traditional law firms, but is also spreading geographically to both developing and developed jurisdictions in a way that potentially threatens existing patterns of work allocation and employment even in mature legal markets such as the United States.

Even when local norms have produced more resistance to Anglo-American models than convergence with them, the resulting synthesis underscores how the spirit of "*jugaad*" – a common phrase used to capture the ability of Indians to find a creative work-around to seemingly intractable problems – can create novel approaches that produce surprisingly effective results. Gingerich, Khanna, and Singh (Chapter 17) present a perfect example of this prized character trait in their discussion of the inventive recruiting system in India's National Law Schools. As the authors argue, these elite law schools were originally set up largely to encourage talented Indian students to enter government service or to provide access to justice for India's millions of poor citizens. Nevertheless, as the authors document, in recent years the overwhelming majority of the top students at these institutions now pursue work in corporate law firms and other areas of the corporate ecosystem (see also Gingerich and Robinson Chapter 16). At the same time, much of the faculty remains hostile to this corporate turn in employment patterns, and therefore has little interest in setting up a formal recruiting system to accommodate these new employers. Even those faculty members who are sympathetic to the students' desire for corporate jobs have little relevant experience that would lead them to be able to establish anything like the kind of recruiting system found in law schools in the United States and United Kingdom. As a result, students in India's National Law Schools have created their own recruiting process that ingeniously combines formal process with informal peer pressure to produce an efficient system for matching students to jobs, As the authors explain, this student created system goes beyond basic functionality and avoids many of the problematic issues (e.g., students hogging offers) that plague contemporary Anglo-American recruiting models while building a unique camaraderie among graduates that will assist their future careers.

Basheer, Krishnaprasad, Mitra, and Mohapatra's account of "Increasing Diversity by Increasing Access" (Chapter 18) offers a final compelling example. As any observer of the US and UK legal scene can attest, diversity has become a hot-button topic for law schools and law firms in the West, yet relatively little attention has been paid to finding ways to get more students from severely disadvantaged backgrounds to apply to law school in the first place. Precisely because India increasingly relies on a single examination, the Common Law Admission Test (CLAT), to sort applicants – which itself is administered only in English and which rewards the kind of expensive "cram courses" only available to India's upper classes – Basheer and his colleagues have chosen to develop a program that works with India's poorest ethnic and religious minorities to increase the pipeline of students with a realistic opportunity to attend one of the country's elite National Law Schools. The results underscore what might be achieved if a similar program were instituted in countries like the United States, where entrance tests are increasingly playing a similarly decisive role in restricting access to the legal profession.

In addition to documenting that the growth of India's corporate legal hemisphere is more than a simple diffusion story, the chapters in this volume also provide some important clues as to why the ecology of the corporate legal system in this country has evolved in such a hybridized form. Principal among these reasons is the continuing importance of the state in the development of India's new corporate legal sector. As several chapters underscore, the state has played a key role in the development of the ecology of India's new corporate legal sector, including the creation of the National Law Schools, which have provided the lion's share of the talent and intellectual capital that has fueled the growth of the new corporate elite (Gingerich and Robinson, Chapter 16), the promotion of the country's legal capacity building in the areas of trade and trade remedies (Shaffer, Nedumpara, Sinha, and Bahri, Chapter 20; Wu, Chapter 21) and in the growing area of bilateral investment (Papa and Sarkar, Chapter 22), and in supporting the regulatory structure that has allowed the Indian corporate bar to develop relatively free from foreign competition (R. Singh Chapter 12).

Paradoxically, other chapters highlight the role played by the relative weakness of the Indian state. For example, Galanter and Robinson's (Chapter 14) account of India's Grand Advocates underscores that there are some members of the Indian bar that are arguably even more powerful than the state – and certainly more powerful than India's new corporate legal elite. As the authors demonstrate, these traditional appellate advocates –many of whom can date their influence back to the time of independence –are as, if not more, important than India's top judges in interpreting the law. As a result, they command compensation and prestige that far exceeds that of even the most highly paid and regarded partner in an Indian law firm or GC of a major Indian company. Significantly, the authors also document that in this rarified sector, traditional gender hierarchies – as well as hierarchies of caste, class, and communal ties – are as important as they ever have been.

At the opposite end of the professional hierarchy, Mamidi (Chapter 15) documents how India's "small-town lawyers" are playing a critical role in the land acquisition efforts of major Indian and multinational companies. Although these traditional practitioners can be described in one respect as agents of globalization, as Mamidi makes clear the source of their effectiveness lies in their pre-globalization ties to the country's underdeveloped legal system that rewards local ties, particularly where land is at stake. Once again, it is the infirmities and not the strength of the state that is driving the hybridization that Mamidi presents.

In the end, the chapters in this volume present a complex picture of globalization and localization interacting to produce a glocalized hybrid ecosystem for India's new corporate legal elite. The next section examines how this ecosystem is in turn affecting the rest of India's legal profession, its social structure and political economy, and the global market for legal services generally.

D. *The Implications for India of a Glocalized Corporate Ecosystem*

As Gupta, Khanna, and Wilkins make clear in the Overview (Chapter 2) that completes this introductory section, notwithstanding its recent growth, the corporate legal sector still remains a tiny fraction of India's more than one million lawyers. Nevertheless, its influence is already being felt in parts of the legal profession that extend far beyond the formal boundaries of the corporate ecosystem. Galanter and Robinson's analysis (Chapter 14) of India's Grand Advocates underscores these effects. Although as the authors point out these senior lawyers retain much of their traditional power, the development of litigation departments in India's top law firms (Nanda, Wilkins and Fong, Chapter 3) and increasingly sophisticated in-house legal departments in both foreign and Indian companies (Wilkins and Khanna, Chapter 4) are beginning to reshape the balance of power between India's version of Advocates and Solicitors in much the same way that Flood (Chapter 10) argues has happened in the United Kingdom. Indeed, in a GLEE conference during the early stages of this research, the managing partner of one of India's top law firms warned, in the presence of one of India's most revered Grand Advocates, that these forces could result in the marginalization of the Advocate profession if these senior lawyers did not modernize the way that they treat both junior lawyers and clients.

At the opposite end of the professional hierarchy, Mamidi describes (Chapter 15) how India's "small-town lawyers" are being transformed through their engagement with the process of land acquisition by Indian and foreign companies. As Mamidi documents, not only are these largely solo practitioners being introduced into the corporate ecosystem by companies seeking to use their social networks and knowledge of India's antiquated and byzantine land laws, but some are being directly hired as in-house lawyers to do this work on a full-time basis, or are forming their own law firms to serve this new corporate clientele. The fact that some of India's ordinary lawyers, who have traditionally scraped by on a subsistence income earned by literally hustling cases on the court house steps (Gupta, Khanna, and Wilkins, Chapter 2), now have the opportunity to transition from the "individual" to the "corporate" hemisphere has important implications for both access to justice for those individuals living in rural India where finding a lawyer is already difficult, and for the social structure of the Indian bar as a whole.

The rapid rise of India's corporate legal sector has also generated something of a "war for talent" because the number of lawyers who have the skills and training to do corporate work is not large enough to meet the nearly insatiable demand. One can see the effects of this in a number of chapters. Most directly this is visible in the stratospheric growth of law firms and in-house departments, and in the concomitant rise in compensation for associates and partners in law firms and legal budgets for companies (Nanda, Wilkins, and Fong, Chapter 3; Wilkins and Khanna Chapter 4). Moreover, one explanation for the findings of greater gender equality in Indian law firms (Ballakrishnen, Chapter 7) and the increasing interest in pro bono (Gupta, Chapter 8) is that these have been driven in part by the need to attract and retain talent in a world where there are not enough male lawyers, or lawyers who care only about financial rewards, to go around. The fact that lawyers with training and experience in corporate law are in such high demand relative to their supply may also help to explain why so many Indian lawyers have been able to "peel off" from India's Big 5 law firms and open successful firms of their own, notwithstanding their lack of communal connections, such as family ties, or a pre-existing reputation that, as we have seen, are still critical in the Indian environment. (Krishnan and Thomas, Chapter 6)

Indeed, the mismatch between the growing demand for corporate lawyers in India and the relatively modest supply of those who possess the requisite credentials and experience for these positions appears to be having an important effect on who is deciding to go to law school. As both Gingerich and Robinson (Chapter 16) and Kumar (Chapter 19) note, in the years following Independence and continuing until the beginning of the new millennium, law was regarded as a low-status occupation by most educated Indians. (As one of the authors in this volume explained when his mother told her friends that he had decided to go to law school the response was often: "I thought he was a good student!") Indeed, one of the primary reasons that the government created the National Law Schools was to counter this perception for the purpose of encouraging more top students to obtain a legal education, thereby improving access to justice for ordinary Indians and modernizing the country's legal system. Although the National Law Schools have succeeded in raising the prestige of a career in law and the caliber of the applicant pool, they have done so in large measure by giving their students access to lucrative corporate careers (Gingerich, Khanna, and Singh, Chapter 17). This fact is, in turn, likely to affect which students decide to apply to law school, and what they expect to receive from their careers, much in the same way that the tremendous increase in law-firm hiring during the boom years in the US legal services market transformed the expectations of American law-school applicants.

These latter changes highlight how the growth of India's corporate ecosystem is also helping to reshape the country's long-embedded social structure. It is important not to overstate this effect. As several chapters underscore, communal ties of caste, clan, family, religion, and region remain hugely important in the Indian corporate ecosystem (Nanda, Wilkins, and Fong, Chapter 3; Wilkins and Khanna, Chapter 4; Krishnan and Thomas, Chapter 6). But it is also important not to understate this effect either. As Gingerich and Robinson (Chapter 16) document, the fact that those who are able to obtain admission to one India's top National Law Schools have access to career opportunities in the corporate sector that are increasingly difficult to obtain for those without this credential is creating a new hierarchy in which elite educational credentials count as much – or in some cases even more – than communal ones. (The explosion in the number of "personal ads" that emphasize elite educational credentials over caste or communal status suggest that this may be a changing feature of Indian social and cultural life that extends well beyond the legal profession.) As Gingerich, Khanna, and Singh (Chapter 17) explain, the ties that the students form with their "batch mates" can confer the kind of continuing advantages on career development that graduation from an elite law school currently confers in the United States or United Kingdom – advantages that in the Western context have been shown to mitigate, although certainly not to eliminate, the impact of social characteristics such as religion, gender, race, and social class.

To be sure, as Basheer (Chapter 18) persuasively argues, there is considerable overlap between this new educational elite and the traditional income and language markers that have always defined India's traditional elites. And, as Basheer goes on to note, even the few members of India's lower socio-economic classes or castes who do manage to be admitted to India's National Law Schools often do not have the social skills or capital to succeed in the corporate world. Nevertheless, the fact that corporate employers in both law firms (Nanda, Wilkins, and Fong, Chapter 3) and in-house legal departments (Wilkins and Khanna, Chapter 4) appear to be placing increasing value on elite educational credentials – driven in part by the growing number of returning second and third generation Indians who have grown up in environments where traditional communal markers are less important – suggests that India's new corporate sector has the potential to help restructure the country's social hierarchy. The growth of new corporate forms, such as LPO, which depend even less on traditional social connections than traditional law practice seems likely to accelerate this trend (Mamidi, Chapter 15).

The presence of India's new corporate legal elite is likely to have a similarly mixed effect on the country's political economy. As we indicated at the outset of this Introduction, there is an important debate in the literature about whether corporate lawyers in emerging economies are likely to see themselves primarily as "agents of globalization," whose primary interest is to advance the free market principles of the old Washington Consensus, or whether they will be more loyal to the model of the developmental state that countries such as India, China, and Brazil have used to transform their economies following the global shift of the 1990s. The empirical studies in this volume contain evidence for both sides of this argument.

Given the role that the state has played in supporting the development of India's corporate ecosystem, it is perhaps not surprising that the lawyers who have benefited from this assistance feel a greater loyalty to the state and its goals than the "agents of globalization" argument would seem to suggest. Thus, as Gupta (Chapter 8), Zaveri (Chapter 9), and Wilkins and Khanna (Chapter 4) document, corporate lawyers often provide free legal services to India's legislative and administrative bureaucracy as part of their commitment to pro bono or law reform activity. Similarly, in the area of international trade and antidumping remedies, Wu (Chapter 21) describes how several of the lawyers who have been instrumental in India's success in this area were motivated to do so – at least in part – because they believed helping the government create such a regime was "the right thing to do." Moreover, they continued to hold free seminars to educate government officials long after they themselves had transitioned from public service to private practice – where they often represent foreign clients whose interests are opposed to those of the government. As both Wu (Chapter 21) and Papa and Sarkar (Chapter 22) emphasize, this process has created valuable "feedback loops" between Indian and global practitioners that have helped India develop legal capacity in the trade area even when Indian law firms successfully represented foreign interests against the government.

Needless to say, not all corporate actors are loyal to the government or to its policies. Indeed, given the history of the "License Raj" that proceeded India's global shift in 1991, many corporations and their lawyers undoubtedly remain deeply skeptical of the government's interest in, or ability to, protect corporate interests. For example, as Papa and Sarkar's (Chapter 22) document, many Indian companies showed little interest in the government's attempt to create a regime that would protect a company's outbound investments, particularly in countries even less developed in India.

Moreover, the efforts by corporate lawyers on behalf of the state documented in this volume have also undoubtedly helped advance the overall interests of the new corporate elite. The fact that law-firm partners and GC have increased their influence in Delhi has obvious advantages for both these lawyers and the powerful corporate interests that they represent. The fact that these actions are often taken outside of the formal legislative or administrative process – and out of the public view – only accentuates these effects. The example recounted by Galanter and Robinson (Chapter 14) of companies retaining top Grand Advocates in order to conflict them out of representing the other side underscores how the influence of corporate money in India can have the same kind of corrosive effect on the development of legal doctrine that many argue it is having in the United States.

As Gupta, Khanna, and Wilkins (Chapter 2) note in their Overview, however, even if they are driven primarily by self-interest, India's corporate lawyers have an important stake in fostering a legal system inside the country that at least has the patina of the rule of law. As the authors document, prior to liberalization there was very little need for the kind of complex drafting, analytical, and negotiating skills possessed by corporate lawyers. Economic matters were either settled by regulatory fiat or naked influence pedaling – or both. It was only when India moved to a more or less open economy, with a more or less transparent legal structure that India's corporate ecosystem began to blossom. It is therefore not surprising, as Zaveri (Chapter 9) documents, that the outgrowth of the "lobbying" efforts by India's corporate lawyers has tended to produce greater legalization of the Indian economy, whether in the context of greater liberalization or imposing new restrictions on foreign entry.

Only time will tell whether this greater legalization actually benefits the Indian economy – and a broad section of the Indian people – as much as it benefits India's new corporate lawyers. We close by saying a few words about what we might expect in the coming years with respect to the development of India's corporate legal ecosystem and its effect on the rest of Indian society, and on the global economy generally.

5. LIBERALIZATION 2.0

As this book goes to press, India is entering the third year of a new majority government led by Prime Minister Narendra Modi. As Gupta, Khanna, and Wilkins (Chapter 2) indicate in their Overview, one of the Modi government's announced priorities is to further liberalize the Indian legal sector by allowing greater entry of foreign law firms for carrying out arbitration in India (Mehra 2015). Although it remains uncertain whether any significant reforms will be implemented soon, the chapters in this volume provide some important clues to what a more liberalized legal regime might look like, both for India and for the global legal services market more broadly.

Several chapters underscore the potential disruption that the entry of foreign law firms might bring. Thus, A. Singh (Chapter 11) and R. Singh (Chapter 12) speculate that the entry of foreign law firms would significantly drive up the salaries for lawyers working in India's newly expanded corporate ecosystem. Nanda, Wilkins, and Fong (Chapter 3) and Krishnan and Thomas (Chapter 6) argue that it would also put pressure on Indian law firms to adopt less "communal" (and more "professional") systems of recruitment, promotion, and compensation. Wilkins and Khanna (Chapter 4) agree, noting (along with Galanter and Robinson Chapter 14) that global law firms and clients might also put greater pressure on India's Grand Advocates to improve the quality and the customer focus of their services. Global law firms might also put pressure on India's National Law Schools to expand and improve their business law curricula (Gingerich and Robinson, Chapter 16) and to formalize their recruiting systems (Gingerich, Khanna, and Singh, Chapter 17).

Whether these and other consequences materialize depends in large part upon how many global law firms take advantage of India's new openness and actually establish significant offices in the country. As Nanda, Wilkins, and Fong (Chapter 3) indicate, it is not clear how many will do so, particularly with respect to firms based in the United States that have a much larger domestic legal market than those that come from either the United Kingdom or Europe, particularly after the global financial crisis (Flood Chapter 10). Moreover, as Varottil (Chapter 5) underscores, even if foreign law firms are able to take some of the business away from India's corporate firms, these firms have an opportunity to ride the wave of globalization in the opposite direction and increase their business by following the growing number Indian companies that are investing outside of India in much the same way that Anglo-American firms followed their clients into India and other emerging economies.

The effects of India's continued liberalization, both of its legal profession and of its economy generally, on the global market for legal services are similarly uncertain. As Khanna (Chapter 13) notes, there has been considerable fear in recent years that the rise of LPO in India and other jurisdictions is going to produce a significant reduction in the employment of US lawyers. But, as Khanna argues, by reducing the overall cost of legal services to Western clients, it is possible that LPOs and other similar "disruptive innovations" could end up increasing the demand for legal for services in a way that creates employment opportunities for lawyers (or those with legal training) both in the United States and India. Similarly, as both Wu (Chapter 21) and Papa and Sarkar (Chapter 22) document, as Indian companies turn their attention to outbound investment, both public and private actors involved in international trade and investment may very well take a different view of India's role in institutions of global governance such as the WTO and ICSID than what we have seen to date.

Although much of the future of India's new corporate ecosystem and its influence both within and outside of India therefore remains uncertain, what is clear is that the influence of India's new corporate legal elite is likely to grow in the coming years. As the socio-legal scholar Robert Nelson documented almost three decades ago in the context of America's corporate lawyers, large law firms and in-house legal departments serve as "partners with power" with major corporate interests. As India's public and private companies – and the growing number of companies around the world that seek to serve the Indian market – continue to increase in size and influence, it stands to reason that their "partners" in the corporate ecosystem will rise in importance as well. While the empirical studies in this volume cannot predict with certainty where this influence will take India's new corporate elite, they do provide a number of important indications about the terms and conditions under which this influence will be created, negotiated, and deployed.

References

Abel, Richard and Philip Lewis, eds. 1988. *Lawyers in Society: The Common Law World*. Berkeley: University of California Press.

1988. *Lawyers in: The Civil Law World*. Berkeley: University of California Press.

Baker, George and Rachel Parkin. 2006. "The Changing Structure of the Legal Services Industry and the Careers of Lawyers." *North Carolina Law Review* 84 (5): 1635–1682

Bayly, C.A. 2002. *Indian Society and the Making of the British Empire*. Cambridge: Cambridge University Press.

Bayly, Susan. 2001. *Caste, Society and Politics in India from the Eighteenth Century to the Modern Age*. Cambridge: Cambridge University Press.

Bhagwati, Jagdish. 2004. *In Defense of Globalization*. New York: Oxford University Press.

Birla, Ritu. 2009. *Stages of Capital: Law, Culture and Market Governance in Late Colonial India*. Durham: Duke University Press.

Cavanagh, John and Jerry Mander. 2004. *Alternatives to Economic Globalization: A Better World Is Possible*. San Francisco: Berrett-Koehler Publishers.

Chandavarkar, Rajnarayan. 1994. *The Origins of Industrial Capitalism in India: Business strategies and the working classes in Bombay, 1900–1940*. Cambridge: Cambridge University Press.

Coates, John, Michele DeStefano, Ashish Nanda and David Wilkins. 2011. "Hiring Teams, Firms, and Lawyers: Evidence of the Evolving Relationships in the Corporate Legal Market." *Law & Social Inquiry* 36 (4): 999–1031.

Daley, Mary and Carole Silver. 2007. "Flattening the World of Legal Services? The Ethical and Liability Minefields of Offshoring Legal and Law-Related Services." *Georgetown Journal of International Law* 38 (3): 401–449.

Damodaran. Harish. 2008. *India's New Capitalists: Caste, Business, and Industry in a Modern Nation*. Ranikhet: Permanent Black.

Dezalay, Yves and Bryant Garth. 2002. *The Internationalization of Palace Wars: Lawyers, Economists and the Contest to Transform Latin American States*. Chicago: University of Chicago Press.

2010. *Asian Legal Revivals: Lawyers in the Shadow of Empire*. Chicago: University of Chicago Press.

Dinovitzer, Ronit, Robert L. Nelson, Gabriele Plickert, Rebecca Sandefur, and Joyce S. Sterling. 2009. *After the JD II: Second Results from a National Study of Legal Careers*. Chicago: The American Bar Foundation and the NALP Foundation for Law Career Research and Education.

Dirks, Nicholas B. 2001. *Castes of Mind: Colonialism and the Making of Modern India*. Princeton: Princeton University Press.

Drezner, David. 2007. *All Politics is Global: Explaining International Regulatory Problems*. Princeton: Princeton University Press.

Dutt-Majumdar, N. 1974. *Conduct of Advocates & Legal Profession: Short History*. Calcutta: Eastern Law House.

Eaton, Richard M. 1993. *The Rise of Islam and the Bengal Frontier 1204–1760*. Berkeley: University of California Press.

Ekbote, Gopalrao. 1973. *Educational System in India and Legal Education*. Sir Alladi Krishnaswami Aiyer Endowment Lectures, Andhra University Press.

Ellickson, Robert C. 1991. *Order Without Law: How Neighbors Settle Disputes*. Cambridge: Harvard University Press.

Epp, Charles. 1998. *The Rights Revolution: Lawyers, Activists, and Supreme Courts in Comparative Perspective*. Chicago: University of Chicago Press.

Flood, John. 2011. "The Re-Landscaping of the Legal Profession: Large Law Firms and Professional Re-Regulation." *Current Sociology* 59 (4): 507–529.

Flood, John. 2013. "Institutional Bridging: How Large Law Firms Engage in Globalization." *Boston College Law Review* 54 (3): 1087–1121.

Galanter, Marc and Thomas Palay. 1991. *Tournament of Lawyers: The Transformation of the Big Law Firm*. Chicago: University of Chicago Press.

Galanter, Marc and William Henderson. 2008. "The Elastic Tournament: A Second Transformation of the Big Law Firm." *Stanford Law Review* 60 (6): 1867–1918.

Galanter, Marc ed. 1968. *Special Issue Devoted to Lawyers in Developing Societies with Particular Reference to India*." *Law & Society Review* 3(2/3): 191–468.

Galanter, Marc. 1984. *Competing Equalities: Law and the Backward Classes in India*. Berkeley: University of California Press.

Gambetta, Diego, 1996. *The Sicilian Mafia: The Business of Private Protection*. Cambridge: Harvard University Press.

Ghandhi, J.S. 1988. "Past and Present: A sociological Portrait of the Indian Legal Profession." In *Lawyers in the Common Law World* edited by Richard Abel and Lewis, Philip. Berkeley: University of California Press.

Gilson, Ronald. 1988. "The Devolution of the Legal Profession." *Maryland Law Review* 49 (4): 866–916.

Hadfield, Gillian. 2014. "The Cost of Law: Promoting Access to Justice Through the (Un)Corporate Practice of Law." *International Review of Law and Economics* 38 (1): 43–63.

Heinz, John and Edward Laumann. 1982. *Chicago Lawyers: The Social Structure of the Bar*. Chicago: Northwestern University Press.

Heinz, John, Robert Nelson, Rebecca Sandefur and Edward Laumann. 2005. *Urban Lawyers: The New Social Structure of the Bar*. Chicago: University of Chicago Press.

Held, David and Anthony McGrew, eds. 2003. *The Global Transformations Reader. 2nd ed*. Cambridge: Polity Press.

Held, David & Anthony McGrew, eds. 2007. *Globalization Theory: Approaches and Controversies*. Cambridge: Polity Press.

Jaffrelot, Christophe. 1996. *The Hindu Nationalist Movement and Indian politics*. London: C. Hurst & Co. and Penguin India.

Jaffrelot, Christophe. 2003. *India's Silent Revolution: The Rise of the Lower Castes in North India*. New York: Columbia University Press, C. Hurst & Co. and in New Delhi Permanent Black.

Jaffrelot, Christophe. 2011. *Religion, Caste, and Politics in India*. Oxford: Oxford University Press.

Jayal, Niraja Gopal. 2013. *Citizenship and Its Discontents: An Indian History*. Cambridge: Harvard University Press.

Karns, Margaret & Karen Mingst. 2004. *International Organizations: The Politics and Processes of Global Governance*. New York: Lynne Rienner.

Khanna, Vikramaditya. 2009. "Corporate Governance in India: Past, Present & Future?." *Jindal Global Law Review* 1 (1): 171–196.

Krishnamurthy, Chandra. 2008. "Legal education and legal profession in India." *International Journal of Legal Information* 36(2): 245–257.

Krishnan, Jayanth. 2004. "Professor Kingsfield Goes to Delhi: American Academics, the Ford Foundation, and the Development of Legal Education in India." *American Journal of Legal History* 46:447–499.

2007. "Outsourcing and the Globalizing Legal Profession." *William and Mary Law Review* 48: 2189–2246.

2010. "Globetrotting Law Firms." *Georgetown Journal of Legal Ethics* 23 (1): 57–102.

Krueger, Anne O. & Sajid Z. Chinoy. 2003. *Reforming India's Economic, Financial and Fiscal Policies*. Stanford: Stanford University Press.

Liu, Sida. 2013. "The Legal Profession as a Social Process: A Theory on Lawyers and Globalization." *Law & Social Inquiry* 38(3): 670–693.

Liu, Sida & Honqgi Wu. 2016. "The Ecology of Organizational Growth: Chinese Law Firms in the Age of Globalization." *American Journal of Sociology* 122 (3): (forthcoming).

Maddison, Angus. 2006 "A Millenial Perspective." *OECD*, 261.

Mehra, Puja. 2015. "Foreign Law Firms Will Soon Carry Out Arbitration in India." *The Hindu*. June 30, 2015. Available at: www.m.thehindu.com/news/national/bci-agrees-to-centres-propsal-to-open-up-arbitration-legal-services-to-foreign-law-firms/article7368041.ece.

Mendelsohn, Oliver. 2006. "The Indian legal profession, the courts and globalisation, South Asia." *Journal of South Asian Studies* 28(2): 301–320.

Menon, Madhava 2009. *Turning Point: Memoirs of Padmashree Prof. N.R. Madhava Menon*. New Delhi: Universal Law Publishing.

Mukherjee, Mithi. 2010. *India in the Shadows of Empire: A Legal And Political History 1774–1950*. New Delhi: Oxford University Press.

Morrison, Reese. 2006. "What's the Difference between General Counsel and Chief Legal Officer?" Law Department Management Blog, March 22. www.lawdepartmentmanagementblog.com/law_department_management/2006/03/whats_the_diffe.html.

Munshi, Kaivan & Mark Rosenzweig. 2001. "Traditional Institutions Meet the Modern World: Caste, Gender and Schooling Choice in a Globalizing Economy." *American Economic Review* 96 (4): 1225–1252.

Nayyar, Deepak. 2010. "China, India, Brazil and South Africa in the world economy: engines of growth?." In *Southern Engines of Global Growth*, edited by Amelia U. Santos-Paulino & Guanghua Wan. New York: Oxford University Press.

Paul, John J. 1991. *The Legal Profession in Colonial South India*. Bombay: Oxford University Press.

Quack, Sigrid. 2012. "Recombining national variety: internationalisation strategies of American and European law firms." *Journal of Strategy and Management* 5(2): 154–174.

Raza, Moonis, eds. 1991. *Higher Education in India: Retrospect and Prospect*. Association of Indian Universities.

Regan, Mitt and Palmer Heenan. 2010. "Supply Chains and Porous Boundaries: The Disaggregation of Legal Services." *Fordham Law Review* 78 (5): 2137–2191.

Ribstein, Larry. 2012. "The Death of Big Law." *Wisconsin Law Review* 2010 (3): 749–815.

Rodrik, Dani and Arvind Subramanian. 2004. "From 'Hindu Growth' to Productivity Surge: The Mystery of the Indian Growth Transition." *IMF Working Paper* 04/77.

Rosen, Robert. 1989. "The Inside Counsel Movement, Professional Judgment and Organizational Representation." *Indiana Law Journal* 64(3): 479–553.

Rostain, Tanina. 2008. "General Counsel in the Age of Compliance: Preliminary Findings and New Research Questions." *Georgetown Journal of Legal Ethics* 21 (2): 465–490.

Rostain, Tanian and Mitt Regan. 2014. *Confidence Games: Lawyers, Accountants and the Tax Shelter Industry*. Cambridge: MIT Press.

RSG Consulting. 2010. "Top 40 Indian Law Firms." www.rsgconsulting.com/rsg-india.

Rudner, David West. 1994. *Caste and Capitalism in Colonial India: The Nattukottai Chettiars*. Berkeley: University of California Press.

Sarkar, Sumit and Tanika Satkar. 2013. *Caste in Modern India: A Reader* (2 vols.). New Delhi: Permanent Black.

Sathe, S.P. 1989. "Access to Legal Education and the Legal Profession in India." In *Access to Legal Education and the Legal Profession* edited by Rajeev Dhavan, Neil Kibble, & William Twining. Butterworth Legal Publishing.

Sathe, S.P. 2002. *Judicial Activism in India: Transgressing Borders and Enforcing Limits*. New Delhi: Oxford University Press.

Schmitthener, Samuel. 1968. "A Sketch of the Development of the Legal Profession in India." *Law and Society Review* 358 (2/3): 337–382.

Scholte, Jan Aart. 2000. *Globalization: A Critical Introduction*. London: Macmillan.

Schukoske, Jane. 2009. "Legal Education Reform in India: Dialogue Among Indian Teachers." *Jindal Global Law Review* 1 (1): 251–279.

Shankar, Shylashri and Pratap Bhanu Mehta. 2008. "Courts and Socioeconomic Rights in India." in *Courting Social Justice: Judicial Enforcement of Social and Economic*

Rights in the Developing World edited by Varun Gauri and Daniel M Brinks. Cambridge: Cambridge.

Sharafi, Mitra. 2014. *Law and Identity in Colonial South Asia Parsi Legal Culture, 1772–1947*. Cambridge: Cambridge University Press.

Silver, Carole, Nicole De Bruin Phelan & Mikaela Rabinowitz. 2009. "Between Diffusion and Distinctiveness in Globalization: U.S. Law Firms Go Global." *Georgetown Journal of Legal Ethics* 22 (4): 1431–1471.

Srinivas, M.N. 1964. *Caste in Modern India and other Essays*. Bombay: Asia Publishing House.

Steger, Manfred. 2003. *Globalization*. New York: Oxford University Press.

Susskind, Richard. 2008. *The End of Lawyers?: Rethinking the Nature of Legal Services*. New York: Oxford University Press.

Swaine, Robert. 1946. *The Cravath Firm and Its Predecessors, 1819–1947*. New York: Ad Press.

Tomlinson, B.R. 2003. *The Economy of Modern India 1860–1970*. Cambridge: Cambridge University Press.

Trubek, David, Yves Dezalay, Ruth Buchanan, & John Davis. 1994. "Global Restructuring and the Law: Studies of the Internationalization of Legal Fields and the Creation of Transnational Arenas." *Case Western Reserve Law Review* 44 (2): 407–498.

Trubek, David. 1984. "*Where the Action Is: Critical Legal Studies and Empiricism.*" *Stanford Law Review* 36(1/2): 575–622.

Wald, Eli. 2009. "The Other Legal Profession and the Orthodox View of the Bar: The Rise of Colorado's Elite Law Firms." *University of Colorado Law Review* 80 (6): 605–683.

Weberstaedt, Jakob. 2013. "English Alternative Business Structures and the European Single Market." Available at: www.papers.ssrn.com/sol3/papers.cfm?abstract_id=2333174.

Wilkins, David B. 2012. "Is the In-House Counsel Movement Going Global? A Preliminary Assessment of the Role of Internal Counsel in Emerging Economies." *Wisconsin Law Review* 2012 (2): 251–304.

Wilkins, David B. and Mihaela Papa. 2012. "Globalization, Lawyers, and India: Toward a Theoretical Synthesis of Globalization Studies and the Sociology of the Legal Profession." *International Journal of the Legal Profession* 18 (3): 175–209.

Wilkins, David B. and Mihaela Papa. 2013. "The Rise of the Corporate Legal Elite in the BRICS: Implications for Global Governance." *Boston College Law Review* LIV (3): 1149–1184.

2

Overview of Legal Practice in India and the Indian Legal Profession

Arpita Gupta, Vikramaditya S. Khanna, and David B. Wilkins

I. INTRODUCTION

As we begin to explore the impact of globalization on corporate legal practice in India, and on the Indian legal profession more generally, it is critical to obtain a deeper understanding of the pre-existing structure of Indian corporate law practice. Such an understanding not only provides the context against which we can more fully explore the changes that have occurred but also aids in constructing a relatively common factual base, which is shared by other chapters in this book. In light of that, this chapter maps the current state of corporate legal practice in India beginning with an historical exploration of business, law, the state, and the legal profession in India. This is because corporate legal practice is often closely associated with developments in these areas, which drive the demand for corporate legal work and structure how it is provided. Indeed, as we shall see, the fortunes of the corporate legal sector in India have ebbed and flowed over time as developments occurred in these areas. Finally, our analysis enables us to provide a detailed typology of corporate legal practice in India as well as identifying the key areas of general legal practice. This further aids in constructing a common reference point for other chapters in this book.

Parts II–IV examine pre-Independence India. Part II discusses pre-British India, focusing on the Mughal Empire, to highlight the early evidence we have on the development of the legal profession in India. A profession of pleaders (*vakils*) had developed by this time and occupied an important role. Part III explores the impact of the arrival of the British East India Company (the "Company"). The Company developed its own courts and continued to rely on *vakils* in many matters, but reserved the more formal Supreme Court for British attorneys. The system of two types of pleaders would be a feature of Indian legal practice for quite some time. There was also evidence of the development of early law firms in India at this time (primarily to serve British clients whose business interests were expanding in India). Part IV describes how the advent of the British Raj influenced the legal profession in India. The multiple classes of pleaders continued, and Company courts were subsumed into a more official judicial structure. In addition, as British business and Indian family groups grew, we witnessed the growth of many more law firms (many of which continue to exist today) with strong connections to business communities in India. Moreover, Indian legal education began in earnest during this time to serve the expanding needs of the Raj. Indeed, as the prestige of the profession increased, many more Indians decided to pursue legal study.

Part V examines the developments following India's Independence, in 1947, to 1991. The government of India took over parts of the economy and engaged in a heavier form of state planning involving the creation of a detailed license regime with strong restrictions on foreign investment. This had numerous effects on the legal profession. First, the state directly overhauled the legal profession with the enactment of the Advocates Act, 1961, which abolished the multiple categories of pleaders and created a national regulator (the Bar Council of India). Second, because the apex court (the Supreme Court) was now in Delhi rather than London, litigators based in India prospered as more and more matters were being decided locally. Third, these developments limited the growth prospects for law firms because many of the skills associated with law firms (e.g., fine contract drafting, addressing intricate cross border matters) took a second seat to the skills needed to comply with, and challenge judicially, the large array of regulatory proscriptions.

Part VI discusses the first decade of liberalization (1991–2000) and how that influenced the corporate legal sector. As regulations were pared back, the demand grew for fine contract drafting and other skills associated with law firms. In addition, as restrictions on foreign investment were relaxed, the amount of cross border work increased, which also enhanced the demand for the skills associated with law firms. Further, the increase in demand for transactional work triggered the growth of in-house departments, which now focused on more than just compliance with regulations. Finally, litigators also experienced substantially increased demand as issues associated with the retraction of the state began to get addressed in the courts. The overall increase in demand for lawyers skilled in relatively newer areas of law led to increased pressure on legal education in India, and we witnessed the creation and growth of the National Law Schools.

Part VII hones in on developments from 2000 until now. As India's global interactions continued to increase, so did the law firms and in-house departments. Moreover, new players – such as legal process outsourcers – entered the fray. These developments led to ever-growing demand for lawyers and to even further demand for law schools to train these lawyers. Now, with a new government, it appears that further changes are anticipated for the development of corporate legal practice in India.

Part VIII concludes with a typology of Indian corporate legal practice that builds upon the typology developed in the United States. A number of later chapters take up some of the issues noted in this chapter and explore them in greater depth thereby enriching our understanding of the complex and multihued tapestry that is corporate legal practice in India in the age of globalization.

II. PRE-BRITISH INDIA

India has a long and successful history of business, with the subcontinent accounting for roughly 25 percent of global GDP until as late as the beginning of the eighteenth century.[1] Indeed, there is substantial evidence throughout much of Indian history of a wide variety of fairly advanced and significant business entities that were regulated by a combination of community norms (e.g., caste and kinship ties), contract (or contract-like) arrangements, and numerous religious, quasi-religious, law, and law-like codes (Khanna 2005). In spite of this, there is limited evidence to date on the presence and activities of a legal or pleader profession (or a functional equivalent) until the Mughal Empire. In light of this, we begin our inquiry with them.

The Mughal Empire ruled over large parts of India for the better part of three hundred years until the mid-1700s. Although this period witnessed much upheaval on many fronts, there is also substantial evidence of economic growth and the operation of a judicial system (Raychoudhuri et al. 1982, 172–477).

Under the Mughals, the emperor was the head of judicial administration (Baillie 1875; Scrafton; Rankin 1946; Shahidullah 2012). However, this function was largely carried out by a series of imperial officials and their subordinates. Justice was speedy, and settlement was common and quick. The Mughals maintained both secular and ecclesiastical courts, but in matters relating to "nonbelievers" (e.g., Hindus, Christians), they generally allowed them to be resolved under Hindu or Christian law and, in cases in rural environments, often allowed matters to be determined by local customs as understood and applied by village and caste-based adjudicators (often called *panchayats*). Indeed, it may be safe to say that for the vast majority of people in the subcontinent (who were living in villages), most disputes were settled under local customs and usages as applied by local adjudicators without much intervention from the Mughals. However, within the rest of the Mughal system there was substantial discretion given to the decision makers (often called *qazis*), and there was concern that corruption was an increasing problem.

As a disputant, you could have a representative present your petition or argument before a court or local decision-making body. This person was usually called a *vakil*, even though the term originally refers to a very high government official (at one time considered second only to the emperor). Although *vakils* may not always have had legal training, they were usually people with good advocacy skills who understood the local political, administrative, and judicial structures.[2] Indeed, some British observers seemed to have measured praise for the system, which appeared to protect and favor, in some respects, foreign trade, a matter the British East India Company would have greatly valued.

III. THE BRITISH EAST INDIA COMPANY

As the Mughal Empire weakened, regional powers rose in significance and brought with them an even greater vigor in economic activity (Chandra 1986; Prakash 2002). India witnessed many developments including the increase of external trade, primarily with Europe, which in turn attracted many from Europe to come to India (e.g., the English, French, Portuguese) (Bayly 2002). The European traders usually kept large militias that often supported various successor states as they battled one another for supremacy and influence in the waning days of the Mughal Empire. Over time, the English and French trading companies became key powers in India. Indeed, by the mid-eighteenth century, the British East India Company was the most powerful military force in the subcontinent and was essentially ruling over large parts of it. The Company reigned, in effect, from 1757 to 1857. This was quite a profitable arrangement for the Company as witnessed by the estimate that one single province (that of Bengal) produced 60 percent of the total English imports from Asia (Gupta 1962; Lawson 1993).

The Company established its own courts (addressing matters of relevance to it) as well as provincial and appellate courts. In addition, in the three presidency regions (i.e., Bombay, Madras, and Bengal), the British created Supreme Courts of Judicature (via British Regal Charter), which appeared to apply common law principles to matters primarily occurring in the jurisdiction of the presidencies.[3]

In spite of de facto Company rule, the Mughal Empire still cast a long shadow in the form of its administrative institutions and practices, which were, by in large, continued by the Company and various successor states (Eaton 1993). For example, when the Company established the provincial and appellate courts, it permitted *vakils* or other native pleaders to enroll, creating "for the first time a regular legal profession for the Company's courts" (Schmitthener 1968–1969).[4] But the supreme courts of Bombay, Madras, and Bengal were the sole preserve of British legal professionals (barristers, advocates, and attorneys), completely excluding the indigenous legal practitioners. The development of two groups of pleaders (e.g., *vakils* and British barristers) is something that would become ensconced in India for some time to come.

The vast majority of *vakils* and attorneys were engaged in litigation and court (or adjudicatory fora) related work. It was only toward the end of the third decade of the nineteenth century that the first law firms of colonial India appear to be founded. Crawford Bayley & Company, established in 1828, is considered one of India's oldest law firms and one of the few nineteenth-century firms that continues to exist today. It engaged in work that seemed closest to what solicitors did at the time (e.g., commercial contracts, conveyancing, real estate) and often served British clients operating in India (Schmitthener 1968–1969; Galanter and Rekhi 1996). Little & Company, established in 1856, also continues to function today. Over the long period of its existence, it represented a number of prominent clients such as the British East India Company, Bombay Presidency, State of Maharashtra, and Tata Iron & Steel Company, among others.

IV. THE "BRITISH RAJ"

The Company's reign effectively ended with the revolt of 1857, which led to the British Parliament passing the Act for the Better Government of India, 1858, bringing "British India" under its direct sovereignty.[5] The British then set about establishing a highly centralized system of revenue, judicial, and military administration, which was headed by the governor general and his council.

A new hierarchy of courts was established where the Company's courts and the supreme courts were abolished and their jurisdictions subsumed under the high courts. There were three kinds of legal practitioners in these courts: attorneys, advocates (mainly the members of the Bar of England/Ireland/Scotland), and native *vakils* (those holding law degrees from Indian universities), who were the lowest-ranking high court practitioners (Schmitthener 1968–1969; Paul 1991). The rules on specific requirements for enrollment varied from court to court. A system of various subordinate courts was established, where legal practitioners such as pleaders, *mukhtars*, and revenue agents could litigate, even without holding a law degree (Dutt-Majumdar 1974, 30).[6]

Initially, only British barristers and solicitors could plead on the original side in most of the high courts. This distinction between advocates and *vakils* was resented by the latter, who from time to time used to demand an all-India bar, with no distinction between the two kinds of legal practitioners.[7]

In addition to this, there was also a remarkable shift, over time, in the constitution of legal practitioners. For instance, in 1891, out of twenty-four advocates in the Bombay High Court, only seven were Indians. However, by 1911, out of 250 advocates, 234 were Indians (Dutt-Majumdar 1974, 33.) At the same time many new law firms were formed. Between 1872 and 1943, no fewer than ten new law firms were formed, all of which continue in some form today: Tyabji Dayabhai, Wadia Ghandy & Company, Kanga & Company, Mulla & Mulla, Fox Mandal, Khaitan & Company, Amarchand Mangaldas, Anand & Anand, Desai & Diwanji, and Majmudar & Company.

Most of these firms were based in Bombay and had deep connections to various business communities (e.g., Gujaratis, Marwaris, Parsis) in the major business hubs in India at the time (Bombay and Calcutta). In addition, many of these firms started as family-run businesses, or were run by those with other close personal connections with one another (e.g., community, caste). The prevalence of family or community connections is due to many reasons ranging from cultural to religious to greater ease of enforcing arrangements, but regardless of the reasons for their existence, the presence of family-run enterprises meant that more than just legal norms influenced how these enterprises operated (Birla 2008; Sharafi 2010, 2014). Recent studies of these firms have brought to the fore some fascinating insights into how the communities they served often avoided interaction with the official legal system, preferring their own methods of resolving disputes (Birla 2008). Although not uniform across communities – the Parsis were quite willing to interact with the legal system and took leading positions in it – these experiences underscore the complex reality of the interaction between the legal system the British had begun to put in place and the responses of the citizens of India (Sharafi 2010, 2014).

In any case, these firms were primarily involved in commercial matters, real estate, and dispute resolution – leaving the bulk of litigation work to the individual practitioners. In addition, some businesses hired those with some legal training to work within their firms in the company secretary's office. Although these nonlitigation venues were increasing, the vast majority of legal practitioners were individuals focused on litigating in specific courts.[8]

With all these developments, the legal profession became an increasingly popular choice among educated Indians. As a group, lawyers were very active in the public sphere and took up leadership roles. This is amply demonstrated through the predominance of lawyers in all stages of the Indian independence movement.[9] For example, Gandhi, Nehru, Patel, Jinnah, and Ambedkar were lawyers and all had obtained some legal training in the United Kingdom.[10]

To sustain such a large increase in the legal profession, it was necessary to have a concerted effort to increase legal education and training. The earliest roots of the modern legal education system in India can be traced to the recommendation for the introduction of studies related to jurisprudence in colleges, made by a committee constituted pursuant to the issuance of "Macaulay's Minute" in 1835. The first class for regular classroom teaching of law as a course was constituted in 1855 in the Madras Institution and in Elphinstone College (Bombay). Gradually all the major Indian universities established law colleges (Ekbote 1973).[11] This did not happen without criticism – many considered legal education unduly focused on examinations and not on the needs of Indian society – but that did not abate its growth. By the time of Independence (in 1947), 116 law colleges were in the country (Raza 1991).

The popularity of legal studies under the British Raj led to it become a most cherished and prestigious profession. However, the British Raj was coming under increasing pressure from many corners (Sen 1981; Ray 1994; Bandyopadhyay 2004; Bagchi 2010). By the 1940s, and perhaps earlier, it was increasingly clear that the days of the British Raj were numbered.[12]

5. INDEPENDENCE TO LIBERALIZATION (1947–1991)

As India gained Independence in 1947, the new government pursued policies where the state took a much more active and central role.[13] Economic policy and development were pursued primarily through centralized planning via the Planning Commission of India in five-year plans. The state took a key role in running basic industries and strictly regulated private industries via licenses and legislation (Khanna 2009).

The Nehru–Mahalanobis strategy provided the analytical framework for growth in the first fifteen years after Independence (Mahalanobis 1960). The focus was on development of balanced agricultural and industrial growth, establishment of heavy industries, movement toward import-substitution industrialization for self-sufficiency purposes, limits on foreign investment, promotion of science and technology research, and construction of basic infrastructure necessary for agricultural and industrial growth (Anant and Mitra 1998). Although progress was made on some fronts, the rate of economic growth was below the anticipated rate (Ibid). This led the state to gradually shift away, in the mid-1980s, from active state-run economic growth, including placing limits on the role of the public sector, deregulating the industrial sector, and liberalizing imports.

From the perspective of the Indian legal profession there were a number of important developments. First, the government enacted the Advocates Act in 1961, which abolished the distinction between *vakils* and barristers that had persisted for more than two hundred years. There would be only one class of advocates who could practice across India in any court.

Second, in 1961 the Bar Council of India (BCI) was constituted as a central body, unifying the bar throughout the country. The BCI was made the primary body responsible for governing, promoting, and providing standards for legal education in India, as well as recognizing universities whose law degrees satisfied the requirements to qualify for enrollment as an advocate (Advocates Act 1961, S. 7h–i). Indeed, by the beginning of the 1990s there appeared to be more than four hundred law schools throughout the country (many perceived to be of poor quality) and a sense that reform was desperately needed in legal education.[14]

The third development was the increasing role of the state and the rise of the so-called License Raj, because that shaped the nature of legal work. The government of India adopted policies that gave the state control over large parts of the economy (often via state-owned enterprises [SOEs]), imposed many regulations that appeared to operate as entry barriers (thereby reducing competition), tightly limited foreign investment and competition, and made the state the primary provider of debt and equity capital among other things (Anant and Mitra 1998; Khanna 2009). The combined effect of these policies was that the scope for transactional work in India became more limited.

In such tightly regulated markets, the skills commonly associated with corporate law firm practice (e.g., fine contract negotiation, deal making, and drafting) were less important than compliance with regulatory proscriptions. In light of this, skills were needed in compliance and in managing governmental affairs – tasks usually carried out by company secretaries or CFOs (who often were not lawyers) rather than law firms. This was especially true for SOEs, who were the major players in many sectors in India.

Other factors also conspired to limit the scope for corporate law firm work. First, given the prevalence of family-run businesses in India, law firms often engaged in matters related to the issues facing family business (e.g., real estate, inheritance) rather than typical corporate law matters. Second, the restrictions on foreign investment and currency dealings limited the scope for cross border work, which was another area where corporate law firm skills might be valuable. Third, given the slow-to-moderate economic growth during this period, the opportunities for high-frequency domestic commercial work (an important factor in aiding the development of a law firm market) were limited.[15]

A fourth development was the creation of the apex court (the Supreme Court of India) in 1950 in Delhi, as opposed to London, leading to even more attention being focused on the practicing bar in Delhi.[16] The mandate of the Supreme Court was vast – India's constitution is the longest-written constitution in the world and there are a large number of statutes often effectuating government policy. In addition to this, the birth of a new nation raises many questions that are often addressed in an apex court. The Supreme Court thus had many critical decisions in this formative period (e.g., on property rights, the ability of the state to regulate in certain spheres, affirmative action, social justice litigation, and many others, including the emergency state) that led to an even greater focus on it.[17]

In light of this, the caseload at the Supreme Court (and the judicial system in general) increased substantially, which contributed to the now well-known delays in the Indian judicial system.[18] With these delays and the importance of the court, the ability of an attorney to get the audience (face time) of the court became critical. Over time the better attorneys did not necessarily specialize by substantive area but rather in a specific court (e.g., the Supreme Court, the Bombay High Court, and so forth) because the returns came from there.

Although later chapters address the structure of the Supreme Court in greater detail, here we provide a thumbnail account of the operation of the Supreme Court. There are two key sets of attorneys at the Supreme Court. First, the advocates-on-record (AoR), who are the only people who may file any matter or document in the Supreme Court.[19] However, it is usually not the AoR who argues in front of the court. This role largely falls at the feet of the senior advocates. These individuals are designated by the Supreme Court or any high court as advocates who, based on their reputation, ability, knowledge of the law, and standing at the bar, merit a designation as a senior advocate.[20] Although as discussed in a later chapter, being a senior advocate carries with it the potential for substantial earnings and great influence,[21] senior advocates are not entitled to appear in the Supreme Court without an AoR.[22]

However, in spite of the increased focus on the litigating bar in Delhi, there was an overall decline in the reputation and prestige of litigating attorneys. The reasons for this are complex, but suffice to say that the very large increase in qualified attorneys in India was not perceived to be associated with an increase in average quality. The estimated number of attorneys increased from roughly 88,000 at Independence to around 450,000 by the mid-1990s. Given the structure of the court system and the delays endemic in it, the returns to most attorneys would not have been very high (with the highest returns largely available for senior advocates). This would have led many of the best and brightest to consider careers besides law, leading to a drop in the average quality and prestige of an attorney relative to that in pre-Independence India.

VI. LIBERALIZATION TO GLOBALIZATION (1991–2000)

In 1991 India faced a balance of payment crisis (brought on in part by the large debt taken on under the state planning model), culminating in a large drop in the Indian rupee and a severe shortage of funds in India's international reserves (Anant and Mitra 1998; Nayar 1998; Cerra and Saxena 2002). The response was swift, with the government initiating the process of economic liberalization and taking large strides to deregulate the economy (Anant and Mitra 1998). Over the medium to longer term the government began to remove the industrial license system, open up predominantly state-run sectors to private competition, liberalize FDI norms and trade, and implement various financial sector and currency reforms (Ibid).

Although the reforms have proceeded gradually, it is undeniable that there has been a higher and more stable economic growth rate and a substantial reduction in poverty.[23] In addition to this, these reforms laid the foundations for the process of rejuvenation in the legal profession.

A. *Law Firm Growth*

On the heels of liberalization there was a considerable influx of foreign capital into India along with a need to devise new contractual arrangements to fill the gaps left by the excising of regulations. This resulted in an unprecedented demand for transactional advice on complex deals like mergers and acquisitions, often involving multinational entities. This milieu provided the space, opportunity, and demand for law firms to emerge as indispensable service providers to the major domestic and foreign players in the Indian economy.

Indeed, in less than ten years at least nineteen new firms were started, and some of the preexisting firms (e.g., Amarchand Mangaldas, Luthra & Luthra, Nishith Desai) began to grow at an almost exponential rate.[24] These firms have become known for a high degree of sophistication and expertise in multiple practice areas, as evidenced by the kind of deals they handle, the clients they serve, and the highly technical areas of law with which they deal.[25] Nonetheless, this growth seems largely concentrated in just a handful of large-sized (along with some medium-sized) firms, located in large metropolitan cities like Delhi, Mumbai, Bangalore, Chennai, and Kolkata.

Even within the large metropolitan cities, some law firms have either maintained their position (without much growth) or lost some of their business. Some firms like Kanga & Company, Crawford Bayley & Company, and others – formed many years ago – continued to work primarily with their preexisting book of clients on matters related to real estate, inheritance, and tax, as well as to focus on the relationships they had with the larger business houses/families in India. Most of these firms did not (prior to 2000) attempt to develop much of a corporate or capital markets practice. The reason that some firms decided to take advantage of the opening market and others chose to defer is complex and the subject of further discussion later in this book.

In any case, those firms that did grow quickly were, by and large, fairly progressive, all-service (multispecialist), well-paying, and profitable entities. They were staffed with bright young lawyers who had been educated at the best law schools in India and abroad, many of whom had worked in some of the biggest foreign law firms. This knowledge and experience would prove valuable as much of the newer work in India involved cross border issues and multinational clients. Moreover, even though Indian law currently prohibits foreign lawyers from advising on Indian law or practicing in the Indian courts, Indian law firms have established loose business ties with prominent foreign law firms.[26]

Given the growth of these Indian law firms, it might be natural to examine how similar they are to their Western counterparts. Indeed, there are similarities, but there are also important differences especially relating to size, turnover, and organizational structure. These can be attributed in part to the significant time gap between the establishment of Indian and Western corporate legal markets – the former mostly came into being post-1991 and thus are less than twenty-five years old, whereas the latter date back at least to the middle of the twentieth century (RSG Consulting 2015). In addition, there are fundamental differences in context rooted in the nature and role of the state, legal environment, and culture. The myriad interaction between these local specificities and global forces calls for an increasingly nuanced approach to the study and analysis of the legal profession in India.

In terms of size, Indian law firms are smaller than Western ones. According to RSG India Law Centre data, for the top forty Indian law firms in the year 2013, the largest firm had 600 lawyers, the second largest firm had 300 lawyers, the next ten largest firms employed between 150 and 300 lawyers each, and the head count for the rest of the firms ranged between 8 and 150 (Ibid). These figures are substantially smaller than those of their Western counterparts. For instance, the head count for the top 100 US law firms ranged between 489 and

4,036. Further, twenty-one of the top hundred US law firms employed more than one thousand lawyers each (AmLaw 100 2013).

In terms of gross annual turnover, the cumulative size of the commercial legal market in India in 2012 was US$1.075 billion (Vyas 2013). This figure is low compared with that of law firms in the West. For instance, the gross revenue earned by the top hundred law firms in the United States was around US$73.4 billion.[27]

The basic organizational structure of Indian law firms is similar to Western firms, that is, a two-tiered partnership model, distinguishing between equity and nonequity partners. However, there are three major differences. First, US law firms usually take the form of limited liability partnerships. Indian law firms were by and large general partnerships until 2008, when the Limited Liability Partnership Act was enacted, and since then many have converted. Second, firm ownership is more concentrated in Indian firms compared with US firms. In 2012 the average ratio between the number of partners (including both equity and nonequity partners) and associates for the top forty law firms in India was 1:6.2, whereas the ratio between the number of equity partners and the number of lawyers for the top forty law firms in the United States was 1:5.29.[28] Lastly, along with a greater concentration of ownership, family succession and kinship ties among the partners of a firm are more common in Indian law firms.

B. *In-House Departments*

Another area in which substantial change occurred was in in-house departments at Indian corporations. As with law firms, the peeling back of the License Raj and the relaxing of restrictions on foreign investment increased the need for corporations to work with people who have stronger contracting skills, were creative in drafting, and had the necessary skills for facilitating deals in a changing marketplace. Initially, corporations looked to their company secretaries and CFOs to meet these needs. In particular, the CFOs were pivotal because for many firms, most legal and compliance matters were within the CFO's office. Satisfying these needs, however, would prove challenging. CFOs could have approached litigators, but these attorneys had little expertise with commercial matters, and perhaps little inclination to work in-house. In light of this, CFOs frequently began to send this kind of work to outside law firms, which in turn led to the company secretary becoming less significant.[29] However, law firms also had only a handful of people with whom to try to meet the large demand, and that, along with a desire to have a legal advisor familiar with the business, would lead to even greater pressure to develop in-house departments. This formed the base from which in-house departments would both grow and gain in influence, as discussed in Chapter 4.

C. *Litigation*

The litigating bar also benefited from liberalization as new cases arose involving new arrangements drafted with parties from both outside and inside India. Traditionally these issues might have been determined by a regulator, but with the paring back of regulation under liberalization, they began to fall to the already overburdened Indian courts.

This provided litigators in India with more work (and new, often foreign, clients), as well as new challenges, because they were now litigating more commercial matters as compared with constitutional law, tax law, criminal law, real estate, and inheritance. The increase in demand was met by an increase in the fees they charged. In addition, other groups of litigators also experienced growth (e.g., government attorneys and attorneys dealing with inheritance, matrimonial law, and real estate).[30] Indeed, the higher fees for litigation and arbitration have led some law firms to explicitly state that they intend to develop (or increase) their litigation and arbitration departments.

D. *Legal Education*

The growth across so many sectors of the legal profession put great pressure on legal education in India to meet these demands. Immediately before liberalization, the BCI began to take a few steps toward reform with the establishment of the first national law school in Bangalore in 1987, which offered a five-year integrated degree (BA/LLB) to undergraduate students.[31] The development of the national law school was accompanied by reforms in curriculum, pedagogy and teaching methods, accreditation of law schools, law school entrance criteria, and so forth. The motivation underlying these reforms was that Indian legal education needed a considerable overhaul in order to successfully tackle the challenges unleashed by the forces of globalization (Bar Council of India 2010). However, the BCI did not start out to train corporate attorneys but rather to train leaders and lawyers in the public interest. This changed over time – as discussed in papers in this volume – leading to the rising popularity of the five-year integrated degree model. The next set of national law schools (i.e., NALSAR [Hyderabad], NUJS [Kolkata], NLIU [Bhopal], and NLU [Jodhpur]) all opened in the late 1990s as it became clear that the demand for lawyers in the corporate sector was soaring. Overall, the national law schools have proved quite successful with their highly competitive selection procedures and market-oriented curriculum, and they have come to be regarded as premier legal institutions, with their graduates actively pursued by law firms and corporate in-house departments.

VII. GLOBALIZATION TO BRICS (2000–NOW)[32]

With its growing economy and increasing interaction in the global marketplace, India is considered the "I" within the fast-growing BRICS countries (Kobayashi-Hillary 2008; World Bank 2011). Perhaps in recognition (and anticipation) of this, the BRICS countries themselves have banded together in various fora, including the closely followed annual BRICS summits (Kramer 2009; Fourth BRICS Summit 2014).

A. *Continuing Growth as Globalization Grows*

As India's interaction with the global economy increased and as more sectors were liberalized, the demand for corporate legal services grew even stronger. Many new law firms were started, and those in existence continued to grow and morph even faster.[33] Their number, size, and work specialties have grown exponentially (Galanter and Palay 1990).[34] There has also been a stunning growth in specialized law firms that target specific areas of law (e.g., intellectual property, foreign private equity, hedge funds, competition laws) as well as specific business sectors (e.g., infrastructure). Part of this reflects India's continued growth but also a certain degree of reregulation of business as India marches toward the next century.

This growth has occurred along with parallel changes in Indian firms' in-house departments. Increasing globalization and reregulation of certain areas has put pressure on Indian firms to become more familiar with the laws of other countries and come to grips with new developments in India. Of course, firms could simply hire Indian or foreign law firms for some of those needs, but Indian law firms may not be able to provide both the scale and talent levels desired, and foreign law firms, even if they could practice in India, may not have the familiarity with the Indian firm's business and culture. In this situation expanding in-house departments appears desirable.[35] This is precisely what many firms have done, with some in-house departments becoming larger than the largest law firms.[36] The increasing role of in-house departments has been a critical development in many Western economies and may well be in the offing in India, a matter explored in a later chapter.

There were also new developments in the legal services market. As with other professional services, legal services also began to be outsourced to India.

LPO has become a new growth area for Indian attorneys; the largest employer of transactionally oriented attorneys in India is an LPO. The LPO market, as with many global supply chains, is also changing and morphing as we speak and is the subject of another chapter in this book.

Although the corporate sector has grown, the litigation sector is not far behind. Now, the top senior advocates' fees and earnings are regularly referenced in Indian magazines and have become a source of fascination for the news media. Moreover, the presence of arbitration (domestic and foreign) has been growing in India.[37]

The growth in the legal profession in India has been impressive, but we should not lose touch with the ground realities. The corporate legal sector represents – across law firms, in-house departments, and LPOs – a small subset of attorneys (maybe ten thousand or so) out of the 1.3 million plus attorneys registered with different state bar associations in India.[38] Moreover, most law firms are run by partners with close familial or community ties to one another (Galanter and Rekhi 1996). Nonetheless, it is the corporate sector that is the fastest growing and on average the most remunerative.[39] The growth of the corporate sector alongside the presence of globalization has created a sea change in attitudes toward the legal profession in India.

Perhaps nowhere is this seen more starkly than in the growth of law schools and the intense competition to obtain admission and pursue the study of law. At least twelve new national law schools have been established since 2001, and countless other law schools have opened their doors across the country. New private schools – some offering global legal education, such as the Jindal Global Law School – have also entered the fray. Although there is still much to be done to reform legal education, recent developments indicate much optimism for the future.

B. *Modifying the Indian Legal Profession*

In the May 2014 Indian national elections, a new government – led by Prime Minister Narendra Modi – was elected with a clear majority. The new government has promised to push forward with a number of further economic reforms. For our purposes, the most critical has been the recent discussions to allow foreign law firms to enter in some form in India (Mehra 2015). Although discussions have occurred under prior governments, the current discussions have moved much more quickly and seem very likely to eventuate. They appear to allow for foreign law firms to provide advice and engage in arbitration in India. These steps would lead to a substantial opening of the market and to further seismic changes in the Indian legal profession. We are awaiting these further developments with great anticipation.

VIII. CONCLUSION: A TYPOLOGY OF THE INDIAN CORPORATE LEGAL MARKET

We conclude by offering a typology of the Indian legal market that is similar to – but as we will see, different in important respects from – the one that we utilized for categorizing the current state of the Western corporate legal market. Although one could construct a typology in many different ways, we base ours on the one developed for the US corporate legal market. This is for a number of reasons.

First, because Western corporate law firms and in-house departments were the first to develop and are generally acclaimed as being the best in the world, they become a reference point for comparing developments elsewhere. Second, even Indian lawyers who prefer not to adopt the American model often define their approach in opposition to the American model, making the comparison more relevant. Third, given India's increasing interactions with the global marketplace, Indian law firms, their employees,[40] and their clients are likely to have more direct exposure to US and UK corporate law firms and legal departments. Finally, to the extent that the new corporate legal market in India has developed in part in response to perceptions about the Anglo-American corporate legal market, changes in the latter market may foretell changes that will affect the Indian legal market in coming years. This is particularly of interest because some of the realignment of corporate legal services markets in the United States and the United Kingdom are precipitated by globalization – which is one of the key drivers of change in the Indian market.

In light of these considerations, we use as our starting point the five categories used to define the Western corporate legal market: global firms; national, regional, and local firms; focused firms and boutiques; in-house legal departments; and new players. Although we use these categories as a starting point, we highlight where the Indian market contains important variations.

A. *Global Indian Law Firms*

At the moment, India has no truly global law firms. Although a few Indian law firms have a presence outside of India, these "offices" are little more than outposts with little independent significance. This does not mean, however, that there are no Indian firms with global ambitions. To the contrary, prior to its splitting in two, India's largest law firm, Amarchand Mangaldas, had expressly declared that it intends to reach one thousand lawyers and open several foreign offices by 2015. Whether after its split those same ambitions hold true remains to be seen, but the public declaration indicates that the top Indian law firms are grappling with their response to globalization and whether to follow their clients or to compete with the growing presence of Western global law firms in India.

B. *National, Regional, and Local Law Firms*

The top of the Indian legal market is occupied by what we have characterized as large national firms. It is useful to distinguish three variations within this category.

The first are the most elite Indian firms. Traditionally five firms routinely occupy the top of the various rankings with respect to size, revenue, and profitability: Amarchand Mangaldas, AZB Partners, J. Sagar & Associates, Luthra & Luthra, and Khaitan & Company. With the splitting of Amarchand into two, there are now six elite firms. Each of these firms has at least 240 lawyers. And each consistently ranks at the top of the prestige rankings by both clients and law students. There are important differences among these firms in terms of their pedigree, size, structure, specialization, and practices. Each grew significantly following liberalization and played an important role in facilitating the entry of foreign direct investment into India. And each of these firms has explicitly adopted the American model of production of law, albeit with important variations, as we will see.

The elite firms, however, were not the first "national" corporate law firms in India. That distinction belongs to the second category of colonial era solicitor firms. Several of these firms continue to exist today, most notably Crawford Bailey & Company, Bashin & Company, Mulla & Mulla, Rajinder Narain & Company, and Udwadia & Udeshi. Although large by Indian standards, typically between 100 and 200 lawyers, the firms are significantly smaller than the elite firms. The practices of these firms differ significantly as well. Whereas the elite firms tend to concentrate on representing foreign clients in transnational matters, particularly FDI, the colonial era firms tend to represent Indian corporations in domestic matters, particularly real estate, inheritance, and dispute resolution. Finally, unlike the elite firms – some of which can also trace their history to colonial times – the firms that remain in this category have not adopted the American mode of production and instead are structured as a hybrid between the older English model and the model of traditional Indian law firms that existed in the period leading up to Independence.

Finally, there is a third group of national firms that can neither claim the elite mantle, nor the historical pedigree (and client relationships) of the colonial era firms. These firms are also large by Indian standards – typically more than 100 lawyers – and many have offices in cities outside of the major commercial centers of Mumbai, Delhi, and Bangalore, where the elite and colonial era firms tend to be located. These firms tend to represent primarily Indian corporations and family-owned businesses, many of which are themselves regional as opposed to national. Prominent firms in this group include Fox Mandal, Dua Associates, ALMT, Kochhar & Company, Singhania & Company, Desai & Diwanji, DSK Legal, and Wadia Ghandy & Co.[41]

C. *Focused Firms and Boutique Firms*

In the latest rankings of Indian law firms, boutique and specialized firms received some of the highest marks from both international and Indian clients with respect to innovation, client satisfaction, and quality of service. Unlike in the West, where this category contains a mix of some of the oldest and most established firms (e.g., Cravath, Slaughter & May) and new firms, in India the firms that comprise this group, with a few notable exceptions, were almost all formed during what we have characterized earlier as the globalization era beginning in 2000.

These firms, which range in size from a few dozen lawyers to more than 100, tend to specialize in high-end fields of modern corporate practice: private equity, infrastructure and project finance, tax, intellectual property, and arbitration. They have made strong inroads in attracting international clients but also are increasingly popular with Indian corporations engaged in international transactions. They pride themselves on being "modern" in both their internal structure and the way that they conduct their work, and aggressively market themselves to both clients and talent as being much closer to the Anglo-American model than the elite firms. Indeed, as we will discuss in Chapter 6, several of these firms were started by lawyers who left the elite firm in search of opportunities they felt they could not obtain there. Other firms were started by lawyers who were educated in the United States or United Kingdom and/or who already had significant experience working in international firms. Prominent examples in this group are Trilegal, Nishith Desai Associates, Anand & Anand, Phoenix Legal, Platinum Partners, and Talwar Thakore & Associates.

There is, however, another category of "focused" firms that does not exist in the American context, although there is an important analogue in the United Kingdom. These are the advocates-on-record, who often organize as firms and work with senior advocates. As we indicated earlier, and as further described in Chapter 14 of this volume, senior advocates are quite important in the Indian context, often earning incomes that far exceed those of even the most highly compensated elite law firm partner. Although senior advocates – like their UK barrister counterparts – are solo practitioners, they must be briefed and supported by an AoR.[42] Some of the colonial era firms act in this role, particularly for important cases, thus giving them preferred access to some of the most powerful senior advocates.

D. *In-House Departments*

As we indicated above, in-house legal departments are becoming increasingly important in India. As is elaborated on in Chapter 4, in analyzing this rapidly growing sector of the Indian corporate bar, it is useful to distinguish four kinds of companies: foreign multinational national companies (FNCs), Indian state-owned enterprises (SOEs), family-owned or promoter-driven Indian companies, and publicly controlled Indian companies. Because these types of companies reflect different governance structures and have differing degrees of exposure to the global business environment, we would expect that their in-house departments will differ in important ways.

E. *New Players*

India is the birthplace of one of the most important new players in the global corporate legal market: LPO. India's LPO industry is the oldest and largest in the world – although in recognition of the growing importance of "unbundling" legal work and applying technology and process management to reduce costs, this industry has now spawned a number of important competitors around the world, including "near-sourcing" facilities offering similar services in low-cost cities in Western legal markets such as Wheeling, West Virginia, and Belfast, Northern Ireland. The rise of the LPOs and the emerging global supply chain for legal services is discussed in Chapter 13 of this volume.

F. *Global Law Firms*

Although India does not yet have global law firms of its own, a number of global players are actively trying to serve the Indian market. Notwithstanding the fact that under the Advocates Act only Indian citizens are legally permitted to practice law within the country, a number of foreign law firms are actively engaged in representing foreign multinational corporations and Indian corporations in both transactions and disputes. These foreign firms either do their work on a "fly in, fly out" basis – working from offices in Hong Kong, Singapore, London, or New York and then flying in to consult with clients or close deals – or by affiliating with an Indian firm who can perform the local parts of the work. These latter relationships, however, have tended to prove quite unstable. Chapters 3 and 10 explore these alliances and why several have not succeeded.[43]

Finally, the Big Four accounting firms are also active in India, bringing their brand of multidisciplinary practice and offering globally integrated business solutions to all kinds of firms operating in India. With this typology in mind, we now turn our attention to the individual chapters.

Notes

1 For a discussion of commercial activities in ancient India c. 1500 BCE–c. 1200 CE, see Giles 1923; McCrindle 1960; Das 1980; Thaplyal 1996; Kenoyer 1997. For a discussion of the period 1200–1750 AD, see Raychoudhuri et al. 1982; Arasaratnam 1986; Gopal 1986; Das Gupta 2001. For GDP, see Tomlinson 2003; Maddison 2006.

2 Lawyers (those with legal training) did not normally appear on behalf of claimants. These lawyers were more likely to be the decision makers or perhaps the experts to whom the decision maker may refer a matter (e.g., a *mufti*) (Cleveland and Bunton 2013).

3 Supreme courts were established in the presidencies of Bengal, Madras, and Bombay under Royal Charters in 1773, 1801, and 1823, respectively. These courts were to apply English law (common law and statute law) that was introduced into these settlements by the Charter of George I in the year 1726 (Home Intelligence 1927; Sturman 2012).

4 The Bengal Regulation VII of 1793 also regulated legal fees and appointments of government pleaders among other matters (Schmitthener 1968–1969; Dutt-Majumdar 1974). One of the more important sets of rules were contained in Regulation XXVIII of 1814, which addressed licensing and disciplining of the nonbarrister legal professionals (e.g., *vakils*).

5 Though, even prior to taking this formal step, the British Crown was actively involved in overseeing Indian affairs through the Company (Cain and Hopkins 1993; Lawson 1993).

6 The Legal Practitioners Act of 1879 (Act XVIII of 1879) contained further details on these various categories.

7 This would eventually happen with the enactment of the Advocates Act, 1961, which abolished the distinctions between different classes of legal practitioners and entitled only one class of legal practitioners, namely, advocates, to practice in the courts of India.

8 Litigators tended to specialize in particular courts where familiarity with the judge or justices was important (e.g., face time), although specialization in specific areas of law was not that critical.

9 For example, eleven out of sixteen presidents of the Indian National Congress between 1885 and 1909 were lawyers (Mukherjee 2010).

10 Gandhi studied at University College, London and as a barrister at Inner Temple. Nehru studied at Trinity College, Cambridge for his honors degree and then proceeded to study law for two years at the Inns of Court School of Law (Inner Temple) and was admitted to the English Bar in 1912. Patel studied at Middle

Temple Inn in London after having practiced as an advocate in India. Jinnah was trained as a barrister at Lincoln's Inn in London. Ambedkar completed graduate work at Columbia University and doctoral work at the London School of Economics while also completing the bar exam at Gray's Inn.

11 The Indian Bar Council's Act of 1926 (Act XXXVIII of 1926) was also important because it established the bar councils (one created by each high court), which were responsible for legal education and matters related to admitting individuals to the practice of law and its regulation.

12 For an introduction to India's independence movement, see Bandyopadhyay 2004.

13 India faced the Herculean task of initiating economic development of a country afflicted with large-scale poverty, low per-capita income, food scarcity, capital deficiency, low social overhead capital, and abysmal levels of technological and industrial development (Tomlinson 2003, 101; Bandyopadhyay 2004, 133).

14 Although the establishment of the first National Law Schools (in Bangalore in 1987) and accompanying reforms were significant, we defer discussion of it until the next section because the vast majority of national law schools were established after the liberalization program began in 1991.

15 There were some new law firms formed, but they were narrowly focused on specialized areas (e.g., Parekh & Company, specializing in litigation; Nishith Desai Associates, specializing in tax).

16 Prior to Independence, the court of final appeal for India was the judicial committee of the Privy Council in London.

17 Substantial scholarship explores the increasing role of the Supreme Court within India and how it is considered one of the most independent and activist supreme courts in the world (Baxi 1987; Sathe 2002; Shankar and Mehta 2008). In particular, the genesis of public interest litigation (which relaxes standing rules for initiating certain suits), for example, *S.P. Gupta* v. *Union of India*, AIR 1982 SC 149) and the response of the court during the emergency have generated substantial scholarship (Cunningham 1987; Guha 2007; Mehta 2007; Deva 2009).

18 It is worth noting that the delays have only been worsened by an increasing tendency of government departments to litigate issues rather than resolve them with the citizens directly. Indeed, recent studies indicate that the government is the largest and most frequent litigant in the Indian courts. See National Legal Mission to Reduce Average Pendency Time from 15 Years to 3 Years, 2009. A partial explanation for this might be that a court decision provides greater legitimacy and perhaps political "cover" (Khanna 2015).

19 For more on this, see Supreme Court of India Rules available at: http://llbl.webs.com/Files/rulespdf.pdf.

20 The process of designating senior advocates has recently become the subject of a public interest litigation (PIL) filed in the Supreme Court of India (Ganz 2015a).

21 Senior advocates (and most litigating advocates in India) do not charge on an hourly basis, but rather they charge an "appearance" fee.

22 This appears to re-create, in part, the multiple categories of litigators that the 1961 Act seemed to abolish.

23 The average rate of economic growth of India in the two decades preceding the 1991 economic reforms was merely 3.5 percent (Basu 2004; Kotwal et al. 2011; Ministry of Finance 2011; World Bank 2012).

24 Galanter and Rekhi argue that these large law firms emerged because their multi-speciality practices provided one-stop shopping for the kinds of commercial matters relevant to India at the time, the ability to pool resources and specializations to provide complex legal advice, and the ability to combine senior and junior talent in a potentially symbiotic relationship (Galanter and Rekhi 1996).

25 The top corporate Indian law firms are routinely roped in to advise on important domestic and cross border business deals, including a number of multibillion-dollar deals that often employ a consortium of foreign and domestic law firms (*India Business Law Journal* 2013).

26 The agreements come with various monikers: best friends agreement, exclusive/nonexclusive referral relationship, tie-ups, etc. Though a number of high profile tie-ups between Indian and foreign firms ended in breakups (e.g., AZB–Clifford Chance, Trilegal–Allen & Overy, TTA–Linklaters), many new tie-ups have appeared recently, such as J. Sagar–DLA Piper, Ashurst–Indian Law Partners (ILP); Beachcroft–Khaitan, Jayakar Sud–Vohra; and Lex Forska Solutions LLP–Shah Peerally Law Group PC).

27 The top US law firm by revenue earned US$2.4 billion in this period, more than the entire Indian commercial market (AmLaw 100 2013).

28 India data is derived from RSG Top 40 Indian Law Firms (RSG Consulting 2012). US data is derived from the AmLaw 100 2012 dataset.

29 A CFO might have considered hiring attorneys from law firms to work in-house, but in the early days of globalization the pay might not have been comparable to working at a law firm and law firm attorneys may have thought that working in-house could send poor signals about their quality.

30 Litigating on behalf of the government provided one with excellent experience and contacts to branch out into private practice (as it does in developed countries as well).

31 The BCI considered this to be significant, kick-starting "the next level of evolution in legal education in the country" (Bar Council of India 2010).

32 The acronym BRICS for Brazil, Russia, India, China, and South Africa was coined by Jim O'Neill, the chief economist of Goldman Sachs (O'Neill 2001).

33 Amarchand & Mangaldas & Suresh A. Shroff was India's largest law firm in 2014 with more than 600 attorneys, even though it had fewer than thirty attorneys in 1991, and AZB, with more than 250 attorneys, came into its current form only in 2004. Amarchand has morphed again in 2015 after the matriarch of the family passed away and the firm split into two firms – Shardul Amarchand Mangaldas and Cyril Amarchand Mangaldas – both with aggressive expansion plans. For more, see Chapter 3 of this volume.

34 India did not have any organization representing the collective interests of law firms until the Society of Indian Law Firms (SILF) was formed in 2000. It now represents more than one hundred corporate law firms (Krishnan 2010).

35 The in-house counsel is better suited for this role than most CFOs (who understand business but not necessarily the shifting regulatory structures) and outside law firms (who appreciate legal issues but do not present with firm-specific knowledge and skills).

36 One can envision in-house departments taking on a more strategic role as the legal and regulatory issues blend with the business ones in a shifting global environment.

37 Some top senior advocates have begun to offer their services in arbitration as has a newer breed of lawyer who also focuses on trade law services (Ganz 2013).
38 This aspect of the Indian legal profession has been widely studied. For an overview of the traditional organization of legal services in India (Galanter 1968–1969; Schmitthener 1968–1969).
39 Starting salaries at most of the top law firms have increased dramatically in the last decade (as have increases in salaries for more senior associates) – all of which contributes to increased interest in the legal profession.
40 Often the employees have studied or worked in the United States or United Kingdom.
41 For example, according to RSG data on the split of work between international and domestic clients, the proportion of domestic clients of Kochhar is 70% and Wadia Ghandy & Co 60% (RSG Consulting 2015).
42 Senior advocates often employ several "juniors" or trainees in their chambers.
43 The UK firms are the most active in the Indian market, but the US firms are showing increasing interest, as are firms from Australia, Canada, and Singapore.

References

AmLaw 100. 2013. "The 2013 AmLaw 100." *The American Lawyer*. http://www.americanlawyer.com/id=1398584264919/The-2013-Am-Law-100/slreturn=20170018081701

Anant, T. C. A., and N. L. Mitra. 1998. "The Role of Law and Legal Institutions in Asian Economic Development: The Case of India Patterns of Change in the Legal System and Socio-Economy" (development discussion paper no. 662, Harvard Institute for International Development).

Arasaratnam, Sinnappah. 1986. *Merchants, Companies, and Commerce on the Coromandel Coast 1650–1740*. New Delhi: Oxford University Press.

Bagchi, Amiya Kumar. 2010. *Colonialism and Indian Economy*. Oxford: Oxford University Press.

Baillie, N. E. B. 1875. *A Digest of Mohummudan Law*. London: Smith, Elder & Company.

Bandyopadhyay, Sekhar. 2004. *From Plassey to Partition: A History of Modern India*. Delhi: Orient Longman.

Bar Council of India. 2010. *Legal Education*. www.barcouncilofindia.org/about/legal-education/.

2010. *Reform of Legal Education in India: Note on Proposed Directions for Reform*. www.barcouncilofindia.org/wp-content/uploads/2010/07/LegalEducationReformRecommendations.pdf.

Basu, Kaushik, ed. 2004. *India's Emerging Economy: Performance and the Prospects in the 1990s and Beyond*. Cambridge: MIT Press.

Baxi, Upendra. 1987. "Taking Human Suffering Seriously: Social Action Litigation Before the Supreme Court of India." In *The Role of the Judiciary in Plural Societies*. Edited by Neelan Tiruchelvan and Radica Coomaraswamy. New York: St. Martin's Press.

Bayly, C. A. 2002. *Indian Society and the Making of the British Empire*. Cambridge: Cambridge University Press.

Birla, Ritu. 2008. *Stages of Capital: Law, Culture and Market Governance in Late Colonial India*. Durham: Duke University Press.
Cain, P. J., and A. G. Hopkins. 1993. *British Imperialism: Innovation and Expansion 1688–1914*. London: Longman.
Cerra, Valerie, and Sweta Chaman Saxena. 2002. "What Caused the 1991 Currency Crisis in India?" *IMF Staff Papers* 49 (3): 395–425.
Chandra, Satish. 1986. *The Eighteenth Century in India: Its Economy and the Role of Marathas, the Jats, the Sikhs and the Afghans*. Calcutta: Centre for Studies in Social Sciences.
Cleveland, William L., and Martin P. Bunton. 2013. *A History of the Modern Middle East*. Boulder: Westview Press.
Cunningham, Clark D. 1987. "Public Interest Litigation in Indian Supreme Court: A Study in the Light of American Experience." *Journal of the Indian Law Institute* 29 (2): 494–523.
Das, Santosh Kumar. 1980. *The Economic History of Ancient India*. Allahabad: Vohra.
Das Gupta, Ashin. 2001. *The World of the Indian Ocean Merchants*. New Delhi: Oxford University Press.
Deva, Surya. 2009. "Public Interest Litigation in India: A Critical Review." *Civil Justice Quarterly* 28 (1): 19–40.
Dutt-Majumdar, N. 1974. *Conduct of Advocates and Legal Profession: Short History*. Calcutta: Eastern Law House.
Eaton, Richard M. 1993. *The Rise of Islam and the Bengal Frontier 1204–1760*. Berkeley: University of California Press.
Ekbote, Gopalrao. 1973. *Educational System in India and Legal Education* (Sir Alladi Krishnaswami Aiyer Endowment Lectures, 1973). Waltair: Andhra University Press.
Home Intelligence. 1927. *The Asiatic Journal and Monthly Register for British India and Its Dependencies*. London: Black, Kingsbury, Parbury, & Allen.
Galanter, Marc. 1968–1969. "Introduction: The Study of the Indian Legal Profession." *Law and Society Review* 3 (2/3): 201–217.
Galanter, Marc, and Thomas M. Palay. 1990. "Why the Big Get Bigger: The Promotion to Partner Tournament and the Growth of Large Law Firms." *Virginia Law Review* 76 (4): 747–812.
Galanter, Marc, and V. S. Rekhi. 1996. "The Impending Transformation of Indian Legal Profession." Draft.
Ganz, Kiran. 2013. "Breaking: Harish Salve to Join English Bar & London's Blackstone Chambers," www.legallyindia.com/201307193848/Bar-Bench-Litigation/harish-salve-to-join-blackstone-chambers.
2015a. "Only 1 Dalit, 2 Muslims in Last 15 Years: Jaising Files PIL Against Opaque and Nepotistic Senior Counsel Appointment Process," *Legally India*, July 7, www.legallyindia.com/Bar-Bench-Litigation/jaising-vs-beauty-parade-senior-process.
2015b. "Realities for Cyril Shroff," *Live Mint*, May 11, www.livemint.com/Companies/ZDcSquacgFaUIrOnk8iZDN/New-realities-for-Cyril-Shroff.html.
2015c. "The Road Ahead for Shardul Shroff's New Law Firm," *Live Mint*, May 14, 2015, www.livemint.com/Companies/5Dm9pBUAoDdoPdlKOCiEuI/Expanding-abroad-and-11-other-things-Shardul-Shroff-plans-to.html.
Giles, H. A. 1923. *Travels of Fa-hsien*. Cambridge: Cambridge University Press.

Gopal, Surendra. 1986. "A Brief Note on Business Organisation of Indian Merchants in Russia in the 17th Century." *Journal of the Economic and Social History of the Orient* 29 (2): 205–212.

Guha, Ramachandra. 2007. *India after Gandhi: The History of the World's Largest Democracy*. New York: Harper Collins.

Gupta, B. K. 1962. *Siraj-ud-daullah and the East Asia Company 1756–1727: Background to the Foundation of British Empire in India*. Leiden, The Netherlands: E J Brill.

Kenoyer, Jonathan Mark. 1997. "Trade and Technology of the Indus Valley: New Insights from Harappa, Pakistan." *World Archaeology* 29 (2): 262–280.

Khanna, Vikramaditya. 2005. "A New View of the Economic History of Business Organizations: Evidence from Ancient India" (discussion paper no. 2005–2014, University of Michigan Law School Program in Law and Economics working paper no. 14).

2009. "Corporate Governance in India: Past, Present, and Future?" *Jindal Global Law Review* 1 (1): 171–195.

2015. "An Analysis of the Delays in the Indian Judicial System." Draft.

Kobayashi-Hillary, Mark. 2008. *Building a Future with BRICs: The Next Decade for Offshoring*. Berlin: Springer Verlag.

Kotwal, Ashok, et al. 2011. "Economic Liberalization and Indian Economic Growth: What's the Evidence?" *Journal of Economic Literature* 49 (4): 1152–1199.

Kramer, Andrew K. 2009. "Emerging Economies Meet in Russia." *The New York Times*, June 16. www.nytimes.com/2009/06/17/world/europe/17bric.html?_r=0.

Krishnan, Jayanth K. 2010. "Globetrotting Law Firms." *Georgetown Journal of Legal Ethics* 23 (1): 57–102.

Lawson, Phillip. 1993. *The East India Company: A History*. London: Longman.

Maddison, Angus. 2006. A *Millennial Perspective*. Organization for Economic Co-operation and Development, 261.

Mahalanobis, P. C. 1960. *Talks on Planning*. Calcutta: Indian Statistical Institute.

McCrindle, J. W. 1960. *Ancient India as Described by Megasthenes and Arrian* (revised ed. R. C. Majmudar). Calcutta: Chuckervertty, Chatterjee.

Mehta, Pratap Bhanu. 2007. "The Rise of Judicial Sovereignty." *Journal of Democracy* 18 (2): 70–83.

Mehra, Puja. 2015. "Foreign Law Firms Will Soon Carry Out Arbitration in India," *The Hindu*. June 30. www.m.thehindu.com/news/national/bci-agrees-to-centres-propsal-to-open-up-arbitration-legal-services-to-foreign-law-firms/article7368041.ece.

Ministry of External Affairs. 2014. Fourth BRICS Summit, Delhi Declaration, Ministry of External Affairs, India. www.mea.gov.in/mystart.php?id=190019162.

Ministry of Finance. 2011. *State of the Economy and Prospects, Economic Survey 2011–2012*. Ministry of Finance, Government of India.

Mukherjee, Mithi. 2010. *India in the Shadows of Empire: A Legal and Political History 1774–1950*. New Delhi: Oxford University Press.

Nayar, Baldev Raj. 1998. "Political Structure and India's Economic Reforms of 1990s." *Pacific Affairs* 71 (3): 335–358.

O'Neill, Paul. 2001. "Building Better Global Economic BRICs." *Goldman Sachs Economic Working Paper* 66. www.goldmansachs.com/our-thinking/archive/archive-pdfs/build-better-brics.pdf.

Paul, John J. 1991. *The Legal Profession in Colonial South India*. Bombay: Oxford University Press.

Prakash, Om. 2002. "Trade and Politics in Eighteenth-Century Bengal." In *The Eighteenth Century in India*. Edited by Semma Alavi. New Delhi: Oxford University Press.

Press Information Bureau, Government of India. 2009. *National Legal Mission to Reduce Average Pendency Time from 15 Years to 3 Years* (national litigation policy document). www.pib.nic.in/newsite/erelease.aspx?relid=62745.

Rankin, George C. 1946. *Background to Indian Law*. Cambridge, England: Cambridge University Press.

Ray, Rajat K. 1994. *Introduction to Entrepreneurship and Industry in India 1800–1947*. Oxford: Oxford University Press.

Raychoudhuri, Tapan, Irfan Habib, and Dharma Kumar, eds. 1982. *The Cambridge Economic History of India: c. 1200–c. 1750*. Cambridge, England: Cambridge University Press.

Raza, Moonis, ed. 1991. *Higher Education in India: Retrospect and Prospect*. New Delhi: Association of Indian Universities.

RSG Consulting. 2012. "India Report," www.rsg-india.com/reports.

2015. "India Report," www.rsg-india.com/reports.

Sathe, S. P. 2002. *Judicial Activism in India: Transgressing Borders and Enforcing Limits*. New Delhi: Oxford University Press.

Schmitthener, A. Samuel. 1968–1969. "A Sketch of the Development of the Legal Profession in India." *Law and Society Review* 3 (2/3): 337–382.

Scrafton, Luke. 1770. *Reflections on the Government of Indostan*. London: William Strahan ivn. for G. Kearsley and Thomas Cadell.

Sen, Amartya. 1981. *Poverty and Famines: An Essay on Entitlement and Deprivation*. New York: Oxford University Press.

Shahidullah, Shahid M. 2012. "Islamic Jurisprudence in Practice: Criminal Justice in Two Historical Empires." In *Comparative Criminal Justice Systems: Global and Local Perspectives*. Edited by Shahid Shahidullah. Burlington: Jones & Bartlett Learning.

Shankar, Shylashri, and Pratap Bhanu Mehta. 2008. "Courts and Socioeconomic Rights in India." In *Courting Social Justice: Judicial Enforcement of Social and Economic Rights in the Developing World*. Edited by Varun Gauri and Daniel M. Brinks. New York: Cambridge University Press.

Sharafi, Mitra. 2010. *Colonial Parsis and Law: A Cultural History. Government Research Fellowship Lectures 2009–2010*. Mumbai: K. R. Cama Oriental Institute.

2014. *Law and Identity in Colonial South Asia: Parsi Legal Culture, 1772–1947*. New York: Cambridge University Press.

Sturman, Rachel. 2012. *The Government of Social Life in India-Liberalism, Religious Laws and Women's Rights*. New York: Cambridge University Press.

Thaplyal, K. K. 1996. *Guilds in Ancient India: A Study of Guild Organization in Northern India and Western Deccan from c. 600 BC to c. 600 AD*. New Delhi: New Age International.

Tomlinson, B. R. 2003. *The Economy of Modern India 1860–1970*. Cambridge, England: Cambridge University Press.

Vyas, Maulik. 2013. "Slowdown, Competition from Smaller Players Force Law Firms to Offer Heavy Discounts." *ET Bureau*, October 29, 2013.
World Bank. 2011. *Multipolarity: The New Global Economy (Global Development Horizons)*. World Bank.
2012. *Global Economic Prospects: Uncertainties and Vulnerabilities*. World Bank.

SECTION II

THE GROWTH OF THE CORPORATE CORE

3

Mapping India's Corporate Law Firm Sector

Ashish Nanda, David B. Wilkins, and Bryon Fong

At the core of India's new corporate hemisphere is the emergence of a small but influential group of relatively large commercial law firms. A quarter century after liberalization, there are now more than 150 Indian firms that specialize in providing services to corporate clients, the largest of which employ several hundred lawyers and have multiple offices within India, and even some abroad (RSG Consulting 2015). In this chapter, we explore the rise of India's new corporate law firm sector and describe the challenges that these firms are likely to face as India actively considers the next phase of liberalization – the liberalization of the legal services market to allow the entry of foreign law firms, and the resulting integration of India's large law firms into the broader ecology of the global corporate legal services market.

In addressing these questions, we concentrate on five firms: Amarchand & Mangaldas & Suresh A. Shroff & Co., AZB & Partners, Khaitan & Co., Luthra & Luthra, and J. Sagar Associates (JSA). These firms, collectively dubbed the "Big 5" or India's "Magic Circle," have come to dominate the Indian corporate legal market in the quarter century since liberalization. As such, they constitute the most tangible manifestation of the Indian legal profession's attempt to capitalize on the country's global shift toward free markets and greater engagement with the world economy. Moreover, as we document below, all five firms have self-consciously sought to portray themselves as modern by adopting some – but, as we will also see, far from all – of the Cravathist and neo-Cravathist policies and practices of Anglo-American law firms. By examining each firm's history, structure, culture, and strategy, we can see how difficult it is to translate these Western practices to the Indian context and evaluate whether these dominant players have developed their own distinctly Indian approach to the production of corporate legal services.

To investigate these questions, and to understand how India's Big 5 are attempting to capitalize on, and respond to, the challenges of globalization, we call on four sources of data. First, the research team conducted formal, in-depth interviews in 2011–2012 with lawyers from four major India law firms: JSA, Khaitan & Co., Luthra & Luthra, and Nishith Desai Associates. These interviews were supplemented by numerous background interviews with lawyers from a broad range of Indian law firms, including Amarchand & Mangaldas & Suresh A. Shroff & Co., AZB & Partners, and Trilegal. Second, the chapter also draws on robust data provided by RSG Consulting, publisher of the RSG India Report, which is widely regarded as the world's leading rating service for Indian law firms. Since 2008, RSG Consulting has published a biannual comprehensive report on the Indian legal market, including rankings of the top forty firms.[1] RSG also provided background data – for instance, on the revenues of the Big 5 – specifically for this chapter. Third, the authors conducted a number of on- and off-the-record interviews with expert sources on the Indian legal market. Finally, the chapter draws on publically available sources of information, often from the Indian legal press.

In the remainder of this chapter we use this data to explore three questions. First, why were the Big 5 able to rise to prominence, surpassing – but, as we will see, not completely supplanting – a group of older British Raj commercial law firms that were arguably better positioned to take advantage of the new legal work that accompanied liberalization? Second, to what extent have these firms sought to adopt Cravathist and neo-Cravathist policies and practices of Anglo-American large law firms, and how successful have they been in translating these structures to the Indian context? Third, given their relative success over the past twenty-five years, what challenges are the Big 5 likely to face in the coming years, particularly from "second generation" Indian corporate law firms seeking to challenge their supremacy and by global law firms pushing to serve the Indian market? Finally, we conclude by offering some tentative thoughts about what the challenges of India's Big 5 law firms can teach us about the future of the Indian corporate legal market – a future that has become even more complex and uncertain in light of the recent fracturing of India's largest and most successful law firm, Amarchand Mangaldas, into two separate law firms run by brothers intent on asserting their dominance on the Indian corporate legal market – and beyond.

We begin, however, with the surprising failure of India's oldest and most respected law firms to capture the market opportunity presented by liberalization.

I. THE FAILURE OF INDIA'S MOST "ANGLICIZED" FIRMS TO ADAPT TO THE ANGLO-AMERICAN MODEL

As indicated in the Overview to this volume, there were important commercial law firms operating in India long before liberalization. Among the oldest were the British Raj legacy law firms, often established by British lawyers several years prior to India's independence in 1947 (Krishnan 2010). Two of the best-known firms in this category were Crawford Bayley & Co. (est. 1830), Little & Co. (est. 1856), and Mulla & Mulla (est. 1895). When India liberalized its economy in 1991, these three firms were without question the leading corporate law firms in India (Nath 2010). Yet in less than twenty years, these legendary giants had been clearly surpassed by the Big 5, several of which did not even exist before the turn of the new millennium. As we indicate in this chapter, notwithstanding the scant – and often dismissive – attention that these colonial-era firms receive in many descriptions of the contemporary Indian corporate legal market, British Raj firms continue to play a prominent role in certain areas. Nevertheless, it is surprising that they were not able to capitalize on the enormous advantages in reputation, client relationships, and global experience with which they entered the postliberalization period to maintain their leading position.

There are undoubtedly many reasons underlying the British Raj firms' failure to flourish in the years since liberalization. Key among them, however, was their failure to appreciate the need to transcend their traditional British roots to respond to a new "disruptive innovation" in the Indian legal market – a disruption, ironically, that had its roots in part in Britain's own transformation from an imperial economy to one based on the delivery of cutting-edge professional services in an increasingly globalized market. That innovation was the neo-Cravathist model of the large law firm, with its emphasis on transactional work, particularly in "new" fields such as mergers and acquisitions, project finance, and capital markets; a commitment to a professionalized ownership and management structure; and an active and agg ressive embrace of the market for both clients and talent.

As John Flood documents in Chapter 10 of this volume, following the "Big Bang" in which the United Kingdom liberalized its own financial services sector, Britain's Magic Circle firms – Allen & Overy, Clifford Chance, Freshfields, Linklaters, and Slaughter & May – embraced important aspects of this neo-Cravathist model as a means of competing with the US firms organized along these lines that were increasingly crossing the Atlantic. By the 1990s, both UK and US law firms organized along these neo-Cravathist lines were spreading this Anglo-American model around the world as they followed their clients into new markets in search of growth and profitability. India's British Raj firms were slow to pick up on these changes, instead choosing to cling to the gentlemanly understanding of law as a noble profession in which a handful of distinguished senior partners dispensed sage advice to their established Indian clients, with the aid of juniors who were seen but not heard, that had been the norm in the imperial era in which they were formed. In so doing, these firms left the door open for a new entrepreneurial group of Indian lawyers who were willing to embrace new forms of practice and managerial technologies of the new Cravath model – or at least to be seen as embracing them.

In particular, Crawford Bayley & Co., Little & Co., Mulla & Mulla, and other British Raj firms were slow to realize the implications of India's liberalized economy for law practice and that, in order to compete in this new environment, they had to abandon – or at least loosen – the common practice of concentrating ownership and decision making in the hands of a very small, unchanging, and autocratic elite who exerted an iron grip on the firm's management and profits. Thus, even though in the 1990s Crawford Bayley & Co. had approximately 100 lawyers, it was widely believed that equity was shared among only six partners (RSG Consulting 2008). A partner of one leading Indian law firm commented, "Between 1976 and 2001, Crawford Bayley & Co. did not introduce any new equity partners, and so it lost at least two generations of quality lawyers" (ibid., 51). According to RSG Consulting, by 2008 there had still been no new equity promotions, leading to a general perception that the firm was ossifying under the weight of its controlling elite: "There is no retirement age, and there is a perception amongst other firms that some of the senior partners who take home the biggest pay packets aren't pulling their weight (ibid.). That same year, RSG reported that the equity partnership at Mulla & Mulla was similarly concentrated in the hands of a few older partners. Even the firm's famed shipping, insurance, and transport practice – which traces its roots to Mulla & Mulla's representation of the East India Company – is kept vibrant through the efforts of a single dynamic partner (ibid., 106).

Given this structure, it is not surprising that British Raj–era firms had an increasingly hard time attracting and retaining top talent, even though, as we indicate in this chapter, the promise of "partnership" in many of the Big 5 Indian firms that began to challenge these established players following liberalization proved to be less attainable than many of those recruited into these firms were initially led to believe. Moreover, this talent deficit in turn made it more difficult for British Raj firms to keep up with the newly emerging areas of legal practice, such as mergers and acquisitions (M&A), initial public

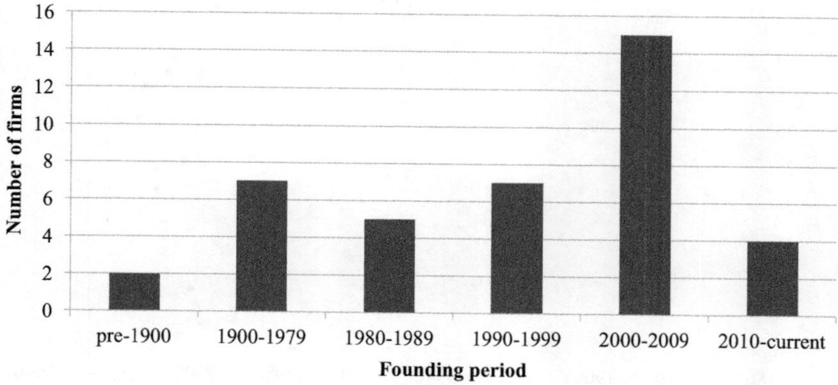

CHART 1 Top 40 Indian law firms by founding period

offerings, and project finance, that foreign multinationals and rising Indian corporates increasingly wanted from their Indian law firms. And the fact that these firms were not prominent in these "modern" practice areas reinforced their image as bastions of "tradition," further diminishing their attractiveness to both lawyers and clients in a world in which the rest of the Indian corporate legal profession was trying to portray itself (whether accurately or not) as embracing global standards of legal practice.

In short, India's British Raj firms fell victim to what the American business theorist Clayton Christensen calls in his influential book of the same name "the innovator's dilemma" (Christensen 1997). Like manufacturers of mainframe computers such as Digital Electronic Corporation and Wang Computers, British Raj firms continued to pursue a model of law practice that had been enormously successful for more than a century long after it had become clear that the alternative neo-Cravathist model being offered by a growing number of new entrants to the market was "disrupting" the traditional patterns by which commercial law firms in India competed for both clients and talent. As a lawyer who had worked at a British Raj firm for more than twenty years, becoming a full equity partner and one of the firm's leading rainmakers, confided when asked why he had nevertheless left to join one of India's Magic Circle firms: "I could no longer credibly tell either my clients or my best talent that this firm was the right platform for me to run my practice" (Interview with Mumbai lawyer, 2012).

Chart 1 documents the net effect of this disruptive transformation. Of RSG's top forty law firms in 2015, less than 20 percent (nine) were founded before 1980, with only two founded in the nineteenth century. Instead, the overwhelming majority of today's top firms – 65 percent – were founded between 1990 and

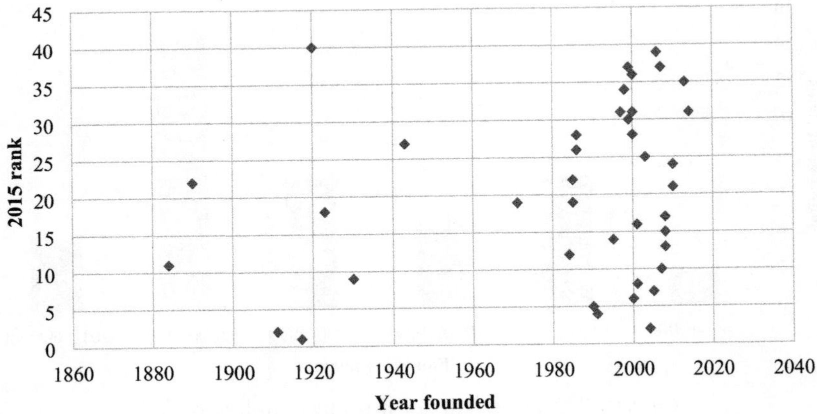

CHART 2 Top 40 Indian law firms by founding date

today. Significantly, of the twenty-six firms founded after 1990, 73 percent (nineteen) were begun in the new millennium. We return to the importance of this proliferation of top firms in Part III.

Finally, as chart 2 demonstrates, with the exception of Amarchand and Khaitan, which were founded in 1917 and 1911 respectively, none of the remaining seven firms founded before 1980 rank above ninth on RSG's 2015 list, with five of the seven faring no better than eighteenth. Clearly, the first-mover advantage that virtually all the British Raj firms had has not translated into lasting success.

Contrary to what many observers of the Indian legal market appear to believe, however, British Raj firms have not totally been displaced by the new Indian Magic Circle disrupters. To be sure, these firms are typically not represented in the top tier in terms of size or profitability. Indeed, by 2015, Crawford Bayley & Co., the most prestigious and successful of the British Raj firms in its heyday, had fallen completely out of RSG's rankings of the top forty Indian law firms (RSG Consulting 2015). Nor do the lawyers working for these firms tend to be represented in the top echelons of important practice areas, such as M&A. Nevertheless, British Raj firms continue to occupy an important niche in the market, particularly in areas where old-line connections and prestige remain salient.

For example, both Crawford Bayley & Co. and Mulla & Mulla continue to represent many important Indian companies in their real estate transactions, particularly when there are sensitive regulatory issues involved. These firms also have long-standing relationships with many of India's top Grand Advocates and high court judges. As Marc Galanter and Nick Robinson document in

Chapter 14, these relationships are extremely valuable given the difficulty that both Indian and multinational companies often have in securing the time – and more importantly the attention – of these critical actors in the Indian legal system. As one knowledgeable informant who worked for several years in a British Raj firm explained: "When the matter is really sensitive and the CEO needs someone he can really trust to navigate the bureaucracy or the courts, he is much more likely to call our firm than even the top Indian Magic Circle firm" (Interview with Mumbai lawyer, 2012). As we indicate in Part III, this kind of service might become even more important when the Indian legal market opens to foreign law firms.

Although British Raj firms are therefore still an important part of the Indian corporate legal services market, as Christensen's theory predicts, their willingness to retreat to an increasingly narrow – albeit important and high-value – form of legal practice opened the door for the firms who would become India's new Big 5. These firms promised to deploy their "new" model of legal practice to disrupt existing patterns of hierarchy, both internally within their firms and externally on behalf of their corporate clients. As we demonstrate in the next part, however, notwithstanding their success in achieving a market-leading position, each of the five leading Indian Magic Circle firms has been far less successful at disrupting the very traditional patterns of organization and control that precipitated the marginalization of the British Raj firms than their rhetoric would lead one to believe.

II. THE RISE OF INDIA'S BIG 5

As chart 3 demonstrates, by the beginning of 2015 five firms had come to dominate the Indian corporate legal market: Amarchand Mangaldas, AZB & Partners, Khaitan & Co., JSA, and Luthra & Luthra. These same five firms have consistently been ranked as the top firms in India in each of RSG's surveys, the first of which was completed in 2008. As chart 4 indicates, the Big 5 are significantly larger than other top Indian firms, boasting more than one hundred more lawyers than their nearest competitors. As we indicate here, these firms also have many of the primary attributes – multiple offices and practice areas, structured recruiting, promotion, compensation, and formal governance systems – traditionally associated with Anglo-American law firms organized on the Cravath model. As such, the success of these firms seems to suggest the triumph of the diffusion of this model in the Indian context. A closer examination of the history, structure, and practices of these institutions, however, demonstrates that the reality of the Indian corporate legal marketplace even for these top firms is more complex than this simple explanation would

Name	Founded	Rank 2015	Rank 2008	# lawyers 2015	# lawyers 2008	# partners 2015	# partners 2008
Amarchand Mangaldas	1917	1	1	655	300+	84	40
Khaitan & Co.	1911	2	5	354	190	81	28
AZB	2004	2	1	295	150	20	17
JSA	1991	4	3	337	150	79	27
Luthra & Luthra	1990	5	3	292	155	42	24
Trilegal	2000	6	5	172	95	23	7
S & R Associates	2005	7	18	53	20–25	8	4
Economic Laws Practice	2001	8	13	127	80*	25	9
Desai & Diwanji	1930	9	7	187	100	27	14
Talwar Thakore & Associates	2007	10	18	26	4	4	2
Wadia Ghandy & Co.	1884	11	13	153	100	34	12
Nishith Desai Associates	1984	12	7	82	80**	8	5
Platinum Partners	2008	13	NR	45	27 (2011)	9	5 (2011)
Kochhar & Co.	1995	14	NR	176	180 (2011)	36	20 (2011)

* Three economists, twenty accountants; ** Lawyers and professionals; *Source:* RSG Consulting

CHART 3 RSG Rankings of Top 15 Indian Law Firms

suggest. To examine these complexities, we explored each of these firms in greater depth along three dimensions: origins and clients, ownership structure and compensation, and growth and development. As the following sections reveal, there are important differences among the Big 5 on these dimensions, and among all of the Indian corporate firms and the neo-Cravathist model

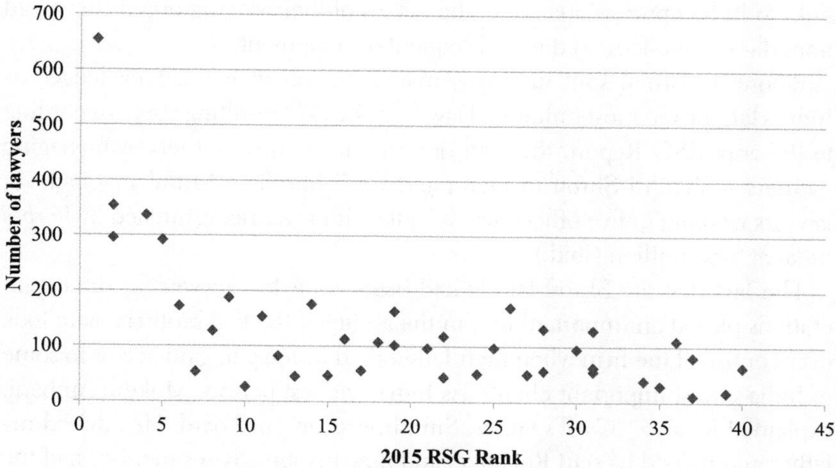

CHART 4 Number of lawyers by ranking

employed by the Anglo-American firms that these Indian corporate law firm leaders were trying to emulate.

A. *Origins and Clients*

Although the Big 5 now share the spotlight as part of India's Magic Circle, they came to this position from very different origins. As Reena SenGupta, the founder of RSG Consulting and an expert on the Indian legal market, notes, "It is quite a complex and layered story. Even when we are talking about the Big 5 firms, they are all quite different" (Interview with Reena SenGupta, 2015). Two of the five – Amarchand Mangaldas and Khaitan & Co. – can trace their roots back almost as far as British Raj firms, with founding dates of 1917 and 1911 respectively. In contrast, AZB & Partners (2004), JSA (1991), and Luthra & Luthra (1989) all were started about the time of liberalization.

This difference in pedigree, however, is less significant than these founding dates might lead one to believe. For instance, although AZB & Partners is the newest of the five, its founding partner, Zia Mody, is the daughter of India's famed Attorney General Soli Sorabjee. Similarly, Jyoti Sagar, the founder of JSA, is the nephew of Dr. Vidya Sagar, who is considered by many to have been the father of intellectual property law in India (Bar and Bench 2011b). Even Rajiv Luthra, the founder of Luthra & Luthra, practiced as a tax accountant in his father's firm before going to law school and opening his own law firm in 1989. Nevertheless, while all of the Big 5 have strong historical links to India's professional elite, the details of their varying origins have had important influences on their subsequent development.

Before its formal split in 2015, Amarchand was widely acknowledged as India's largest and most influential law firm (RSG Consulting 2015). According to the 2015 RSG Report, the firm, jointly run by two brothers as managing partners – Shardul Shroff in Delhi and Cyril Shroff in Mumbai – had 655 lawyers working in five offices across India with revenues estimated by *Forbes India* at $100 million (ibid.).

The fact that the Shroff family had been respected lawyers for three generations played an important role in the ability of the two brothers, who took over control of the firm when their father died in 1994, to gain access to some of India's most important clients. As India's richest person, Mukesh Ambani, explained in 2010, "Cyril's father, Suresh, was on our board. He advised my father and helped us start Reliance, and now his son advises me. I've had the good fortune of growing up with Cyril" (Nath 2010). K. V. Kamath, chairman of ICICI Bank, observed, "They grew and so did we. A whole lot of new institutions got built in this country in the 1990s, and Amarchand was there guiding us and holding our hand. Every new business we built we relied on them to provide us that stamp that this is what we could do, and how to do it" (ibid.). Reflecting the deep and sustained connection between Amarchand, the Shroff family, and the Gujarati business community, Amitabh Jhunjhunwala of Reliance ADAG – itself an Amarchand client founded by the Ambani family – whimsically notes, "You always get good, homemade *gujju* (Gujarati) food when you visit their office around lunch" (Gupta 2012).

The success of Khaitan & Co. can similarly be traced to its long history in Kolkata and its connections to the Marwari business community in that region. When Haigreve Khaitan took control of the family firm shortly after liberalization, he was able to build on the important connections that his uncle had forged with another Indian family business, the Aditya Birla Group. At the time, most prominent law firms operating in India rose in stature through their associations with British organizations. Pradip (Pinto) Kumar Khaitan, the current managing partner of the firm's Kolkata office, explained that this was not an option: "All the British firms used to go to British lawyers, so we ended up working for the Indian community. So it was not a thought process but a logical consequence" (Saluja 2012). As with the Shroff family's early connections to the Ambanis and other Gujarati industrialists, the Khaitan family's connection to the Aditya Birla Group and other Marwari businessmen would continue to play a critical role in the firm's development from a small but influential family firm in Kolkata to one of India's most important and fastest-growing national corporate firms with 354 lawyers in four offices in Bangalore,

Delhi, Mumbai, and Kolkata, and more than $50 million in revenues in 2015 (RSG Consulting 2015).

The origins of the three more recently founded firms have also played an important role in shaping their strategies in the postliberalization period. Zia Mody intended to follow in her father's footsteps and become a Grand Advocate and perhaps a public servant as well. Before doing so, however, her father encouraged her to study abroad at Cambridge University in England and then at Harvard Law School, where she received her LLM in 1979. This experience gave Mody the opportunity to work in Baker & McKenzie in New York City, where she learned firsthand about the Cravath model of the law firm and the corporate transactional work on which it is based.

When the Indian economy began to open up in the 1990s, Mody, who had returned to India to start a traditional advocate's practice, started getting calls from friends and colleagues from the United States and United Kingdom asking for her help. As she explained:

> After about ten years of wearing my band and gown every day, India started opening up to foreign investment, new policies and laws were being formulated, my friends and clients [from my time studying and working in the United States and United Kingdom] started referring foreign clients to me who wanted to invest into India. So, much to my father's dismay and eternal regret, I hung up my gown and switched to table practice.
>
> (*Legal Era* 2012)

Moreover, the kind of "table practice" Mody and the firm she anchors have specialized in also grows directly out of this formative experience. AZB & Partners is best known for its M&A practice, typically on behalf of non-Indian companies. Many of these clients came to the firm through contacts Mody formed during her time at Cambridge, Harvard, and Baker & McKenzie, or through relationships that flowed through these networks. In just over ten years, Mody has been able to parlay these connections into a firm of more than 295 lawyers with offices in Mumbai, Delhi, Bangalore, Pune, and Gurgaon, and even more importantly, one of the most profitable in India.

Jyoti Sagar's early experience with his uncle Dr. Vidya Sagar also played a critical role in shaping the firm that he would go on to found. Sagar spent almost two decades working as an associate in his uncle's firm. But when he finally asked his uncle whether he could become an equity partner, his uncle only offered him a 10 percent partnership interest in the firm – and only then on the condition that his nephew pay a buy-in equivalent to sixty times his annual salary. "I was stunned," Sagar recalled. "I would not work at all if I had that kind of money. Having given nineteen years to the firm in the hope of it being my home someday, I was disappointed that my uncle felt that I had not contributed sufficiently to the firm's goodwill and would need to buy in to the partnership" (Interview with Jyoti Sagar, 2011). Sagar decided to leave and found his own law firm with a different vision – one that has played a critical role in shaping the firm.

Dr. Vidya Sagar's parsimoniousness ended up enriching his nephew far beyond what he likely would have been able to achieve if he had stayed in traditional firm. When he was forced to leave in November 1991, the younger Sagar was able to capitalize on the opening of the Indian market. At his uncle's firm, Sagar's practice had predominantly involved noncontentious corporate and commercial work and IP. Many clients for whom he had worked transferred their files to the new firm of JSA upon its founding, including big-ticket clients such as Pepsi, Gillette, Reebok, Levi Strauss, and Orica, all of whom needed immediate help in obtaining approvals from the newly created Foreign Investment Promotion Board to do business in India. As these clients expanded their presence in India, Sagar and his firm grew with them, eventually expanding into areas such as telecommunications, infrastructure, project finance, and disputes. As of 2015, the firm has 337 lawyers in offices in Delhi, Mumbai, Bangalore, Chennai, Hyderabad, and Gurgaon and total revenues approaching $50 million in 2015 (RSG Consulting 2015).

Rajiv Luthra's timing was also fortuitous. During the 1980s Luthra had a fairly successful tax practice within his father's firm, with clients that included companies such as Rolls-Royce and Bank of America. However, disillusioned with the Indian tax system, Luthra commenced studying for a law degree at age 32. He joked that he chose a career in law "because the competition was low; in spite of how many lawyers there are in India, there are very few good ones, and I thought it would be a cakewalk to establish myself as a good lawyer quickly!" (Bar and Bench 2011a).

Upon graduation, Luthra set up a sole-proprietorship law firm in Delhi in 1989. Given his accounting background, Luthra decided to focus on corporate law, particularly in the power sector. At the time, corporate law firms were uncommon in India. "My initial strategy was to provide legal advice to international companies interested in investing in India," Luthra explained (ibid.). The novelty of this strategy would be acknowledged in 2008, when Luthra was presented the National Law Day Award in "recognition of his singular contribution to the practice of Corporate and Commercial Law in India and for being the country's earliest pioneer in International transaction lawyering" (Luthra & Luthra 2015). Luthra's accounting experience proved to be an asset to his career as a lawyer. "When we negotiate a power purchase agreement, we not only look at the pure legal issues, but we also analyze its implications for the

IRR [internal rate of return], profits, and other risk matrix," Luthra told Business Today in 2003 (Sahad 2003). And because the tax authorities were based in Delhi, Luthra began his firm close to the government officials who were creating the new laws and regulations that would govern these transactions.

Recently, the firm has been recognized as India's "law firm of the year" by several prestigious ranking services, including India Business Journal (2009), the International Financial Law Review (2010 and 2011), and Chambers Asia Pacific Awards (2012), particularly for work where government connections are at a premium. As with the other four, these roots have helped Luthra build one of India's top law firms, with 292 lawyers spread across offices in Delhi, Mumbai, Bangalore, and Hyderabad with revenues of close to $40 million in 2015 (RSG Consulting 2015).

B. *Ownership Structure, Governance, and Compensation*

The varying origins of the Big 5 have also had an important impact on their resulting ownership structure – one that each firm has trumpeted as a means of differentiating itself both from British Raj firms and from one another. Once again, however, these differences have proven less significant and more complex than these various claims would indicate.

The move from "family" or "founder" ownership structure, where a small group of owners control virtually all of the profits and decision making, to a "dispersed" and "professionalized" form of ownership and management is one of the key hallmarks of the Cravath model of the large law firm (Galanter and Palay 1991; Wald 2009). Although India's Big 5 all endorse this ideal in principle, their actual ability to implement this transition in practice has been fraught with difficulty.

1. From Promoters to Partnership?

Given their history stretching back to India's colonial roots, it is not surprising that in 1991 both Amarchand Mangaldas and Khaitan & Co. were 100 percent family-owned businesses controlled by the Shroff and Khaitan families respectively. Although both firms have continually expressed a desire to move toward a more dispersed and professionalized ownership structure, neither has been able to make this transition fully.

Amarchand's experience in dealing with this challenge has been the most extensive and – given the events – the least successful. As late as 1995 the firm remained 100 percent owned and controlled by the Shroff family. That year, renowned litigator M. P. Bharucha and his wife, corporate lawyer Alka

Bharucha, joined Amarchand's Mumbai office with the understanding that they would receive 10 percent of the firm's profits (Nath 2010). "It was the first time an outsider was joining what was essentially a family-run business," noted Bharucha in a 2008 interview (Vallikappen 2008). Although the experiment lasted for thirteen years, it ultimately proved unsuccessful. In 2008 the Bharuchas left Amarchand to start their own firm, taking nine associates with them. A few months later, another high-profile lawyer who had been promised an equity partnership left Amarchand to join Clifford Chance, allegedly because he was unhappy with the equity he was slated to receive (Nath 2010).

Partly in response to the departures, and partly with an eye toward future growth, from 2008 to 2010 Amarchand implemented "Project Moses." Under the plan, the Shroff family's equity decreased to 75 percent, and several nonfamily partners were granted equity stakes, increasing the total number of equity partners to seventeen. Project Moses was able to convince some partners that the Shroffs wanted them to build ownership stakes in Amarchand. Nevertheless, the perception remained that Amarchand was still a family firm.

But the Shroff brothers strongly rejected this characterization. Viewing themselves as entrepreneurs who provided vision, direction, and an appetite for risk similar to "what a Tata, Birla, or Ambani family does," the Shroffs argued that the firm was like "two wheels of a bicycle," with the "wheel" of family ownership providing the stability and continuity that clients sought and needed (ibid.).

Nevertheless, in 2010 the Shroffs commissioned another consultant, Boston Consulting Group (BCG), to help the firm set its strategy moving forward. In September 2011, BCG delivered its report, popularly known as Amarchand 3.0. One of BCG's key recommendations was to empower nonfamily partners and reduce the family's equity holding to around 40 percent by 2017 (Gupta 2012). In October 2011 the firm began implementing BCG's recommendations by promoting five associates to the firm's noncore equity pool on modified lockstep (Ganz 2011).

As with Project Moses, the firm's response appeared to calm the fears of some lawyers about the firm's family ownership. In 2012 an Indian financial newspaper spoke with five partners at AMSS who said that Amarchand 3.0 had given them a greater voice in decision making (Gupta 2012). Yet skeptics described Amarchand 3.0 as "new bottle, old wine" (Ganz 2012). In keeping with the plan's promise, between 2013 and 2015, Amarchand added fifteen partners – an increase of 22 percent of the overall partnership – putting them in the top fifteen firms for that period. Nevertheless, while the exact size of the family's share of the core equity pool was never fully disclosed, at the time of the firm's official dissolution in 2014, most knowledgeable observers believed that it was well more than 50 percent (Interview with Reena SenGupta, 2015).

Although Khaitan & Co.'s history as a family-run firm is similar to Amarchand's, it has tried to take a more direct approach to reducing the family's ownership interest. Like Amarchand, during the early years following liberalization, the Khaitan family gave small amounts of equity to various partners as a means of inducing star lawyers to join or remain with the firm. Yet even as the firm expanded beyond its original base in Kolkata, the family's influence continued to loom large. "Two of the most prominent partners in Delhi were from the family," Haigreve Khaitan noted (Interview with Haigreve Khaitan, 2013). "Delhi was not Kolkata, but it was still very much a Khaitan operation" (ibid.). For Haigreve Khaitan, real change came in 2001 with the opening of the Mumbai office. "That's when there was a conscious transition from a family to a professional law firm," he said (ibid). At that time, the family owned roughly 50 percent of the firm; by 2012, their ownership hovered closer to 20 percent. "There is no role for Khaitans besides that of partner," Haigreve Khaitan maintained (ibid). "We never had any rights in favor of family members making decisions for the firm." RSG's SenGupta agrees, explaining that,

> Even though Khaitan was once a family-dominated firm, its growth and explosion into the Big 5 has been because it has moved away from family in the higher echelons of power. The firm's current managing partner, Haigreve Khaitan, is a very flat, democratic leader who is trying to move the firm to becoming much more modern.
>
> (Interview with Reena SenGupta, 2015)

Nevertheless, the family's influence and heritage remain important. In 2011 the firm hired a branding consultant. One of the questions asked was whether the firm should keep the Khaitan name in its title. Ninety-nine percent of surveyed employees said it should. To celebrate Khaitan & Co.'s one-hundredth birthday in 2011, the firm hired a journalist to write a nearly four-hundred-page history of the firm, a large portion of which focused on the Khaitan family. Although he said he wanted the firm's success to continue regardless of his family's involvement, Haigreve stressed the importance of the family's history to firm culture, noting, "We couldn't be where we are today without our attitude of a family firm" (Interview with Haigreve Khaitan, 2013).

Although all three remaining firms in India's Magic Circle were not officially founded as family firms, each remains dominated by its founding partners. Thus, Zia Mody remains the dominant force behind AZB & Partners, along with her cofounders Bahram Vakil and Ajay Bahl. According to a 2008 report, the firm's equity partners were each assigned a percentage of the firm's total profit pool by the partnership deed, with a small group receiving a significant portion of the profits. According to competitors, the named partners, who brought in most of the business, were collectively entitled to a very large share of the equity. Mody, whose share was rumored to exceed over half of the total, was identified in 2006–2007 as a "prominent tax payer in India" (Robinson 2009).

The influence of AZB's founding partners over every aspect of the firm's management and operation has proven to be a key element in its success. Bharat Vasani, the general counsel of the Tata Group, India's largest business group, reflected:

> There are other very competent firms, but my management found that the response time with Zia was faster. In an M&A, where everything is predicated on timelines, time is of the essence. The determinant is her availability. It is like in a hospital – you feel most comforted when a senior doctor examines.
>
> (Dubey 2011)

Although there are reports that "AZB junior lawyers are getting accolades from international and Indian clients who are very happy to instruct them with Zia in a more supervisory role, in the last analysis all major sign-offs came from the managing partners, particularly Mody, whom several clients referred to as a 'one-woman tornado'" (Nath 2010). As Mody acknowledged, "What a client wants is to flash a piece of paper saying, 'This is Zia's opinion,' then I must write what I believe in" (Gupta 2012).

Rajiv Luthra occupies a similarly dominant position in the firm he began in 1989. "I believe strongly that a law firm is like a family," reflected Luthra, and "my role here is that of a 'benevolent dictator'" (Interview with Rajiv Luthra, 2011). As the firm grew and its ownership structure became more complex – at one time being comprised of separate partnerships for each of the firm's four offices – Luthra and his primary partner, Mohit Saraf, remained the largest shareholders in the firm. Although the firm had other equity partners – and others who in Saraf's words were "equity-like" in that their returns were linked to firm performance – in the end, Saraf made it clear that he and Luthra controlled the firm:

> Whereas law firms in the West tend to have lockstep or modified lockstep structures, in India the situation is different because certain partners have usually contributed much more than other partners would under a traditional

> lockstep. Unlike law firms in the West that usually have long histories, Luthra & Luthra was only established in the 1990s. Rajiv and I funded the entire offices, paid the salaries, and took on the entrepreneurial risk. Therefore, the equity model is different. That's the reason we're the largest shareholders.
>
> (Interview with Mohit Saraf, 2011)

Even the firm Jyoti Sagar founded because his uncle refused to share equity with him remained wholly owned and control by Jyoti Sagar until 1998. However, when Sagar expanded the firm from a sole proprietorship to a partnership of three that year, he did not want the new partners to have to buy in to the partnership the way his uncle had demanded of him. Instead, he established a structure in which Sagar continued to own the goodwill and the new partners began receiving a share of the profits at an agreed percentage.

In 2003, when Sagar brought in another group of partners, he again made clear that there would be no buying or selling of equity. "We didn't want any capital payments or valuations," explained Sagar (Interview with Jyoti Sagar, 2011). "Because our partners don't buy in to equity, they don't get paid out either. Instead, the value of the goodwill was invested in a trust. The trust is funded by the firm annually from firm profits, and beneficiaries of the trust are retired partners, heirs of deceased partners, and disabled partners." Equity levels were agreed to with the consent of the partnership. Two-thirds of the equity was shared between Sagar and Berjis Desai, whom Sagar brought in shortly after founding his firm. One-third was shared among the other nine partners.

But Sagar and Desai wanted to go even further in distancing themselves from the traditional Indian approach to familial control of law firms that forced Sagar to form his own law firm in the first place. Harkening back to the original Cravath model, Sagar instituted a formal antinepotism policy for Jyoti Sagar & Associates under which no two family members can work at the firm. Although, as indicated in the introduction to this section, such policies were once the hallmark of how Cravath-model firms in the United States distinguished themselves from their nineteenth-century competitors that were largely family businesses, these policies have been largely abandoned by their neo-Cravathist successors. This is particularly true with respect to spouses, as large numbers of female lawyers have entered US and UK law firms. At Sagar's firm, however, "the policy applies even when two associates marry," explains Dina Wadia, a partner at the firm. "One of them will need to leave the firm. That might seem extreme, but it comes out of a culture where sons or daughters who may be complete idiots automatically become part of a firm and are given an unfair advantage" (Interview with Dina Wadia, 2011). Sagar summarized the policy as "genius would matter and genes would not" (Interview with Jyoti Sagar, 2011).

These antinepotism rules had an important effect on recruiting. Venkatesh Prasad, who did not come from a legal family, recalled that the firm's reputation for having no family attachments and for being a merit-driven organization were key reasons for his decision to join as an associate in 2000. "The firm's culture is like a collegiate, professional family," Prasad said (Interview with Venkatesh Prasad, 2011). He was made an equity partner in 2009.

To ensure that this "collegiate" and "professional" culture remained vibrant, as part of their 2003 reforms, Sagar and Desai instituted an additional restriction that harkens back to the traditional Cravath model but has also been abandoned by many neo-Cravathist firms: mandatory retirement. Under the new policy, partners are required to retire from the firm at age 65 – with Sagar and Desai required to leave the firm even earlier, at age 60. This meant that Sagar agreed to retire in April 2013. This was unprecedented – indeed, no other firm in India has ever adopted such a policy. "People who found law firms in India don't usually leave," Wadia notes. "What Jyoti and Berjis are doing is laudable" (Interview with Dina Wadia, 2011). In anticipation of Sagar's and Desai's departures, in 2011 J. Sagar Associates formally rebranded itself as "JSA." Sagar commented at the time, "We are popularly known as JSA in the industry. So we want to move to this name so that we have a much broader platform and not be reliant on one or two individuals all the time" (Bar and Bench 2011a).

These reforms have had a significant effect on the firm's growth and profitability. From 2003 to 2012, Sagar and Desai ceded additional equity to incoming partners as the firm grew from eleven equity partners to twenty in 2012. By this time, Sagar and Desai collectively held only 13.5 percent of the firm's equity, with the next rung of partners holding just 0.75 percent less than the two founders (Mitra 2012). Desai noted that this equity structure means that "the firm belongs to everybody rather than any one body" (Ganz 2015). Sagar and Desai believed that the distribution of equity at JSA helped them attract star lateral partners from other firms, such as Chambers and Partners–ranked lawyers from AZB & Partners and Little & Co. Indeed, between 2008 and 2015, JSA added fifty-two new partners, an increase to the total partnership of more than 65 percent.

JSA also created a unique management structure in which most of the formal power was vested in a five-person executive committee – not the managing partner, which until recently was either Sagar himself or his close confidant Desai. Reflecting on the governance structure, Desai notes, "Excom functions like the [UN] Security Council, and the equity partners [are] like a General Assembly" (ibid.). In another twist, voting for new equity partners was done by secret ballot. As we document here, these decisions have helped protect JSA from the most extreme secession issues currently plaguing some of its Big 5 rivals.

2. Compensating "Partners"

Regardless of how much of the firm's total equity they were willing to distribute, the leaders of India's Big 5 also had to determine how they would compensate those lawyers who were deemed "partners" in the firm. Once again, firms looking to adopt what they considered to be the best global standards employed by Anglo-American firms faced a shifting and ambiguous target. Traditionally, Cravath-model firms were governed as true partnerships, in which all partners shared equally in the firm's profits and losses (through a lockstep compensation system) and were entitled to equal participation in the firm's decision making. As India's Big 5 were coming to prominence in the 1990s and early 2000s, however, this traditional governance and compensation model was changing significantly, particularly in the United States.

Although all US firms are still formally organized as partnerships, few of these institutions retain the egalitarian decision-making structure and lockstep compensation that formed the heart of the traditional partnership model of Cravath-model large law firms (Galanter and Palay 1991). Instead, with the exception of a handful of top-performing New York law firms (including Cravath itself), most US law firms are organized bureaucratically, with an increasing amount of decision-making authority concentrated in the hands of formal managers – many of whom are not lawyers – and employ an "eat what you kill" compensation system that rewards partners on the basis of their individual contribution to firm profits (Chambliss and Wilkins 2002; Regan 2004; Wilkins 2007; Chambliss 2009). UK firms – particularly those in the Magic Circle – however, have largely retained their commitment to lockstep partner compensation, albeit typically with various modifications such as "gates" or "bonuses" designed to reward (or punish) performance (Flood 2013). India's Big 5 have struggled with whether to adopt the US firm's more performance-driven compensation system or to emulate the more egalitarian framework used by UK firms – all while grappling with the implications of a move toward either policy on the dominant role that the current generation of founders (whether "family" or simply "promoters" in the style of India's promoter-led conglomerates like the Tatas and the Ambanis) continues to occupy in each of these organizations.

Luthra & Luthra's experience underscores the difficulty many of India's Big 5 firms have experienced with this issue. As indicated here, Luthra and his cofounder initially eschewed the idea of lockstep compensation in favor of a promoter-driven compensation model in which the founders controlled the lion's share of compensation and decision rights. However, in the mid-2000s Luthra & Luthra began considering expanding its equity and adopting a modified lockstep compensation model. "Management realized that if we want to retain people, there's a need for equity to be shared," said partner Nividita Tiwari (Interview with Nividita Tiwari, 2011). One managing associate emphasized, "Reform to the partnership structure is not so much about remuneration of partners, which I think would be on par with other law firms. It's the sense of ownership that is important" (Interview with Luthra & Luthra associate, 2011).

A London consultancy was initially engaged by Luthra & Luthra to advise the firm about different equity-structure options. "We had a town-hall-style meeting with all the partners and managing associates where the consultant explained how lockstep versus modified lockstep works, as well as issues such as tax implications," said Luthra (Interview with Rajiv Luthra, 2011). "We had extensive meetings to discuss the pros and cons of different models over three or four days," recalled Tiwari (Interview Nividita Tiwari, 2011). "This was followed by one-on-one meetings between each partner and the consultant to discuss any issues the partners had." Underscoring the control he retains over the firm, however, Luthra added: "The issue has been discussed extensively within the firm, but ultimately I decide" (Interview with Rajiv Luthra, 2011).

Reflecting the attempt to balance between the US and UK models, the firm elected to adopt a modified lockstep system in 2009 (Ganz 2009a). "There was a feeling that we should have a performance component rather than a system where people can reach a certain number of years of experience and then hang around and not bring in much revenue," said Tiwari (Nividita Tiwari, interview with the authors, 2011). "We want a system that promotes performance," explained Luthra (Interview with Rajiv Luthra, 2011).

Nevertheless, reflecting the complexity of grafting this hybrid system onto a promoter-led Indian law firm, implementing the modified lockstep system has proven to be far more difficult than formally adopting it. In July 2009, *Legally India* reported Saraf as saying that the modified lockstep system was "unlikely to be implemented before the end of the year as structural details of the conversion still needed to be worked out" (Ganz 2009b). By the beginning of 2012, the structure had still not been implemented. As a result, in March 2012, Luthra & Luthra engaged McKinsey to advise the firm on how to put the system in place by the middle of that year (Heine 2012). "We want to get this process right rather than have to change it later," explained Luthra (Interview with Rajiv Luthra, 2011). Saraf added, "I'm the partner responsible for coordinating the equity restructure, which is obviously a challenge in addition to my practice and other management responsibilities. That's why we're seeking input from consultants (Interview with Mohit Saraf, 2011). By 2015, however, Luthra & Luthra had still not announced that the new compensation system had been put in place.

Jyoti Sagar & Associates, on the other hand, has chosen to move more toward the US model but in doing so has experienced its own challenges. The partnership agreement that was approved in 2003 when Desai and his team joined JSA specified that the firm would engage in discussions to decide partnership remuneration. Mercer Consultants was hired to develop a system, which resulted in PROPEL (Performance, Reward, Partner Excellence, and Leadership) being introduced in 2005.

Under PROPEL, partners' salaries were based on an equity component and a performance component. Underscoring the firm's attempt to use the most modern practices, the performance component was initially determined using the Robert Kaplan balanced scorecard system, which assessed partners' performance with respect to internal, external, financial, and learning and development criteria – a system that at the time many Anglo-American law firms were discussing, but few actually employed. Not surprisingly given its novelty, the firm's decision to employ this standard attracted criticism from partners who were accustomed to a more traditional system for determining compensation. "We want to reward numerous behaviors other than billing, such as firm values, education, and marketing. But these soft factors can be hard to measure and complex," said equity partner Akshay Chudasama (Interview with Akshay Chudasama, 2013). "It can be a bit of a lottery in some respects" (ibid.). Moreover, as Sagar acknowledged, the results could be "different each year" (Interview with Jyoti Sagar, 2011).

In response to such criticism, the firm eventually abandoned this cutting-edge innovation and implemented a more traditional modified lockstep model in which each partner's compensation is set within one of four bands and remains fixed for three years. Although the basic elements of the system are therefore both traditional and stable, the firm did not wholly abandon its commitment to integrate more modern elements. Thus, while the largest factor in determining a partner's compensation, around 40–45 percent, is the revenue a partner and his or her team generates, there are additional points awarded based on how much the partner's firm-wide practice area contributes to the firm's overall bottom line. In addition, Desai reports, partners receive points for committee work, marketing, internal training, and a "subjective evaluation for what we call JSA values" (Ganz 2015). There is even "virtually a full 360" appraisal, which includes self – and peer – assessment and a determination by an elected compensation committee. By introducing these elements into the compensation formula, the firm is trying to capture the full range of a partner's contribution to the firm while at the same time reducing subjectivity, since, as Desai makes clear, "the more subjectivity you have, the more people are disgruntled, particularly in a setup like this where Jyoti and I both will not be there" (ibid.). As we discuss later in this chapter, Desai and Sagar were right to worry about how a subjective system might operate in the Indian context in the absence of the firm's founding partners at the helm.

C. *Growth and Development*

As with their US and UK counterparts, pressures surrounding partner compensation have only intensified as India's Big 5 have grown in both size and geographic scope, particularly as this growth has been through mergers and lateral hiring. In response each firm has developed modern forms of bureaucratic management and control, some of which exceed even those adopted by the Anglo-American firms that the Big 5 sought to emulate.

In the original Cravath model, firms were committed to "organic" growth through the promotion of associates who were hired directly out of law school and spent their entire careers at the firm. Cravath-model firms also embraced "nonprofessional" management in which leaders were selected from the ranks of existing partners for their legal skills, as opposed to their managerial ones, and formal bureaucratic structures were kept intentionally light (Wilkins 2015). As the size, scale, complexity, and competitiveness of large law firms in the United States, United Kingdom, and Western Europe increased dramatically in the later years of the twentieth century, these traditional practices became increasingly rare.

Law firms began to engage in extensive lateral hiring of associates and partners, with several firms sourcing the majority of their lawyers in this way (Henderson and Bierman 2009). Even more surprisingly, law firm mergers have become increasingly common, including a growing number of global combinations involving firms from different countries (Wilkins 2015). In addition, virtually all large Anglo-American law firms employ formal management structures, often administered by full-time managers, many of whom are not lawyers (ibid.). By the time India's newly emerging corporate elite looked to create "modern" Anglo-American corporate law firms in the years following liberalization, it was clear that "inorganic" growth and "bureaucratic management" were integral to running a successful law firm. Each of India's Big 5 has tried to adapt this neo-Cravathist paradigm to fit the Indian context, as well as to fit its culture and strategy.

1. Mergers and Acquisitions for Law Firms

AZB & Partners typifies India's Big 5's embrace of the neo-Cravathist paradigm of inorganic growth. In 2002, Zia Mody and Bahram Vakil, who, like Mody, was a second-generation lawyer, merged their practices (Gupta 2012). The firm grew through another merger with Akshay Chudasama's Lex Lude in 2002, after which the firm was named CZB & Partners.[2] Soon, the firm decided it needed a presence in Delhi. In April 2004, CZB & Partners merged with Delhi-based Ajay Bahl & Co. to form AZB & Partners.

When asked how she felt about growing through mergers, Mody told Bloomberg UTV:

> The main thing one has to deal with is synergizing the cultures. Most people are good lawyers, and most people are smart. The real issue is how do you get everybody locked into the DNA of the firm? . . . So it's not that it doesn't have its ups and downs, but I think at the end of the day, it's all about communication, communication, communication. There are certain things, which you just can't compromise on.
>
> (Bloomberg UTV 2011)

Like many of its Anglo-American counterparts, however, AZB & Partners found that achieving full integration is sometimes easier said than done. In July 2009, Anup S. Shah Law Firm, a Bangalore-based law firm known for its prominent real estate practice, and AZB & Partners decided to merge, with Shah being installed as head of the merged firm's Bangalore office. However, less than two years later, in December 2010, Anup S. Shah Law Firm and AZB & Partners announced a "realignment" of their partnership to take effect beginning January 2011 to "allow both AZB & Partners and Anup S. Shah Law Firm to leverage their brand equity in corporate/M&A and real estate segments in Bangalore." Although both sides characterized the breakup as friendly, the fact remains that the potential synergies that both sides believed would occur through the merger had failed to materialize.

Recognizing the difficulties of integrating separate firms – particularly in the Indian context where so many firms are either family or promoter driven – Khaitan & Co. has largely eschewed mergers when moving into new markets in favor of a more traditional strategy of organic growth, supplemented in recent years with a significant amount of lateral hiring and reinforced by centralized and professionalized management. In 1993, Rajiv Khaitan was tasked with establishing a firm office in Bangalore, dubbed after liberalization as the "Silicon Valley of India" because of its ability to attract top IT companies. Allowed the freedom of a fresh start, the office hired an advertising consultant and adopted a new logo and brochure. At the time, there was not much competition for law firms in the area – Amarchand Mangaldas was among the few to have a presence in Bangalore. Almost immediately, Khaitan & Co. received an assignment from foreign retailer Littlewoods, and it was not long before IT companies also came calling.

When in November 2001 Haigreve Khaitan moved to Mumbai with two other lawyers to start an office, he recognized the firm faced taller odds than it had in Bangalore. Haigreve recalled some of the challenges of starting an independent office there:

> There was a lot of hesitation about Mumbai. Unlike Bangalore at the time we started there, Mumbai had a very competitive legal market, and as a family firm from East India, there were fears about our ability to attract top talent. Would we still be considered a Kolkata firm? Would lateral recruits trust they could ascend the firm ladder without the Khaitan name?
>
> (Interview with Haigreve Khaitan, 2013)

Given these challenges, at first the firm looked into the possibility of a merger or an alliance with an existing Mumbai-based farm. But in the end, Haigreve believed that the risks of such a merger were too great and settled on trying to build from the ground up. The process was difficult, but eventually the firm began to impress with its work, and business and lateral recruits followed, beginning with the luring away of Ravi Kulkarni, who was the senior partner at Little & Co. when the firm was taken over by Fox Mandal in 2006. As SenGupta notes, when Kulkarni, a respected corporate lawyer with close ties with the Mahindra Group, joined Khaitan & Co., it was a "stamp of approval" for the firm's fledgling Mumbai operations (Interview with Reena SenGupta, 2015).

This trend toward lateral hiring has increased across all offices in recent years. Between April 2009 and April 2012, Khaitan & Co. increased the size of its partnership by 70 percent, from thirty-two to fifty-five partners. Eighteen of the twenty-three new partners were lateral hires, while only one Khaitan & Co. partner left the firm to join another during that period (Ganz and Shrivastava 2012). Although helping to increase the firm's presence and profitability, this wave of lateral hiring also created important issues of integration and coordination, particularly across offices. Borrowing a page from the neo-Cravathist practices of many of the Anglo-American firms with whom it was working,

Khaitan & Co. responded to these challenges by increasing its reliance on professionalized managers. Thus, beginning around 2005, the firm took pains to streamline communication across its four offices. It introduced national practice groups and common operating systems, aligned recruitment strategy and pay scales, and made sure that each office was complying with the same policies. It also introduced a firm-wide chief financial officer (CFO) and chief operating officer (COO). Finally, Khaitan & Co. ensured that its six-person management committee included two partners from Mumbai, two from Delhi, and one each from Bangalore and Kolkata, thereby not only giving every office a meaningful voice but also clearly signaling that it had grown beyond its Kolkata roots. As Haigreve noted, "There are some cultural differences across the offices, but whereas we used to feel like four distinct offices in four different locations, now we feel like one office across four locations. The look and feel of each office is similar, and we are motivated from the same principles" (Interview with Haigreve Khaitan, 2013).

Although modern managerial practices have therefore played an important role in the firm's success, a large part of the glue that has held the firm together through this period of rapid growth remains traditional: the family. Of the six members of the firm's management committee during this critical period, three were Khaitans.

2. Associate Hiring, Evaluation, and Promotion

In the traditional Cravath model, lawyers were hired directly out of law school, where they were expected to stay for six to ten years receiving training from senior lawyers on how to do the work of the firm's corporate clients. At the conclusion of this probationary period, the best of these lawyers were promoted to partnership in an up-or-out system in which those not promoted were asked to leave the firm – and, in all likelihood, the large law firm sector altogether, since Cravath-model firms hired virtually no lateral partners or associates (Wilkins 2015). As Anglo-American–style law firms have grown in both size and geographic scope, many have abandoned these traditional hiring and promotion practices. As indicated above, virtually all large law firms now hire associates and even partners "laterally" from other law firms (and, to a lesser extent, government agencies and in-house legal departments). Many have also abandoned their traditional up-or-out promotion policy, creating new categories of professionals such as "permanent associates" and "nonequity partners" (Wilkins and Gulati 1998; Henderson 2006).

Indian firms seeking to emulate the Anglo-American model during the period since 1991 have found themselves caught in this transformation. Many started out with an associate development model that resembled the traditional Cravath system. As Cyril Shroff reported about Amarchand:

> Associates evolve through three stages: as an associate, a senior associate, and then a principal associate. The initial phase of associate to senior associate takes about three or three-and-a-half years, a senior associate to a principal associate is a minimum of two years, and then from a principal associate to a nonequity partner would be a minimum of two years. It all adds up to seven-and-a-half years. In special cases it could be faster; in other cases it could be longer or could be never – moving from one stage to another.
>
> (Rainmaker 2011)

However, faced with the pressures of both rapid growth and increasing competition, some of the Big 5 have decided to further rationalize their hiring and promotion practice – rationalizations that in important ways go beyond even those typically employed by neo-Cravathist firms, particularly in the United States.

Khaitan & Co.'s system demonstrates how some Indian firms are creating a new Indian model of associate recruitment and development that hybridizes elements of traditional, neo-Cravathist, and novel Indian practices, often with the help of sophisticated management consultants. In 2009, Khaitan & Co. hired the consulting firm Hewitt Associates to perform an independent assessment of the firm's career progression structure. Given its history as a family firm and the evolving legal marketplace, Khaitan & Co. wanted to create and share with law school and lateral recruits a transparent and rewarding career path that would allow for only the best lawyers, regardless of their surname, to advance within the firm. Partners spent significant time with Hewitt consultants discussing long-term goals. "They asked us, 'Where do we want to go?'" Haigreve Khaitan recalled (Interview with Haigreve Khaitan, 2013). "We decided that while we wanted to grow, what was most important to us was quality. We wanted to stay selective with whom we hired and promoted" (ibid.). Doing so, however, was easier said than done – and gaining the respect of the marketplace, even harder. Nevertheless, the objective was clear.

To accomplish it, the firm ultimately decided on a five-tier system, each with clear benchmarks: associate, senior associate, principal associate, associate partner, and equity partner. In some respects the system harkened back to traditional Cravathist practices. For example, under the system an associate has eight years to make associate partner. If the associate exceeds that time frame, he or she will not be considered for partnership. Those who make associate partner are then expected to make equity partner within two years. Other aspects of the system, however, move beyond even neo-Cravathist models.

Prior to the reform, Khaitan & Co. had adopted the neo-Cravathist practice of paying associates a "performance bonus" based on such factors as the associate's formal evaluation or billings. As many firms who have employed similar practices have discovered, the result was that associates had the incentive to focus on their individual performance, sometimes at the expense of the performance of the team as a whole. Under the new system, bonuses were pegged to the performance of the associate's entire practice group, thereby encouraging collaboration. Although many neo-Cravathist Anglo-American firms talk about promoting teamwork, few have gone so far as pegging associate compensation to produce this result (Gardner 2015). As a result, this system for encouraging collaboration may constitute the kind of innovation that could have reverberations on the practices of large law firms outside of India. We return to this possibility in the Conclusion.

Khaitan & Co.'s approach to hiring displays a similarly hybridized approach. Borrowing from traditional Cravath-model practices, Khaitan & Co.'s plan commits the firm to hiring only top performers from the most prestigious Indian law schools. Unlike the traditional Cravath model – and even the contemporary practices of most neo-Cravathist firms, particularly in the United States – the firm does not simply rely on these traditional credentials. In addition, Khaitan & Co. also requires that all potential recruits take a battery of firm-administered technical and behavioral exams. Although a few UK firms also test their potential recruits, Khaitan & Co.'s extensive reliance on testing appears to go well beyond the norm in the vast majority of Anglo-American firms.

Not surprisingly, these changes in the way that Khaitan & Co. recruits, evaluates, and promotes its lawyers proved controversial to some within the firm. Faced with this new environment, a small number of lawyers left the firm. Haigreve Khaitan is adamant that although the departures were difficult, in the end it was a price worth paying. "We wanted to be honest," Haigreve recalled. "Our standards have become higher. We wanted to be firm and objective, and clear about our expectations from the beginning" (Interview with Haigreve Khaitan, 2013).

Looking to the future, Haigreve was adamant that family members would be held to the same standards as other lawyers. Referring to the members of the Khaitan family who were currently associates, the family's unquestioned current leader and the firm's managing partner stated adamantly that nothing was guaranteed. "They may not qualify for partner," Haigreve declared flatly (ibid.).

Of course, whether Khaitan & Co. – or for that matter, any of the Big 5 – can successfully keep to this promise and transition themselves from family- or promoter-driven organizations to true professional partnerships remains to be seen. Nor is this the only challenge these firms are likely to face by the end of India's third decade as a relatively open market economy. Both internal and external forces threaten to destabilize the delicate balance between the Cravathist and neo-Cravathist policies that the Big 5 thought they should pursue to become modern and professional law firms, and the traditional family and communal structures that the leaders of these organizations have, to a greater or lesser degree, attempted to graft on to the new corporate firms that they created. These challenges will only intensify as the Indian legal market further integrates into a global legal market that is itself being fundamentally transformed. Subsequent chapters will explore many of these challenges in depth. We therefore conclude by briefly highlighting three changes that are likely to be of particular relevance to the future of India's Big 5.

III. THE FUTURE OF INDIAN LAW FIRMS IN THE GLOBAL AGE OF MORE FOR LESS

Three related challenges loom large for India's large law firm sector: *succession*, and the transformation from family or promoter ownership and client relationships based largely on personal and/or communal ties; *domestic competition* from second-generation Indian corporate firms that claim to have moved beyond the Big 5's approach to ownership and control; and *foreign competition* from global firms seeking to serve the Indian market. All of these challenges are likely to be accentuated by the tremendous changes currently roiling the entire global legal services market.

A. *Succession*

Many law firms around the world are facing succession issues. This is particularly true in the United States, as the baby boomer and generation X lawyers who have been running these organizations are being asked to transition responsibility for their firms and particular clients to a new generation of lawyers whose views about work and family may be quite different from their own (Wilkins 2015). This issue, however, is likely to be particularly acute for India's Big 5, where this generational shift is also closely intertwined with the shift from family or promoter control to a more dispersed, democratic, and professional form of organization and control. The recent split of India's largest and most successful law firm underscores just how difficult it may be for Indian's Big 5 to manage this transition successfully.

On August 24, 2014, Bharati Shroff, the matriarch of the Shroff family that founded and still continues to run Amarchand Mangaldas Suresh A. Shroff & Co., passed away at age 82. Although she had not been active in the firm for many years, upon her death it was revealed that she was the largest single owner of equity in Amarchand, controlling 22.5 percent of the firm – 5.5 percentage points more than either of her sons, Shardul and Cyril (each of whom held 17 percent stake). Moreover, in her will Bharati Shroff left all of her equity in the firm, as well as all of her other assets – reported in total to constitute more than $100 million – to Shardul (Business Standard 2015).

Not surprisingly, Bharati Shroff's actions sent shockwaves through the family and through the Indian market. In addition to the personal ramifications, which were understandably severe – the two brothers ended up fighting over the division of the estate – the mother's action highlighted thinly veiled tensions between the brothers. For many years, the Mumbai and Delhi operations of the firm had been run as virtually separate practices, with Cyril holding de facto control over the Mumbai office and Shardul over the Delhi office. In bequeathing 22.5 percent of the firm to Shardul along with her other assets in her will, Bharati upset what had been an uneasy balance of power. Although the mother's attempt to give Shardul overwhelming control over the firm was ultimately set aside by a court per a Family Framework Agreement, under which her shares were divided equally between the two brothers (Shardul received all of the mother's other assets), by this point the fate of the firm was already sealed. Less than a year after their mother's death, the two brothers agreed to split the firm into two parts: Cyril Amarchand Mangaldas (CAM), consisting of the old firm's Mumbai, Bangalore, and Hyderabad offices; and Shardul Amarchand Mangaldas (SAM), formed from the firm's prior Delhi, Ahmedabad, and Kolkata offices. The two firms formally commenced operations in May 2015.

At the time this chapter is being written, it is too early to tell what will become of these two new firms – and whether either will ever achieve the prominence of the old firm, or its promise for the future. Two years before Bharati Shroff's death, Amarchand announced an ambitious plan to nearly double the number of its lawyers to one thousand and to have one hundred partners by 2017 (Lin 2012). The firm also planned to add new Indian offices and even hinted that it would likely expand overseas. After the breakup, however, CAM and SAM are more focused on building capacity in the domestic markets where each lost offices and market share to the other. For instance, CAM is keen on opening an office in Ahmedabad – the existing office in the city went to SAM – a city close to the family's Gujarati origins. And Cyril, for one, still hopes to build CAM into a thousand lawyer law firm by 2018.

Although the future of the two firms is uncertain, the breakup of Amarchand stands as a cautionary tale for the rest of the Big 5 about the difficulty of transitioning from a family- or founder-controlled firm to a professionally managed one – and how quickly and dramatically these issues can emerge. As late as 2012, both Cyril and Shardul believed that succession was not a pressing issue for the firm. As Cyril stated: "Shardul and I hopefully have a nice ten years to go at least, unless we suddenly drop dead, but except for that we are good to go for a long time. And by that time the firm will be something else." As the story containing this quote concluded: "Leadership, therefore, is likely to be a question that will become important only when the younger Shroffs come of age" (Ganz 2012). Clearly, both the Shroffs and many observers underestimated the inherent instability of creating "something else" out of a family-owned firm.

Nor are the other Big 5 firms immune from this risk. Although the control over equity and management held by the Shroff family was arguably more extensive than in any of the other firms, Khaitan & Co., AZB, and Luthra & Luthra all continue to be run by founding family members or promoters who exercise outsized control over the management and client base of their respective firms. Should one of these leading figures leave the firm for any reason, the ability of the organization to continue to thrive or even survive could be in significant jeopardy. RSG's SenGupta notes, "Luthra and AZB are what might be called 'ego-run firms,' in the sense of having a dominate founder who has found it difficult to delegate power in any meaningful way. You have this very top-heavy structure, where you have these dominant figures in Rajiv Luthra and Zia Mody, and underneath it you have a paucity of equally strong partners" (Interview with Reena SenGupta, 2015).

Indeed, even with their founders still present, a common complaint by clients levied against all of India's Big 5 is that they lack "bandwidth" beyond the considerable talents of their founders. As a general counsel of a leading company said of Amarchand before the split: "When I go to Amarchand, I ask for this lawyer on this project. It is very personality driven. And that's because I don't feel comfortable unless it is being supervised" (Nath 2010). According to the 2013 RSG India Report, some multinationals had even stopped using Amarchand because of lack of access to quality partners. In response, Amarchand ramped up its training and knowledge management programs, but the worry that the firm had failed to transition from the reputation of its top partners remained.

Nor was Amarchand alone in the perception of clients about this issue. According to media reports, AZB & Partners was built around one person: Zia Mody (Robinson 2009). For instance, she looked after several major client relationships, including Reliance Industries and Bharti Airtel. She was seen as the face of, and dominant force behind, AZB, which was commonly referred to as "Zia's firm" (Heine 2012). When asked what clients look to her for, Mody told Bloomberg UTV:

> I think that what they want from me at the end of the day is my judgment call. There are so many gray areas in today's world, and regulation is not black, it's not white. . . . They're looking to say, "Should I do it, Zia – how bad is it going to be for me – how will this look?"
>
> (Bloomberg UTV 2011)

Even though Mody no longer reads every word of each draft that leaves the firm, as she was reputed to do in the firm's early years, she still finds it difficult to let go, particularly "on strategic issues or crisis calls or closing some point when the deal is about to fall away, or when the client says, 'Look, I really want you to walk into that room because I think your presence is required'" (ibid.). Although clients appreciate Mody's skill and dedication – many calling her the single best lawyer in the Indian market – these same qualities have made it more difficult for other lawyers to develop. As a case in point, in 2014, Abhijit Joshi, then the CEO of the firm, left to start up a new law firm, Veritas Legal. Similarly, the defection of AZB's head of M&A and his chief deputy in September 2015 highlights the difficulty of retaining bandwidth in a firm with such a dominant founding partner.

Only Jyoti Sagar and his partner, Berjis Desai, appear to have properly anticipated these issues. Anticipating Sagar's retirement, in 2009 the firm put a succession plan in place under which Desai would succeed Sagar as "founding partner," and upon his retirement, the firm would elect a new leadership team. Much to the surprise of many observers in the Indian market, the firm has followed through on this plan. In 2013, Sagar retired and was replaced by Desai, who in turn announced his own retirement from leadership in 2015, leaving the firm completely in 2017. With the absence of both Sagar and Desai, the firm elected Mumbai-based partner Dina Wadia and Gurgaon-based Shivpriya Nanda as the first women to lead the firm, and its first comanaging partners.

Given the difficulty that Amarchand and other firms have had around this issue, Sagar and Desai are understandably proud of this transition. As Desai reflected:

> I am proud to say [when we] started in 2003, the combined equity percentage of Jyoti and me was 66%. When Jyoti retired, [our] combined equity was 13%. And today, my equity is only 6%. So, at least [with] this experiment, whatever it is, we have not followed the route of bankrolling ourselves to the grave but to play with this experiment. Some of our junior partners, depending on their

> assessment and evaluation, have earned and are earning more money than me. . . . I don't think at any other firm this would be accepted.
>
> (Ganz 2015)

Moreover, throughout this transition period, the firm has continued to thrive, even gaining in size and profitability on the other Big 5 firms. Thus, according to the RSG India Report, over the past two years JSA has been both the fastest-growing firm (adding ninety-seven new people – a 40 percent increase) as well as the firm that has added the most new partners (twenty-nine – a 50 percent increase). The report notes that "JSA [is] closing what has been a clear gap between the top two and the rest of the market" (RSG Consulting 2015, 15). Nevertheless, while SenGupta praises the firm's commitment to establishing a true professional firm, she cautions that it is too early to tell what the ultimate impact of the loss of the firm's two top founding partners will be:

> While too many Indian founding partners will prove to have left too late, the question is whether Jyoti Sagar and Berjis Desai may have left too early. His old firm is doing well today, but the challenges for tomorrow are going to be more than anything that the market has seen so far.
>
> (Interview with Reena SenGupta, 2015)

The fact that in their survey of general counsels Wilkins and Khanna find no mentions of JSA as being one of the top three law firms mentioned by Indian or multinational companies highlights that there is reason for the firm to worry about whether it has peaked too soon (see Chapter 4 of this volume). As the following two sections indicate, these worries are likely to only intensify as JSA and the other firms in the market face growing competition from both inside and outside the traditional Indian legal market.

B. *Second-Generation Indian Corporate Firms*

As chart 3 indicates, the Big 5 have dominated the Indian legal market for the past decade. Not surprisingly, this success has produced new competitors – competitors who have been spurred on by the failure of the Big 5 to fulfill their promise of creating fully modern and professional law firms. In Chapter 6 of this volume, Jayanth Krishnan and Patrick Thomas examine these firms in some detail. We therefore concentrate only on two, Nishith Desai Associates (NDA) and Trilegal, which exemplify the pitfalls and the promise of challenging the Big 5.

When we first began studying India's new corporate law firms in 2011, NDA was aggressively challenging the Big 5 for supremacy. With only six partners and seventy-one lawyers, it was less than one-third the size of the smallest of India's Magic Circle firms. However, the firm was a strong performer in its focus areas of tax, telecommunications, and intellectual property. It was the highest-performing firm in RSG India's 2011 Client Satisfaction survey and was ranked number eight among Indian law firms overall in that report. By 2015, RSG Consultants estimates that its gross revenues were $20 million (RSG Consulting 2015).

Established at the cusp of liberalization in 1990, from the outset NDA tried to establish itself as a new and different kind of firm, with an emphasis on cutting-edge technology and research. As Desai explained with pride, "Research and academics are part of the DNA of the firm. No other law firm in the world has its foundation in research and development" (Interview with Nishith Desai, 2012). Although Desai acknowledged that "some of our research won't bring tangible financial rewards," he staked his claim on this activity bringing attention to the firm, particularly among technology-focused clients and a new generation of top talent (ibid.).

For more than a decade, the strategy paid off. In 2000, NDA established an office in California's Silicon Valley to be close to US technology companies. In 2006, NDA became the first Indian law firm to establish an office in Singapore. In 2011 the firm was ranked as Indian Firm of the Year for Technology, Media and Telecom (TMT) by the *International Financial Law Review* and number one in TMT by Chambers and Partners. That same year, the firm was able to recruit Pratibha Jain, formerly the legal head of Goldman Sachs India and before that a lawyer with Sullivan & Cromwell and Skadden Arps Slate Meagher & Flom, to establish its Delhi office. As Jain explained, "The opportunity to undertake extensive research at NDA is exciting. When I was an academic, I missed legal practice, but in the past as a practitioner, I missed academia. NDA gives me a balance between academic work and legal practice" (Interview with Pratibha Jain, 2012).

Indeed, NDA was so committed to producing cutting-edge research that the firm planned to establish its own research center on 4.5 acres of land in the coastal region of Raigad. The center, which was being designed by an architect based in New York, was intended to include space for people within NDA and external visitors to conduct original research and generally engage in "blue sky thinking," as well as a meditation center and tennis courts. To get its lawyers and guests back and forth between Mumbai and the new facility, the firm even invested in a solar-powered boat designed in Germany. Asked why he was investing so heavily in developing the research center, Desai responded, "It enhances the firm's excitement quotient and happiness quotient" (Interview with Nishith Desai, 2012).

In the end, however, it was Desai who has been unhappy in the past few years – in part because of the unhappiness of some of the firm's top lawyers with the firm's ownership structure. Notwithstanding cutting-edge practices that went well beyond what even the most sophisticated Anglo-American firms were investing in research and technology, in one important respect NDA has remained a traditional Indian law firm. Despite the firm's egalitarian philosophy, Nishith Desai remains effectively the sole proprietor at NDA, with all other "partners" having very small ownership stakes, and even less power. This fact, combined with the difficulty of funding real R&D from a traditional law firm model – particularly in the midst of a slowing economy – has taken its toll on the NDA model. Although the firm continues to be praised for innovation – winning RSG's *Financial Times* award for Innovative Law Firm of the Year in 2014 and 2015 – NDA has failed to keep pace with the Big 5 in terms of revenue and profitability. As of 2015, the firm had dropped out of RSG India's list of the top ten leading Indian firms.

Trilegal, although less innovative, has done a better job of incorporating neo-Cravathist policies to produce a more credible promise of improving on the traditional Indian model of family and promoter control. Trilegal was founded in 2000 by a group of graduates from the National Law School of India – Bangalore. Initially, the founders established three offices – Bangalore in 1998, Delhi in 1999, and Mumbai in 2000 – which functioned independently. After a few years, however, the partners agreed to merge the three offices into one, adopting the name Trilegal – a name emblematic of the firm's aspiration to break away from the family- and promoter-driven models of the Big 5.

Trilegal has worked hard to distinguish itself from India's Big 5 and other family- and promoter-driven firms. Anand Prasad, one of the four cofounders of the firm, repeatedly has made clear that his main purpose in setting up the firm is to break the glass ceiling of family firms, establishing an organization that solely considers a lawyer's merit. That goal is reflected in Trilegal's structures. For example, according to *Legal India*, the firm has no "managing partner" (Legal India 2016). Rather, the firm is managed via committees, whose members are selected via election. Each committee is appointed for a different task in order to ensure that all the partners actively contribute in the working of the firm. A coordination committee supervises all the committees.

In addition to its governance structures, Trilegal is one of only two firms with a pure lockstep model in India – a structure that the firm borrowed from UK Magic Circle firm Allen & Overy. In this system, new partners start at 10 points and are awarded 2.5 points per year for thirteen years until they reach a maximum of 40 points – the same amount as each of the firm's founding partners, who are "plateaued" at that level. Finally, to ensure a smooth transition when the original partners step down, the firm worked with a foreign consultant to devise a succession plan designed to ensure that the next generation will be able to take over the firm successfully.

The results have been impressive. In 2015, Trilegal was India's sixth largest firm, with 172 lawyers, 23 of whom are equity partners, spread over four offices in Delhi, Mumbai, Bangalore, and Hyderabad (RSG Consulting 2015). The firm currently does about 60 percent of its business with foreign companies, including global juggernauts such as Heineken, Microsoft, Mitsubishi, Vodafone, and BP. The 2015 RSG India Report notes, "The firm was once seen as firmly entrenched in the second tier, but many now see it as a top-tier firm, alongside JSA, Khaitan, and Luthra & Luthra" (ibid., 189). For the first year ever, more clients named Trilegal as a "top tier" than a "second tier" law firm. The report continues, "Clients also commented on the firm's structure, which visibly sets them apart from more traditional and family-dominated law firms. They are seen as part of a wave of new, more modern firms, which has started to disrupt the established market" (ibid., 189). Indeed, apart from Khaitan & Co., Trilegal was mentioned by clients as the most improved law firm in the report.

Of course, whether Trilegal can maintain its newfound status – particularly after the founding partners do turn over the reins to the next generation – remains to be seen. In the eyes of many, the firm has already demonstrated how hard it is to make this transition when it failed to promote – or more accurately, refused to accelerate the promotion of – three talented junior lawyers who promptly left the firm to set up Phoenix Partners, which in just a few short years has already established itself as a rising star in the market. In trying to maintain, and perhaps even improve, on its leading position in the coming years, however, Trilegal has one notable advantage over many of its Big 5 rivals: the firm worked closely and successfully with Allen & Overy for many years. Although the two firms ended their formal strategic alliance in 2012, the knowledge the firm acquired over the years as a result of its close connection with a top-tier UK law firm may prove to be very valuable as India finally liberalizes the market for legal services.

C. *Preparing for Liberalization – and Protecting Against it*

Ever since the Indian economy liberalized in 1991, there has been an intense debate both inside and outside of the country about whether the market for legal services should follow suit by allowing the entry of foreign law firms. Subsequent chapters explore this debate directly, along with the resulting strategies pursued by foreign firms, particularly the UK Magic Circle firms, to serve the Indian market from afar. As these chapters underscore, although the standard prediction that the Indian legal market will open "in two years" has now been repeated for more than a decade, recent actions by the Modi government appear to signal that this long-awaited opening may in fact take place soon, beginning with allowing foreign law firms to participate in international arbitration in India.

In the meantime, however, some Indian law firms have tried to prepare for what they believe to be the inevitable opening of the market by forging alliances – often dubbed "best friends" arrangements – with foreign law firms. UK Magic Circle firms, who have long had designs to reenter the legal market of the former jewel in the British crown, have been particularly interested in such arrangements. Indeed, UK Magic Circle firm Linklaters was so anxious to establish a toehold in the Indian market that in 2006 it engineered the creation of a new firm by encouraging Suresh Talwar, a senior partner at Crawford Bayley & Co., and Shobhan Thakore from AZB & Partners to create a new firm called Talwar Thakore & Associates, with whom Linklaters would enter into a nonexclusive referral agreement.

Two years later Trilegal entered into a similar nonexclusive referral agreement with Allen & Overy, another of the UK Magic Circle firms eager to participate in the Indian market. One of Trilegal's founding partners later described the circumstances that convinced the firm to enter into the relationship:

> In 2007 it sounded as if the Indian legal market would open up in the next few months. A host of international firms started moving in and looking at Indian firms for tie-ups. There were a few that spoke with us. We took a view that, as an establishment, we would be better off if we teamed up with an international firm.
>
> (Interview with Venkatesh Prasad, 2011)

One year later, the trend toward tie-ups between Indian and Magic Circle firms reached the Big 5 when AZB & Partners announced that it was entering into a "best friends" relationship with the UK Magic Circle firm Clifford Chance. Clifford Chance partner Rahul Guptan explained why the firm found the deal so appealing:

> We thought, compared to our competitors who got smaller firms, that we got a full-service firm with a pan-India presence. This is exactly how we would have liked our office to be. AZB is professionally managed and is well known in the market. AZB ticked all the boxes, and we probably did the same for them.
>
> (Interview with Rahul Guptan, 2011)

The AZB–Clifford Chance friendship, however, proved to be short-lived. In January 2011 the firms announced that the relationship had ended. Guptan explained:

> The agreement ended in the backdrop of the financial crisis. We had entered into the agreement expecting there to be a two- to three-year horizon when deregulation would take place, but that did not happen. . . . We realized we may have been a bit premature in doing this.
>
> (ibid.)

The failure of the Indian legal market to open up as predicted has undoubtedly also undermined the potential of the Linklaters–Talwar Thakore and Allen & Overy–Trilegal alliances, although the former alliance is still functioning. Nevertheless, these alliances highlight four trends that have the potential to further destabilize the dominance of India's Big 5, particularly if the Modi government follows through on its promise to allow foreign firms at least partial entry into the Indian market.

First and most obviously, these alliances have given Linklaters, Allen & Overy, and to a lesser extent Clifford Chance an important head start in establishing their position with Indian clients for when the market finally opens up. As a Trilegal senior partner admitted, the agreement augmented Allen & Overy's ability to present itself to clients as an integrated full-service setup in relation to India-related work and has consequently made Allen & Overy "as near local as it can be under the current legal structure" (Interview with Venkatesh Prasad, 2011).

Second, these arrangements reinforce the argument by second-generation firms like Talwar Thakore and Trilegal that they have broken free from the family- and promoter-driven structure that continues to dominate India's Big 5 and therefore are a more modern alternative for both clients and talent – a perception that reinforces the argument for further liberalization of the Indian legal market. As Sandeep Katwala, regional managing partner for Europe, Middle East, and Africa and national head of the India group at Linklaters, stated in explaining why Linklaters' tie-up with Talwar Thakore was even better than Allen & Ovary's arrangement with Trilegal:

> By tying up with an existing firm, you are accepting the level of quality within the firm. TTA was set up from scratch. It is a meritocratic partnership without any founder or family equity. What we aspire to do in conjunction with TTA is try to mirror the model that operates at Linklaters. We are trying to achieve a certain quality of offering and what we think makes that happen is a certain model. So they've borrowed from us in terms of how they're setting themselves up.
>
> (Interview with Sandeep Katwala, 2011)

Katwala's last point reinforces a third benefit from "best friends" arrangements – even when temporary – that has wider implications for the Indian legal services market: knowledge transfer between the UK and Indian partners. One of Trilegal's senior partners underscores the many new systems and practices that Allen & Overy has helped the firm install:

> Allen & Overy helped improve our IT and email systems. They assisted us with HR processes. They have been very active in their support and have people in their London office who are instructed to work with Trilegal advising us. We are currently working with Allen & Overy to put together a knowledge management system with training conducted by Trilegal and vice versa. Allen & Overy assisted us in devising our performance evaluations. We didn't have any HR personnel at that time and sought advice from Allen & Overy about issues such as how to reconcile differences between staff and remuneration. Before these processes were established with Allen & Overy, it felt like the founding partners were always "fighting fires" to handle HR and other issues in addition to building the practice.
>
> (Interview with Venkatesh Prasad, 2011)

Finally, these "best friends" arrangements have brought more than just knowledge into the Indian market. They have also brought people – particularly previously nonresident Indians (or NRIs, as they are popularly called) who have decided to return home after many years of practice abroad. Thus, when Talwar Thakore started operations in January 2007, Feroz Dubash joined the firm after spending eight years at Linklaters. In November 2009, TTA hired two partners, including Thakore's son, and two managing associates from Linklaters. Similarly, on August 31, 2009, Allen & Overy announced that Srinivas Parthasarathy, a capital markets partner, would relocate from Allen & Overy's Singapore office to Trilegal's Mumbai office. These and other returning Indians with their extensive engagement with the more professionalized and at least formally meritocratic norms of neo-Cravathist Ango-American law firms are likely to be less willing to accept the traditional patterns of family and promoter control that continue to typify India's Big 5 law firms.

D. *Segmentation, Elimination, or Glocalization?*

The Indian corporate law firm market has matured considerably in the quarter century since the country's global shift in 1991. The question remains whether this sector will see even more volatility in the next quarter century – and if so, whether the result will be even further segmentation and differentiation among the country's top corporate law firms, or whether we will see a growing homogenization as Indian law firms are absorbed, whether literally or figuratively, into broader global neo-Cravathist networks. Or, alternatively, will the parts of the hybridized model that currently characterizes India's Big 5 not only survive but expand as India moves from being an "inbound" to an "outbound" economy? Although it is certainly too early to predict which of these futures is the most likely, our research does provide some clues about what those with an interest in these questions should be watching for as they seek to chart the course that this important sector is likely to follow in this increasingly important country.

As indicated earlier in this chapter, the Big 5 has already become either a "Big 6" or a "Big 4" depending upon what happens with the two parts of the old Amarchand firm. SenGupta predicts that both will become top firms – and that Trilegal may join them as well. "Assuming that the market remains closed, in the next five years, I think that the Big 5 will probably be a Big 6 or 7. I think Trilegal will move into the top bracket, along with both Shardul Amarchand (SAM) and Cyril Amarchand (CAM)" (Interview with Reena SenGupta, 2015). But SenGupta also predicts that the distance between the Big 7 and other leading Indian firms might be closing. "I also think that the work will start getting spread around a bit more," she speculates, "so the second tier will look a lot stronger" (ibid).

Whether this is likely to occur, however, will depend upon how successful the Big 6 or 7 are at retaining their talent. As chart 3 indicates, and as Chapter 6 on "peel off" firms confirms, many of the firms in India's second tier have been started since 2000 by top partners who have left the Big 5 – many of whom have self-consciously set up organizations with names like Economics Law Practice and Platinum Partners that are designed to distance themselves from the family- or promoter-driven model still used by all of the Big 5. If this trend continues, it could not only strengthen these new entrants but also weaken – and perhaps even destroy – some of the firms at the top. SenGupta sees this as a possibility,

> I think in ten years, some of the names that we currently have won't be in the top tier anymore. Just as Amarchand could split in two, other firms could implode overnight and second-tier firms could merge and become serious contenders. The problem with all the Indian firms is, until they have a proper institutional foundation, the danger of dissolution is always there. That's why it is so interesting that someone like Akshay Chudasama moved. He could potentially have been the next managing partner of JSA and had been on the Executive Committee. But he chose to go to SAM. So you have these really counterintuitive moves, where senior players could just go for whatever reason – ambition or sheer founder fatigue. The Indian market is very fluid. (ibid.)

Indeed, ironically it could be that the two (now three) original family-run law firms – CAM, SAM, and Khaitan & Co. – could end up separating themselves from the rest of the other top firms to form a new and smaller elite tier. As chart 3 underscores, this was precisely what seemed to be happening between 2008 and 2015, with Amarchand and Khaitan & Co. growing at a much faster pace than the remainder of the Big 5. Although the Amarchand split problematizes its future, it is entirely possible that both parts of the firm could emerge even stronger than before, embracing the kind of commitment to modernization that has helped Khaitan & Co. move from fifth to second place in RSG's rankings.

To be sure, all three firms are likely to retain an important degree of family control. But this structure may in the end turn out to be well suited to the Indian market, where most important Indian businesses have a similar structure, and where a strong deference to seniority and authority, and deep bonds of communal affiliation and loyalty, remain an important part of the culture. By way of analogy, in the United States since 2008, the top fifteen to twenty firms on the *American Lawyer* profit-per-partner index have been moving steadily away from even the next twenty firms, let alone the average for the top hundred (American Lawyer 2015). Moreover, almost all of those in the top tier are firms based primarily – if not exclusively – in New York City with norms and practices that are much closer to the traditional Cravath model than the neo-Cravathist practices that have become so widespread in the US corporate legal market. It is possible that this form of segmentation, based on the fit between an established organizational form and the needs of particular clients, will come to define the Indian corporate legal market as well.

Of course, whether this "glocal" Indian hybridization of the neo-Cravathist model survives and prospers will depend in part whether – and to what extent – India liberalizes its market for legal services. "If that happens," SenGupta posits, "it will turn the market upside down" (Interview with Reena SenGupta, 2015). As indicated in Chapter 11 of this volume, some form of liberalization is likely in the next few years. As SenGupta puts it, "I think liberalization is more likely to happen under Modi than anyone else, and the consequences are likely to depend upon how 'liberalized' the market is allowed to become, and how both global firms and India's Big 5 respond to this opening" (ibid.).

It is possible that the future for India's Big 5 could be bleak. SenGupta hypothesizes:

> The parallel I would draw would be the German market, when the British firms started to go in. Within about two years, out of the top firms, only Hengeler Mueller retained its independent status and brand name. Out of

> the remaining top firms, three merged with UK firms, with two losing their names and identities altogether. More than likely, given where the firms are now, that could easily happen in India as well.
>
> (ibid.)

Even if this were to occur, however, it is doubtful that the global firms would be interested in taking over – or able to take over – the entire Indian corporate legal market. Given the complexity and interconnectedness of the Indian economic, political, and social structure, there will likely always be a place for local knowledge and expertise. Paradoxically, the British Raj–era firms with their deep connections to India's traditional hierarchies might actually be seen as more valuable in this new reality than the Big 5 firms, whose primary business has typically been handling the Indian law aspects of transactions for foreign clients that these companies trusted global advisors would now be able to handle on their own. Again, by way of analogy, this is why Marc Galanter and Nick Robinson say (Chapter 14, this volume) that India's Grand Advocates have been the group that has arguably profited the most from the country's liberalization to date.

Moreover, it is also possible that global firms will be less interested in establishing a direct presence in India than many Indian law firms currently fear, particularly if they continue to be barred from practicing Indian law. Thus, even though foreign firms are able to set up offices in Brazil to practice their "home country law," relatively few have chosen to do so, and the top Brazilian firms continue to dominate the local legal market (Cunha et al. forthcoming).

Finally, the German experience cited by SenGupta also highlights one other possible future for the top firms in India's corporate legal market. As SenGupta rightly states, many of the leading German corporate law firms were swallowed up by Anglo-American global firms after Germany liberalized its legal market. But the lone prominent survivor, Hengeler Mueller, has not just survived as an important German firm but thrived by pioneering a new global model based on an alliance of top independent firms around the world. Interestingly Amarchand – and now both CAM and SAM – are a part of this alliance, the goal of which is to create a hybridized and glocalized model that combines the best global practices from the Anglo-American model with the innovation and dynamism being developed by law firms in emerging markets. As economic power shifts to these markets, we are already beginning to see firms based in these rising powers following their clients into new markets, particularly in Asia-Pacific and Africa. Indeed, before the split, Amarchand was rumored to be considering opening an office in Singapore, and perhaps elsewhere in Asia as well. As Africa, with its large Indian diaspora, becomes more important, it is possible that Indian firms will go there as well. The global expansion of the Chinese law firm King & Wood into Australia and Europe represents another possible future for at least some Indian law firms.

Once again, which of these futures will come to pass will depend on a wide range of factors both within and outside of India. Given the current size of the Indian economy and the country's growing importance in the world, however, what does seem clear is that the contest between India's current Magic Circle firms and those seeking to displace them – whether from within India or from outside the country – will only grow more intense over the coming years.

Notes

1 The 2015 RSG India Report and rankings consisted of fieldwork, phone interviews, and survey data collected between December 2014 and April 2015. According to RSG, this included client satisfaction reviews from 514 clients of Indian law firms, 50 phone interviews with a control group of legal purchasers, analysis of 167 India law firms, submissions from 80 law firms, interviews with 27 Indian managing partners, on-the-ground research with firms and clients, interviews with foreign law firm India practice heads, and analysis of published deals databases and tables. More information on the 2015 Report as well as all previous reports can be found on the RSG India website: www.rsg-india.com.

2 In 2005, Chudasama left the firm to join J. Sagar Associates (JSA).

References

American Lawyer. 2015. "The 2015 Am Law 100: Rich and Richer." *American Lawyer*, April 27. www.americanlawyer.com/id=1202489912232/The-2015-Am-Law-100-Rich-and-Richer.

Bar and Bench. 2010. "20 Years of JSA: Conversation with Jyoti Sagar, Founder Partner J. Sagar Associates." *Bar and Bench*, December 13. www.barandbench.com/20-years-jsa-conversation-jyoti-sagar-founder-partner-j-sagar-associates/.

2011a. "Conversation with Luthra & Luthra Law Offices Managing Partner, Rajiv K. Luthra." *Bar and Bench*, January 17. www.barandbench.com/conversation-luthra-amp-luthra-law-offices-managing-partner-rajiv-k-luthra/.

2011b. "Founder of Remfry & Sagar Dr. Vidya Sagar Passes Away." *Bar and Bench*, March 3. www.barandbench.com/founder-remfry-amp-sagar-dr-vidya-sagar-passes-away/.

2011c. "Rebranding of Indian Law Firms; JSA Is the New Entrant." *Bar and Bench*, September 23. www.barandbench.com/rebranding-indian-law-firms-jsa-new-entrant/.

Bloomberg UTV. 2011. "Interview with Zia Mody – Pathbreakers." www.wn.com/The_Date__Pathbreakers_In_coversation_with_corporate_attorney_Zia_Mody.

Business Standard. 2015. "Amarchand Mangaldas Split Is Now Official." *Business Standard*, May 7. www.business-standard.com/article/companies/amarchand-mangaldas-split-is-now-official-115050600702_1.html.

Chambliss, Elizabeth. 2009. "New Sources of Managerial Authority in Large Law Firms." *Georgetown Journal of Legal Ethics* 22 (1): 63–95.

Chambliss, Elizabeth and David B. Wilkins. 2002. "Promoting Effective Ethical Infrastructure in Large Law Firms: A Call for Research and Reporting." *Hofstra Law Review* 30 (3): 691–716.

Christensen, Clayton. 1997. *The Innovator's Dilemma: When New Technologies Cause Great Firms to Fail*. Cambridge: Harvard University Press.

Cunha, Luciana Gross, Daniela Monteiro Gabbay, José Garcez Ghirardi, David M. Trubek, & David B. Wilkins, eds. Forthcoming. *The Brazilian Legal Profession in the Age of Globalization: The Rise of the Corporate Sector and Its Impact on Lawyers and Society*. Cambridge: Cambridge University Press.

Dubey, Rajeev. 2011. "The Art of the Deal." *Business World*, August 20.: www.businessworld.in/businessworld/businessworld/content/Art-Deal.html.

Flood, John. 2013. "Institutional Bridging: How Large Law Firms Engage in Globalization." *Boston College Law Review* 54 (1): 1087–1121.

Galanter, Marc and Thomas Palay. 1991. *Tournament of Lawyers: The Transformation of the Big Law Firm*. Chicago: University of Chicago Press.

Ganz, Kian. 2009a. "Luthra Goes Lockstep, Modernises Management Structure." *Legally India*, June 13. www.legallyindia.com/2009061251/Law-firms/luthra-goes-lockstep-modernises-management-structure.

2009b. "Luthra Looks to Bangalore: Delays Lockstep Conversion." *Lawyer*, July 31. www.legallyindia.com/20090731118/Law-firms/luthra-looks-to-bangalore-delays-lockstep-conversion.

2011. "3 Women, 2 Men Enter Amarchand Side Equity as BCG Says: Grow to 1,000 by 2017 with 11 Practice Heads." *Legally India*, October 16. www.legallyindia.com/l201110162385/Law-firms/3-women-2-men-enter-amarchand-side-equity-as-bcg-says-grow-to-1000-by-2017-with-11-practice-heads.

2012. "India's Biggest Law Firm Prepares for Next Stage of Evolution." *Livemint*, February 17. www.livemint.com/2012/02/17011534/India8217s-biggest-law-firm.html.

2015. "Berjis Desai Talks about the JSA Experiment." *Legally India*, June 3. www.legallyindia.com/Law-firms/talking-the-talk-with-berjis-desai-extended-edition.

Ganz, Kian and Prachi Shrivastava. 2012. "3 Years of Khaitan: 70% Growth, 18 Lateral Partners." *Legally India*, April 2. www.legallyindia.com/201204022706/Law-firms/3-years-of-khaitan-a-co-70-growth-18-lateral-partners-this-year-no-partner-promoted-9-new-sas-in-new-career-track.

Gardner, Heidi. 2015. "Teamwork and Collaboration in Professional Service Firms: Evolution, Challenges, and Opportunities." In *The Oxford Handbook of Professional Service Firms*. Edited by Laura Empson, Daniel Muzio, Joseph Broschak, and Bob Hinings. Oxford, Oxford University Press. upta, Deepali.

2012. "The Five Fundamental Differences between India's Top Two Corporate Law Firms Amarchand & Mangaldas and AZB Partners." *Economic Times*, March 15. www.articles.economictimes.indiatimes.com/2012–03–15/news/31197164_1_azb-partners-zia-mody-shardul.

Heine, Friederike. 2012. "Top Indian Law Firms Aim to Modernise as Market Grows." *Legal Week*, March 2. www.legallyindia.com/20090731118/Law-firms/luthra-looks-to-bangalore-delays-lockstep-conversion.

Henderson, William. 2006. "An Empirical Study of Single-Tier versus Two-Tier Partnerships in the Am Law 200." *North Carolina Law Review* 84 (4): 1691–1750.

Henderson, William and Leonard Bierman. 2009. "An Empirical Analysis of Lateral Lawyering Hiring Trends from 2000–2007: The Emerging Equilibrium for Corporate Law Firms." *Georgetown Journal of Legal Ethics* 22 (4): 1395–1430.

Interview with Akshay Chudasama. 2013.

Interview with Anand Prasad. 2011.

Interview with Dina Wadia. 2011.

Interview with Haigreve Khaitan. 2013.

Interview with Jyoti Sagar. 2011.

Interview with Luthra & Luthra associate. 2011.

Interview with Mohit Saraf. 2011.

Interview with Mumbai lawyer. 2012.

Interview with Nishith Desai. 2012.

Interview with Nividita Tiwari. 2011.

Interview with Rahul Guptan. 2011.

Interview with Rajiv Luthra. 2011.

Interview with Reena SenGupta. 2015.

Interview with Sandeep Katwala. 2011.

Interview with Venkatesh Prasad. 2011.

Interview with Pratibha Jain. 2012.

Krishnan, Jayanth. 2010. "Globetrotting Law Firms." *Georgetown Journal of Legal Ethics* 23 (1): 57–102.

Legal Era. 2012. "In Conversation with Zia Mody." *Legal Era*, November 12. www.legalera.in/legal-articles/item/30-in-conversation-with-zia-mody.html.

Lin, Anthony. 2012. "Amarchand Opens Up." *American Lawyer*, June 4. www.americanlawyer.com/id=1202556958287/Amarchand-Opens-Up.

Mitra, Moinak. 2012. "How Jyoti Sagar & Berjis Desai Made JSA Partners in Profit." *Economic Times*, February 10. www.articles.economictimes.indiatimes.com/2012–02–10/news/31046381_1_law-firm-equity-partners-azb.

Nath, Shloka. 2010. "India's Biggest in Law, Amarchand Mangaldas." *Forbes India*, February 8. www.forbesindia.com/article/boardroom/indias-biggest-in-law-amarchand-mangaldas/15382/1.

Rainmaker. "The Mandate with Cyrill Shroff." www.youtube.com/watch?v=x4kNMu6gfLM.

Robinson, David. 2009. "India's Elite Law Firms." *Chambers Magazine* 30. www.chambersmagazine.co.uk/Article/1616.

RSG Consulting. 2008. India Report.

2015. India Report.

Regan, Milton. 2004. *Eat What You Kill: The Fall of a Wall Street Lawyer*. Ann Arbor, MI: University of Michigan Press.

Sahad, P. V. 2003. "Law's One-Stop Hot-Shops." *Business Today*, July 6. www.archives.digitaltoday.in/businesstoday/20030706/features3.html.

Saluja, Pallavi. 2012. "Conversation with Pradip Kumar Khaitan and Haigreve Khaitan." *Bar and Bench*, December 13. www.google.com/search?q=Conversation+with+Pradip+Kumar+Khaitan+and+Haigreve+Khaitan&rlz=1C1CHFX_enUS508US508&oq=Conversation+with+Pradip+Kumar+Khaitan+and+Haigreve+Khaitan&aqs=chrome.69i57.213j0j7&sourceid=chrome&es_sm=122&ie=UTF-8.

Vallikappen, Sanat. 2008. "Mum on Split M P Bharucha Takes 'Law' into His Hands." *DNA India*, March 28. www.dnaindia.com/money/report_mum-on-split-m-p-bharucha-takes-lawinto-his-hands_1157744.

Wald, Eli. 2009. "The Other Legal Profession and the Orthodox View of the Bar: The Rise of Colorado's Elite Law Firms." *University of Colorado Law Review* 80 (2): 605–683.

Wilkins, David B. 2007. "Partner Shmartner! EEOC v. Sidley Austin Brown & Wood." *Harvard Law Review* 120 (5): 1264–1277.

2015. "Law Firms." In *The International Encyclopedia of the Social and Behavioral Sciences*. Edited by James D. Wright. Oxford: Elsevier, 578–584.

Wilkins, David B., and Mitu Gulati. 1998. "Reconceiving the Tournament of Lawyers: Tracking, Seeding, and Information Control in the Internal Labor Markets of Elite Law Firms." *Virginia Law Review* 84 (8): 1581–1681.

Wilkins, David B. 2015. "Law Firms." In *International Encyclopedia of the Social & Behavioral Sciences*. Edited by James D. Wright. Amsterdam: Elsevier.

4

Globalization and the Rise of the In-House Counsel Movement in India

David B. Wilkins and Vikramaditya S. Khanna

I. INTRODUCTION

As documented in the introduction to this volume, by almost any measure one of the most significant developments in the corporate legal services market in the United States over the past thirty years has been the growth in the size, stature, and influence of internal legal counsel. This "in-house counsel movement," as the American legal scholar Robert Eli Rosen aptly labeled this transformation to signal the key role that internal lawyers themselves were playing in furthering their growing economic power and professional standing, has in turn played a critical role in the transformation of the structure, norms, and practices of large law firms and other actors that comprise the corporate hemisphere of the US legal profession (Chayes and Chayes 1985; Rosen 1989; Gilson 1990; Daly 1997; Wilkins 2012).

In this chapter, we explore whether some version of this in-house counsel movement has come to India. To investigate this question, we conducted three kinds of research. First, from 2011 to 2012, we conducted in-depth, semistructured interviews in India with internal counsels. Second, from 2014 to 2015, we administered a comprehensive survey directed toward the general counsels (GCs) of companies operating in India. With respect to both the interviews and the survey, our goal was to collect data from a wide range of companies, including large Indian conglomerates controlled by an individual promoter or family (hereinafter "business groups"), Indian state-owned enterprises (hereinafter "SOEs"), Indian companies that are neither business groups nor SOEs (hereinafter "private companies"), and foreign multinationals operating in India (hereinafter "FMCs"). We eventually completed more than seventy interviews and collected seventy-four completed surveys. Both samples include a significant number of companies from each of the four targeted firm types and represent a large percentage of the market capitalization of companies operating in India. Finally, we supplemented this original research with a review of publicly available information about the Indian corporate market, which we use both to test the representativeness of our sample and to more comprehensively describe the Indian legal market.

Based on this data, we find that there has been substantial change in the role of in-house counsel in India, with these lawyers becoming considerably more important both within their companies and within the Indian legal profession generally. However, while the processes through which these changes have occurred bear some similarities to those in the West, there are important differences between the in-house counsel movement in India and its Western counterpart. As a result, we conclude that the development of this part of the Indian corporate legal sector cannot be explained by a simple diffusion model and instead must be seen as a hybrid of global, primarily Anglo-American practices, and local Indian practices that respond to important aspects of India's unique corporate, legal, and institutional structure. We test this conclusion by examining whether our data about the structure, function, and norms of internal counsel in India supports four hypotheses grounded in the development of the in-house counsel movement in the US context.

Our argument proceeds in three parts. Part II begins by reviewing the benchmarks by which the development of the size, sophistication, and importance of in-house counsel has been measured in the United States. We then explore the global and local factors that may be producing similar developments in India, as well as the features of India's history, culture, and legal marketplace that may affect the scope and content of how the in-house counsel movement develops in this country. We conclude this part by presenting four hypotheses that we will explore through our data: (1) the overall size and importance of in-house legal departments at Indian companies is likely to have increased significantly in the past decade and GCs will expect these departments to grow further in the coming years; (2) among Indian companies there will nevertheless be substantial variation in the size, status, and functioning of in-house departments on the basis of differences in ownership structure, industry type, and social structure and status; (3) those Indian companies that have greater integration with the global economy will be more likely to adopt a model of internal lawyering that resembles the Western model; and (4) GCs will become "change agents" who press for changes in the Indian legal profession and society in general. Part III then presents our data and methodology, and summarizes our key findings with respect to each of the benchmarks for evaluating the development of the in-house counsel movement in India. Part IV uses these findings to assess each of our four hypotheses. Part V concludes by discussing the future of the in-house counsel movement in India and the potential consequences for the Indian legal market.

II. BACKGROUND AND HYPOTHESES

A. *The Benchmark: Six Parameters for Measuring the in-House Counsel Movement in the United States*

To understand why the in-house counsel movement might be moving to India, it is important to briefly recall why GCs in the United States and other Western jurisdictions have been so successful in transforming their power and status, both within their organizations and within the legal marketplace, in such a relatively short period of time. As we documented in the introduction, the rise of the in-house movement in the United States was predicated on three interlocking claims: an *economic* argument that taking work inside would save costs; a *substantive* justification that because of their proximity to the business, the advice inside lawyers give corporate managers is likely to be better than the advice given by outside counsel; and a *professional* argument that because they are the guardians of the company's long-term interests and reputation, GCs are better able to fulfill the gatekeeping role of insuring that companies comply with both the letter and the spirit of the law than their counterparts in large law firms who have largely abandoned this role in the pursuit of short-term profits per partner. These arguments, in turn, have helped to spur six important changes in the organization of internal counsel offices in the United States – and the relationship between these offices and other key constituents both inside and outside the organization – that are consistent with the basic tenets of the inside counsel movement (Wilkins 2012). We summarize these six changes below:

1. **Size**, with many GC offices now rivaling the size of major law firms (Baker and Parkin 2006; Coates et al. 2011);
2. **Credentials and identity**, with internal law departments becoming a premier employment destination for top associates and partners from large law firms, especially among women (Dinovitzer et al. 2012; Neil 2011);
3. **Control over the legal function**, with inside lawyers now acting as the primary diagnostician of the company's legal problems and the chief purchasing agent for outside legal services (Schwarcz 2008; Coates et al. 2011);
4. **Expanded responsibility and membership in senior leadership**, with most GCs reporting directly to the CEO, overseeing functions adjacent to the legal department (e.g., public relations, government affairs, human relations, compliance), and serving on senior leadership teams

with jurisdiction over strategy and other major corporate decisions (Morrison 2006; Coates et al. 2011);

5. **Professional status**, with GCs increasingly viewed as equal – and in many respects dominant – members of the legal profession who exercise significant authority over the profession's norms and practices (Wilkins 2012); and
6. **Influence over public policy**, with GCs in the United States exercising important influence, both individually and through collective action by the Association of Corporate Counsel and other similar organizations, over important public policy issues, both domestically and globally (Rostain 2008; Coates et al. 2011).

Collectively these six changes provide empirical support for the economic, substantive, and professional claims made by in-house counsel in the United States, and increasingly in the rest of the Global North. In this chapter, we explore whether similar arguments are being deployed by GCs in India and if so, whether they are likely to be as persuasive as they have been in the West.

B. *Why Globalization is Likely to Spur the in-House Counsel Movement in India*

The three forces of globalization identified in the introduction to this volume provide good reasons to believe that some version of the in-house counsel movement is likely to come to India. As indicated in the introduction of this volume (Chapter 2), a key reason that India has "emerged" in recent years is that it has adopted a series of regulatory reforms that have opened its economy to the global market and opened up sectors that were previously closed off to private entities (Bhagwati 2004). Among other important changes, this opening has meant that a growing number of multinational companies have operations in India. It is plausible that these companies will want in-house lawyers who will support their Indian operations in the same way that their existing operations are supported in more-established markets. The emphasis on the importance of internal counsel by multinational companies is, in turn, likely to encourage the growing number of Indian companies being created – or growing larger – as a result of these forces of *economic globalization* to adopt similar expectations for their own in-house lawyers. The imperative to upgrade their in-house counsel function is likely to become all the more urgent as these Indian corporates expand their operations into new markets, particularly markets such as the United States and Europe, where the regulatory environment is both complex and challenging.

This process of diffusion is likely to be spurred by the *globalization of knowledge*. A growing number of the lawyers working in companies based in India have been educated in the United States, United Kingdom, or Western Europe.[1] Along with learning about US securities laws and other substantive issues, these students are also likely to have absorbed at least something about the ideology of the in-house counsel movement during their time in the West.[2] Formal education, however, is only one mode for the dissemination of knowledge – and arguably not the most important when it comes to lawyers. Since 2000, organizations such as the Association of Corporate Counsel, and publications and websites such as *The Lawyer* and *Legally India*, have devoted significant attention to in-house counsel in India. By trumpeting examples of the importance of in-house legal departments, these new professional associations and publications further the dissemination of the tenets of the in-house counsel movement.

The last process of globalization – the *globalization of governance* – is likely to help drive home the value of these tenets, both to in-house lawyers and to the managers and shareholders these lawyers serve. As many scholars have observed, international and transnational regulation increasingly plays a key role in governing the affairs of companies that compete in the global economy (Drezner 2007). At the same time, these supranational regulations interact and compete with a growing proliferation of national laws that regulate similar conduct. All of this is likely to increase the demand for the kind of knowledge about law, regulation, and the institutions of national, regional, and global governance that in-house lawyers credibly claim to possess and deploy. Companies are therefore likely to look for internal lawyers capable of engaging in the kind of sophisticated analysis about the interplay of legal and nonlegal solutions and the opportunities for regulatory arbitrage or damage control that typify the style of internal lawyering trumpeted by the in-house counsel movement.

The situation will be even more complex for Indian companies when venturing beyond their borders. Consider the complex array of interconnected laws, regulations, and standards that fall under the general heading of corporate governance. Indian companies will need to understand the full range of laws in this area even if some of these restrictions do not immediately apply to their operations in their home jurisdiction (Tomasic and Fu 2005). This regulatory complexity between the global and the local levels arguably places a premium on a certain kind of internal legal expertise and familiarity with the corporate client. (For an analogous argument, see Chapter 13 of this volume.) As a knowledgeable observer asserted in the context of the growth of sophisticated in-house lawyers in Latin America: "As the scale and severity of regulatory oversight in the United States increases across the board, Latin

American GCs are facing the next significant compliance challenge – conducting rigorous internal investigations which don't cost the earth" (Bolton 2010).

Indeed, the fact that Indian companies are just as likely to expand into other emerging economies as into the more developed markets of the Global North is only likely to make the growing globalization of governance even more salient. As an Indian GC who has been schooled in the ways of the in-house counsel movement through receiving an LLM in the United States and by working for both Indian and multinational companies – and who for the past two years has been hosting a monthly discussion group for other Indian in-house lawyers from both Indian and multinational companies – summed up his understanding of his role:

> [A]s an in-house you are working closely with your business colleagues, understanding their challenges and finding creative ways of achieving business objectives in a legal and ethical way. The in-house lawyer must take on a leadership role, take calculated risks, and stick his or her neck out by giving clear and insightful guidance to the business.... You many times end up crisscrossing between thinking like a business person and a lawyer in dealing with this challenge.
>
> (Kurunathan 2011, 32–33)

Needless to say, there is certainly no guarantee that economic globalization, the globalization of knowledge, and the globalization of governance will *necessarily* produce sophisticated in-house counsel in India, let alone that the GCs that do emerge from this context will look exactly like their US counterparts. To the contrary, we hypothesize that there are likely to be significant differences between the model of internal counsel that develops in India and the one that the United States produced. The next section explores why we believe there are likely to be important differences in the Indian context.

C. *How India's History is Likely to Shape this Movement*

When India gained independence, in 1947, it had a fairly well-established private corporate sector (Khanna 2009). However, as Chapter 2 of this volume documents, from 1947 to 1991 India developed a more closed, state-centered, and state-run economy with considerably greater regulation and limits on both domestic and foreign competition. In light of these features, Indian companies had very little need to employ skilled or sophisticated transactional lawyers. To the contrary, compliance with India's arcane regulatory requirements was far more important than the fine art of contract negotiation and drafting. Most of this compliance work was therefore carried out by company secretaries or within the finance division, as many of the regulations directly impacted their work. These corporate functionaries were rarely lawyers. This was especially true in Indian SOEs (which, in the Indian context, are often called public sector undertakings, or PSUs) who were major players in this more tightly regulated economy (see Chapter 2 of this volume). Only a handful of firms had well-established GC positions, and often the tasks of the legal department were subsumed within larger departments and more limited to compliance.

The liberalization of the Indian economy in 1991 changed – but did not completely erase – these old patterns. As corporations looked to meet the new demands of India's more open economy, they initially tended to rely on those functionaries who were already providing their other legal or compliance services. Specifically, the CFOs started taking a greater role in the process of addressing legal issues. This probably made a great deal of sense because all the other legal and compliance matters were largely within the CFO's purview, so adding on additional matters seemed appropriate. However, because they lacked legal expertise, CFOs often turned to India's rapidly developing corporate law firms to provide the necessary legal competence, particularly in areas where the overall decrease in regulatory fiats was increasing the importance of fine contract drafting and negotiation. When the cost of sourcing the company's increasing legal needs from outside firms began to rise steeply in the new millennium, it was often the CFO who stepped in to build an internal legal department to rein in these expenditures. Not surprisingly, when they did so, they often sought to keep control over the new fixed cost of running an in-house legal function, and the even greater variable cost of hiring external law firms, by continuing to have the legal function report to the CFO. This was particularly true for India's large business groups, where the CFO tended to be a close confidant of the promoter or family that controlled the group and was charged with exercising tight control over all the important functions of the organization.

Although the rapid growth and further globalization of the Indian economy since 2000 has continued to put pressure on these traditional patterns – particularly with respect to Indian companies with greater exposure to the global economy – we do not expect these practices to disappear entirely. Indian CFOs are simply too powerful, particularly in business groups where the typical CEO is likely to want the CFO to remain in control. At the same time, distinctive features of the Indian corporate law firm market are likely to lead both Indian corporates and FMCs to invest more in developing sophisticated internal legal expertise than comparable companies operating in the United States or other jurisdictions. As is documented elsewhere in this volume, notwithstanding its tremendous growth since 1991, the Indian corporate law firm sector remains relatively thin in terms of both the total number of law firms and, even more importantly, the number of lawyers within these firms who have the requisite expertise and experience to do sophisticated corporate work. When this fact is coupled with the ban on foreign law firms practicing in India, it is likely to give both Indian companies and FMCs an incentive to rely even more heavily on their own internal legal resources than companies in jurisdictions such as the United States, where the external market is more well developed. It may also lead these companies to be more willing than their Western counterparts to outsource their work to providers other than law firms, for example, in areas such as compliance.[3]

All these unique features of the Indian legal market are likely to influence the development of internal legal departments and the role of the GC. Table X below provides a pre-2000 snapshot of what in house departments looked like in the US and in India as a starting point for our analysis.

In-house legal departments in comparison

Variables	US model	India pre-2000
Size	Grown dramatically since 1980s; large corporations have GC offices that rival the size of large outside law firms.	Quite small, although beginning to grow
Credentials and Identities	Almost all are lawyers and members of the bar. A large number of people working in-house are women.	Not all lawyers; many have backgrounds as company secretaries. Very few are or were members of the bar as rules require in-house lawyers to suspend membership.
Control over the legal function	Largely select outside counsel and manage the relationship	Limited say in determining who is outside counsel and in managing that relationship
Internal reporting relationships	Commonly report to the CEO	Generally report to the CFO rather than the CEO or board
The profession	Important players in the profession with increasing influence throughout	Limited influence in the profession; suspend bar membership (if applicable) when enter in-house department
Public policy	Active role in public policy with regular interactions with government	Very limited role in influencing public policy

D. *Hypotheses*

Given this combination of global and local factors, we developed four interrelated hypotheses that we used to guide our empirical research about the state of the Indian in-house counsel movement in the second decade of the twenty-first century: (1) the overall size and importance of in-house legal departments at Indian companies is likely to have increased significantly in the past decade across all sectors, and GCs will expect these departments to grow further in the coming years; (2) among Indian companies there will nevertheless be substantial variation in the size, status, and functioning of in-house departments on the basis of differences in ownership structure (e.g., business groups, SOEs, private companies, and FMCs), among other things (e.g., industry, social, cultural, or regional status and norms); (3) those Indian companies that have greater integration with the global economy – for example, because they have sizeable export earnings, operate in markets with significant foreign competition, or have important operations outside of India – will be more likely to adopt a model of internal lawyering that resembles the Western model; and (4) GCs will become "change agents" who press for changes in the rest of the Indian bar, including law schools, law firms, senior advocates, and even traditional solo and small-firm practitioners, as well as exerting increasing influence on legal and public policy debates both within India and within the formal and informal institutions of global governance.

The following section presents our data and discusses the support provided, if any, for each hypothesis.

III. QUALITATIVE INTERVIEWS AND SURVEY RESPONSES – KEY FINDINGS

A. *Data and Methods*

In order to explore our hypotheses and learn more about the evolving role of the GC in India, we gathered detailed data and information from three sources: (1) semistructured qualitative interviews with more than seventy GCs working in a broad range of companies operating in India; (2) survey questionnaires completed by seventy-four GCs, once again from a broad range of companies operating in India; and (3) publicly available information on the Indian corporate market, including financial information on Indian firms available from the Prowess online database maintained by the Centre for Monitoring the Indian Economy.

The interview data was obtained through individual interviews (or sometimes interviews in small groups) with GCs at Indian firms between October 2011 and March 2012 in Mumbai, New Delhi, and Bangalore (the "interview" data). The individuals were primarily either the GC or the equivalent senior legal officer (or for some US multinational companies, the person in charge of the company's legal operations in India). We also interviewed a few lawyers who were more junior in these organizations. For expositional ease we refer to these interviewees collectively as "GCs," although not all of them had that title. They were contacted either by phone or email or via "snowball" sampling and were told that the interview would discuss their views and experiences on the changing role of the GC in postliberalization India. All were told that their responses would be confidential. We oversampled those sectors, or groupings, of Indian business that were most likely to have a greater demand for legal services (and larger in-house departments) and to be more impacted by the changes wrought by globalization and liberalization. The interviewed GCs come from a broad cross section of companies operating in India (including US multinationals, large promoter- (controller-) driven conglomerates, SOEs, and small- and medium-sized entrepreneurial Indian firms) across a number of sectors (including mining and minerals, construction, banking and finance, media and high tech, and consumer goods).

The survey questionnaires were primarily completed from 2014 to 2015. Most respondents completed the questionnaire as part of an in-person interview with our research team at AC Nielsen India, and the remaining respondents through the online questionnaire. The questionnaire was quite detailed – with more than one hundred questions – and often required GCs to look back into their records. Like the interview data, we oversampled the sectors or groupings of Indian business that had a greater demand for legal services (and larger in-house departments) and greater interaction with globalization. The GCs were contacted either by phone or email or via "snowball" sampling and again were provided a brief description of the topic of the survey (and some requested the questionnaire in advance of meeting). The respondents were told their responses would be confidential with results reported in aggregate form only.

Survey respondents worked at firms representing about 27 percent of the market capitalization of publicly traded Indian firms. This is almost certainly an underestimate, because some of the responding firms are private firms – even though they are very large – and hence their financial information is not available to us. The responding firms also represent a broad cross section of ownership groups (e.g., business groups, SOEs, foreign firms, and nonbusiness-group firms) and provide a good representation of the Indian

TABLE 1. *Sample compared to the market*

	Responding firms	Market (BSE)	Percent of sample/market
Market cap	INR 1,667,863.68	INR 6,226,491.35	27%

corporate market, especially those with legal departments most likely to be impacted by globalization and liberalization.

Finally, we obtained financial data on publicly traded Indian firms from the online Prowess database maintained by the Centre for Monitoring the Indian Economy (the "Prowess" data). Prowess provides a wealth of information about financial performance including variables from the income statement, balance sheet, and cash flow statement among others. For some of our survey sample firms, Prowess did not maintain data because either these firms were not listed as separate firms (e.g., subsidiaries of FMCs) or they were unlisted Indian firms (even though they may have been large).

In the next few sections we describe our key findings from the interview data and the survey data as supplemented by the Prowess data. We begin with a brief description of our survey respondents and a discussion of the rise in legal expenditures for Indian firms.

B. *Description of Survey Respondents and Firms' Expenditures on Legal Charges*

As indicated here, for the survey questionnaires we geared our efforts toward approaching the GCs of the larger firms. As table 1 indicates, this resulted in our respondents representing about 27 percent of market capitalization of Indian firms. Table 2 presents the composition of our sample, which is roughly 46 percent business-group firms (thirty-four), 11 percent

TABLE 2. *Ownership structure*

Ownership structure	Percent of sample	Number of firms	Number of firms by type in market (%)	Market cap of each type in market (%)
Business group	46%	34	33%	49%
Nonbusiness group	11%	8	58%	10%
FMC	26%	19	6%	12%
SOE	18%	13	3%	28%

non-business-group firms (eight), 25 percent foreign firms (nineteen), and 17 percent SOEs (thirteen). The breakdown of ownership types closely tracks the market capitalization of these groups, but results in an oversampling of foreign firms and an undersampling of SOEs relative to their market capitalizations. This relative distribution, however, arguably reinforces the overall value of our findings, since foreign firms are likely to be particularly important to an understanding of the role of globalization, and because SOEs, as our data confirms, are likely to have unique operating conditions and concerns that set them apart from other Indian companies. We try to account for these and other possible biases of our sample in our analysis.

The large proportion of Indian market capitalization – 27 percent – represented by our seventy-four respondents underscores the heavy concentration in the Indian markets. Even though there may be more than four thousand publicly listed and traded firms in the Prowess database, the very largest of them represent the vast majority of market capitalization. The importance of this concentration is highlighted by our nonrespondent analysis in table 3. Firms that were approached and responded were larger in profits and assets (and similar in sales) to firms that were approached but did not respond.

Finally, with the exception of FMCs, our respondent firms primarily have their headquarters in India. However, well over one-third of them (37 percent) have more than 20 percent of their operations overseas – capturing the growing number of Indian corporates that have a very active interaction with globalization. This is further highlighted by approximately 42 percent of respondents indicating that they had engaged in significant cross border activity in the past three years and respondents noting that around 54 percent of their activity was directed to projects outside of India.

In sum, the survey sample provides a good representation of Indian firms (in both market capitalization and ownership structure), as well as capturing the companies most likely to be impacted by globalization. We therefore believe that it provides a good basis for testing our four hypotheses.

TABLE 3. *Responding firms compared to nonresponding (but approached) firms*

	Responding firms	Nonresponding firms[4]
Assets (average)	INR 59,737.02	INR 33,374.94
Sales (average)	INR 8,521.68	INR 8,844.83
Net income (average)	INR 6,264.26	INR 3,178.20

All amounts in rupees crores (USD 1 ~ INR 60) unless otherwise stated. A crore is 10 million rupees.

FIGURE 1 Increase in legal charges outside of India

Before doing so, however, a few words about the growth in Indian business firms' legal expenditures provides important context. Figure 1 presents data from Prowess about the increase in the amount firms report spending on "legal charges" (a data field representing amounts spent on outside legal services – e.g., advocates, outside law firms). As figure 1 shows, these charges have increased dramatically over the past decade. From 2004 to 2015 "legal charges" by Indian companies increased by more than 270 percent. Indeed, from 2010 to 2015 – a period in which India was recovering from the global financial crisis – legal charges increased by almost 60 percent. Moreover, even this impressive growth in legal charges undoubtedly underestimates the total amount that Indian companies are spending on legal services, because it does not include expenditures on in-house departments, which, as later tables show, has grown substantially. Finally, the overall growth in legal spend – both internally and to external providers – by Indian companies and FMCs operating in India is likely to continue its rapid growth as Indian law reforms carve out new areas for more legal work (e.g., the proposed bankruptcy code, the land acquisition reforms, and the proposed Goods and Services Tax), Indian firms expand more deeply into global markets, and the policies of the new Modi government potentially leading foreign firms to increasingly view India as an attractive investment option. If the US experience is any indication, this continued growth in the demand for legal services is likely to further the development of the in-house counsel movement in India.

To test this proposition, the following sections explore nine issues where our quantitative and qualitative data shed light on key tenets of the in-house counsel movement. The first two – credentials and demographics (section C), and size and structure of Indian in-house departments (section D) – provide details on who works in the GC's office, where they are hired, and the structure and size of in-house departments. The next section examines the relationship between the GC and other important internal players at the firm (section E). Section F provides an overview of the GC's work and responsibilities. The next three sections detail the GC's status and interaction with important constituents outside the firm, specifically, outside law firms (section G), the bar (section H), and the government (section I). Finally, section J concludes by discussing how the data presented in the prior eight sections bears on the four hypotheses presented in Part II.

C. *Credentials and Demographics*

As indicated in Part II, a central feature of the in-house counsel movement in the United States has been a shift in the credentials and demographics of GCs and those who work in internal legal departments. As table 4 documents,

TABLE 4. *Demographics and credentials*

	All	Business group	Nonbusiness group	FMC	SOE
Percent of male GCs	89%	85%	100%	89%	92%
Age of GC	48	49	43	47	51
LLM earned	24%	15%	38%	32%	31%
Mother's education (college+)	47%	38%	38%	74%	39%
Father's education (college+)	74%	76%	63%	79%	69%
No one in immediate family with legal education	53%	59%	50%	53%	38%
Current/former member of the Indian bar	59%	47%	63%	68%	77%
Never a member of the Indian bar	30%	35%	38%	26%	15%
Currently a member of another country's bar	4%	3%	13%	5%	0%

the qualitative and quantitative evidence from our research reveals a more complex reality in India.

Overall, our data indicates that there has been a general upgrading in the credentials and experience of in-house lawyers across all companies operating in India. There are, however, important differences with respect to age and company type. These differences came out clearly during our qualitative interviews. The older GCs we interviewed were much more likely to be graduates of less prestigious Indian law schools, with some not having law degrees at all. Most of these older GCs had limited or no international experience and had worked in the in-house world (often at the company where they were now the GC) for most of their career. This was particularly true of GCs working in SOEs. The credentials and experiences of the younger GCs we spoke to, however, differ significantly from this pattern. GCs who were in their 40s were much more likely to have gone to one of India's elite National Law Schools, to have significant international experience (including in many cases an LLM from a US or UK law school), and to have spent at least part of their career in a law firm. Not surprisingly, this was particularly true of GCs in US multinationals.

Our survey data confirms this general trajectory. As a preliminary matter, GCs tend to come from relatively advantaged families. Nearly 75 percent of respondents came from families where the father had obtained a college or postgraduate qualification, with nearly 50 percent coming from households where the mother had a similar level of education. The fact that GCs tended to have educated parents is not surprising given the general status and income associated with these positions. However, there was one noticeable difference between the GCs we surveyed and the other prominent lawyers discussed elsewhere in this volume. Less than 50 percent of the GCs in our sample have other lawyers in their families. Although this percentage may seem high relative to other jurisdictions, given the importance of family connections in other prestigious parts of the Indian legal profession – particularly large law firms and "Grand Advocates" – documented elsewhere in this volume, the fact that most GCs do not come from families with legal credentials may have something to do with why some Indian lawyers find the in-house career track an attractive one. We will return to this issue later.

With respect to their own credentials, nearly 92 percent of GCs responding to our survey (sixty-eight out of seventy-four) had some form of law degree (e.g., LLB, JD, or LLM), signifying a significant change from the period prior to liberalization. However, only about 60 percent of the lawyers in our sample were actually members of the Indian bar – with only a small minority (4 percent) holding membership in a foreign bar. This last statistic was particularly surprising, since almost a quarter of the respondents (24 percent) have an LLM from a foreign law school, presumably giving them the chance to sit for a foreign bar. Indeed, only 12.5 percent of the GCs at FMCs were members of a foreign bar.

Collectively, this pattern suggests that while educational credentials – including those from foreign law schools – are valuable, bar membership is less so. This is consistent with anecdotal information that we have received from Indian LLM students at our respective institutions who have reported that while their employers are happy for them to get an LLM, they provide little or no support for the extra time and expense it takes to sit for the bar. This suggests that the push for professional standing within the organized bar that characterized the in-house counsel movement in the United States may be less important in India, at least to date.

Indeed, the GCs in our sample had relatively little experience outside of the in-house world before assuming their current positions. As seen in table 5, a little less than half of our respondents (46 percent) report that they were promoted to GC from within their firm. We suspect, however, that this may underreport the number of GCs who have essentially been promoted from "within" since several of the GCs at business-group firms came to their positions from other companies within the overall group. But even a 50/50 split between internal promotions and lateral hires suggests that the process of selecting a GC remains more insular in India than in the United States and other Western markets.

This appears to be especially true for SOEs. For example, while the average age of the GCs in our sample was 48, GCs at SOEs tended to be older, with

TABLE 5. *Job history*

	All	Business group	Nonbusiness group	FMC	SOE
Mean tenure of GC at firm (years)	9.74	9.38	5.71	9.06	13.69
Mean tenure of GC as GC (years)	5.35	5.56	4.71	6.71	3.38
GC promoted from within	46%	41%	43%	38%	69%
Previously worked at another company	57%	59%	50%	63%	46%
Previously worked at a law firm	11%	9%	13%	16%	8%
Previously worked at other (e.g., government)	26%	27%	25%	11%	46%

an average age of 51. Consistent with our interviews, this pattern suggests a continuation of the traditional pattern in SOEs of promoting on the basis of seniority. The data with respect to a GC's average tenure with their company also supports this interpretation. Thus, the average tenure of GCs in our sample was five years in the position as GC, and almost ten years as employees in their current firm. The exception to this general pattern were GCs at SOEs, who averaged only 3.38 years in their position as GC but nearly 14 years as employees of the SOE.

Moreover, even GCs who come from the outside are far less likely to have law firm experience than their Western counterparts. Only 11 percent of the GCs in our sample came to their current position directly from a law firm, with only 31 percent having any law firm experience at all, typically less than three years. Instead, most of the GCs in our sample came to their current jobs after substantial experience working in another in-house department (57 percent). This pattern differs significantly from jurisdictions where many GCs are hired directly from top law firms, and almost all have had at least some significant law firm experience before going in-house (Heineman 2016). In our qualitative interviews, many GCs justified the preference for internal promotions and external hiring from other legal departments on the grounds that lawyers in Indian law firms were particularly ill suited for the requirements of a GC position. As we indicate later on, however, new hiring practices may be changing these traditional patterns.

The skepticism toward law firm experience with respect to the GC position is an interesting contrast to the responses on hiring lower-level lawyers into the in-house department. Here more than half the respondents indicated that Indian law firm experience would be desirable (though even more preferred prior in-house experience). Indeed, when asked what factors might be most important to hiring internally, the top five responses were law firm experience, in-house experience, graduating from an elite law school, strong English skills, and business training.[5] These are all consistent with the work of the GC's office becoming more complex and global. However, this does suggest that law firm experience might be seen more in the next cohort of GCs.

Moreover, the constraints on the supply of qualified lawyers in India may be beginning to break down traditional hiring patterns. When we asked survey respondents what factors might influence their hiring decisions going forward, the top three factors – significant international experience, more in-house experience, and greater negotiations training – are all consistent with what one sees when looking at the development of in-house legal

TABLE 6. *Hiring legal department lawyers*

	All	Business group	Nonbusiness group	FMC	SOE
If hire straight from law school, what percentage of new entrants	1–10%	11–20%	1–10%	1–10%	11–20%
Do not hire straight from law school	54%	48%	71%	63%	46%
If new hires are not straight from law school, what was their immediate prior employer?					
Foreign law firm	33%	53%	25%	20%	23%
Domestic law firm	54%	46%	75%	43%	71%
Other company	77%	76%	0%	86%	15%

departments in the United States and other developed markets. At the same time, filling these positions is becoming ever more difficult, with few candidates possessing the desired characteristics and a large number of potential employers seeking the services of those who have them, which may be leading some in-house departments to become more willing to hire directly from law school.

In the United States, direct hires from law school into an in-house department are rare, but in India, as table 6 indicates, a little fewer than half the firms we surveyed were open to hiring directly from law schools, albeit only from top schools, and on average only for less than 10 percent of the new entrants into their departments. Indeed, many of the large in-house departments now recruit at the National Law Schools and other prestigious educational institutions, as one of us documents in Chapter 17 of this volume. Of course, it remains to be seen whether these new recruits will stay with their new corporate employers long enough to be promoted to GC or other top positions, or whether they will leave after a few years to join law firms or other employers. We anticipate, however, that the level of competition for high-end legal talent will only continue to increase in India, particularly as these departments increase in size and take on more-complex structures.

There is one other characteristic of those who currently occupy GC positions that also may change in the future – gender. To our surprise, the vast majority of the GCs in our survey sample are men (89 percent overall). This percentage stands in sharp contrast to the overall gender demographics of the legal department as a whole, where more than one-third of all lawyers are female. Moreover, this paucity of women GCs stands in contrast to the experience in the United States, where 21 percent of the GCs in *Fortune* 500 companies are female (Khorasanee 2014). More importantly, this dearth is at odds with the growing presence of women in top positions in Indian law firms (see Chapter 7 of this volume).

It remains to be seen whether this difference is simply a matter of time – as indicated here, the evolution of India's GC offices has lagged behind the development of important commercial law firms as providing important and desirable positions for top Indian lawyers – or signals a deeper difference between the norms, practices, and opportunity structures of law firms and in-house legal departments in the new Indian corporate legal sector. Indeed, it is not difficult to imagine that both explanations may be working at the same time.

For example, the relative "newness" in the perceived importance of GC offices compared to law firms may lead many talented individuals to consider working at Indian law firms over taking a position as a GC, at least for the time being. The structures of the markets in which these respective segments of the corporate legal bar compete may also be important in explaining this difference. Notwithstanding their traditional patriarchal and hierarchical structure, the forces of economic globalization are increasingly forcing Indian family-controlled corporations to compete globally in a manner that places a premium on being more efficient – and as a result, more "professional" – with respect to the promotion and development of talent within the organization. This helps explain why junior lawyers often perceive that they have more opportunities in these organizations than they do in India's family-owned and -run law firms, which have been able to shield themselves at least partially from global competition as a result of rules that restrict the entry of foreign law firms.

At the same time, however, precisely because the promoters and other CEOs who currently run Indian companies face increasingly stiff competition, they often seek to surround themselves with trusted advisors, often from clan, caste, or family networks, whose loyalty is unquestioned. Not surprisingly, those who come from outside the organization – for example, law firm partners – or "outside" traditional social networks, from which women in India have often been excluded, are likely to find it difficult to obtain this kind of position of trust. The combination of the "newness" of the rise of GC offices, the increasingly professional nature of Indian business firms, and the desire to keep trusted advisors in top positions may help explain, along with other factors, why a growing number of women are entering GC offices in India, but why so few have been promoted to GC.

D. *Size and Structure of Indian in-House Departments*

One of the key areas of interest for our inquiry is what has been happening to the size and structure of in-house departments at Indian companies as they engage more with globalization in the context of a liberalizing economy. We begin this inquiry by examining the changes in the budgets for in-house departments in India. Table 7 provides our key findings. It appears that across the board the budgets for in-house departments have substantially increased. On average in-house budgets increased well more than 50 percent just between

TABLE 7. *Budget of in-house department*

	Mean (INR)	Mean (USD)*	Median (INR)	Percent change	Range of budget spent on outside lawyers
All					
2009	69,600,000	1,160,000	24,800,000		41–50%
2012	106,000,000	1,766,667	44,000,000	52.30%	51–60%
2014–2015	130,000,000	2,166,667	50,000,000	22.64%	51–60%
Change 2009–2015				86.78%	
Business group					
2009	69,900,000	1,165,000	21,200,000		51–60%
2012	92,900,000	1,548,333	35,000,000	32.90%	61–70%
2014–2015	132,000,000	2,200,000	45,000,000	42.09%	61–70%
Change 2009–2015				88.84%	
Nonbusiness group					
2009	20,000,000	333,333	20,000,000		11–20%
2012	27,500,000	458,333	30,000,000	37.50%	11–20%
2014–2015	35,000,000	583,333	35,000,000	27.27%	31–40%
Change 2009–2015				75.00%	
FMC					
2009	87,200,000	1,453,333	30,000,000		61–70%
2012	161,000,000	2,683,333	50,000,000	84.63%	51–60%
2014–2015	184,000,000	3,066,667	55,000,000	14.29%	51–60%
Change 2009–2015				111.01%	
SOE					
2009	51,400,000	856,667	12,500,000		51–60%
2012	89,000,000	1,483,333	44,000,000	73.15%	51–60%
2014–2015	93,700,000	1,561,667	40,000,000	5.28%	51–60%
Change 2009–2015				82.30%	

* 1 USD ~ 60 INR

2009 and 2012 with further increases thereafter (for a total increase of 87 percent on average from 2009 to 2015). The firms with the largest increases are FMCs. Although our data does not allow us to provide a definitive answer as to why the budgets of these companies are growing especially rapidly, we suspect that both increasing business in (or with) India and the growing importance of antibribery and anticorruption regulation, including the US Foreign Corrupt Practices Act (FCPA) 1977 (where enforcement was ratcheted up in the mid-2000s) and the newly enacted UK Bribery Act, are likely to be playing an important role.[6] Further, over the past five years the trend among all companies in our sample has been for about half of the overall legal budget to be spent on outside lawyers.[7] This data is therefore consistent with the general escalation in "legal expenditures" documented in figure 1, as well as with the capacity constraints at in-house departments discussed here.

Although Indian companies continue to spend a sizeable portion of their total budget on outside counsel, the size and structure of legal departments have also grown substantially. Table 8 documents this significant expansion. The average size of the in-house department of our survey respondents was 28.83 people, which represented a 64 percent increase over the prior three years (with the GCs reporting that they hired an average of 16.25 people in the past three years). Going forward, the GCs reported that their department would likely grow another 66 percent over the next three years. Among the various types of firms, the SOEs have the largest in-house departments. This is likely due to SOEs being subject to various rules and regulations that may not be applicable to other firms. However, it is noteworthy that the SOEs also have large numbers of nonlawyers in their in-house departments (averaging about seventeen). Several informants in our qualitative interviews told us that these are primarily compliance specialists and corporate secretaries.

These averages, however, hide much variety. In our interview data it was clear that most in-house legal departments are small by Western standards. A small number of the GCs we interviewed were the only lawyer in their department, and for several others the total number of lawyers was fewer than five. This was particularly true of multinationals, which often had small India teams linked to larger regional centers in Hong Kong, Singapore, or elsewhere in Asia. In a sign of India's growing importance, in one or two cases these other regions sometimes reported to the Asia GC who now sits in India.

Other departments, however, were by these standards quite large. These were often in the resources, construction, or banking areas. For example, a GC of a large infrastructure company reported that he had sixty-six lawyers in his department, while the head lawyer at a mining company reported that his

TABLE 8. *Size of in-house department*

	All	Business group	Nonbusiness group	FMC	SOE
Average number of lawyers in India	28.83	27.09	8.88	16.33	69.18
Median number of lawyers in India	12	10	7	13.5	60
Average number of lawyers worldwide	119.88	34.65	56.63	345.71	76.40
Median number of lawyers worldwide	15	12	7	75	74.5
Average number of lawyers outside of India	91.05	7.56	47.75	329.38	7.22
Percent of lawyers in India	24%	78%	16%	5%	91%
Percent of lawyers outside of India	76%	22%	84%	95%	9%
Percentage of in-house lawyers in India who are women	32%	32%	34%	32%	34%
Increase in number of lawyers in legal department in India (past three years)	64%	65%	75%	53%	69%
Expected increase in number of lawyers in India (next three years)	66%	74%	63%	63%	54%
Number of nonlawyer professionals in legal department	7.22	3.85	1.00	8.47	17.18

department employed around eighteen to twenty lawyers. Indeed, a handful of departments were large by any standard. The Tata Group, for example, has four hundred in-house lawyers around the world, and ICICI Bank has well more than one hundred. Not surprisingly, these companies are significantly more integrated into the global economy than their peers.

Although the majority of Indian in-house departments are relatively small, most GCs we interviewed boldly predicted that their departments would grow quite substantially over the next few years. Whether these bold predictions turn out to be true, of course, remains to be seen, but it raises interesting questions about the relationship between size of the GC's office and its relative importance in the firm. Although a large legal department has traditionally been one of the hallmarks of the in-house counsel movement, as one of us found in a prior study of US companies, some of the largest legal departments are located in banks and other financial institutions where many lawyers are engaged primarily in low-level legal or regulatory work (Coates et al. 2011). Both our survey and interviews suggest that there is a similar pattern in India as well.[8] The fact that most Indian GCs (85 percent) maintain a strong role in compliance activities is likely to exacerbate this trend. As we indicated in this chapter, prior to liberalization most in-house departments were largely relegated to ensuring compliance with regulatory and legislative requirements rather than fine contract drafting (because many things were mandated by the state). As the state liberalized, deregulated, and then reregulated, many of the compliance activities stayed with the GC's office. Thus, one may need to probe more deeply into the functioning of the GC's office in India to obtain a better understanding of its rising importance – it is to this question that we now turn.

E. *Relationships With Internal Corporate Players*

As the size of in-house departments has grown, there is corresponding evidence that the internal influence of the GC has grown as well. Prior to 2000 most GCs in India reported to the CFO, thereby confirming their subordinate status to this central corporate function. In recent years, however, more GCs have been moved away from this reporting structure. As table 9 indicates, nearly half the GCs in our sample report to the CEO, with an additional 10 percent reporting to the board. To the extent that reporting relationships are a good indicator of importance, the GC has clearly moved up in the corporate hierarchy.

It is important to note, however, that directly reporting to the CEO in a business group will often mean reporting to the controlling shareholder of the firm. Although arguably signifying more stature than reporting to the CFO, it may not signify the same level of independence that reporting to the CEO has taken on in the United States and other Western jurisdictions. As suggested

TABLE 9. *GC reporting structure*

	All	Business group	Nonbusiness Group	FMC	SOE
Board	10%	9%	14%	6%	15%
CEO	49%	59%	43%	35%	46%
Global/regional GC	17%	6%	14%	47%	8%
CFO	10%	13%	14%	6%	8%

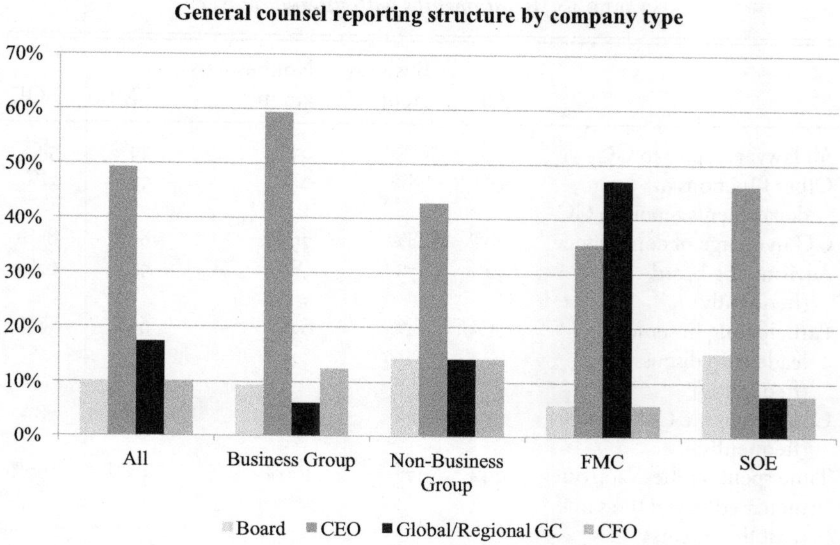

FIGURE 2 GC reporting structure

here, strong controlling shareholders are likely to demand even more loyalty from their GCs than the typical Western CEO. As a result, it is important not to automatically take proximity to the CEO as a measure of independence, even if it is a measure of influence.

Although this distinctive feature of many important Indian companies complicates any straightforward diffusion story about the in-house counsel movement in the Indian context, several other pieces of data taken together support the conclusion that across all company types the role of GC is becoming more important in India. For example, table 10 indicates that approximately 51 percent of our respondents had all lawyers within the company report to the GC directly (as opposed, for example, to reporting to both the GC and the CFO or another corporate officer). Significantly, 31 percent of GCs say other departments report to them. Moreover, the overwhelming majority of GCs in our sample claim that they play a key role in senior leadership decisions. Indeed, 74 percent of survey respondents claim that they either frequently or very frequently advise the CEO, 61 percent assert that they participate in senior leadership discussions, and about 50 percent report that they advise the board at least on a fairly frequent basis.

Of course, GCs may have many reasons for exaggerating their importance to senior business leaders, particularly on an anonymous survey. We therefore spent considerable time during our qualitative interviews investigating this issue to try to probe beyond this kind of self-serving rhetoric. Not surprisingly,

TABLE 10. *Relationships with internal players*

	All	Business group	Nonbusiness group	FMC	SOE
All lawyers report to GC	51%	53%	63%	39%	54%
Other functions or departments report to GC	31%	38%	0%	32%	31%
GC in charge of compliance	86%	88%	75%	89%	85%
Advising the board (frequently)	50%	47%	38%	52%	62%
Participating in senior leadership discussions (frequently)	61%	64%	63%	68%	38%
Counseling the CEO (frequently)	35%	38%	38%	26%	38%
Time spent on these activities increased/stayed the same (past three years)	99%	97%	100%	100%	100%
If increased, how much more time do you spend on these activities	41%	36%	24%	48%	56%

the GCs we interviewed articulated a broader range of views about whether they were valued members of the senior management team in their organization. Ironically, those who were most likely to see themselves as highly valued members of management were also the least likely to act as traditional lawyers. These internal lawyers tended to work for one of the important family-owned business groups where they have a very strong relationship, often cemented by social or familial bonds, with the controlling shareholder. As a result, these lawyers function more as trusted business advisors or consigliore than as traditional lawyers, leaving that function to more junior lawyers situated within the various businesses, or to outside counsel.

At the opposite end were several GCs who struggled to get their senior managers to understand the importance of law and legal issues at all. As one GC in a SOE confided, his biggest challenge is to convince his managers, all of whom are senior government officials, that legal restrictions have to be taken as seriously as political ones in operating the company.

Nevertheless, there was a general sense among our interviewees that GCs are slowly beginning to take on a more strategic role within their companies. This appears to be particularly true in businesses with an immediate and significant interaction with law (e.g., infrastructure development), where the company is large and outward facing, or where the particular GC in question has been able to demonstrate the "value add" of integrating legal services into broader business objectives.

Finally, there is one area in which Indian GCs may be ahead of their US and Western counterparts with respect to integrating legal and business objectives. In some companies, the GC office is not simply a staff function for providing legal services to the organization but also a profit center selling services to outside clients. For example, one respondent suggested that his company might be bundling legal and other services and selling them to clients. Although the respondents who admitted that they might be engaged in this practice were understandably reluctant to discuss it in detail (since it is not clear whether such conduct is permissible under present Indian, or international, regulations), it does raise important questions about whether the combination of technology and culture will produce a new model of in-house practice in India and other emerging economies – and the effect that such new models might have on existing practices.

F. *Overview of Work, Role, and Concerns*

With expanded influence in their firms and larger budgets, one anticipates that Indian GCs would see their work portfolio increase. Table 11 provides details on the job responsibilities and requirements for GCs in our sample.

Consistent with the fundamental tenet of the in-house counsel movement that the GC should have control over the company's legal needs, virtually all the GCs in our sample indicated that they have primary responsibility for managing the legal department staff (95 percent), hiring outside lawyers (91 percent), and managing outside lawyers (88 percent). Closely following these core managerial duties, 84 percent of the GCs in our sample indicated that they were primarily responsible for contract design and negotiation, suggesting that Indian GCs also continue to have direct responsibility for substantive legal work. Finally, 82 percent of the GCs in our sample indicated that they have primary responsibility for compliance in their company. Given, as we indicated in this chapter, that compliance had typically been the responsibility of the CFO in most Indian companies, the fact that the overwhelming majority of GCs now have primary responsibility for this function is another indication of the shifting balance of power between these two positions in Indian companies. The fact that most of the GCs in our sample placed compliance among their top three priorities, along with managing the legal department staff and

TABLE 11. *Primary responsibilities of the GC*

	All	Business group	Nonbusiness group	Foreign	SOE
Managing legal department staff	95%	94%	100%	95%	92%
Hiring outside lawyers and law firms	91%	91%	88%	89%	92%
Managing outside lawyers and law firms	88%	85%	100%	89%	85%
Company representative in public policy debates	4%	6%	0%	5%	0%
Compliance with domestic regulations	82%	82%	75%	84%	85%
Compliance with regulations arising out of cross border interactions	74%	76%	63%	89%	54%
Contract design and negotiation	84%	82%	88%	84%	85%
Managing IP assets	69%	74%	50%	74%	62%
Designing or implementing corporate social responsibility policies	43%	44%	38%	37%	54%
Ensuring compliance with antibribery/similar policies	64%	62%	50%	79%	54%
Other area(s)	34%	21%	38%	53%	38%

contract negotiation, underscores just how much this area has become a core part of the GC's role in companies operating in India. Indeed, 57 percent of respondents indicated that the time they spent on these three priorities had increased significantly in the past three years.

As we move away from core legal and compliance-related duties, there was less consensus among respondents about the areas for which GCs are primarily responsible. Thus, 69 percent reported that they oversee their company's IP assets, with only 50 percent of nonbusiness-group GCs indicating that they have this responsibility. At the same time, although only 64 percent of the sample overall claimed primary responsibility for antibribery and corruption efforts, 79 percent of the GCs in foreign companies reported having this responsibility – indicating that this is a particular concern for these entities. Finally, while 31 percent of the sample reported having other functions or departments reporting to them, none of the GCs of nonbusiness-group Indian companies indicated that they had this kind of responsibility.

The fact that the role of the GC in India is still primarily focused on managing and delivering legal services, as opposed to the broader vision of the role championed by many GCs in the United States, is confirmed by how they spend their time. The top five areas where GCs in our survey spent their time were commercial contracts (31–40 percent of their time), civil liability/arbitration (21–30 percent), regulatory compliance (11–20 percent), consumer issues (11–20 percent) and M&A (11–20 percent). This was largely consistent across all types of firms. How this legal work was sourced is explored in section F.

This portrait of GCs in India as serving a primarily "legal" role situated these actors somewhere in between their US counterparts, who frequently see themselves as "entrepreneurs," to borrow Nelson and Neilsen's term, whose job is to "further the business interests of the company," and GCs in Russia, who, according to Kathryn Hendley's classic study are "reluctant to exercise" even the basic gatekeeping role of policing their company's legal conduct (Nelson and Neilsen 2000, 463–464; Hendley 2010, 7). From our interviews, we saw no evidence of the self-identified powerlessness that Hendley found among Russian GCs. To the contrary, virtually all of the Indian GCs we interviewed claimed to be playing an important role in their organizations. Indeed, nearly all expressed that understanding their client's business was a key part of their role. Nevertheless, when we probed more deeply, it was not clear how many of these internal lawyers were actually involved in strategic counseling or decision making that went beyond legal issues. The fact that the three most important changes GCs would like to see in their role in their company were a greater role in the business side, more compliance efforts, and a better in-house department – all indicate GCs wanting more influence but not yet having it at the level seen in the United States.[9]

Although this focus was true for most of the GCs in our sample, those in strong promoter-driven companies were the most likely to assert that they played a more "entrepreneurial" role in key strategic decisions, particularly when these lawyers shared a common cultural or caste identity with the promoter. At the same time, it was not clear how many of them conceived of their role as going beyond informing corporate managers about the law to actively police company conduct. In an interesting development, those located in strong promoter-driven companies were the least likely to talk in terms of policing the promoter, suggesting a tradeoff between their role as consigliore with significant influence in strategic decision making and their willingness or ability to act as a gatekeeper policing client misconduct. This outcome is similar to that found in a study by one of us on independent directors in India (Khanna and Matthew 2010).

G. *Relationships With Outside Law Firms*

The interaction between the in-house department and outside law firms is one that animates much of the discussion of the changes in the in-house role (Rosen 1989; Coates et al. 2011). Given the critical importance of this relationship, we asked our survey respondents a number of questions about this relationship.

1. Purchasing Outside Legal Services and Areas of Work

We began by asking GCs how their firms' top five areas of legal work were sourced. Their responses (see table 12) indicate that our respondents tended to keep the majority of the commercial contracts and regulatory compliance work in-house (both at 51–60 percent of the work), whereas civil liability/arbitration, consumer issues, and M&A was largely sourced from outside providers (61–70 percent for all three). We further asked GCs what portion of their outside legal expenditures by area of law was fulfilled by domestic law firms, foreign law firms, and other types of firms (e.g., outsourcing entities, compliance specialists, accounting firms). Not surprisingly, Indian domestic law firms tend to do the lion's share (around 80 percent) of all of the outside legal work in civil liability/arbitration, regulatory compliance, and consumer law. This was consistent with our interviews where most GCs reported that they sent the majority of their litigation-related work outside. What was surprising to us was how much these companies also turned to foreign law firms for M&A and commercial contracts, which were ranked in the top five areas of a typical company's legal needs. The fact that more than 40 percent (42.65 percent) of the respondents to our survey stated that they were increasingly involved in

TABLE 12. *Sourcing of the top five categories of legal work*

	Commercial contracts	Civil liability/ arbitration	Regulatory compliance	Consumer	M&A
		Inside/outside split			
Inside	51–60%	31–40%	51–60%	31–40%	31–40%
Outside	41–50%	61–70%	41–50%	61–70%	61–70%
		Outside sourcing			
Domestic law firm	72.02	82.69	78.85	88.60	74.25
Foreign law firm	40.28	31.39	27.86	23.33	46.67
Other provider (e.g. LPS)	23.33	28.33	26.00	13.33	5.00

significant cross border work, with more than 50 percent (53.79 percent) indicating that their company had significant activities outside of India, suggests that the amount of work going to foreign law firms is likely to continue to increase in coming years.[10]

We then asked whether the amount of legal work going to outside providers had changed significantly in the past three years and 31 percent said it had. We further probed whether these changes were the result of more work going in-house or to domestic law firms or foreign law firms. The majority of respondents (52.38 percent) indicated that the change was doing more work in-house, while 33.33 percent indicated the change was giving more work to domestic law firms and 14.29 percent giving more work to foreign law firms.

In light of the importance of outside legal services, we inquired how decisions to purchase outside legal services were made. The results are provided in table 13. It appears that the majority of all surveyed firms use preferred provider lists for domestic firms (74 percent), with business-group firms being somewhat less likely to do so (65 percent) than other company types. Although our survey data does not allow us to determine the precise reason for this difference, it is consistent with reports from some of our key respondents that in business groups the controlling family will often have its own lawyers that it uses for personal matters, who will then be used for business purposes too, particularly for sensitive matters where personal and business interests are most likely to be intertwined.

The average size of a company's preferred provider list is about seven firms (except for SOEs, which have many more). Not surprisingly, this is much smaller than what one of us found when we studied large US companies, where the average company tended to have more than twenty firms on its list of preferred providers – although, as we also found, most companies tended

TABLE 13. *Hiring domestic law firms*

	All	Business group	Nonbusiness group	FMC	SOE
Use preferred provider list	74%	65%	88%	79%	85%
Number of firms on list*	10.75	7.68	6.71	7.20	24.27
List made by GC*	91%	86%	100%	93%	91%
List in 2010*	71%	68%	57%	73%	82%
Percentage of work to list*	61–70%	61–70%	51–60%	61–70%	51–60%
Change since 2010 (same or more to list)*	97%	100%	100%	91%	100%

* of those with list at time of survey

to give 80 percent of the business that went to these providers to ten firms or less (Coates et al. 2011).[11] Indian SOEs deviate from this general pattern. These companies tended to have much larger lists, consisting of twenty-four law firms on average. Again, we can only speculate about the reasons for this difference. Our interview data suggests, however, that both the breadth of the legal services these large entities need, as well as the heightened political need to appear not to be captured by any particular provider, and the political scrutiny that is likely to be applied to many of their decisions, have led these Indian companies to be somewhat more expansive in the number of law firms with whom they regularly work.

Whatever the size of the list, consistent with the tenets of the in-house counsel movement, the overwhelming majority (91 percent of the GCs in our survey) reported that they were primarily responsible for putting it together. Moreover, consistent with what we have seen in the United States, survey respondents also report that a healthy majority (61–70 percent) – although not all – of the company's legal work goes to law firms on the list. Nor is this an entirely recent development. Although very few of our interviewees reported that their companies had such a list in the early 2000s, our survey respondents confirm that by 2010 a large number of companies (71 percent – just more than 3 percent less than we found in 2015) had already put such a list in place.

Finally, when asked to name the three Indian law firms with which they worked the most, the majority of GCs tended to cite the best-known firms in the marketplace, particularly Amarchand & Mangaldas & Suresh A. Shroff, Khaitan & Co., AZB, JSA, and Luthra & Luthra, with Amarchand and Khaitan being named most frequently. This confirms Nanda, Wilkins, and Fong's finding in Chapter 3 of this volume that from 2014 to 2015, when we conducted the survey, these so-called Big 5 firms had come to dominate the Indian marketplace.

Although the Big 5 continue to constitute a near oligopoly for top work, many of the GCs we interviewed expressed a strong desire to change this reality. In interview after interview, we were surprised at the bitterness that many GCs expressed toward the major law firms and, in particular, at their senior partners – even senior partners who were the company's primary outside lawyer, and who had been so for years. On more than one occasion we were told that in order to get their work done, it was sometimes necessary for the GC to go to the senior partner's office (as opposed to the other way around), where the chief legal officer might have to wait for hours before gaining a brief audience with the "great man or woman," before being shunted off to a more junior partner who, in the eyes of the GC, was typically far less skilled

TABLE 14. *Hiring foreign law firms*

	All	Business group	Nonbusiness group	FMC	SOE
Use preferred provider list	45%	52%	38%	69%	23%
Number of firms on list	8.31	9.73	15.00	5.64	4.33
List made by GC	79%	94%	67%	55%	100%
List in 2010*	64%	63%	33%	73%	67%
Percentage of work to list	61–70%	61–70%	91–100%	41–50%	61–70%
Change since 2010 (same or more)*	95%	90%	100%	100%	100%

in the transaction than the senior partner. Indeed, for many GCs the largest problem in the Indian legal market is that there simply are not enough Indian lawyers with the requisite skill to handle the increasingly complex transactions that Indian companies and multinational companies operating in India find themselves confronting. As a result, when GCs do have a choice about which law firm to select, they tend to choose one with the ability to "scale up" to handle a complex deal. Not surprisingly, this tends to lead them back to the top established players.

We also asked whether companies operating in India maintained a similar list of preferred providers for foreign law firms. Table 14 provides the results. The overall number was substantially less than the percentage of companies with preferred provider lists for domestic Indian law firms, but still quite substantial. A little less than half of the companies in our sample (45 percent) kept such lists for foreign law firms, with a fairly high percentage (79 percent) of GCs claiming that they were responsible for putting the list together. The average size of the list of foreign firms was slightly larger (eight) than it was for domestic Indian firms (seven), with approximately the same percentage (61–70 percent) of total work going to firms on the list. The foreign law firms most likely to appear on these lists were well-known global firms such as Baker & McKenzie, DLA Piper, Clifford Chance, and Allen & Overy, with Reid Smith and Herbert Smith (now Herbert Smith Freehils) being frequent choices as well.

Both Indian and multinational companies used their list of preferred providers to negotiate "preferred discounts" or otherwise put downward pressure on fees. Indeed, Indian GCs seemed to be particularly active in this area, often boasting in our interviews that they paid fees that were significantly lower than the ones that were paid for similar work by foreign companies. As a result, in the opinion of several informants, the major Indian law firms make the bulk of their profits on work for foreign clients. As more than one interviewee noted, this is why the Indian law firms are so anxious to keep foreign law firms from entering the Indian legal market.

With respect to foreign law firms, our interviews revealed strong support among a broad cross section of companies operating in India in favor of allowing these firms to enter the Indian market. Not surprisingly, this sentiment was particularly pronounced among FMCs, who expressed a strong desire to be able to use the same law firms in India that they use elsewhere in the world. At the same time, many of these same GCs signaled their distaste for the fees that the global law firms are already charging them for specialized or cross border work. As a result, it is not clear from our interviews how much companies based in India would actually use international law firms if they were able to enter the market. This is particularly true for Indian companies, some of which expressed an interest in having their Indian law firms expand internationally so that these Indian law firms could provide them with services on their oversees transactions at the Indian price level that these GCs have been able to negotiate for domestic work, as opposed to what they consider the "outrageous prices" charged by global firms.

Finally, given the importance of Grand Advocates in India, we asked GCs which Grand Advocates they tended to hire. Here there was a clear set of common choices: Harish Salve, Gopal Subramanium, Mukul Rohatgi, and Abhishek Manu Singhvi. Once again, the frequency with which these well-known advocates were chosen underscores the claim made by Marc Galanter and Nick Robinson in Chapter 14 of this volume that there are a small number of Grand Advocates who dominate the Indian advocacy market. Our interviews confirmed this pattern. Several respondents, however, went on to express great frustration with the quality of these top advocates. Although they were happy to use a range of advocates for low-stakes work, virtually all our respondents felt compelled to hire one of the top Grand Advocates when the stakes were high. These advocates, many GCs reported, are even more difficult to deal with than top law firm partners. Yet because of their perceived special relationship with top judges and arbitrators, even the most powerful GCs appear to feel that they have little or no choice but to hire these Grand Advocates in important matters.

2. Significant Versus Routine Work

Although there are a number of areas of legal work in-house departments in India typically give to outside law firms, we know that not all such work is of equal importance. In particular, we know from our experience in other markets

TABLE 15. *Routine legal work*

	All	Business group	Nonbusiness group	FMC	SOE
Percentage of legal budget on routine matters	46%	43%	27%	511%	52%
Percentage of routine work sent to various providers					
In-house lawyers	49%	43%	63%	44%	69%
Outside law firms	66%	71%	67%	54%	66.6%
Non-law-firm providers (e.g. LPO)	30%	22%	10%	20%	65%

that GCs often distinguish between how they source "very significant" legal work and work they view as being more "routine." We therefore asked survey respondents a series of questions designed to see whether this distinction was significant in the Indian context, as well as to identify the factors, processes, and players involved in sourcing these two general types of legal work.

As a preliminary matter, it is significant to note that nearly half of the budget of the companies in our survey sample (46 percent) was spent on routine legal work. In addition, respondents indicated that about 66 percent of this routine work was sent to outside law firms, as opposed to just less than 50 percent being kept inside. Also consistent with findings explored by one of us in a subsequent chapter in this volume on legal outsourcing, close to 30 percent of the budget that companies are spending on routine legal work is going to non-law-firm providers. As our interviews made clear, many companies use a combination of in-house, law firm, and outsourcing companies to do their routine work, which explains the overlap in percentages found in table 15.

With respect to "very significant" matters, which we defined as an important transaction or a significant piece of litigation, the patterns look very different. Whereas most of the routine work sent to outside law firms pertained to civil litigation or low-level arbitration, the majority of the very significant work sent to Indian law firms pertained to civil liability and contracts, while foreign firms were more likely to handle important matters involving M&A, and civil liability and arbitration. In both cases, the GC is the person who primarily made the choice of whom to hire (76 percent of GCs chose the domestic law firm and 86 percent chose the foreign law firm). Once again there was convergence toward a small subset of law firms – domestically it was Amarchand, Khaitan, and AZB and for foreign firms, it was DLA Piper, Clifford Chance, and Baker & McKenzie.

We were also interested in learning how GCs decided whom to hire for very significant matters. GCs indicated, much as they did in the United States, that for domestic law firms, "prior experience with a lawyer or firm," "the reputation of the lawyer/firm," and "results in similar cases" were key determinants in hiring both Indian and foreign law firms. In addition, however, Indian GCs reported that "ethical infrastructure" and "quality control systems" were important when hiring domestic firms and that "geographic scope" was an important consideration when engaging foreign law firms. None of these factors was considered important by the average GC in a US S&P 500 company (Coates et al. 2011).

Indian GCs differ from their US counterparts with respect to these factors, providing important clues about the current state of in-house legal departments operating in India. For example, Indian GCs are concerned with a law firm's internal quality-control systems, which appears to reflect that GCs are concerned, as noted earlier, about the quality and depth of the lawyers at even the best Indian law firms. The fact that GCs are also concerned with the "ethical infrastructure" in India's domestic law firms may also reflect this concern, since weak ethics may have deleterious effects on quality.

However, even independent of quality concerns, the exasperation voiced by many GCs at the state of affairs in India's legal system also leads us to think that ethical concerns are independently important, since companies – particularly FMCs – may fear being embroiled in ethical issues that arise from a law firm's attempt to navigate the byzantine, and too often corrupt, workings of India's judicial and administrative processes. Moreover, as foreign countries continue to enhance enforcement of laws targeted to foreign corruption, such as the FCPA and the UK Bribery Act, both FMCs and Indian corporates are becoming more attuned to ethical considerations. Finally, the fact that Indian GCs consider a foreign firm's "geographic reach" suggests that they are less confident than their US counterparts at selecting law firms in particular foreign markets and therefore tend to look for more "global" firms with a broad geographic reach. Global powerhouses such as Baker & McKenzie and DLA Piper tend to top the list of foreign firms hired by Indian corporates, reinforcing this intuition.

In terms of where Indian GCs obtained information on the factors that most interested them when hiring Indian firms, our survey results indicate that the primary sources of information were personal knowledge (83 percent) and information from colleagues within their organization (43 percent). Only 56 percent indicated that they consulted with people outside of their organization, with 34 percent saying that they looked at public sources of data, such as the kinds of rankings put out annually on law firms or individual lawyers by firms such as Chambers & Partners and RSG Consulting. Although these percentages are directionally similar to what one of us found in our study of the legal purchasing decisions of large US companies, it is interesting to note that both the percentage of GCs in India who claimed to rely on their personal knowledge in making these decisions was significantly less than their US counterparts (82 percent, as compared to 97 percent in the United States), and the willingness of the former group to consult public sources of data was significantly higher (34 percent in India versus 24 percent in the United States) than we found in the US companies. This suggests that either India's GCs are less confident in their knowledge of the Indian legal market or they generally have a greater willingness to rely on data in making legal purchasing decisions. The fact that more than a third of respondents indicated that they thought they would be more likely to rely on "external" sources of information (e.g., conversations outside of their own organization and public sources of data) in the future suggests that the latter explanation may be more plausible. This fits with a general trend that one of us has documented toward a greater use of metrics and other objective data in the legal services market (Wilkins 2016).

This trend is even more pronounced with respect to the hiring of foreign law firms. Although traditional factors such as "reputation," "prior experience," and "results in similar cases" continue to dominate in importance, the GCs in our survey rated "rankings in periodicals" as only slightly less important to size and geographic scope (3 on a 5-point scale, where 1 is "very important" and 5 is "not important at all," compared to 2.87 and 2.65) when hiring a foreign law firm for a very significant matter. Similarly, only 72 percent of GCs indicated that they relied on "personal knowledge" when selecting foreign law firms in these matters, while 60 percent said they consulted experts outside of their own organization and 44 percent consulted publicly available data. The fact that 60 percent of respondents believed these "external" sources would be even more important in making similar decisions in the future underscores the growing importance of these factors in the global market.

3. Terminating or Adjusting Relationship with Outside Legal Service Providers

In addition to asking about hiring, we also queried both interviewees and survey respondents about when they terminated law firms they were using for very significant work. As figure 3 indicates, the results parallel what we know about the US market but also underscore that relationships between companies and their important law firms may be more stable and enduring in

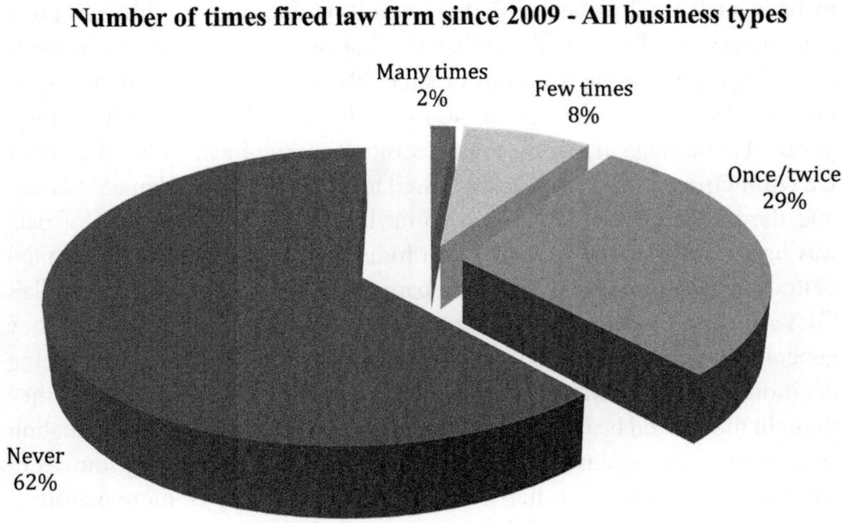

FIGURE 3 Number of times fired law firm since 2009

emerging markets such as India than they are in a developed market such as the United States.

As we indicated in this chapter, one of the hallmarks of the in-house counsel movement in the United States is the claim that GCs have "broken up" the long-standing relationships between companies and their principal outside law firms, and that they enforce this new "spot contracting" regime by frequently switching legal providers to obtain the best service and price. When one of us studied the legal hiring and firing decisions of large US companies in the years before the global financial crisis, we discovered that the reality was a good deal more complex than this simple story would suggest (Coates et al. 2011). Although GCs had moved from the kind of bilateral monopoly relationships that companies traditionally had with their top outside law firms and were generally exercising more control over the law firms that were hired, it was not true that they were switching important law firm relationships frequently as the spot market contracting analogy would imply. Instead, we found that important law firm relationships were changed relatively infrequently. Rather than terminating the relationship altogether, GCs used the strategy of reducing work when they were upset with either the quality or the price of the services they received. These work reductions, however, were typically neither just at the level of the individual lawyer with whom the company was upset nor across the board to the entire firm. Instead, GCs most often reduced work to the entire "team" or "department" where the offending lawyer worked, leaving other teams or departments alone. As a result, we concluded that US GCs considered neither the "lawyer" nor the "firm" the correct unit of analysis, but rather were beginning to see firms as collections of semiautonomous teams or departments who would be expected to take responsibility for the conduct of their individual team members, but who were not themselves responsible for the conduct of other parts of the firm if they were working well.

Our survey data in India shows a similar pattern, but one where firm-level relationships continue to play a larger role. As in the United States, the vast majority of companies in India rarely terminate important law firm relationships. Indeed, fully 62 percent have not done so at all between 2009 and 2015, with another 29 percent having only done so once or twice during this period. These percentages are significantly higher than what we found in the United States, where only 31 percent of companies had not terminated a significant law firm relationship and 48 percent had done so once or twice during a comparable period (Coates et al. 2011). The fact that less than 10 percent of respondents in India claimed that they terminated important law firm relationships relatively frequently – compared to the 21 percent who reported doing so in our US sample – underscores how stable these relationships still are in India. This is consistent with what we heard during our qualitative interviews about the relative thinness of the Indian large law firm market. The fewer alternatives, the less likely a GC is to terminate an important law firm relationship.

This dimension of the Indian corporate legal market may also help explain why GCs operating in India do not seem to have substituted work reductions for terminations. Unlike US GCs, who reported that they placed firms "in the penalty box" by reducing work when they were displeased, less than 40 percent of GCs in India reported taking similar action at least once or twice since 2009, with more than 60 percent reporting that they had not done so at all during this period. Although this could be because of the consistently superior service these GCs are receiving, the many GCs we interviewed who expressed extreme displeasure with how they had been treated by India's top law firms suggest that the thin market for lawyers with both the experience and reputation to take on challenging corporate assignments – and the fear that alienating one of these top lawyers will make it difficult for a company to work with a given firm in the future – is the more persuasive explanation.

Finally, as in the United States, when GCs did reduce work, they were more likely to do so with respect to the entire team and/or department (65 percent), as opposed to just the individual lawyer with whom they were upset (22 percent). These numbers are roughly similar to what we found with respect to GCs in large US companies and suggests that while relationships are still "sticky" in India at the level of the entire firm, GCs in this jurisdiction may be beginning to follow their US counterparts in penalizing the team and department level as well. This understanding could have important implications for the creation of the kind of second-generation corporate law firms described in Chapter 6 of this volume, which are often formed by "peeling off" important partners – and more recently, whole practice groups – from India's Big 5 law firms.

H. *Relationships with the Bar*

In the United States, one of the key goals of the in-house counsel movement has been a quest for legitimacy and status within the organized bar. We therefore examined whether GCs in India have engaged in any similar project and how the creation of new in-house organizations, either within India or globally, has impacted this quest. Although the process is clearly still developing, both our interview and survey data suggest that Indian GCs still have a long way to go to gain the recognition and respect within the profession that their US and even Western European counterparts have achieved.

At the most basic level, GCs in India occupy a formal status that lies somewhere in between the full professional standing they enjoy in the United States and the clear second-class citizenship their predecessors in India traditionally occupied prior to liberalization, where many of those doing the company's legal work were not trained as lawyers. Although we encountered a few people functioning in the GC role who had only the traditional "company secretary" qualification, the overwhelming majority of those in both our interview and survey samples had been educated as lawyers. However, as we saw in table 4, only about 60 percent of GCs who responded to our survey are either current or former members of the Indian bar, suggesting that while legal education is important to the role as currently understood, actual bar membership is not.[12] Interestingly, GCs in business-group firms had the lowest percentage of bar membership, with less than half (about 47 percent) ever having been a member of the Indian bar. Once again, this is consistent with the observation that many of those in these positions are chosen for reasons other than their technical legal skills or qualifications.

Moreover, even when they are formally members of the bar, Indian GCs are not fully equal to lawyers practicing in law firms. Like their counterparts in Europe, in-house lawyers in India are not entitled to the benefit of the attorney–client privilege when speaking with their corporate managers (Varottil 2012). Interestingly, however, this deficit does not seem to be as critical as it has been in Europe given that so few cases ever get to the full decision state in Indian courts due to the extreme backlogs and delays that permeate that system. It will be interesting to see whether this issue becomes more significant as Indian GCs find themselves engaged in more transnational work that may subject them to litigation or arbitration in non-Indian courts. At present, the fact that Indian GCs are not covered by the lawyer–client privilege may also help explain why US multinationals prefer GCs who are dually qualified as American lawyers and therefore entitled to the full professional standing that in-house counsel in the United States enjoy.

With respect to professional organizations specifically focused on GCs, both Association of Corporate Counsel (ACC) and domestic organizations appear to be growing but are still at a relatively early stage of development. The most active group is the Indian Corporate Counsel Association (ICCA), but even this group appears to be relatively small and fragmented. Given the diversity among the kinds of companies and ownership structures, it may be difficult to put together all the various kinds of professionals who work as internal counsel – across all the various kinds of domestic and international organizations in which these counsel work – to create an association that can effectively promote the collective professional interests of India's in-house lawyers. Whether or not either international or domestic GC organizations are able to bridge these traditional divides will go a long way toward determining whether internal counsel in India achieve the kind of professional status enjoyed by their counterparts in the United States. Given the role that these professional organizations in the United States have played in amplifying GCs' political clout, it seems plausible that similar organizations would need a stronger footing in India for GCs there to play a similarly significant role in broader policy and legal debates.

At present, therefore, the quest for professional status seems to be a less important goal of the in-house counsel movement in India than it has been in the United States. As a result, it is not surprising that relatively few of the GCs in our survey reported that they participate frequently or very frequently in debates on the regulation of the legal profession (27 percent) – notwithstanding their expressed displeasure about the exclusion of foreign lawyers.

I. *Relationships with Government*

The story, however, appears to be quite different with respect to GCs' participation in broader public policy debates on behalf of their corporate clients. As table 16 indicates, a far higher percentage of GCs report actively engaging in concerted activity designed to influence public policy in India, and increasingly around the world. Thus 43 percent of our survey respondents reported that they commented frequently or very frequently on pending legislation. Thirty-four percent indicated that they participate in trade organizations relating to their company's activities, much of which undoubtedly involves seeking to affect government action. Perhaps most significantly, a third of respondents

TABLE 16. *Relationships with the bar and government*

	All	Business group	Nonbusiness group	FMC	SOE
Comment on pending legislation	43%	44%	13%	47%	53%
Interact with agency officials	33%	30%	26%	37%	38%
Speak out on public policy issues on behalf of the company	26%	24%	13%	31%	31%
Participate in debates over the regulation of the legal profession	27%	32%	13%	26%	23%
Participate in any trade group organizations	34%	33%	26%	47%	23%
Percent change in time spent on participation on politics and legislative matters	24%	21%	16%	26%	36%

indicated that they frequently or very frequently interact with government officials on behalf of their company.

Although these percentages are undoubtedly lower than one would find in the United States in response to similar questions, they confirm the findings in other research, both in this volume (Chapter 9 on lobbying in India) and elsewhere (Khanna 2016), that GCs in India are beginning to play a more active role in policy and economic development. Our interview data confirms this trend. In one particularly striking example, the GC of a prominent Indian company reported that he had been intimately involved behind the scenes in drafting an important piece of business legislation and that he had begun spending about half of his time in Delhi, where he regularly meets with lawmakers and regulators. The fact that a quarter of our survey respondents indicated that the time they spent on these issues has increased significantly in the past three years underscores just how important this kind of activity has become to GCs in India.

Given India's political economy, it is not surprising that GCs are finding themselves increasingly drawn into public policy debates. As indicated earlier, the government sector is arguably even more important to the corporate legal market in India than it is in the United States. Similarly, as Indian companies become multinationals, including operating in countries in Asia, Latin America, and Africa that have yet to emerge, the in-house lawyers working within these organizations will also likely find themselves creating private ordering schemes that may affect issues of public concern.

Of course, even if Indian GCs decide to play this kind of role, it is far from clear whether they will be able to do so effectively – or that they will be the primary ones who are asked to perform this important function. For example, only 26 percent of the respondents in our survey indicated that they are frequently called upon to speak publicly on behalf of the company on important issues. Indeed, it is quite possible that the influence that GCs (and GC organizations such as the ACC) have in the United States is as much a function of America's highly legalistic culture as it is the power of in-house lawyers. The fact that UK GCs have been far less successful at pushing their regulatory agenda than their US counterparts is at least an indication that context may play a key role in the success of this last aspect of the in-house counsel movement.

IV. HYPOTHESES

Given this overall picture of Indian GCs, we find substantial evidence to support each of the four hypotheses with which we began this chapter. We also, however, find evidence that complicates each hypothesis and raises additional questions worthy of further inquiry.

A. *Hypothesis 1: In-House Departments in India are Growing in Size and Importance*

Our data provides strong support for the hypothesis that in-house departments in India have increased substantially in both size and importance. In particular, the growth in the budgets of Indian in-house departments from 2009 to 2015, the growth in outside legal expenditures over the same period, and the increase in the number of people working within in-house departments provides strong support for this hypothesis. The expectation of the GCs responding to our survey that both budgets and internal hiring will continue to grow further substantiates this initial hypothesis, as does the increasingly important role that many GCs are playing within their organization.

The growth across all respondents is really quite dramatic. For example, table 7 reports that in-house legal budgets at the firms responding to our survey have soared an average of 87 percent from 2009 to 2015, with foreign firms having the highest growth over that period (111 percent) and nonbusiness-group private firms growing 75 percent. Figure 1 provides evidence that the legal expenditures on outside legal service providers have accelerated so that in the past five years (from 2010 to 2015), there was a 62 percent growth in such expenditures. Table 8 allows us to view this growth from the perspective of the size of the in-house division, which over the three years prior to the survey (from 2011 to 2014) had grown 64 percent (on average) in the number of employees, with nonbusiness-group private firms growing the fastest in head count (75 percent) and foreign firms growing the slowest (53 percent). Moreover, when asked how much they expected their departments to grow over the next three years (from 2015 to 2017), our respondents on average said they expected a 66 percent increase in the size of their departments, with business-group firms leading the charge (74 percent) and SOEs being the slowest (54 percent).

To further explore the increase in size of in-house departments, we examined the difference in means (t-tests) for a number of variables, and the results are reported in the appendix. We find that the differences in the means of the legal budgets of 2009 and 2012, the legal budgets of 2012 and 2014–2015, and the growth in legal budgets from 2009 to 2012 and 2012 to 2014–2015 are significant at the 1 percent level. This adds further evidence in support of the increasing size of in-house departments. Moreover, the increase is secular and largely consistent across ownership types, with the exception of foreign firms, whose average legal budgets grew more than the rest of the firms in 2012 (although this result is only marginally significant at 10 percent). As we indicated, this might be associated with greater expenditures to ensure compliance with antibribery laws in their home countries (e.g., the FCPA and the UK Bribery Act). Similarly, the appendix also reports that the increase in the size of in-house departments is across all ownership types.

In addition to size, there is considerable evidence from our survey responses that the importance of the in-house department has grown substantially. Perhaps the most direct evidence is in table 9 and figure 2, where respondents indicated that on average about 60 percent of GCs reported to either the board or the CEO. This stands in marked contrast to the information provided by interviewees about what the traditional (i.e., pre-1991) reporting structure was (i.e., the GC reported to the CFO or the company secretary). Further, the results in the appendix indicate that this change is across the board, with the exception of the mean percentage of foreign firms having their GCs report to the board or the CEO being lower than that of the rest of the firms. This seems largely driven by the fact that many foreign firms' GCs report to global GCs rather than the local or global CEO. Collectively, these reporting patterns provide strong evidence of a change in the GC's importance and status within the company.

These findings are bolstered by the other responses in table 10, which indicate that about 50 percent of our respondents advise the board frequently or very frequently, 60 percent participate in senior leadership discussions frequently or very frequently, and about 74 percent counsel the CEO frequently or very frequently. Indeed, of our survey respondents, all but one indicated that the amount of time they spent on these activities had either increased or stayed the same in the past three years. Further, we asked, if there had been an increase in time spent, how much more of their time was spent on these activities. The average was slightly more than 40 percent. Moreover, when we look at the t-test differences in means reported in the appendix, the increase in time is secular, with GCs at SOEs being the ones reporting the greatest increase in time spent on these activities. These findings are all consistent with our hypothesis about the increasing importance of GCs' offices.

Finally, table 13 also provides supportive evidence by noting that most firms have preferred provider lists for domestic law firms (75 percent), 91 percent of GC respondents are responsible for making such lists, and about 61–70 percent of the outside legal work goes to those on the list. Our interview data, collected in 2011 and 2012, indicated that GCs had been increasing in importance, but that managing the relationship with outside providers was not entirely within their control at that time. The survey results indicate that in the past three years Indian GCs have gone a long way toward gaining control over these decisions. Once again, the data reported in the appendix indicates that the preferred provider lists are now the norm across all company types, with business-group firms being less willing to have preferred provider lists for domestic firms as compared to other companies.

B. *Hypothesis 2: Ownership Structure Influences Size and Importance of in-House Departments*

Our data also supports the hypothesis that there are important differences in the structure and functioning of in-house legal departments across the four different kinds of ownership structures we discuss. For example, as table 7 illustrates, although all types of companies have increased their legal budgets, FMCs did so at a rate that is significantly higher (111 percent) than the rate of increase of the average nonbusiness-group company (75 percent). Although there may be many potential explanations for this difference, it is consistent with the intuition outlined in section III D that the growing importance of anticorruption initiatives and compliance have caused FMCs to invest more in strengthening their legal budgets than their Indian counterparts.

Our data also reveals other important differences across ownership structure. For example, in table 13 we see considerable variation in the use of preferred provider lists by ownership type, with business-group firms being the least likely to have such a list (65 percent), and nonbusiness-group firms being the most likely (88 percent). Yet another area of considerable variation is in how often firms terminate important law firm relationships. With respect to this variable, business-group GCs were the least likely to report having done so – with 77 percent stating that they had not terminated a single such relationship since 2009 – and FMCs being the most likely to terminate such relationships, with only 38 percent stating that they had not done so during this same period. Once again, although there are many possible explanations for these differences, business groups appear to have more personal and stable relationships with their outside law firms, providing some support for the claim that notwithstanding the size and complexity of these organizations, they still tend to be dominated by important relationships based on communal or personal affiliations. As we have indicated, this is one of the unique features of the Indian environment that is likely to continue to affect the diffusion of the Western model of the in-house counsel movement.

The data also underscores the unique features of GCs at SOEs. As the appendix documents, the GCs' tenure at these companies, and time as the GC, tend to be longer than in other types of companies. Similarly, GCs at SOEs are significantly more likely to be promoted from within than at other companies, and in-house departments at SOEs are larger (in terms of employees) than in-house departments at private Indian companies (both business group and nonbusiness group) and FMCs. Finally, GCs at SOEs are significantly more likely than their counterparts in the other three categories to have increased the amount of time they spend on high-level activities, such as counseling the CEO or advising the board.

Taken as a whole, these differences provide some support for the anecdotal reports we received in our qualitative interviews that the government is in the midst of an ongoing effort to upgrade the legal capacity of these important quasi-state actors, but that these efforts must take place within the context of organizations that are also subject to many of the same bureaucratic rules as other parts of the government on such issues as seniority and promoting from within. Once again, identifying these differences in how state-owned and/or managed companies operate will be critical to understanding how features of the in-house counsel movement that were developed in the United States, where such entities are relatively rare, will be translated and adapted in emerging economies such as India, where such entities are common.

C. *Hypothesis 3: Firms Interacting with the Global Economy Will Have Larger and More Important In-House Departments*

Our data also provides support for our hypothesis about the connection between a company's interaction with the global economy and the size and importance of its in-house legal department. As an initial test of this hypothesis

TABLE 17. *Export earnings, legal budget growth regressions*

	Legal_bdgt_ growth	Legal_bdgt_ growth	Legal_bdgt_ growth	Legal_bdgt_ growth	Legal_bdgt_ growth	Legal_bdgt_ growth
	[1]	[2]	[3]	[4]	[5]	[6]
Export earnings	0.008	0.013	0.013	0.013	0.012	0.016
	[2.53]**	[3.41]***	[3.38]***	[3.31]***	[2.57]**	[2.05]**
Ln (sales)		0.017	0.001	0.004	0.007	0.09
		[0.37]	[0.02]	[0.06]	[0.11]	[0.46]
Ln (profits)			0.052	0.026	−0.023	0.191
			[0.85]	[0.11]	[−0.09]	[0.32]
Ln (assets)				0.029	0.053	−0.211
				[0.12]	[0.20]	[−0.34]
SOE						0.072
						[0.05]
Foreign					−0.22	−0.603
					[−0.62]	[−0.42]
Non-BG					−0.3	
					[−0.53]	
BG					−0.099	−0.311
					[−0.27]	[−0.23]
Legal charges						0.003
						[0.55]
Constant	1.31	1.05	0.805	0.715	0.965	1.26
R-squared	0.138	0.2938	0.306	0.3064	0.3234	0.405
Observations	42	31	30	30	30	18

we gathered data from Prowess on export earnings of firms and then scaled it by dividing by sales. This was then used as an independent variable in a regression where the dependent variable was the geometric mean on the growth in the legal budget for in-house departments. These results (along with the addition of more control variables) are reported in table 17. As the regressions demonstrate, companies with greater export earnings to sales are associated with a faster growth rate in in-house legal budgets in our time frame. This is consistent with increasing interaction, with the global economy being associated with a larger in-house department.

Other measures of a firm's connection to the global economy show weaker results. Our survey asked two questions that bear on this connection: (1) whether more than 20 percent of the company's operations are located outside of India; and (2) whether the company engaged in any cross border transactions in the prior three years. These responses were then used as independent variables in regressions on various measures of in-house department size. For example, we found that in simple regressions (without controls), the variables reflecting whether the firm had substantial operations outside of India and whether there were important cross border transactions in the past three years were positively associated (albeit at the marginally significant 10 percent level) with the number of employees in the in-house department. However, as we added control variables, this association lost statistical significance. Similarly, we examined whether these two measures of a firm's interaction with the global economy were associated with measures of the GC's importance in the organization (e.g., advising the board, participating in senior management discussions). Once again, the simplest regression (without controls) provided some support for a positive association (again at the marginally significant 10 percent level). However, as control variables were added, this statistical significance largely disappeared.

Thus, the results on the connection between firms with stronger global ties and the size and importance of the GCs' offices in India suggest a positive relationship but are not robust across our measures of stronger global ties. Only the results for export earnings to sales are quite consistently significant and positive. These findings provide suggestive evidence at best that a connection may exist. Further study would be necessary to obtain more convincing evidence and to determine how much of the secular increase in size and importance of GCs' offices may be attributable to connections to the global economy. Indeed, it will be interesting to see whether larger differences will emerge as India's companies become even more deeply enmeshed in globalization.

D. *Hypothesis 4: In-House Departments are Becoming "Change Agents"*

Finally, in the survey we asked a number of questions to explore whether GCs were becoming more active as "change agents," either at the level of government policy or within the Indian bar. Table 16 provides some support for this hypothesis – e.g., 43 percent of respondents comment on pending legislation frequently or very frequently, 33 percent interact with agency officials frequently or very frequently, and 26 percent speak on public policy issues on behalf of the company. But while these percentages are impressive by historical Indian standards, they are nowhere near the level of engagement with public policy that we see from GCs in the United States and Western Europe. Our interview data confirms this general picture, with relatively few of the GCs we talked to claiming that they spend a great deal of time on general policy issues. And, as indicated in this chapter, neither our survey nor our interview data suggests that GCs in India are spending a great deal of time on influencing debates over the legal profession.

Nevertheless, as we indicated in section IIG, an important minority of GCs now see engaging in public policy debates and advocacy as an increasingly important part of their role. Given that the process of commenting on laws as we think of it in the United States is fairly new in India – and, as documented in Chapter 9 of this volume, continues to be considered of questionable legal or moral validity by many in India – the fact that so many prominent GCs were willing to claim that this is an important part of their role is, we argue, significant in and of itself. The fact that many GCs reported that the amount of time they were spending on these activities had increased significantly in the past three years indicates that this part of the GC's role may become even more important in the coming years.

Finally, we also note that the appendix indicates that across most of these activities it is the nonbusiness-group firms that are the least involved in these kinds of activities. Given that these firms tend to be smaller than either business groups or SOEs, we suspect this may reflect a capacity constraint at these firms, which then pulls down the overall level of involvement in our sample. As these firms grow larger and more enmeshed in India's rapidly changing political and legal environment, it is certainly plausible that their GCs will also increase their involvement in policy work.

Variables	US model	India pre-2000	India post-2000
Size	Grown dramatically since 1980s; large corporations have GC offices that rival the size of large outside law firms.	Quite small, although beginning to grow	Increased dramatically in size and in budgets; some large corporations have GC offices that are as large or larger than Indian law firms. Some differences across different types of firms.
Credentials and identities	Almost all are lawyers and members of the bar. A large number of people working in-house are women.	Not all are lawyers. Many have backgrounds as company secretaries. Very few are, or were, members of the bar (Bar Council of India Rules require in-house to suspend membership). Most are not from families working in the law.	Almost all are now lawyers, and the number of women working in-house has increased substantially (though few are GC). Still few are members of the bar. Most are not from a family working in the law.
Outside counsel	Largely select outside counsel and manage the relationship	Limited say in determining who is outside counsel and in managing that relationship	Most GCs now appear to have substantial influence in selecting and managing outside counsel. Business-group GCs have somewhat more limited say in this area.

(*cont.*)

Variables	US model	India pre-2000	India post-2000
Internal reporting relationships	Reporting to CEO is very common. Regularly advise top corporate players.	Generally report to the CFO rather than the CEO or board. Limited advising of top corporate players.	Nearly 60 percent now report to the CEO or the board. Frequently advise top corporate players.
The profession	Important players in the profession with increasing influence throughout	Limited influence in the profession; suspend bar membership (if have it) when enter in-house department	Influence in profession is increasing; still suspend bar membership (if have it) when enter in-house department
Public policy	Active role in public policy, with regular interactions with government	Very limited role in influencing public policy	Increasing role interacting with government, though not yet as pervasive as in the United States

V. THE FUTURE OF THE IN-HOUSE COUNSEL MOVEMENT IN INDIA

From the data presented in this chapter, it is clear that some version of the in-house counsel movement has come to India. Whether measured against the baseline of the status of internal counsel in India prior to liberalization in 1991 (or indeed, the practices of the early years of the new century), or even the admittedly still more-advanced benchmarks used to assess the in-house counsel movement in the United States and other Western economies, there has been a dramatic growth in the size, status, function, and power of GCs working in large companies operating in India. It is also clear, however, that this development is not a simple story of the diffusion of the US model to India. Historical and cultural forces unique to the Indian context have shaped – and mostly likely will continue to shape – the development of internal lawyering in India, even as the forces of economic globalization, and the globalization of knowledge and governance, continue to put pressure on both Indian corporates and FMCs operating in India to conform to more Western norms and practices.

Given this complex "glocal" dynamic, as we have labeled this general phenomenon in the introduction to this volume, it is likely that GCs in India will play an increasingly important role in the development of the Indian legal profession, and the Indian political economy in general, albeit in ways that are likely to differ from the role these actors are playing in the United States and other more developed economies. Thus, while we expect GCs in both Indian and foreign companies to continue to push for reform of the India legal services market – with respect to both the entry of foreign law firms and the quality and price of the services that companies receive from the growing number of domestic corporate law firms – we do not expect that even the most powerful GCs will soon become the kind of change agents we are currently seeing in the United States. As one of us has documented, since 2008, GCs in the United States have begun pushing aggressively for a series of changes that are expressly intended to bring "disruptive innovation," to borrow the business law scholar Clayton Christensen's evocative (and provocative) phrase, to the corporate legal services market (Christensen 1997). As a result, these increasingly sophisticated purchasers have been turning to a range of new providers, from LPOs and electronic discovery companies at the low end, many of which are ironically located in India and other emerging economies (see Chapter 13 of this volume), to the Big 4 accounting firms and other multidisciplinary firms offering to integrate law, business, strategy, and risk management into "globally integrated business solutions" that threaten to destabilize the legal profession's existing economic, organizational, and human capital models (Wilkins and Esteban 2016). Although, as we have seen, Indian GCs are taking some important steps to gain greater control over Indian corporate law firms and the Indian legal market in general, we see no evidence in favor of the kind of sweeping reform that we are beginning to see in more developed legal markets – at least not yet.

At the same time, as Indian companies continue their expansion into new markets – particularly markets in other emerging economies in East and South Asia, Latin America, and Africa – we expect that they will have to develop their own innovative ways of helping their companies drive growth while reducing risk in these challenging environments. This will require Indian GCs to incorporate a broad range of new knowledge and skills – including supply chain and project management, risk and talent assessment, and cross cultural awareness and fluency – that will take them far beyond the "legal" domain that has been their primary focus.

Only time will tell how successful India's in-house legal departments will be in attracting, developing, and retaining the kinds of lawyers who will be able to navigate these complex dynamics. What is certain is that any credible future account of the development of India's corporate legal market must pay close attention to how these increasingly important actors understand their position in India's legal profession in the age of globalization, and how they try to shape that age to fit both their and their powerful clients' interests.

APPENDIX – DIFFERENCE IN MEANS

Variables	Business group vs. field	Business group vs. nonbusiness group	Business group vs. FMC	Business group vs. SOE	FMC vs. field	SOE vs. field	Nonbusiness group vs. field
Tenure of GC at firm (years)	0.679	3.661	0.316	−4.317	0.903	**−4.87****	4.48
Tenure of GC as GC (years)	−0.4	0.848	−1.14	**2.18*****	−1.8	**2.42*****	0.705
GC promote from within (%)	−0.094	0.022	−0.031	**0.286*****	−0.106	**0.292*****	−0.03
Budget – 2009	−7768000	4.99^7	(1.73^7)	1.85^7	(2.87^7)	1.83^7	5.00^7
Budget – 2012	2.25^7	6.54^7	(6.84^7)	3972727	**(7.67^7)*****	2.14^7	8.49^7
Budget Growth (2009–2012)	0.494	−0.555	0.198	−1.24	0.636	−1.251	−0.3
Budget – 2014–2015	2403038	9.67^7	(−5.25^7)	3.8^7	(7.49^7)	4.69^7	1.04^8
Budget growth (2012–2014/2015)	−0.094	−0.199	0.091	0.178	0.049	0.16	−0.273
Budget growth (2009–2014/2015)	−0.229	−0.87	0.504	0.256	0.506	0.169	−1.07
Geometric growth legal budget (2009–2014/2015)	−0.186	−0.041	0.26	0.155	0.214	0.059	−0.16
Number of lawyers in-house in India – mean (median)	3.34	18.21	23.37	**−42.09****	16.74	**−47.75***	22.49
Increase in number of lawyers in legal department over the past three years	−0.16	0.022	**0.313*****	0.032	**0.303*****	−0.065	−0.071
Increase in percentage of lawyers in legal department over the past three years	−8.18	3.333	1	19.39	−4.26	18.599	−1.17
Increase in number of lawyers in legal department over the next three years	−0.146	0.11	0.124	0.197	0.062	0.145	0.037

GC reports to board and CEO (%)	−0.174	0.116	**0.276***	0.072	**0.242***	−0.026	0.025
Advising the board: frequently	0.046	0.154	−0.102	−0.086	−0.104	−0.074	0.201
Participating in senior leadership discussions: frequently	−0.081	0.081	−0.084	**0.321**	−0.171	**0.337**	0.042
Counseling the CEO: frequently	−0.103	**0.353**	−0.042	0.161	−0.131	0.127	**0.333**
Percent time spent on these (change)	8.26	**11.94**	−11.62	**−20.32**	−9.34	**−18.71**	19.44
Use preferred provider list for domestic law firms (%)	**−0.182***	0.165	**0.228***	0.136	0.168	0.046	0.075
Do you make the list? (%)	−0.076	0.136	0.07	0.045	0.033	0	0.104
Percentage work to those on list	−0.456	0.817	−0.136	1.01	−0.569	0.939	0.611
Percent of legal budget went to these routine areas	4.34	16.74	−7.31	−8.59	−6.29	−8.56	20.26
Since 2009 ever terminated LF relationship	**−0.28**	0.195	**0.382**	**0.256***	**0.295**	0.102	0.054
First time working with this firm	**0.539***	**−0.75**	**−0.528**	**−0.464***	−0.222	−0.11	−0.42
Since 2009 ever reduce amount paid	0.06	−0.038	0.033	−0.16	0.08	−0.162	−0.008

(cont.)

Variables	Business group vs. field	Business group vs. nonbusiness group	Business group vs. FMC	Business group vs. SOE	FMC vs. field	SOE vs. field	Nonbusiness group vs. field
Since 2009 ever reduce amount work	0.006	0.029	0.062	−0.092	0.082	−0.11	0.036
Comment on pending legislation	−0.025	**0.375****	−0.079	−0.038	−0.124	−0.063	**0.405****
Interact with agency officials	0.047	0.103	−0.121	−0.032	−0.128	−0.008	0.144
Speak out on public policy issues on behalf of the company	0.031	0.169	−0.127	−0.014	−0.148	0.004	0.208
Participate in debates over the regulation of the legal profession	−0.107	0.257	0.014	0.152	−0.059	0.113	0.223
Participate in any trade group organizations	0.018	0.132	−0.197	0.152	**−0.252****	0.195	0.159
Percent time increase/decrease	−0.021	0.096	0.023	−0.029	0.016	−0.049	0.095
Percent change in time spent on participation on politics and legislative matters	5.52	1.82	−7.35	−9.18	−5.42	−7.43	5.91
	2012 v. 2009	**2014–2015 v. 2012**	**2014–2015 v. 2009**	**Growth 2012–2015 v. 2009–2012**			
Budget	**3.37*****	**2.017*****	**4.87*****	**−0.677***			

Note: *1% level; **5% level; ***10% level

Notes

1 Carole Silver has been the most important legal scholar documenting the growing importance of LLM programs in the United States and elsewhere (Silver 2007, 2009).

2 It is important not to exaggerate the amount of specific information about the GC's role that the typical LLM student in the United States or United Kingdom is likely to absorb. Notwithstanding the triumph of the in-house counsel movement, there is very little actual discussion of the role of internal counsel in American law schools (Wald 2012). Nevertheless, even if students do not learn much about what in-house lawyers actually do, our first-year law students now understand that these are important and – for many students – desirable positions in the US legal services industry.

3 Some GCs we interviewed suggested that there have been outsourcing firms specializing only in compliance with company law and other similar matters for quite some time.

4 This column refers to all firms that were approached but did not respond except for BP because its size and profits are very much larger than virtually all other firms in this group.

5 One might treat graduating from an elite law school and strong English skills as being highly correlated because most of the candidates at elite law schools come from backgrounds where their English skills are likely to be quite strong (see Chapter 18 of this volume).

6 Having said that it is clear that some of these increases are being driven by a few firms with very large expenditures (i.e., the medians are often below the mean increases which suggests outliers in the data), but it is clear that there is a secular trend to increase legal expenditures.

7 This is not inconsistent with our interview data where GCs reported spending around 60% of their budget on in-house matters. Our interviews were conducted about two years before the surveys, so the mild discrepancy (60% in the 2012 interviews and 40–50% in the 2014 surveys) is understandable.

8 A recent study of Brazilian GCs reveals similarly ambiguous evidence (Gloncalvez and Gloncalvez 2010).

9 Moreover, when asked what reforms these GCs would most like to see in the Indian justice system, the three most common responses were reducing delays in court, improving lawyer quality, and providing better judges. These also underscore that GCs in India still tend to most identify with the traditional legal functions of their jobs.

10 Although not reported in the text, we found that Indian companies place most of their criminal law–related legal needs (representing 1–10% of their total legal needs) with Indian and foreign law firms suggesting that in-house legal departments have little capacity to do this kind of work internally. It also underscores that criminal law matters are important to companies doing business in India, both domestically and on the global stage. This is consistent with India's use of criminal law to accomplish regulatory objectives that are made difficult to achieve civilly because of the country's glacial court system, as well as the growing importance of criminal law issues such as corporate crime and corruption on the global stage.

11 There are also fewer law firms in India than the United States, so one might expect a shorter list in India.
12 This is in part due to the expectation that lawyers working in-house will suspend their bar membership (see rule 49, section VII, chapter II, part VI of the Bar Council of India Rules), but our survey question was whether the respondent had ever been a member of the Indian bar, to which about 40 percent answered no.

References

Baker, George and Rachel Parkin. 2006. "The Changing Structure of the Legal Services Industry and the Careers of Lawyers." *North Carolina Law Review* 84 (5): 1635–1682.

Bhagwati, Jagdish. 2004. *In Defense of Globalization*. Oxford: Oxford University Press.

Bolton, Clare. 2010. "Internal Investigations: The Next Big Challenge for In-House Resourcing." Latin Lawyer. August 16. www.latinlawyer.com/news/article/40785/internal-investigations-the-next-big-challenge-in-house-resourcing/.

Chayes, Abram and Antonia H. Chayes. 1985. "Corporate Counsel and the Elite Law Firm." *Stanford Law Review* 37 (2): 277–300.

Christensen, Clayton. 1997. *The Innovator's Dilemma: When New Technologies Cause Great Firms to Fail*. Cambridge: Harvard Business Review Press.

Coates, John C., Michele DeStefano, David B. Wilkins, and Ashish Nanda. 2011. "Hiring Teams, Firms and Lawyers: Evidence of the Evolving Relationships in the Corporate Legal Market." *Law and Social Inquiry* 36 (4): 999–1031.

Daly, Mary. 1997. "The Cultural, Ethical, and Legal Challenges in Lawyering for a Global Organization: The Role of the General Counsel." *Emory Law Journal* 46 (3): 1057–1112.

Dinovitzer, Ronit, Robert L. Nelson, Joyce S. Sterling, and Bryant G. Garth. 2012. *After the JD 2: A Longitudinal Study of Careers in Transition, 2007–2008*. Ann Arbor: Inter-university Consortium for Political and Social Research.

Drezner, Daniel. 2007. *All Politics Is Global: Explaining International Regulatory Regimes*. Princeton, NJ: Princeton University Press.

Gilson, Ronald. 1990. "The Devolution of the Legal Profession: A Demand Side Perspective." *Maryland Law Review* 49 (4): 869–916.

Gloncalvez, Marco and Alessandra Gonçalvez. 2010. "Brazilian Study on the Relationship between Legal Departments and Law Firms." *Martindale-Hubbell*, June 17. www.community.martindale.com/legal-groups/Geography/brasilia_lawyers/m/brasilia_lawyers-mediagallery/17147.aspx.

Heineman, Ben. 2016. *The Inside Counsel Revolution: Resolving the Partner-Guardian Tension*. New York: Ankerwycke.

Hendley, Kathryn. 2010. "The Role of In-House Counsel in Post-Soviet Russia in the Wake of Privatization." *International Journal of the Legal Profession* 17 (1): 5–34.

Khanna, Vikramaditya. 2009. "Corporate Governance in India: Past, Present and Future?" *Jindal Global Law Review* 1 (1): 171–195.

Khanna, Vikramaditya and Shaun J. Mathew. 2010. "The Role of Independent Directors in Controlled Firms in India: Preliminary Interview Evidence." 22 *National Law School of India Review* 22: 35–66.

Khanna, Vikramaditya. 2016. "Can Two Wrongs Make a Right? Insights From the Development of the Home Mortgage Market in India." Draft.

Khorasanee, Gabrielle. 2014. "Women GCs Leading Fortune 500 Companies on the Rise." FindLaw Corporate Counsel Blog, March 26. www.blogs.findlaw.com/in_house/2014/03/women-gcs-leading-fortune-500-companies-on-the-rise.html.

Kurunathan, Mahalakshmi. 2011. "Special Report – India." *Asia Counsel Magazine* 8 (9): 30–46.

Madsen, Michelle. 2008. "High Profile but Low-Key – Has GC100 Lived Up to Its Promise?" Corporate Counsel, January 29. www.corpcounsel.com/id=900005501840/HighProfile-but-LowKey-Has-GC100-Lived-Up-to-Its-Promise?slreturn=20160218134812.

Morrison, Reese. 2006. "What's the Difference between General Counsel and Chief Legal Officer?" Law Department Management Blog, March 22. www.lawdepartmentmanagementblog.com/law_department_management/2006/03/whats_the_diffe.html.

Neil, Martha. 2011. "Some Corps Cut Costs by Hiring Law Grads to Work In-House Instead of Using BigLaw Associates." *ABA Journal*, August 11. www.abajournal.com/news/article/some_corps_cut_costs_by_hiring_attorneys/.

Nelson, Robert and Laura Nielsen. 2000. "Cops, Counsel, and Entrepreneurs: Constructing the Role of Inside Counsel in Large Corporations." *Law and Society Review* 34 (2): 457–494.

Rosen, Robert Eli. 1989. "The Inside Counsel Movement, Professional Judgment and Organizational Representation." *Indiana Law Journal* 64 (3): 479–553.

Rostain, Tanina. 2008. "General Counsel in the Age of Compliance: Preliminary Findings and New Research Questions." *Georgetown Journal of Legal Ethics* 21 (2): 465–490.

Schwarcz, Steven. 2008. "To Make or to Buy: In-House Lawyering and Value Creation." *Journal of Corporation Law* 33 (3): 497–575.

Silver, Carole. 2007. "Local Matters: Internationalizing Strategies for U.S. Law Firms." *Indian Journal of Global Legal Studies* 14 (1): 67–93.

2009. "Educating Lawyers for the Global Economy: National Challenges." *Kyung Hee University Law Review*.

Tomasic, Roman and Jian Fu. 2005. "Regulation and Corporate Governance of China's Top 100 Listed Companies: Whither the Rule of Law?" The Research Committee on the Sociology of Law Annual Conference, Paris, July 11–13. www.reds.msh-paris.fr/communication/docs/tomasic-fu.pdf.

Varottil, Umakanth. 2010. "Delaware Ruling on Indian In-House Counsel and Legal Privilege." IndiaCorpLaw Blog, December 20. www.indiacorplaw.blogspot.sg/2012/12/delaware-ruling-on-indian-in-house.html.

Wald, Eli. 2012. "In-House Myths." *Wisconsin Law Review* 4 (2): 407–462.

Wilkins, David. 2012. "Is the In-House Counsel Movement Going Global? A Preliminary Assessment of the Role of Internal Counsel in Emerging Economies." *Wisconsin Law Review* 4 (2): 251–304

Wilkins, David, and Maria Jose Esteban. 2016. "The Role of the Big Four Accountancy Firms in the Reconfiguration of the Global Market for Legal Services." Center on the Legal Profession Working Paper Series 2016–01.

5

The Impact of Globalization and Cross-Border Mergers and Acquisitions on the Indian Legal Profession

Umakanth Varottil

I. INTRODUCTION

The phenomenon of globalization has generated a greater flow of capital, goods, and services across borders. While a substantial part of that flow in the twentieth century was from the developed world into the emerging markets, the reverse trend has recently become quite prominent as well. This has given rise to a wide variety of cross-border transactions in which law firms in the participating jurisdictions are called upon regularly to advise. One such transaction is the cross-border merger and acquisition (M&A), which involves the merger of two companies across borders, or the acquisition by one of the businesses or the control of another.

The impact of globalization on the legal profession has been the subject matter of academic study (Flood 2007; Silver 2007; Sokol 2007; Faulconbridge et al. 2008; Henssler and Terry 2012). A large part of the existing literature has focused on how international law firms from the developed markets (particularly the United States and the United Kingdom) have dealt with the effects of globalization. There is, however, burgeoning literature on the manner in which the legal profession in the emerging markets is adapting itself to meet with newer opportunities and challenges that emanate from globalization (Liu 2008; Krishnan 2010; Papa and Wilkins 2012). This chapter seeks to add to that body of knowledge with specific reference to India in the backdrop of cross-border M&A, which is an archetypal transaction that fully exemplifies the various facets of globalization.

Cross-border M&A in India is of recent vintage, as it only began in earnest during liberalization in 1991. While the initial thrust for the first decade of liberalization was by way of inbound acquisitions by foreign companies, since India entered the period of more intense globalization in 2000, it has witnessed frenetic activity by Indian companies engaging in outbound acquisitions. As this chapter documents, this activity has, in turn, produced a major shift in the Indian legal profession. Through constant interaction with international law firms and international clientele, there has been a transfer of knowledge, systems, and practices to Indian law firms such that they are able to undertake a larger role in cross-border transactions such as M&A. Although the relationship between Indian law firms and international law firms began as one of collaboration and mutual cooperation, the gradual capacity-building efforts by the Indian law firms have partially converted that relationship into one of competition.[1] While the international law firms began the cross-border deal decades ago with a largest shares of the pie, this study finds that the Indian law firms have expanded their role significantly into territories that were once exclusively within the domain of international law firms. The outbound foray of Indian companies has required lawyers to adopt an international outlook and obtain familiarity in dealing with laws, practices, and cultures not only in common law jurisdictions in which they have a working knowledge but also to cross new frontiers while transacting with other emerging economies with civil law traditions from countries as far as Latin America.

However, the Indian legal profession also faces crucial challenges that need to be addressed before it can fully benefit from the effects of globalization. The lawyer's role is shifting from that of a legal technician to one of a "trusted advisor" with commercial flair and managerial skills to effectively hand-hold the client during the deal-making process. Given that cross-border transactional practice is relatively recent in India, this study finds a lack of widespread availability of these skills and the required sophistication, which generates significant pressure on star lawyers, within the corporate legal profession in India. Although there is arguably a greater need for policy reforms that would grow the cross-border market for M&A in India, the debate regarding the entry of international law firms continues to be unresolved.

From a methodological perspective, a large part of the findings in this chapter are based on a qualitative survey that involved a series of interviews with eighteen different practitioners in the India cross-border M&A space. These include senior partners (several of whom are managing partners) from thirteen law firms in India across various bands,[2] three in-house legal counsel (two of whom are general counsel to India's large business houses active in cross-border M&A), and two lawyers from Indian practice groups of international law firms. Eleven interviews were conducted in person in Mumbai, and seven were telephonic interviews. The questions were open-ended and semistructured. The average interview time lasted more than one hour.[3] The author's previous experience as a corporate and M&A practitioner in a Band 1 law firm between 1995 and 2006 (which is much of the relevant time period of study) facilitated the interviews and contributed to a firsthand knowledge and experience of the issues discussed in this chapter.

Part II analyzes the evolution of cross-border M&A activity in India and examines current trends. While there has been variation in the levels of inbound and outbound activity, the general increase in size and complexity has placed unique demands on the Indian legal profession. Part III tracks the revolutionary changes in the role of corporate and M&A lawyers in India within the span of two decades. It also identifies the challenges that continue to preoccupy Indian lawyers in this space. Part IV looks at the institutional changes that Indian law firms have effected to deal with these challenges, including appropriate steps to build capacity and skills and to acquire the requisite human capital. Part V discusses the manner in which Indian law firms procure cross-border M&A work and how they price their services. Part VI finds that globalization and cross-border M&A provide both opportunities and challenges to in-house legal departments of Indian companies. Part VII examines some of the normative issues in terms of policy reforms required to boost cross-border M&A activity in India, and changes required to the structure of the legal profession to deal with enhanced activity.

II. TRENDS IN CROSS-BORDER M&A[4]

India presents significant opportunities for cross-border M&A. It is among the top acquisition destinations attracting buyers from other markets on inbound deals, particularly in comparison with other emerging markets (Merger market 2011, 11). It is also among the leading countries whose companies are actively acquiring targets and assets overseas through outbound deals (Grant Thornton 2011, 8–9; Allen & Overy 2012, 22).

The origin of the spate of cross-border M&A involving Indian companies can be traced to the liberalization of India's economic policies in 1991 that followed decades of state domination in business activity, which was accompanied by slow growth. In the initial years following liberalization, there was a flood of foreign investments into India, primarily in the form of greenfield investments (through joint ventures), but also through acquisitions and buyouts of Indian target companies. The emphasis was almost entirely on inbound acquisitions and investments, with hardly any outbound activity on the part of Indian companies.

However, at the turn of the century, India witnessed a new trend whereby Indian business houses began foraying abroad through outbound investments and acquisitions of overseas targets. Having obtained the required confidence during the liberalized economic regime, and having been exposed to global competition, Indian business houses went "from being passive resisters to active promoters of globalization" (Kumar 2009, 12). This phenomenon was also facilitated effectively through changes in India's legal regulations that eased restrictions on foreign acquisitions by Indian companies.[5] The tide completely turned in 2006, when outbound investments by Indian companies surpassed inbound investments by foreign companies (Kumar 2009, 12).

The recent sentiment regarding Indian M&As has, however, been one of cautious optimism. In the wake of the global financial crisis, there was a significant drop in volumes of M&A deals, both globally and with those involving Indian companies (Simhan 2012). At the same time, that Indian M&A activity has already begun to witness a strong resurgence (Grant Thornton 2015).

Within the M&A space, cross-border deals have gradually acquired prominence over purely domestic deals. The trends over the last few years indicate that while domestic deals are higher in number, the cross-border deals are larger in size (Srividya 2011). This suggests that most of the domestic deals are generally within the mid-to-small segment. In any event, there is overall consensus that a substantial part of M&A in India involves a cross-border element.[6]

Within cross-border deals, the recent activity since 2011 suggests a perceptible tilt towards inbound deals, shifting from the previous domination of outbound acquisitions.[7] This has been attributed to the valuations of businesses in India, and the generally relative stability of Asian businesses in comparison with European and other economies (Srividya 2011). Although the overall drop in inbound deals is understandable given global market conditions, the steeper drop in outbound deals and its surrounding circumstances reveal an interesting story that has implications on the manner in which Indian corporate legal practice is evolving and the challenges it is likely to pose going forward.

First, the blockbuster outbound acquisitions witnessed during the period from 2006 to 2008 have failed to return. During that period, several leading Indian conglomerates made multibillion-dollar acquisitions of companies in the United Kingdom, the United States, and Germany.[8] Not only have the acquirers been leading industrial houses, but several of the targets were larger than them in size (Afsharipour 2011, 1041). However, since then, the global turn of events has questioned the profitability of several of these acquisitions as they have not performed up to expectations ("Running with the bulls" 2012). Furthermore, as outbound Indian acquisitions have largely been leveraged through offshore borrowings, the lack of freely available financing due to adverse market conditions has added to the inability of Indian firms to make large-sized acquisitions abroad.[9]

Second, and linked partly to the previous reason, the profile of Indian acquirers and the size of their acquisitions have undergone change. While reasonably sized deals are still prevalent in Indian acquisitions of assets in the resources sector overseas, most other deals are in the midmarket sector and spearheaded by medium-sized Indian firms (Bajaj 2011). The more substantial acquisitions are by either government-owned companies or established business groups in industries such as power, telecom, mining, and natural resources (Confederation of Indian Industry and Ernst & Young 2011). The midsize deals are either in the manufacturing space or in consumer services, where Indian companies are looking toward obtaining access to international markets for their products (and sometimes services) (Confederation of Indian Industry and Ernst & Young 2011).

Third, there has been a sea change in the geographic distribution of Indian outbound deals. While nearly all of the initial deals involved acquisitions in developed markets such as the United Kingdom and the United States and a handful in continental European countries such as Germany, the latest round of acquisitions target either developing countries or emerging markets, as well as such developed countries that are resource-rich (Afsharipour 2011, 1042–1043). While the manufacturing and consumer-related acquisitions span across markets such as Africa, Latin America, and Eastern Europe (the former Soviet Union countries), the resource forays also include Southeast Asia (particularly Indonesia) and Australia (Bajaj 2011). This new trend of "South-South" deal making presents different types of opportunities as well as challenges for the Indian corporate and M&A legal fraternity as they are not accustomed to business dealings in those regions to the extent they have been in the leading developed markets (see below).

In analyzing M&A trends in India, it is clear that cross-border M&A continues to play an important role in the Indian economy and the corporate sector. While there may be fluctuations in the volume of activity and in the mix of inbound and outbound transactions, the corporate legal sector in India will need to continue with its process of reinventing itself to meet the demands of increased cross-border M&A, both in terms of its size and complexity. With this background, I now discuss how the Indian legal profession has adapted itself to meet the complexities of the new environment.

III. CROSS-BORDER M&A AND THE CHANGING ROLE OF LAWYERS IN INDIA

There is no doubt that globalization has significantly impacted the way of doing business in emerging economies such as India. Similarly, it has impacted the way in which corporate lawyers practice in the M&A and related fields. In order to assess and more objectively measure the impact, in this part, I seek answers to a series of key questions. (a) What is the role of a lawyer generally in an M&A transaction? (b) How is the legal profession in India positioned to discharge this role? (c) How has the Indian legal profession's role altered to suit circumstances occasioned by the phenomenon of globalization? (d) What are the differences in roles between inbound deals and outbound deals? (e) What are the challenges that the profession must address in order to more fully benefit from globalization?

A. *Role of Lawyers*

Lawyers are called upon to perform several, often complex, tasks in an M&A transaction. The initial task relates to *deal structuring*, which involves the creation of the path that helps achieve the clients' goals in a manner that is not only in compliance with applicable law but also cost-effective.[10] In this role, lawyers ensure that a transaction complies with applicable laws such as corporate and securities law, and that it also involves minimal outflow in the form of taxes, stamp duties, and similar costs. Once the parties display their intention in principle to proceed with the transaction, the acquirer's lawyers (along with other advisors) undertake a *due diligence* exercise to obtain relevant information regarding the target. This helps reduce the information asymmetry between the acquirer and the seller, and better educate the acquirer about the appropriateness of the price being paid for the transaction (Gilson 1984). In other words, it is a method by which the acquirer affirms its view of the target's value. *Contract drafting and negotiation* are key roles lawyers play. The legal contracts in an M&A transaction reduce uncertainties between the parties by stipulating the terms on which the deal will be carried out. More importantly, the key terms such as representations, warranties, covenants, and indemnities carry out the task of allocating the various risks among the parties. These are often the most heavily negotiated terms in M&A deals.[11] In large and complex M&A, lawyers are called upon to undertake the task of *specialized compliance*. This includes compliance with takeover laws in public M&A involving listed companies, and compliance with competition/antitrust laws and sector-specific regulations. Finally, in the event of disputes between the parties, *litigation* acquires a prominent role to be carried out by lawyers.

Although these tasks can be fairly straightforward in small and private deals, they acquire tremendous complexity in large transactions, particularly where public-listed companies are involved. In that scenario, it ceases to be a private matter, and the interests of shareholders and other stakeholders acquire importance. In the next section, I examine how the Indian legal profession has organized itself to perform these tasks in cross-border M&A involving Indian companies.

B. *Structure of the Indian Legal Profession: Servicing Cross-Border M&As*

The Indian corporate and M&A legal practice is evolving at a rapid pace, and there is vast heterogeneity in the backgrounds and structures of Indian law firms that are actively involved in the corporate and M&A sphere.[12] The 2013 Chambers Asia Pacific Guide ranked thirty-four law firms in India under the category of "Corporate/M&A" (Chambers and Partners 2013).[13] The Guide also ranked ninety-six individual practitioners in that category who are associated with either these law firms or others. Among the law firms, five were included under Band 1 and therefore considered to form part of the "elite" circle.[14] They are law firms with a substantial size and national presence. As for firms in other bands, while a few of them are of a substantial size and have a national presence, others have lean operations with offices in one or two cities only.[15] Many such firms are also boutique operations carving a niche for themselves in the area of M&A or private equity and venture capital investments. In cross-border M&A transactions, while it is difficult to arrive at precise estimates, most law firms represent both international clients as well as domestic clients, although the ratio of representation may vary (sometimes significantly) from firm to firm. While some law firms overwhelmingly represent international acquirers, others focus on sellers or targets in India, such as the Indian business houses or government enterprises.

Apart from the domestic Indian law firms, several international law firms from the United States, the United Kingdom, and a few other countries (notably Germany, Switzerland, Singapore, and Japan) have been actively participating in the Indian cross-border M&A activity, at least during the last two decades, if not longer. These firms are active through their "India practice groups" or "India desks" that comprise lawyers whose role (either fully or in part) relates to procuring and servicing clients on India-related M&A deals.[16] The India practice groups operate either as multilocational teams or through specifically assigned offices. A substantial number of international law firms handle their India work out of Asian offices in Singapore or Hong Kong, whereas others are content to handle that out of their principal offices in London or New York.

In 2013 Chambers and Partners ranked thirty international law firms under the head "Corporate/M&A" for India and nineteen lawyers who are associated with either these firms or others (Chambers and Partners 2013). Despite the lack of offices in India, these firms continually advice clients on India M&A deals and also staff themselves with India-qualified lawyers whom they proactively recruit either from law school campuses in India or laterally from the Indian legal practice.

A third category of practitioners relevant for cross-border M&A in India consists of in-house legal counsel. Here, I confine myself to the in-house counsel of Indian companies that participate in cross-border M&A, as it is the impact of globalization on this constituency that is relevant. The in-house legal community in India has also taken steps to meet with the challenges of globalization. The community has grown in stature from the position of a supporting role to the finance team to that of a gatekeeper as far as legal issues are concerned. While some of the leading Indian business groups have large in-house legal teams led by a group legal counsel, others have much smaller teams.[17]

While recently there has been an exponential growth of law firms and practitioners specializing in cross-border M&A, their numbers continue to be limited relative not only to the size of the legal community in India as a whole but also to the demands of companies (both international and domestic) in carrying out these transactions. Trends suggest that a substantial part of cross-border M&A work in India is carried out by a small number of firms and specific practitioners with them.[18] Furthermore, there is a significant concentration of high-value and complex M&A transactions among the elite firms and those in relatively higher bands in the ranking.[19]

C. *Role of the Indian Legal Profession Since Liberalization*

Globalization and the consequent surge of cross-border M&A activity have had a profound impact on corporate legal practice in India within a span of only two decades, and that is evident from the manner in which M&A lawyers' roles have undergone a metamorphosis. In the initial phase of cross-border M&A activity (which spanned the early- to mid-1990s), which was replete with inbound deals, the Indian lawyers primarily undertook the role of advising on the Indian leg of the transactions and on matters of transaction structures and contractual arrangements purely from the perspective of Indian law. The lead role in cross-border M&A was usually played by an international law firm, often the one that represented the acquirer as its relationship firm on a worldwide basis. While the international law firm conducted all of the drafting and much of the due diligence, the Indian law firm reviewed the documentation from the point of view of enforceability under Indian law, and assisted in the performance of due diligence. Transaction structures and customary contractual provisions that were commonplace in the Western markets were dealt with a sense of novelty in the Indian markets. For example, during that period, foreign acquirers of Indian companies or their assets were met with stiff resistance from Indian sellers or targets when they were asked to provide detailed representations and warranties that are customary in cross-border M&A transactions.[20] Negotiations became protracted, due not just to commercial and contractual disagreements, but often to the asymmetry in the appreciation of the scheme of the legal documentation and the risk allocation it entailed.[21] Indian lawyers had the additional onerous task of apprising their clients, who were also unfamiliar with these contractual arrangements due to their limited experience with cross-border activity.

However, all that was to change quite rapidly thereafter. Over the years, due to the effects of globalization, the Indian corporate legal fraternity has acquired tremendous exposure to international standards and practices. This is substantially the result of the experience gained from the cross-border transaction boom that has occurred in India since the 1990s. Constant interactions by law firms in India and their clients with international law firms has resulted in a transfer of knowledge, systems, and practices to Indian law firms, such that Indian law firms now undertake a significantly expanded role in cross-border M&A transactions. As we will see subsequently, several cross-border deals (particularly on the inbound side) are now undertaken by Indian law firms to either the exclusion of international law firms altogether or their limited participation. A number of factors are attributable to this rapid transformation. In her work relating to outbound acquisitions from India, Professor Afsharipour lists three benefits of the Indian legal system that may have contributed to the growth in such transactions, and they apply equally in the inbound context as well: (i) common law origins, (ii) the use of English as the language for law and business in India, and (iii) the training of corporate lawyers in India (Afsharipour 2011, 1047–1052).[22]

First, since India follows the common law system, having inherited it from the British colonial rule, Indian lawyers and their clients have had little difficulty in acclimatizing themselves to Western concepts and practices both in the commercial and legal spheres (Afsharipour 2011, 1048–1049; "Law and globalization" 2010). In both the inbound and outbound sides, most of the pioneering transactions involved companies from the United States and the United Kingdom, which share similar legal traditions with India.

Second, the use of the English language for law and business in India has facilitated a more direct (and firsthand) exchange of knowledge between Indian law firms and their international counterparts (Afsharipour 2011, 1049–1050).

Third, Indian legal education has been strongly influenced by the West, particularly the United States (Krishnan 2005; Afsharipour 2011, 1051–1052). Being familiar with general legal principles arising under common law, Indian lawyers were better able to absorb the sophistication in M&A processes and documentation.

Consequently, Indian law firms have expanded their role in cross-border M&A transactions beyond merely advising on Indian law issues pertaining to structuring and enforceability. The current offerings of Indian law firms include the entire range of services including structuring, due diligence, drafting and negotiating documentation, and specialized compliance, especially in inbound transactions, which are essentially driven by Indian lawyers as the target is domiciled in India. This role of Indian law firms varies significantly between inbound deals and outbound deals, each of which requires separate examination, a matter to which I now turn to.

D. *Deal Specifics: Inbound Versus Outbound*

Indian lawyers are called upon to perform vastly different roles in inbound transactions on the one hand, and outbound transactions on the other. Although Indian lawyers developed cross-border M&A expertise through inbound deals, they have been required to translate some of that learning into practice while advising Indian clients on outbound deals. While the lay of the land is familiar to Indian lawyers in an inbound deal, they are required to "feel their way" on several outbound acquisitions that take them to territories that were previously unchartered from an Indian perspective.

1. Inbound Deals

Since inbound deals are domiciled in India, the Indian law firms on the transaction have a significant role to play on all aspects. This includes advice on legal issues (primarily under Indian law), due diligence, drafting and negotiation of documents, and specialized compliance.[23] Although the involvement of an international law firm on the acquirer's side was prevalent in the initial years of liberalization, interview evidence suggests that such role is now the exception rather than the rule. Wherever international law firms are involved, their participation is occasioned due to some specific reasons.

International law firms with India practices are called in to advise an acquirer without prior deal experience with India. It is the lack of knowledge of the Indian market, legal system, and legal profession that compels first-time acquirers or investors to rely heavily on an international law firm, usually their relationship firm at a global level or sometimes locally within their own jurisdiction. In such situations, the international law firm plays a significant role and might even control the entire transaction and oversee the work of the Indian law firm (to the extent of Indian law issues), much in the same way business was carried out in the initial years following liberalization. However, once acquirers become familiar with the Indian markets and the legal system,[24] they are more likely to work extensively and directly with Indian law firms.[25] Repeat transactions appear to build the requisite trust between foreign acquirers and their Indian law firms.[26] Apart from preventing any duplication of work, this approach also helps reduce cost, which incentivizes the creation of direct relationships that appear to be largely the market practice on inbound deals.[27]

Another instance where international law firms continue to play a significant role is when the acquisition is tied to the availability of financing to the acquirer overseas, such as in a leveraged transaction. Since the acquisition and its financing must proceed seamlessly, the international law firm will have a significant bridging role to play.[28] This could also be the case when the acquirer is raising monies through issue of securities overseas to finance its acquisition. In other instances, international law firms become active when the acquirers are from non-English-speaking countries that have a civil law system. The international law firm acts to bridge legal differences and to break language and cultural barriers. In such a case, the international law firm will typically staff the transaction with lawyers from the acquirer's jurisdiction in case they operate an office there.[29] The final instance where international law firms are involved is when they are required to perform a gatekeeping role on behalf of the foreign acquirer that routinely undertakes transactions in India. Here, the role is fairly limited as the bulk of the transaction is handled by the Indian law firm representing the acquirer. The international law firm reviews the transactional structure and documentation at a broad level principally to ensure that all matters that are customary to the acquirer in global transactions are adequately addressed.

This discussion leads me to the impact of globalization on the relationship between international law firms and Indian law firms. Are they collaborators or competitors? In a related context, it has been found that the development of the Chinese corporate legal market has witnessed "a process of boundary-blurring and hybridization" whereby "local firms become structurally global-looking and global firms receive localized expertise" (Liu 2008, 771). When this theory is juxtaposed in the Indian context, the discussion earlier indicates a different result, at least in the inbound situation where the boundaries are becoming somewhat clearly drawn between the roles of international law firms and Indian law firms in the cross-border M&A space. To this limited extent, the Indian experience is arguably at variance with the Chinese experience.[30]

2. Outbound Deals

The strong emergence of outbound deals by Indian companies in the last decade has impacted the Indian legal profession fairly significantly, and in ways that are different from the impact of inbound deals. There is no uniformity in the impact of outbound deals on the Indian legal profession: as we shall see, the opportunities and challenges present themselves in varying ways for Indian law firms at different ends of the spectrum. Interestingly, the midtier firms appear to have embraced the outbound flurry to their advantage, more than the elite firms. One may surmise that a continuation of this trend could bring about significant changes to the structure of the legal profession that services cross-border M&A, particularly on the outbound side.

At the outset, in terms of the traditional role of an Indian lawyer, it is arguably minimal in an outbound acquisition by an Indian company. Although somewhat restrictive in nature, the Reserve Bank of India's (RBI) rules pertaining to outbound investments by Indian companies are clear-cut and do not provide much scope for interpretation. There is little room to maneuver in terms of structuring transactions in ways that are more commercially beneficial to the Indian acquirers. Conversely, most of the legal action is situated in the jurisdiction of the target. The transaction structuring and legal documentation are more likely to be governed by the laws of the target's jurisdiction. Moreover, deal processes such as due diligence are likely to be localized there, too. Given these circumstances, it is entirely reasonable to assume that a substantial part of the transactional process will be undertaken by the local law firm representing the acquirer in the target's jurisdiction. At most, the Indian law firm may be expected to take on a broader role (such as a gatekeeping role) on deals for first-time outbound acquirers, with that role diminishing progressively as the Indian acquirer obtains greater international transaction experience. This simply mirrors the trend evident in inbound deals, where the Indian law firms now take on the bulk of the role. However, as we shall now see, matters have acquired greater complexity and do not represent a trend that is simply the reverse of what occurs in an inbound deal.

Two distinct trends are evident on outbound deals, and this split is created by differences in the nature of the law firms and the clients they represent. Surprisingly, the Indian law firms in Bands 4 and 5 of Chambers and Partners's classification are more active in the outbound space than the firms in the higher brackets (Appendix 1).[31] In other words, the current trend demonstrates a greater role for Indian law firms that represent midsize outbound Indian acquirers doing midsize outbound deals with lesser complexity. On the other hand, larger Indian outbound acquirers (that are typically represented by the elite law firms) carrying out blockbuster deals with higher levels of complexity demonstrate a distinct preference to carve out a greater role (of leading the transaction) to an international law firm, thereby leaving a marginal role for the Indian law firm. Consequently, while the larger and more prominent Indian law firms are less sanguine about their role on outbound deals, the midsize law firms display greater ambition from a strategic perspective to undertake outbound deals. These results merit some greater explanation, which also speaks to the structure of the corporate legal profession in India and the nature of the market for corporate legal services.

I begin with the elite law firms and others in the higher bands. First, the clientele they represent are more sophisticated with greater international exposure. Consequently, the clients enjoy relationships with international law firms, having worked with them extensively. This relationship enables such outbound acquirers to tap easily into the resources of the international law firms, who are often also familiar with the workings and requirements of the client.[32] Second, given the larger sizes of the transactions and the prominence of the acquirers, the legal cost is less of a concern. Such Indian outbound acquirers are willing to bear the costs of appointing an international law firm and allowing it to perform the lead role on the transaction.[33] Third, interview evidence suggests that the elite law firms and others in the higher bands are operating at high capacity on deals requiring their greater involvement (such as inbound deals), so they do not possess the required bandwidth to undertake outbound deals. Moreover, these law firms strategically believe in carrying out the role that they are best positioned to, which is to handle inbound deals and other aspects involving matters of Indian law, rather than to extend themselves into a new territory that might require additional skill-building efforts. For these reasons, the Indian law firms higher in the band order are less likely to receive instructions for a larger portion of outbound deals. Apart from that, these law firms display less interest in undertaking these deals on account of lack of capacity (and related reasons) and do not seem to vie for that market by competing with either the international law firms or law firms at the lower bands.

Moving to Bands 4 and 5, the position seems to change drastically. *First*, the clientele they represent is relatively inexperienced in the outbound acquisitions sphere. These clients do not have significant prior experience of dealing with international law firms or local firms in the target's jurisdiction. They require hand holding from the Indian law firms on key aspects of the transaction. In such a case, comfort levels are high when Indian law firms take control of the transaction on a turnkey basis and parcel out portions that are relevant to the target's jurisdiction to a local law firm therein. The Indian law firm plays a key role in the appointment of the local law firm and in instructing it on various matters and overseeing the delivery of its services. *Second*, the midsize outbound acquirers are acutely cost-conscious and do not find it efficient to consult multiple law firms. Hence, they prefer to have their relationship law firm in India carry out a substantial part of the assignment, including structuring the transaction, drafting and negotiating the legal documentation, and handling a substantial part of the due diligence. The local law firm in the target's jurisdiction is involved only to the extent of commenting on the enforceability of the arrangements under its local law.[34] Similarly, if the transaction is to be governed by a neutral legal system such as the United Kingdom, then English lawyers' involvement would be limited to commenting on the enforceability of the structure and legal documentation under English law. In this manner, the Indian acquirer is able to keep legal costs low by providing an effective role to the Indian law firm with whom it has a relationship and is therefore able to obtain a preferred rate of billing. By keeping the local target jurisdiction law firm's role to a minimum, their billings do not result in skyrocketing costs, and the client derives the benefits of cost arbitrage. *Third*, interview evidence reveals a great sense of enthusiasm and entrepreneurship among the law firms in Bands 4 and 5 to undertake outbound acquisitions. These firms seem more prepared and willing to undertake the role of managing the transaction even if most of the legal aspects are alien to Indian law.[35] There is also a mild geographical or regional correlation. Law firms and offices based in cities other than Mumbai (being the commercial capital) and New Delhi (being the political capital) tend to display a keener interest in undertaking a larger role in outbound transactions, as opposed to law firms headquartered in those two cities. That is because, on a relative basis, the regional law firms and the regional offices of national law firms tend to represent midsize companies who are more likely to confer that role on the Indian law firms.

The execution of work by Indian law firms on outbound deals abounds with novel challenges. As discussed earlier, while the initial outbound euphoria was directed toward the West and the developed nations in the United States, the United Kingdom, and Western Europe, the current trend of Indian outbound acquisitions points toward other emerging markets. Indian law firms have been able to meet with the demands of the transactions with a lesser level of difficulty due to the similarities in the markets and legal systems between India and those developed nations. In addition, given that these jurisdictions have developed legal systems that promote transparency and certainty in the legal process, there is relative ease in predictability of outcomes. However, in the altered scenario that currently applies, Indian companies are training their guns on other emerging markets in Africa, Latin America, and Southeast Asia. Apart from the use of civil law to deal with transactional issues, which Indian lawyers are less familiar with, these economies present additional difficulties such as the lack of transparency and certainty within the legal system. Other barriers creep in, too, such as differences in language and culture, which introduce further complexity in deal making. Indian law firms are increasingly being called in to perform the role of a "cultural translator" to bridge the gap in legal understanding, especially in the case of midlevel acquirers who may lack sophisticated legal teams (Interview 1 with a partner of a Band 1 firm in Mumbai, 2012). That leads to the key question: What are the capabilities of Indian law firms to play a lead role in advising outbound acquirers embarking upon deal-making activity in previously unchartered territories? As one practitioner poignantly notes, the Indian law firms see themselves as "explorers," especially in relation to deals involving targets in unfamiliar jurisdictions, as is increasingly the case on "South-South" deals (Interview 2 with a partner of a Band 4 firm in Bangalore, 2012).[36]

To be sure, the Indian law firms undertaking lead roles on outbound deals are conscious of the limitations of such roles. All such firms admit their inability to pass judgments or provide opinions on matters of local law in target jurisdictions. To that extent, they do not consider the local firms as dispensable. It is only the process-driven matters, such as structuring, due diligence, and documentation, that are handled by the Indian firm. As far as local matters are concerned, even on due diligence and enforceability of the documents under local law, they receive the final sign-offs from target jurisdiction firms. What the Indian law firm appears to bring to the table are skills relating to management of the deal as a whole and acting as a "single point advisor" to the Indian client, which does not require a mastery of local laws in various jurisdictions.

While the elite and large law firms do not generally see a significant role for themselves on outbound transactions and appear somewhat indifferent to that type of practice, the firms in the lower bands servicing midtier clientele, often at a regional level, possess a diametrically opposite outlook on outbound deals and are wasting no opportunity to ride on the outbound bandwagon. Of course, there are logical reasons for these differing approaches, as we have seen.

After having seen the radical transformation of Indian legal practice within a span of two decades on both the inbound and outbound sides, it is only appropriate to consider the challenges that face Indian corporate law firms and to discuss some of the measures they have been adopting (or should adopt) to meet these challenges head-on.

E. *The Challenges of Globalization*

The demands of globalization and cross-border M&A have required Indian law firms to adapt themselves in ways that were relatively unknown even in the recent past. Currently, the legal skills of corporate and M&A lawyers in India are almost taken for granted. What seems to matter is the ability of practitioners to master the commercial and financial aspects of deals and to act as deal managers or project managers in order to take the transaction to fruition on behalf of their clients. In the Indian context, these additional skills, which operate as significant differentials, are not in adequate supply, with the resulting dearth of law firms and practitioners that are able to meet with these demands.

1. Commercial Savoir Faire; "Trusted Advisor"

Previously, the role of the Indian law firm was clearly limited to advising on legal issues. All business and commercial issues were dealt with directly by the corporate clients or by their investment banks. That boundary has considerably blurred in more recent transactions. It is inadequate for corporate and M&A lawyers to simply advise on the legal matters and leave the decision making to the clients. Lawyers are becoming internalized into the decision-making process of corporate clients and becoming an intrinsic part thereof. At the initial stages of cross-border M&A, law firms are invited to express their view on commercial and business risks in the transaction, apart from the legal risks that were traditionally within their domain.[37] They are required to advise companies on what risks are fairly acceptable. The risk perception of law firms and practitioners acquires utmost importance, and lawyers cannot be seen to be entirely risk-averse. For example, structuring transactions in the Indian scenario can be fairly challenging. On many areas of cross-border investment, the legislation, rules, and regulations in India continue to carry several areas of ambiguity. Even when they are somewhat clear, regulators tend to take views that differ vastly from what the industry and legal community believe the position to be.[38] This not only requires lawyers to take considered positions on matters of law, but that may have to be buttressed through discussions and interaction with the regulators. Where clear answers may not be forthcoming, lawyers will need to opine on whether the risk of uncertainty is acceptable or not. In that sense, the market settles for nothing less than a solution-based approach.

The market places significant premium on corporate and M&A lawyers to provide "deal wisdom." In a general sense, lawyers are expected to provide their views on several commercial matters: for instance, whether the valuation appears to be broadly in order or in an acceptable range, whether the multiples used in the valuation are appropriate, and the like. Additional inputs include the level of risk that is acceptable given the findings of a due diligence conducted on the target. Often, commercial and legal matters are inextricably linked and require law firms to apply their commercial judgment. Even during the drafting and negotiation of legal documentation, the commercial wisdom of lawyers in appropriately devising the terms and conditions so as to protect the client from unacceptable risk acquires importance. Lawyers are, more often than not, called upon to advise on commercial terms and conditions. Lawyers are repeat players in the M&A markets, while buyers and sellers may enter into either one-off transactions, if they are strategic players, or with some level of regularity, if they are financial players. Hence, a lawyer's wisdom on "market practice" is continually sought after while determining the terms of an acquisition: What should be the nature of representations and warranties sought? Should there be a cap on indemnities, and if so, what is an appropriate percentage? Should there be deferred consideration or an earn-outs structure? These are common questions now faced by M&A lawyers in India.

In all, the role of a corporate and M&A lawyer has become one of a "trusted advisor."[39] This role is a key differentiator of star M&A lawyers in India from others in the field. The star lawyers tend to play this role to a greater extent given their wealth of experience handling complex cross-border M&A transaction and their reputation and standing with the regulators.

2. Deal Management

The role of deal management has become the need of the day with cross-border transactions, and Indian law firms are being compelled to include this within their scope of services. "Deal management" broadly refers to the responsibility of the law firm for managing the transaction and the process in order to achieve successful completion.[40] This includes managing the various players involved in the transaction such as the principals and other advisors; controlling the legal documentation, due diligence, and related processes; and ensuring the deal is completed.

This requires varied skills, including a deep understanding of the transaction and its individual elements, and an appreciation of various legal regimes in jurisdictions across which the transaction is spread. Law firms undertaking this role need to put in place internal systems and practices that efficiently manage the process. Needless to say, the individual lawyers involved in deal management need to receive adequate training and be experienced in that role. Indian law firms are increasingly under pressure to take on this function due to their larger role in inbound deals and their gradually expanding role in outbound deals (at least with the midtier law firms). While matters may be relatively straightforward with inbound deals, as they are domiciled in India, they may be somewhat thorny on outbound deals. Indian lawyers handling deal management functions on outbound deals are not only required to obtain familiarity with laws and practices in the target's local jurisdiction but also need to deal with issues of cultural sensitivity. While historically Indian lawyers have evolved through inbound acquisitions where the deal management function has been carried out by international law firms, this role reversal (particularly on outbound deals) has compelled Indian law firms to acquire these additional skills to manage and oversee the role of the local law firm in the target's jurisdiction, seek answers to the right questions, and obtain advice in a timely manner.

Despite the increasing demands on Indian law firms to carry out a wider role on deal management, questions remain on their ability as well as interest in meeting those expectations. Indian lawyers are not adequately trained, if at all, in deal management aspects of cross-border transactions, essentially because this was not considered to be a requisite skill of a corporate or M&A lawyer until very recently. For similar reasons, systems and practices within Indian law firms are also yet to be developed to meet deal management needs. Doubts have been expressed regarding the availability of bandwidth to carry out such a role, at least at senior levels. For example, the corporate and M&A partners at Indian law firms are somewhat overstretched in their resources to be able to commit significant time to deal management efforts.[41] On the other hand, the more junior lawyers may lack the capability and experience to carry out such a function effectively. This presents a dilemma: although the Indian market for cross-border M&A places high demand on deal management services, the skills, systems, practices, bandwidth, and interest seem inadequate to effectively carry out that function. While awareness regarding this concern exists, it is not clear if there is enough motivation among Indian law firms to take deal management to the next level. Indian law firms will continue to countenance this key challenge that globalization and cross-border M&A have hurled at them.

3. Constraints of Disproportionate Resources

Although the demands for high-quality legal services in cross-border M&A deals have increased exponentially in the recent years due to the effect of globalization, the supply of quality lawyers and law firms in India has not grown at the same pace to meet with the demands. The number of law firms and lawyers in India is this space is low, relative not only to the needs of the Indian cross-border M&A market but also in comparison with the corporate and M&A bar in other countries (particularly the developed markets). Even within law firms in the cross-border space, only a few individuals carry the reputation and weight in servicing cross-border M&A transactions and in maintaining the requisite quality. Moreover, the star lawyers who are capable of advising on the most complex cross-border deals are even fewer. All of those issues puts enormous constraints on the time and resources of a handful of lawyers within the entire corporate bar in India. This requires the lawyers to handle several transactions at the same time, the result being that their services are commissioned on the more crucial and sensitive aspects of the transaction while the day-to-day running of the transactions is left to mid- and junior-level lawyers. This is a complex issue with no easy solution. This constraint can be expected to disappear, if at all, at a gradual pace as more and more trained lawyers move up the ranks within law firms to take on a lead role in cross-border M&A transactions, or if more peel-off law firms with experienced partners are to be created to fill this gap.

While the international law firms have the advantage of a more balanced gearing with respect to resources, their role in the Indian market is somewhat limited given the constraints within which they operate. They are not permitted to establish a presence in the Indian markets, yet the boundaries regarding their role (particularly on inbound transactions) have been drawn more clearly.

In concluding this part, I find that the role of the Indian legal profession has been subjected to a paradigm shift within a period of two decades, whereby it has been required to reinvent itself constantly. At an overall level, the participation of Indian law firms in cross-border transactions has increased significantly. Large inbound transactions, which continue to dominate the Indian cross-border M&A markets in terms of size, are handled by the elite Indian law firms, who maintain a hefty market share. On the outbound side, barring some exceptions, the key players are the law firms in Bands 4 and 5. While these transactions are increasing in number, their sizes are not comparatively significant. For this reason, in terms of deal value, complexity, and overall market share, the elite firms are key players in India's cross-border M&A legal market.

While the role of the Indian legal profession in cross-border M&A has greatly expanded, a few challenges remain to be addressed before it can fully absorb the benefits of globalization.

IV. INSTITUTIONALIZATION AND SKILL BUILDING

This part deals with how the Indian legal community has reacted to meet the challenges of globalization in the cross-border M&A sphere. It is necessary to consider how Indian legal practices have taken steps at an institutional level to build the requisite skills and capacity to manage cross-border transactions to meet the demands of clientele, both in terms of bandwidth to effectively carry out the work and in maintaining the requisite quality of the work product.

A. *Building Domain Expertise*

The radical changes in the legal regime pertaining to cross-border transactions in India, and the growing levels of sophistication in the deal-making process, have compelled Indian law firms to build expertise in emerging areas.[42] This has thrown the spotlight onto two specific aspects. The first pertains to the need for greater legal expertise in emerging areas of M&A in India (such as merger control regulation) or those traditional areas of law that are acquiring greater complexity in the cross-border context (such as taxation and dispute resolution). The second pertains to expertise required on various sectors (or verticals) that enhances the quality offering of the law firm to the client.

1. Technical Legal Expertise

Certain areas of the law dominate in cross-border M&A transactions. This has compelled law firms to build their expertise in such areas.

The first such area is merger control regulation (or competition law, as it is referred to in the Indian context). Due to changes in the law that accompanied India's liberalization in 1991, the cross-border M&A regime in India had been devoid of any merger control regulations during the growth phase.[43] Transactions could be carried out without any fear of scrutiny from antitrust regulators regarding the impact of the transaction on the consumer market. However, coming into effect in 2011, a new merger control regime has been established with the Competition Commission of India (CCI) as the regulator. A regime for prenotification of M&A transactions (both cross-border and domestic) beyond certain quantitative thresholds has witnessed frenetic capacity building within the Indian legal profession to meet with these new demands. Several law firms have established competition law practices, hiring specialists in the field. As of October 2013 the CCI had already handled more than 130 M&A proposals (Competition Commission of India 2013). The experience thus far has been positive, primarily because the cases before the CCI have been straightforward, with no significant dispute regarding the economic aspects such as market share. The merger control system and the capacity of the legal profession are likely to be tested further in the future as more-complex transactions come up for consideration before the CCI. Although merger control is considered to be a crucial emerging area of expertise for Indian law firms, it is limited to a few key law firms. While most of the firms in the upper bands are building competencies in merger control, other firms consider it a less important practice area. That is also consistent with the markets these law firms service. The law firms in the higher bands are more likely to advise on large and complex transactions, which will almost always trigger merger control scrutiny, but the law firms servicing the midsize and smaller deals display attenuated interest as such deals are likely to stay below the radar screen from an antitrust perspective. While this area of expertise has brought about drastic changes to the cross-border M&A process, the interest in this area of the law is limited to a few of the firms.[44] In any event, it is too early to evaluate the implications as the merger control regime change is fairly recent.

The second area is tax structuring on cross-border M&A. Taxation on such transactions is not only complex but also extremely controversial.[45] Despite the importance of tax in M&A transactions, the acquisition of tax capabilities in the Indian legal profession has not been structured. Historically, the domain expertise on tax (especially on cross-border matters) has remained with certain specialized tax law firms and solo practitioners, apart from a significant play in this area by specialist accounting and tax advisory firms.[46] Although several full-service law firms, who are active in the cross-border M&A space, are building their own internal tax competencies by laterally hiring tax practitioners at senior levels, these developments are not adequately meeting the demands of the industry. For example, the Indian legal profession is far from undermining the relevance and importance of specialist tax practitioners, including the accounting firms. This survey indicates that even though taxation issues are critical to M&A transactions, capacity building within Indian law firms to deal with the complexities is not universal. There are only some honorable exceptions. Unlike merger control, which has a greater impact on large transactions, tax issues have implications across the board. In order to enhance cross-border M&A practice to the next level, Indian law firms will have to build stronger tax practices to meet with the needs of the industry.

Dispute resolution forms an integral part of certain jurisdictions, where high-profile M&A deals are likely to be litigated before the courts. However, instances of litigation involving M&A deals in India (whether cross-border or domestic) are few and far between. Very few acquisition agreements have been questioned before courts of law. The roles of boards and directors have also not been subject to close scrutiny as they are in other developed jurisdictions (such as Delaware in the United States). Hence, historically, cross-border M&A has been heavily transaction oriented with little emphasis on dispute resolution aspects.[47] Going forward, however, cross-border M&A transactions could likely become litigated in courts of law. Moreover, it is now common for M&A deal documentation to provide for arbitration, with the seat of arbitration being in India or elsewhere (in arbitration centers such as Singapore, London, and Paris). Even though the dispute resolution practice is not significant yet, Indian law firms will have to build capacity to deal with litigation that may emanate from failed cross-border M&A deals.

2. Expertise in Verticals

Domain expertise that spans a specific industry sector or vertical has hardly been prevalent in India. Expertise in verticals can be advantageous, especially because it provides industry-specific knowledge and experience that can be useful in structuring transactions and more importantly in matters of due diligence. This survey indicates a preference among some law firms to build expertise on specific verticals, while others believe that the Indian market is still too nascent to require such industry specialization.[48] On inbound transactions, the preference lies in sectors such as pharmaceuticals, defense equipment (including aerospace), financial services, retail trade, and infrastructure. On outbound transactions, expertise is sought on energy and resources, telecom, and consumer retail.

Another trend that is gradually emerging is the need for geographical or regional expertise, especially on outbound transactions. A greater understanding of specific target jurisdictions can help Indian law firms service acquirers more effectively on outbound acquisitions in those jurisdictions. While this trend appears in the planning and thought process of Indian law firms, it is not clear whether any of the law firms have indeed begun to create such geographical expertise, or whether such expertise in fact exists yet.[49]

B. *Building Systems and Practices*

In addition to domain expertise, cross-border M&A requires law firms to meet with high standards of service. The clientele is usually sophisticated and has extensive experience dealing with law firms around the world. This places tremendous pressure on law firms to maintain stellar quality of output as well as superior service standards[50] and new types of demands on Indian law firms. Traditionally, Indian law firms and practitioners have been relied upon for technical expertise and their knowledge of, and experience with, the Indian legal system. As there is a more general growth in technical expertise within the corporate bar in India, service standards are increasingly becoming the distinguishing factor between firms hired to advise on cross-border M&A. Matters such as accuracy and standardization in drafting legal documentation, knowledge of commercial issues, and responsiveness to client needs are all crucial skills to acquire and enhance.

The lack of standardization in offerings is a function of the manner in which the corporate legal profession in India has evolved. As discussed earlier, the expertise on specialized practice areas such as cross-border M&A resides in a few individuals, and such expertise is not capable of being easily replicated across the firm. As there is great emphasis on individual capabilities, it leads to heterogeneity in the offerings of a law firm, with limited standardization in output. For example, different opinions issued by a law firm, or different legal documents drafted by a law firm, may not necessarily carry the same "look and feel."[51]

On this count, there was general agreement among my interviewees regarding the continuing gap between the standards of service and responsiveness of international law firms and those of Indian law firms. They recognize the need for Indian law firms to build further on service standards so as to match international standards. I sought to understand how the Indian law firms set their benchmarks on service standards. While some of them aspire to match international standards, several others prefer to set their own benchmarks rather than to merely emulate other law firms (whether internationally or within the domestic arena).

Indian law firms have more recently taken steps to enhance service standards. Some of them seek to address the gap through the establishment of sophisticated knowledge management systems aided by modern technology. This includes the management of a central database of precedents and knowledge generated by the firm's practitioners. Another effort being taken by Indian law firms is to introduce more structured training of their lawyers. Although a substantial part of training of Indian lawyers in the past has been somewhat ad hoc in the absence of formal requirement for continued professional development (CPD) or continued legal education (CLE), several law firms are instituting internal training programs that lawyers are mandated to take. This is to enhance the expertise and quality offerings by law firms and to raise the standards in a more competitive environment that has been engendered by globalization and cross-border M&A.

C. *Recruitment Strategy*

Building an adequate base of human capital is essential for law firms handling cross-border transactions. Due to the impact of globalization, lawyers in the cross-border M&A space can no longer be content with their expertise in the home jurisdiction and must possess a broader international outlook. As we have seen, although expertise within the home jurisdiction is crucial (relevant in inbound transactions), they must also be generally familiar with other jurisdictions they generally transact in (relevant in outbound transactions). That leads me to the question of how law firms can devise their recruitment strategy so that they can build the requisite human capital. Given the requirements of cross-border M&A, I hypothesize that the cross-border nature of legal practice requires lawyers (within both international law firms and Indian law firms) to acquire knowledge and expertise not only of their home country laws but also of other jurisdictions in which they regularly transact.

Contrary to my preliminary assumption, the knowledge of laws in multiple jurisdictions or qualification in multiple jurisdictions is not a factor that Indian law firms consider to be critical while recruiting lawyers. My interviewees were unanimous (barring one significant exception) in their position that knowledge of, or qualification in, other jurisdictions is not essential to handle cross-border M&A in an Indian law firm. While such wider knowledge is certainly considered to be an advantage, recruitment decisions are not made primarily on that ground.[52] Greater importance is given to the specific knowledge and experience of the candidate rather than multiple qualifications.[53] The belief among Indian law firms is that knowledge and expertise on laws in other jurisdictions can be obtained through local law firms appointed in those jurisdictions.[54]

Although Indian law firms do not seem to be intentionally seeking out foreign qualified lawyers, the recent boom in cross-border M&A (and other) activity has attracted a number of returnee lawyers who were previously practicing with international law firms in centers such as London, New York, and Singapore. Although not followed consciously as a strategy by Indian law firms, it has resulted in several internationally experienced lawyers being recruited by some Indian law firms on a lateral basis, many of whom service the firms' cross-border M&A needs.

In concluding this part, I find that globalization and cross-border M&A have propelled the Indian legal profession to acquire domain expertise in several practice areas such as competition law and taxation, while I find weak signs of specialization across industry verticals. The continuing gaps in service standards between international law firms and Indian law firms have led to the latter focusing on standardization of systems and practices, and greater emphasis on training. However, when it comes to recruitment strategies, there is no specific approach determined by Indian law firms to meet with the challenges of globalization by hiring dually qualified lawyers, although several law firms have been able to hire lawyers with international experience to boost their cross-border practice.

V. MARKET COMPETITION: SELECTION AND PRICING

This survey identifies trends on how law firms are chosen to represent clients in cross-border M&A and how they price their services.

A. *Selection of Law Firms*

I seek to explore the key factors that companies (both international and domestic) utilize to determine their choice of law firm to represent them on a cross-border M&A transaction. These factors are: (i) expertise and quality (usually judged by reputation); (ii) ongoing relationships; (iii) availability; and (iv) price competition. Often, it is not a single factor but a combination of them that clinches the appointment of a law firm. Nevertheless, some preferences become evident in the cross-border M&A space. Moreover, certain factors bear greater relevance with the nature of the client that appoints the law firm.

1. Expertise and Quality

Given the usually sophisticated and complex nature of cross-border M&A, it is not surprising that expertise and quality are the key factors that determine the choice of law firms.[55] This is even more important in an emerging market such as India, where there is considerable variation in expertise and quality across law firms and even across individual lawyers within each law firm. Expertise and quality are almost indispensable in large and more complex transactions where they are sole determinants of law firm choice.

There appear to be differences in the manner of judging the expertise and quality of Indian law firms for selection purposes. Local companies as well as international companies with prior Indian experience are conversant with the Indian law firms to judge for themselves. When it comes to first-time players in the cross-border M&A market, particularly when they are international companies with limited India experience, expertise and quality is judged through proxies. In such cases, reliance is place heavily on the reputation of law firms, which is signified through rankings of law firms by agencies such as Chambers and Partners and Mergermarket. Apart from that, an international law firm representing such a company may intermediate the choice of law firm based on its knowledge and experience of the Indian law firm market. However, often, the recommendations of international law firms are also guided by alliances that some Indian law firms are part of.[56]

2. Relationship

When several law firms possess the requisite capability (in terms of expertise and quality) to represent companies on a transaction, relationship becomes an important distinguishing factor. Repeat transactions may have generated mutual trust and confidence in a specific law firm, or even a specific partner or team of lawyers within a law firm. In such cases, familiarity with the client's needs will facilitate a more efficient representation by the law firm. For instance, the law firm's awareness of the standard clauses that are acceptable to the client's organization will facilitate uncomplicated negotiation of legal documentation, and an understanding of the risk appetite of the client will aid in structuring and due diligence.

Relationship plays an even greater role in the Indian context, where several large businesses are owned by business families, many of which are listed on the stock exchanges. Several Indian law firms have been representing business groups for a substantial period of time, and this establishes a bond that makes the choice of law firms somewhat straightforward for such businesses. Relationship is found to be a significant factor even in professionally managed businesses, but to a lesser extent than for family-owned businesses.

3. Pricing

Given the complexity of cross-border M&A transactions, the pricing policy and fee estimates of law firms have a much lesser significance in the choice of law firms, compared with other practice areas. Since the stakes involved in large and complex transactions are high, and so is the attendant risk, companies are less concerned about the costs incurred in legal representation. This survey indicates that price is hardly a criterion for the selection of law firms in cross-border M&A. The only exception appears to be in the case of midsize "plain vanilla" deals, where pricing might be accorded some importance.

There is additional sensitivity in selecting law firms through a bidding process that is common in certain other practice areas. Since most M&A transactions, particularly public M&As, are price sensitive in nature, confidentiality of the deal becomes critical. Hence, companies are unable to approach several law firms for fear of a wider dissemination of the information regarding a potential deal. These transactions are also extremely time sensitive in nature. However, pricing continues to be a key factor on deals involving government companies or public-sector undertakings. In such situations, often proposals are invited from various law firms as part of a bidding process. This might be relevant since several government companies are active in the M&A market either in the form of divestment by the government as a form of privatization of the business or for acquisition of businesses overseas (particularly in the resources sector).

Curiously enough, there are signs that pricing is sometimes a significant factor even for international acquirers. However, that appears to be due to a lack of familiarity of the Indian legal market and the heterogeneity of its offering.[57]

4. Availability

The availability of individual specialists within law firms is relevant, but not to the extent as the other factors. In large and complex transactions, companies are willing to approach lead partners in law firms, who might not commit their time to the transaction on a day-to-day basis. There is recognition that the deal will be driven largely by a junior partner or a senior associate, but also that the lead partner will be involved to a limited extent on crucial aspects of the transactions, such as complex structuring, tricky negotiations, or liaisons with the regulators. The clients obtain the comfort that they can rely on the lead partner when required even though such partner is not actively involved in the deal.

In midsize or plain-vanilla deals, however, the availability of the handling partner and the team becomes more important. The choice of law firm in such circumstances may be driven by factors such as responsiveness and enhanced service standards, particularly because of the lack of complexity.

The above discussion indicates strong correlation between the type of clientele and their use of specific factors in the choice of law firms, which I summarize below in Table 1.

B. *Pricing and Billing Policies*

The complexity involved in cross-border M&A transactions commands a premium for law firms in comparison with other practice areas. However, there

TABLE 1. *Type of clientele and the factors for the choice of law firms*

Type of clientele	Factors for choice of law firm
Multinational company International acquirer	• Expertise and quality • Reputation • Rankings
Indian business group Repeat acquirer (international)	• Relationship
Government company	• Bidding • Pricing and commercials

are varied polices when it comes to the determination of legal fees on a transaction. While hourly billing rates for different professionals were previously the norm, particularly for international clients, the use of uncapped hourly rates is increasingly the exception rather than the norm. It is only a small fraction of international clients who accept a fee arrangement that is based entirely on hourly rates.[58]

The other fee arrangement that is favorable to companies, but somewhat disadvantageous to law firms, is a fixed-fee arrangement. The risk of exceeding estimated hours of work and number of lawyers staffed on the transaction is borne by the law firm rather than the client. Interview evidence indicates a significant pressure on law firms to move toward a fixed-fee arrangement. This is especially the case where clients have established relationships with law firms and offer economies of scale through repeat transactions. Such tendencies are also witnessed in medium-sized deals that carry tight budgetary constraints for legal and other advisory costs in connection with the transaction.

The prominent arrangement, however, that has evolved in the Indian context is an intermediate type of fee structure, which is based on a fixed fee or a capped hourly rate, and based on certain assumptions (regarding the number of hours of professional work involved and the duration of the project). If the assumptions are breached, then an additional fee is charged on a default hourly rate, unless the law firm and the client are able to agree upon an additional fixed fee.

Not every M&A transaction that is initiated results in fruition. Several deals fall through before they are completed, although significant legal work has been carried out and legal costs incurred. That poses challenges to how billing arrangements are structured. In India, a practice has developed where the law firm agrees to provide an ad hoc discount that is negotiated if the deal is not consummated.[59] This is a smoother process in the case of established relationships, where the possibility of repeat transactions will facilitate an offer for discounts from the law firm.

One method of addressing clients' needs would be to enter into a "success fee" arrangement with law firms so that there is no downside if the deal fails to be consummated as the law firm would then not receive any fee. In order to compensate for this possibility, a higher fee could be offered if the transaction was to be completed, and this is sometimes computed as a percentage of the transaction value. However, such contingency fee arrangements are not popular in India. Furthermore, they are proscribed by the rules governing legal practice in India. There is limited flexibility in structuring alternative fee arrangements in the Indian context.

Overall, while cross-border M&A transactions form a lucrative area of practice due to the premium they command, there is limited flexibility for Indian law firms to structure fee arrangements.

VI. IMPACT ON IN-HOUSE LEGAL COUNSEL

Globalization and cross-border M&A transactions have had a major impact on the in-house counsel movement in India.[60] Prior to this, the in-house legal departments within Indian companies played a less active role on transactions. The in-house legal department was considered primarily as a support function and usually reported to the chief financial officer (CFO) or the head of the finance function. However, given the greater exposure to international transactions and global practices, the in-house movement has picked up considerable steam in India, and the general counsel of leading Indian companies are exerting themselves actively and becoming influential on various aspects of cross-border M&A in which their companies are involved. This survey indicates, however, that the role of the Indian in-house counsel in these transactions is a "mixed bag," with a wide variation in the roles of the in-house counsel depending on the nature of company they represent, as well as the preferences, enthusiasm, and motivation of the different individuals occupying the position.

The primary role of the in-house counsel in cross-border M&A (as in other practice areas) is to select external law firms to represent them, particularly in large and complex transactions. The more sophisticated in-house counsel enjoy close working relationships with a preferred set of external law firms they can call upon to advise on specific deals.[61] Such in-house counsel perform the role of appropriately instructing the law firms and setting their expectations up front, which would minimize gaps in obtaining better-quality services from external law firms. In-house counsel are also foisted with the role of managing the legal cost and thus play a significant role in negotiating fees with external law firms.

As far as the substantive aspects of the transaction are concerned, the survey indicates mixed reactions regarding the extent of involvement of in-house counsel. The in-house counsel of larger business groups and those who are more sophisticated play a more integral part in the transaction. They are closely involved in structuring the transaction, assessing the risk, and ensuring that the interests of the client are protected. They perform the role of bridging any gap between the commercial expectations and goals of the client from the transaction on the one hand and the outcome of the transaction and the advice of the external law firm on the other hand. In that sense, they are required to "market the risks of the deal to the business and compliance folks" (Interview with a partner of a Band 3 firm in Mumbai, 2012). Conversely, they play the role of a "guide or gatekeeper" to the external law firm by overseeing the work product (Interview 4 with partner of a Band 5 firm in Bangalore, 2012). The nature and level of involvement of the in-house legal counsel vary based on a number of other factors, such as whether the deal is significant to the company and often whether the in-house legal team is occupied in handling other pressing matters relating to the company. When the in-house teams are unable to be involved for those reasons, they rely more extensively on the external law firm to protect their interests and entrust them with the entire transaction with minimal oversight.

The in-house counsel participation is fairly active in structuring the transaction and in identifying the potential risks that could arise from the transaction structure. The possibility of costs such as taxes and stamp duties is a significant concern for in-house counsel as it directly affects the commercial viability of the deal. Another area where in-house counsel are active is due diligence. Although the due diligence itself is usually carried out by an external law firm, the in-house teams are keen to analyze the finding of the due diligence and to identify key risks they can take back to their management for assessment. Regarding legal documentation, they are primarily drafted by external law firms and rarely by in-house legal counsel. However, the in-house teams are often closely involved in the negotiation process to ensure that the interests of the client are adequately protected in the documentation, especially on issues that may have commercial implications.

An interesting trend I noted in the survey is that a handful of in-house legal teams have executed cross-border M&A transactions without the use of an external Indian law firm. That is sometimes the case when a company with a sophisticated legal team enters into a midsize or small transaction that is devoid of any complexity, particularly if the company is the seller of business or shares to an international acquirer. More importantly, the in-house legal team of at least one large Indian business group has successfully completed outbound acquisitions without engaging an Indian law firm for the purpose. The in-house team in that situation manages and oversees the transaction and hires local law firms in target companies' jurisdictions whom they instruct directly. However, it is unlikely that this phenomenon will be witnessed soon in midsize companies that lack sophisticated in-house legal teams.[62]

Outbound acquisitions also present organizational challenges within in-house legal departments. For instance, when an Indian company acquires an overseas company that is much larger in size, how will the target's legal department be integrated with that of the Indian acquirer? How are the legal reporting lines redrawn after the acquisition? Will the legal functions be centralized at the headquarters in India? These are intriguing questions to which answers are still evolving as such developments involving Indian companies are only a few years old. However, with at least two large Indian business groups that have undertaken substantial outbound acquisitions, the integration of the in-house legal teams was found to be straightforward. The general counsel of these groups decided to leave the legal organizational structure of the target companies intact, without significantly altering the authority or functioning of the in-house legal teams in those jurisdictions. They also consciously avoided imposing the acquirer's own standards on the target companies and instead sought to learn from the target's in-house team with an open mind. This type of cooperative management of legal functions has engendered smooth functioning. However, as discussed earlier, this only represents the initial experience, and the solutions to some of these issues are only likely to evolve over a period of time with more lessons in the future.

Globalization and cross-border M&A therefore provide both opportunities as well as challenges to the Indian in-house legal community.

VII. CROSS-BORDER M&A AT THE CROSSROADS: WHERE TO NOW?

In the final part, I examine some of the normative issues that need to be considered for the creation of a more vibrant and effective cross-border M&A market in India.

A. *Bottlenecks in the Regulatory Regime*

Although there has been a significant liberalization of laws and policies in India during the last two decades, the regulatory regime in India continues to be restrictive compared with countries in the developed world. While several aspects of cross-border M&A transactions, particularly on the structuring side, are taken for granted in developed markets, they pose insurmountable hurdles while effecting a cross-border M&A deal involving an Indian company. This is due to a combination of the policies promulgated by India's central bank, the Reserve Bank of India (RBI), and the securities regulator, the Securities and Exchange Board of India (SEBI).[63] Some of the key hurdles are as follows:

1. There are a number of restrictions on outbound investments by Indian companies. For example, it is not possible to issue shares of the Indian acquirer in consideration for the acquisition. Therefore, acquirers are compelled to use cash (through a combination of internal accruals and borrowings overseas) to fund the acquisitions, thereby constraining the options available to structure overseas acquisitions. Moreover, there are limitations on the use of multiple layers of subsidiaries overseas to effect the acquisitions (Khan 2012, 14). An option for dual listing of securities is not available, thereby making a cross-border merger of equals difficult.[64]
2. Indian banks and financial institutions face regulatory obstacles in lending to, or otherwise financing, an acquisition of shares by Indian acquirers.
3. Leveraged buyouts of Indian companies are prohibited due to the rules against financial assistance.[65] Although other jurisdictions carry whitewash provisions that enable shareholders to approve the financial assistance as long as the company continues to be solvent thereafter, such a facility is not available to Indian companies. The only exception available is in the case of private companies, but this is not altogether attractive, as targets in large leveraged buyouts are likely to be public companies.
4. The takeover regulations in India that regulate tender offers have been recently overhauled and the new Substantial Acquisition of Shares and Takeovers (SEBI) Regulations, 2011, came into effect only in October 2011. There is limited clarity regarding the working of these provisions. A related aspect, the squeeze out of minority shareholders, has its own share of difficulties in implementation, too.

5. As far as inbound acquisitions are concerned, several key sectors are not fully open to foreign acquirers. Sectors such as retail trading, insurance, banking, and defense are subject to caps on foreign investment, which makes a buyout impossible.
6. There has been an upheaval in the taxation implications of cross-border M&A transactions due to a high-profile dispute between the Indian income tax authorities and Vodafone, which resulted in a ruling of the Supreme Court of India in favor of Vodafone (Vodafone 2012). However, subsequent legislative efforts to enhance the scope of taxability of cross-border M&A transactions have exposed parties to uncertainty regarding their tax liability (Ministry of Finance 2012).

The current level of cross-border M&A involving Indian companies has been accomplished despite these constraints. Expectations are that the activity will grow exponentially if appropriate reforms are introduced to address some of these issues. If that were to occur, even on a gradual basis, the increase in activity will pose additional opportunities and challenges for the legal profession in India, for which it will have to be prepared.

That leads to the question of when and how the anticipated changes might occur and what role the legal profession plays in bringing about legal reforms that will facilitate greater cross-border M&A activity.

B. *Legal Reforms and the Role of the Legal Profession*

Respondents in the survey generally agree that reforms are overdue. Although there have been some significant reforms such as the enactment of the new Companies Act, 2013, few believe that wholesale reforms to liberalize cross-border M&A activity will be forthcoming soon. But, in the context of this chapter, I am keener to analyze the role of the Indian legal profession in attempting to bring about facilitative legal reforms. Traditionally, the legal profession in India hardly had any direct role to play in legal reform, at least in the corporate space. More recently, however, lawyers are displaying greater interest in participating in the reform process.

Such participation is achieved on the one hand by commenting upon draft proposals of the governmental bodies for reform. Increasingly, some regulatory authorities in India are implementing a participative process of rule-making. A practice, thus far unknown in the Indian context, has developed where key regulators put up discussion papers on key policy issues before they are legislated. Examples of these are the government of India on matters relating to the foreign investment policy, and SEBI on matters of securities regulation and takeovers. Law firms and in-house counsel regularly send in their recommendations, which are considered by the regulator. Even when law firms are not motivated enough to make direct recommendations, they are called upon by industry bodies and chambers of commerce[66] to assist in preparing position papers on the policy reforms. Although this type of participation by law firms in law reform is gradually on the upswing, it is unstructured in nature. It is not possible to gauge the impact of the legal profession's recommendations and their acceptability (or otherwise).

Another method is for lawyers to be represented on special committees formed for specific reform processes. For instance, during the preparation of the policy and legislation on key aspects of cross-border M&A such as takeover regulations and merger control regulations, key lawyers were represented on the panels and were able to directly contribute to the lawmaking process.

Despite the availability of those avenues, the impact of the legal profession on the reform process is arguably thin. Several regulatory authorities do not follow the practice of public consultation during reform process, much less consult with the legal community.[67] Moreover, the process of lobbying has not received express recognition and is far from the type of influence that lobbyists command in jurisdictions such as the United States.

C. *Structure of the Legal Profession*

Finally, I consider the direction in which the structure of the legal profession is likely to move in the future. As discussed earlier, the legal market in India in the cross-border M&A space is dominated by a few law firms and practitioners. Two trends are evident. *First*, there is likely to be greater institutionalization of the law firms in the higher bands. Several law firms have set up formal management structures and are poised for growth in size. *Second*, the emergence of peel-off law firms is likely to continue, as the market appears broad enough to accommodate a larger number of players.

However, there is a need for clarity, certainly on certain aspects regarding regulation of the legal profession. The largest uncertainty thus far that has an impact on servicing cross-border M&A pertains to the position regarding the entry of international law firms into the Indian market directly. While the government has been vacillating on its position for a long time, some clarity is emerging regarding the regime governing international law firms' involvement in Indian cross-border M&A deals largely by way of judicial pronouncements. It is clear that international law firms are not allowed to establish offices in India even if they do not undertake litigation and limit their practices to transactional work. A judgment of the Bombay High Court in 2009 (Lawyers Collective 2010) called into question the establishment of liaison offices by three international law firms in previous years. However, a judgment of the Madras High Court (A. K. Balaji v. Government of India 2012) has preserved the role of international law firms in transactional work, such as cross-border M&A, as long as they do not establish their offices in India and only travel in and out of India. In addition, they are not allowed to advise on matters of Indian law and must confine themselves to the laws of their home jurisdiction or international law.[68] The debate regarding the allowing international law firms into India raises several arguments on both sides. Further clarity will reduce the uncertainty in the current environment within which the international law firms are operating in the context of cross-border M&A involving Indian companies.[69]

VIII. CONCLUSION

The globalization of the legal profession has caused a profound impact on Indian law firms as it has on international law firms. The Indian law firms and in-house legal community have reinvented themselves to deal with changing roles in cross-border M&A transactions. The boundaries between the role of international law firms and Indian law firms have been redrawn. While other emerging markets have seen the process of boundary blurring, the Indian market displays clearer boundaries. This is due to the peculiarities of the Indian market, with a rising local corporate bar on the one hand and concurrent limitations on international law firms' ability to establish themselves on Indian soil on the other hand.

The analysis of the Indian legal practice relating to cross-border M&A provides the platform for further study relating to the impact of globalization on other emerging economies. A comparison of the impact on economies such as Brazil and China might reveal subtleties and contrasts that are intrinsic to our understanding the legal profession in a transnational world. To that extent, this chapter seeks to study one single specific practice area in a single emerging economy, with the hope that its contribution can be meaningful in a more wide-ranging study on globalization and its effects on the legal profession in emerging economies.

Appendix 1 – Indian law firms listed according to the Chambers Asia Pacific Guide 2013 in the category "corporate/M&A"

Band 1	Band 2	Band 3	Band 4	Band 5
Amarchand & Mangaldas & Suresh A. Shroff & Co.*	Desai & Diwanji	Bharucha & Partners*	ALMT Legal (Indian Advocates)*	ARA LAW
AZB & Partners*	Platinum Partners*	DSK Legal	Mundkur Law Partners	Crawford Bayley & Co.
J. Sagar Associates*	S&R Associates	Dua Associates	Phoenix Legal	Fox Mandal
Khaitan & Co.*	Talwar Thakore & Associates	Economic Laws Practice	Rajani Associates	HSA Advocates
Luthra & Luthra Law Offices*	Trilegal*	Kochhar & Co.	Vaish Associates	IndusLaw*
		Majumdar & Partners*		Kanga & Co.
		Nishith Desai Associates		Link Legal
		Samvad Partners*		Singhania & Partners
		Seth Dua & Associates		
		Tatva Legal		
		Wadia Ghandy & Co.*		

* Interviewed for this chapter.

Notes

1 The limitation on international law firms from establishing offices in India is also a contributing factor, as I discuss subsequently.

2 A list of the law firms interviewed is contained in Appendix 1.

3 The interviewees were forthcoming with their views. There was also a sense of contribution to this project on the part of the lawyers in that the result of this effort would help generate a better understanding of the legal profession in India, which will benefit the various players.

4 A brief discussion of the evolution of cross-border M&A activity in India is necessary, as it suitably correlates with the manner in which the role of corporate lawyers in India has evolved over the years.

5 In 2000 the Reserve Bank of India (RBI) promulgated a set of regulations that govern outbound acquisitions by Indian companies. This set of regulations has been further liberalized over the years on an ongoing basis.

6 This is generally evident from practitioner interviews.

7 Recent years have also witnessed the resurgence of joint ventures as a form of inbound investment. Examples of this are Tata-Starbucks in beverages and Reliance-BP in oil and gas. Many of the dynamics involving the impact of globalization on the Indian legal profession work in the same way with joint ventures as they do in cross-border M&A. Moreover, while some interviewees saw a fifty-fifty split in their practice between inbound and outbound deals, others saw as much as a ninety-ten split. No interviewee experienced more outbound deals in their practice in 2011 than inbound ones.

8 The noteworthy acquisitions are Tata's acquisitions of Corus and Jaguar Land Rover, Hindalco's acquisition of Novelis, and Suzlon's acquisition of REpower. Bharti's acquisition of the African assets of Zain followed soon thereafter (The Economist 2012).

9 Most of the large outbound acquisitions by Indian companies are financed through borrowings overseas secured on the assets of the target and the shares in the target, often coupled with a guarantee by the Indian parent. A small portion of the acquisition price might come from internal sources of the acquirer (such as retained earnings), but shares of the acquirer are not used as consideration for the acquisition (Khan 2012, 11).

10 In that sense, corporate lawyers have long been referred to as "transaction cost engineers" (Gilson 1984).

11 There is no uniformity regarding the stage at which lawyers are involved in an M&A transaction. Lawyers often counsel clients of the importance of their involvement at an early stage – for example, at the time of drafting the term sheet or letter of intent itself – so that all legal issues are broadly addressed in a timely manner, saving subsequent embarrassment, costs, and delays to parties. However, concerns of costs and confidentiality often play in the minds of firms that prevent the early involvement of lawyers on all deals.

12 The historical evolution of corporate law firms in India is discussed in the Overview chapter of this volume.

13 An extract of the list of law firms across various bands is set out in Appendix 1. The categorization of law firms and lawyers by Chambers and Partners poses some difficulty to my analysis because they combine general corporate work with M&A in their ranking category. However, I believe this is unlikely to distort the position significantly as the law firms and lawyers in this category have the necessary capabilities and experience to carry out M&A transactions, although that might not be their sole practice area.

14 These are: (1) Amarchand & Mangaldas & Suresh A. Shroff & Co., (2) AZB & Partners, (3) J. Sagar Associates, (4) Khaitan & Co., and (5) Luthra & Luthra Law Offices. Note, however, that this is based solely on the Chambers and Partners rankings and that other ranking guides might potentially reveal a modified elite circle.

15 A few also have international offices, primarily in locations such as Singapore, London, and Silicon Valley.

16 Some Indian law firms also enjoy "best friends" arrangements with international law firms, such as Talwar Thakore & Associates and Linklaters. Although other high-profile arrangements did exist in the past, they have since been terminated. They are Trilegal and Allen & Overy, and AZB and Clifford Chance.

17 In-house legal counsel is the subject matter of Chapter 4 of this volume, although I return to the specific role they play in cross-border M&A deals in part VI of this chapter.

18 This is borne out overwhelmingly through interview evidence.

19 This trend is evident even in the United States (Krishnan and Laux 2008).

20 The standard US-style representations and warranties in M&A documentation ran into dozens of pages, while the UK-style documentation was less lengthy.

21 As interview evidence, and the author's own experience as a legal practitioner in India during a part of that period, reveals, episodes such as the following were not entirely uncommon. When presented with drafts of legal documentation by the acquirer's international law firm, the sellers and the lawyers representing them simply deleted all the detailed representations and warranties while returning the draft with their markups. This caused significant delays and difficulties in the negotiation process. Such instances also created mistrust between the parties: while the sellers and their lawyers refused to provide detailed representations and warranties, partly due to their lack of familiarity with such documentation structures, such a stance was taken by the foreign acquirer and its advisors as a sign that the sellers were unwilling to open their cards and be transparent. It would take some time and several rounds of discussions before the fence was mended and the transaction proceeded further.

22 It is, however, also the case that several cross-border M&A deals do involve companies from non-English-speaking countries that follow the civil law system, where some of these benefits may not directly apply.

23 One interviewee remarked that "the role of the Indian lawyer on inbound transactions, as the master of the law governing the investment, is almost complete" (Interview with a partner of a Band 1 law firm in Mumbai, 2012).

24 One interviewee referred to this as the process by which the foreign acquirer becomes "Indianized" (Interview with a partner of a Band 1 law firm in Mumbai, 2012).

25 Rare instances have been reported where even first-time foreign acquirers have worked directly with an Indian law firm. In such cases, there is direct and extensive involvement of the general counsel of the acquirer on a day-to-day basis (Interview 3 with a partner of a Band 3 law firm in Mumbai, 2012).

26 In that sense, financial acquirers such as private equity houses tend to be repeat players working directly with Indian law firms with increasing regularity. Conversely, this trend is less likely with strategic acquirers whose deals in India are onetime, or at best sporadic.

27 Preliminary interview evidence from international law firms indicates the lack of interest among them to undertake the role that essentially belongs to Indian law firms. One interviewee from an international law firm even remarked that "inbound M&A is a dying practice for international law firms" (Interview 5 with an international lawyer in Hong Kong, 2012).

28 The role of US law firm Kirkland & Ellis in advising IGATE and a consortium of private equity funds on the acquisition of Patni Computers in India through a public tender offer typifies this example (Huddleston 2011).

29 For example, in an acquisition of an Indian company by an Italian acquirer, the Milan office of a Magic Circle firm (or its affiliate) could potentially advise the acquirer, along with an Indian law firm that advises on Indian law issues.

30 A number of reasons could be proffered for this, including the different legal regimes that regulate legal practice in the two jurisdictions, with China permitting international law firms to open offices on their soil (with certain restrictions), and with India prohibiting the same.

31 Bands 4 and 5 consist of traditional law firms as well as the newer peel-off (or splinter) law firms (for more, see Chapter 6 of this volume.

32 It is well known that Herbert Smith represents the Tata Group on all of its significant outbound acquisitions.

33 It has been found that there are some instances that buck this trend. For example, at least one elite law firm is known to represent a leading industrial group extensively on outbound acquisitions, although not necessarily the most complex ones. Other law firms also seem willing to undertake a more overarching role to prized clients with whom they have a well-entrenched relationship. This is usually driven by the clients' desire to maintain some limits on costs, as Indian law firms charge lower charge-out rates than their international counterparts.

34 This is the converse of the trend witnessed in the early days of inbound investment into India, where international law firms used to play the role that these Indian law firms now play on outbound acquisitions. Similarly, the local law firms in the target's jurisdiction play the role that Indian law firms used to formerly play.

35 One partner of a Band 4 firm emphatically stated that he would accept work on an outbound deal only if his firm were given the role of the lead firm handling the entire transaction and in turn instructing the local law firm in the target's jurisdiction on specific local law matters (Interview with a partner of a Band 4 law firm in Bangalore, 2012).

36 In jurisdictions such as the United States and the United Kingdom with common law legal systems where some level of familiarity exists, the Indian law firms see themselves as "flag bearers" instead (Interview with a partner of a Band 4 firm in Bangalore, 2012).

37 One trend is gradually emerging whereby Indian companies are willing to embark on a cross-border M&A transaction without the assistance of an investment bank. Companies are building up substantial in-house commercial capabilities, especially when they are active in the cross-border M&A market. The absence of an external investment bank makes the role of the law firm on the transaction somewhat more onerous as the corporate client may look to the law firm for "hand holding" on commercial matters as well.

38 Some instances where clarity has been long elusive in Indian regulations are: (1) the enforceability of options (put and call) on securities on Indian companies, (2) the enforceability of transfer restrictions in shareholder agreements, and (3) whether the existence of supermajority or veto rights in favor of certain shareholders will trigger the mandatory public offering requirements under takeover regulations on account of a change in "control" of the company. Although some recent legislative and regulatory efforts, including the enactment of the Companies Act, 2013, might have the effect of addressing some of the concerns, the ambiguities have not disappeared.

39 The importance of this role is exemplified by the fact that nearly half the interviewees saw themselves as "trusted advisors" (or were mindful of the need to play such a role) and unilaterally used the very same expression when describing their role. This is also echoed by the corporate sector in India. For instance, the chief executive officer (CEO) of a leading cross-border M&A player in India stated this to be one of his key expectations of a law firm representing his company (Piramal 2012).

40 Other expressions used in this context are "project management" and "transaction support services."

41 As one interviewee said, "Indian lawyers are highly leveraged at a partner level. They are involved in so many deals at the same time. They will be less motivated to do deal management work. But, international law firms have the bandwidth. Their partners do few deals at the same time, and they can therefore carry out deal management functions and put everything into the deal" (Interview 7 with a partner of a Band 1 firm in New Delhi, 2012).

42 Specialization within the corporate legal practice is a concept that is itself of recent vintage in India. A clear-cut distinction between courtroom lawyers and transactional lawyers emerged not too long ago. Even within the transactional bar, specialization among various practice areas such as corporate, M&A, capital markets, banking, and project finance has occurred only in the last decade and a half.

43 The Monopolies and Restrictive Trade Practices Act, 1969, was amended to remove the provision of presanctions on mergers.

44 The introduction of a merger control regime has been described to create a "0 to 180 degree change" in M&A transactions (Interview with a Band 1 law firm partner based in Mumbai, 2012).

45 Multiple tax rulings on cross-border taxation, including one from the Supreme Court of India in the *Vodafone* case that favored the assessed, coupled with subsequent attempts by the government to amend the law with retrospective effect, have all added a greater level of uncertainty. I discuss this in part VII A.

46 All of the Big Four accounting firms have strong tax practices, apart from other Indian accounting firms that are active in this space.

47 The only exception involves amalgamations, demergers, or other forms of corporate restructuring that are initiated through "schemes of arrangement" under the Companies Act, 1956 (and now as reenacted in 2013), that require the sanction of the court. Occasionally, the schemes are challenged before courts by parties whose interests are affected, and this could result in prolonged litigation. A section of the corporate litigation bar in India does exist that specializes in handling these matters before the courts.

48 Some interviewees believed that the industry expertise can be garnered from the clients that the law firms represent, and it is not necessary to build separate in-house expertise on that count.

49 It is a different matter that several Indian lawyers have previously practiced in other jurisdictions, and hence can be said to command some level of expertise in respect of those jurisdictions. However, such expertise is created more on an ad hoc basis rather than in a structured manner. For a discussion of such foreign-qualified lawyers, see part VIIC.

50 One observation was that "clients are becoming ruthless when it comes to service standards. They want value for money" (Interview 1 with a Band 1 law firm partner in Mumbai, 2012).

51 As one group general counsel observed: "The drafting of international law firms is consistent. There is a lot of variation within the domestic firms" (Interview 8 with a general counsel in Mumbai, 2012).

52 One interviewee noted that having a number of lawyers qualified in other jurisdictions can be a "good marketing pitch for the law firm. For example, having a New York–qualified lawyer on the team may be useful only in showing the availability of such capability with the firm" (Interview 4 with a partner of a Band 5 firm partner in Bangalore, 2012).

53 Some interviewees expressed concern with dually qualified lawyers, as they fear a dilution in the knowledge and expertise on matters of Indian law, which are considered crucial, especially when the lawyer has spent a prolonged period of time outside India.

54 The consensus is that the use in outbound acquisitions of law firms in the target's jurisdiction cannot be dispensed with, and therefore hiring a lawyer with expertise in that jurisdiction does not add much value.

55 Here, I refer to expertise in terms of domain knowledge and experience, and to quality in terms of superiority in service standards and delivery.

56 While there are broader alliances such as Lex Mundi, some Indian law firms also enjoy "best friends" arrangements with international law firms.

57 At least two interviewees reported the existence of this trend. One noted: "Since international clients are habituated to dealing with standardized offerings from a number of their international law firms, they assume some level of commonality in the offerings of Indian law firms, and hence use price as the distinguishing factor. They do not realize that the quality differential among law firms and lawyers in India is quite high" (Interview 9 with partner of a Band 2 firm in Mumbai, 2012).

58 Several respondents suggested this to be around 10 percent of all fee arrangements.

59 One law firm, however, offers a "busted deal discount" up front in the fee arrangement itself, whereby it agrees to charge a percentage of the overall fee in case the transaction does not materialize (Interview 6 with a partner of a Band 4 firm in Bangalore, 2012).

60 The in-house counsel movement is the subject-matter of Chapter 4, and here I confine myself to the role of in-house counsel in the cross-border M&A space.

61 In companies with less sophisticated in-house legal teams, however, the choice of outside legal counsel is made by the business head (CEO or promoter) based on a direct relationship enjoyed with a law firm or a specific partner.

62 This finding resonates well with my previous analysis that the midsize and small outbound acquirers rely more heavily on Indian law firms to handle their overseas acquisitions on a "turnkey" basis.

63 This is largely due to the concerns of the RBI to protect the economy against the adverse effects of capital flows and those of SEBI to protect the interests of investors in the stock markets.

64 At least one highly anticipated outbound acquisition is said to have failed on account of this limitation (Shah 2009).

65 Section 67(2) of Companies Act, 2013, prohibits a company from providing financial assistance to a person in relation to the acquisition of its own shares.
66 Some of the leading industry bodies are the Confederation of Indian Industry (CII), the Federation of Indian Chambers of Commerce and Industry (FICCI), the Bombay Chamber of Commerce and Industry, and the National Association of Software and Services Companies (NASSCOM).
67 A regulator such as the RBI, whose policies are crucial to cross-border M&A, is known not to formally consult with the public or with lawyers when it considers policy changes.
68 The court stated its opinion on matters involving transactional practice: "In the light of the scheme of the [Advocates] Act, if a lawyer from a foreign law firm visits India to advice his client on matters relating to the law which is applicable to their country, for which purpose he "flies in and flies out" of India, there could not be a bar for such services rendered by such foreign law firm/foreign lawyer. We are persuaded to observe so, since there may be several transactions in which an Indian company or a person of Indian origin may enter into [a] transaction with a foreign company, and the laws applicable to such transaction are the laws of the said foreign country. There may be a necessity to seek legal advice on the manner in which the foreign law would be applied to the said transaction, for which purpose if a lawyer from a foreign law firm is permitted to fly into India and fly out advising their client on the foreign law, it cannot be stated to be prohibited. The corollary would be that such foreign law firm shall not be entitled to do any form of practice of India law either directly or indirectly" (Ibid.).
69 I do not propose to deal with the merits of this debate, as it is not intrinsic to my analysis. However, the debate has been analyzed in Krishnan, 2010.

References

A. K. Balaji v. Government of India. 2012.

Afsharipour, Afra. 2011. "Rising Multinationals: Law and the Evolution of Outbound Acquisitions by Indian Companies." *UC Davis Law Review* 44 (3): 1029–1089.

Allen & Overy. 2012. "M&A Index, Q4 2011." www.allenovery-event.de/files/m_a_index_q42011.pdf.

Bajaj, Vikas. 2011. "With Growing Confidence, India Pursues Mergers Abroad." *DealB%k, New York Times*, September 28, www.dealbook.nytimes.com/2011/09/28/;with-growing-confidence-india-pursues-mergers-abroad/?_r=0.

Chambers and Partners. 2013. "Chambers Asia Pacific 2013 (Corporate/M&A)." www.chambersandpartners.com/110/354/Editorial/8/1.

Competition Commission of India. 2013. Orders of the Commission. www.cci.gov.in/index.php?option=com_content&task=view&id=171.

Confederation of Indian Industry and Ernst & Young. 2011. "Transactions 2011: Setting the Stage for the Next Era of M&A." www.ey.com/Publication/vwLUAssets/Transactions-2011/$FILE/Transactions_2011.pdf.

Faulconbridge, James R., Jonathan V. Beaverstock, Daniel Muzio, and Peter J. Taylor. 2008. "Global Law Firms: Globalization and Organizational Spaces of Cross-Border Legal Work." *Northwestern Journal of International Law and Business* 28 (3): 455–488.

Flood, John. 2007. "Lawyers as Sanctifiers: The Role of Elite Law Firms in International Business Transactions." *Indiana Journal of Global Legal Studies* 14 (1): 35–66.

Gilson, Ronald J. 1984. "Value Creation by Business Lawyers: Legal Skills and Asset Pricing." *Yale Law Journal* 94 (2): 239–313.

Grant Thornton. 2011. "Mergers and Acquisitions: Global Prospects for Growth." *International Business Report*. www.gt.com.sg/publications/articles/MA%20Prospects%20for%20growth%202011.pdf.

Grant Thornton. 2015. "Private Equity and M&A Activity Hits Three Year High as Investor Interest in India Increased." *Grant Thornton Media Centre*. January 16. www.grantthornton.co.uk/en/news-centre/private-equity-and-ma-activity-hits-three-year-high-as-investor-interest-in-india-increases/.

Henssler, Dr. Martin and Laurel S. Terry. 2012. "Lawyers without Frontiers – A View from Germany." www.personal.psu.edu/faculty/l/s/lst3/lawyerswithoutfrontiers.pdf.

Huddleston Jr., Tom. 2011. "Kirkland Advises iGATE on Patni Acquisition." *American Lawyer*. January 10. www.americanlawyer.com/id=1202481773703/Kirkland-Advises-iGATE-on-Patni-Acquisition?slreturn=20150907081042.

Interview 1 with a partner of a Band 1 firm in Mumbai, 2012.

Interview 2 with a partner of a Band 4 firm in Bangalore, 2012.

Interview 3 with partner of a Band 3 firm in Mumbai, 2012.

Interview 4 with a partner of a Band 5 firm in Bangalore, 2012.

Interview 5 with an international lawyer in Hong Kong, 2012.

Interview 6 with a partner of a Band 4 firm in Bangalore, 2012.

Interview 7 with a partner in a Band 1 firm in New Delhi, 2012.

Interview 8 with a general counsel in Mumbai, 2012.

Interview 9 with partner in a Band 2 firm in Mumbai, 2012.

Khan, Harun R. 2012. "Outwards Indian FDI – Recent Trends and Emerging Issues." Address at the Bombay Chamber of Commerce and Industry, Mumbai. March 12.

Krishnan, C. N. V., and Paul A. Laux. 2008. "Legal Advisors: Popularity versus Economic Performance in Acquisitions." *Corporate Ownership and Control* 6 (2): 475–500.

Krishnan, Jayanth K. 2005. "Professor Kingsfield Goes to Delhi: American Academics, the Ford Foundation, and the Development of Legal Education in India." *American Journal of Legal History* 46 (4): 447–449

Krishnan, Jayanth K. 2010. "Globetrotting Law Firms." *Georgetown Journal of Legal Ethics* 23 (1): 57–103.

Krishnan, Jayanth K. 2013. "Peel-Off Lawyers: Legal Professionals in India's Corporate Law Firm Sector." *Socio-Legal Review* 9 (1): 1–59.

Kumar, Nirmalya. 2009. "India Unleashed." *Business Strategy Review* 20 (1): 4–15.

The Economist. 2010. "Law and Globalization: Not Entirely Free, Your Honour." July 29. www.economist.com/node/16693882.

Lawyers Collective v. Bar Council of India. 2010. 112 Bombay Law Reports 0032.

Liu, Sida. 2008. "Globalization as Boundary-Blurring: International and Local Law Firms in China's Corporate Law Market." *Law and Society Review* 42 (4): 771–804.

Mergermarket. 2011. "Global M&A Survey: An Outlook on Global M&A Activity." www.intralinks.com/articles/2011/intralinks_global_ma_report.pdf.

Ministry of Finance. 2012. *Union Budget 2012–2013*. March 16. www.indiabudget.nic.in/.

Papa, Mihaela, and David B. Wilkins. 2012. "Globalization, Lawyers, and India: Toward a Theoretical Synthesis of Globalization Studies and the Sociology of the Legal Profession." *International Journal of the Legal Profession* 18 (2): 175–209.

Piramal, Ajay. 2012. "The Indian Story in Global Mergers and Acquisitions." Address at the International Bar Association Conference, Mumbai.

The Economist. 2012. "Running with the Bulls: Are Indian Firms Really Going to Take Over the World?" March 3. www.economist.com/node/21548965.

Shah, Ajay. 2009. "Deeper Lessons of Bharti/MTN Dual Listing." *Financial Express* October 5. www.mayin.org/ajayshah/MEDIA/2009/mtn.html.

Silver, Carole. 2007. "Local Matters; Internalizing Strategies for U.S. Law Firms." *Indiana Journal of Global Legal Studies* 14 (1): 67–93.

Simhan, T. E. Raja. 2012. "More M&A, PE Deals Last Year but for Less Value." *The Hindu Business Line*. January 9. www.thehindubusinessline.com/markets/more-ma-pe-deals-last-year-but-for-less-value/article2814622.ece.

Sokol, D. Daniel. 2007. "Globalization of Law Firms: A Survey of the Literature and a Research Agenda for Further Study." *Indiana Journal of Global Legal Studies* 14 (1): 5–28.

Srividya, C. G. 2011. "2011: Inbound M&A Bucks the Trend!" The Firm–Corporate Law in India. December 16. www.thefirm.moneycontrol.com/story_page.php?autono=635079.

Vodafone International Holdings. 2012. B. V. v. Union of India. 6 Supreme Court Cases 613.

SECTION III

NEW ACTORS AND FUNCTIONS WITHIN THE CORPORATE CORE

6

Being Your Own Boss: The Career Trajectories and Motivations of India's Newest Corporate Lawyers

Jayanth K. Krishnan and Patrick W. Thomas[1]

I. INTRODUCTION

The Indian law firm sector clearly has experienced great growth since the country liberalized in 1991, and this chapter seeks to discuss this point in four steps. Section II briefly discusses the emergence of postliberalization corporate law firms and how they have fared in the aftermath of the global recession, particularly in comparison to their more established counterparts. The demographics and attitudes toward globalization of the Indian lawyers who have been part of the postliberalization process are described as well. Section III then moves to a discussion of how and why Indian corporate lawyers – after 1991, but really within the past decade as India has increasingly transitioned from liberalization to globalization – have been motivated to forge their own career paths in a different way than their predecessors. Here, the resource-based desires of this newer generation of corporate lawyers are emphasized, specifically as they relate to their ambition of forming their own firms.

Section IV adds another layer to this analysis by presenting a set of psychological motivations that have spurred these young lawyers to establish their own enterprises. The social psychology literature has long been sensitive to how employees can often be driven to great unhappiness, and even departure from the workplace, when the professional culture tolerates hazing, verbal abuse, and bullying. As will be discussed, many of the younger, newer generation of Indian corporate lawyers have decided to leave what would appear to be secure places of employment because they were in a hostile work environment. But as Section V, the conclusion highlights, while there can be rewarding aspects accompanying such a decision, serious challenges for these lawyers can exist after they are out on their own. The study ends by noting that liberalization and the globalization of the Indian economy have forever changed the Indian corporate law firm landscape.

II. BACKGROUND ON PRE- AND POST-1991 INDIAN CORPORATE LAW FIRMS

As indicated in the Overview and in Chapter 3, India's corporate legal sector has grown significantly since 1991. Moreover, as indicated in Chapter 5 on the key corporate law front of mergers and acquisitions (M&A), even though a decline in work since 2008 is often mentioned, the total value and number of deals completed in the immediate aftermath of the financial crisis (2009–2011) remained impressive, with post-1991 Indian law firms making their mark here as well. The same is true with respect to infrastructure and project finance deals. According to a recent report, in 2011 ten Indian law firms were involved in the representation of 186 infrastructure and project finance deals that were worth more than 79 billion US dollars (Shrivastava 2012).[2] Significantly, the ten firms represent an admixture of old and new. Three of the most prestigious Indian law firms – Amarchand (1917), Luthra & Luthra (1989), and Fox Mandal (1896) – were part of this group. So too, though, were several postliberalization newcomers, including Clasis Law (2010), India Law Services (1998), Link Legal (1999), R&A Associates (1999), Trilegal (2000), and SJ Law (2008) (Krishnan 2013). And one of the firms, KJSV, formed in 1996, is an interesting combination of old and new, serving as a recent offshoot of the historic Khaitan & Company, which was founded in 1911.

These examples highlight how a variety of firms with a range of histories are doing lucrative corporate law work in India. Although their histories may differ, the manner in which they have historically governed themselves has tended to follow one of two models: the family-based, kinship approach or the personality-driven approach. Kinship firms typically have adhered to deeply wedded rules and norms that limit upward mobility for the vast majority of their lawyers. In addition, although these firms are often wealthy and prestigious, there is great disparity in compensation between those (relatively few) who are equity partners (typically family members) and the rest who are not. Personality-driven firms tend to have a single lawyer (or perhaps two or three) serve as the defining figure of the particular law firm. This individual must approve most major executive decisions, including compensation, work assignments, significant client-related matters, and the hiring, firing, and promotion of other lawyers in the firm. Yet kinship and personality-driven firms can overlap in how they operate, with some of these firms affirmatively implementing strategies meant to adapt to the changing times, including embracing principles such as greater inclusiveness and participation, transparency in governance, and meritocracy (Krishnan 2010).

Since the opening of the markets, the dynamics of this traditional legal services space has changed the face of the Indian law firm sector. Within the past decade – although really dating back to 1991 – a new generation of firms have become important providers of legal representation to a greater array of clients. These firms, with purposefully bold names like Platinum Partners, Phoenix Legal, IndusLaw, and Tatva Legal, have been in the thick of several noteworthy corporate and transnational deals during the past decade. So too have firms like S&R Associates, Talwar Thakore & Associates, and Bharucha & Partners, each with lawyers who have tremendous corporate experience (Krishnan 2013, 27–31).

Moreover, contrary to conventional wisdom, the corporate law firm sector in India is *not* restricted to just three or four dozen firms. The website www.HG.org lists approximately six hundred Indian corporate law firms in its directory. Admittedly, this site is imperfect because lawyers pay a small fee (less than $200) to list their firms on it, thus contributing to a possible overinclusive element to the database.(There is also under inclusiveness to the site, as several well-known firms are not on it.) But even if a fraction – say 20 percent – are actual law firms (rather than an individual Indian courtroom advocate calling himself or herself a firm), then already the number of such Indian firms present in the marketplace exceeds one hundred.

As an alternative source, the authors of this chapter mined every news story from *Legally India*, the most in-depth electronic magazine of its kind that covers Indian law firms, from August 12, 2012, back to 2009, when this e-daily first appeared. They also conducted searches from other databases, and during the ethnographical research in India, the first author learned of additional firms as well. The results suggest that there are more than two hundred corporate law firms within the country, with many more likely. Furthermore, more than 50 percent of the firms have emerged just since 2000, with virtually all have lawyers who had worked at another corporate firm beforehand. Hence, India's corporate legal sector continues to grow, and one reason is because many lawyers have decided to break away from their previous employers and form new entities. This has made the market increasingly exciting and promising for clients, law school graduates, and the lawyers themselves.[3]

These entrepreneurial lawyers are mostly in their late twenties and early thirties. (Although that is not always the case – three of the most prominent of these lawyers in recent years were senior partners in highly reputed firms [Krishnan 2013, 31–32].[4]) Furthermore, those who have departed the traditional corporate law firms generally are graduates from the more highly reputed

Indian law schools. They have also had some international experience – as a student in an international moot court competition, or as a holder of a foreign law degree, or having done work abroad while a lawyer in a former firm. Additionally, these lawyers typically favor liberalizing India's legal services market. In fact, they see themselves as global lawyers, as professionals who are intimately familiar with the global legal landscape.[5]

This phenomenon, while seeming to occur in greater numbers today, is not entirely a recent occurrence, however. One of India's largest and most successful and respected firms, Jyoti Sagar Associates, has been described by its founder as a firm that was a start-up in the 1990s, after this lawyer broke off from his uncle's firm, which was and remains a well-known outfit in its own right (Mitra 2012). Although its attrition rates are comparatively not as high as those of other firms, JSA has become a type of establishment firm, where lawyers leave and pursue their own path – much in the same way as the organization's original breakaway lawyer, Jyoti Sagar, did years ago.

Thus, to better understand today's landscape, interviews were conducted between 2010 and 2012 mainly with lawyers from the 200-plus firms described earlier. To protect the anonymity of the respondents, they will not be identified and have been coded. In total, interviews with thirty-six lawyers representing twenty-five family and personality-driven firms were completed. In addition, interviews occurred with twenty-five new-generation lawyers. Most of these lawyers have indeed formed their own firms, but interestingly not all have, which will be discussed later. Furthermore, beyond just the interviews, the first author was allowed to shadow several of these newer-generation lawyers and spend time within their settings. This methodological technique of "soaking and poking" (Fenno 1978, 249–250) rendered a greatly nuanced picture of the respective environments. The two next sections will shed insights into both the culture of the Indian corporate firm sector and the motivations for this departure phenomenon.

III. RESOURCE-BASED MOTIVATIONS

Lawyers who have left firms that are more traditional (family-based) or personality-driven to form new firms of their own cite several resource and institutional justifications for their decisions. Without exception, one key contributing factor to the departures was the perception of the inequity in compensation packages. As one lawyer who left a prominent law firm stated, "From the moment we started, our salaries were so low. We made in a year what first-year associates in Western firms make in a month" (Interview 3, 2010).

From the interviews, as well as from data gathered by another resource, it appears that yearly starting salaries for entering associates within the country's traditional and more established personality-driven firms range from $15,000 to $25,000 (Lin 2012; Legally India, n.d.; Ganz 2013). These figures do not include potential bonuses or year-end raises based on performance, but even accounting for these additions, a first-year associate is unlikely to earn more than $30,000 per year.

To counter the charge that first-year associates are underpaid, senior-level partners at four different established firms argued that the comparison to American or British salary structures was not appropriate. For one thing, they contended, the purchasing power of Indian associates is far greater than that of their counterparts in the United States or United Kingdom. "10 lakhs a year [roughly $20,000], plus benefits, plus a mobile [phone] is a bloody lot here," decried one partner (Interview 16, 2012). Moreover, there is a market and fairness-to-clients issue. According to these different partners, in the Indian context clients are unwilling to pay exorbitant hourly rates for the work product of junior lawyers – who, while smart, often do not know much substantive law and tend to be adequate writers at best (Interview 3, 2010; Interview 4, 2010; Interview 16, 2012). Partners at such firms who are in charge of billing rates do not, as one lawyer suggested, seek to bill clients (Interview 16, 2012). Generating comparatively less revenue than American and British firms, such Indian firms have to adjust their compensation packages to associates, which is why salary structures are what they are. A final defense given is twofold, namely that Indian associates are not saddled with as much law school debt as American graduates and thus do not demand such high salaries, and as Indian associates continue their tenure within the firm, salaries do escalate. As one partner commented, "especially if they are good, they can be very well-off without even being a partner" (Interview 16, 2012).

Many new-generation lawyers, though, scoff at these arguments. Kinship and personality-driven firms by their very nature, they suggest, are not flat but rather pyramid structures where disproportionate influence is vested by those who control the reins. (A senior partner at a smaller but well-known family-based firm conceded as much.[6]) Take salaries, for example, which in these firms are not uniformly distributed but discretionary. Even a senior-level associate can expect only a percentage of his or her salary to be fixed at the start of the year, leaving a portion (sometimes upwards of 40 to 45 percent) to be determined at the end of the fiscal year by the partners in charge. Otherwise put, there are built-in glass ceilings for those who are not family members or who are not part of the "in-control" group. Thus, a key motivation for lawyers who leave is to be part of – or to create – a more transparent, merit-based organization where there is satisfying and predictable remuneration (Interview 12, 2011; Interview 13, 2011).

The idea that firm governance and the decision-making processes should be less top-down and more transparent goes beyond salary. The manner in which traditional and personality-driven firms delegate work assignments also can be frustrating, particularly for already disaffected associates. This point plays out in two cross-cutting ways. On the one hand, some lawyers who depart do so because they feel too pigeonholed and intellectually constrained. These lawyers wish to be exposed to a range of legal areas and often also want to do pro bono work. Instead they find themselves limited to certain practice sectors where the pressures of billing and meeting client and partner demands prevent them from experiencing other opportunities.

On the other hand, some lawyers break away because they want to move in a much more specialized direction. These lawyers seek to maximize their time working in areas they especially enjoy, without having to answer to superiors who may not be attuned to, or interested in, these particular sectors. Three examples highlight this point. The first involves a boutique that focuses mainly on two legal sectors. This firm has just a handful of equity partners and associates, and a small number of staff assistants. One of the founders was at a traditionally elite law firm before forming this partnership, and the motivation was clear. This person wanted to be independent, to be a boss, and to focus exclusively on those practice areas that were the individual's inspiration for becoming a lawyer from the outset. At his former place of employment, the lawyer was spread too thin, describing it as "wearing ten different hats" (Interview 11, 2011). Another partner at this same firm stated it another way: he was constantly (and poorly) multitasking for different partners who worked in different departments (ibid.). When they finally could work on their areas of interest, they were not given opportunities to interact with the clients because of their status as associates.

Second, this idea of leaving to concentrate on specific areas has made public news for another firm, Verus Advocates. Started in February 2011, Verus has already opened four offices (in Delhi, Mumbai, Kolkata, and Hyderabad) and has fifteen lawyers – five equity partners and ten salaried lawyers (Ganz 2012). The story of Verus is one of exciting entrepreneurialism. The founding partner is Krishnayan Sen, a graduate of the elite NALSAR law school in Hyderabad, who spent time apprenticing under the famous Supreme Court lawyer, V. R. Reddy. Sen then took over his father's kinship-based firm, Udayan Sen & Company, in Kolkata (Ganz 2011). In 2009, Krishnayan Sen decided to close the family firm and join the highly regarded Bharucha & Company, whose two founding partners are the extremely well-respected husband-wife team of Marezban and Alka Bharucha (ibid.). (The Bharuchas were formerly partners at Amarchand & Mangaldas until they broke away in 2008 [Vallikappen 2008].)

Less than two years into his tenure, however, Sen left the Bharuchas to start his own firm, Verus (Ganz 2012). Boldly, Sen opened three offices at the same time, in Mumbai, Delhi, and Kolkata. He soon added an office in Hyderabad. He made this decision to focus on his two passions, corporate law and litigation – where he could be the leader of his own organization and pursue his dream of creating a firm that could be of value to domestic and foreign clients on these two fronts (Ganz 2011, 2012). In 2012, Sen attracted two associates away from his former employer to join Verus as equity partners and two other litigators from Delhi to lead his office in the capital city (Ganz 2011, 201). For the entire Verus team – particularly the equity partners – not only is the firm now national and a prime example of how there are different layers to the start-up process, but there is also a focus and in-depth commitment toward the two areas of the law that most appeal to the group. As Sen has noted, "I think it's possibly going to be a distinguishing factor, having a very strong balance of both corporate [lawyers] and litigators" (Ganz 2012). And Verus's Jay Parikh (one of the new equity partners) has commented, "It was the entrepreneurial bug that bit me.... This was always something on the backburner in a sense, because I had always thought of doing something on my own and it came up as a brilliant opportunity" (ibid.).

Beyond seeking to practice more generally or, alternatively, in a more specialized manner, some lawyers leave their previous jobs for other reasons. Some depart to pursue higher educational degrees in hopes of entering academia, whether in India or abroad.[7] Others leave to be part of a policy think tank or nongovernmental association, or to try their hand working as a solo practitioner or litigator in the courts. Still others depart but stay in the corporate world, by lateralling to another firm or joining a corporation as an in-house counsel lawyer. For this last set, the decision to remain in the corporate sector is based upon two factors: being able to maintain a similar or even better standard of living and having the assurance that they will have greater time, flexibility, and opportunities to engage in the not-for-profit causes to which they are committed.[8]

One other institutional and resource-based reason for why these lawyers leave relates to gender. Nearly three-quarters of the respondents interviewed here were men. It is not known for certain whether this percentage reflects the situation throughout the country, but given information received from informed participants, the figure may indeed be representative. Of the women lawyers from whom data was gathered, several left their employers to join a new-generation firm because it offered greater institutional support for starting a family. One married lawyer said that because of how few women were in her former workplace, let alone in positions of power, there was a sheer lack of understanding of the pressures she faced at home, at her job, among her extended family, and within her social community (Interview 17, 2012). Another expressed frustration that time away to have a baby counted against her in terms of salary, promotions, or both (Interview 18, 2012). By finding firms that accommodated family-leave policies, these lawyers were able to have a much better work-family balance.

At the same time, several women lawyers at certain traditional and powerful personality-driven firms have had chances to leave for promising positions elsewhere, but they have opted to say no. For some of these women lawyers, they are simply not interested in having a family and their main ambition is moving up the professional ladder (Interview 6, 2010). They are satisfied with their remuneration, the prestige of the firm, and the work they are doing. For others who have family ambitions, they remain because their present firms provide institutional benefits, including maternity leaves and accommodating environments that allow for success at work and the opportunity to have a family (ibid.). A few firms even provide day care centers (or what in India are called "crèches") for employees' children.

In reflecting on the difference between women lawyers who leave and those who do not, the latter tend to be in firms that are at the very top of the "elite law" pyramid. Those less satisfied with their circumstances, by contrast, can be in a range of other places. However, when women lawyers do depart, a common reason is because they perceive their respective settings as having insufficient institutional support and resources dedicated to the issues that are important to them. Their motivation to leave, therefore, tends to be based on a desire to be in a climate that is structurally committed to providing them professional and personal satisfaction.

IV. PSYCHOLOGICAL MOTIVATIONS

From the earlier discussion it is clear that within the corporate legal sector, visible hierarchical cleavages are present. Indeed in many corporate law firms lawyers must climb multiple layers before reaching the top of the leadership pole.[9] A first-year lawyer is referred to as a new associate and upon promotion can move to senior associate, then to principal associate, then to salaried partner, and finally to equity partner. The time it takes to make these upward jumps varies, and in several kinship and personality-driven firms it is difficult to become an equity stakeholder without being part of the family or the founding team of lawyers.

It is palpable that lawyers who depart feel frustration at this hierarchy. Knowing that the odds of making partner – salaried or equity – are long, junior-level lawyers are resigned to accept that this is part of the corporate firm system in which they work. Yet what they have difficulty accepting, and ultimately what helps to contribute to their departures, is that the hierarchy is reified by the incorporation of emotionally harmful norms into the workplace. These hurtful behaviors reflect a workplace bullying culture that the social psychology literature has been describing over the years (Leymann 2000; Einarsen 2000; Jennifer et al. 2006; Krishnan 2013, 13–19), and the application to the Indian corporate legal sector, in particular, appears to manifest in different ways.

Yet before detailing these accounts, it is crucial to note the extreme sensitivity that lawyers who break away have toward publicly discussing the impact of workplace bullying. Repeatedly they emphasized that they would never publicly acknowledge the ill treatment they felt at their former firms. In press releases announcing their departures, for example, several of them noted how they happily touted their terrific relationships with their ex-colleagues and the amount that they learned while working in their previous posts.[10]

These lawyers frequently take extra efforts to stay in contact with those for whom they formerly worked; they send holiday cards, invite their former colleagues to social gatherings, and even sometimes refer business to them. The reason is simple and often is one of self-interest: the lawyers wish not to burn bridges and believe that maintaining good relationships (at least publicly) will reap benefits for them as they pave their new career paths. Given that many of these lawyers are young and part of a new generation, and that the legal services market in India is a series of interconnected networks, they simply cannot afford to alienate colleagues who may be helpful to them in the future.[11]

That said, the motivation to depart, along with seeking material gains, is also tied to a keen desire to be in a more emotionally conducive environment that fosters professional development and personal fulfillment. To begin on the professional side, by far the most frequently cited frustration by these departing lawyers is a feeling that workwise they are in situations where they cannot succeed. Examples within various levels of the law firm pyramid highlight this point. Consider those instances where an upper-level associate is given an overabundance of responsibilities with unreasonable deadlines and little staff support. Here such work can include managing multiple partners' case files, drumming up client business, mentoring junior associates and law student interns, serving on various firm committees, and being expected to participate in a range of external bar association activities. Upper-level associates with these tasks are often told by their superiors that it is because the firm has faith in them that they are in charge of so much. "We believe in you, we trust you, and we need you," recounted one upper-level associate's conversation with a partner who repeatedly saddled the former with multiple tasks (Interview 8, 2010).

And certainly this type of comment is not always gratuitous. Upper-level associates who receive such responsibilities frequently are highly respected within the firm. They are seen as smart, personable, multitalented, and hard-working. They receive these large workloads because they are known "to get things done" (ibid.). After all, they have made it as a senior or principal associate – a feat accomplished by only a select few within Indian "elite law" – because of their intelligence, impressive work product, and political skills. It is only rational then for partners in charge to rely upon these lawyers to do the necessary (albeit more time-consuming) work of the firm.

Yet many upper-level associates are skeptical that increased responsibility is a reward for being appreciated. In fact, they believe it is just the opposite. One lawyer's story serves as a nice representation. This lawyer started as a first-year associate at a well-known but smaller family firm and progressed up the ladder to an upper-level associate in a shorter-than-usual span of time. His ambition for becoming an equity stakeholder, he concedes, was well known, which he claims led to the imposition of a glass ceiling upon him by the partners (Interview 9, 2010). Because these partners knew that they could not legitimately cast him as incompetent or as rendering poor services, this lawyer contended that they instead saddled him with an extraordinary amount of busywork (ibid.).

As such, he routinely would work at the firm for seventeen to eighteen hours a day. Yet he still would not be able to complete all his assignments. As the social psychology literature might call it, this lawyer was literally "mobbed' with work" (Leymann 1996, 2000; Einarsen 2000; Einarsen et al. 2003; Jennifer et al. 2006; Bartlett and Bartlett 2011; Krishnan 2013, 13–19). The lawyer's inability to meet the demands of his superiors soon resulted in negative feedback. At first the comments were snide – implied remarks that if he could not handle this amount of work now, how would he be able to make it as a partner, where the responsibilities are that much greater? The criticism intensified, and although the lawyer knew it was pretext, he could not help but begin to doubt his abilities. This insecurity became especially pronounced when his superior would berate him in front of others. Finally, he decided to submit his papers, informing his superiors that he would be leaving to join another recent start-up firm (Interview 7, 2010).

When there is intense pressure from the top, it is not surprising to see similar behavioral patterns trickle down. As another upper-level lawyer mentioned, although he sometimes felt badly about it, he was very demanding on his juniors. Not only would he give them difficult projects, but he would be critical and at times yell at them (Interview 2, 2010). Senior associates at other firms acknowledged they behaved similarly, and they too conceded that they verbally accosted their younger colleagues. Too often the standard of behavior would be to scream first and listen or ask questions later. While not seeking to be excused, their explanation was that as upper-level associates they were being squeezed by their supervisors, and as a means of seeking relief they delegated matters to those beneath them. However, frequently these junior-level associates were only one to two years out of law school, and they were too inexperienced. Their writing was poor, and they had little ability to grasp key legal concepts. Simply put, they were untrained, and because their immediate superiors were under intense pressure themselves, these young lawyers ultimately received great amounts of scrutiny and scolding and little of what they needed most – mentorship.[12]

Indeed, consider two other younger lawyers who were each previously in smaller but respected firms. The patterns for these junior lawyers were similar. Work would be assigned, but it would be in an area of the law with which the associates had little familiarity. In each case, they would study and research the respective subject matters, but they inevitably would have questions and need assistance. E-mails would be sent to supervisors, but replies were rare. "Getting an audience" with the superior, as one of them mentioned, was difficult because of how infrequently the latter was in the office (Interview 3, 2010).[13] In the beginning, these junior lawyers also sought help from others in their cohort, but this was not a reliable source of assistance; fellow associates either had little time to aid or were also clueless on the legal matter being researched. Moreover, there was a general fear that asking too many questions – whether to peers or supervisors – might lead people to make assumptions about the lawyer's competency levels (ibid.).

The ramification of such absentee mentorship was that the work product, which was often a memo or draft of a client letter, was inadequate. Even the junior lawyers conceded as much (ibid.). But to them, the lack of tutelage signaled something more, especially when their supervisors were frustrated over the poorly submitted product. Namely, it represented a deliberate tactic where the junior lawyers believed they were being set up to fail. In the eyes of these associates, they were being placed in a sink-or-swim environment. They knew they were cheap to hire and expendable. Those few who "got it" – because they knew how to politic, learned quickly on their feet, or for some other reason – remained, and those who struggled left, which is exactly what happened to these two lawyers (ibid.).

If being buried with assignments and suffering – as well as engaging in – castigation represents one set of experiences of lawyers who departed, there are other ways lawyers can feel alienated. For example, both junior- and senior-level associates can often feel as though they are not given proper credit by their respective superiors when jobs are performed well and, as already stated, are too frequently blamed when projects go awry.[14]

In addition, lawyers can experience frustration because of how *little* work they are given, a sign they can perceive to be as purposive. In particular, when business in the firm has been slow, associates often find themselves without much work to do.[15] Then, when a project does emerge, the dynamics of work assignments become more than just routine delegation. Those who are given projects from their higher-ups tend to be "repeat receivers" (assuming their performance is good), while those who are passed over continue to remain idle. A climate of dissonance ensues between those who are busy and those who are not, where the latter feel shunned by their superiors and resentful toward their fellow associates. In fact, unbusy lawyers firmly believe that they are being ignored because of personal politics, not because they lack talent or are in the wrong department. The perception is that they simply are not part of the in-group.[16]

Add to this the fact that concurrently such supervised lawyers can face a range of personal indignities. Such put-downs might include charges of stupidity and an overall lack of intelligence to derogatory comments on their appearance. One lawyer, for instance, remarked how his boss was known to say harshly, "How can you be so dumb?" (Interview 2, 2010). Another commented that he was regularly denied permission to be a part of client meetings because the superior bluntly stated that the junior would not make a good physical impression (Interview 3, 2010). (According to this associate, he felt the real reason for exclusion was based on the supervisor not wanting to share the spotlight [ibid.].) Other direct insults cited by different subordinates involved laughing at an associate's use of the English language, being teased (in front of others), given only negative reinforcement, and, relatedly, being constantly yelled orders at, all of which effectively eroded the individual's dignity and self-worth.[17] Even one upper-level associate remarked that in all his time at his firm, he could not recall his boss ever using the words "may" or "please" (Interview 11, 2010). Instead, harshly stated phrases such as "get me this" or "do that" were regularly employed (ibid.).

For anyone familiar with Indian workplaces, these accounts will not appear to be the least bit surprising. Several of the lawyers interviewed resignedly noted that most people simply accepted the persistence of such demeaning behavioral patterns. There also appears to be a significant and worrying amount of *indirect* personal attacks that breed insecurity among those targeted. There are numerous forms that this particular behavior can take. When it occurs, however, especially over a prolonged period, it contributes to an enormous lack of confidence for those who endure it, and the overall effect on firm culture is negative. Cleavages develop and fester and feelings of ostracism grow, resulting in an inharmonious climate.

Much of this behavior described by the respondents was based on subtle, often tacit, and difficult-to-quantify metrics. These were their impressions and perceptions, but they mattered and affected why these lawyers were unhappy and sought to depart their workplace environment. Moreover, while many of the attacks were discussed in terms of superiors vis-à-vis subordinates, they were occasionally cited as occurring laterally among peers as well.

To begin, most of the associates who felt passively bullied from the top down stated that they were ignored or received subtle verbal jabs from their supervisors. The comments could range in nature, but fundamentally they caused the associates to feel as though they were not part of the same social circles or socioeconomic backgrounds as their bosses. If the subordinates came from elite schools and their bosses did not – or vice versa – that might prompt a series of indirect, snide, and offensive comments. If the subordinates were from economically privileged backgrounds while their bosses were not – or vice versa – that too might generate subtle verbal accosting. Or if there were differences based on language or gender, mild but still hurtful and repetitive insults might ensue. Or, simply put, when personalities did not mesh, that could be enough to foster passive-aggressive, negative comments from the superior.[18]

Feelings of exclusion and inferiority could be bred through different types of social encounters. So superiors might dine, go for drinks, or just have pleasant visits during office hours with only those who were like the superiors themselves.[19] Relatedly, those associates who were part of the in-group, as opposed to those who were not, would be privy to more information on such matters as the business state of the firm, who the new hires and fires were, as well as random gossip ruminating within the office (ibid.). And within group settings, the self-perceived excluded lawyers regularly could feel isolated, believing that superiors subtly (but purposely) would undermine them or dismiss their input in front of the others, which would only further lower the targeted associates' confidence levels. Again, for these subordinates it was nothing their superiors overtly did; rather, it was the subtle, implied, but still real conduct that left them insecure.

Advantaged associates also participated in diminishing the identity of the targeted lawyers. Such lateral bullying could be seen as an adult form of what is referred to in India as "ragging." In these cases, the advantaged lawyers could team up on the marginalized individuals by engaging in the same subtle actions the superiors were described as doing. Targeted associates might experience the quiet jokes, sarcasm, and affirmative exclusion. They might also see their peers whispering or glaring in an intimidating manner. Here too these behaviors, while not overtly aggressive, could still shake the confidence of the marginalized lawyers. These hostile, disruptive actions surreptitiously clothed in indirect conduct were difficult to complain about.

Clearly then these targeted lawyers felt serious barriers to remedying their circumstances. In theory, this group could organize and form a clique of its own. They could mock, chide, and openly stand up against their peers. But there was no evidence of such collective, rebellious behavior occurring based on the research conducted. The reason seemed simple enough: these lawyers already felt they were in a tenuous spot; were fragmented; had little political, economic, or social capital; and were afraid of losing the little they had.

Still, this is not to say that those who were the targets did nothing in response. Both as a means of coping as well as exhibiting some defiance, these lawyers employed different passive forms of resistance (Scott 1985). Within their own circles, some privately ridiculed those who hazed them. Imitating idiosyncrasies, gestures, and accents of superiors or advantaged peers was not uncommon. Others looked to staff workers or those lower on the hierarchical ladder for support, airing their complaints about those whom they disliked.[20] Then there was the tactic of gossip and hearsay. In one case, a disgruntled associate took pleasure in telling a story he had heard about another associate submitting a purposely faulty assignment to a group of partners and then blaming the poor work product on improper instructions from the immediate supervisor, who apparently was thereafter disciplined. In another instance a lawyer claimed to know that favored associates received "money under the table" (Interview 17, 2012) as an incentive to join the firm. (The money would then not have to be reported as taxable.) Neither of these two instances could actually be proved during the research for this project, but the point is that the first author heard permutations of both of these episodes during other unrelated conversations with different parties in different firms. Each time, the conveyors of the stories exuded confidence and a sense of empowerment in being able to cast their colleagues in such a bad light.

Notwithstanding these forms of passive resistance, for those who felt on the periphery, they by and large endured until the lack of professional satisfaction *combined* with the personal unhappiness reached a level they could no longer bear, leading them to pursue another career path. For those who went to another firm or created their own firm, their desires could not be clearer. They wanted exciting work, but just as importantly, they yearned for less hierarchy, more mentoring, and greater collegiality, and their view was that being part of a new-generation operation offered such an opportunity.

V. CONCLUSION

While there is much excitement and anticipation from these lawyers about starting a new chapter of their lives, it is important to realize that not all have had the same experiences after leaving their former places of employment. This concluding section will focus on the challenges these lawyers face in their new corporate law firms.

For those who have left to work in a newer firm, there are three dimensions to their departure. First, lawyers can move to existing firms that are not new entities. One recent and high-profile example involves Sumes Dewan and his shift from Fox Mandal to Desai & Diwanji. Both of these firms trace their roots to preindependence times, and Dewan, prior to joining Fox Mandal, was at K. R. Chawla & Company, established in 1996 by Harvansh Chawla, which boasts offices in Delhi, Bangalore, and Singapore. Dewan's most recent lateral move is especially important to note for this study because it highlights that lawyer departures from one firm to another do not necessarily mean starting anew.[21]

Second, lawyers can depart from one firm to a firm that was formed as a result of lawyers departing to create a new venture, rather than an older, established firm. These types of firms can vary; when the firm is longer-standing, the transition is less likely be dramatic compared with going to a newer start-up. And third, lawyers can depart to form their own firms.

Lawyers going to firms that fall in the second and third categories often face similar challenges. Initially, many from both camps may envision less hierarchy. They may believe that there will be greater merit-based evaluations, enjoyable camaraderie, and exciting opportunities to engage in diverse legal matters, including pro bono work. Also, they may imagine that this new enterprise means more democracy and participation in terms of how the firm functions on a day-to-day basis.

To be sure, for some lawyers these expectations are met at their new workplace environments. For others, though, the outcomes do not manifest in the ways they anticipated. Consider several instances of junior lawyers departing their places of employment to existing, albeit younger new-generation firms. One lawyer described the firm to which he was moving as having "no big-name lawyers" (Interview 18, 2012). Apportioning the little work that existed by the partners among the associates was difficult and always political. Another mentioned that he felt pressure to bring in business for which he had no training (Interview 15, 2011). Still another lawyer relayed that it was impossible not to see partners privileging certain associates over others (Interview 14, 2011). And multiple lawyers recounted workplace bullying episodes – occurring in similar ways as was discussed earlier.[22] Overall, for those who felt disaffected after joining a new-generation firm, the sentiment was that it was a struggle to find professional satisfaction, to work on diverse legal matters, and to be free from interpersonal politics. Furthermore, because they were now in much smaller environments, when tensions did arise, the whole office had the potential for becoming poisoned with bad feelings, which has been the result in some of these situations.

For those who have left to start firms, there have been challenges as well. So much of how the transition unfolds depends upon the professional reputation of these lawyers. "Big-name lawyers" find the change to be less financially worrisome, mainly because they are often able to bring a lucrative client base to their new setting. An endowed portfolio brings instant credibility and social capital, and having financial security allows for energies to be devoted to other necessary matters.[23] Conversely, lesser-known lawyers can struggle not just to attract clients but also to manage the day-to-day affairs of the office.

Regardless, both types of lawyers can and do encounter difficulties. For several of these lawyers, they have never been rainmakers or the public face of their place of employment. To be sure, having this opportunity can be what motivates lawyers to start their own practices. But once that reality sets in – that they are responsible for bringing in business, meeting payroll, overseeing staff, and the like – the pressure to perform can be intense. As some of these lawyers have learned, there is a different suite of skills between being a good lawyer with legal talent and being an effective administrator and leader.[24]

These lawyers can also face management conflicts in their new environments. Recall that many of these lawyers left their former employers because of a desire to be part of a more democratic and transparent system of evaluation and accountability. However, in their new legal settings they are now the ones responsible for ensuring that there is openness, and as several lawyers (now the main partners) have come to learn, they are often unable to satisfy the different constituencies on this front (ibid.).

Take two cases that, although different, are similar in the types of experiences felt by such partners. The first is of a former associate from a small, well-known firm who left to form a new firm where he is partner. This person shares power with a group of other colleagues but has come to believe that egalitarianism is not always the best method of running a law firm. He and the leadership have made a number of unpopular decisions. Certain associates have been promoted in an accelerated manner to the outrage of those who have not. Some associates are relied upon for important projects more heavily than others, and input is sought from specific associates while contributions from others are impliedly ignored or dismissed (Interview 10, 2011).

This partner insisted that these decisions were based on justifiable reasons. At his previous job this lawyer was not involved heavily in the governance of the firm. Presently, however, these responsibilities are part of his portfolio. He has learned that some associates are simply better, more likable, more dependable, and more hardworking than others. To not distinguish the stronger associates from the weaker ones, he argues, would hurt the firm financially, demoralize the productive personnel, and ultimately affect how clients are treated. Yet he now recognizes the impact such differentiation can have and how it can be negatively interpreted by his junior colleagues (ibid.).

The case of a second partner who started his own firm some years back sheds further light. This office has a handful of equity partners and a group of associates, as well as a small number of staff assistants. In addition to the tough choices this lead partner must make, perhaps the most difficult is how he feels a need to be top-down in much of the decision-making process. He is conflicted all the more because at his previous position he was an associate who struggled and felt excluded from the governance of the firm. That was his motivation to leave. But being in a leadership role has led him to do things that he never anticipated. He admits he often cancels or cuts short appointments with people who are "low priority" (Interview 5, 2010). He frequently ignores what he categorizes as unimportant e-mails or texts. He delegates assignments and expects immediate results, even when he knows he has not given proper instructions or been a good mentor. He often finds himself micromanaging matters in an unpredictable fashion, which can shake the confidence of associates and staff-members (ibid.).

If this lawyer's only drawbacks were that he was a bad manager of his time, he could probably justify his behavior along cost–benefit lines. But he also yells. He screams and makes demands in often rude and unpleasant ways. He can treat subordinates poorly, harshly, and derogatorily (ibid.). While surely not universal, the same patterns were observed among other partners who broke away and formed their own firms. Otherwise put, and conscious or not, these partners can and do engage in workplace bullying, which is, of course, sadly ironic.

Many partners were not willing to discuss this aspect of their management style. Some took great offense when questions were raised about why there appeared to be such a culture of aggressiveness toward subordinates. Compared with how they were treated at their old firms, a few partners retorted, their current workplace environments were serene.[25] Yet the observations of different firms showed the definite presence of a bullying culture. Many partners engaged in behavior that they abhorred while at their former places of employment. However, the bullying culture they experienced and sought to escape appeared within the new workplace settings. Despite the rhetoric of wanting a more flat governing structure, hierarchy can and did persist and was enforced in part through the same types of hazing techniques described earlier. And when there was pushback from junior colleagues unhappy with this treatment, partners responded by reverting to behavior with which they were familiar – bullying, which then led to even more deepened cleavages.

This study has sought to describe the pluralism and diffusion within the Indian corporate law firm sector, including the impact psychological forces play. One natural follow-up question – for another day – is why, when it comes to bullying in particular, do those who have suffered and been victims often participate in these demeaning tactics against those who are less powerful than them? Should these victims not be more sensitive, especially since they know how debilitating these actions can be? Briefly, for those familiar with the literature on this subject, the answers are mixed (Widom 1989, 1989a; Widom and Wilson 2009).[26] Some studies have found a relationship between being a victim and then having that victim become an abuser (ibid.). The theory is that victims are socialized to believe that the treatment they received is acceptable, and thus repeating this behavior too is acceptable. Other studies, however, show less of a causal connection (ibid.).

Alternative answers may emerge as being more India-specific. One might be the notion that in India nothing ever gets done unless people are prodded and aggressively pushed. As this argument might follow, because there is such inertia within Indian society, verbally accosting subordinates is necessary in order to have basic – let alone more complicated – tasks completed. Another response might be that given India's historic caste structure, it is not surprising to see such variations of hierarchy manifesting in the workplace. Still others may suggest that it is unfair to judge Indian workplace actions through a single normative lens. Believing that Indians ought to act a certain way toward one another in professional settings, without recognizing there may be cultural nuances and accepted understandings among the negotiating parties, ignores the reality that Indians might well operate under different norms than those found in other societies.

Obviously these essentialist and culture-based arguments will resonate with some. For example, might certain lawyers be guilty of bullying others on the basis of caste? Perhaps. But caste is complicated because while traditional upper castes may have advantages in some settings, in other contexts this is not the case. Rather, as discussed earlier, being a member of a particular family or religious community, or linguist group, or coming from a specific law school or region of the country, may be more indicative of what is behind the relationship between a superior and subordinate. Surely caste can be intertwined with all these factors, but, simply put, more research and subtle investigation of caste are needed before blanket conclusions can be made.

There is also a response to the claim that Indian workplaces are distinct and should not be normatively judged. The fact is that the data shows that bullying is not something that victims enjoy. For these victims, bullying is a transgression of their human dignity. That it continues in newer contexts by newer perpetrators only confounds those striving to end its dominance.

For the new generation of Indian lawyers, there are now more ways out than ever before. Because of liberalization and globalization, increased opportunities exist for Indian lawyers. More such lawyers have real hope that they too can become part of the "haves" (Krishnan 2013). To be sure, achieving this goal remains difficult,[27] yet that is what makes studying the Indian legal services sector so interesting. Yesterday's legitimately disgruntled recipient of bullying may be tomorrow's aggressor – but tomorrow's victim may respond by leaving again. If this pattern continues, the number of lawyers who go it alone will only further increase, which will spawn even greater competition within this space. Moreover, consider if foreign law firms are introduced into the market – something that even various Indian opponents predict will occur: more players will be in the arena, which will likely mean more and newer norms emerging, with a hopeful one being the reduction of bullying as a standard practice (Krishnan 2010). For many, this development would be welcomed by victims enduring such hardship, as well as by those who seek a greater level of professionalism and respect within the workplace.

Notes

1 This chapter extracts from and draws upon work that first appeared in Jayanth Krishnan's "Peel-Off Lawyers: Legal Professionals in India's Corporate Law Firm Sector" (Krishnan 2013). Given the limitations of space here, readers are asked to consult this article when seeking to review references, footnotes, tables, and other data mentioned in this chapter.

2 Citing data from Dealogic, Shrivastava notes that "[i]n seventh place on the list is one-year-old project Clasis Law, where Mumbai-based projects partner Ishtiaq Ali completed 14 deals worth $3.6bn, after it broke away from ALMT Legal" (Shrivastava 2012).

3 For a list of all the firms that the authors compiled, as well as a detailed discussion of the methodology, accompanying sources, and databases referenced during the course of this compilation, see Krishnan 2013.

4 Some examples of prominent senior lawyers departing their former places of employment include Suresh Talwar, Alka and M. P. Bharucha, and Ciccu Mukhopadhaya (ibid., 31–32).

5 This attitudinal information comes from a summation of the interviews, which will be discussed in the next two sections.

6 This lawyer observed that "most of the law firms are proprietary in nature [being dominated by one individual or in some cases by two or three members of the same family]. The firms are styled as partnership firms but the control vests with one individual at the top or with the family" (e-mail correspondence, 2012).

7 For a discussion on Indians coming to the United States to obtain LLM degrees, see Swethaa Ballakrishnen's "Homeward Bound: What Does a Global Legal Education Offer Indian Returnees?" (Ballakrishnen 2012)

8 For a recent article on the growth in in-house counsel within Indian companies, see Vyas et al., "India Inc in Favour of Setting-Up in House Legal Team" (Vyas 2012). In addition, for the changing dynamics of corporate in-house counsel, see Chapter 4.

9 This information and the information in the remaining part of this paragraph are based on cumulative years of study on the Indian law firm sector undertaken by the first author.

10 This point was repeated in almost all of the multiple interviews the first author had with the different respondents. For more information on these sources, refer to the earlier discussion on methodology.

11 These consistent patterns, again, came through in the multiple interviews the first author had with the different respondents.

12 This account was reflected during the interview with the lawyer, but was also a pattern cited during interviews with other similarly situated lawyers.

13 This quote has been collected from just one of these two lawyers' responses.

14 These consistent patterns, again, came through in the multiple interviews the first author had with the different respondents.

15 This trickles down to interns as well, who may go many days without any assignments at all.

16 These consistent patterns, again, came through in the multiple interviews the first author had with the different respondents.

17 These points are based on multiple conversations the first author had with different interviewees over the course of the information-gathering process.

18 All the circumstances described in this paragraph are based on multiple conversations the first author had with different interviewees over the course of the information-gathering process.

19 This argument is based on multiple conversations the first author had with different interviewees over the course of the information-gathering process.

20 This turning to lower-ranking people also gave the confidants a sense of importance, which in turn produced a certain level of trust, loyalty, and respect – feelings otherwise absent in the targeted lawyers' daily professional lives.

21 For more information on this newer firm setting, see Ganz (2012a). (Note that Dewan was not interviewed for this project.) In addition, according to Ganz, Fox Mandal traces its roots back to 1896, Desai & Diwanji traces its roots to 1930, and Dewan's departure from KR Chawla seems to have been somewhat contentious according to *Legally India* (India Business Law Journal 2009; Ganz 2012a).

22 This information is based on multiple conversations the first author had with different interviewees over the course of the information-gathering process.
23 These lawyers can seek to gain lines of credit from banks. They are also more easily able to lease office space, hire staff, and purchase necessary technological equipment, including the much-needed backup electricity generators. Such partners, therefore, can have an easier time, especially in comparison to those who do not have such initial resources.
24 This information is based on multiple conversations the first author had with different interviewees over the course of the information-gathering process.
25 This information is based on conversations the first author had with different interviewees over the course of the information-gathering process.
26 Cathy Widom has discussed the cycle of violence as it relates particularly to children and abuse (Widom 1989, 1989a)
27 This may explain also why once they attain a certain amount of power, these lawyers seek to consolidate their position through the tactic that they so despise – bullying.

References

Ballakrishnen, Swethaa. 2012. "Homeward Bound: What Does a Global Legal Education Offer Indian Returnees?" *Fordham Law Review* 80 (6): 2441–2480.

Bartlett, James E. and Michele E. Bartlett. 2011. "Workplace Bullying: An Integrative Literature Review." *Advances in Developing Human Resources* 13 (1): 69–84.

Einarsen, Stale. 2000. "Harassment and Bullying at Work: A Review of the Scandinavian Approach." *Aggression & Violent Behavior: A Review Journal* 5 (4): 379–401.

Einarsen, Stale, Helge Hoel, Dieter Zapf, and Cary Cooper. 2003. *Bullying and Emotional Abuse in the Workplace: International Perspectives in Research and Practice*. New York: Taylor & Francis.

Ganz, Kian. 2010. "Fox Mandal Recovery: 2 Partners, Office Leaseback." *Legally India*, www.legallyindia.com/201001111383/Law-firms/foxmandal-delhi-recovery-2-partners-office-leaseback.

2011. "Young Entrepreneur Krishnayan Sen Starts Forthright 3 City Firm Verus." www.legallyindia.com/201102161808/Law-firms/young-entrepreneur-krishnayan-sen-starts-forthright-3-city-firm-verus.

2012. "4 NUJS Partners Join 4 City Start-Up Verus from Courts and Bharucha." www.legallyindia.com/201203312699/Law-firms/breaking-4-nujs-partners-join-4-city-start-up-verus-from-courts-and-bharucha.

2012a. "Fox's Sumes Dewan Bolster Desai & Diwanji Delhi, Says Clients Will Join." www.legallyindia.com/201207052936/Law-firms/foxs-sumes-dewan-bolsters-desai-a-diwanji-delhi-says-clients-will-join.

2013. "LI Salary Survey Results (pt. 2): How Much Do & Will Your Law Firm Batchmates Make?" www.legallyindia.com/201211233261/Analysis/li-salary-survey-results-pt-2-how-much-do-a-will-your-law-firm-batchmates-make.

Fenno, Richard E. 1978. *Home Style, House Members in Their Districts*. Boston: Little, Brown.

India Business Law Journal. 2009. *Directory of Indian Law Firms* www.indilaw.com/pdfs/2009%2520Directory%2520of%2520Indian%2520Law%2520Firms.pdf.

Interview 1, February 19, 2010.
Interview 2, May 17, 2010.
Interview 3, May 18, 2010.
Interview 4, May 19, 2010.
Interview 5, November 8, 2010.
Interview 6, November 10, 2010.
Interview 7, November 10, 2010.
Interview 8, November 13, 2010.
Interview 9, November 13, 2010.
Interview 10, June 2, 2011.
Interview 11, July 11, 2011.
Interview 12, July 12, 2011.
Interview 13, July 13, 2011.
Interview 14, July 15, 2011.
Interview 15, September 3, 2011.
Interview 16, February 18, 2012.
Interview 17, February 19, 2012.
Interview 18, March 13, 2012.

Jennifer, Dawn, Helen Cowie, and Katerina Ananiadon. 2006. "Perceptions and Experience of Workplace Bullying in Five Different Working Populations." *Aggressive Behavior* 29 (6): 489–496.

Krishnan, Jayanth K. 2010. "Globetrotting Law Firms." *Georgetown Journal of Legal Ethics* 23 (1): 57–102.

2013. "Peel-Off Lawyers: Legal Professionals in India's Corporate Law Firm Sector." *Socio-Legal Review* 9 (1): 1–59.

Correspondence to author, March 27, 2012.

Legally India. n.d. "Indian Lawyers Salaries." Accessed July 2012. www.legallyindia.com/wiki/Indian_lawyer_salaries.

Leymann, Heinz. 1996. "The Content and Development of Mobbing at Work." *European Journal of Work and Organizational Psychology* 5 (2): 165–184.

2000. "Mobbing and Psychological Terror at Workplaces." *Violence & Victims* 5 (1): 119–126.

Lin, Anthony. 2012. "Not Just a Family Matter." *The Asian Lawyer* Summer 2012: 22–27.

Mitra, Moinak. 2012. "How Jyoti Sagar and Berjis Desai Made JSA Partners in Profit." www.articles.economictimes.indiatimes.com/2012--02--10/news/31046381_1_law-firm-equity-partners-azb.

Scott, James C. 1985. *Weapons of the Weak: Everyday Forms of Peasant Resistance*. New Haven, CT: Yale University Press.

Shrivastava, Prachi. 2012. "Amarchand Replaces Luthra at Top of 2011 Project Finance League Table." www.legallyindia.com/201202082558/Projects/amarchand-replaces-luthra-at-top-of-2011-project-finance-league-table.

Vallikappen, Sanat. 2008. "Mum on Split, M. P. Bharucha Takes 'Law' into His Own Hands." www.dnaindia.com/money/report-mum-on-split-m-p-bharucha-takes-law-into-his-hands-1157744.

Vyas, Maulik, M. V. Ramsurya, and Kala Vijayraghavan. 2012. "India Inc in Favour of Setting-Up in House Legal Teams." www.articles.economictimes.indiatimes.com/2012--02--10/news/31046258_1_legal-advisors-legal-team-aditya-birla-group.

Widom, Cathy S. 1989. "Does Violence Beget Violence? A Critical Examination of the Literature." *Psychological Bulletin* 106 (1): 3–28.

1989a. "The Cycle of Violence." *Science* 244 (1): 160–166.

Widom, Cathy S. and Helen W. Wilson. 2009. "How Victims Become Offenders." In *Children As Victims, Witnesses, and Offenders: Psychological Sciences and the Law*. Edited by Bette L. Bottoms, Cynthia J. Najdowski, and Gail S. Goodman. New York: The Guilford Press.

7

Women in India's "Global" Law Firms: Comparative Gender Frames and the Advantage of New Organizations

Swethaa S. Ballakrishnen

I. INTRODUCTION

In this chapter, I focus on the comparative careers of women in India's legal profession, which have, in a short span of a few decades, witnessed a marked divergence from expected gender norms. Traditionally, legal practice in India, as in the rest of the world, has been predominantly male dominated. And this continues to be the case in most of the country's professional spaces. However, over the past two decades, especially in elite corporate law firms across the country, this dynamic has undergone a discernable change. While courtrooms and litigating bars continue to be predominantly male and typically hierarchical, women within the enclaves of these firms seem to be entering and succeeding on par with their male peers, often without having their gender status questioned. This combination of gender-neutral promotion, remuneration, and advancement to partnership is empirically interesting in itself, but it is particularly compelling in the context of what we know about professional careers globally and in India specifically.

At the core of this chapter is the exploration of one such mechanism that might account for this comparative advantage and negotiation of hierarchy. If gender is in fact irrelevant in these spaces, how do we account for this privileged inconsequence? To this end, I ask three broad questions – first, broadly, given what we know about the legal profession and India (both together and separately), what factors contribute to the emergence of firms as petri dishes for gender-agnostic professional rewards? Second, how has this emergence survived only in certain specific (and unexpected) career tracks against the odds of an otherwise gender-inhospitable professional backdrop? And, finally, how has this success been concentrated in domains where you'd least expect to find them, i.e., large corporate firms that in most other contexts are least favorable for affording such parity to its female constituents?

In Part II, I trace the literature on gender in professional workplaces and the case of high status work more generally in India. In Part III, I outline the crucial emergence of these elite firms that came into prominence after 1991 and contrast them structurally with other organizational forms that populate the Indian legal market. I suggest that it is this peculiar context of emergence that is vital in being able to afford this institutional backdrop for egalitarianism[1]. In Part IV, I contrast the case studies of women in these different firms to speak to some of the contrasting advantages that women in different organizations enjoy. Finally, in part V, I use a specific theoretical framework to set these contrasting data in context and to offer a possible explanation for why women might be institutionally advantaged in these firms. I offer, borrowing from a line of social psychological research, that one explanation for this advantage (to the extent that is exists) could be that these global organizations are seen as new institutions with little or no coherent gender-based stereotypes attached to them and therefore no frames of reference within which women can immediately be discriminated and/or disadvantaged. At the core of this chapter, then, is the proposal that the ambiguity of gender frames at "new sites of innovation" – i.e., women in these newly-constructed corporate law firms – allow for a particular renegotiation of hierarchy. I suggest that the Indian case of elite law firms offers a good example of broader theory that in novel sites where background frameworks are weak or challenged by other concerns, there is the capacity to question existing forms of privilege (Ridgeway 2009, 2011).

II. THE UNLIKELY CASE OF FEMINIZATION

At the outset, it should not be that surprising that women are reaping high workplace rewards. The substantial increase of women in the workplace has been an important achievement of the gender movement, especially over the past few decades, even if the evidence for this feminization has not been uniformly optimistic. We know that across the globe women have been entering the professions in greater numbers than ever before, but that the pace of advancement is slow and uneven in different countries and cultures (Davidson and Burke 2011). Research consistently shows that women match or outnumber men in higher education, including professional schools, even in countries not known for their gender egalitarianism (Bell 2011; Rosin 2012). Yet there is also simultaneous evidence of the stalling out of the gender egalitarian project in many of the late-industrial countries (England 2006, 2010). In terms of the workplace, this has meant that keeping credentials and expectations constant, career paths between men and women diverge quickly, leaving women at the unequal end of workplace rewards such as promotions, pay, and bonuses (Burke and Nelson 2002).

Research mapping gender dynamics and hierarchies in the legal profession follows a similar trajectory. For instance, we know that there are more women lawyers now than ever before, a rise that has been heralded as "revolutionary" in the history of the profession (Abel and Lewis 1989; Mather 2003). We know that there are now considerably more women graduating from law schools and that this rise in feminization is consistent across nations (Schultz and Shaw 2003; Wilder 2007; Michelson 2013). At the same time, while recent workplace accounts are not as drastic as early accounts riddled with discrimination and ceilings, there continues to be evidence of gender-typed biases and treatment within law schools and legal work spaces (Granfield 1992; Epstein 1993; Pierce 1996; Kay and Gorman 2008) alike.

A. *The Unique Case of Success: Women in Global Law Firms*

Existing and recent research all point to a consistent and increasing global feminization of the legal workforce (Schultz and Shaw 2003; Michelson 2013). But although these accounts have suggested that certain Asian countries have been lagging in this trend, it isn't until recent comparative research on the demography of the legal workforce internationally that we have some grasp of how vast the disparity is, particularly in the Indian context (Kay and Gorman 2008; Michelson 2013). Not only has India – like its other Asian counterparts – had a lower rate of feminization of the profession, this research suggests that it has the *lowest* rate of feminization. Women in most Western countries represent 30 percent (United States) to 50 percent (Finland) of the workforce, and while representation in other Asian countries is lower (about 10–20 percent), the percentage of women in the Indian professional landscape has remained flat at about 5 percent (Michelson 2013).[2]

Thus, at both of these levels of entry and success, the particular and limited case of Indian women working in large, global-style corporate law firms offers an interesting contrast to traditional accounts. First, the Indian legal profession is a notable exception to this otherwise consistent trend of feminization within the profession globally. Second, in spite of this context of a highly male professional workforce (or, as one can argue, because of it), these elite Indian firms seem capable of delivering highly egalitarian advantages to its women lawyers, not just at the level of entry but at the levels of advancement and success. This is a rhetoric that is salient not only in the general context of what we know from the women and professions literature, but particularly in the context of India, where women are so poorly represented in other positions of power within the profession. Together, this sets up a unique context for understanding the negotiation of gendered hierarchies in these spaces.

B. *Existing Explanations for Feminization*

There are two main explanations for the feminization of any workforce. The first is a pure functionalist argument that suggests that intrasegregation is led by microessentialism (Charles and Bradley 2009). Thus, women are thought to be better at different tasks. The skill sets needed for these tasks are primed in certain jobs, even in otherwise male workplaces (for example, secretaries in traditionally male, hierarchical companies), and to respond to the need for these skills, women have the advantage, to a limited extent, within these occupational spheres (Reskin 1993). Thus, more doctors in the medical profession don't necessarily mean more doctors uniformly within the profession; it is likely to mean more doctors in certain fields where female essentialist skills and preference are primed and preferred (e.g., pediatrics). The second explanation that is prevalent for sudden feminization is that the occupation is disregarded or devalued in some way, either because the occupation is not prestigious or because the tasks associated with it are not "pure" (Sandefur 2001). Thus, it is possible that more women are in these jobs not because there is actually a commitment to gender egalitarianism, but because these jobs are just not wanted by men who have access to higher-prestige work (England 1992). As an extension of this general theoretical framework, the organizational literature concerning gender and globalization in the developing world has so far limited its attention to either low-prestige workforces, such as factory work or sex labor, or positions that have become feminized like the "pink collar" labor in the Caribbean (Freeman 2000; Piper and Roces 2003; Salzinger 2003). Naturally, both of these situations are problematic for gender scholars because they give an unfair representation of advantage and egalitarianism where they don't exist.

In the Indian context, too, studies on women and work outside of agriculture remain primarily concerned with the informal sector and low-wage employment (Paul 2009; Raju and Swaminathan 2012). With the advent of liberalization, there has been some indication of an increase in different types of workforces that were available to women, but this too has been confined largely to routine, segregated, and task-intensive labor within sectors like IT, outsourcing, foreign export, and telemarketing (Jeyaranjan and Swaminathan 1999; Gothoskar 2000; Jhabvala and Sinha 2002; Patel 2010; Mukherjee 2004). To the extent that there is research on professional workforces, there is confirmation to an essentialist prejudice to feminization in select family-friendly subfields such as obstetrics/gynecology for women doctors, friendly "customer-relations" human resource positions for women managers, or communication-related manager posts for female engineers (Gupta et al. 1998; Patel and Parmentier 2005; Chadda and Sood 2010). In addition, research on women within high-prestige professional tracks shows that they are subjected to persistent gender role expectations and penalties for deviance. For instance, research by Patel and Parmentier shows that female engineers from India's elite engineering schools (the "IITs") continue to be on the periphery of employing organizations compared with their male peers (Patel and Parmentier 2005). Research shows that there is a strong *partifocal* bias to female participation and promotion within elite organizations (Gupta and Sharma 2003). Other research on highly educated women reveals that while women match – and sometimes surpass – men at entry levels within prestigious organizations, they advance at rates that are much less significant than their male peers who started with them (Kumar 2001). Similarly, research on women in the Indian managerial workforce testifies to strong entry constraints, fewer opportunities for within-organization training and education, a resistance to women in positions of power, and an overall male bias, even among managers who think of their organizations as meritocratic (Jain 1975; Desai 1977; Gulhati 1990; Gupta et al. 1998; Buddhapriya 1999; Naqvi 2011).

Thus, in the Indian case, workforce feminization has followed this expected trend of being either essentialism-driven or low-prestige work. For instance, in the Indian example of legal reorganization and firm formation, the LPO example is less persuasive as a true site of innovative gendering of work because these firms are relatively low prestige compared with large law firms and corporate practice. Much like other examples of feminization, this concentration of women in lower-prestige work is not uncommon (England 1992). The case of large concentrations of women in Indian LPOs is still noteworthy, but it is not as unique because it is circumscribed by the lower prestige of these jobs. And in the few cases where highly educated women have managed to break entry barriers into prestigious workforces, their advancement and value has varied significantly from their male peers.

However, India's global law firms are by no means low prestige, and the demand for entry into these firms is high among men and women alike (Papa and Wilkins 2011). Further, these firms are not just notionally high prestige but also have very high-paying jobs that service highly prestigious clients, factors that together confirm the continuing position of prestige these firms occupy (Sandefur 2001). And women within these firms report advantages that are in line with their male peers not only at the level of entry but also at higher levels of advancement. It is *this* exception to the gender and feminization literature that makes the case of these global lawyers especially salient. In spite of this heavily gendered environment, how are women entering and succeeding within these high-pay, high-prestige global firms without having the nature of the work or their own positions within this work devalued? How is this departure from traditional accounts of sex segregation and gender-based devaluation made possible in this Indian case? This research pursues explanations to these central questions and offers one set of explanations for this possibility.

Existing data, to the extent it exists, deals with either descriptive data on these firms, limited accounts, or policy recommendations (RSG Consulting 2011; Ganz 2012; Rainmaker India 2012). In this chapter, I use data from extensive fieldwork and substantive interviews to pursue a more theoretical line of argument that investigates the individual and organizational circumstances that empower this advantage. Particularly, I ask: What characteristics of these firms or of lawyers make this high and successful feminization possible in an otherwise hostile environment? What do these new firms offer to provide a respite from the background of strong gender bias and discrimination?

III. GLOBAL LAW FIRMS

As Gupta, Khanna, and Wilkins set out in the Overview, since 1991 India has developed its own brand of global law firms, in part by successfully keeping out their truly global competitors. Although by some estimates there are as many as 150 such law firms in India today, like the authors in Chapter 3, I restrict my main point of interest to the most globally salient of the firms that respond and cater to the most sophisticated legal transactions in the country, many of which involve foreign clients and/or international transactional counterparts. As the authors make clear in Chapter 3, these firms differ markedly from their more traditional peers, as well as from the smaller "corporate" firms that have also developed during this period. The following chart captures these differences:

The tracing of the evolution of these firms from an organizational perspective in Chapter 3 of this volume is necessary because it holds the key for understanding the set of factors that have created and fostered new kinds of professional work spaces. Particularly, these firms were attractive to new entrants in the profession, who pitted them against the clique-friendly litigation practices. Unlike older practices, which were rigid and preferential toward ascribed networks, these new legal organizations were set up structurally like Anglo-American law firms, allowing at least some entry and opportunity to

	Organizational structure	Type of legal practice
Traditional practice	Stand-alone practice, employing family/close kin	Litigation; appearing in court
Corporate law firm	Firm with entry and opportunity to outsiders	Transactional
Global law firm	Large firm with entry and opportunity to outsiders (India's Big Law)	Transactional; high domestic and global significance

CHART 1

nonfamilial members within it, although, as documented in prior chapters, family and other communal relationships continue to exist even in these organizations. Entry and success was seemingly meritocratic within these firms, and this career choice was appealing to many graduates from the national law schools – newly elite schools from which these firms were posed to recruit and that championed the cause of meritocracy. In other words, unlike in traditional litigating practice, where charismatic authority and close kinship ties were valued above all else, corporate firms were organized to embrace at least the appearance of the assumption of rational authority. These large, hyperelite law firms seemed to particularly champion these values compared with more traditional practices. And perhaps this setting offers some insight to the salience of these firms for understanding the negotiation of gender.

A. *Why are Global Firms Salient to the Gender Discussion?*

Although demarcation of subclasses within the professions is a global phenomenon, the magnitude of stratification within the Indian legal profession is a more extreme representation of a "winner takes all" philosophy (Frank and Cook 1995). As indicated in Chapter 1, while a few successful lawyers have high prestige in the community and flourishing legal practices, most of India's law graduates work for meager wages and low (if any) prestige. Not surprisingly, virtually all these lawyers were men. With the professional rewards out of reach and the steep academic time commitment (law in India was traditionally a graduate degree, which conflicted with what was considered to be an appropriate marriage age for women), few women went to law school and even fewer joined the profession after graduation (Michelson 2013). As a result, courthouses and litigation firms were (and to a large extent continue to be) workplaces strongly dominated by men. This strong sex segregation meant that traditional litigation firms in India were environments where gender was deeply salient. From accounts of lawyers who recount the "old days," the few women who worked in these litigation offices were secretaries or stenographers and most of these traditional firms continue to display similar hegemonic practices, unequal interactions, and gender stereotypes similar to other ethnographic observations of the legal profession (Pierce 1996).

As I outline here in section III A, by the end of the twentieth century, the landscape had changed yet again, and India was beginning to emerge as a developing power. Alongside, and in response to, a larger international call for egalitarian merit, the profession was forced to reevaluate its structure. Two broader changes in the legal profession are particularly relevant for the current analysis of this transformation as a "site of innovation." First, as indicated in Chapter 1, the 1990s, due to the creation of the national law schools, witnessed an increase in the quality of domestic recruits these law firms could employ. Moreover, these schools were dedicated to increasing the number of women in the profession. Although the number of women enrolled in law schools had increased in the decades following Independence, women role models in the profession were still few and far between. The few women law firm partners were either spouses or daughters of famous male lawyers. In time, however, the success of these national law schools (which offered women a five-year undergraduate degree in law) ushered new and ambitious female talent into the legal profession, which was responding, in part, to an increasingly international marketplace. Women lawyers started gaining access into law firms and legal practices that, until then, had been off limits.

Second, this wave of educational reform was well timed with broader changes in the Indian economy. In 1999, India opened its markets for foreign direct investment, resulting in the first spate of global investors and, thus, clients. This spearheaded a decade of institutional reform and readjustment that resulted in law firms that structurally resembled their Western counterparts. Note that traditionally, law firms were small family-run practices whose recruitment was basically through word of mouth or known networks. Non-family members rarely were promoted to partner track positions, and equity was never shared to "outsiders." Modeled after the normative egalitarian prototype of the Anglo-American law firm, the new firms, in contrast, had egalitarian recruitment, promotion opportunities, and equity-sharing compensation. Although part of this restructuring was in response to a sudden increase in transactional work (and, potentially, the dearth of family members or networked "others" who could efficiently respond to this spate of international sophisticated work), some of it must have also been the need to fit the global standard of an achievement-based system.

Yet, even given these changes in the corporate legal market, recent success stories within the Indian legal profession have been predominantly male dominated, and the enrollment and promotion figures within the litigating bar offer some comparison. A brief look at the numbers confirms that the gender hierarchy within this sample is more reflective of what we'd expect from a profession that is more than 90 percent male. Women are, as traditional accounts of the professions would suggest, even more sparsely distributed in positions of power than in the profession overall. For instance, as of 2012, of the 294 lawyers who have been promoted to the position of senior advocate in the Indian Supreme Court, only 5 (or about 2 percent) have been women (Supreme Court of India s 2012). If we were to take into account the demographic history of judges in the Supreme Court, the story remains depressing as far as female representation is concerned: among the 204 judges in the 63-year-old history of the Supreme Court, only 5 (or less than 2.5 percent) have been women (Supreme Court Official Statistics 2012). And, of course, accounts of "grand advocates" who transform the courts and receive disproportionate rewards and prestige do not include stories about women (see Chapter 14 by Galanter and Robinson on this topic).

In other words, everything we know about the Indian legal profession and the success of women within it has been within elite corporate law firms, particularly among firms that I categorize as "global."[3] From industry reports (International Business Law Journal 2012), we know that the biggest and most prestigious of these global firms, Amarchand & Mangaldas & Suresh A. Shroff & Company (AMSS) and AZB & Partners, have a significant women representation in their partnership. Twenty-one of Amarchand's fifty-nine partners are women, including nine out of the thirteen (almost 70 percent) recent ascenders to partnership in March 2012. AZB & Partners does not disclose numbers but confirms that almost half its partners are female. Both firms have strong women in the managing partnership (three out of five of AMSS's controlling partners are women – even if within the same family – and AZB & Partners was founded initially by Zia Mody, commonly championed as the leading Indian expert on corporate M&A and one of India's foremost businesswomen) and senior lawyers and key partners in both firms don't acknowledge gender as being a differentiating factor in their professional rewards and trajectories. J. Sagar Associates, another elite law firm, even more recently (2015) elected two women to become the firm's joint managing partners and even though slightly less "global" elite firms like Trilegal have a skewed gender ration at partnership, the few women who do "make it" continue to talk about their experiences in ways that diverge from their international peers[4]. This gendered representation in these prominent, high-prestige global firms is particularly unique because it places itself in rich contrast to the general experience of the global legal profession as well as the experience in Indian litigation, company boards, other firms, and newer law practices (Schultz and Shaw 2003; International Business Law Journal 2012; Galanter and Robinson 2017).[5]

IV. NOTES FROM THE FIELD: EMPIRICAL EVIDENCE OF COMPARATIVE ADVANTAGE

Gender scholars, as I outline earlier, have offered distinct accounts at different levels of analysis – individual, interactional, and institutional – to explain how gender-based inequality at the workplace is created and reinforced. Most inclusive of these accounts have been those that integrate all three levels, urging us to think of gender not as something that operates to people or institutions in a vacuum but instead as a reinforcing "structure" or "frame" that operates constantly (Risman 1998; Ridgeway 2011). These explanations are compelling because they illustrate the persistent nature of accepted gender hierarchies and the challenge of overcoming set of societal beliefs and expectations. My research design was grounded on the premise that structural reinstating of gender applied to advantage as much as to disadvantage[6]. And to this extent, my fieldwork focused on the ways in which gender was imagined and experienced to tease out these mechanisms that reinstated and resisted traditional hierarchies. In my interviews (Table 1), I focused on variation across these different levels of analysis amongst lawyers in different kinds of legal practice[7]. I was descriptively curious, at the individual level, about the social and cultural factors (e.g., their family background, educational training, etc.) that shaped these lawyers' potential for success – particularly, how these professional women evaluated their place within these elite firms and responded to their structured expectations. At the interactional level, I was interested in the interactions these women had and/or were capable of leveraging. I asked them what they thought of their peers (e.g., how did clients respond to having a senior woman lawyer in the transaction, how did peers?), their mentors, their referents or/and superiors, and, in turn, how this affected their expectations and experience within these organizations. And by also interviewing male colleagues, clients and superiors, I placed these findings in the context of expectations that similarly placed men had for their own careers.[8] At the macro level, the impetus was to hone in on the innovative structural factors these global firms were offering that were capable of diverting the persistent effects of a deeply hierarchical gendered profession. I attempted to investigate what law firm management thought of these women (i.e., how "good" lawyers or "productive" lawyers were defined) and what factors were seen as

TABLE 1. *List of interviews*

	Women	Men
Main interviews (n = 71)		
Pilot: 2011–12		
Senior lawyers in "global" law firms	15	–
Senior lawyers in litigation practice	4	
Senior lawyers in other law firms	3	
Phase 1: 2013		
Lawyers in "global" law firms	20	6
Lawyers in litigation practice	8	
Lawyers in other law firms	6	4
Lawyers in in-house practice	5	
Key informant interviews (n = 9)		
Pilot: 2011–2012		
Senior lawyers in "global" law firms		3
Senior law firm lawyers		2
Senior litigating lawyers		2
Phase 1: 2013		
Clients		2
Total interviews	61	19

necessary for advancement within the firm. Particularly, I was interested in the ways in which essentialist values like deference played out in these interactions and, how these organizational limitations and advantages contrasted with other institutional factors peculiar to India (for example, the abundance of household help, extended family, etc.).

Elsewhere, I have detailed the importance of these descriptive data for the global law firm, but here I only use these descriptions to make meaningful comparative inquiry between different workplace sites (Ballakrishnen 2013). This is crucial because this comparative scenario between interviews with women lawyers in global law firms and in more-traditional legal practice settings offers an important lens to dissect the role of globalization in shaping and evolving new institutional norms with gender-neutral advantages to its lawyers.

A. *Thematic Comparative Findings*

Before I discuss themes of distinction between these sites, it is useful to establish similarities across these samples. For one, gender-neutral advantage in certain kinds of workspaces was not just an imagined reality. Across the board, lawyers identified the broad exceptions to hierarchical, gender-hostile environments but usually this was in the form of "othering" in relation to litigation. People would say things like "India is not so bad for women – at least, there is no discrimination in fields like law and the media . . . By law, I mean corporate law, not litigation, of course" or "I don't think firms have that sort of problem – it's only in the courts," essentially marking the clear boundaries between traditional litigation practice and other kinds of work. Second, there was a clear agreement that this demarcation was a function of liberal markets, and most respondents referred to the ways in which globalization had changed the way work was done – specifically in terms of how firms (as a large, inclusive category) had modernized work and changed the practice of law. Finally, and most significantly, there seemed to be a general consensus – by both people who worked in these firms and those who did not – that the firms I refer to here as global were not just significant, important firms, but firms that were used to defining this gender egalitarian advantage. So lawyers within these firms would say things like "Gender? I don't think it has ever been an issue here" or "Look around – more than half of us are women. Gender is not something that even comes up as an issue" or "I work in an all-woman team, my boss is a woman – if anything, I am the minority."

But lawyers who didn't work within these global firms would use it as a hallmark for why gender didn't matter in these new types of organizations. For example, litigating lawyers would refer to the advantage in law firms and say "I don't think the corporate world or firms have it bad at all. I mean, in a place like Amarchand or Zia, it definitely doesn't seem to matter if you are a man or a woman." In almost every one of these interviews, there was some hand-waving to these firms, making them indispensable to the conversation about gender and new organizational evolution. What is more, these large prominent firms became the hallmark for the egalitarian advantage in general of all firms. I am not just arguing here that firms in general were better spaces for women than traditional legal practice, but also that in the relative (and sliding) scale of advantage global firms had a spot reserved at the pinnacle.

This sketch of the grander legal market aside, comparative narratives of women across organizations were distinctly different. Women in more traditional practice, as expected, brought up stories about how the profession was male-centric and deeply hierarchical, about how networks and associations still mattered, and how, for the most part, it operated as an "old boys" club. Still, most lawyers had chosen the field because of the value that being in the courtroom gave them personally. To the extent that they saw structural advantage in their professional careers, it was usually because they were practicing in chambers where they felt valued by their seniors (almost all male) or had proved to their peers, the bench, and clients, through a variety of ways, that they were worthy counsel. Often this meant that they "toughen up" and not "act like an emotional woman," but for many of these women, that was not something they had to learn. They were told by mentors and seniors in the field to reconsider their decision about joining the profession because of their gender, and stories were rampant with advice to "join the corporate sector" instead, but they had chosen to do it anyway, because of individual persuasion and perseverance.

On the other hand, women in different kinds of corporate practice – corporate legal departments in companies and banks, law firms, and large global firms (and, I will argue, in that order) – met with less organizational hostility and did not start their careers with the expectation that gendered hierarchies would operate against them. To some extent, this distinction was because they were not in litigation. Yet, on deeper perusal, it seemed clear that while most kinds of careers were better than tracks in litigation, there was still resistance to gender-neutral ascending across each of these paths. While women in firms, especially global firms, had successes such as promotions and pay that were on par with their male peers, more-personal decisions such as balancing family and work or choosing where to live applied, to varying degrees, across the sample. This data can speak to rich, independent narratives about each of these legal career tracks in India, but I use it here to focus on the three main comparisons that emerged from the data across the sites of legal practice, one at each of these levels, to help discover the differences in experiences across settings and to highlight the unique circumstantial advantages offered by the workplace settings these women operate within: (1) the effect of socialization and resultant gender-typing, (2) the creation and perception of doing "emotional" labor, and (3) organizational boundary formation and the conceptualization of gender as "diversity."

1. Socialization and Gender Typing at Work

At the level of the individual, socialization accounts (e.g., Babcock and Laschever 2007 argue that the sex-appropriate socialization of children (e.g., "girls are coy," "boys will be boys"), even if without intention, shapes identity and expectations as adults (e.g., "women are communal," "men are agentic"). The reason this distinction on the axis of gender is problematic is because it has a tendency to valorize these dichotomies, often to the detriment of women (Sprague and Zimmerman 1993). Following the extension of this micro-level account is essential because these resultant identities temper interactions by creating norms of appropriateness and traditional gender roles. These norms become especially relevant in the mixed-sex workplace setting where they form prescriptive sanctions with penalties for transgressions from these expected roles, such as the backlash that agentic women face (Rudman and Glick 2001). Because compliance with these norms is the path of least resistance, men and women are socialized into acting in different ways, *even* when they think they are not individually affected by existing gender stereotypes (e.g., through a stereotype threat). In the Indian case, this socialization account was as expected – men and women across institutional sites confirmed that they were brought up to be different – but there were strong distinctions between how this was viewed in the courtroom versus the boardroom. Women in law firms admitted to "being quieter" or "talking differently" than men, but rebuffed the assumption that this necessarily disadvantaged them. Take, for example, this explanation by a senior lawyer in a global law firm about the distinction in her socialization and its resultant effects:

> I don't think not being aggressive is being deferent. I think it is just a matter of speaking. For instance, when I go to a meeting with someone who is at my level and we are both trying to communicate something, I won't say he is more articulate – because I am also articulate – but I think when I am trying to say the same thing as he is, I tend to tone down my thoughts. I will modulate my voice and those kinds of things. And the male lawyers I work with, I guess they either don't realize it or they just don't do it. And it is not conscious. I don't think "Oh, I am a woman, I should talk like this," but it is just natural – all our lives we have spoken and behaved in a particular way.
>
> (Interview 6 with a senior associate in a global law firm, 2012)

In contrast, accounts from women in litigation seemed to suggest that there was a certain assumption about gender that was not only pervasive but also problematic to their performance in the courtroom. Take, for instance, this example of a litigating lawyer in the Mumbai High Court with a flourishing practice, a young woman in her twenties who was described by her colleagues as "successful" and "doing very well" although at the start of her career. Despite her own environment, she explains how gender is being "done" in these courts, stemming from learned essentializing behavior that disadvantages women:

> I find that very, very often, especially around Bombay, girls are used for PR while boys are in general secretary and treasurer positions. So girls are volunteers that get sent to counsel's chambers because they are pretty and nice, and they are giving invitations to these lawyers, saying "Please come, sir . . ." It happens; it is very sad. And all these girls will have pretty, long, straight hair, with colored barrettes, and I know – it seems like they are

> playing up to that circumstance.It started with them in college. It was a learned behavior – you know, you are a pretty girl and you will be sent to a senior counsel's chamber to invite him for something, and the senior counsel will notice you because you have come to invite him to something, whereas the fact is that the senior lawyer has not really given her a second look. It's all in their head. They are building this [recognition] up in their head – because you are a pretty girl, you should do hospitality work, and that, unfortunately, carries over when they graduate and come into the profession as well. They will wear their collars open like this <motions to her collar with a front button open> and they will wear their hair in a particular way <flips her hair and motions in this flippant fashion> and flicking their hair – and it drives me insane. Because I am like "nobody is falling for it – nobody is paying attention to you – this is literally all in your heads."
>
> (Interview 14 with a litigating lawyer 2013)

This rhetoric of "women lawyers" being seen as a distinct identity was common among many of the interviews with litigators and in conversations about them. Like the young lawyer above who distinguishes herself from the others who "play up to the circumstances," some of this identity is structured around resistance and reframing, but even as women personally disassociated with this identity of being seen as women first, they recognized that it was something they had to counter with. For example, many women spoke about how they just needed to "show ___ that we are serious about this" or "the [bar] is just testing us – but once we've won their confidence, *then* it does not matter." Thus, being able to accept these fixed labels (even if only in resistance) as an integral part of the culture was necessary to surviving within the environment. And this, to some extent, is the hurdle of established workforces: with the identities of successful and unsuccessful workers already set, new entrants face strong assumptive judgments and association that necessarily needs to be countered.

On the other hand, women who were counsel in companies didn't have the same sort of general stereotyping about what a "woman lawyer" was like but, instead, had to deal with more individual-level assumptions while interacting with people within the institution. Women who worked within legal departments of banks and financial institutions, for example, were commonly subjected to gender-related assumptions given that most of their clients were men. One senior woman in-house lawyer, vocalizing the sentiment of many of her other peers whom I had interviewed, characterized a large percentage of her work as "gatekeeping," where she had to keep the commercial arm of the company – often seen as more mainstream – informed about and guarded from regulatory and legal causality. She said this often made her seem like the "bad cop" who was constantly telling business/commercial teams that they couldn't do things. She understood that this was the nature of the job, but she also felt that she was being judged as someone who was stopping transactions from going ahead because she was a woman who "didn't get the commercials" or wasn't "commercially savvy." She, like other lawyers in similar positions, felt like if she were a man, this would not have been the reaction since there remains an assumption that men naturally understand commercials. But mostly, because the supply of legal services within a company was seen as an ancillary support function, women felt that while they were adept at playing a "gatekeeping" role, it was also attached to an assumption of caretaking.[9]

In contrast, women in firms – especially large global firms – fairly consistently reported the relative gender neutrality in their perceived identities. Given that many of these women came from similar backgrounds – English-speaking, private-school-trained women from middle-class families – the environments they were introduced into played a big role in creating and fostering these assumptions about gender. Of course, not all firms were equal in being able to provide this sort of environment where gender wasn't primed, and women in smaller firms who had a lot of "traditional clients" (who were, surprisingly, often described the same way) were subject to some of this gendered backlash, but it certainly wasn't comparable to the recurring assumption that women in traditional litigation practice faced. For example, women in smaller, less elite firms spoke about the one-off chance that a "traditional client" would be "uncomfortable about talking to a woman" or ask in particular for another lawyer. But usually, because this was an aberration and not a recurring reality, women were able to shrug it off and react to it with amusement and distance. To the extent this happened, women spoke about how it made them want to work harder at proving these clients wrong (usually to the point where the client would never ask for another lawyer), and others spoke about how it was just a matter of "putting them in place" the few times that gender was made salient in a transaction.

Women in global firms, on the other hand, consistently reported having sophisticated and/or international clients where the question of being thought of as a woman was never in dispute. As the face of a large, globally important organization, they saw themselves – and, in turn, were seen – as the given firm's lawyer and not as a woman or a "woman lawyer."

Thus, gender typing existed across sites, and its prevalence was deemed sustainable by varying degrees. Many of the women dealt with it either by ignoring it or making light of it when it was an aberration and, in other cases, working hard to prove that it was a misconception. But much of this leverage to deal with it was connected to the kinds of institutional support they received at their worksites. Thus, while similar women existed across these different sites, the type of organization they worked for afforded different types of advantage and buffering from the patriarchal assumptions about their identity.

2. Emotional Labor

Women across sites did work differently and interacted with their peers, superiors, and clients in ways that were in line with traditional accounts of socialization and gender typing. Yet, in these different situations, this labor and attitude were received differently. The most valuable comparison that fleshes out this distinction in this data is the way women across these sites interacted with clients. While many women shared stories about clients "not caring" about their gender, the "preference" for women, even in global firms, seemed to be for reasons that were traditionally thought to be gender-typed. Thus, it was not just that people in law firms were doing things differently, but instead, that the same things were given different values in different interactions. Male colleagues and clients alike described the preference for women in the interests of the "work being done well" or the "matter being taken care of." In addition to this preferred behavior, clients of senior lawyers in global law firms preferred female lawyers and partners because they were more confident about women in these firms being careful and dedicated to ensuring quality:

> Yeah, I think my clients would.... That is what I hear... [Clients say,] "I want women on my team. Guys are careless and overconfident."... it does not mean that women are underconfident but women are more careful with their work. *They care.* I was talking to a client about our team [the team in question had more women than men], and he said, "Oh, it is good you have that composition because I would much rather have a woman partner or senior associate [than a man]... because that ensures quality."
>
> (Interview 7 with senior associate in a global law firm, 2012)

At the same time, these preferences on account of "better" behavior, politeness, and care are all examples of feminized qualities in the workplace that are not typically not known to advantage women in high-pressure corporate environments. Take this illustration by a senior female associate explaining the advantage of transactions with a senior lawyer in a global law firm:

> I have worked with a male partner and a female partner. One negotiation, I went with a male partner, and at the end of the negotiation, everyone was really angry, and it ended on a bad note. The next time, I went with a female partner [with the same team, clients], and the experience was much different – it was not as charged. They realized they were negotiating with

two women, and they were much more polite than they were when they were dealing with a man and a woman. So I do think it happens that being a woman helps in a transaction like this.

(Interview 7 with senior associate in a global law firm, 2012)

The fact that being helpful or "not charged" would "help" in a transaction is, in itself, not something that would typically advantage professional women. In fact, given everything we know about women in the workplace, lack of aggression was detrimental to success within high-prestige organizations. Yet this did not always seem to amount to disadvantage in the Indian setting. Women partners agreed that they had different styles of lawyering and negotiating – even within their firms – but that this effect of socialization differentiated, instead of necessarily disadvantaging, them. For example, this partner at a global firm spoke about her trajectory compared with her male peers:

I would never kick up a fuss about a raise or demand to be put on a certain matter. And because I am not pushy like that, it is more likely to be given to me, the [managing partner] is more likely to work with me, more likely to give me the matter, than he is with X [the male partner peer], who is "being an ass" by asking for these things.

(Interview 5 with partner at global law firm, 2011)

This feminization of work in itself is not uncommon. There are several accounts of female labor being preferred for reasons of care and precision (e.g., the feminization of the Mexican factory worker in Salzinger 2003). However, this preference in a high-pressure work environment, where you would imagine aggression and competitiveness (traditional male-typed values) rather than good behavior and commitment to detail (female-typed values), seemed rather novel. On the other hand, in company legal departments, this advantage and preference was blunted by client preference for lawyers they were traditionally used to, that is, men.

I have done well – but I know that sometimes it hurts to not be a man. When we travel on transactions, for example. It is such a man-friendly company that I feel like I come in the way of people doing what they would otherwise do. They would never tell anyone that, of course. But I know if they could choose between me and a man, they would – in an instant.

(Interview 9 with in-house lawyer with 5 years of experience, 2011)

One argument is that it was something about the nature of this work that made this caretaking especially salient. While "taking care" of things might seem particularly important to transactional practice – common in law firms and corporate settings – it could be less relevant to traditional litigation practice, where aggression in the courtroom was superior to just "getting things done." Still, litigators made reference to this emotional labor in their practices, too:

> No, clients don't care. Genuinely, they don't care. . . . At one point in time, there was a *genuine* problem with women getting briefs in the high court. I don't really know what changed – and I was really concerned about it. I was talking to a friend of mine who was doing corporate work, and he said, "See, the old guard is gone – I can name maybe three really good male junior counsel and I can also name three really good female junior counsel. And if I pit one against the other, I know who is more hungry and who is working harder and who the one is who will be there five minutes before the case is being heard versus the man, who will be strolling in late. She will be there, she will have her matters ready and her case ready. *Women will just take care of it, you know?*
>
> (Interview 14 with a litigating lawyer, 2013)

Even so, this lack of aggression, while useful in ensuring work is taken care of, was less helpful in the courtroom, where it actually mattered. Interactions in actual practice – where performance and resultant assumptions were crucial in determining success – were more gendered. Take the case of this young lawyer who explained the implicit tensions in both the harmful, gendered ways in which judges perceived women as well as the ways in which her peers dealt with this perception to their detriment –

> . . . But most judges won't yell at a woman who is making these mistakes. . . . They won't yell in the way they might have yelled [to teach] a man: they don't give any woman their time. They are always afraid that the girl is going to break into tears. And they test these boundaries; they don't just assume them. I have seen a lot of sensible male judges testing a woman to teach, but with girls they start off very slow and they stop listening and back off completely when they think they might cross the line. *So the emotional reaction that you might have to something the judge might say – or their expectation of it – could hinder your professional growth.* And women really have to learn to control their emotions. You can't just be that person who bursts into tears in a professional environment. Girls are taught that if you cry, you will get things done: it is just sad, but it is the way it is.
>
> (Interview 19 with a litigating lawyer, 2013)

What is also interesting here is that the lawyer who reported it, herself a young women in her twenties, saw not just this gendered assumption – but also the actual gendered behavior by her peers – as a source of this tension. Similar interactional assumptions and reactions were much less stark in the other sites where the performance of gender was much less a part of professional identity.

And while there certainly were assumptions about women that were primed in interactions, people were hard pressed to describe the ways in which gender substantively mattered (especially negatively) in the global firms. Thus, across sites, it seemed that while the visions of labor and the characteristics that were primed in similar ways, they were being received and valorized differently by the host institutions within which they operated. And it is within this framework that the case of interactive gender gains comparative salience.

3. Women and (as) Diversity

At the macro level, institutionalist accounts have suggested that jobs become institutionally gendered (Acker 1990), with specific gender expectations of the "right" worker (e.g., Salzinger 2003). In the Indian case, as I suggest above, gender certainly remains constructed by workplace expectations and reception. And this distinction was even clearer in a contrast between how this question about diversity was treated by a senior partner in a corporate law firm and a corresponding peer in a litigation practice. When asked about how each of these firms were diverse, both partners recounted details about associates from different parts of the country, who spoke different languages, but were varied about how gender accounted for this diversity. On the one hand, the head of a litigating practice was quick to rationalize the gender exception:

> Women lawyers? Yeah, we have some – but they all get married and go away. Once they have a <makes a hand movement to indicate a baby>, they cannot stay, no? Who will do all the work at home?
>
> (Interview 18 with a senior male litigator, 2012)

On the other hand, the partner at the global law firm saw the diversity in his firm as not needing to include women because, as he put it, women were not really diverse within the context of his firm:

> But how are *women* diverse? We don't think of these lawyers as "women" associates and partners – they are just associates and partners. I guess it's because we have so many women lawyers, we don't think of a minority or . . . a diversity, as you call it.
>
> (Interview 17 with a senior male partner at a global law firm, 2012)

Yet, it was not just at the level of partnership that these distinctions were made clear. Women in litigation recognized that the choice they were making was to be lawyers within a strongly male, hierarchical structure: one that they had been warned against by their referents and close ties in the profession. This common example of having been warned against this career path is a good illustration of this demarcation across sites:

> My father still suggests certain kinds of practice to me. He will say, "Why don't you consider doing corporate litigation?" or "Why don't you consider doing conveyance or other nonlitigation work?" and he has always said this to me.
>
> (Interview 36 with a litigating lawyer, 2013)

Speaking to lawyers across different kinds of legal institutions was educational in throwing light on the ways in which there was a constructed expectation for certain firms – which I call "global" – to be different, by both people who work in these firms as well as those who don't. In particular, women in these global firms felt the clear distinction between their counterparts in litigation and how gender was salient in their context in reference to these women in litigation. This senior lawyer who had worked both in litigation and in a global law firm made the case for this comparison clear:

> People don't think of it [gender] as an issue [in global firms] – I get the perspective [that it] would have been different if I had been a litigating lawyer.... [speaking about a previous internship in a litigation practice]... my senior was a woman and I know that judges looked at a case differently when a male lawyer was arguing instead of a female lawyer. So if I had been in litigation, it would have been different... but not here, never here.
>
> (Could you give me an example?) Yeah... If there were particular cases, and they needed a specific result before a specific judge, they [senior women lawyers] would send certain male lawyers. I guess you could use being a woman to an advantage – but the way you talk to them and handle them doesn't work the same way in court as it does in a law firm.
>
> (Interview 13 with principal associate at a global law firm, 2012)

In addition to individual assumptions and resultant interactional dynamics, institutional environments are equally consequential in allowing these relationships to flourish. This "othering" of the experience throws light on the ways in which global firms are different for its inhabitants. They paint the picture of these organizations as sites where distinction was neither considered nor tolerated – both by people working in these firms as well as those viewing them from the outside. While women in litigation would talk about gender as salient organically in interviews, I would have to often prime it explicitly in conversations with women in large law firms, again speaking to the clear contrast among the different sites of work. Women – and men – spoke of gender in these firms not only as something that did not exist but, instead, as something that never had any scope to flourish. Of course, an important part of this emergence must have been that the largest and most prestigious of these firms had key partners who were female, drawing some reference to the ability for core role models to structure these institutions a certain way. But there was also a more organic expectation that these firms, for whatever reason, never were like the rest. Independent of whether people were in these firms or outside of them, they were discussed and referred to as places where gender did not matter, making them a separate coherent category that was indispensable to this discussion. It is to this comparative institutional framework and the theoretical possibility of egalitarian emergence that I turn to now.

V. THEORETICAL EXTENSIONS: THE ADVANTAGE OF NOVEL FRAMES

Even though gender stereotypes are created at the individual level, with interactional and institutional reinforcement, they are created and cemented, forming a social structure where disadvantages to women are not only accepted but also expected. This multidimensional analysis of the way gender is "done" (West and Zimmerman 1987) is important because it lends insight to the different ways in which the distinction between men and women is repeatedly made salient in a variety of social settings. Social psychologists have argued that one such argument for the way gender is "done" is construction and attachment of a persistent gender frame. I use this premise of gender frames and supplement it to globalization expectations to offer one explanation for why gender in the Indian global law firm setting works so differently despite all odds.

A. *The "Frame" Argument*

Ridgeway and Correll (2004) make an imperative argument that this repetitive salience extended to gender makes it a "background identity." They argue that this is especially problematic in the workplace because the "common knowledge" that is drawn from stereotypical gender-based distinction influences how men and women are differentially evaluated and legitimized (Ridgeway and Correll 2004). Ridgeway (2011) further extends this conceptualization of a background identity to what she refers to as a "primary gender frame" for coordinating social relationships. By infusing gendered meanings into the structures and practices by which work and home are organized, gender becomes an all-pervasive frame of reference with embedded beliefs about gender status and difference. In this way, the inescapable multilevel construction of identity and difference makes gender-based inequality persistent even in the seemingly more egalitarian modern workplace (Ridgeway 2011).

This conception of persisting gender frames in the workplace offers a multilevel theory for not only current institutional arrangements but also future institutions that emerge out of existing blueprints. Since the modern world demands constant reconstruction of social institutions that reflect the ongoing social, political, and economic changes in society, workplaces are constantly changing. However, Ridgeway argues that changes in cultural beliefs about gender lag behind changes in material circumstances between men and women (Ridgeway 2011). As a result, even in these "sites of innovation" (her term for new forms of social interaction and institution), a threat of persisting gender inequality remains because these new institutions are organized based on existing gender-unequal blueprints of their predecessors. However, in particular sites of economic and social innovation, she offers an exception. While background frames are likely to help organize new activities in these sites of innovation, she argues that the exact effect of these activities depends on the salience and relevance of gender to the new setting. When the basic framework of the job is not particularly gender typed, the background gender frame is only diffusely relevant. Since these sites of innovation do not have a persisting blueprint that enforces strong gender stereotypes to the new organization, there is the chance that it creates only modest disadvantages for the women who are employed in these organizations. On the other hand, more male-typed jobs, even in sites of innovation, are restricted by the constraints of the background gender frame they operate within. Thus, women employed in sites of innovation with a diffuse gender stereotype have relative advantages over both women in traditional workplaces, as well as women in other sites of innovation where the gender frame is less diffuse.

These new sites of innovation, then, under some limited circumstances, offer an opportunity for gender constructs to be renegotiated and problematic gender-unequal frames to be revised. This potential for escape from the otherwise monotonous reconstruction of gendered hierarchies is imperative because it not only affects the particular institution but also offers broader implications for gender inequality. In this chapter, I suggest that newly emergent global-style law firms in India are "new sites of innovation" and this reconstruction offers advantages to young Indian female lawyers who have traditionally been excluded from the rewards of the Indian legal profession.

B. *Indian Global Law Firms as New Sites of Innovation*

These global law firms in India are prime sites for studying the gender frame within innovative institutions for three main reasons. First, these institutions are new and innovative within the country's legal labor market. Unlike their earlier law office and litigation chamber counterparts that were closely tied by "old boys" networks, these new postliberalization firms are organized much more like their global counterparts. This sort of organizational setup might not

TABLE 2. *Organizations of interest and their representative characteristics*

	"New site" characteristics		Preexisting gender frame		
	Innovative work	Innovative structure	Gendered work	Gendered structure	
Law firm	Yes	Yes	Ambiguous	Ambiguous	Innovative site with diffuse gender frame
Litigation practices	No	No	Yes	Yes	Traditional structure with strong gender frame
Company legal department	Yes	No	Ambiguous	Yes	Partially gender typed

be innovative per se, but it was very novel in the context of the historical Indian legal workforce. Second, at the time of their incorporation, not only were these firms structurally novel, they were also dealing with global transactional work that the country was not familiar with. This is relevant because unlike litigation work (that one could argue was strongly tied to a gender stereotype because of the history of the male advantageous profession), transactional work that was done by these law firms was such a new form of work that it had no attachment to a predominant gender frame. Finally, the work itself was so intimately associated with being prestigious global work that it is likely that this association to the West helped blunt what might otherwise have been a stronger gender frame.

Of course, this advantage of these global firms is especially relevant in light of their comparative context. Unlike litigation firms that are still largely organized as lawyers' offices where gender roles and male hegemony are persistent, these law firms do global transaction work. Similarly, unlike legal departments of companies where the actual work has been changed because of liberalization and an increase in transactional work, these global law firms are not located within hierarchical organizations. As an extension, the gender frame of reference is not an active, established (and previously male-dominated) company (Table 2). Surely, this comparison is more ambiguous than the stark difference between litigating lawyers and global law firm associates, but as the accounts show, there is still a difference in expectation and performance among clients and associates alike. There is no "preference" for a male transactional M&A lawyer in a large global law firm because there is no preconceived notion of what an M&A lawyer ought to be, look, and act like. Because there isn't a set expectation, there is more negotiation of that image in interactions and, over time, construction of the new image.

In this chapter, I argue that one plausible mechanism at play that might account for this unique advantage women in large law firms have is that gender stereotypes are *not* yet set (and, arguably, were not set even at inception) and subsequent gendered expectations had not yet been formed. As a result, it is possible that in this case, the otherwise diffuse background characteristic of gender, especially in a country like India, is not as salient as it otherwise might be. In turn, this allows for some leeway in negotiating new gender expectations that do not have a precedent for gender-based inequality. But this argument, while efficient to a degree, does not satisfy the peculiar advantage of the firms at the very top of institutional hierarchy. What about these large, elite law firms that I call "global" is particularly capable of leveraging this advantage? If it was only a matter of new work and new kinds of institutions, all corporate firms that do new kinds of transactional work would be completely gender neutral. Yet we know this is not the case. It is this extension to the frame argument that applies specifically to global firms that I address next.

C. *Extension of the Frame Argument*

There is no doubt that these global firms are new sites of structural innovation. But there are two additional extensions that make this frame argument particularly salient within global firms. First, these firms are not just set at the level of occupational entry. Most global firms recruit from highly elite national law schools, which then predate this frame argument well before the level of entry into these firms. Thus, part of the mechanism of gender neutrality that is at work here is the framing that happens at these schools. As graduates of gender-neutral cohorts, these men and women are organically socialized to not find gender balanced professional sites as novel or problematic. And their environments aren't seen as particularly "diverse" because these firms grew alongside these schools, in a symbiotic dynamic that was gender balanced without especially setting it up to be so.

The second extension to this argument is that these global firms are, by definition, firms that have been created as a response to globalization. Being situated in India, a country whose development has rapidly been marked by factors of globalization, they are new sites that are reacting and emerging in response to global stimuli. In particular, these global law firms, because of the restricted entry of actual global practice in India, are responding to an expectation of globally competitive legal service firms. They are not just doing international work for international clients within new firms; they are doing work in ways that are meant to reflect their competitiveness in a world market. Thus, clients viewing them as meritocratic and modern, with women partners and senior lawyers, signals not necessarily a gender egalitarian workplace but a meritocratic one. In turn, this aspiration to be and, more importantly, seem like modern work spaces might be an image construction that is not meant to be gender egalitarian but just happens to appear that way independent of intent. In turn, women, who have relatively few advantages in the legal workplace, are eager to do well in the few avenues for gender-neutral work spaces that are available to them. Thus, one explanation could be that it is not just a new "frame" mechanism that is at work here, but instead the operation of a novel frame alongside a frame in response to globalization. Since these global firms are most relied on to be the face of this response, their assumptive adherence to meritocracy isn't as surprising.[10]

Yet why do I not argue that this advantage is couched among the senior female role models within these firms (another characteristic that is common across these global firms)? Naturally, with ethnographic interview data like this, causality necessarily has to be drawn with caution. At the same time, while it is true that both of the largest and most prominent global firms have strong, powerful women at their helm – accounting for big role models at the partnership level – this has, like other factors, not worked as only an advantage. While women certainly felt like gender wasn't a determinant in their success because of the composition of the senior partners in the firm, this composition also had other problems. Younger male associates, in particular, had a characterization of the "difficult woman boss" that was similar to other narratives of this kind of situation.[11] And women at different stages sometimes felt like they had to work harder to not prime gender because they felt it would not be accepted.[12] There certainly was a general sense of "If she can do it, why can't I?" that worked to both encourage junior women as well as create a space where potential gender-based excuses for nonperformance would not be tolerated.[13] One area where this was particularly salient was in how women spoke about balancing family and work. The advantage of starting careers in their early twenties meant that these women were well on partnership track by the time they had to make serious life course decisions about starting a family. And many women waited – much to their advantage – till they were in these positions of power before they had to negotiate time commitments and client expectations[14]. But while many of the women I spoke with were married or in committed partnerships, there was still a general sense that doing it was difficult and complicated – especially when it necessarily was at odds with the kind of commitment that was needed to do well in these firms, as set by more-senior female partners.

VI. CONCLUSION: ARE THESE WOMEN IN GLOBAL LAW FIRMS REALLY ADVANTAGED?

In her seminal essay on feminization and the legal profession, Menkel-Meadow (1989) argues that scholars researching these issues should employ frameworks that recognize the impact of gender-constructed social difference. Because gender is not just a "woman's issue" and "success" is not a gender-neutral measure, research truly committed to unpacking women's experiences in the profession is required to examine the role that gender difference and social construction of this difference plays in professional practice. In this chapter, I have tried to begin a possible inquiry into the experience of these women lawyers in India by employing a comparative framework across fields and over multiple levels of analysis.

These findings are certainly imperative to shed light on the differences in the way gender is constructed and experienced across different sites, but this is only one axis of enquiry. For example, this entire story of advantage could be conflating a deeper class narrative: women in global law firms do better because they self-select from an elite pool of similarly qualified and socially advantaged women. Like one law firm lawyer offered (for why she would never be mistaken for a secretary or a paralegal by a client): most of the people who come here would never be mistaken for anything but a lawyer because they come from a certain strata of society. This advantage of class was particularly salient when it came to balancing family and work. While women across sites spoke about having to navigate choices and paths about children, it was clear that certain kinds of women were best able to leverage this balance. Typically, these women worked in cities where they had large social ties and networks (often, these cities also happened to be their hometowns), which often also meant that they had certain class advantages, including the liberal cultural freedom to make choices such as marrying partners of their choice and making their own decisions about starting (or not starting) families. Thus, one possible explanation could be that these women might not be priming and championing a gender narrative at all – they might be championing a class narrative. Even so, women from a certain strata with class advantages have always existed (and continue to exist), and my broader research on elite professional women shows that not all elite firms – including other kinds of "global" firms – advantage women in the same ways and it is something about *these* firms that seems to offer them particular advantage. This is not to say their class frame is not advantaging them, but that their class frame alone has not been enough to advantage them in the past or even now, in other contexts. When holding the individual-level advantages constant, women across different work spaces continue to be differently advantaged upon entry into these different firms, and it is this novelty of advantage – even if only to a cross section of the population of lawyers capable of leveraging it – that sets these global firms apart.

Even so, this offers only a preliminary framework to understand these new sites of innovation and the extensions of their frameworks. And what I offer here is only one set of macro-level explanations for differences that might explain why women in large global firms are particularly advantaged. There are umpteen other explanations, of course. For instance, the processes of hiring and career trajectories are inherently distinct across these kinds of practice, so women *and* men face different challenges in these different sites.

Second, women in different stages in their career have very different narratives about gender – it is entirely likely that women are overreporting their success and experience within these firms because these firms are so much better than any comparative sites they could be working in. It is certainly optimistic that these women are doing so well, but at least part of the explanation could be the uniqueness of the opportunity given the general hostility in the professional markets in India. Since this is the only environment within which their hard work is valued and rewarded independent of strong organizational assumptions that are attached to their gender, these firms attract better-qualified and harder-working women. Taken to the extreme, this could slight the "advantage" of egalitarianism we seem to be seeing.

Third, perhaps the women in these firms are actually much better qualified and better prepared than their male counterparts and the fact that they are doing *only* as well as their male peers (while working harder) is a sign that the frameworks are not as egalitarian as they seem. To test this, again, comparative and systematic data between men and women is necessary. On the other hand, it could be the case that women do better simply because more women stay on – i.e., women do better not because they are better than their male counterparts but because men are leaving for better opportunities. These global firms are certainly highly prestigious sites within India, but with international opportunities and the capacity for transfer, perhaps more men leave these firms for better work pastures.

Similarly, clients are important to understanding this self-reported advantage better – what do clients really want and how are they vocalizing this preference?

Is deference and "good behavior" in a negotiation really valued by clients? And if yes, is it valued from women more because it is expected from women (so, in turn, are they responding to core microessentialism demands created by the clients)? Another explanation could be the kinds of clients that these firms serve and the ways in which that reiterates meritocratic advantage across these sites differently. Thus, institutional frameworks and structural advantages are important and necessary to understand this advantage, as I suggest. But equally necessary is an understanding of how these institutional frames are emerging and responding to global expectations of modernity and preferences for visible egalitarianism.

Another distinctive characteristic of the women in these global firms is their family demographic. Family and children are still, at the moment, only part of the imagination of many of the women I interviewed in these global law firms. While many of them were in partnerships or married, few had children. Certainly the advantage of age (most national law school graduates join these firms in their early twenties and have eight- to ten-year partnership tracks) helped make this decision less pressing, but we know from other accounts from the profession[15] that motherhood and planning families are core barriers to advancement. Of course, India's joint family structure and general culture of dependence meant that there were avenues to rely on these ties for child care and assistance. These women – and women like them who have achieved partnership without having to make motherhood decisions – will no doubt have to start thinking about this at some point, but there is certainly some remainder optimism that age offers that will help them as they navigate these balances.

Finally – and depressingly – this could well be a short-lived advantage. These firms are new, and as I argue here, this novelty is instrumental to their ability to deliver egalitarian advantage. At the same time, this newness also means that these firms are still smaller than their comparative counterparts in other countries, and more likely to have a culturally homogenous lawyer population and to change over time. While it is certainly promising that early cultural constructions of these firms are egalitarian, we will have to wait and see what happens as India's global legal landscape continues to expand and change.

Notes

1 Note that for the purposes of typology, I refer to these firms that Gupta, Khanna, and Wilkins set out in the Overview of this volume, as "global" firms. Yet, the firms in which women are reaping these unprecedented advantages are not Indian offices of global firms or even firms large enough to look like global firms in other

parts of the world. Instead, these elite firms are consistently considered *the* industry leaders in their organizational demographic. As I will argue later in this chapter, I use the term *global* because a combination of regulatory and historical factors have deemed that these firms evolved as the country's response to the global impetus of a booming international market and competition.

2 Even the less conservative estimates by the Bar Council of India stagnate this number at about 10 percent (Bar Council of India 2010).

3 There has been some more recent news about elevations of women lawyers in the Indian Supreme Court.

4 Trilegal, for example has only two female partners but they talk about partnership and the challenges they face in an interestingly non-gendered way. While female partners acknowledge the stress of balancing work and home, they think of it more as a professional life choice rather than a function of their gender.

5 In 2010, out of a total of 1,112 directorships in companies on the BSE-100 index, only 59, or 5.3%, were held by women. The boards of about half the companies had no women at all. In contrast, 14.5% of company directors in the United States were women, compared with 12.2% in the United Kingdom, 8.9% in Hong Kong, and 8.3% in Australia (Asia Business Report 2010). Trilegal, which was set up only twelve years ago, took nine years to promote its first woman into partnership, and today only two of its nineteen partners are women.

6 Between 2011 and 2013 (see Table 1), I conducted full-length, semi-structured interviews with more than eighty lawyers in different levels and positions within law firm practices, within litigation, and within company legal departments. Note that the initial project that these data come from was not focused on gender differences between sites but, instead, modified to respond to themes from fieldwork that followed a grounded theory approach (Glaser 1992, Charmaz 2003). As a result, interviews with earlier respondents served more as key-informant interviews rather than substantive interviews and in the pilot stage (July 2011– March 2012). I conducted twenty-two "main" interviews, all with senior women lawyers (and mostly in global law firms) as well as seven male lawyers in senior positions. These interviews set the stage for Phase 1 of the project (May 2012–September 2013) when I conducted fifty-one full-length (Total N = 51 + 29 pilot = 80) interviews across the three sites of my interest with both men and women, but oversampling women lawyers.

7 All the phase 1 interviews were in Mumbai, India, and face-to-face. Once the project began to focus on gender differences, I Instead of speaking with only women in large law firms, I tried to vary the organizations as well as the cohort of the respondents to tease out differences in experience. And while I spoke to many male lawyers across different stages in their careers, I oversampled women lawyers. I employed this comparative sampling strategy only once I had analyzed the findings in my pilot project for a range of theoretical sampling reasons. First, I was interested in the general law firm effect – to see if women in law firms were experiencing their jobs the same way as women in litigation and company law. Was there a marked difference in the way lawyers in certain types of organizations felt about their experience? Second, I wanted to tease out if it was just the law firm effect that was advantaging women, or if there was something peculiarly advantageous about being in a certain kind of large global firm. Third, I wanted to be able to find out not just what women thought of their jobs but, instead, how their peers considered

the women's careers. Finally, I spoke with women across different stages in their careers; I wanted to make sure that it was not just women in positions of power who felt advantaged. The findings presented here are a comparative analysis of this data as well as from informant data in less structured conversations with several lawyers and important spokespersons in the industry.

8 Currently, there are only 17 interviews (including seven with key informants) with male lawyers in my sample. However, this contrast, especially after I had analyzed a considerable number of the current interviews, helped place some of the data in context and was a good way of fleshing out the experience of women lawyers in these firms.

9 This assumption and extension of legal work and success as caretaking in itself is not novel. In her work on American legal practice, Pierce relays how the role of women paralegals as "caretakers" of their male bosses is seen as key to their success within firms. Women and men both depend on the "emotional labor" and the subsequently reliant relationship of care as essential to well-functioned working (Pierce 1996; 1999).

10 As I have argued elsewhere, even in cases where egalitarian workplace settings align, it is hard to replicate it if you are constantly faced with clients who do not respect egalitarian frameworks (Ballakrishnen 2015).

11 A first-year associate in one of the global firms confessed that he had been warned by his slightly senior friends about female bosses. He said, "I was told by friends in years three or four who had female bosses themselves that women bosses could be quite hard. They were very nice for some time, but then they could get crazy." Later in the interview, he mentioned that he himself had no problems, but he'd noticed that "female associates do change. They go from being nice and friendly to curt and formal when they get promoted.... The real change happens when they go from being principle associates to partners." It might well be that women felt like they had to keep their guard and protect their identity from becoming "too friendly," but it was still being received by their male juniors a certain way (Interview 73 with male junior associate, global law firm in Mumbai, 2013).

12 As one senior (married) lawyer who was on track to be partner said, "The evidence is all around. There aren't any nursing mothers in [the global firm I work at], and I can count the number of women with children. It is almost like women in firms like these want to prove that you aren't soft... that you are not shackled by family and other things that society says women are supposed to take care of" (Interview 82 with senior associate in a global law firm in Mumbai, 2013).

13 Many women spoke about this general culture of resistance to excuses and rhetoric that were seen as "womanly." Junior associates, in particular, spoke about how gender was so neutered in these global firms that they didn't think it right to make excuses that would make them seem like they were "using the gender card" (Interviews with global firm in Mumbai, 2013).

14 For instance, this senior associate in a global firm, who was referencing the advantage of not being on a parent track, commented: "We [referring to her peer group of senior lawyers] are at a stage where there are many women, but most of us don't have children and aren't immediately planning on having children. There is no immediate sense of this *parenthood culture* <gestures with air quotes>. If you look at the women in senior positions, they are either not married or married and don't

have children yet.... But three partners right now are pregnant, and it is the first time this is happening" (Interview 6 with senior associate in a global law firm, 2012).

15 The Rainmaker Report, which focused on a slightly more senior demographic of women (the average age was thirty-four years in that sample with more than a third of the population having more than ten years of practice), seemed to give the impression that most women lawyers *did* think that motherhood was a strong barrier to career rewards. For instance, 75 percent of women in law firms who took the survey agreed that the maternity break did have an adverse impact on their career (as compared with 52 percent of women in litigation and 43 percent of women who worked in companies) (Rainmaker Report 2011, 72).

References

Abel, Richard L., and Philip Simon, and Coleman Lewis. 1989. *Lawyers in Society: Comparative Theories*. New York: Beard Books.

Acker, Joan. 1990. "Hierarchies, Jobs, Bodies: A Theory Of Gendered Organizations." *Gender & Society* 4 (2): 139–158.

Babcock, Linda and Sara Laschever. 2007. *Women Don't Ask: The High Cost of Avoiding Negotiation – and Positive Strategies for Change*. New York: Bantam.

Ballakrishnen, Swethaa. 2013. "Why is Gender a Form of Diversity?": Rising Advantages for Women in Global Indian Law Firms." *Indiana Journal of Global Legal Studies* 20 (2): 1261–1289.

Ballakrishnen, Swethaa. 2015. Same Same (But Different): Accidental Feminism And Unintended Parity In India's Professional Firms. PhD Dissertation. Stanford University. www.purl.stanford.edu/wt907gt9034.

Bar Council of India. 2010. Statement of Total Number of Advocates Enrolled with the State Bar Councils as of January 2. www.120.138.244.28/advocates/num-advocates .php.

Bell, Myrtle P. 2011. *Diversity in Organizations*. Mason: South-Western Educational Publishing.

Buddhapriya, Sanghamitra. 1999. *Women in Management*. New Delhi: APH Publishing.

Burke, Ronald J. and Debra L. Nelson, eds. 2002. *Advancing Women's Careers: Research and Practice*. New York: Blackwell Publishers.

Chadda, Rakesh and Mamta Sood. 2010. "Indian Research on Women and Psychiatry." *Indian Journal of Psychology* 52 (7): 229–232

Charles, Maria and Karen Bradley. 2009. "Indulging Our Gendered Selves? Sex Segregation by Field of Study in 44 Countries." *American Journal of Sociology* 114 (4): 924–976.

Charmaz, Kathy. 2003. "Grounded theory." In *Qualitative Psychology: A Practical Guide to Research Methods*. Edited by Jonathan A. Smith. New York: Sage Publishing.

Davidson, Marilyn J. and Ronald J. Burke. 2011. *Women in Management Worldwide: Progress and Prospects–An Overview*. Surrey: Gower Publishing.

Desai, Neera. 1977. *Women in Modern India*. New Delhi: Vora and Company.

Epstein, Cynthia Fuchs. 1993. *Women in law*. University of Illinois Press.

England, Paula and Su Li. 2006. "Desegregation Stalled: The Changing Gender Composition of College Majors, 1971–2002." *Gender & Society* 20 (5): 657–677.

England, Paula. 2010. "The Gender Revolution Uneven and Stalled." *Gender & Society* 24 (2): 149–166.

Frank, Robert H. and Philip J. Cook. 1995. *The Winner Takes All Society*. New York; London and Toronto.

Freeman, Carla. 2000. *High Tech and High Heels in the Global Economy: Women, Work, and Pink-Collar Identities in the Caribbean*. Durham: Duke University Press Books.

Galanter, Marc and Nick Robinson. 2017. "Grand Advocates: The Traditional Elite Lawyers." In *The Indian Legal Profession in the Age of Globalization*. Edited by David B. Wilkins, Vikramaditya S. Khanna, and David M. Trubek. Cambridge: Cambridge University Press.

Glaser, Barney G. 1992. *Emergence vs. Forcing: Basics of Grounded Theory Analysis*. Sociology Press.

Gandhi, Jogindra Singh. 1987. *Sociology of Legal Profession, Law, and Legal System: The Indian Setting*. New Delhi: Gyan Books.

Ganz, Kian. 2012. "Law Firm Rankings." *Legally India*. www.legallyindia.com/wiki/Indian_law_firms.

Gothoskar, Sujata. 2000. "Teleworking and Gender." *Economic and Political Weekly* 35 (26): 2293–2298.

Granfield, Robert. 1992. *Making Elite Lawyers: Visions of Law at Harvard and Beyond*. New York: Routledge.

Gulhati, Kaval. 1990. "Attitudes toward Women Managers: Comparison of Attitudes of Male and Female Managers in India." *Economic and Political Weekly* 25 (7/8): M41–M48.

Gupta, Ashok, Manjulika Koshal and Rajindar Koshal. 1998. "Women Managers in India: Challenges and Opportunities." *Equal Opportunities International* 17 (8): 4–18.

Gupta, Namrata and Arun K. Sharma. 2003. "Patrifocal Concerns in the Lives of Women in Academic Science: Continuity of Tradition and Emerging Challenges." 2003. *Indian Journal of Gender Studies* 10 (2): 279–305.

India Business Law Journal. 2012. "*India Business Law Directory*." www.indilaw.com/pdfs/India%20Business%20Law%20Directory%202012–2013.pdf.

Interview 5 with partner at global law firm, 2011.

Interview 7 with senior associate in a global law firm, 2012.

Interview 6 with a senior associate in a global law firm, 2012.

Interview 9 with in-house lawyer with 5 years of experience, 2011.

Interview 13 with principal associate at a global law firm 2012.

Interview 14 with a litigating lawyer, 2013.

Interview 17 with a senior male partner at a global law firm, 2012.

Interview 18 with a senior male litigator, 2012.

Interview 19 with a litigating lawyer, 2013.

Interview 36 with a litigating lawyer 2013.

Interview 73 with male junior associate, global law firm in Mumbai 2013.

Interview 82 with a female senior associate, global law firm in Mumbai 2013.

Jain, D., ed. 1975. *Indian Women*. New Delhi: Ministry of Information and Broadcasting.

Jeyaranjan, J. and Padmini Swaminathan. 1999. "Resilience of Gender Inequities: Women and Employment in Chennai." *Economic and Political Weekly* 34 (1): 16–17.

Jhabvala, Renana. and Sinha, Shalini. 2002. "Liberalization and the Women Worker." *Economic and Political Weekly* 37 (21): 2037–244.

Kay, Fiona and Elizabeth Gorman. 2008. "Women in the Legal Profession." *Annual Review of Law and Social Science* 4 (2): 299–332.

Kumar, Neelam. 2001. "Gender and Stratification in Science: An Empirical Study in the Indian Setting." *Indian Journal of Gender Studies* 8 (1): 51–67.

Legal 500. "India Law Firm Rankings." Accessed February 11, 2013. www.legal500.com/c/india.

Mather, Lynn. 2003. "Changing Patterns of Legal Representation in Divorce: From Lawyers to Pro Se." *Journal of Law and Society* 30 (1): 137–155.

Menkel-Meadow, Carrie. 1989. "Exploring a research agenda of the feminization of the legal profession: theories of gender and social change." *Law & Social Inquiry* 14 (2): 289–319.

Michelson, Ethan. 2013. "Women in the Legal Profession, 1970–2010: A Study of the Global Supply of Lawyers." *Indiana Journal of Global Legal Studies* 22 (3): 1071–1137.

Mukherjee, Mukul. 2004. "Marketable Skills in the Wake of Globalisation: A Study in the Indian Context." *Women's Studies Research Centre Working Paper*.

Naqvi, Farah. 2011. "Perspectives of Indian Women Managers in the Public Sector." *Indian Journal of Gender Studies* 18 (3): 279–309.

Papa, Mihaela and David B. Wilkins. 2011. "Globalization, Lawyers and India: Toward a Theoretical Synthesis of Globalization Studies and the Sociology of the Legal Profession." *International Journal of the Legal Profession* 18 (3): 175–209.

Patel, Reena. 2010. *Working the Night Shift: Women in India's Call Center Industry*. Stanford: Stanford.

Patel, Reena and Mary Jane C. Parmentier. 2005. "The Persistence of Traditional Gender Roles in the Information Technology Sector: A Study of Female Engineers in India." *Information Technologies and International Development* 2 (3): 29–46.

Paul, Tinku. 2009. *Women Empowerment through Work Participation*. New Delhi: New Century Publications.

Pierce, Jennifer L. 1996. *Gender Trials: Emotional Lives in Contemporary Law Firms*. Berkeley: University of California Press.

Piper, Nicola and Mina Roces. 2003. *Wife or Worker? Asian Women and Migration*. Oxford: Rowman and Littlefield.

Rainmaker India. 2011. "Challenges Faced by Indian Women Professionals." Accessed February 11, 2013. www.scribd.com/doc/102128508/Challenges-Faced-by-Indian-Women-Legal-Professionals-Full-Report.

Reskin, Barbara. 1993. "Sex Segregation in the Workplace." *Annual Review of Sociology* 19 (1): 1-41.

Ridgeway, Cecilia L. 2009. "Framed Before we Know it How Gender Shapes Social Relations." *Gender & Society* 23 (2): 145–160.

Ridgeway, Cecilia L. 2011. *Framed by gender: How gender inequality persists in the modern world*. New York: Oxford University Press.

Ridgeway, Cecilia L. and Shelley J. Correll. 2004. "Unpacking the Gender System a Theoretical Perspective on Gender Beliefs and Social Relations." *Gender & Society* 18 (4): 510–531.

Risman, Barbara. 1998 "Gender as Structure." In *Gender Vertigo: American Families in Transition*. Edited by Barbara J. Risman. New Haven: Yale University Press.

Rosin, Hannah. 2012. *The End of Men*. New York: Penguin Books.

RSG Consulting. 2011. "India Law Firms." www.rsg-india.com/rankings.

Rudman, Laurie A. and Peter Glick. 2001. "Prescriptive gender stereotypes and backlash toward agentic women." *Journal of social issues* 57 (4): 743–762.

Salzinger, Leslie. 2003. *Genders in Production: Making Workers in Mexico's Global Factories*. Berkeley: University of California Press.

Sandefur, Rebecca L. 2001. "Work and Honor in the Law: Prestige and the Division of Lawyers' Labor." *American Sociological Review* 66 (3): 382–403.

Schultz, Ulrike and Gisela Shaw, eds. 2003. *Women in the World's Legal Professions*. London: Hart Publishing.

Sprague, Joey and Mary K. Zimmerman. 1993. "Overcoming Dualisms: A Feminist Agenda for Sociological Methodology." In *Approaches to Qualitative Research: A Reader on Theory and Practice*. Edited by S. N. Hesse-Biber & P. Leavy. New York: Oxford University Press.

Supreme Court of India. Supreme Court Advocate on Record List as on 22.05.2012. Accessed on February 11, 2013. www.supremecourtofindia.nic.in/circular/advocateonrecord.pdf.

Supreme Court of India. Supreme Court List of Senior Advocates Designated by the Supreme Court as on 17.12.2012. Accessed February 11, 2013. www.supremecourtofindia.nic.in/outtoday/sradv17122012.pdf.

Wilder, Gita Z. 2007. "Law School Debt and Urban Law Schools." *Southwestern University Law Review* 36 (2): 509.

West, Candace and Don H. Zimmerman. 1987. "Doing Gender." *Gender & Society* 1 (2): 125–151.

8

Pro Bono and the Corporate Legal Sector in India

Arpita Gupta

I. INTRODUCTION

This chapter is the first qualitative empirical study of pro bono practices of elite corporate law firms in India in a global context. I collected and analyzed data on five major aspects: the range of pro bono work and other socially oriented initiatives; their shared understanding of the term *pro bono*; the institutionalization of pro bono; the perceived advantages of doing pro bono work; and the factors limiting the amount of pro bono at these firms. It is important to analyze the surveyed law firms' responses to these questions against the backdrop of the specific regulatory, historical, economic, and sociocultural milieu of India to understand the dialectical complexity of the interaction between global and local forces, which leads to the distinctively Indian vision of pro bono and socially oriented practices at these law firms.

This study focuses on elite corporate law firms because they are more exposed to global forces relative to other parts of the Indian legal profession and pro bono work has become an important and increasingly institutionalized part of global corporate law firm culture, especially in the United States and the United Kingdom, raising the question of how India has received that culture (Cummings 2004). Moreover, Indian corporate law firms have recently experienced quite spectacular growth, thereby spiking greater interest in their activities. In light of this, and the paucity of studies relating to it, there is a great deal of curiosity about the various aspects of Indian law firm pro bono practice as compared with that of global law firms.

The survey responses provide interesting findings. First, globalization has had an important effect on the culture of pro bono practices at Indian corporate law firms. In particular, the globalization of knowledge and practices is manifest in a gradual move toward institutionalization of pro bono at most surveyed law firms, as well as in the recent emergence of matchmaking organizations (both domestic as well as foreign) that seek to connect practitioners with people who need legal advice, such as social entrepreneurs, public interest organizations, and nonprofit organizations. Second, the external notion of pro bono is not received in a vacuum in India. The contextual specificity of Indian public interest law (PIL) and litigation, the predominantly transaction-based work of most top-tier Indian law firms, and the traditionally embedded beliefs, practices, and cultural values relating to the notion of "doing good" have shaped the currently evolving understanding and practice of pro bono in India. This suggests that pro bono in India is taking on something of a "glocal" flavor, or a mix of global and local.

Indeed, the use of the term *pro bono* is fairly recent in India. The current understanding of the term is amorphous and overlaps with other socially driven initiatives like corporate social responsibility (CSR). Beliefs such as "giving back" and "doing good" underlie these concepts and give them broad definitional parameters. Unlike the United States, initiatives like pro bono and CSR do not have clearly distinct meanings and spheres of operation in India.

The chapter is organized as follows: Section II describes the qualitative research methodology used for this study. Section III maps out the salient characteristics of PIL in India and develops a typology of the means of furthering public interest causes. This typology helps to understand the distinctive pro bono involvement of the law firms described in section IV. Section IV reports and analyzes the results of the qualitative study on the pro bono activities of Indian law firms, primarily in these three broad categories: litigation based, transaction based, and non-transaction based. Legal advice on transactional matters is considered to be the most predominant form of pro bono Indian law firms undertake and thus is dealt with in detail. This section also identifies various factors encouraging and/or discouraging Indian firms from undertaking pro bono work. Section V details the main characteristics of an India-specific model of corporate pro bono and highlights issues needing further research.

II. RESEARCH METHODOLOGY

The qualitative research in this chapter is based on a survey that was supplemented with telephonic interviews and e-mail correspondences with partners of some of the respondent law firms. First, I undertook a preliminary survey of the top forty law firms in India through e-mail to find out how many firms regularly pursued pro bono work. Although most of the firms disclosed doing some kind of pro bono, only eleven firms reported regularly performing it. Seven of those firms are top-tier firms (ranked between 1 and 10) and four are midtier firms (ranked between 11 and 40), as per the classification by the RSG India Centre (RSG Consulting, 2013).

Second, I asked those eleven firms to fill out a detailed Pro Bono Questionnaire (Appendix 1), which constituted the most important research tool for this study. The questionnaire included both fact-based and opinion-based questions and was loosely based on the survey developed by Cummings and Rhode for studying US pro bono practices (Cummings and Rhode 2010). The structure and substance were significantly modified to suit the Indian context. (See Appendix 2 for a list of the law firms that participated in this study.)

Third, to obtain additional insights, I engaged in further e-mail correspondence and telephonic interviews with some of the respondent law firm partners, who are pioneers and leaders of the corporate legal sector.

Fourth, I surveyed students at one of India's elite law schools – the National University of Juridical Science in Kolkata – on their views on pro bono work in India (Appendix 3).

III. PUBLIC INTEREST IN INDIA: LAW AND BEYOND

PIL in India exhibits both *sui generis* traits acquired through its unique evolutionary path in India, as well as the more general characteristics of its global counterparts. The indigenous innovations include the dilution of procedural requirements like *locus standi* (due to the introduction of epistolary jurisdiction by the Supreme Court of India), making it easier for suits to be brought forth,[1] and the Indian government's belief that it is important to provide the needy with access to free legal aid. PIL in India has also been influenced by various socially inclined international law conventions and practices on issues of global concern, such as human rights (especially women's rights) and environmental protection; and references made by the Indian judiciary to foreign case law where the domestic law is insufficient, ambiguous or archaic.[2]

The public interest and social welfare causes in India are promoted through both social action litigation (SAL) and non-litigation-based means,[3] both of which essentially focus on providing access to justice to the underprivileged.

PIL in India is largely dominated by SAL[4] and is often used synonymously with it. SAL first developed in the late 1970s, when the Supreme Court of India began to initiate and encourage it when the legislature failed to sufficiently protect the vulnerable and the executive failed to enforce existing legal protections. Justice P. N. Bhagwati, who made the pioneering move to introduce SAL in India, succinctly summarized the underlying purpose: "to promote and vindicate public interest which demands that violations of constitutional or legal rights of large numbers of people who are poor, ignorant or in a socially and economically backward position should not go unnoticed and unaddressed" (*People's Union for Democratic Rights and others v. Union of India and others*, AIR 1983 SC 1473 at 1476). Subsequently, social activists and some lawyers – referred to by Baxi as "sociolegal entrepreneurs" – initiated SAL at the Supreme Court, which highlighted the excesses committed by state agencies and officials; their disregard for the principles of administrative law, such as the rule of law; and their failure to protect the vulnerable from injustice committed against them by those in power (Baxi 1985, 117).

In addition, Article 39A of the Constitution of India directs the state to "provide free legal aid . . . to ensure that opportunities for securing justice are not denied to any citizen by reason of economic or other disabilities." In consonance with this provision, the Parliament of India enacted the Legal Services Authorities Act, 1987, which provides for free and competent legal service to the weaker sections of society through *Lok Adalats*(translated as "People's Courts") to be established throughout the country.[5] *Lok Adalats* are special courts that resolve disputes more quickly and ease the burden on the delay-ridden Indian courts by handling easily resolved cases and helping parties reach a final settlement.[6] Although started with noble intentions, various impact assessment reports and academic empirical studies conducted on these courts have revealed significant deficiencies with the quality of justice imparted, frequent violation of procedural rules, and widespread laxity in enforcement of judgments (Galanter and Krishnan 2003–04).[7] Most of these observations are, however, equally applicable to the regular court system and should not be used to discredit the idea of *Lok Adalat*, but rather to improve its performance.

But any approach focusing on litigation as the primary means of forwarding public interest is bound to have limited efficacy because of the Indian court system's delays and operation (Deva 2009, 33). Choosing other methods beyond litigation is imperative for substantively forwarding this cause.

Relying primarily on reformatory and preventive means of action, non-litigation-focused measures address the root causes underlying limited access to justice, especially for people in weak or vulnerable positions. Since these root causes could be attributed to many factors, such as social norms, patriarchy, caste consciousness, entrenched customs and beliefs, and peculiar historical settings, an integrated set of responses is necessary to address the problems holistically.

Although this aspect of PIL has not traditionally received as much attention as the litigation-based approaches, policy makers and civil society organizations are increasingly recognizing its importance. Some of the non-litigation-focused approaches include enacting social legislation, spreading legal awareness, promoting public interest–focused ethics as core elements of legal education, and ensuring effective enforcement of existing social legislation (Cooper 1999).

Social legislation refers to laws that benefit and protect those individuals who, due to factors like race, sex, health, disability, or social standing, have traditionally been discriminated against and are not in a position to successfully defend their interests against the centers of entrenched power (Chekki 1969). India has one of the most progressive sets of socially focused laws in the world with numerous welfare laws, policies, and social action programs for the poor, socially backward classes, laborers, children, senior citizens, women, people suffering from a physical or mental disability/handicap, and so forth. These measures seek to address important issues such as land reforms, illiteracy, hunger, housing, public health, and rehabilitation (Chekki 1969). To minimize social inequality and injustice, most of these laws have a two-pronged approach. First, they seek to create a level playing field by explicitly laying down provisions on equality. Second, by adopting affirmative action measures, they seek to address past injustices. Third, laws such as the Right to Information (RTI) Act, 2005, which do not directly fall under the category of social legislation, have helped immensely to enforce numerous social legislations by requiring the state to provide information on the implementation and enforcement of these laws.

Closely related is the assessment of the impact of existing laws and social policies and suggestions for policy and legal reform. In India a number of civil society organizations, research and policy think tanks, social activists (further empowered by the RTI Act), and government-appointed committees are active in this sphere. But this measure is grossly underutilized because these laws and policies are often not implemented and enforced.

Other non-litigation-based approaches include spreading legal awareness and reforming legal education. Frequently, individuals who are protected by this legislation are unaware of their rights, which often renders a well-intentioned legislation ineffective. This scenario is aggravated by the fact that about 24 percent of the country's population (around 290 million people) is illiterate (Census of India 2011). Because most of these people reside in rural areas, are part of migrant labor communities, and are located across the country, spreading legal awareness is very difficult. Several nongovernmental organizations (NGOs) primarily focus on this very cause. Also, the Legal Services Authorities Act of 1987 has mandated the formation of district-level legal service authorities, requiring them to spread legal awareness and facilitate access to justice (Legal Services Authorities Act, 1987, Chapter IV, § 10 and § 11).

The litigation and non-litigation-based measures provide options to Indian law firms to design innovative, efficient, and high-impact pro bono programs aimed at furthering the cause of public interest. Given the magnitude of the problems and the inadequacy of relying solely on the government to resolve them, law firms, with their legal expertise and resources, can make a substantial contribution in furthering public interest causes.

IV. CORPORATE LAW FIRMS IN INDIA AND PRO BONO

In this section, I aim to describe various aspects of pro bono practice by elite law firms in India; and to discover and analyze the factors particular to India that either assist or impede the participation of law firms in pro bono activities. This part is largely based on the qualitative empirical research I conducted through a detailed pro bono questionnaire, supplemented by e-mail correspondence and telephonic interviews with partners of major firms and representatives of public interest organizations in India.

Through a preliminary inquiry, I found that although most law firms do some kind of pro bono work, the top-eight-ranked firms and some of the midtier firms as ranked by RSG Consulting's 2013 India Report mainly undertook pro bono work on a large scale and on a comparatively regular basis (RSG Consulting 2013). These eleven firms all responded to the pro bono questionnaire. Instead of law firm partners filling out the questionnaire separately, they filled out just one questionnaire that represented the firm's views. Most of these firms are full-service firms that specialize in multiple areas of commercial law.

The partners of the surveyed law firms constituted the foci of this qualitative research as they represent one of the fastest-growing sectors of Indian legal profession. The entire research was directed at getting information based on two fundamental themes: first, organizational information regarding the current pro bono practices, involvement in socially responsible activities, and linkages with public interest organizations; and second, attitudinal information regarding the perceived advantages of pro bono, factors impeding or encouraging pro bono work, the desirability of institutionalized pro bono practice, and the likely impact of potential foreign law firm entry.

A. *Extent of Institutionalization of Pro Bono*

To find out the extent of the institutionalization of pro bono work, I analyzed the responses to the questions regarding the existence of a pro bono department/committee, budgetary allocation, and firms' opinions on the hours spent doing pro bono work considered billable. The pro bono culture among Indian law firms is not as institutionalized as in the West, mostly because of the remarkable difference in the average size of Indian and Western law firms.

1. Pro Bono Department

Most of the firms did not have a separate department or committee to coordinate pro bono activities, but four of the top-tier firms had a partner heading the pro bono practice. (Out of those four firms, only one [survey respondent 2] has a partner dedicated specifically to supervising pro bono work.) One of the firms had a separate "social sector practice" department through which pro bono activities were conducted, which advised social businesses and entrepreneurs in legal, tax, and strategic issues on a pro bono basis. The partner heading this department spent 15–20 percent of his total work time on pro bono and quasi pro bono activities, and all members of the firm were expected to work in this department for some time. The quasi pro bono work was charged on the basis of "happiness billing" by "letting a client pay whatever he deemed appropriate" (Survey respondent 6).

Generally pro bono activities were undertaken on an ad hoc basis, usually at the behest of one or more of the partners. Six of the surveyed firms opined that although pro bono started in their firm on an ad hoc basis, they were in the process of systematizing it (survey respondents 1 and 3–7). It must be clarified that taking up pro bono work in an ad hoc manner does not imply doing less of it or doing it irregularly. One of the respondent firms aptly remarked that although the firm performed pro bono work on an ad hoc basis, they regularly undertook such work (survey respondent 5).

2. Budget for Pro Bono Activities

None of the firms surveyed had a fixed budgetary allocation for pro bono activities; they released funds as and when required. A top-tier firm was discussing an initiative with GiveIndia Foundation in which the firm's lawyers "will be donating part of their salaries to NGOs through GiveIndia by a process through which each individual's donations are collected and then routed to various NGOs of that person's choice – GiveIndia has a large list of NGOs that are categorized by the type of cause that they work for, such as child rights, women's rights, and rights of elderly people" (Survey respondent 5).

By making monetary contributions to an organization dedicated to a particular social cause, the firm members are performing more than mere charity. As most of the corporate law firms in India focus on transaction work, the individual members of the firm do not have many opportunities to be directly involved with litigation-based pro bono work. Thus, allowing individual members to connect with legal and social reform–focused public interest organizations is an innovative strategy that allows them to engage with the cause(s) they are connected to and to perform pro bono work by proxy. This would establish a donor-recipient link between the firm and the recipient organization, so the latter would be more likely to approach the former for advice relating to transaction-based legal issues it encounters. Indeed, most Indian law firms did not consider pro bono, CSR, and other socially oriented activities as hermetically insulated because these concepts were considered to be different manifestations of "doing good" and carrying on "responsible business." For instance, one of the firms was collaborating with Grameen Creative Lab to establish a fund exclusively for social business, particularly for providing microfinance facilities to small social entrepreneurs (survey respondent 6).

3. Pro Bono Work as Billable Work

Four of the firms counted hours spent doing pro bono work as billable hours (survey respondents 1–3 and 6). This was done to incentivize the law firm members to take up work other than regular for-profit work and to allay concerns about their inability to complete the minimum number of billable hours as a result of taking on pro bono work. In the year 2010–2011, one of the firms spent a total of eight thousand hours on pro bono work (survey respondent 1). The fact that only four out of eleven firms count pro bono work as billable indicates that the pro bono culture among law firms in India is fairly recent, voluntary, and largely informal. Three out of the four firms that count pro bono work as billable are much larger than the other firms, which contribute less in part because of their smaller size.

Though most firms agreed that pro bono work should be institutionalized and systematized, they also felt that it should not be forced upon the firm or employees because the voluntary aspect is important. Further, making it compulsory would not ensure quality contribution.[8] One of the firms favored making it mandatory for all law firm employees to earmark a specific number of hours for pro bono work. The rationale for this was that " . . . without an institutionalized system where a certain number of hours are mandatory, you risk a situation where employees engaging in pro bono work may feel disadvantaged compared to other colleagues who are close to achieving the firm's financial targets" (survey respondent 5).

In addition, the president of the Society of Indian Law Firms (SILF), Lalit Bhasin, disclosed that the SILH has issued a guideline requiring all member law firms to perform at least ten hours of pro bono per week, and most of the hundred-plus member firms had been adhering to this commitment (e-mail correspondence with author, 2012).[9]

B. *Range of Pro Bono Activities Undertaken*

Law firms engage in pro bono activities ranging from litigation to transaction based, as well as education, water conservation, and so forth. I have prepared a typology of the broad categories under which these activities could be classified. These categories are not watertight, and activities can fall under more than one head or even under the category of CSR. The non-litigation-based categories are further divided into transactional and nontransactional activities.

1. Litigation-Based Activities

Litigation-based pro bono work forms the smallest constituent of the overall pro bono work done by the respondent firms. I came across just a handful of court cases in which any corporate law firm participated on a pro bono basis. Some of the law firms were or had been involved in litigation for a social cause or on behalf of individuals in need. For instance, on behalf of the SILF, one of the firms filed a public interest petition before the High Courts of Bombay and Delhi, seeking a response from the central and state governments on antiterrorism measures to ensure a terror-free life for citizens (Lalit Bhasin, e-mail correspondence with author, March 12, 2012).

In another example, a firm represented a group of fishermen who fished in an area near Nhava Sheva (a seaport close to Mumbai) in the Bombay High Court. Some companies handling dangerous chemicals in the port area had petitioned the court to direct the state pollution control board to permit them to handle those chemicals where the fishermen fished. But with the law firm intervening on behalf of the fishermen, the companies withdrew their petition. The firm acknowledged that it involves itself in such causes "selectively," based on "strong feeling about a particular issue" (survey respondent 11). Such instances of pro bono activity are rare because a law firm's services are mostly transaction based, not litigation focused. Most cases are litigated by law-focused public interest organizations that specialize in litigating such matters.

But with the emergence of matchmaking organizations, which seek to connect those who need legal advice with law firms (on a pro bono basis), the trend seems to be changing. For instance, at the behest of Lex Mundi Pro Bono Foundation (a matchmaking organization), lawyers of a leading law firm in India represented a social entrepreneur who had developed a bamboo gasifier to produce cheap and environmentally clean electricity for a village in India.

But, after several people having vested interests filed a complaint against this initiative, the state pollution control board canceled the project for violation of environmental regulations. The law firm challenged this in the Patna High Court and managed to obtain a favorable decision for the electricity generation project.

Explaining why litigation-based activities form a very small part of the overall pro bono activities of Indian law firms, Bhasin stated:

> (T)he Central government has constituted the National Legal Services Authority (NALSA) under the Legal Services Authorities Act, 1987 to provide free legal services to the weaker sections of the society and to organize *Lok Adalats* for an amicable settlement of disputes. Since the Supreme Court and State High Courts have already entrusted the pro bono legal services to Legal Aid Committees, and the fact that the same are aided and funded by government, the bulk of the pro bono court cases go to the litigation lawyers.
> (email correspondence with author, March 12, 2012)

Additionally, socially minded independent litigation lawyers, who provide free court-based legal services to the needy in both individual matters (e.g., domestic violence, divorce, alimony) and matters concerning a group of individuals (e.g., human rights, housing, rehabilitation of displaced population, human trafficking), have created numerous organizations in India.[10] But notably, none of the respondent firms had any links with such organizations. One reason is that these organizations are staffed with lawyers specializing in litigation. Suhaan Mukerji, then a pro bono partner at Amarchand & Mangaldas & Suresh A. Shroff & Co., notes that they are largely self-dependent and do not need legal advice or aid from corporate law firms (Interview with Mukerji 2012).

Also, when asked about their preferred mode(s) of performing pro bono, almost all the law firms chose "providing their regular transactional services to not-for-profit/social entrepreneurial clients for free/at reduced rates" over "participating in litigation matters involving those in need" (survey respondents 1, 2, 4, 5, and 6). There seems to be a clear division of labor in the case of the preferred mode(s) of doing pro bono between corporate law firms and public interest organizations providing legal advice or aid.

2. Transaction-Based Activities

Most of the law firms disclosed providing transactional services to not-for-profit public interest organizations, individuals, and the government on a pro bono basis. Although it used to be quite challenging to match lawyers with matters suited to their expertise, this is gradually becoming less problematic with the matchmaking organizations, which verify that an individual or organization working for socially useful ends genuinely needs legal services and lacks the resources to pay for them.

Some recently started matchmaking organizations include TrustLaw Connect, iProbono, and UnLtd India. The first two organizations have international links and receive international funding, while the third one is entirely India based. TrustLaw Connect is a Thomson Reuters Foundation Service, and iProbono is a UK-based "nonprofit online network" seeking to develop an active pro bono culture among Indian law firms. Some of the respondent firms are connected with these organizations and have undertaken pro bono work through them, but presently Indian law firm involvement with these entities is quite limited. More firms should be encouraged to register with such organizations.

a. ADVISING PUBLIC INTEREST ORGANIZATIONS. Some transactional issues for which social enterprises, NGOs, charities, and advocacy groups need legal advice are: setting up a trust/society or any other appropriate organizational structure under Indian law; routing investments from Indian and/or foreign investors; obtaining venture capital; drafting commercial contracts; general corporate matters; protection of intellectual property; and certain important tax-related matters, such as compliance with requirements under the Foreign Contribution (Regulation) Act, 2010 and tax benefits under the Income Tax Act, 1961.

Some firms also provided innovative solutions to socially oriented entrepreneurs. For instance, one firm was closely involved with the poverty-alleviation activities of the Grameen Foundation, USA. The firm advised Grameen on some unique initiatives to provide financial and nonfinancial support to microfinance companies and other social businesses such as the growth guarantee scheme and implementation of software and social performance measurement indices (survey respondent 1). The firm disclosed doing "deeply discounted work for small and medium companies in the microfinance sector," including not-for-profits such as the Cashpor Micro Credit and Friends of Women's World Banking. Acknowledging the future fee-generating incentive in providing legal assistance to social businesses today, Vineetha MG of AZB & Partners stated that "[w]hen law firms work with social businesses at the inception stage, they grow with them and they grow to become important clients of the firm" (Interview 1 with Vineetha 2012).

The organizations that respondent firms have advised range from small to large in size, and from domestic to international in their areas of operation, and cover a wide range of social and economic issues. By providing legal advice on a pro bono basis, law firms perform a valuable function for society. This kind of service forms the biggest constituent of the total pro bono work done by firms largely because it is aligned with the firms' core work and can be easily performed through the firms' regular channels of work.

b. ADVISING SOCIAL ENTREPRENEURS.[11] Most firms gave pro bono advice to social entrepreneurs and social ventures–promoting organizations. For instance, one firm advised the National Innovation Council (NIC) on an INR$75 billion social venture fund to be set up under Project Innovate to establish a financially viable venture capital model to "significantly affect the bottom of the pyramid" (survey respondent 3).

One of the firms developed three very innovative strategies to advance social business in the country: establishing a large fund for social businesses; creating strategies for facilitating mergers and acquisitions among nonprofit businesses; and setting up a social stock exchange for trading of businesses that value social impact more than mere financial profitability (survey respondent 6).

Social entrepreneurs can also gain a great deal from matchmaking organizations. As opposed to organizations like NGOs, which due to their organizational capacity can easily approach legal practitioners for pro bono advice, small social entrepreneurs find it difficult to approach entities that are willing to aid them on a pro bono basis. The opposite is equally true – it is difficult for those willing to aid these individuals to find them. UnLtd India is exclusively dedicated to providing social entrepreneurs with financial and advisory services (including legal services) from the first stage to the last stage. Ravistan Anthony, operations manager, UnLtd India, notes that law firms could offer to advise social entrepreneurs listed by these organizations and help set up more organizations "... by helping them in registration and various other subregistration processes" (e-mail correspondence with author, March 12, 2012).

Largely owing to the work of these organizations, voluntary services offered by law firms to social entrepreneurs have commendably increased. For instance, one firm provided transactional advice to an Ashoka Fellow who helped conceive and establish the Rickshaw Bank, a project that enables rickshaw pullers in India to own the rickshaws they pull. This firm also assisted Drishtee, a social enterprise that provides services to rural India through village kiosks that are run and managed by local entrepreneurs.

c. ADVISING THE GOVERNMENT. Prima facie, advising the government on legal matters, might not be regarded as falling within the ambit of pro bono work. But given the specific nature of the state in India and the intention with which the legal advice is given, free advice to the government could be seen as pro bono work. Socialism and welfare orientation might constitute the two most defining characteristics of the Indian state. One of the key rationales behind pro bono work is to give back to society, and one might consider the state to be the foremost representative of Indian society. Relinquishing legal fees for advice given to the state by law firms can be seen as a way of contributing that amount toward social welfare spending by the state, especially for advice related to the enactment of a legislation/rule with wide social implications.[12] Apart from forwarding the social cause, by advising the government on a pro bono basis, the firms are also developing contacts within the government.

Most respondent law firms counted providing free/reduced rate legal services to the government as a pro bono activity. One firm helped the government of India with a number of World Trade Organization disputes and assisted some of the government ministries in drafting/reviewing policies and legislations (survey respondent 5). Other firms gave free advice to various government departments on business law–related matters (survey respondents 1 and 2). Another firm gave pro bono advice to the government on the implementation of the Providing Urban Amenities in the Rural Areas (PURA) scheme, designed to empower villages economically, bridge the urban-rural gap, and improve the quality of life in rural areas by intensifying physical, electronic, and knowledge connectivity between rural and urban parts of the country (survey respondent 3).

3. Non-Transaction-Based Activities/Proxy Pro Bono

Apart from contributing indirectly to the public interest cause by providing litigation and transaction-based services, most law firms also reported direct engagement in promotion of various social causes. These activities are more akin to the CSR activities undertaken by corporations in general. Due to the primarily corporate nature of most of the work of the elite Indian law firms and the widespread prevalence of corporate culture among them, most of the respondent firms emphasized conducting "responsible business" (survey respondent 3). CSR and pro bono are not viewed as being mutually exclusive but as united by the underlying notion of giving back to the society. Also, the same department and institutional apparatus of the firm are often used to conduct both pro bono and CSR work.

a. POVERTY ALLEVIATION AND ECONOMIC DEVELOPMENT. Almost all respondent firms agreed that poverty alleviation, the biggest bane afflicting Indian society, was the most important cause for pro bono activity. When asked, "If you are required to dedicate certain number of work hours to pro bono work, which area(s) would you prefer to work with?" each firm listed issues it desired to promote through pro bono. Nearly all respondents indicated poverty alleviation as their foremost priority (survey respondents 1, 3, 5, 6, and 11).

The respondent firms detailed their involvement with a number of poverty-alleviation programs. For instance, one firm procured gifts for employees and corporate clients on festivals and special occasions from Himjoli Products Pvt. Ltd., a social enterprise that seeks to create sustainable employment in rural areas of Himachal Pradesh by partnering with various self-help groups producing handmade products (survey respondent 4).

The contribution made by these firms is not confined only to India. For instance, a firm recently "seconded one of its associates (for a period of two months) to Grameen Foundation USA's Philippines office on a pro bono basis to assist Grameen Foundation in Philippines to analyze the regulatory regime governing mobile money and microfinance in Philippines and devise innovative solutions to foster financial inclusion" (survey respondent 1).

b. HUMAN DEVELOPMENT. The firms are contributing toward the ideal of human development in multiple ways by supporting causes like education, legal awareness, and human rights. One firm reported its tie-up with Teach for India by encouraging its associates to volunteer to teach in municipal schools. One of the firm's founding partners is also actively involved with several charitable, philanthropic, and developmental activities and a member of various charitable trusts, schools, and an NGO dedicated to the progress of rural women (survey respondent 1). Another firm collaborates with the Pan Himalayan Grassroots Development Foundation, a nonprofit organization working in Uttarakhand and Himachal Pradesh to promote sustainable, self-reliant development at the village level to construct sanitation facilities by harvesting rainwater in Uttarakhand schools (where many girls drop out due to lack of sanitation facilities) (survey respondent 4). Indeed, many firms mentioned initiatives ranging from firm members teaching in various law colleges of India (survey respondent 6) to being involved with socially oriented organizations (e.g., Naaz, for HIV-positive individuals; Help Age, for the elderly; and Asha, an awareness campaign on child sexual abuse) and running in-house education programs for its office assistants and support staff (survey respondent 5) to making donations to certain causes (survey respondent 6) to participating in a drive to stick reflector tapes on cycle rickshaws to minimize accidents (survey respondent 3).

These examples underscore that in India the concept of doing good is quite broad, and pro bono is usually thought to include activities that would be labeled as CSR or charity in the United States. I will discuss the history context for this shortly.

C. LAW REFORM PROPOSALS. Due to their experience and high degree of expertise in commercial laws, corporate law firms can be good candidates for advising the government on reforming business laws. It is not unusual for government-appointed law reform committees to seek recommendations from these firms. For instance, one firm had submitted a series of regulatory reform proposals on a pro bono basis to a Reserve Bank of India–appointed committee on microfinance.[13] Some of its recommendations were accepted and incorporated by the bank. The firm also suggested that the Companies Bill be amended to permit a new hybrid entity through which social entrepreneurial activities could be carried out profitably (similar to benefit corporations in the United States and community interest corporations in the United Kingdom) (survey respondent 1).

C. *Defining Pro Bono in the Indian Context*

It is difficult to develop a universally applicable definition of the term *pro bono* because its literal meaning ("public good") can mean different things in different contexts. Indeed, in India, unlike the United States and many European countries, the term *pro bono* is not defined officially in any statute, rule, or code of conduct. By analyzing the activities enumerated earlier and the viewpoints expressed by the respondent firms performing pro bono work, a better understanding of the term *pro bono* and its connotations can be reached. The concept of pro bono in India reflects both indigenous and global elements.

The indigenous element has two important aspects: the belief that the legal profession is a noble profession, and the specific meaning and intricate connotations that the phrase "doing well" has acquired in Indian society over a long period of time. The legal profession in India is not synonymous with business (which is considered to be driven by profit motive alone). This distinction appears to be primarily rooted in the regulations that entrust lawyers with ethical duties toward the court (Rules 1–9, § I, Chapter II, Part IV, Bar Council of India Rules), client (Rules 11–32, § II, Chapter II, Part IV, Bar Council of India Rules), opponent (Rules 34–35, § III, Chapter II, Part IV, Bar Council of India Rules), colleagues (Rules 36–39, § IV, Chapter II, Part IV, Bar Council of India Rules), and society in general. This notion of nobility raises the expectation of onerous conduct on the part of lawyers, even at the cost of their self-interest at times. In light of these considerations, the Bar Council of India Rules note that lawyers have a duty to render legal aid to those who are "genuinely in need of a lawyer" as "free legal assistance to the indigent and oppressed is one of the highest obligations an advocate owes to society" (Rule 46, § VI, Bar Council of India Rules).[14] The law firm partners and lawyers I interviewed and corresponded with also emphasize the link between professionalism and performance and their duties toward society in providing free legal advice.

Unlike the regulations just described, the second aspect coloring the understanding of the term *pro bono* in India is not explicitly mentioned in a particular source. It is implicit in the understanding of the concept of "doing good" that has evolved in the Indian cultural context. Numerous literary and oral sources composed and/or translated in different Indian languages in varying historical time periods (some of them dating even before 1000 BC) exposit the meaning, characteristics, rationale, and implications of "doing good."[15]

Over time, these beliefs have become embedded in the social conscience. Some of the fundamental traits associated with doing well for others forms the leitmotif of the basic message: there should be no expectation of any favor in return from the person who is being helped (Bhagavad Gita, Chapter 17, Verse 11); the action should not be merely a lip service or done with an eye on reaping any benefits out of the act (ibid., Verse 12); it should not be done for mere fame, honor, or personal aggrandizement (ibid., Verse 18); it should not be done with a hope of being rewarded (ibid., Verse 21); it should be done with a sense of duty (ibid., Verse 20); and lastly, it should be done for a person genuinely in need and not for a person of means who can easily afford it (ibid., Verse 22).

These beliefs, which have become the guiding principles behind the kind of donation, philanthropy, CSR, etc., practiced in India, also permeate the understanding of pro bono.[16] Many of the partners held similar views. They did not quote from any specific text or literary source, but gave their general understanding of the meaning and implications of pro bono. This understanding corresponded with the set of beliefs found in various literary sources and thus reflects a process of unconscious internalization of long prevalent cultural beliefs. Some of the important characteristics of pro bono that were emphasized were: (1) high-quality legal services should be provided; (2) pro bono should be done for the benefit of the society, not the firm; (3) every free legal service cannot be counted as pro bono, especially when done for friends, family, or long-standing clients, as in most of these instances, they expect to receive a return favor and can afford legal services on their own); (4) it should not be done merely for creating a positive image and drawing in more clients; and

(5) it should not be limited to a onetime advice session or monetary donation, and attention should be paid to ensure sustainability of the benefits accruing from conducting pro bono activities. Some of the respondent firms refused to give a list of the organizations they had supported through pro bono work or requested anonymity based on the ideology behind the Indian concept of *gupt daan* ("anonymous help")[17] that emphasizes anonymity of the donor to ensure that the act was not done for the sake of honor, fame, self-aggrandizement, etc. For some firms, disclosing their pro bono activities would defeat the larger purpose for which they undertook it.

Moreover, it is not always possible to fit the "traditional ways of engaging in socially beneficial activities within the parameters of the definition of 'pro bono' and CSR initiatives, as generally understood in the Western countries" (survey respondent 7). In particular, one firm noted that historically in India such activities were undertaken on an individual rather than an institutional basis and thus depended on the conscience of the individual.

But, due to globalization, these indigenous cultural beliefs have come to share space with the notions and practices associated with pro bono at the international level, especially for elite Indian law firms that are increasingly making their presence felt at an international level. Their attempt to keep pace with the pro bono practices at the global level is apparent from the steps they are taking to institutionalize pro bono. As discussed earlier, some of these firms have already made an initial move toward making pro bono practice more systematic, formal, and well-coordinated by adopting measures like setting up a separate pro bono department in the firm, making a partner in charge of supervising the firm's pro bono work, considering the hours spent on pro bono work as billable hours, and linking up with organizations promoting public interest and social entrepreneurship.

D. *Factors Contributing to the Growth of Pro Bono Among Law Firms in India*

The growth in pro bono and related activities in India is heartening. In this section, I explore some of the factors leading to its growth.

1. Availability of Resources

The fact that large corporate law firms are more actively involved in doing pro bono can be explained in part through the availability of resources necessary to undertake large-scale and organized pro bono activities.[18] As India's economy and law firm business has grown, so has its available resources. A larger resource base implies more funding, infrastructure (e.g., departments dedicated to pro bono), research capability, and human capital (e.g., the capability of transferring a pro bono matter from one advocate to another).[19] A firm can create "an enabling environment for pro bono and foster a culture of giving back to the society" (survey respondent 1). Even if it is not mandatory for a firm's members to do pro bono work, by creating such an environment, the cumulative pro bono output of the firm is bound to increase, as compared with a situation where there is no institutional support.[20]

2. Peer Pressure

Law firms operate in a very competitive environment where they vie for the same pool of clients and law school graduates. A comparative analysis of the last few years' law firm rankings show that seven to eight firms compete closely for the top spots (RSG Consulting 2013). In such an environment every parameter that reflects on a firm's level of professionalism,[21] including pro bono involvement, counts. This is apparent from the considerable attention the firms have recently started paying to their pro bono programs and activities. These firms are adopting comparable pro bono initiatives and thus creating some competition in doing pro bono work. Such competition is expected to increase with the opening up of the Indian legal market to foreign lawyers and law firms.

3. Perceived Benefits

The law firms that responded to the pro bono questionnaire were asked to rate, on a scale of 1 to 5, various reasons that made doing pro bono important for the firm (Question 17, Pro Bono Questionnaire, Appendix 1). The two reasons that were most favored showed predominantly altruistic motives. These were (1) "[h]andling a matter with positive social impact would give a sense of achievement to the lawyers working in law firms" (option c) and (2) "such a work gives a sense of 'giving back' to the society" (option a). These were followed by the option: "[i]n an overtly competitive environment, such work serves to distinguish the firm and gives it a good reputation" (option e). Next in line was the understanding that "[i]t would diversify the work portfolio of the firm employees and act as a breather to the mundane corporate life, and thus contribute to job satisfaction of the employees" (option b). The least favored factor was "[s]uch work provides good legal and interpersonal training (by providing opportunities for group work, coordination, and interaction) to the firm employees, benefiting the firm in the long run" (option d).[22]

The following chart shows how the firms rated five options about the perceived benefits of doing pro bono:

	Option A	Option B	Option C	Option D	Option E
Respondent 1	1	5	2	3	4
Respondent 2	4	2	3	1	1
Respondent 3	5	5	5	5	5
Respondent 4	5	4	4	3	3
Respondent 5	5	3	5	4	2
Respondent 6	5	4	5	4	5
Respondent 7	5	1	5	1	5
Respondent 8	4	1	5	1	1
Respondent 9	1	1	4	1	1
Respondent 10	2	2	2	3	4
Respondent 11	2	2	3	2	3
Total	39	30	43	28	34

CHART 1 Perceived advantages of doing Pro Bono work (on a scale of 1–5)

The reason mentioned least – pro bono work provides good training to the newly recruited lawyers – though considered very important in the United States, did not find much favor in India (Cummings and Rhode 2010). This is because, unlike the United States, the culture of sending firm employees to public interest organizations for performing pro bono work where they get trained while working does not exist in India because the primary area and mode of work done by corporate law firms (transactional work) is different from that of public interest organizations (social issues and litigation, lobbying, researching, and spreading awareness about such issues). One of the major contributory factors behind such a situation in India is the large-scale government involvement in providing free legal aid, which eclipses the relatively few public interest organizations in this space. None of the survey participant firms had links with any public interest organization. Another perceived benefit of doing pro bono, which is less favored by Indian law firms, is that such work provides good publicity to a firm and attracts clients in the overtly competitive market for legal services (ibid.). This difference can be explained on two grounds. First, the Bar Council of India imposed a ban on any kind of advertisement by lawyers (including law firms); and second, as explained by Suhaan Mukerji, the TITLE, the consciousness about doing large-scale pro bono is still developing among firms and the quality of legal services provided by any firm is the most relevant determining factor a client considers when deciding which firm to hire (Interview 2 with Mukerji 2012).

4. Global Influences

All the law firms operating at the global level have developed well-institutionalized pro bono and corporate responsibility departments. In the United States, statutory provisions (Rule 6.1, ABA Model Rules of Professional Conduct) exhort lawyers to perform pro bono work for a minimum number of hours, and there are law firm rankings based solely on the quantity and quality of pro bono work.[23] Pro bono culture is becoming well entrenched in most of the developed parts of the world.

Elite Indian corporate law firms that have business links with foreign law firms and international clients are increasingly paying attention to pro bono work. Many law firms responded yes to the question, "In the eventuality of opening up of Indian markets to foreign law firms, do you think that to remain competitive, there would be a pressure on Indian law firms to make pro bono a formal, systematic and institutionalized practice of the firm" (survey respondents 1, 3, and 4). One can see the effects of these global influences in some Indian law firms as they learn and adopt global pro bono best practices. For instance, Allen & Overy supported a major law firm in India in their pro bono and community service by sharing its best practices and working together on some projects, like countering online child exploitation (Pro Bono and Community Affairs Report 2009).

Further, a petition was recently filed against the presence of foreign law firms in India, countering a claim that foreign law firms are mere businesses while the Indian legal profession is considered to be a "noble" profession. The respondent foreign firms argued that they do not treat their profession as mere business and perform pro bono and community services on a much larger and wider scale than their Indian counterparts (A.K. *Balaji v. Government of India and others*, Writ Petition No. 5614/2010, Madras High Court). This statement is bound to trigger introspection about this issue among Indian law firms.

Although currently a law firm's pro bono profile is not considered to be an important factor affecting recruitment of law graduates by Indian law firms, says Suhaan Mukerji, it might become important when foreign law firms, with a well-developed pro bono culture, are allowed to enter the Indian legal market (Interview with Mukerji 2012). Such practices might be appealing for law graduates who wish to do public service while having the benefits of working in a corporate atmosphere. Somewhat disagreeing with this view, one law firm partner commented that even if the Indian market is opened to foreign lawyers, "the foreign law firms will take their time in getting to know the Indian market, context, and milieu before committing to any local pro bono efforts" (ibid.). Initially, even the foreign law firms would, in all likelihood, "focus on getting their operations sorted and achieve business continuity before embarking on pro bono work" (ibid.). But most firms agree that in the long term having a pro bono environment would be beneficial for Indian firms.

As part of a research project on the inclination of law school students in India toward pro bono, the results of a survey conducted in one of the top three elite law schools of India (National University of Juridical Sciences) are relevant.[24] Seventy students in their fourth and fifth years of law school participated in the survey. Out of these, about 70 percent of the students (forty-nine) indicated that having pro bono work as part of the work profile "will make the job more interesting and satisfactory." They also opined that when there is not much difference between pay packages and perks being offered by different law firms, they would prefer to join a law firm that gives them an "option to do pro bono work along with the regular firm work and count the time spent doing pro bono as billable work." Thus, in the long run, having a well-structured pro bono program would seem to benefit Indian law firms.[25]

E. *Factors Limiting Pro Bono Involvement of Indian Law Firms*

As has been observed before, compared with their Western counterparts, pro bono culture is not as formally incorporated and as widely prevalent among Indian law firms. Some of the important factors for this are as follows:

1. Recent Spread of Modern Law Firm Culture

The recent origins of the law firm culture in India is one of the most important factors behind the present limited involvement in pro bono work. According to a response to the pro bono questionnaire, "[t]he present focus of Indian law firms is to establish their practices" (survey respondent 4). Another firm commented that, at this juncture, it is a little premature to expect the newly established Indian corporate sector to devote extensive time and resources to pro bono work and undertake full-fledged pro bono work like Western firms, because most of the law firms are currently "focused on arriving at an equilibrium/structure that affords the maximum efficiency for a firm for their size, which means largely focusing on billable work" (survey respondent 7). Additionally, as socially driven initiatives in India have traditionally been "personally driven, law firms would probably not take this [large-scale institutionalization of pro bono work] up with any sense of urgency" (survey respondent 7).

Nevertheless, many of the firms have engaged in several pro bono activities and served various social causes. According to another response, although pro bono initiatives are not formalized as they are in the United States or United Kingdom, some Indian law firms are beginning to institutionalize pro bono (survey respondent 3).

2. Lack of Awareness

Apart from some large corporate law firms, law firms are not generally aware of pro bono (survey respondent 1). A partial explanation for this is the absence of any statutory definition or minimum requirement to do pro bono by the Bar Council of India. In the United States, both federal and state bar associations are actively involved in promoting pro bono work. Firms also strive to climb up in the rankings based on pro bono work[26] and eagerly advertise their pro bono profile and social responsibility initiatives. As yet, these trends are not visible in India.

3. Extensive Involvement of the State in Providing Legal Services

This emphasis on private assistance for pro bono in the United States is partially a result of the rollback of government-led legal aid.[27] The US Congress has banned "federally funded programs from engaging in a range of activities including litigation involving class actions, alien's and attorney's fees" (Cummings and Rhode 2010). But in a socialist-leaning country like India, where there is a constitutional and statutory duty to provide free legal aid to the needy, the state is heavily involved in providing such services, creating the perception that there is less opportunity for private participation.

4. Smaller Average Size of the Firms

Apart from a handful of large law firms, most firms in India are small or medium sized. Compared with the average size of law firms in the United States and United Kingdom, even the so-called large law firms of India would fit under the medium-sized category. Small size implies limits in terms of resources, infrastructure, and the ability to take up large-scale pro bono work. Indeed, a law firm partner stated that these firms are typically driven by their bottom lines, are fairly stretched for resources, and are rarely able to dedicate their time to pro bono matters (survey respondent 9).

5. Information Asymmetry

There is wide information asymmetry between those who need legal advice and those who can provide it. Although matchmaking organizations are attempting to connect law firms with those needing legal advice, the overall extent of such efforts is very limited, partly because most people who need legal advice do not live in big cities, where most law firms are located. This further narrows the opportunity for beneficial pro bono work undertaken by law firms.

V. CONCLUSION

Given the indigenous and global influences on the meaning and practice of pro bono in the Indian corporate legal sector traced in this chapter, three concluding remarks can be made.

First, there is a conscious move toward formalizing, institutionalizing, and expanding pro bono practice along the lines of global pro bono practices, at least with elite corporate law firms in India.

Second, simple transplantation of the global pro bono model would have limited efficacy in the Indian context. The precise form and content of the corporate pro bono model in India needs to consider the country's specific socioeconomic concerns, and the availability of the most effective means of redressing them. Given the magnitude of poverty, the fact that the majority of the population (68 percent) inhabit the rural areas, the specific role and nature of the state, and the sheer number of people who need access to justice in the country, the state's role in providing pro bono services is pivotal. Private corporate pro bono cannot seriously supplant the state's role. At most, it can supplement the government's efforts. Even in the United States, the impact and functioning of private pro bono is far from satisfactory and has been criticized in a number of academic studies (Arcia 1994; Rhode 2004).

Third, in India there is no watertight compartmentalization between concepts like pro bono, CSR, and other public interest–oriented acts as they quintessentially share the notion of "doing good" as their fundamental core. The understanding of the term *pro bono* in the Indian corporate legal sector is more holistic as opposed to its Western counterpart, which strictly equates pro bono with providing legal help through the means of litigation- and transaction-based work. Legal help usually constitutes just one dimension of addressing a societal concern, and providing legal help would likely only partially resolve the issue. Although, at the moment, there is no official policy on pro bono framed by either the government or the Bar Council of India, if a policy were formed, it should encompass a holistic view of pro bono to respond to the country's particular challenges. This chapter contributes toward developing a *sui generis* model of pro bono by extending the definitional parameters of the term *pro bono* and developing an integrated approach of "doing good."

This study constitutes an initial inquiry into the nature of pro bono practice among corporate law firms in India. Although it describes and analyzes a number of significant aspects of corporate legal pro bono practice in India, including its meaning, range, and institutionalization, it also tangentially touches upon a range of issues needing further research, such as the relationship between pro bono and professionalism, individual-led versus institution-led pro bono, and the ways in which pro bono can be performed more effectively.

APPENDIX 1 – SURVEY – PRO BONO PRACTICES OF CORPORATE LAW FIRMS IN INDIA

I. *Firm and Personal Information (These Details Would Remain Confidential)*

1. Name of the firm, year of establishment:
2. Firm location (city):
3. Your name (optional):
4. Your contact details – e-mail/mobile no. (optional):
5. Your designation in the firm:
6. Department/area(s) of law you are working in:

II. *Status of CSR/Pro Bono Initiatives Undertaken by the Firm*

7. Does the law firm participate in any:
   a. Pro bono activity (**Yes** or **No**):

If **Yes**, then elaborate/enumerate those activities:

b. Corporate social responsibility (CSR) activity (**Yes** or **No**):

If **Yes**, then elaborate/enumerate those activities:

III. *Socially Oriented Involvements of the Firm*

8. Has the firm been involved with any legal aid organization? If **Yes**, which?
9. Has the firm represented any group/organization in the court on pro bono basis?

10. Has the firm supported movements geared toward legal education, gender equality, environmental protection, assistance to the elderly, HIV awareness, etc.?

If **Yes**, enumerate:

11. Does the firm run any special program or project relating to particular issues like education, employment, etc.?

IV. *Collaborations with Not-For-Profit Organizations*

12. Does the firm have any dealings with a not-for-profit organization/social entrepreneurial organization (**Yes** or **No**)?
    a. If **Yes**, is this purely a business relationship?
    b. Are there cases where the firm's advice has been given to these organizations free of cost/without any fee?

Name of the nonprofit organization	Matters in which the firm assisted the not-for-profit organization
1.	
2.	

13. Has the firm worked with legal aid organizations like Majilis, Alternative Law Forum, Lawyers Collective, etc.?

V. *Institutionalization of Pro Bono*

14. Is there a fixed portion of the firm's revenue reserved for pro bono activities?
15. Is there someone responsible for coordinating pro bono activities of the firm?
    a. Name and contact information of the person(s):
16. Are pro bono activities conducted on ad hoc basis *or* is there a systematic effort?
    a. Why do you think that the law firms in India are not very keen upon doing pro bono work (underline/highlight)?

The firm employees are already overloaded with work.
Such activities are seen as a burden on the firm's finances.
Any other reason:

VI. *Perceived Advantages of Pro Bono*

17. Rate on a scale of 1 to 5 the following reasons you think would make pro bono important for a firm (5 for the most important reason(s) and 1 for the least important reason):
    a. Handling a matter with positive social impact would give a sense of achievement to the lawyers working in law firms.
    b. It would diversify the work portfolio of the firm employees and act as a breather to the mundane corporate life, and thus contribute to job satisfaction of the employees.
    c. Such work gives a sense of "giving back" to the society.
    d. Such work provides good legal and interpersonal training (by providing opportunities for group work, coordination, and interaction) to the firm employees, benefiting the firm in the long run.
    e. In an overtly competitive environment, such work serves to distinguish the firm and gives it a good reputation.

VII. *Opinion of the Firm Employee on Some Issues Dealing with Pro Bono*

18. Did you participate in any legal aid program in your law school?
19. Were you aware that most of the successful law firms in United States and United Kingdom, as well as those operating internationally, are adopting an institutionalized pro bono/CSR initiative?
    a. If **Yes**, then, in the eventuality of opening up of Indian markets to foreign law firms, do you think that to remain competitive, there would be a pressure on Indian law firms to make pro bono a formal, systematic, and institutionalized practice of the firm (**Yes** or **No**)?
20. Do you think that Indian law firms should also make pro bono/CSR practice an important component of their business strategy? Why?
21. Do you think that a minimum number of work hours out of the total number of work hours expected of a law firm employee should be made compulsorily dedicated to doing pro bono work (**Yes** or **No**)? Briefly explain why you think so.
22. If you are required to dedicate a certain number of hours to doing pro bono work, which area(s) would you prefer to work with (e.g., child rights, gender equality, economic development, environmental issues, better access to education, legal awareness)?
23. Which mode(s) of performing pro bono would you prefer (please highlight/underline your preferred mode):

– Participating in litigation matters involving those in need
– Carrying out legal research/suggesting improvement in laws
– Collaborating with nonprofit legal groups/organizations in particular social causes
– Providing your regular transactional services to not-for-profit/social entrepreneurial clients for free/at reduced rates.
– Suggest any other mode you think to be appropriate:

24. What do you think is/are the best way(s) in which the lawyers working in law firms can contribute to the society/social causes?

Confidentiality

Your personal details will remain confidential. Your responses would be used to carry out a focused study on the level of involvement of Indian corporate law firms with pro bono work.

Indicate if you wish to be attributed for the comments you have made in this survey (**Yes** or **No**):

APPENDIX 2 – LIST OF THE LAW FIRMS THAT PARTICIPATED IN THE SURVEY

Name of the firm	Survey respondent number
AZB & Partners	1
Amarchand & Mangaldas & Suresh A. Shroff & Co.	2
J. Sagar Associates	3
Trilegal	4
Luthra & Luthra	5
Nishith Desai Associates	6
Khaitan & Co.	7
Bhasin & Co.	8
Anonymous	9
Anonymous	10
D.H. Law Associates	11

APPENDIX 3 – SURVEY: PRO BONO AND LAW STUDENTS IN INDIA

Law school: National Academy of Juridical Sciences, Kolkata, India

Year at the law school:____

Definition of pro bono: working for a larger social cause/underrepresented constituencies of people/indigent person(s) who cannot afford legal service.

Q1. What are the most important criteria when you decide/will decide to join a law firm?
- High pay package and perks
- High opportunities of growth
- Work satisfaction in terms of work quality, diversity, and satisfaction
- Any other criterion:

Q2. In case there is not much difference between pay packages and perks being offered by different law firms, would you prefer to join a law firm which gives you an option to do pro bono work along with the regular firm work and count the time spent doing pro bono as billable work?

Q3. Do you think that having pro bono work as part of your work profile will make your job more interesting and satisfactory?

Q4. Given a choice to do pro bono along with the regular dealings at your law firm, what issue(s) of pro bono work would you prefer (tick mark)?
- Gender equality
- Child rights
- Poverty mitigation, e.g., by providing social entrepreneurs setup business/service
- Environmental issues
- Better access to education and legal awareness
- Tribal rights
- Any other issue you feel for:

Q5. Given a choice to do pro bono work by your law firm, what mode(s) of performing pro bono would you prefer (please tick mark):
- Taking up pro bono cases and representing them in the courts
- Carrying out legal research/suggesting improvement in laws
- Collaborating with nonprofit legal groups/organizations in particular social causes
- Providing your regular transactional services to not-for-profit/social entrepreneurial clients for free/at reduced rates
- Any other mode that you may choose:

Notes

1 The concept of PIL was first introduced in India in the case of *S.P. Gupta v. Union of India*, 87 SCC 1981, in which the Supreme Court of India diluted the rigors of

locus standi doctrine. For a detailed discussion on this particular aspect (Susman 1994).

2 For instance, in the landmark judgment of *Vishakha v. State of Rajasthan*, AIR 1997 SC 3011, the Supreme Court of India ruled that in the absence of any law protecting women against sexual harassment at the workplace, the provisions of the Convention on the Elimination of All Forms of Discrimination Against Women (CEDAW) should be used.

3 This definition is very close to the understanding of PIL as described in the Globalization, Lawyers, and Emerging Economies (GLEE) topic paper: "legal activities that advance interest of and causes of constituencies of disadvantaged" (Cummings et al. 2011).

4 Upendra Baxi first drew attention to the difference between the PIL of India and the United States. On the grounds of certain fundamental differences, he used the term *social action litigation* in the case of India (Baxi 1985).

5 As required by the Legal Services Authorities Act of 1987 most states have enacted the State Legal Services Authorities Act to provide easy, free, and extensive access to justice to the weaker sections of society.

6 According to the data released by the Supreme Court of India, as of December 2010 more than thirty-two million cases were reported to be pending in various courts of India.

7 For instance, see "Twenty Sixth Report on Demands for Grants (2008–09) of the Ministry of Law and Justice," Department Related Parliamentary Standing Committee on Personnel, Public Grievances, and Law and Justice, 11, www.cjponline.org/judiciary/26thCommitteeReport-Law&Justice.pdf.

8 Scholars have different opinions about whether pro bono should be voluntary or compulsory. See Boyle (2007, 415–426) and Davis (2006–2007, 85–96).

9 The SILF's rationale for issuing this guideline can be gauged from one of the SILF's important goals: "promoting and providing legal aid and assistance to the needy." The interaction with various international bar associations that actively encourage pro bono among law firms and lawyers is another important factor behind issuance of this guideline.

10 Public interest organizations like Majilis, Lawyers Collective, and others are some of the major NGOs in India aiming to facilitate access to justice for the vulnerable sections of the population.

11 Even in the United States, providing free legal assistance to social entrepreneurs and carrying on day-to-day operations are becoming important aspects of pro bono services provided by the corporate law firms. Matchmaking organizations such as the Lex Mundi Pro Bono Foundation play an important role in this respect.

12 This is not the trend in the United States. The advice given to the government in India on certain matters can be seen as pro bono because of the larger political context of the country – India is a welfare state, which is fundamentally different from the United States, which has a more adversarial role in policy making.

13 The sub-committee of the Central Board of Directors of Reserve Bank of India to Study Issues and Concerns in the MFI Sector related to the entities regulated by the bank (popularly known as the Malegam Committee).

14 The legal system in India is largely based on the British legal system. Various provisions of the Bar Council of India Rules on Professional Conduct can be traced as far back as AD 13.

15 Among other sources, the topic of doing well for others or for a social cause figures in Ishavasya Upanishad (ca. 1000 BC), Mahabharat (ca. 600–300 BC), and Bhagavad Gita (ca. 200 BC–AD 200).

16 This survey, which was conducted before the provision for mandatory CSR was introduced u/s 135 of the new Companies Act, 2013, showed that law firms hardly distinguished between the notions of CSR and pro bono. Nevertheless, as seen from the perspective of corporate legal sector, there are three important points of overlap between these notions in India. The first point is the underlying notion of "doing good." Second, both of these concepts have a strong indigenous influence and can be traced backed to works composed around five thousand years ago. From Vedanta (ca. 1500 BC) to Kautilya's Arthashastra (ca. 350 BC) to Gandhi's concept of Trusteeship, there are detailed discussions on the ethical ways of conducting business and doing social good. Due to this influence, there are certain important points of departure from how these concepts are construed in the West. See Muniapan and Dass (2008). Third, both of these concepts have been subject to similar debates, the most important of which being whether these should be made compulsory.

17 In Indian tradition *gupt daan* (e.g., anonymous giving) is considered to be the most superior of all kinds of donations/help. The identity of the one who is helping is kept completely anonymous (including from one's own family members and friends). Making an act of helping others public is thought to belittle the nobility and goodness of such an act.

18 Similar observations have been made with regard to pro bono practice in U.S. law firms (Cummings and Rhode 2010).

19 The advantages of carrying pro bono work through large law firms have been widely discussed in the context of the United States. Many of these observations would be applicable in the case of large law firms in India, which now share many characteristics with their Western counterparts (Josef 2009, 619–621).

20 For these very reasons, the Pro Bono Institute has come out with a Law Firm Pro Bono Challenge specifically for large law firms (i.e., firms having fifty or more lawyers).

21 Scholars hold differing views as to whether doing pro bono counts as an element of professionalism (Sossin 2008).

22 The issue of job satisfaction of the law firm employees needs to be seen in the larger context of how the corporate law firm sector in India is broadly structured. The comparatively larger partner-to-associate ratio (leverage) in the Indian firms is specifically relevant to this issue.

23 The role of ranking (based on pro bono performance by the law firms) in attracting law students to join firms with substantial pro bono contribution in the United States is considered to be significant (Cummings and Rhode 2010, 2371).

24 The number and extent of clinical programs being run in the law schools in India are increasing, and law school students are being encouraged to regard pro bono culture prevalent in the law firms as an important factor in choosing which firm to join.

25 Unlike in the United States, as of now, Indian law firms' corporate clients are not pushing firms to perform pro bono work. The most important consideration for corporate clients when choosing a law firm is the quality of work a law firm delivers in the area(s) of its specialization.

26 Law firm rankings based on pro bono can have a positive or negative impact on the pro bono performance of law firms. One example of a negative outcome is "the 'Heisenberg effect': the rankings changed the phenomenon they claimed to measure" (Cummings and Rhode 2010, 2372).

27 Various pros and cons of rollback of the US government participation and an increase in private participation in providing legal aid to the indigent and public service organizations have been discussed (Regan 1999; Abel 2009).

References

Abel, Richard. 2009. "Paradoxes of Pro Bono." *Fordham Law Review* 78 (5): 2443–2449.

Arcia, Omar J. 1994–1995. "Objections, Administrative Difficulties and Alternatives to Mandatory Pro Bono Legal Services in Florida." *Florida State University Law Review* 22 (3): 771–798.

Baxi, Upendra. 1985. "Taking Suffering Seriously: Social Action Litigation in the Supreme Court of India." *Third World Legal Studies* 4 (1): 107–132.

Boyle, Leslie. 2007. "Meeting the Demands of the Indigent Population: The Choice between Mandatory and Voluntary Pro Bono Requirements." *Georgetown Journal of Law and Ethics* 20 (4): 415–426.

Chekki, D. A. 1969. "Social Legislation and Kinship in India." *Journal of Marriage and Family* 31 (3): 165–172.

Cooper, Jeremy. 1999. "Public Interest Law Revisited." *Commonwealth Bulletin* 25 (1): 135–153.

Cummings, Scott L. 2004. "The Politics of Pro Bono." *UCLA Law Review* 52 (1): 1–149.

and Deborah L. Rhode. 2010. "Managing Pro Bono: Doing Well by Doing Better." *Fordham Law Review* 78 (4): 2357–2442.

Fábio de Sá Silva, and Louise G. Trubek. "The Ties That Bind: Mapping Arenas of Engagement between Corporate and Public Interest Law in Emerging Economies." Unpublished manuscript, October 8, 2008. (draft for GLEE Conference: The Legal Profession in the Age of Globalization, New Delhi, India, October 8, 2011).

Davis, Jessica. 2006–07. "Social Justice and Legal Education: Mandatory Pro Bono Legal Services." *Charleston Law Review* 1 (1): 85–96.

Deva, Surya. 2009. "Public Interest Litigation in India: A Critical Overview." *Civil Justice Quarterly* 1 (1): 19–40.

Galanter, Marc and Jayant K. Krishnan. 2003–04. "'Bread for the Poor:' Access to Justice and Rights of the Needy in India." *Hastings Law Journal* 55, (4): 789–834.

Interview 1 with Vineetha 2012.

Interview 2 with Mukerji 2012.

Josef, Ellyn H. 2009–10. "Is Bigger Better? The Large Law Firm Model of Meeting the Pro Bono Obligation." *South Texas Law Review* 51 (3): 605–621.

Muniapan, Balakrishnan and Mohan Dass. 2008. "Corporate Social Responsibility: A Philosophical Approach from an Ancient Indian Perspective." *International Journal of Indian Culture and Business Management* 1, (4): 408–420.

Regan, Francis. 1999. "Legal Aid without the State: Assessing the Rise of Pro Bono Schemes." *University of British Columbia Law Review* 33 (3): 383–403.

Rhode, Deborah L. 2004–05. "Pro Bono in Principal and in Practice." *Hamline Journal of Public Law and Policy* 26, (3): 315–330.

RSG Consulting. 2013. "India Report." www.rsg-india.com/roving-rsg/2013-rsg-india-report.

Sossin, Lorne. 2008. "Public Interest, Professionalism and Pro Bono Publico." *Osgoode Hall Law Journal* 46 (2): 131–158.

Susman, Susan D. 1994. "Distant Voices in the Courts of India: Transformation of Standing in Public Interest Litigation." *Wisconsin International Law Journal* 13 (1): 57–100.

The Bhagvad Gita, trans. W. J. Johnson. New York: Oxford University Press, 1994.

9

How India's Corporate Law Firms Influence Legal, Policy, and Regulatory Frameworks

Bhargavi Zaveri

I. INTRODUCTION

As I wait outside the office of a senior bureaucrat of the Finance Ministry of the Indian government in Delhi, I notice two impeccably dressed gentlemen waiting for him. Requesting them to wait even longer, the bureaucrat allows me into his office, and I silently thank my university affiliation and good luck for the priority I receive. After ushering me in, the bureaucrat volunteers that the people waiting outside are senior-level associates with a prominent Delhi-based corporate law firm. They had sought a meeting with him to justify why the private security agency that one of their foreign clients proposes to start in India deserved exemption from the protracted approval process that would otherwise have to be followed under the Indian foreign investment laws. If they succeed in making a case for exemption, it may well be a precedent for other foreign investors proposing to invest in a similar business format in future.

This experience perhaps best describes the subject of this chapter by illustrating one of the many ways in which corporate law firms are influencing the country's policy frameworks. Worldwide, scholars and the general population traditionally perceive the lawyer as an inherently political actor (Dezalay and Garth 2010; Krishnan 2013). Successful legal professionals often have relationships with government officials and political connections (Krishnan 2013). Although the Indian legal profession has been widely acclaimed for leading sociopolitical movements during the country's Independence era, it has since been perceived as largely aloof from policy advocacy, having been accused of restricting its advocacy role to courtrooms (Galanter 1989; Krishnan 2003). The litigating bar is often applauded for limited policy outcomes achieved through public interest litigation (PIL) (Anant and Singh 2002; Krishnan 2003, 100; Perry-Kessaris 2008). The government also regularly consults senior lawyers, most notably the attorney general and the solicitor general, on proposed legislation.[1]

As documented in the Overview of this volume, until very recently the corporate bar constituted a small segment of the Indian legal profession. Moreover, it has been frequently criticized for its lethargy in policy activism (Krishnan 2010). The influence on law and policy of Washington law firms in the United States and Magic Circle firms in the United Kingdom and the eurozone has been extensively documented by the academia and media. Subject to a few exceptions, the Indian corporate bar has traditionally been much less developed as policy and political actors (Interviews 1, 2, and 4 with law firms, 2014; Chatlani 2013).

However, there has been a remarkable shift over the past half decade, during which Indian corporate law firms have begun taking a much deeper and sustained interest in the formation and reform of the country's and legal frameworks. By increasingly showcasing policy affairs in their suite of transactional and advisory services, they are following the footsteps of their American and British counterparts. As this chapter documents, notwithstanding both formal restrictions and informal norms that appear to limit lobbying by Indian lawyers, current policy frameworks in fact allow wide latitude for the corporate legal services sector to influence law and policy formulation and implementation in India. Unlike in the period prior to liberalization, in 1991, and even in the first decade thereafter, when governance and legislation involved minimal public participation, the last decade has witnessed increasing institutionalization of such participation in India's law and policymaking processes. Indeed, the inauguration of a new national government in 2014, which emphatically promotes public participation in governance, gives this subject even greater significance. With a swelling demand for professional representation before legislative and policymaking bodies, Indian law firms have strategically started to use these new access opportunities to influence policy frameworks, and even to obtain specific policy outcomes for their clients. Deviating from courtroom and boardroom advocacy, Indian law firms are increasingly starting to optimize interface platforms with executive and legislative bodies in India and have successfully negotiated policy-level decisions for their clients

This chapter seeks to understand the implications of this new public role for India's corporate law firms by analyzing the practices of these firms and comparing them to law firms in the United States and United Kingdom. What has triggered the corporate lawyers' interest in policy formulation? How do they influence policy regimes? How significant is their impact? How do law firms distinguish themselves from other policy advocates, and how do they view the future of this practice? Equally as important, how has the relatively new, albeit rapidly growing, Indian corporate legal services sector sought to influence the country's policy frameworks, and how are these law firms interfacing with the government and policymakers in the course of their practice? By benchmarking the advocacy practices and policy impact of India's emerging corporate legal elite against those of their more advanced counterparts in the United States and the United Kingdom, the chapter both documents the extent of these changes and provides a window into the future for the corporate sector in this area.

To investigate these questions, in 2014 I conducted in-depth and semistructured Interviews with fifteen corporate practitioners spread across six Indian law firms in Mumbai and New Delhi, as well as with officials of the finance and commerce ministries of the government of India, and with leading representatives from a policy center and an industry association.[2] Interviewees were asked about their experience interfacing with different regulatory authorities and policymaking bodies, and the areas in which that interfacing influenced policy and their views on the future of the practice area and the lobbying industry in general. Interviewees have been promised personal confidentiality and are therefore referred to only by their affiliation (e.g., as being from a law firm, the government, a policy center, or an industry association).

In addition to conducting interviews, the author also gathered information from law firm websites (where available) and from periodicals and other publicly available sources of data on Indian law firms and the Indian public policy arena. Finally, the author gained extensive personal experience in interfacing with policymakers and regulators while working in the corporate department of a law firm from 2006 to 2012. Collectively, this information provides unprecedented insight into the role that India's corporate law firms are currently playing in policymaking.

Before proceeding, it is important to make three caveats about the limitations of this chapter. First and foremost, given cultural taboos and sensitivities associated with lobbying in India and elsewhere, although the paper includes examples of law firms pursuing advocacy initiatives before executive, legislative, and administrative bodies, it does not suggest the use of corruption or monetary inducement. Only legitimate interfacings with the government that law firms have used to press for policy-related issues on merit are included. In a similar vein, this chapter takes no position about whether even the legitimate forms of advocacy described here should – or should not – be legally permissible. India's approach to lobbying is broad and complex, and beyond the scope of this chapter. Finally, as indicated later, several Interviewees make claims about the effectiveness of their policy advocacy. Although the author has endeavored to verify such claims through additional Interviews or other publicly available sources, this has frequently not been possible. In such cases, the claim of influence is reflected as having been "reported."

Part II gives an overview of the professional policy advocacy sector in India in comparison to more-established advocacy markets such as the United States and the United Kingdom, traces trends among Indian corporate law firms fostering a policy advocacy practice, and records law firms' self-perceptions with respect to this practice. Part III outlines the general law- and policymaking processes in India, and identifies stages that law firms have used, or might use in the future, to influence law and policy. Part IV uses the country's FDI policy and regulatory framework as a case study to demonstrate some creative and aggressive advocacy strategies law firms have used to achieve policy outcomes for their clients. Part V compares the policy footprint of Indian law firms to law firms in the United States and the United Kingdom, and suggests that trends similar to those witnessed in these jurisdictions are manifesting themselves among India's BigLaw. Part VI concludes, arguing that the Indian corporate legal services sector is beginning to exhibit significant traits of "strategic" lawyering, much like its American counterparts. With government-stakeholder interface at an all-time high, it predicts that heightened demand for representation before policymakers will propel this practice among professionals. As a result, the corporate legal services sector is poised to play a deeper role in formulating and implementing law and policy in India.

II. THE PROFESSIONAL ADVOCACY LANDSCAPE IN INDIA: EMERGENCE OF A DATA-ORIENTED ADVOCACY PRACTICE IN INDIA

The practice of lobbying has always had an uncomfortable status in liberal democracies. On the one hand, it is frequently associated with political scandals, corruption, and political funding (Ray 2008; Hindustan Times 2010; Hazarika 2011; Khilnani 2011; Thakurta 2012). On the other hand, it is also deeply connected with the rights of citizens to petition their government and participate in the lawmaking process (*Rumley v. United States* 345 US 41 (1953), *Eastern Railroad Presidents Conference v. Noerr Motor Freight* 365 US 127 (1961), and *Regan v. Taxation with Representation of Washington* 461 US 540 (1983)).

In the United States and the United Kingdom, this balance has been struck in favor of extensive and open policy advocacy by the private sector, albeit under equally extensive regulation (Allard 2008). In both of these countries, much – although certainly not all – of this policy advocacy work is done by law firms. Thus, in the United States, the proverbial "Washington lawyer" is the "go to" lobbyist for many corporations and interest groups (Goulden 1971; Fatka and Levien 1998; Allard 2008; Hoe 2011). But even many traditional corporate firms engage in significant lobbying activities. For instance, the website of Skadden, Arps, Slate, Meagher & Flom notes, "Attorneys at Skadden have long-standing relationships with representatives from the US government, including the executive branch agencies that comprise CFIUS – a critical element to a successful outcome." Similarly, the Jones Day website notes that the firm "successfully lobbied both the Australian and Chinese governments resulting in the Chinese security forces conducting raids against a large group of trade secret infringers." Similarly, lobbying features in the marketing material of most UK-based Magic Circle law firms under different names, albeit not as prominently as with the US lobbying law firms. For instance, the public policy practice area of Clifford Chance claims to have expertise in "shaping law and policy as it evolves" and comprises "legislative process and legislative drafting,"[3] "political intelligence and monitoring," and "public consultations and policy papers." A 2013 press release issued by the firm announcing the appointment of the new head of its public policy practice proclaimed that the new appointee would provide strategic advice to "clients in . . . influencing legislative and regulatory developments as well as other governmental activities in the United Kingdom and across the European Union."

By contrast, until recently India has struck a balance against extensive lobbying by private parties – at least on the surface. While Indian law does not explicitly regulate lobbying, Indians have traditionally equated lobbying with corruption, and the practice is often perceived as being unorganized and dominated by a "safari-suited man with an attaché meeting a client in a rundown government guesthouse" (Hindustan Times 2010; Sanyal and Kalra 2013). Nevertheless, while there is no official account of the number of lobbyists in the country, much less an account of those who actually wield any form of influence, the practice is ubiquitous in the form of advocacy, public relations, and corporate communications (Ventakesh 2013; Zaveri 2013a).

Two lobbying-related episodes and their nationwide media coverage have, however, brought the professionally managed lobbying industry in India to the forefront since 2012. With the enactment of protransparency legislation and an emphasis on transparent decision-making processes, there is emerging consensus that lobbyists are employing "case-law-style advocacy" to effect policy changes in India (Giridharadas 2006; Chandramouli and Malik 2007). The Right to Information Act, 2002 (RTI Act) requires covered public authorities to make extensive public disclosures. This includes an obligation to proactively publish the procedures they follow in decision-making processes and the arrangements they use for holding public consultation on proposed policies. The possibility of their decisions being publicly scrutinized has resulted in the bureaucracy insisting upon legal and technical factual data to support requests for administrative decisions.[4]

On the demand side, the recent public outcry over a professional agency lobbying for allocation of the national telecom portfolio to a candidate favored by one of its clients has made corporations wary of using noncredible "agents" or opaque methods of interacting with governmental agencies (Chandramouli and Malik 2007). This culture is particularly evident among foreign enterprises that have invested in the country's booming economy in the postliberalization period. Often bound by antibribery statutes with extraterritorial operations, such as the US Foreign Corrupt Practices Act and the UK Anti-Bribery Act, foreign enterprises largely rely on professionals to communicate with governmental agencies. As a result, traditional techniques of making financial contributions to political parties and using informal political connections, grass-root mobilization, and media coverage to influence policy in India are now supplemented with formal and informal stakeholder consultations with policymakers; formal representation before legislative, executive, and regulatory bodies; and the strategic use of Indian judicial activism. Results of a survey that examined the popularity of various lobbying techniques in India indicate that providing technical information to the government was the third most popular lobbying tool after financial contributions and public demonstrations (Anant and Singh 2002; Krishnan 2003; Ayyar 2009). These circumstances, coupled with unprecedented levels of stakeholder inclusion in law and policymaking processes, have led stakeholders to both develop in-house expertise and resort to financial and legal advisors to support their endeavors in influencing policy and administrative decisions (Ray 2008).

A. *Showcasing Policy Expertise*

The Indian legal services sector has slowly but consistently responded to this demand as evident from the manner in which Indian law firms are gradually positioning themselves as being experts in policy advocacy. Law firms are increasingly dedicating parts of their marketing material to policy affairs. For example, in 2014, according to its website, Policy, Law and Regulation Chambers (PLR Chambers), a newly found Delhi-based law firm, positions itself as focusing on "legal and public policy and legitimate lobbying services." Similarly, Amarchand Mangaldas has marketed their policy and government affairs practice group on Lex Mundi. The group is described as "the point of first contact for Indian and foreign industry chambers, parliament, think tanks, and government departments." The firm claims to have expertise in "complex negotiations with the executive and legislative branches of the government," in navigating "the inherent political and public affairs hurdles," and in influencing policy and legislation. Similarly, J. Sagar Associates (JSA) and Dua Associates have marketed their policy practice areas.

Law firms are also increasingly leveraging off positions held by their members on government-constituted committees and their ongoing relationships with government agencies. For instance, JSA's website notes the ongoing support, advice, and views that the firm provides to Indian securities regulators' various committees as well as the regular interaction their partners have with regulators on the evolution of regulations in the capital markets. The official website of Luthra & Luthra, a Delhi-based Band 1 law firm, states that the firm is often engaged by "various departments of the government of India . . . to advise on various WTO disputes and policy issues" and is "regularly involved in advising on policy issues, including India's position in international trade matters."

The trend of showcasing policy and government affairs expertise is not restricted to marketing efforts among law firms. Their expertise in the advocacy space has started gaining recognition outside the law firm circle. For instance, since 2011, the Indian *Business Law Journal* has hosted a Policy and Regulation Award category for law firms.[5] The journal has recognized law firms for their capacity to act as "an adviser to policymakers and those looking to influence policy," for their "knowledge of sentiment in the corridors of power," for "having the ear of the regulator," and similar such capabilities (Indian Business Law Journal 2014).

Building policy-facing practice areas is also reflected in law firm recruitment practices. For example, over the past five years, several firms have recruited former members of the administration and specific sector regulators (Ganz 2009; Chauhan 2010; Shrivastava 2012; Chatlani 2013). In particular, with the introduction of a new antitrust regulator, several Indian law firms are reported to have started their competition law practice by recruiting senior staff of the former competition regulatory authority.

Putting this together, two new trends are emerging among corporate law firms in India. First, the organized corporate bar is consciously and actively participating in the country's law- and policymaking processes. Second, policy advocacy is gaining traction as a distinct practice area among Indian law firms, some of whom are already offering such services either specifically or as part of their general transaction and advisory services. It is, however, important to qualify these propositions by adding that advocacy endeavors made by law firms presently constitute a small part of the overall professional policy advocacy sector in India, which is currently dominated by public relations agencies, in-house public relations departments of corporations, and chartered accountants.

B. *Self-Perceptions*

Any analysis of this area would be incomplete without recording how the sector perceives itself vis-à-vis this practice area. In the author's Interviews with law firms, they unanimously concurred that they extensively interface with governmental agencies and regulators to influence proposed or existing laws or policies, and have actively and strategically taken up policy-related hurdles that their clients face with regulators and policymaking bodies.[6] They were, however, equally unanimous in their apprehension of being perceived as lobbyists. As such, many Interviewees qualified their policy impact by emphasizing that policy-level changes resulting from their advocacy initiatives benefited an entire industry, as opposed to a particular client. One interviewee noted:

> We do not run to the policymaker every time the client wishes to tweak the policy or regulations. . . . such conduct only works to the detriment of the law firm, which loses creditworthiness before the regulator. The idea is . . . if there is a particular policy that is adversely affecting the industry in general, we will try and convince the policymaker to change his mind and make it see reason.
>
> (Interview 8 with a law firm, 2014)

In other cases, however, Interviewees emphasized that advocacy mandates were accepted by the law firm on a "best efforts" basis only, and before accepting the mandate, they inform the client that neither meetings with officials nor policy outcomes can be guaranteed (Interview 3 with a law firm, 2014).

Although there was no standard policy among law firms for billing clients for advocacy, most law firms reported that they charged clients on an "effective hours spent" basis, except in cases where the advocacy involved presenting or arguing informal or formal applications for exemptions or approvals before legislative, executive, or regulatory authorities, in which case the firm typically charged on a per-application basis (Interviews 1, 3, 4, 6, 8, and 9 with law firms, 2014). When advocacy efforts were taken in response to general solicitation from the government, they were not billed or billed nominally.

All law firms Interviewed claimed to have "go-to people" for particular matters, either because of specific skill sets or because of their rapport with different regulators and government officials. However, only one of the six law firms interviewed had a dedicated policy advocacy team and was looking to build more capacity in that practice area (Interview 3 with law firm, 2014). The other five firms considered policy advocacy as part and parcel of their overall transaction and advisory services (Interviews 1, 4, 5, 8, and 10 with law firms, 2014). While more than 50 percent of the law firms interviewed believed that the demand for policy advocacy by law firms would intensify in the immediate future, two of them insisted that they would not systematically build capacity in this area in the absence of a legal framework allowing lobbying in India (Interviews 2, 3, 4, 5, 8, and 9 with law firms, 2014).

Despite the different forms and varying extents of policy advocacy, all the law firms Interviewed indicated a general hesitation toward systematically building advocacy capacity. First, advocacy efforts undertaken at the behest of the government or industry associations do not form a major source of revenue for the firms, as most firms accept policy-related mandates on a pro bono or nominally charged basis. Moreover, such efforts are largely viewed as part of a relationship-building exercise with the government and industry associations. Secondly, while law firms do market their advocacy expertise to clients, they remain wary of being tagged as *lobbyists*, a term that remains taboo.

Notwithstanding law firms' self-perceptions with respect to this practice, the data nevertheless shows that the corporate legal services sector in India is playing a significant role in law and policy formulation and is poised to continue doing so. As a natural corollary, policy advocacy as a practice area will gain prominence as law firms adopt an "all services under one roof" approach. Continued state intervention in the Indian economy and increasing institutionalization of stakeholder participation in lawmaking processes will also propel a demand for technical and legal expertise in business-government interface. As demonstrated later, the Indian legal services market is already capitalizing on this demand and will likely become more aggressive in doing so.

III. LAWMAKING PROCESSES AND ACCESS POINTS

Before considering the techniques and platforms that law firms use to interface with policymakers and influence policy in India, it is helpful to provide an overview of the law- and policymaking processes. In doing so, one sees that the involvement and impact of Indian law firms is limited when primary legislation is considered on the floor of the Parliament. However, law firm policy advocacy is more impactful in influencing delegated legislation and the administration of policy. Moreover, because a more open and participatory approach is increasingly being adopted by policymaking and regulatory bodies in India, there is increased space for policy advocacy.

A. *Overview*

India follows a federal system of governance and has a bicameral legislature comprising the president, the Lok Sabha (literally the house of the people), and the Rajya Sabha (the upper house). Although the formal path of a bill introduced in Parliament allows opportunities for access for stakeholders and the general public, law firms rarely intervene or exercise substantive influence at this stage of the lawmaking process. When the bill is on the floor, members of Parliament are entitled to vote as per their individual choice. In reality, however, they vote on party lines as failure to do so would generally result in them losing their parliamentary membership.[7] At this stage, advocacy efforts are usually taken before the political party or, practically speaking, party leaders (Yadav 2008). This manner of advocacy generally requires strategies that parties could use to appease larger sections of their electorate, such as political donations, large-scale dissemination of information, and media campaigns, rather than technical information and support (ibid., 72). Moreover, consideration of legislation in the Indian Parliament is largely driven by political exigencies, meaning that bills are often passed without much policy-oriented debate or discussion (Jalan 2007). Since the advocacy efforts of Indian law firms are largely oriented toward expertise and technical support, law firms are not typically known to engage with political leaders when a bill is on the floor of the house.

Recently, the Indian government has started following the practice of prelegislative scrutiny of bills, or seeking feedback from the public on draft bills before they are sent to the cabinet for approval and introduced in Parliament. For example, the government recently released a draft Regulatory Reform Bill that seeks to overhaul infrastructure regulation for public feedback before introducing it in Parliament. The Women and Child Development Ministry did the same thing with a draft of a proposed Protection of Women from Sexual Harassment at the Workplace Bill. In these cases, law firms have played more of a role, particularly when the subject of the bill pertains to a law firm's key practice area. Indeed, one of the Interviewees noted that her law firm, deviating from usual practice, provided detailed feedback on the draft Regulatory Reform Bill when it was released for prelegislative scrutiny as the bill dealt with infrastructure sectors such as coal, oil, and telecommunications, all of which are crucial practice areas for the firm (Interview 3 with a law firm, 2014).

This route of access, however, suffers from some limitations. First, until recently, a ministry introducing a bill in the Parliament was not obligated to engage in prelegislative scrutiny – although, as of the time this study was completed, considerations were being made to require prelegislative scrutiny of all bills. Also, access does not ensure influence, and since there is no system of publicizing feedback received or reasons for rejecting some suggestions and accepting others, it is difficult for lawyers and their clients to gauge the efficacy of this access route.

Another opportunity of access in the formal path of a bill is accessing parliamentary committees and subcommittees considering the bill. Parliamentary committees in India regularly seek expert advice and engage in stakeholder discussions. Industry and trade associations often engage law firms to respond to such invitations on their behalf, particularly if the discussion is likely to involve technical aspects of the bill (Interview 12 with industry association, 2014; Interview 3 with law firm, 2015). Parliamentary committees also have the discretion to hold hearings with stakeholders. On some occasions, law firms "having a good reputation" have proactively intervened and obtained hearing opportunities in connection with bills under consideration. For instance, while considering the provisions of the Prevention of Sexual Offences Against Children Bill, one of the law firms Interviewed was specifically invited to orally represent their views on the provisions of the bill (Interview 3 with a law firm, 2014).

While this avenue of policy influence exists, given that voting in the house is largely political, even at this stage, the role of law firms is restricted to drafting written representations and, where invited, making oral representations to the committee members (Celestine 2009). Also, given that much of the primary legislation deals with broad-level policy, leaving operative guidelines to delegated legislation, law firms do not make a conscious effort to intervene at the stage of the primary legislation itself, unless the subject matter of the primary legislation directly affects a large portion of their typical clientele, such as the new Tax Code and Companies Act.

B. *Access to Bureaucracy*

Most policy and legislative initiatives are taken by the prime minister and individual ministers within the council of ministers.[8] The need for a new policy or modification to an existing policy is brought up in a variety of ways, including meetings between stakeholders and ministers or senior bureaucrats, memoranda addressed or presentations made by industry associations before the relevant ministry or its officials, and even public feedback conveyed in different ways such as media reports (Interview 11 with policy center, 2014; Interview 13 with government, 2014).[9] This broad spectrum of influence is in part a reflection of the way ministers are selected. Ministers have always enjoyed a very close relationship with the Indian bureaucracy (Perry-Kessaris 2008). Since the allocation of portfolios to ministers is largely based on political standing and popularity, ministers do not always have expertise on the portfolio assigned to them (Jalan 2007).

Members of the bureaucracy, however, all of whom have cleared the highly competitive Indian Administrative Services examinations, are equipped with experience and expertise on administering the ministry to which they are assigned. In those cases in which the minister lacks subject-area expertise, he or she normally relies on senior bureaucrats for advice on policy and administration (Kochanek 1974, 59–60).In this backdrop, the upper echelons of Indian bureaucracy have emerged as one of the principal points of access for influencing policy.

Law firms typically approach the secretary or other relatively senior bureaucratic, make policy recommendations, and urge them to take up the matter and endorse their case to the minister (Interview 4 with a law firm, 2014). For instance, a foreign trade association recently retained a law firm to engage the Commerce Ministry on the liberalization of the e-commerce retail sector. The law firm made extensive representations on behalf of its client before a senior official of the Commerce Ministry. Shortly thereafter, the ministry released a discussion paper seeking public feedback on liberalization of India's e-commerce sector (Interview 3 with a law firm, 2014).

1. Direct Access

In interviews conducted with law firms interfacing extensively with the government, respondents reported varied levels of rapport with government officials. Some noted, however, that they had developed strong enough relationships to telephone officials for policy-related clarifications (Interviews 4, 5, and 6 with law firms, 2014). Law firms have also been recruited by regulators to draft specific sections of delegated legislation. For instance, the task of drafting regulations on the standards for the manufacture, storage, and distribution of alcohol under the Food Safety and Standards Act was assigned to Amarchand Mangaldas (Food Safety and Standards Authority of India 2010).

Similarly, Interviewees reported regulations under the Competition Act, India's relatively new antitrust regulatory framework and the legal framework for insider trading, as having been drafted almost entirely by law firms (Interview 7 with a law firm, 2014). Interviewees also noted instances in which the government had requested law firms to help administer new legal frameworks, such as training officials in new laws, strengthening enforcement mechanisms, and building judicial institutions (Interviews 2 and 3 with law firms, 2014).

2. Indirect Access

In addition to interfacing directly with the administration, law firms interface with the government indirectly through industry associations like the Confederation of Indian Industries (CII) and the Federation of Indian Chambers of Commerce and Industry (FICCI), which heavily engage in advocacy on behalf of their members.[10] Most Band 1 and Band 2 law firms are members of these associations and are often called upon by them to advise on legislation and prepare written presentations. Industry associations often request well-known partners from member law firms to represent their cases before ministries and regulatory authorities as "having them represent our stand may make the regulator more comfortable" (Interview 12 with an industry association, 2014).

What is noteworthy is that this relationship is symbiotic. While associations have used the expertise of their law firm members to advocate before authorities, law firms have also used their association membership to advocate the interests of individual clients (Interviews 1, 2, and 8 with law firm, 2014). When a client comes across a policy-related issue, firms have reported taking the issue before an industry association, thereby giving it a generic appeal, before engaging with policymakers through the association. The idea, according to Interviewees, is that a regulator or policymaker is more likely to entertain the policy concerns of an industry association more than those of just an individual corporation.

To give an example, a client of one of the Interviewee law firms was having difficulties complying with a contract with a public sector undertaking (PSU), under which the client was a supplier-cum-service provider. Since the contract contained provisions for multilevel inspections and approvals before any performance-related installment was disbursed to the supplier, the supplier was finding it economically unviable to continue performing his part of the contract. When the client supplier brought up the matter before the law firm, instead of seeking to renegotiate the contract with the PSU, the firm took the issue before a trade association and convinced them that the industry's and the client's interests were aligned. The association, in turn, took up the issue before the government, advocating a revision of the templates of the contracts (Interview 2 with law firm, 2014)

3. Open-Door Policymaking Processes and Future Trends

As indicated earlier, even in the years following liberalization India allowed very limited formal public participation in policymaking. As a result, attempts to interface with the government were viewed suspiciously.[11] Stakeholders usually found the government to be "remote" and "unapproachable," and access to decision makers was often sought through personal connections rather than organized means (Kochanek 1974). However, post-1999, there has been a remarkable change in the frequency, quality, and efficiency of government-industry interface, with government officials making conscious and extensive efforts to improve and increase interface with businesses and stakeholders.[12] Indeed, a survey on government-stakeholder interface conducted in 2003 found bureaucrats in India to be progressive, helpful, and friendly to businesses and civil-society actors (Perry-Kessaris 2008). As demonstrated later, this decision to connect with businesses and stakeholders gave an opportunity to law firms – as well as other actors – to actively influence the formation and implementation of policies (Interview 10 with a law firm, 2014).

4. RTI and Technological Capacity Building

The RTI Act helped foster a culture of transparency and accountability among public authorities (Ministry of Personnel, Public Grievances and Pensions 2005). This, coupled with the increased technological sophistication within the government, facilitated the widespread dissemination of information and institutionalized digital connections between government and stakeholders. In sharp contrast to the pre-1999 era, the websites of corporate affairs and commerce ministries have sections dedicated to discussion papers, draft policies, and regulations seeking feedback from the public. For instance, in 2014 the Commerce Ministry adopted a creative approach toward interfacing with the public by initiating an interactive online chat facility with the public and bulletin board systems that offer clarifications on implemented policies on a regular basis. Most Interview participants found these feedback systems to be an important mechanism for interfacing with government officials. Stakeholders and legal advisors regularly post specific queries on the bulletin board to obtain answers within an average response time of thirty-six business hours, thereby encouraging even more communication between lawyers and government officials. Similarly, the interactive chat service function on the DIPP website allows public access to a DIPP official during office hours, once again encouraging stakeholders and their legal advisors to engage these regulatory officials in dialogue about important policy matters.

5. Voluntary and Compulsory Inclusion in Policymaking Processes

Several new Indian regulators have voluntarily institutionalized systems for stakeholder consultation in their policymaking processes. For instance, the telecom regulator releases all draft regulations for feedback and, with a response, displays the comments on its website. Similarly, the Securities and Exchange Board of India (SEBI), the regulator for the securities markets; the Reserve Bank of India (RBI), the banking regulator; and the Competition Commission of India (CCI), the antitrust regulator, generally seek public comments on most policies of a substantive nature

In addition to these voluntary endeavors, the last decade has also witnessed the enactment of legislation and directives obligating regulators to engage in stakeholder consultations before enacting policies and delegated legislation. For example, the Airports Economic Regulatory Act, 2008 mandates that the airports regulator "ensure transparency in exercising its powers and discharging its functions" by holding consultations with stakeholders and documenting and explaining all decisions taken. Similarly, the Electricity Act, 2003 requires that all delegated legislation under the act be subject to "previous publication." All of these voluntary and compulsory measures provide important opportunities for law firms to engage in dialogue with public officials about matters of concern to their private clients.

Nevertheless, stakeholder participation has not yet been uniformly and fully institutionalized across all policymaking and regulatory bodies. As several interviewees underscored, consultation processes are largely ad hoc and often done on a selective basis (Interview 4 with law firm 2014; Interview 11 with policy center, 2014). Furthermore, most regulators and ministries do not publish feedback from stakeholders or, where feedback that has been solicited is not ultimately incorporated into the final policy, their reasons for rejecting what had been proposed. As one law firm Interviewee noted, notwithstanding some advances, the entire feedback process remains "very opaque" (Interview 3 with a law firm, 2014).

In 2013 extensive steps were taken to provide for compulsory and in-built stakeholder participation in rule-making processes in the financial services sector. The Financial Stability and Development Council (FSDC), an executive body chaired by the finance minister and comprising representatives of the four main financial regulators in India, resolved to adopt best practices for governance and framing regulations in their respective fields.[13] A FSDC regulation dated October 2013 and accessible on the Finance Ministry website mandates the four financial regulators of the country to publish "all draft subordinate legislation for public feedback before finalization."[14] Moreover, in 2014 the cabinet secretariat adopted a resolution on prelegislative consultation. The resolution mandates that every ministry proactively publish proposed legislations and keep them in public domain for at least thirty days before tabling it in Parliament. It mandates the same rule for all delegated legislation as well. These resolutions break new ground as they are the first initiatives to institutionalize mandatory public participation in the formulation of laws and regulations in India.

6. Law Firm Influence on Delegated Legislation and Policy Administration

Indian corporate law firms have taken advantage of the interface opportunities noted earlier and engaged in heavy advocacy at the rule-making level. For example, when the country's new takeover regulations were drafted and finalized by the securities regulator in 2011, several law firms made extensive written comments in response to the regulator's invitation for feedback on issues, such as the minimum size of a mandatory open offer (Interview 9 with a law firm, 2014). Similarly, all law firms Interviewed reported giving feedback on the government's proposed policy for liberalizing the multibrand retail sector, including the conditions on foreign investors (Interviews 1, 2, 3, 4, 5, and 9 with law firms, 2014). Specific law firms have also been given personal hearings on their proposed policies, particularly due to the firms' expertise in the relevant subject matter (Interviews 4 and 9 with law firms, 2014).

IV. ADVOCACY IN CROSS BORDER TRANSACTIONS

One can examine India's cross border transactional policies as a case study to demonstrate both the methods of interaction as well as the policy impact of law firms in the policymaking process. Using cross border transactional policies as a case study is important in two ways. First, since the partial economic liberalization in 1991, law firms have started generating a large percentage – and in many cases, the majority – of their revenue from cross border transactions (Chapter 5 of this volume). The surge of foreign direct investment into the Indian economy, the pervasive nature of the foreign exchange regulatory regime, and the premium attributable to foreign clients have made cross border M&A and advisory work one of the most "coveted and crowded" practice areas in the Indian legal profession (Zaveri 2013). With firms constantly vying for such mandates, they often innovate their service offerings and have gradually expanded their role in cross border transactions, including through policy advocacy with government authorities. A survey on lawmaking processes conducted in 2004 in Karnataka revealed that foreign investors are becoming increasingly involved in law and policy reformation and that, in doing so, they heavily draw on their local partners – in particular – lawyers and accountants, to interface with the government in India (Perry-Kessaris 2004).

Second, because FDI policy formation is largely an executive-driven process, it provides fertile ground for advocacy by stakeholders, civil society actors, and professionals (Sachdev 2006).[15] Traditionally, the entry, restriction, and operations of foreign players in various sectors of the Indian economy have often been associated with lobbying activity. For instance, the Italian clothier Ermenegildo Zegna is reported to have lobbied the Indian government for liberalizing the luxury-brand retail segment of the economy. Similarly, Walmart is reputed to have lobbied for liberalizing the multibrand retail segment, and Amazon for liberalizing the e-commerce retail sector (Perry-Kessaris 2004).While these instances of lobbying have been largely associated with access to political leadership, professional firms have also been getting into the game.

A. *Advocacy Before Executive Bodies*

Interviewees from law firms unanimously reported having pursued or witnessed creative advocacy efforts before the Foreign Investment Promotion Board (FIPB), the agency responsible for approving foreign investment in restricted sectors. Interviewees noted that the FIPB was a hotbed for advocacy, whether in terms of representing clients on substantive policy changes, claiming exemption from prohibitive requirements, pleading for "regularizing" previous policy violations, seeking clarifications on extant gaps in policy, or merely requesting expeditious disposal of their clients' pending applications. This level of policy advocacy can be linked to the collaborative conduct of the FIPB and the wide discretion it has in administering the FDI policy framework.

The FIPB was originally constituted to "negotiate with large international firms" and to recommend FDI proposals for approval by the finance minister and what is now the cabinet committee on economic affairs (Ministry of Industry 1991). Given the consultative nature and purpose of the body, the FIPB has always been perceived as being more than an application clearance agency, and it frequently collaborates with investors and industry. For example, while most Interviewees noted that there was no fixed procedure for scheduling appointments with the FIPB, requests for informal meetings from law firms are generally accepted when the firm has a client's application pending before the body. Moreover, government officials often proactively reached out to law firms while considering complex applications. Similarly, even on general policy matters – policies without any specific application pending – the FIPB receives representations for policy changes. Indeed, one interviewee showed the author representations made by a tobacco manufacturer's association to the FIPB advocating for liberalization of the tobacco sector in India.

Over time, the FIPB's role has expanded to making substantive policy recommendations to the Department of Industrial Policy and Promotion (DIPP), the primary body responsible for FDI policy formulation and announcements. The FIPB makes policy recommendations to the DIPP on the basis of issues arising in applications and representations made by stakeholders and professionals (Interviews 13 and 14 with government, 2014). Many of these recommendations have subsequently become substantive policy.[16]

Law firms have extensively and strategically used the informal and collaborative attributes of the FIPB to press for policy change and to address policy gaps. For instance, one Interviewee explained how her law firm informally made presentations before the FIPB opposing a policy that required an Indian company having any foreign shareholding to obtain FIPB approval before making a downstream investment in any sector (Interview with a law firm, 2014). The firm approached the FIPB to explain that any client having significant operations would eventually acquire allied or competing businesses by making downstream investments, and the policy therefore risked overburdening companies with foreign shareholding by requiring FIPB approval before making any downstream investment – no matter the size. After several meetings, the FIPB made recommendations to the DIPP on this issue, after which the policy dispensed such approval for Indian companies as long as such companies had genuine business operations. This policy was replaced with substantive rules on calculation of "indirect" FDI in Indian entities.

While the FIPB is empowered to make recommendations for approval or rejection of cross border transactions involving infusion of FDI in India and imposing conditions on them, there is little to no statutory guidance regulating the exercise of this discretion.[17] Their flexibility to adopt a case-by-case approach is another avenue that law firms have strategically used to their clients' benefit. For instance, in the aftermath of the global recession, law firms representing foreign investors made representations before the FIPB seeking a waiver for their clients from compliance with minimum capitalization norms, FDI provisions that require investors to bring in a minimum amount of capital from time to time. The FIPB considered these representations and granted exemption where the representations made out an "extraordinary" case for waiver (Foreign Investment Promotion Board 2009). Thus, the discretionary power of the FIPB to impose conditions on cross border transactions has created unique advocacy opportunities for law firms to advance the interests of their clients.

B. *Participation in FDI Policy Formulation*

Worldwide, investment discourse has emphasized the participation of foreign investors and local stakeholders in the creation and implementation of law (World Bank 2005; Perry-Kessaris 2008). For instance, since the mid-1990s, World Bank surveys have found that the extent to which investors are notified and consulted when their host states undertake legal reform is positively correlated to the credibility of the investment climate of the country. In this regard, the DIPP frequently adopts a consultative process for the formulation of major policies by releasing discussion papers and seeking feedback on draft regulations from the public on its website. For instance, it holds an open annual consultation process before finalizing the annual consolidated FDI policy applicable to the country (Interviews 4 and 6 with law firm, 2014; Interview 14 with government, 2014). Stakeholders, particularly law firms, have wholeheartedly responded to solicitation for feedback on policies that potentially affect their clients.[18]

The DIPP also accepts feedback from stakeholders, both direct and indirect. For instance, the US-India Business Council's website reveals a constant dialogue between bureaucrats, political government actors, and members of the organization including actors representing US investments. While these associations often engage law firms for advisory mandates, their contributions range from mere collation and the recording of stakeholder feedback to substantive advice on the impact of potential policies (Interviews 2 and 3 with law firm, 2014).

Similarly, in 2011 the DIPP issued a notification declaring that shares with built-in options issued by Indian companies to their foreign shareholders would be considered foreign debt, not equity. This effectively meant that Indian companies could not issue shares with crucial "exit" rights to foreign investors unless they complied with the more onerous regulatory framework applicable to Indian companies soliciting foreign debt. The DIPP's pronouncement created a furor in the investor community. As a result, law firms with significant foreign clientele directly approached the DIPP on behalf of their clients seeking a policy reversal. The collective advocacy efforts resulted in the revocation of the pronouncement within thirty days of its introduction.

C. *Reluctance of Courts to Intervene*

Finally, stakeholders aggressively pursue advocacy before investment regulators with policy discretion, like the FIPB and the DIPP, because the FDI regime has practical immunity from judicial review. Courts in India have consistently held that economic policy and decision making are legislative and executive prerogatives and have allowed the freedom of "trial and error" to the government in these matters, unless these decisions violate constitutional limits or are abhorrent to reason (*Balco Employees Union v. Union of India* 2002; *Federation of Railway Officers Association v. UOI* 2003). Particularly in matters of FDI policy interpretation and implementation, courts have steadily dismissed petitions seeking adjudication, holding that "issues pertaining to foreign investment and attendant modalities are largely a matter of executive policy . . . when two views are reasonably possible of an executive order, . . . unless strong and compelling reasons exist, . . . [courts] should not supplant the views of the executive government" (*Putzmeister India Pvt. Ltd. and Ors. v. Union of India and Ors* 2006; *The Federation of Associations of Maharashtra v. Union of India* 2005).[19] This leaves the policymakers and administrators in the Indian FDI regime virtually the last resort for any stakeholder seeking to make any policy impact, thereby necessitating all advocacy initiatives to be pursued at either the political or the bureaucratic level of the policymaking machinery.

V. CONCLUSION

In his thesis on the Indian lawyer and his role in modern society, Galanter has classified the American legal profession in two segments: the strategic type and the service type (Galanter 1989). The strategic type of lawyer does not operate exclusively through litigation or limit himself or herself to tangible legal claims but serves the long-term interests of the client through a series of all-inclusive strategies including pursuing the client's interests before legislative, administrative, and political forums; planning the client's operations to take optimum advantage of the legal environment; and collaborating with the client in decision making and during interfacing with the administration on such forums.[20] On the other hand, the service type of lawyer focuses on fructified legal claims of clients, is driven by existing information, and pursues traditional forms of advocacy before courts. Galanter then concludes that most of Indian lawyering falls in the latter category.

More than twenty years after these observations were made, this article demonstrates how the (then almost nonexistent) corporate segment of the Indian legal profession is now exhibiting crucial attributes of "strategic" lawyering in the Indian context. Indian lawyers are now representing their clients' interests not only before courts and tribunals but also before legislative, executive, and administrative forums; negotiating policy exemptions, waivers, and benefits for them; and actively influencing policy as part of their transactional and advisory work. While the Indian political and economic environment and the rapidly emerging trend toward inclusive governance have made such representation and participation possible, the continued demand for such representation has made it more recurrent. From a policymaker's perspective, this essay offers insights into how the corporate legal services sector in India is slowly beginning to impact policy formulation, development, and implementation in the country.

What do these trends imply for the corporate legal services sector in the times to come? The evolving regulatory frameworks that seek to address the increasing complexities of the Indian economy are only going to propel the demand for expertise-oriented representation before the administration. As witnessed in the United States, the emphasis on transparency will underpin this demand for representation in legal ways, as distinguished from the traditional methods of informal access. As demonstrated, while some law firms have recognized these opportunities and are systematically capitalizing on the demand, a large segment of the corporate legal services sector is hesitant to build capacity until the country has a robust regulatory framework governing lobbying. Indeed, several law firms rely on services of other professionals, such as independent accountants, for interfacing with the administration, as they themselves lack the familiarity or expertise that these professionals could guarantee in dealing with the administration.

Based on these trends, there are two possible directions this practice may take. One direction is where law firms maintain status quo. Under this direction, law firm policy advocacy would occur on a case-by-case, law-firm-by-law-firm basis. This also implies the continued involvement of nonlawyer professionals, who may develop better expertise and familiarity with the administration. The other direction is one in which a segment of law firms build formal and focused policy advocacy capacity and use their experience to represent clients before the policymaking and administrative bodies. Even as most firms hesitate in engaging in aggressive advocacy, it appears that a small segment of the Indian corporate legal services sector is moving in the latter direction.

Notes

1 As recent examples, Gopal Subramaniam, a former solicitor general, was appointed on a government-constituted committee to revise rape laws in India, and Soli Sorabjee, a former attorney general, was appointed on a committee to revise the legal framework governing police institutions in India.

2 Of the six law firms interviewed, three are Band 1 law firms and three Band 2. The reference to "bands" has been made on the basis of their band ranking by popular agency rating law firms such as Chambers and Partners and Legal 500. The specific law firms interviewed have been identified because of their experience in interfacing with different executive, regulatory, and legislative bodies in the past. The ministries were selected because they regulate statutory and policy regimes that

most Indian corporate law firms specialize in. The policy center was interviewed as in the past it has closely worked with the finance and commerce ministries in areas where law firms have extensively interfaced with policymakers. An industry association's views are relevant as industry associations often serve as the platform for government-industry interface, as explained later in the chapter, and the Interviewee association was selected because it had a national presence, a stellar reputation, and easier access.

3 This part of the practice involves advisory "on the process of EU and UK legislation, including the choice of procedure, the timing of legislation, and the parliamentary stages, as well as on the institutions and how they operate. Understanding it is critical to influencing legislation."

4 During an interview conducted in 2003, a senior Indian bureaucrat remarked that "public interest litigation is always on our minds" and the added transparency mandated by the RTI Act means that "we have to be doubly careful, document everything correctly, and get all our facts right to ensure that the danger of a public interest litigation is minimized" (Perry-Kessaris 2008, 112).

5 While acknowledging that law firms are often nominally remunerated when called upon to draft legislation and frame policy for the government, the magazine indicates that Indian law firms nevertheless find it an attractive opportunity to develop long-term relationships with the government and administration.

6 One of the interviewees termed their involvement with the government as "deep and intense" (Interview 2 with law firm 2014). Another interviewee stated that it was common for associates in the law firm to build a sufficiently personal and positive rapport with officials within certain ministries that enabled them to telephone such officials or meet them without prior appointment (Interview 6 with a law firm 2015).

7 Article 102 of the Constitution provides for disqualification from the house of a member who votes or abstains from voting contrary to any direction issued by the political party to which he belongs, unless such member has obtained the prior permission of such party or such voting or abstention has been condoned by such party within fifteen days from the date of such voting or abstention.

8 Although the executive authority of the union is vested in the president, this authority is, in practice, exercised by the prime minister, who is the leader of the majority party in the Lok Sabha, and his council of ministers, who are members of Parliament appointed as ministers by the president on the recommendations of the prime minister (Kochanek 1974; Jalan 2007).

9 As one interviewee reported, a former finance minister he worked with habitually cut out objective policy-related opinion pieces from daily newspapers and sent them to the relevant bureaucrat within the ministry with instructions to prepare a note on the law or policy discussed in the opinion piece and offering solutions to problems highlighted in the piece.

10 Per the CII website, one of the benefits of being a member of the CII is that "... you will access a world of opportunities, from networking with ... to assisting in framing economic and industrial policies through close linkage with the government" (CII 2014). The FICCI and the CII have been known to have aggressively lobbied the government on a range of laws and issues including FDI in e-commerce and multi-brand retail trading, corporate governance regulations, etc. (Mishra and Thomas 2013).

11 For instance, the Industrial Development and Regulation Act of 1951, which was one of the most important and far-reaching pieces of Indian legislation affecting the private sector, provided for the establishment of a statutory committee comprising persons representing business interests and mandated consultation with the committee before framing rules under the IDRA.

12 As one Interviewee put it, "Earlier, approaching the Finance Ministry or the Commerce Ministry was possible only if you knew someone. Now, they are open to having a meeting with you if you have a genuine matter to discuss with them" (Interview 1 with a law firm 2014).

13 The FSDC was constituted by the government of India in 2010 for promoting stability and development of interregulatory coordination in the Indian financial sector. Chaired by the finance minister, it comprises representatives from the Reserve Bank of India, Securities and Exchange Board of India, Insurance Regulatory and Development Authority, and Pension Fund Regulatory and Development Authority.

14 The resolution also states that, "All regulations . . . and all other subordinate legislations (including circulars, notices, guidelines, letters, etc.) . . . must comply with the following requirements: . . . 3. All draft subordinate legislation should be published with a statement of objectives, the problem it seeks to solve, and a cost–benefit analysis (using best practices). 4. Comments should be invited from the public and all comments should be published on the website of the regulator. Regulations will become effective after the Board approves them. Board approval should take into account all comments received."

15 Although the statutory framework directly governing FDI in India is limited to the Foreign Exchange Management Act, 1999 (FEMA), foreign exchange transactions relating to India (including FDI) are directly and heavily regulated by delegated legislation. This delegated legislation is in the form of regulations made by the RBI, which decides the extent of foreign investment allowed in any given Indian sector, the conditions attached to such investment, and all other aspects regulating the investment.

16 During 2009–2010, several Indian companies made applications and representations to the FIPB requesting permission to issue shares to foreign investors for noncash consideration. The FIPB, recognizing that the existent policy was silent on this issue, granted permission to the applicants on a case-by-case basis. Simultaneously, it recommended the formulation of a definitive policy on issuance of shares to foreign investors for consideration other than cash. Soon thereafter, the DIPP issued a discussion paper on the matter and pronounced a policy allowing Indian companies to issue shares for certain kinds of noncash consideration. Similarly, the FIPB has in the past, on the basis of representations made before it, made policy recommendations on the FDI in limited liability companies incorporated in India, in private security agencies, and in the abolition of the policy requiring foreign investors to obtain FIPB approval before investing in a sector in which it already had a tie-up with an Indian investor.

17 The limited guidelines prescribed for consideration of FDI proposals by the FIPB are not legally binding but are prescriptive guidelines that "would not in any way restrict the flexibility or bind the FIPB from considering the proposals . . . on other criteria or special circumstances or features it considers relevant" (Department of Industrial Policy and Promotion 1997).

18 For instance, among the six law firms Interviewed, four of them confirmed having submitted written feedback on the discussion paper on FDI in multibrand retail trading and e-commerce released by the DIPP. At the last annual consultation held by the DIPP on the draft consolidated FDI policy, an estimated forty law firms participated (Interview 14 with government, 2014).

19 Similarly, where civil society actors (not being parties to an approval or transaction) have sought to challenge policy made by the government on FDI, the court has exercised restraint in reversing the policy and has reiterated the discretionary powers of the DIPP and the FIPB, as executive agencies responsible for the formulation and implementation of this policy framework, time and again.

20 Although this characterization was made in the context of delivery of legal aid services, the thesis applies it equally to corporate law practice in America.

References

Allard, Nicholas W. 2008. "Lobbying Is an Honorable Profession: The Right to Petition and the Competition to Be Right." *Stanford Law and Policy Review* 19 (1): 23–68.

Anant, T. C. A. and Jaivir Singh. 2002. "An Economic Analysis of Judicial Activism." *The Economic and Political Weekly* 37 (43): 4433–4439.

Ayyar, R. V. Vaidyanathan. 2009. *Public Policymaking in India*. Delhi: Pearson.

Celestine, Avinash. 2009. "Engaging with Policymakers." PRS Legislative Research. www.prsindia.org/administrator/uploads/general/1250578574~~Engaging%20with%20Policy%20Makers.pdf.

Chandramouli, Balaji and Arman Malik. 2007. "The New Face of Lobbying." *Business Today*, July 15. www.businesstoday.in/magazine/features/the-new-face-of-lobbying/story/22.html.

Chatlani, Vandana. 2013. "Indian Law Firm Awards 2012." *India Business Law Journal*. www.indilaw.com/pdfs/sample3.pdf.

Chauhan, Neha. 2010. "Khaitan & Co Hires IAS Man as Partner, Real Estate Head." *Legally India*, March 9. www.legallyindia.com/20100309565/Law-firms/khaitan-a-co-hires-ias-man-as-partner-real-estate-head.

Decision taken in the meeting of the Committee of Secretaries on the Pre-Legislative Consultation Policy. 2014. www.cabsec.nic.in/about_functions.php.

Department of Industrial Policy and Promotion. 1997. "Guidelines for the Consideration of Foreign Direct Investment (FDI) Proposals by the Foreign Investment Promotion Board (FIPB)." www.dipp.nic.in/English/acts_rules/policy/ip503.htm.

Dezalay, Yves and Bryant G. Garth. 2010. *Asian Legal Revivals: Lawyers in the Shadow of Empire*. Chicago: University of Chicago Press.

Fatka, Stacie L. and Jason Miles Levien. 1998. "Protecting the Right to Petition: Why a Lobbying Contingency Fee Prohibition Violates the Constitution." *Harvard Journal on Legislation* 35 (2): 559–588.

Food Safety and Standards Authority of India. 2010. www.fssai.gov.in/Portals/0/Pdf/CEOsReport.pdf.

Foreign Investment Promotion Board. 2009. *Review* 26. www.fipb.gov.in/Forms/FIPBREVIEW2009.pdf.

Galanter, Marc. 1968–1969. "The Study of the Indian Legal Profession." *Law and Society Review* 3 (2/3): 201–211.

1989. *Law and Society in Modern India*. Oxford, England: Oxford University Press.

Ganz, Kian. 2009. "Vaish Starts Competition with Senior CCI Hire." *Legally India*, August 31. www.legallyindia.com/200908311158/Job-moves/vaish-starts-competition-with-cci-senior-hire.

Giridharadas, Anand. 2006. "India's New Lobbyists Use American Methods." *The New York Times*, May 18. www.nytimes.com/2006/05/18/business/worldbusiness/18iht-lobby.1778893.html?pagewanted=all&_r=0.

Goulden, Joseph C. 1971. *The Superlawyers: The Small and Powerful World of the Great Washington Law Firms*. New York: Dell Publishing.

Hazarika, Sugato. 2011. *Influencing India: Lobbying in the World's Largest Democracy*. New Delhi: Bridging Borders Publications.

Hindustan Times. 2010. "Under Their Influence," *Hindustan Times*, May 8. www.hindustantimes.com/news-feed/views/under-their-influence/article1-541147.aspx.

Hoe, Catherine. 2011. "Lobbying Practices Leave Law Firms for More Independence, Equity for Non-Lawyers." *Washington Post*, December 25. www.washingtonpost.com/business/capitalbusiness/lobbying-practices-leave-law-firms-for-more-independence-equity-for-non-lawyers/2011/12/13/gIQAtmhUHP_story.html.

Interview 1 with law firm, 2014.

Interview 2 with law firm, 2014.

Interview 3 with law firm, 2014.

Interview 4 with law firm, 2014.

Interview 6 with law firm, 2015.

Interview 7 with law firm, 2014.

Interview 8 with law firm, 2014.

Interview 9 with law firm, 2014.

Interview 10 with law firm, 2014.

Interview 11 with policy center, 2014.

Interview 12 with industry association, 2014.

Interview 13 with government, 2014.

Interview 14 with government, 2014.

Jalan, Bimal. 2007. *India's Politics: A View from the Backbench*. New York: Penguin Books.

Khilnani, Sunil. 2011. "The Economy of Influence." *Live Mint*, November 17. www.livemint.com/Leisure/N5onoJSaoditWeGfIo2YWO/The-economy-of-influence.html

Kochanek, S. A. 1974. *Business and Politics in India*. Berkley, CA: Berkeley University of California Press.

Krishnan, Jayanth K. 2003. "Social Policy Advocacy and the Role of the Courts in India." *American Asian Review* 21 (2): 91–124.

2010. "Globetrotting Law Firms." *Georgetown Journal of Legal Ethics* 23 (1): 57–100

2013. "Peel-Off Lawyers: Legal Professionals in India's Corporate Law Firm Sector." *Socio-Legal Review* 9 (1): 1–10.

Ministry of Personnel, Public Grievances and Pensions, Government of India. "Compendium of Best Practices on RTI." www.rti.gov.in/compendium_online.pdf.

Ministry of Industry, Government of India, Department of Industrial Policy and Promotion Office. 1991. Memorandum, August 22. www.eaindustry.nic.in/handbk/chap008.pdf.

Mishra, Richa and Thomas K. Thomas. 2013. "CII Is Building a Partnership with Government, Not Lobbying." *Business Line*, April 16. www.thehindubusinessline.com/industry-and-economy/cii-is-building-a-partnership-with-govt-not-lobbying/article4623944.ece.

Nagar, Anirudha. 2014. "Laws by the People, for the People." *The Hindu*, February 24.

Perry-Kessaris, Amanda. 2004. "Use, Abuse and Avoidance: Foreign Investors and the Legal System in Bangalore." *Asia Pacific Law Review* 12(2): 161–189.

2008. *Global Business, Local Law: The Indian Legal System as a Communal Resource in Foreign Investment Relations*. London: Ashgate.

Ray, Shantanu Guha. 2008. "Forked Tongues and Artful Nudges." *Tehelka Magazine* 5 (4).

Sachdev, Rohit. 2006. "Comparing the Legal Foundations of Foreign Direct Investment in India and China: Law and the Rule of Law in the Indian Foreign Direct Investment Context." *Columbia Business Law Review* 2006 (1): 167–214

Sanyal, Kaushiki and Harsimran Kalra. 2013. "A Case for Democratising Lobbying in India." Oxford India Policy Blog, May 18. www.policyblog.oxfordindiasociety.org.uk/2013/05/28/a-case-for-democratising-lobbying-in-india.

Shrivastava, Prachi. 2012. "SEBI Exec Director Usha Narayanan Joins Amarchand Mumbai as Counsel." *Legally India*, September 25. www.legallyindia.com/201209253133/Law-firms/sebi-exec-director-usha-narayanan-joins-amarchand-mumbai-as-counsel.

Thakurta, Paranjoy Guha. 2012. "Advocacy of Interest or Corporate Bribery?" *Hindustan Times*, December 15. www.hindustantimes.com/delhi/advocacy-of-interest-or-corporate-bribery/story-CWoCbIzrxeKEsxLulOkibN.html.

Ventakesh, Mahua. 2013. "Lobbying May Be Legalized, with a New Tag: Advocacy." *Hindustan Times*, July 5. www.hindustantimes.com/business/lobbying-may-be-legalised-with-a-new-tag-advocacy/story-MPsjMCdeY8TD9sXFqqj6CO.html.

World Bank. 2005. *World Development Report 2005: A Better Investment Climate for Everyone*. www.web.worldbank.org/WBSITE/EXTERNAL/EXTDEC/EXTRESEARCH/EXTWDRS/0,contentMDK:23083004~pagePK:478093~piPK:477627~theSitePK:477624,00.html.

Yadav, Vineeta. 2008. "Business Lobbies and Policymaking in Developing Countries: The Contrasting Cases of India and China." *Journal of Public Affairs* 8 (1): 67–82.

Zaveri, Bhargavi. 2013a. "The Disclosure of Lobbying Activities Bill, 2013." *The Economic and Political Weekly* 48 (24), June 15. www.academia.edu/4421590/The_Disclosure_of_Lobbying_Activities_Bill_Economic_and_Political_Weekly.

2013b. "DIPP and FDI–The Long Road to Clarity, Bar and Bench (July)." Report of the Financial Sector Legislative Reforms Commission, Volume I: Analysis and Recommendations. www.finmin.nic.in/fslrc/fslrc_report_vol1.pdf.

2013c. "India's BigLaw: Metamorphosis from Deal Making to Policy Activism," September 23. blogs.law.harvard.edu/legalprofession/2013/09/23/indias-biglaw-metamorphosis-from-deal-making-to-policy-activism.

SECTION IV

REGULATION AND FOREIGN COMPETITION

10

Theories of Law Firm Globalization in the Shadow of Colonialism: A Cultural and Institutional Analysis of English and Indian Corporate Law Firms in the Twentieth and Twenty-First Centuries

John Flood

I. INTRODUCTION

The final restatement of this chapter should be short. If we ask, "What is the state of foreign law firms in India?," the answer is: there are none because they are banned from India for a variety of political, legal, and professional-cultural reasons. So what is there to say about foreign law firms in India? Perhaps more than may be realized from my opening. Despite a ban on practicing in India, foreign law firms have been strategic, if not canny, in their business with India. For not having a physical presence does not mean foreign law firms are not heavily involved with Indian legal business. My aim in this chapter is to explain empirically and theoretically why we have this nebulous situation.

For a country that is making inroads to the global economy as one of the BRICS (Brazil, Russia, India, China, South Africa), its protectionism is remarkable and the absence of English and US law firms is surprising (O'Neill 2001). Nevertheless, India is the home to radical legal production methods like the legal process outsourcing (LPO) movement (Chapter 13 of this volume; Kuruvilla and Noronha, 2016). Globalization is difficult to envisage without their participation and intercession. India is a big country with thriving business involving both outward and inward investment. Large law firms are necessary both to engineer and design the transactions and to sanctify them in order to translate them into terms acceptable to global capital (Cain 1983 Gilson 1984; Bernstein 1995; Flood 2007 Dent 2009; Howarth 2013). We know Indian general counsel (Chapter 4 of this volume) use the biggest global law firms for many of their deals, including acquisitions and sales Papa and Wilkins 2011; Wilkins and Papa 2013).[1]

II. COLONIAL LEGACY

We should not underestimate the legacy and impact of the colonial dimension in the relationship between the United Kingdom and India. From 1857 to 1947 (if not earlier, around 1757), India was under British colonial rule (see Overview of this volume). Britain created new administrative and professional classes – a western elite – that came to dominate bureaucratic life (Johnson 1972 Iyer 2004, 2). However, Britain failed to westernize India, and the British ruling elite remained apart and separate. Maddison portrays it in a forthright manner: "[the British] developed their own brand of self-righteous arrogance, considering themselves purveyors not of popular but of good government.[2] For them the word 'British' lost its geographic connotation and became an epithet signifying moral rectitude" (Maddison 1971, 6). Despite these rebarbative British attitudes, the new middle class of India – the compradors – the professionals and capitalists, were among the main beneficiaries of British rule (ibid., 23). The contradictions of the British helped promote ambivalent views among those who come into contact with them (Misra 2003). They helped construct the new class but remained detached from it, which was not a healthy portent for future relationships. Future subaltern historians have reinforced this view. Chatterjee has argued for the persistence of "colonial difference," while postcolonial states tried to make sense of their new independent conditions with elites unabashedly remote from their peoples (Chatterjee 1993, 10). However, more recent Whiggish interpretations have reinforced the positive aspects of colonialism and suggested the actions of elites in newly independent countries cannot be solely blamed on their colonial heritage (Guest 2005, 1; Wiener 2013). Whichever view we subscribe to colonialism remains ever present when analyzing future developments in India.

III. THEORETICAL CONSTRUCTS

To understand the resistance to foreign law firms, I adopt two theoretical constructs. First is legal culture, a concept quite elastic and awash with distinctions, yet it provides an interpretive framework (Nelken 2014). The second is the institutional nature of professional service firms (PSFs) and their ambitions to dominate global professional enterprise (Boussebaa et al. 2012; Flood 2012; Muzio and Faulconbridge 2013). To make sense of these approaches, we need to take account of the institutional structures of PSFs and also the strategies they deploy to gain a large global footprint. Although they are two separate and intellectually distinct literatures, I conjoin them to create a narrative that articulates the reasons for the anomaly, for even Nelken questions how distinct they may be (Nelken, 2014, 16–17).

The idea of legal culture provides the overarching framework – essentially a heuristic device – within which the institutional arrangements and strategies provide the sense of agency that drives the narrative. To begin, four relevant categories of culture provide the framework. These are:

1. English legal and large law firm culture and financialization
2. Indian legal and large law firm culture
3. Indian legal professional culture and the rejection of foreign law firms
4. Western PSF culture and globalization, and their impact on India

The reason for largely focusing on English legal and large law firm culture at the expense of United States and other countries' law firms is because the English firms have been conspicuous, and politically active, in seeking entry through the intercession of the UK government's lobbying activities which have been buttressed by a range of key professional lobbying groups (e.g., TheCityUK and UK India Business Council) (Flood 2007; Papa and Wilkins 2011).[3] The United States has never been as evangelical as the United Kingdom in promoting the global benefits of its legal system, courts, and legal professionals (Dezalay and Garth 2002).

Culture, and legal culture, is abstract, slippery, and troublesome (Nelken 2014, 2). Yet it has utility. It enables us to universalize some things, which can be perceived in the four categories mentioned. Both Friedman and Merry refine legal culture into different dimensions that include internal and external aspects, the practices and ideologies, and legal consciousness (Friedman 2006; Merry 2012). Thus we can look at lawyers as individuals and firms as a profession in society within the contexts of agency and structure. As we explore, more of these distinctions are blurred as in the case of large corporate law firms whose identity is becoming more amorphous as global professional service firms (GPSFs) come to resemble one another as they grow. Thus, the Cravath archetype may symbolize an ideal of the law firm, but it no longer embodies the true values of the modern global law firm (Swaine 1948; Galanter and Henderson 2008; Wald 2012, 2015). Furthermore, place this within the context of a liberalizing legal regime such as the Legal Services Act, 2007 in the United Kingdom, and the ideal is further marginalized in light of new structures (Flood 2015a).

It is useful to interpret legal culture along two axes, vertical and horizontal. The vertical refers to the particular cultures of discrete countries and jurisdictions, a type of hard culture formed by courts, institutions, and formal rules. To talk of English legal culture as distinct from various types of Asian legal

TABLE 1. *Interplay between hard and soft legal culture*

		Legal culture (soft)	
		S_s	S_w
Legal culture (hard)	C_s	C_sS_s	C_sS_w
	C_w	C_wS_s	C_wS_w

cultures, such as Indian or Chinese, reminds us of how Weber saw them as being formative of particular types of legal rationality and formality. They were dependent on their legal professions for advancing as they did as well as the level of codification of their legal systems (Weber 1978). Horizontal legal culture is more amorphous and is akin to the way Anne-Marie Slaughter distinguishes between different types of power: command or collaborative (Slaughter 2013). The horizontal axis therefore includes ideas of soft law, globalization, private ordering by law firms and lawyers, transnational law, and regulation and meta-regulation. These do not so much conflict with vertical propositions of law – e.g., legislation and court judgments – as supplement and augment them. Indeed, Gessner argues that the state is now incapable of producing sufficient law for globalization so that it has shifted into a series of (informal although legitimate) public-private partnerships that extend the range and reach of the state while absolving it from the responsibility of direct action (Gessner 2009). One significant example of these partnerships is international commercial arbitration where the state enables *lex mercatoria* to flourish independently, though maintaining some oversight, often through specialized courts, such as the UK Commercial Court (Cranston 2006; Flood and Whyte n.d.).

We represent these cultural dimensions by use of a two-by-two table, where C_{n-1} is the type of hard culture and S_{n-1} is the type of soft law culture. There are similarities here with Weber's conception of rationality in law (Weber 1978, 654–658).

C_s equals a strong level of legal culture, while C_W is a weak level. S_s and S_W are corresponding values in soft law culture. Thus C_sS_W represents a formal legal system that contains elements of soft law such as mediation or arbitration that do not rely on state intervention. Nevertheless, C_s characterizes a formalized system of culture embedded in rational law, while C_W represents less rational modes of lawmaking such as Weber's Kadi justice (ibid. 976). Thus, for example, C_WS_s epitomizes a state where lawmaking is considered unreliable but nonstate forms of law are thought to be dependable. The commercial legal cultures of Russia and China would fit this variant where immature state institutions are supplemented by trusted transnational forms such as international arbitration. Legal cultures including the United Kingdom and the United States would fit into C_sS_s, where institutions of all kinds are used and respected. India may fit C_sS_w, where formal institutions override the use of less formal ones, as can be seen in the attacks on foreign lawyers. C_wS_w represents low trust in any legal institutions, possibly with little recourse to external modes of lawmaking, as in "failed" states like Somalia or some of the Caucasian states.

Culture necessarily bonds to globalization through porous national boundaries. The hegemonic world cultures imposed their impression of a dominant culture on all others, in some form such as the Washington Consensus (or neoliberalism), which endured throughout the latter part of the twentieth century. Now the idea of the consensus is dead, but neoliberalism lives on (Williamson 2013). This simplistic model is now inadequate to explain how politics and economy operate in a postrecession and conflict-ridden world where the search for supplies of natural resources is driving new collaborations and alliances between countries. The world is physically the same, but the "Great Game" has rearranged its contours. North-south divisions remain important but not prevailing. With the rise of the BRICS, south-south trade, for example, is growing fast. Globalization can absorb these distinctions and differences effortlessly. Soft power, through international trade or cultural exports, flows to fill gaps, spaces where conventional normativity is weak (Snyder 1994).

Legal cultures are coerced into adapting and accepting these new forms. Soft power is further reinforced through this "third culture" approach by the rise of new types of international institutions that set standards, regularize transactions in particular fields, and create new communication networks (Nelken 2014, 26). It chimes with the varieties of capitalism literature that emphasize the role of informal norms, soft power, and culture (Hall and Soskice 2001, 13). A striking example here is the rise to global preeminence in the derivatives industry of the International Swaps and Derivatives Association (ISDA) (Morgan 2008; Biggins and Scott 2013). It produces the templates and contracts for transactions and provides a metaregulatory oversight for the industry. When viewed globally the picture is complicated. According to Schneiderman, the global regime for foreign investment is now composed of some 2,800 bilateral and regional investment treaties (Schneiderman 2014, 60). It remains an open question whether globalization is creating a new legal culture that tends toward legal homogenization and convergence or toward divergence and fragmentation. Argentina's recalcitrance over repayments to bond holders in the face of US court decisions voices these tensions (Wolf 2014). Moreover, while the global PSF typifies convergence in some forms, other forms of fragmentation and resistance show otherwise. India's resistance to foreign lawyers is one stark example in contrast to the United Kingdom's apparent willingness to accept many kinds of lawyers and legal innovation. One of the questions that will need addressing in relation to India is whether India's resistance is widespread throughout its legal profession and system or is subject to its own internal dynamic fragmentation.

IV. INDIA AND ITS LEGAL PROFESSION

For Queen Victoria, the Empress of India, India was referred to as the "Jewel in the Crown" (Scott 1996). During the colonial era many English lawyers went to India, where they practiced, joined the Indian Civil Service, or became district administrators (Maddison 1971; Johnson 1972; Corfield 1995). By the time of Independence, in 1947, the Indian legal profession was effectively modeled on the English Bar – robed lawyers in independent, solo practice. As Chapters 12 and 14 of this volume show, the vast majority of Indian lawyers still follow the same patterns. From the time of Independence to around 1991 India was inward looking with little foreign direct investment. After the economic liberalization of 1991 the Indian corporate law firm (see Chapter 3 of this volume) developed into the strong institutional firms they are today, but they are relatively few in number, although powerful in terms of economic and social capital.[4] These law firms are employed on both outward and inward investment business for their clients. In so doing they developed close relationships with western global law firms.

According to the World Bank, with a population of 1.25 billion, India has a GDP of $2 trillion, which is forecast to grow to $6.6 trillion (World Bank 2013). With an economy and population of this scale, it is understandable why foreign law firms would want to establish themselves there.

V. ENGLISH GLOBAL LAW FIRMS AND THEIR FINANCIALIZATION

In this section, I discuss how large law firms have evolved. I do not intend to cover their entire history: that has been covered elsewhere (Flood 1996, 2012). More interesting for our enterprise is the development of the financialized law firm as a distinct and discrete entity within the population of law firms.

The English Magic Circle group of law firms comprises four firms: Allen & Overy, Clifford Chance, Freshfields, and Linklaters (Slinn 1984, 1987; Keenleyside 1999). Usually a fifth is added, Slaughter and May, although is it smaller than the others and has a reduced global footprint (Dennett 1989a). These law firms dominate the UK legal market in numbers of lawyers and revenue generated. Their business includes banking, mergers and acquisitions, and international trade, among others. They have offices in the major cities in the world in addition to a set of "best friends" and networks. Their main competition is the large New York law firms. Two key distinctions that should be noted about these two groups are that in the United States there is no professional distinction between litigators (barristers) and office lawyers (solicitors) as there is in the United Kingdom.

Second, a comparison of the US and UK economies shows that the United States far outweighs the United Kingdom in value as measured by gross domestic product. The net result is that US law firms have a healthy and growing domestic market while UK law firms are compelled to look outside national boundaries for markets because of the relatively small scale of the UK economy. Of course there are US law firms that have global reach: Baker & McKenzie is a prime example along with firms like White & Case and Shearman & Sterling. Yet because of the UK firms' globalizing strategies, there are significant differences between US and UK law firms in relation to their governance and structure. It speaks profoundly to the partnership structure of law firms that it has been their defining symbolic virtue and value for many years. Now, with globalization and more pluralistic workforces, UK firms are moving away from the classic ideal of P^2 partnership toward more-managed bureaucratic ideals of governmentality, which in turn is having an effect on the perceptions of law practice in other countries when UK firms try to establish themselves (Hinings et al. 1999).

Below this group are the Silver Circle law firms, which include firms such as Ashurst, infamous for being one of the very first law firms to attempt to establish in India after the economic liberalization (Slinn 1997).[5] It was a globalizing firm in the nineteenth century when the senior partner, John Morris, traveled the world for his clients. It also provided the founding partners for Slaughter and May (Dennett 1989a, 1989b). Other firms in this group would, for example, include Herbert Smith and Eversheds (Phillips 2007).

The London law firms are among the most global and largest in the world. Clifford Chance has 3,300 lawyers in twenty-six countries with thirty-six offices. DLA Piper has 4,200 lawyers in thirty countries. The newly created Dentons–Dacheng will have 6,500 lawyers. By comparison the largest US law firm is Baker & McKenzie with over 4,200 lawyers in seventy-six offices in forty-seven countries. But its London office is the biggest in the firm with around four hundred lawyers. Most firms organize their work around a mixture of legal fields and industries; thus, for example, although Allen & Overy appears to do most areas of work, its key area is banking, as is, to a large extent, Clifford Chance.

Entry requirements are more or less standardized across the sector. Lawyers qualify after either a degree in law or a graduate diploma in law followed by a legal practice course and a training contract of two years. Upon joining, a lawyer becomes an associate in a particular department and he or she will spend his or her career there. While the Cravath model of the law firm still has traction for many, it was never fully incorporated into the English model. The route to partnership was vague and nebulous, often coming to the fore only two years before a partnership decision would be made. Many of the law firms used "lockstep" remuneration for both associates and partners, and many still do. The idea was that partners would share collectively in the growth of the business rather than competing with one another through merit-based pay. One of the values of the English law firm was its value of collectivization.[6] Lockstep reinforced such values, but it carried a significant cost. Partners were expected to retire early, usually somewhere in their fifties (Galanter and Roberts 2008).[7] When the law firms were smaller, the expectations of the partners were managed collegiately and ideas of fairness and equity obtained (Smigel 1969). But as stories like Regan's tale of Milbank Tweed tell us, institutions transform and create new narratives to justify themselves (Regan 2004).

The late 1990s and early 2000s were, for many law firms, times of profound transformation from the classic collegial partnerships toward a more managed bureaucratic form of professionalism. This came in part because law firms were engaged in merging or taking over other law firms and growing rapidly. DLA Piper's battle with Orrick over acquiring the lawyers from the collapsed wreck of Coudert Brothers is a telling example. Globalization was another pressure exerted on law firms that amounted to the regicide of the ancient regime. The overall effect of these pressures forced law firms into taking more dirigiste approaches to their organization and governance, whereby formerly autonomous partners would give up their power to managing partners, chief executive officers, leadership committees, and the like. Restructuring programs like Freshfields's "Size and Shape" and Linklaters's "Project New World" not only reduced lawyer numbers but consolidated the power of law firms' new leaderships and helped create the ideal one-firm model.

The development of the western large corporate law firm appears a natural development of the legal business as it incorporates itself into the global race for legal domination. McKinsey once proffered a "winner takes all" analysis to explain why some law firms were growing so large (Becker et al. 2001). To some lawyers and firms in other countries, the Anglo-American giant invasion is interpreted as a threat to their ideal of professionalism.[8]

VI. NEW INSTITUTIONALISM AND LAW FIRMS

To understand how professional organizations have evolved in the face of globalization and managerialism, I use Scott's three-pillar neoinstitutionalist framework (Scott 2014). The ideas behind institutionalism, which mesh neatly within cultural frameworks, proposed that formal organizational structure not only reflected technical demands and resource dependencies but was also shaped by institutional forces, including rational myths, knowledge legitimated through the educational system, and the professions, public opinion, and the law. The core idea that organizations are deeply embedded in social and political environments suggested that organizational practices and structures are often either reflections of or responses to rules, beliefs, and conventions built into the wider environment (Powell 2008).

DiMaggio and Powell focused on what they termed coercive, normative, and mimetic processes (DiMaggio and Powell 1983). Coercion came through the state, regulations, and politics, while normativity resulted from professional ideologies and values, and the educational processes used to reproduce professionals, and mimetic forces were the background practices often taken for granted. With the new institutionalism we can look inside the organization and see how it is structured while observing the social and economic changes occurring around it. Jerry Van Hoy revealed how Jacoby & Meyers transformed itself into a networked and highly distributed law firm once the advertising ban on lawyers had been removed by the US Supreme Court (Jerry Van Hoy 1997). Scott advances the analytical framework basing it on three pillars of the institutional order: regulative, normative, and cultural-cognitive (Scott 2014). To this is added the level of field analysis. In this case international law firms constitute a field, and fields are sites of contest over which the competing members debate the key issues (Bourdieu and Wacquant 1992; Hoffman 1999). For Powell there are four stages to field composition (Powell 2008):

1. An increase in the amount of interaction among organizations within a field
2. The emergence of well-defined patterns of hierarchy and coalition
3. An upsurge in the information load with which the members of a field must contend
4. The development of mutual awareness among participants that they are involved in a common enterprise

These are recognizable patterns among global and international law firms (Morgan and Quack 2006a, 2006b). And taking the field level also lets us see the patterns of competition and cooperation between law firms and other types of GPSFs like accounting and management consulting. And because GPSFs cross borders, they engage the political as well as the economic and social. Governments become involved in standards setting and the conditions under which they can establish – if at all – in respect of licensing regimes and the like.[9] In the case of India we see a contest between endogenous and exogenous values fought between governments, regulators, and law firms.

Scott's three pillars begin with hard rules of regulation and move to the soft values of culture. The regulative pillar embodies a sense of obligation as it deals with the legally sanctioned rules that create the framework for actors and organizations to function in. Law is a highly regulated activity because we idealize the rule of law above other activities. The judiciary is considered an independent arm of government, and its decisions cannot be easily brooked. Lawyers have obligations to the court as well as to clients. No matter how zealous the lawyer, the public interest is impossible to ignore, though corporate lawyers can often be in conflict. As one lawyer reported, "I make it happen for the client." His comment focused on the client alone. Yet, more and more, lawyers are forced to abrogate this relationship as money laundering and antibribery rules compel them to report and disclose (Terry 2015).

Muzio and Faulconbridge classify the regulative into two logics: production of producers and production by producers (Muzio and Faulconbridge 2013, 908). In comparing England and Wales with Italy, they find a much higher incidence of regulation in Italy than in England and Wales. So, for example, it is easier for UK firms to keep their names, whereas Italy requires the names of actual partners.[10] UK firms have more freedom to negotiate fees, whereas Italy has fee schedules, and Italy is more restrictive on advertising and marketing of law firms. Global law firms have to attempt to accommodate many such sets of regulations while retaining the ethos of the "single" law firm. Smets (2008, 383) showed, in comparing the London and Frankfurt offices of a global law firm, how German regulators seriously questioned "whether a *Rechtsanwalt* practicing in an international law firm conforms to the conventional image of a *Rechtsanwalt* as an agent of the administration of justice, as postulated by §1 BRAO." The very legitimacy of the English firm was rendered suspicious by regulatory oversight. It is around the regulative pillar that law firms find the most blatant hindrances to their efforts to achieve global status. Clearly regulatory regimes can either advance or hinder institutional change. The English Legal Services Act, 2007 is a striking instance of legislation enabling change (Loughrey 2014).

As organizations, large global law firms have enjoyed considerable success in establishing themselves in foreign territories where regulatory regimes can initially be hostile, as was the case in Germany. In Germany the framework was wider than the country itself – it included the European Union and its Single Market – which helped to ease the transplantation of the English law firm into Germany and by extension relax the rules on office location and dispersion for German law firms.[11] India has a tight regulatory structure that is reinforced by the bar associations using litigation strategies to defeat foreign office establishment. GPSFs are now used to countering these tactics.

Within the organization the normative pillar is key. Here we see standard operating procedures, handbooks, training manuals, compliance regimes, and the like, all designed to instill a common ethos in the firm's lawyers. For the legal profession the normative realm captures the essence of professionalism as a distinct mode of behavior that sets professions apart from other occupational groups in society. Professionalism has at its core the control of production by producers and the control of production of producers, and large law firms invest heavily in creating processes that speak of a "single" firm. Directors of education and quality travel from office to office to ensure that common quality standards in the delivery of legal products are maintained within the firm. General counsel issue internal rules that apply throughout the firm regardless of office location. In one interview a senior lawyer remarked that for most lawyers in the firm, it mattered little where they were educated or trained because the firm created its own knowledge base through the firm's in-house precedents/boilerplate documentation. Knowledge of the firm's documents took precedence over knowledge of law (or legal knowledge was assumed). Gulati and Scott's study of the *pari passu* clause in sovereign debt contracts shows how exactly firm knowledge is paramount over law, with sometimes potentially deleterious consequences (Gulati and Scott 2012). It is the normative pillar that represents the imperial ambitions of the large global law firm at its most stark. The single-firm aspiration attempts to impose a universal consciousness on the firm regardless of partners' origins. This is challenging work as many PSFs have discovered (Maister 1993; Lowendahl 2005; Hitt et al. 2006; Nordenflycht 2010).

The large global law firm presents problems in governmentality regardless of form (e.g., Swiss verein, alliance, or partnership). Law firms were traditionally lean organizations with partners taking on executive and managerial roles as needed. Professional administrators were typically absent.[12] With firms topping four thousand lawyers, the "gentleman amateur" approach is inadequate, and though partnerships are meant to express the values of community, modern firms are adopting classic managerial and bureaucratic responses to their crises in governmentality. Both Wald and Empson et al. have shown how the institutional basis for law firms has shifted in this direction (Wald 2012; Empson et al. 2013). Wald argues that large law firms can adopt a model of "smart growth" that appears to incorporate some of the older values with managerialism and thereby avoids explosive and disruptive growth. His example illustrates the tension in growth as financialization and commercialism assume greater importance than professionalism. Empson's view is different in that large law firms "are experiencing a change which breaks with the institutional field's prevailing institutional logic – a development referred to by law firm partners as the 'corporatization' of partnership" (ibid., 811).

The common feature shared by Wald and Empson is the erosion of partner autonomy within modern global firms concomitant with the rise in the power of executive control and nonlawyer managers to run "multimillion-pound enterprises" (ibid., 816). It is not quite displacement but more a layering of one archetype of control on another – a form of sedimentation (Cooper et al. 1996, 623). Nonlawyers have brought new skills into the law firm around coordinated business development, creation of firm-specific knowledge, establishing interactional relationships with clients through internships and secondments, and business development and marketing on a systematic basis. Their inputs have been felt as firms have reconfigured their partnerships, as in the examples of Freshfields and Linklaters mentioned here, especially in the Great Recession. Senior and managing partners, with specialist knowledge, have been able to relocate the firm's axis of power with the use of sophisticated measures and metrics that enable them to understand the firm's financial position better than most partners. And the boundaries between nonlawyer managers and the senior cadre of lawyers is blurred or made porous as power, authority, and control are seized by nonlawyer others. Thus far developments in professionalizing management are mostly restricted to the few big firms as others try to grasp what this entails for them (Empson 2013). What is clear from the literature on Indian corporate law firms is that none have yet taken this path: they are firmly located within kinship structures as the organizing principle and so prone to fission (Nanda et al. 2012; cf. Ouchi 1980, Hanlon 2004, Galanter and Roberts 2008). They are the functional opposite of the global GPSFs.

The final pillar, the cultural-cognitive element, is considered by some theorists to be the central pillar of institutional theory. It is analytically distinct from the normative pillar, but there are overlaps. Scott asserts, "Our use of the hyphenated label *cognitive-cultural* emphasizes that internal interpretive processes are shaped by external cultural frameworks" (Scott 2014, 67) So if we look at the construction of symbolic orders and processes and cultural systems, there are layers deriving from earlier periods. For example,

Slinn demonstrates the importance of networks for law firms (Slinn 1984, 116–117). Freshfields advised various Indian railway companies in the nineteenth century. The head of the East Indian Railway Company was R. W. Crawford, MP, brother-in-law to Henry Freshfields. Crawford also headed a merchant bank. Crawford, through his networks, was, in addition, chairman of the Imperial Mexican Railway Company and had interests in the Ottoman-Smyrna Railway Company, which redounded to the benefit of Freshfields. Furthermore, Freshfields's senior partners sent their sons to Trinity College, Cambridge, where they mingled with the children of the Rothschilds, Barclays, Hambros, Lloyds, and more (Hanlon 2004, 189). Thus, shared values and reputational capital were paramount in the formation of global markets as both clients could trust each other and could predict stable, lengthy relationships.

The state reinforced these relationships, which allowed the PSFs to flourish. When the state began to unbundle its economic commitments to utilities, transport, and the like through privatizations and reshaped the welfare state in a neoliberal mode, the GPSFs were conduits for much of this work and they expanded enormously.[13] While clan linkages were important, they were inadequate for the governmental procedures of the new economy. Managerialism and bureaucratization became defining symbols of this new era. Still, elements of the older regime have lingered on in, for example, the retention of lockstep remuneration, although it, too, is changing. Compared to Indian law firm arrangements, lockstep seems positively democratic compared to the paternalistic approaches of their law firm governance.

The English and, by extension, American large law firms have evolved, and still are, into a professional sui generis, their own field. They are distinct from smaller firms in their own jurisdictions as they are in others. Moreover, they are now part of the global spatiotemporal assemblages referred to earlier (Faulconbridge and Muzio 2011). GPSFs have both constitutive and regulative roles in that they are part of the global dialogue on regulation – how and where it should be applied – on their own behalf as well as their clients.

VII. INDIAN LARGE LAW FIRMS: AN EMERGING MATURE PROFESSION

I include this section not as a full explication of the Indian big law firm, which is explained in Chapter 3 of this volume, but in order to contrast it with the Anglo-American model discussed here. The Indian legal market was estimated to be worth $1.075 billion, "with the biggest 500 Indian companies each spending an average of $2.15 million on legal fees" (Harris 2013).

Krishnan points out that the vast majority of lawyers in India are solo courtroom practitioners, but there are growing numbers of lawyers working in corporate law firms doing transactional work (Krishnan 2010, 63). He says,

> The elite law firms that house these lawyers have a reputational hierarchy among themselves, but overall they are classified as such because of the volume of revenue they generate, the reputation of the partners in charge, the prestigious clientele whom they serve, and the bright legal staff that they employ.
>
> (ibid.)

Indian corporate law firms operate under archaic rules that restrict growth and competition (Nanda et al. 2012, 3). The firms share common features with Italian law firms of paternalistic governance with limited access to equity and unequal rewards (ibid.; Muzio and Faulconbridge 2013, 909). As described in Chapter 3 of this volume, Cyril Shroff, then a senior partner of Amarchand & Mangaldas (AMSS) described the firm in terms of a "two-wheels-of-a-bicycle" model – one wheel represented the Shroff family and the other wheel the professional lawyers at AMSS. Others remarked that "a law firm is like a family," harking back to the earlier iterations of the English corporate law firms. The culture of Indian corporate law firms is really only changing at the margins as new firms, often split-offs from established firms, emerge adopting more aggressive modes of western practice (Krishnan 2012).[14]

There are, therefore, considerable differences between the Anglo-American model of law firm practice and the Indian. They are separated by fifty years in time and the global space. They possess few of the features that distinguish the big global law firms from the rest. Kinship, inadequate management, monopolistic regulatory environments, opaque remuneration structures favoring the Big Man – all these features have effectively been removed from the GPSF. From a new institutionalist perspective, Indian corporate law firms have not advanced as far as the UK law firms along the normative and cultural-cognitive dimensions. Is it any wonder that the Indian legal profession reacts negatively and rejects foreign infiltration? Their anxieties are underpinned by the same fears that prevent the New York State Bar from permitting nonlawyer-owned UK practices to share fees with New York lawyers.

VI. THE INDIAN REJECTION OF FOREIGN LAW FIRMS

From the time the Reserve Bank of India granted limited practice licenses to Ashurst (UK), Chadbourne & Parke (US), and White & Case (US), the issue of foreign law firms' establishment in India has been the subject of constant litigation by various interest groups and of political haggling, both within Indian and between the United Kingdom and India (Krishnan 2010; Taylor 2011; Divan 2013). Ashurst closed its Indian liaison office in 2010 after the Bombay High Court ruling (Ganz 2010; RSG 2015, 219). Foreign lawyers cannot practice law in India nor can they set up offices in India. And until 2012 they were forbidden to "fly in and fly out" to advise Indian clients, but the Madras High Court has accepted this as a legitimate activity.[15] While the main, most vocal opposition has come from India's solo practitioners, the corporate lawyers through the Society of Indian Law Firms (SILF) have reacted against proposals to admit foreign lawyers (Krishnan 2010, 81–82). They see the situation as less one of a partnership between outsiders and locals and more of a takeover of their business. In connection with this, most of the alliances or "best friend" arrangements between foreign law firms and Indian corporate law firms have collapsed over the years. Indian lawyers could see they were part of a new comprador group being created by these alliances and so rejected their subordinate positions. The result of the extended political argument and litigation is that other centers have captured the "Indian practices" of the global law firms, notably Singapore and London.

In order to avoid problems with establishment, western law firms attempted a number of "best friend" relationships with Indian firms. Examples included Clifford Chance with AZB, Allen & Overy with Trilegal (2008–2012), and ALMT with Clyde & Co. (Ganz 2009), but all have foundered. Although they satisfied foreign law firms' desires, other foreign firms shied away from using these firms tied into best friendships. Indian law firms eventually extricated themselves from these relationships in order to extend their referral networks, especially as liberalization appeared as distant as ever. The 2015 RSG India Report emphasizes the desire of Indian managing partners to remain nonexclusive. But if liberalization were to occur, it is open as to what types of alliances might form (RSG Consulting 2015).

The most recent spate of attacks by Indian bar associations have been on the activities of the Big Four accounting firms, which have been accused of practicing law in alliance with Indian law firms. The SILF has complained to the Bar Council of Delhi against this:

> You can't do indirectly what you can't do directly. These are devices. Also the ownership of the [best friend] firms and all vests with accountancy firms. It is just a facade. Management and control and everything are done by these accountancy firms.
>
> (Shrivastava 2015)

The SILF has now said it might accept a "Singapore-style" foreign lawyer entry through joint ventures with Indian law firms, but it remains vague (*Legally India* 2015). The antipathy against foreign law firms remains strong, even to the extent of preventing foreign lawyers from engaging in arbitrations in India (IANS 2015). The Bar Council of India (BCI) remains strong and influential, which allows the SILF to ride on its policy coattails.

In the next section, I explore the strategies of the foreign law firms to do Indian legal work without being based in India. The two key strategies are to base Indian lawyers in locations close to India and to form informal networks that attempt to not trigger alarms with the BCI.

IX. WESTERN PROFESSIONAL SERVICE FIRM CULTURE, GLOBALIZATION, AND THEIR IMPACT ON INDIA

The fear of Indian lawyers against foreign law firms is due to their size and scale and their domination of the global legal marketplace. How is this developed? The theory of global production networks informs us that many variables come into play when producers foster global plans to disperse production. Two key variables are optimizing cost-capability ratios and customer pressures. Other risks include shifts in markets, new technologies, exchange rate fluctuations, quality management, branding dilution, regulatory risk, and labor and environmental risks (Yeung and Coe 2014). And in constructing global value chains, firms navigate risk that they attempt to mitigate by interfirm and intrafirm coordination. For PSFs and law firms in particular, these are considerable risks as they must ensure quality of service is obtained from each of their offices and suppliers.

It can go wrong, as Arthur Andersen's implosion after the Enron debacle showed (Coffee 2002). Behaviors, norms, and values had yet to be equally distributed throughout Andersen, which led to erratic behavior in parts of the firm. Law firms now spend enormous sums on in-house training, compliance, and quality control, all of which are part of the bureaucratic, financialized corporate law firm and barely comprehensible in the traditional partnership where partners exercised autonomy. Much of the regulation is imposed at state and professional levels, but the main thrust comes from within firms who live in fear of the Andersen aftermath. At the interfirm level more and more firms are moving away from using outsourced legal processes for their own onshore, insourced units, which are easier to manage and supervise. The rise of lawyer unemployment postcrisis and the growth in the numbers of paralegals, combined with relaxed tax burdens in host cities, make intrafirm developments feasible and profitable, and help to reduce the risk in value chains.

Global law firms work hard to present themselves as single firms, as Muzio and Faulconbridge illustrate in their analysis of failed English alliances with

Italian law firms (Muzio and Faulconbridge 2013). The story was repeated in India. Yet, at a deeper level, global law firms are really sets of interlocking networks with common branding and outputs. The difficult part for law firms is to manage expectations of clients that their global production networks will follow through on the implicit service promise. Law firms have increased their use of internal regulatory compliance through the use of general counsel or compliance officers and risk committees that analyze and then issue firm-wide edicts (Chambliss 2009). In the case of England and Wales, all firms are compelled to appoint COLPs and COFAs, who are mandated to report breaches of the agreed risk management plans to the Solicitors Regulation Authority (SRA) each year. The SRA publishes a series of analyses of present and future risk scenarios on a continuing basis, with topics such as "Spiders in the Web: The Risks of Online Crime to Legal Business" and "Catching a Chill: Law Firms and Risks of Group Contagion."

To fully understand GPSFs as global production networks is to constitute them as an autonomous field with its own rules, values, and coalitions (Scott 2014, 219). I have argued in an earlier article that global law firms, especially the English ones, constitute a special class equivalent to the "born globals" (Cavusgil and Knight 2009; Flood 2013). The key attributes of born globals are their speed of action, their quick response times, and their ability to learn. For English law firms an outward aspect to the world has been a necessity in part to satisfy their clients' international expectations and to find ways to expand their markets. In contrast to US law firms that, except for a few – Baker & McKenzie and Coudert Brothers – never faced the same pressures, the English firms had three distinct advantages in the flexibility of English law to adapt to mercantile needs, the use of English as a commercial lingua franca, and the high reputation of their lawyers and the court system (Flood 2007). These characteristics paradoxically were a help to English law firms in navigating a fragmented regulatory world for international and national legal services. And ultimately their culmination came to be embodied in the City of London, which, along with New York, has become the financial locus of the world.

The result of these transformations is the production of a new field of law firms distinct from other big law firms. Seabrooke articulates the theme nicely:

> Global professional service firms are . . . involved in transforming professionalism from a national occupational concern to a transnational organizational and managerial concern . . . The transnational realm is increasingly a place where professionals are being professionalized to organize across jurisdictions, and where professionals are mobilizing to generate demand for their

> skills and knowledge. Some of this transnational activity comes at the expense of national professional associations, who have traditionally been dominant in controlling their own jurisdictions and deciding who gets to do what work . . .
> (Seabrooke 2014, 2)

Indeed, he goes further in positing that professionals create their own markets by constructing their own transnational epistemic cultures or communities that are within general professions yet separated (Knorr Cetina 1999). Thus there are lawyers within firms who also establish communities and network outside of them, as in the creation of the swaps markets and their regulatory frameworks (Morgan 2008; Biggins and Scott 2013). These professionals mediate between different groups and networks and ease knowledge flows where there are gaps. Moreover, they move between and in and out of these groups and organizations. Their knowledge and transnational elite status enables them to float over national boundaries and provide transnational solutions.

For example, Singapore, with the relaxation of its establishment rules, now competes with Hong Kong to be the main Asian hub for legal work. Singapore's proximity to India, its common law rules, and its sophisticated dispute resolution system enable it to be considered the prime location for UK and US India offices. Moreover, these firms have succeeded in hiring many Indian lawyers to their Singapore offices, especially if dually qualified (Chapter 17, this volume; Taddia 2013; Dyas 2014). Some firms now have fifty or more lawyers working on their Indian desks. We also know from Silver's work that the US LLM has become a useful source for US law firms to find trained lawyers who can represent American legal values back in their own countries (Silver 2005).

Despite the success of Singapore as a base from which to do Indian legal work, foreign law firms have continued to persist in "entering" India itself. Garg outlines three models of affiliation (Garg 2012, 1184). The first is through ad hoc referrals where the Indian firm provides services for the foreign law firm as required, but there is no exclusivity in the relationship. Foreign law firms do not invest in these relationships: they are functional. The second model is the surrogate arrangement where a foreign law firm (e.g., Linklaters, helps a team of Indian lawyers set up a new firm). While they cannot invest cash, they can supply IT systems and share clients and practice groups. This model grants considerable control to the foreign law firm. The third model is the "best friends" model discussed earlier, which has diminished. But these are the nodal points where Indian and foreign law firms differ from each other. GPSFs, including law, want those who align with them to subscribe to their values and systems, especially the one-firm model. The inability to form long-term alliances militates against investment over the long term and so weakens the quality of the relationships formed.

The final part of this process has been the rise and growth of the LPO movement (see Chapter 13 of this volume). Although not as big as business process outsourcing, many companies, foreign and domestic, are setting up LPOs. Their success has been brought into stark relief by the threat of litigation from Indian lawyers for the unauthorized practice of law by LPOs. The suspicion is that LPOs are reverse engineering into the practice of law. Companies like Integreon and Pangea3 are perceived as extending their ranges of work "up the value chain" away from mere process-based work. Again, it is an open question whether the big PSFs – accounting and management consulting – will view this route as a means of capturing legal services.

X. CONCLUSION

Despite glimmers of liberalization, the prospect of full openness remains distant (Times of India 2015). Yet canny western law firms have devised multiple ways of circumventing these obstacles – modern technology and air travel enable lawyers to meet with their clients wherever they wish (Silver 2010). I have tried to show that by combining a cultural and institutional analysis, we can capture the dynamics of resistance and change. They offer lenses through which we can discern the processes, people, and institutions that are involved. This is not a story about foreign law firms in India, but rather this paper attempts to explain sociologically why the prospect of foreign law firms must unnerve Indian corporate lawyers, and ordinary ones, too, in ways they do not yet fully comprehend. In comparison to global UK and US law firms, Indian corporate law firms are relatively immature institutions focused on family, paternalism, and market protection. The new field of the global law firm presents a threat to Indian law firms: they are sophisticated, powerful, globally networked, and financially strong with strong internal value systems. There is the ever-present fear that alliances would become mergers and takeovers, which has intensified local resistance. Institutionally UK and Indian law firms once shared common features and values based around partnership and professionalism. Production of producers and production by producers were similar in both, but in the twenty-first century the global law firm has transformed into a new type of professional organization. Its values are no longer similar to those of the traditional Indian corporate law firm. To take the argument to its logical extent, we are in the midst of a new imperialism with the Anglo-American GPSFs constituting the new core while countries like India inhabit the new periphery. As Boussebaa perceptively points out, the new core–periphery hierarchy is not just economic exploitation but, more importantly, cultural domination (Boussebaa 2015).

The clash of institutional logics is explosive, and, in truth, the prospect of challenging the powerful orthodoxy of Indian legal culture is a high bar to overcome, but not impossible. It is clear that the progress of GPSFs is now at a stage where they cannot retrench. Transnational or global professionals and their firms constitute a field separate to those of other firms. Others might believe they occupy the same social and intellectual space, but they soon learn their challenges are defeated by superior power. They operate with distinctive logics more removed from the collegiate professional ethos and closer to market-oriented bureaucratic mentalities. For some Italian and Indian legal professions, this is anathema and is to be resisted and opposed. They have yet to mature to the level of the GPSF. Unless they subjugate themselves to the regime of the global firm, it is difficult if not impossible for them to globalize. At present neither the legal culture nor institutional frameworks are receptive to their imperial ambitions. Is Indian resistance futile? We shall learn. The movement for change will have to come from the Indian legal profession. Just to list the competing institutional logics illustrates the enormity of the task facing Indian lawyers and their professional associations:

- Large law firms versus small law firms
- Transnational practice versus domestic practice
- One-model global law firms versus fragmented family law firms
- Outward-looking legal profession (e.g., Law Society of England and Wales) versus inward-looking (e.g., Bar Council of India)
- Adaptive soft law cultures (United Kingdom) versus formalized hard law cultures (India)

Institutional analysis provides us with a way of viewing these transformations and identifying the elements that are bringing them about. From the production of firm-specific knowledge to the immutable forces of international business, organizations are adopting new strategies to optimize their position in the global arena. They take advantage of their size and scale to be significant players in the determinations of new regulatory spaces at national and global levels. Their growth has compelled them to adapt to managerial and bureaucratic modes of governance, removed from traditional partnership. And the pursuit of the one-firm model has created markets for compliance and firm-wide education and training to reinforce the value of the firm over the individual lawyer. Viewed in this light, Indian lawyers and law firms are located with the ancient regime and are resisting the push to modernity and transformation.

India's legal culture presently provides a protective cloak against incursion by the foreigners (Krishnan et al., forthcoming). Its professional culture reinforces the roles of defensive regulation and litigation, and gives voice to its largely atomized legal profession. India's rapid economic growth and resultant strength buys it breathing space in the global order. It refuses to be pushed into global change unless on its own terms, a reverberation of India's colonial past. Yet moving away from global trade talks means the fragmented but global world is amended piecemeal through the increased number of bilateral talks. For GPSFs this has relatively little negative effect. Their genius is to occupy the gaps and spaces left by this fragmented approach and to provide solutions that overcome difficulties created by gaps. The more India resists being an effective partner in the global dialogue, the harder it will be for it to cope with change on its own terms.

Notes

1 RSG Consulting reported that Allen & Overy "picked up seventeen client mentions for the best reputation in India, two fewer than both third-ranked Clifford Chance and Linklaters . . . RSG said that Indian companies mentioned forty-five different US law firms . . . compared to thirty-three UK law firms, although the UK firms dominated the top of the rankings" (Harris 2013).

2 Compare the Palestine-Israeli experience with the British, which appeared more benign (Frenkel and Shenhav 2003; Frenkel 2008).

3 For more, see, for example, "UK Legal Services Are Key to Boosting Growth," where the Secretary of State for Justice said, "British law has an unrivaled reputation in the world: a decision from a UK court carries a global guarantee of impartiality, integrity and enforceability. Our legal sector is also one of the most open in the world. And the benefits of removing barriers to foreign investment and business are clear, with UK legal exports almost quadrupling in little more than a decade and over 200 foreign law firms now operating in London." www.thecityuk.com/international-trade-policy-and-promotion/overseas-articles/uk-legal-services-are-key-to-boosting-growth/. See UK India Business Council, www.ukibc.com. UKBC events in London are reported to be 'lawyer heavy' (www.rsg-india.com/foreign-law-firms/news/using-ukibc-get-india).

4 The term *shroff*, for example, connotes a banker in India (www.merriam-webster.com/dictionary/shroff), so it is no surprise that the largest corporate law firm in India, Amarchand & Mangaldas & Suresh A Shroff & Co., is also a major banking and corporate firm, although now split between the two Shroff brothers (Ganz 2015). Both are now competing in each other's markets.

5 Ashurst has a "best friend" referral relationship with Indian Law Partners.

6 The law firm histories mentioned earlier show that the early manifestations of law firms in the nineteenth century showed them to be family affairs with the senior partners taking most of the earnings (Hanlon 2004). Collectivism is a twentieth-century phenomenon.

7 Freshfields found itself in litigation with former partners who felt they had been treated unfairly in the firm's pension reforms, which saw some partners aged 54 awarded smaller sums than others aged 55. The firm culled one hundred lawyers from the partnership in its "Size and Shape" restructuring.

8 About 40 percent of the Magic Circle's revenues now come from the United Kingdom (Binham 2014).

9 The field effectively includes transnational governance also as we include the negotiation of treaties between states and regions and states. Recent examples that involved law were the bilateral treaties between South Korea and the European Union and the United States. I suspect the TTIPS bilateral treaty between the United States and the European Union, the largest of its kind, will no doubt include some reference to legal services since the European Union is keen to promote cross-border practice and professionalism, such as the Transatlantic Trade and Investment Partnership.

10 Muzio has noted it is not uncommon for an Italian client to ask who Mr. Clifford and Mr. Chance are (Muzio 2014).

11 Sometimes regulation has strange effects. In order to accomplish similar arrangements regarding tax and governance as English law firms, German law firms had to turn to and adopt the English limited liability partnership structure until the German government introduced its own domestic equivalents.

12 In part this is due to regulations that bar nonlawyers from being partners or fee sharers in law firms, so financial and IT officers would always be inferior to the lawyers. The alternative business structure under the Legal Services Act, 2007 allows nonlawyers to become business owners.

13 During the "Future of the City: Assessing the Future of UK Financial Services and Professional Services" conference held in London in 2014, Angus Knowles-Cutler, senior partner of Deloittes, reported that 70 percent of the firm's revenues were generated in London.

14 Indian corporate lawyers are beginning to adopt lobbying tactics in their practices to influence policy for their clients (Chapter 9 of this volume).

15 Depending on how the judgment is read, it could mean that "fly-in and fly-out" activities are restricted to Tamil Nadu as opposed to being India-wide. There is a strong possibility the case will be appealed, so uncertainty continues (Desai et al. 2012). See also Flood on how the negotiations on the Trade in Services Agreement are being conducted and their attempt to annul the power of countries' institutions to object to the establishment of foreign professionals (Flood 2015b). The BRICS are excluded from the negotiations.

References

Becker, Wendy, Miriam Herman, Peter Samuelson, and Allen Webb. 2001. "Lawyers Get Down to Business." *McKinsey Quarterly* 4 (1): 45–55.

Bernstein, Lisa. 1995. "The Silicon Valley Lawyer as Transaction Cost Engineer." *Oregon Law Review* 74 (2): 239–255.

Biggins, John, and Colin Scott. 2013. "Private Governance, Public Implications and the Tightrope of Regulatory Reform: The ISDA Credit Derivatives Determinations Committees" (research paper no. 57/2013, Osgood Comparative Research in Law and Political Economy Forum, North York, Canada, www.ssrn.com/abstract=2360278).

Binham, Caroline. 2014. "'Magic Circle' Firms See Profits Reappear." *Financial Times*, July 8. www.app.ft.com/cms/s/1d8e0644-03a3-11e4-817f-00144feab7de.html.

Bourdieu, Pierre and Loïc Wacquant. 1992. *An Invitation to Reflexive Sociology*. Chicago: University of Chicago Press.

Boussebaa, Mehdi. 2015. "Professional Service Firms, Globalisation and the New Imperialism." *Accounting, Auditing and Accountability Journal* 28 (8):1217–1233.

Boussebaa, Mehdi, Glenn Morgan, and Andrew Sturdy. 2012. "Constructing Global Firms? National, Transnational and Neo-Colonial Effects in International Management Consultancies." *Organization Studies* 33 (4): 465–486.

Cain, Maureen. 1983. "The General Practice Lawyer and the Client: Towards a Radical Conception." In *The Sociology of the Professions: Lawyers, Doctors and Others*. Edited by R. Dingwall and P. Lewis. New York: Macmillan, 106–130.

Cavusgil, Tamer and Gary Knight. 2009. *Born Global Firms: A New International Enterprise*. New York: Business Expert Press.

Chambliss, Elizabeth. 2009. "New Sources of Managerial Authority in Large Law Firms." *Georgetown Journal of Legal Ethics* 22 (1): 63–95.

Chatterjee, Parta. 1993. *The Nation and Its Fragments*. Princeton: Princeton University Press.

Coffee, John. 2002. "Understanding Enron: 'It's about the Gatekeepers, Stupid." *Business Law* 57 (4): 1403–1420.

Cooper, David, C. R. Hinings, Royston Greenwood, and J. Brown. 1996. "Sedimentation and Transformation in Organizational Change: The Case of Canadian Law Firms." *Organization Studies* 17 (4): 623–647.

Corfield, Penelope. 1995. *Power and the Professions in Britain 1700–1850*. London: Routledge.

Cranston, Ross. 2006. "Theorizing Transnational Commercial Law." *Texas International Law Journal* 42 (3): 597–617.

Dennett, Laurie. 1989a. *Slaughter and May: A Century in the City*. London: Granta.

1989b. *Slaughter and May: A Short History*. London: Granta.

Dent, George. 2009. "Business Lawyers as Enterprise Architects." *Business Lawyer* 64 (2): 279–328.

Desai, Vyapak, Vivek Kathpalia, and Arun Scaria. 2012. "Practice of Foreign Law in India: Foreign Lawyers Can 'Fly-In and Fly-Out.'" *India Law Journal* 5. www.indialawjournal.com/volume5/issue_1/special_story.html.

Dezalay, Yves and Bryant Garth. 2002. *The Internationalization of Palace Wars: Lawyers, Economists, and the Contest to Transform Latin American States*. Chicago: University of Chicago Press.

DiMaggio, Paul and Walter Powell. 1983. "The Iron Cage Revisited: Institutional Isomorphism and Collective Rationality in Organizational Fields." *American Sociological Review* 48 (2): 147–160.

Divan, Anil. 2013. "Restrict Foreign Access to the Bar." *Hindu*. www.thehindu.com/todays-paper/tp-opinion/restrict-foreign-access-to-the-bar/article4531773.ece.

Dyas, Maulik. 2014. "Indian Lawyers in Demand: Foreign Law Firms Queueing Up to Hire India Experts." *Economic Times*. www.articles.economictimes.indiatimes.com/2014-08-06/news/52514675_1_rbs-india-indian-law-firms-allen-overy.

Empson, Laura. 2013. "Who's in Charge? Exploring Leadership Dynamics in Professional Service Firms." www.cass.city.ac.uk/_data/assets/pdf_file/0004/181228/Empson-Exploring-Leadership-Dynamics-in-Professional-Service-Firms.pdf.

Empson, Laura, Imogen Cleaver, and Jeremy Allen. 2013. "Managing Partners and Management Professionals: Institutional Work Dyads in Professional Partnerships." *Journal of Management Studies* 50: 808–844.

Faulconbridge, James and Daniel Muzio. 2011. "Professions in a Globalizing World: Towards a Transnational Sociology of the Professions." *International Sociology* 27 (2): 136–152.

Flood, John. 1996. "Megalawyering in the Global Order: The Cultural, Social and Economic Transformation of Global Legal Practice." *International Journal of the Legal Profession* 3 (1/2): 169–214.

2007. "Lawyers as Sanctifiers of Value Creation." *Indiana Journal of Global Legal Studies* 14 (1): 35–66.

2012. "The Re-organization and Re-professionalization of Large Law Firms in the 21st Century: From Patriarchy to Democracy." *Journal of the Legal Profession* 36 (2): 415–439.

2013. "Institutional Bridging: How Large Law Firms Engage in Globalization." *Boston College Law Review* 54 (3): 1087–1121.

2015a. "The New World Order for Lawyers and the Legal Profession(s)." *Jotwell*, April. www.legalpro.jotwell.com/the-new-world-order-for-lawyers-and-the-legal-professions/.

2015b. "Trade in Services Agreement (TiSA) and Legal Services." www.johnflood.com/blog/2015/06/trade-in-services-agreement-tisa-and-legal-services/.

Flood, John and Whyte, Avis. n.d. "The Construction of a Global Court: The Commercial Court" (unpublished paper).

Frenkel, Michal. 2008. "The Multinational Corporation as a Third Space: Rethinking International Management Discourse on Knowledge Transfer through Homi Bhabha." *Academy of Management Review* 33 (4): 924–942.

Frenkel, Michal and Yehouda Shenha. 2003. "From Americanization to Colonization: The Diffusion of Productivity Models Revisited." *Organization Studies* 24 (9): 1537–1562.

Friedman, Laurence. 2006. "The Place of Legal Culture in the Sociology of Law." In *Law and Sociology*. Edited by M. Freeman. Oxford: Oxford University Press.

Galanter, Marc and William Henderson. 2008. "The Elastic Tournament: A Second Transformation of the Big Law Firm." *Stanford Law Review* 60 (6): 1867–1929.

Galanter, Marc and Simon Roberts. 2008. "From Kinship to Magic Circle: The London Commercial Law Firm in the Twentieth Century." *International Journal of the Legal Profession* 15 (3): 143–178.

Ganz, Kian. 2009. "How to Win a Friend and Alienate People." *Legally India*. www.legallyindia.com/20090728111/Analysis/how-to-win-a-friend-and-alienate-people.

2010. "Interview: Richard Gubbins on Grey Hairs and India without Ashurst Office." *Legally India*. www.legallyindia.com/20100219518/Interviews/interview-richard-gubbins-on-india-without-ashurst-office-and-grey-hairs.

2015. "The Road Ahead for Shardul Shroff's New Law Firm." *LiveMint*, May 14. www.livemint.com/Companies/5Dm9pBUAoDdoPdlKOCiEuI/Expanding-abroad-and-11-other-things-Shardul-Shroff-plans-to.html.
Garg, Christine. 2012. "Affiliations: Foreign Law Firms' Path into India." *New York Law School Law Review* 56 (3): 1165–1191.
Gessner, Volkmar. 2009. "Towards a Theoretical Framework for Contractual Certainty in Global Trade." In *Contractual Certainty in International Trade: Empirical Studies and Theoretical Debates on Institutional Support for Global Economic Exchanges*. Edited by V. Gessner. Oxford: Hart Publishing.
Gilson, Ronald. 1984. "Value Creation by Business Lawyers: Legal Skills and Asset Pricing." *Yale Law Journal* 94 (2): 239–313.
Guest, Robert. 2005. "Africa's Development Challenge: From Predatory to Accountable Government." *Economic Development Bulletin* no. 1. Cato Institute. www.object.cato.org/sites/cato.org/files/pubs/pdf/edb1.pdf.
Gulati, Mitu and Robert Scott. 2012. *The Three and a Half Minute Transaction: Boilerplate and the Limits of Contract Design*. Chicago: University of Chicago Press.
Hall, Peter and David Soskice, eds. 2001. *Varieties of Capitalism: The Institutional Foundations of Comparative Advantage*. Oxford: Oxford University Press.
Hanlon, Gerard. 2004. "Institutional Forms and Organizational Structures: Homology, Trust and Reputational Capital in Professional Service Firms." *Organization* 11 (2): 187–210.
Harris, Joanne. 2013. "A&O Tops List of Foreign India Practices." *Lawyer* 22, April. www.thelawyer.com/news-and-analysis/regions/asia-pacific/ao-tops-list-of-foreign-india-practices/3004008.article.
Hinings, C. R., Royston Greenwood, and David Cooper. 1999. "The Dynamics of Change in Large Accounting Firms." In *Restructuring the Professional Organization: Accounting, Health Care and Law*. Edited by D. Brock, M. Powell, and C. R. Hinings. London: Routledge.
Hitt, Michael, Leonard Bierman, Klaus Uhlenbruck and Katsuhiko Shimizu. 2006. "The Importance of Resources in the Internationalization of Professional Service Firms: The Good, the Bad, and the Ugly." *Academy of Management Journal* 49 (6): 1137–1157.
Hoffman, Andrew. 1999. "Institutional Evolution and Change: Environmentalism and the US Chemical Industry." *Academy of Management Journal* 42 (4): 351–371.
Howarth, David. 2013. *Law as Engineering: Thinking about What Lawyers Do*. Cheltenham, England: Edward Elgar.
IANS. 2015. "Cabinet Clears Amendments to Fix Indian Arbitration (Yet No Sign of Foreign Lawyer Ordinance)." *Legally India*. www.legallyindia.com/Bar-Bench-Litigation/cabinet-clears-amendments-to-fix-indian-arbitration-yet-no-sign-of-foreign-lawyer-ordinance.
Iyer, Lakshmi. 2004. "The Long-Term Impact of Colonial Rule: Evidence from India." www.people.hbs.edu/liyer/iyer_colonial_oct2004.pdf.
Johnson, Terence. 1972. "Imperialism and the Professions: Notes on the Development of Professional Occupations in Britain's Colonies and the New States." *Sociological Review* 20 (S1): 281–309.
Keenleyside, Humphrey. 1999. *Allen & Overy: The Firm 1030–1998*. London: Allen & Overy.

Knorr Cetina, Karin. 1999. *Epistemic Cultures*. Cambridge, MA: Harvard University Press.
Krishnan, Jayanth. 2010. "Globetrotting Law Firms." *Georgetown Journal of Legal Ethics* 23 (1): 57–102.
2012. "Peel-Off Lawyers: Legal Professionals in India's Corporate Law Firm Sector." *Socio-Legal Review* 9 (1): 1–59.
Krishnan, Jayanth, Vitor Dias, and Martin Hevia. Forthcoming. "External Forces, Internal Dynamics: Foreign Legal Actors and Their Impact of Domestic Affairs." *Texas Law Review*.
Kuruvilla, Sarosh and Ernesto Noronha. 2016. "From Pyramids to Diamonds: Legal Process Offshoring, Law Firm Employment Systems, and Law Labor Markets in the US and India." *Industrial and Labor Relations Review* 69 (2): 354–377.
Legally India. 2015. "How SILF Feels about Liberalisation: Not Happy but More or Less Ready for Entry, Wants Singapore Model." www.legallyindia.com/Bar-Bench-Litigation/how-silf-feels-about-liberalisation-not-happy-but-more-or-less-ready-for-entry-wants-singapore-model.
Loughrey, Joan. 2014. "Accountability and Regulation of the Large Law Firm Lawyer." *Modern Law Review* 77 (5): 732–762.
Lowendahl, Bente. 2005. *Strategic Management of Professional Service Firms*. 3rd ed. Copenhagen: Copenhagen Business School Press.
Maddison, Angus. 1971. *Class Structure and Economic Growth: India and Pakistan since the Moghuls*. www.ggdc.net/MADDISON/articles/moghul_3.pdf.
Maister, David. 1993. *Managing the Professional Services Firm*. New York: Free Press.
Merry, Sally. 2012. "What Is Legal Culture? An Anthropological Perspective." In *Using Legal Culture*. Edited by D. Nelken. London: Wildy, Simmonds and Hill.
Ministry of Justice. 2013. "UK Legal Services on the International Stage: Underpinning Growth and Stability." www.gov.uk/government/uploads/system/uploads/attachment_data/file/219802/legal-services-action-plan-0313.pdf.
Misra, Maria. 2003. "Lessons of Empire: Britain and India." *SAIS Review* 23 (2): 133–153.
Morgan, Glenn. 2008. "Market Formation and Governance in International Financial Markets: The Case of OTC Derivatives." *Human Relations* 61 (5): 637–660.
Morgan, Glenn and Sigrid Quack. 2006a. "Global Networks or Global Firms? The Organizational Implications of the Internationalisation of Law Firms." In *Multinationals, Institutions and the Construction of Transnational Practices: Convergence and Diversity in the Global Economy*. Edited by A. Ferner, J. Quintanilla, and C. Sanchez-Runde. London: Palgrave Macmillan.
2006b. "The Internationalization of Professional Service Firms: Global Convergence, National Path-Dependency or Cross-Border Hybridisation?" In *Professional Service Firms*. Edited by R. Greenwood, R. Suddaby, and M. McDougald. Greenwich: JAI Press.
Muzio, Daniel 2014. "Global PSFs and the Challenge of Institutional Complexity." Lecture. www.sbs.ox.ac.uk/faculty-research/professional-service-firms/daniel-muzio-global-professional-service-firms-and-challenge-institutional-complexity.
Muzio, Daniel and James Faulconbridge. 2013. "The Global Professional Service Firm: 'One Firm' Models versus (Italian) Distant Institutionalized Practices." *Organization Studies* 0 (0): 897–925.

Nanda, Ashish, Edwina Smith, and Tanya Aggarwal. 2012. "A Perspective on Leading Indian Corporate Law Firms circa 2011." Harvard Law School.
Nelken, David. 2014. "Thinking about Legal Culture." *Asian Journal of Law and Society*: 1–20. www.ssrn.com/abstract=2466424.
Nordenflycht, Andrew von. 2010. "What Is a Professional Service Firm? Toward a Theory and Taxonomy of Knowledge-Intensive Firms." *Academy of Management Review* 35 (1): 155–174.
O'Neill, Jim. 2001. "Building Better Global Economic BRICs" (paper no. 66, Goldman Sachs Global Economics). www.goldmansachs.com/our-thinking/archive/archive-pdfs/build-better-brics.pdf.
Ouchi, William. 1980. "Markets, Bureaucracies and Clans." *Administrative Science Quarterly* 25 (1): 129–142.
Papa, Mihaela and David Wilkins. 2011. "Globalization, Lawyers and India: Toward a Theoretical Synthesis of Globalization Studies and the Sociology of the Legal Profession." *International Journal of the Legal Profession* 18 (3): 175–209.
Phillips, Tom. 2007. *A History of Herbert Smith*. London: International Financial Law Review.
Powell, Walter. 2008. "The New Institutionalism." In *International Encyclopedia of Organization Studies*. Edited by S. Clegg and J. Bailey. New York: Sage.
Regan, Milton. 2004. *Eat What You Kill: The Fall of a Wall Street Lawyer*. Ann Arbor: University of Michigan Press.
RSG Consulting. n.d. "LPO Accused of Providing Legal Advice. www.rsg-india.com/legal-process-outsourcing/news/lpo-accused-providing-legal-advice.
2015. *RSG India Report*. London.
Schneiderman, David. 2014. "The Global Regime of Investor Rights: Return to the Standards of Civilised Justice?" *Transnational Legal Theory* 5: 60–80.
Scott, Paul. 1996. *Jewel in the Crown*. London: Arrow Books.
Scott, Richard. 2014. *Institutions and Organizations: Ideas, Interests, and Identities*. 4th ed. New York: Sage.
Seabrooke, Leonard. 2014. "Epistemic Arbitrage: Transnational Professional Knowledge in Action." *Journal of Professions and Organization* 1 (1): 1–16.
Shrivastava, Prachi. 2015. "'Liberalisation = Obsolete Subject,' as SILF's Bhasin Vows to Go after Big 4's Best Friends." www.legallyindia.com/Law-firms/silf-to-go-after-pds-advaita-and-ors-in-follow-up-to-big-four-complaints-read-complaints.
Silver, Carole. 2005. "Winners and Losers in the Globalization of Legal Services: Situating the Market for Foreign Lawyers." *Virginia Journal of International Law* 45 (4): 897–934.
2010. "Globalization and the US Market in Legal Services – Shifting Identities." *Journal of Law and Policy in International Business* 31 (4): 1093–1150
Slaughter, Anne-Marie. 2013. "Filling Power Vacuums in the New Global Order." *Boston College Law Review* 54 (3): 919–936.
Slinn, Judy. 1984. *A History of Freshfields*. London: Freshfields.
1987. *Linklaters and Paines: The First One Hundred and Fifty Years*. London: Longman.
1997. *Ashurst Morris Crisp: A Radical Firm*. London: Granta.
Smigel, Erwin. 1969. *The Wall Street Lawyer: Professional Organization Man?* Bloomington: Indiana University Press.

Snyder, Francis. 1994. "Soft Law and Institutional Practice in the European Community." In *The Construction of Europe: Essays in Honour of Emile Noël*. Edited by S. Martin. New York: Kluwer.

Swaine, Robert. 1948. *The Cravath Firm and Its Predecessors 1819–1948*. New York: Ad Press.

Taddia, Marialuisa. 2013. "Singapore's Attraction as a Hub for Western Legal Expertise Creates Tensions." *Law Society Gazette*. www.lawgazette.co.uk/practice/singapores-attraction-as-a-hub-for-western-legal-expertise-creates-tensions/5037616.fullarticle.

Taylor, Phil. 2011. "... And Two Steps Back." International Bar Association. www.ibanet.org/Article/Detail.aspx?ArticleUid=b7c03389-4f52-4f77-9d5b-03d9ea789145.

Terry, Laurel. 2015. "Legal Profession Efforts to Combat Money Laundering and Terrorist Financing." *New York Law Review* 59 (3): 487–518.

Times of India. 2015. "Foreign Lawyers May Get Toehold, but Won't Be Allowed to Fight Cases." www.timesofindia.indiatimes.com/india/Foreign-lawyers-may-get-toehold-but-wont-be-allowed-to-fight-cases/articleshow/47873203.cms.

Van Hoy, Jerry. 1997. *Franchise Law Firms and the Transformation of Personal Legal Services*. New York: Quorum Books.

Wald, Eli. 2012. "Smart Growth: The Large Law Firm in the Twenty-First Century." *Fordham Law Review* 80 (6): 2867–2915.

2015. "Biglaw Identity Capital: Pink and Blue, Black and White." *Fordham Law Review* 83 (5): 2509–2555.

Weber, Max. 1978. "Economy and Law (Sociology of Law)." In *Economy and Society: An Outline of Interpretive Sociology*. Edited by G. Roth and C. Wittich. Berkeley: University of California Press.

Wiener, Martin. 2013. "The Idea of 'Colonial Legacy' and the Historiography of Empire." *Journal of the Historical Society* 13 (1): 1–32.

Wilkins, David and Mihaela Papa. 2013. "The Rise of the Corporate Legal Elite in the BRICS: Implications for Global Governance." *Boston College Law Review* 54 (3): 1149–1184.

Williamson, John. 2013. "What Should the World Bank Think about the Washington Consensus?" www-wds.worldbank.org/external/default/WDSContentServer/WDSP/IB/2013/04/15/000445729_20130415170451/Rendered/PDF/766500JRN0WBRO00B0x374385B00PUBLIC0.pdf.

Wolf, Martin. 2014. "Holdouts Give Vultures a Bad Name." *Financial Times*, September 2. www.ft.com/cms/s/0/bf3bd3f2-31ef-11e4-b929-00144feabdc0.html#axzz3CiGHKjJl.

World Bank. 2013. Data: India. www.data.worldbank.org/country/india.

Yeung, Henry Wai-chung and Neil Coe. 2014. "Toward a Dynamic Theory of Global Production Networks." *Economic Geography*. DOI: 10.1111/ecge.12063.

11

Globalization of the Legal Profession and Regulation of Law Practice in India: The "Foreign Entry" Debate

Aditya Singh

I. INTRODUCTION

Not long ago, the idea that Indian lawyers would be business advisors to big corporations and negotiators for mega deals might have seemed laughable. The Indian lawyer was simply a courtroom advocate, and most lawyers restricted their practices to a single court.[1] However, as India began liberalizing its economy in 1991, businesses began demanding more corporate and transactional legal services to help them take better advantage of the economic opportunities arising locally and globally.

Today, the Indian legal sector is one of the most dynamic in the world. The establishment and growth of law firms in major cities in India primarily focused on transactional and advisory work reflects the rise of the Indian legal market. According to RSG Consulting, a UK-based legal consultancy firm, the Indian legal market is worth about $800 million and expected to top $1 billion in three years (Arackal 2010; Nath 2010). Although the fast-growing corporate legal sector is still a small part of the Indian legal profession (of the estimated 1.2 million lawyers in India, only about 4,000 work in the top forty corporate law firms), corporate spending on legal services is projected to rise substantially over the next five years (RSG Consulting 2010).

All this titillates foreign law firms. Much like the multinational accountancy firms that entered the Indian market postliberalization, global law firms see tremendous opportunities in India. Many Indian lawyers, however, oppose liberalizing the legal services market in India. Some say that in India "the legal profession is not a business and it is not up for sale"; others argue that there is no "pressing need" to liberalize in light of India's "national interest" (Shroff 2007; Bhasin 2009).

This paper examines globalization of the legal profession and the entry of global law firms into India. Should foreign law firms be allowed to operate in India, and if so, under what circumstances? Will Indian businesses benefit? Will Indian lawyers lose their clients and be unable to compete with foreign counterparts? This paper provides a framework for understanding and evaluating this debate.

Part I analyzes the regulatory landscape for law practice in India. Part II confronts the debate as seen by the various stakeholders. I describe and assess the many arguments for and against the entry of foreign law firms into India. Part III discusses the *Lawyers Collective* case, the only Indian judicial decision directly addressing the issue of entry of foreign law firms. Here, I look at the legal arguments raised in court, comment on the myriad interpretations of the term *practice of law* as used in the Advocates Act, 1961, and briefly comment on the developments post–*Lawyers Collective*. Part IV compares the experiences of global law firms in other countries, particularly how liberalization of legal services markets is affecting emerging Asian economies. Part V discusses how global law firms can service clients on India-related transactions without directly entering the Indian legal market. I identify the advantages and disadvantages of the possible modes of entry for foreign law firms. I conclude by proposing how to construct an economically feasible, legally tenable, and politically favorable mode of entry for foreign law firms.

II. THE INDIAN LEGAL PROFESSION'S REGULATORY LANDSCAPE: PAST, PRESENT, AND FUTURE

The current regulation of the legal profession in India is governed by the Advocates Act, which replaced nearly two centuries of regulation by the British as discussed in Gupta, Khanna, and Wilkins (this volume). This part discusses the act and the Bar Council of India Rules, which form the key basis of regulation, as well as likely future initiatives.

A. *The Advocates Act*

Chapter IV of the Advocates Act regulates the right to practice law in India. Section 24 of that act makes clear that any person who is a citizen of India, is age twenty-one or older, and has obtained a law degree from a recognized university is entitled to be admitted as an advocate. However, a national of any other country may be admitted only if duly qualified citizens of India are permitted to practice law in that country.[2] As I discuss later, this principle of reciprocity becomes important in addressing the argument of Indian lawyers against the entry of global law firms into India.

A few other provisions are relevant for our later discussion of how courts have ruled on the scope of the right to practice law in India. Section 29 provides that only advocates are entitled to practice the profession of law. Section 30 confers on these advocates the right to practice before all courts, tribunals, and relevant authorities throughout the territory to which the Advocates Act extends. Section 33 states that only advocates are entitled to practice in any court. Section 45 prescribes penalties for any person who practices in any court or before any authority or person without proper authorization. Surprisingly, the act defines neither "practice the profession of law" nor "practice." What does it then mean to practice the law in India? Is practice restricted to litigation, that is, an appearance before any court, tribunal, or appropriate authority? Or does it also regulate corporate lawyers doing transactional work? These questions have been at the center of the legal debate on the entry of global law firms into India.

B. *The Bar Council of India Rules*

The Bar Council of India is empowered under the Advocates Act to make rules governing the profession and has promulgated the Bar Council of India Rules. Rule 6 in Chapter III, part VI, of the rules states that an advocate whose name has been removed from the rolls "shall not be entitled to practice the profession of law either before the court and authorities mentioned under section 30 of the Advocates Act, or in chambers, or *otherwise*" (emphasis supplied). Although the Advocates Act plainly states that it only seeks to regulate litigation, the use of the term *otherwise* in the Bar Council of India Rules raises the question of whether these rules apply to transactional work not involving practice before courts. The Bombay High Court addressed this contentious issue in the *Lawyers Collective* case, which I discuss in part III.

C. *Future?*

The Legal Practitioners (Regulations and Maintenance of Standards in Professions, Protecting the Interest of Clients and Promoting the Rule of Law) Bill seeks to revamp the regulatory design of the Indian legal profession. Presently in draft form, the bill proposes to set up a legal services board similar to the UK Legal Services Board.[3] Some Indian lawyers have criticized the government for trying to establish a "superregulator" and suspect that this could be a way to get foreign law firms into India.[4]

But how does this bill affect the entry of global law firms?[5] Section 35 of the bill provides that the legal services board "shall function as the regulator for regulatory objectives under this act for legal professionals *other than those covered by the* Advocates Act 1961 *as enumerated in Schedule I*." Schedule I, in articles 1 and 2, includes "qualified lawyers who are not practicing advocates, doing legal services in their Chambers" and "qualified lawyers engaged in drafting and conveyancing." Reading section 35 together with schedule I, "qualified lawyers who are not practicing advocates" and "qualified lawyers engaged in drafting and conveyancing" are a distinct group from the "legal professionals under the Advocates Act, 1961." If enacted, this bill could, by challenging the existing interpretation of the scope of the Advocates Act, change the course of the legal debate around the entry of global law firms into India.

III. THE FOREIGN ENTRY DEBATE: ASSESSING VIEWS OF THE STAKEHOLDERS

A. *The Government of India and Bar Council of India*

On the issue of allowing foreign lawyers to practice in India, the government of India has always found itself, as Jayanth Krishnan puts it, in the middle of a political minefield (Krishnan 2010a, 57). During the past decade, successive governments have followed the same strategy: they have paid lip service to the principle of liberalization but have never taken a formal decision that could anger a section of the legal profession (Krishnan 2010a, 60). However, in 1999, when the Bharatiya Janata Party–led National Democratic Alliance government was in power, Ram Jethmalani, a senior lawyer, was appointed law minister. Jethmalani favored opening up India's legal services market and underscored that the opposition was deliberately misunderstanding the debate over entry of foreign law firms into India (Krishnan 2010a, 70). Facing severe criticism from liberalization opponents, his proposal was shelved. Since then, all law ministers have tiptoed around the issue long enough to have their successors tackle the problem (Brayne n.d.). Apart from the Law Ministry, the Department of Commerce of the government of India has supported opening up the market, arguing that opening up the legal sector will bring in more professionalism and dynamism to the sector and give clients more choice (Singh 2011).

Successive governments seem to have overestimated the political volatility of this issue. The average voter is not directly affected by legal market liberalization, and partisan political parties are less likely to scuttle reform proposals meant largely for corporate and transactional law practice. Lawyers, while powerful, are a relatively small group of the electorate. Therefore, this will not be as politically costly a decision as successive governments think it to be. Indecision, however, is damaging India's legal sector, and political considerations must not paralyze policy on this crucial issue.

B. *The Clients: Businesses and General Counsels*

Indian businesses have grown tremendously over the past two decades, leading to a rise in demand for legal services. Generally, India-based multinationals and large domestic companies welcome foreign law firms' entry because competition among law firms will increase, resulting in better quality and competitive prices (Ganz 2010). Clients will have a broader set of firms from which to choose, and Indian clients with foreign business interests will be able to obtain foreign law advice in India. Presently, Indian clients who deal with foreign governments and partners generally have to work with foreign law firms based in New York, London, Singapore, or Hong Kong. Admission of foreign lawyers and law firms will change this, making it convenient for clients to engage and instruct their lawyers in the same city and time zone (Krishnan 2010a, 78).

Those against liberalization, however, worry that foreign firms may come into India, use their financial muscle and large size to lower the price of legal services, thereby eliminating competition, and set their own price (Frumin 2007, 17–18; Krishnan 2010a, 78).

There has been a bitter debate on whether the entry of foreign law firms will improve the quality of legal services. In my view, the market will answer this question for itself. If foreign firms cannot cater to the specific Indian law requirements, then clients will shy away, forcing them to shut shop. Similarly, Indian law firms will be challenged to match foreign law firms in terms of international best practices and strong knowledge management systems. As Jonathan Brayne, the India group head at Allen & Overy, said, "If the market sees no role for foreign law firms, the harsh realities of international lawyering will soon see them close their offices and leave" (Brayne n.d.).

C. *Society of Indian Law Firms and Traditional Family-Owned Law Firms*

Senior or majority equity-holding partners of Indian law firms generally oppose legal market liberalization (Firm 2009).[6] The Society of Indian Law Firms (SILF), an interest group of elite law firms, is the most vociferous opponent of the entry of foreign law firms. As is clear from Bhasin's "Indian legal profession not for sale" pitch, one of their major arguments is that foreign firms would corporatize law and make law practice in India a business rather than a profession. It is hard to agree with this argument because Indian firms are already increasingly operating like businesses, corporatizing law in their own way (Ganz 2010). Bhasin's argument that the deep pockets of foreign firms will pollute the sacrosanct India legal profession is unconvincing for two reasons. First, foreign law firms are advising both Indian and foreign clients on Indian law and engaging with domestic law firms in distinct forms and, in many ways, are already here. More importantly, India is in the process of preparing new rules for ethics and professional responsibility based on "international principles" (Ganz 2011b). As foreign law firms are admitted, domestic lawyers will get exposure to some international best practices for adhering to ethics rules. For instance, global law firms with hundreds of clients have created "Chinese walls" to prevent conflicts and protect client interests.[7]

But some arguments are more nuanced than others (Shroff 2007). They make a valid point that Indian law firms operate under severe restrictions compared with their foreign counterparts. For instance, Indian law firms have not been allowed to freely advertise and maintain websites.[8] For years, Indian partnership law did not allow more than twenty partners in a law firm. Given these circumstances, admission of foreign law firms should be permitted only after a level playing field is created in the Indian legal sector (Luthra 2007, 17–18). On the other hand, entry of foreign lawyers and increased competition may encourage the government and the Bar Council to level the field. The government has enacted the Limited Liability Partnership Act, 2008, which provides the advantages and flexibility of limited liability. There has also been some activity on the advertising issue – many firms are now maintaining their websites with disclaimers that these are for "informational purposes only" and "not be interpreted as soliciting or advertisement." Moreover, the Bar Council of India has, in a pending litigation, informed the Supreme Court that it is amending the rule that prohibits advertising (Express News Service 2008). As these changes set in, the SILF and its colleagues will find it increasingly difficult to justify their arguments against admission of foreign firms.

Of course, liberalization will make traditional, family-based law firms less profitable and perhaps significantly less profitable for the most senior partners or "family members" at these firms. But except for this miniscule proportion, it is not a bad thing for the Indian legal profession because a more professionalized system will ensure that profits trickle down to associates and that distribution is more equitable.

D. *New-Generation Indian Lawyers and Law Firms*

Young Indian lawyers – the ones who have set up their own firms or are working in big firms at junior levels – usually support the entry of foreign players in the legal sector.[9] Many of them feel trapped because of the existing family-based and proprietorship models, where opportunities for growth are limited. Of course, if and when foreign firms come into India, they will attract some of the best transactional lawyers working in Indian firms since many of the younger lawyers hope to get hired by foreign firms at better terms of service (Ganz 2010).

Opening up the legal market will create an influx of foreign law firms. However, as these firms will be dealing with Indian law and procedure, they will hire mostly local lawyers trained in India. It is financially unviable for foreign law firms to send expatriate lawyers from their home countries to foreign countries. As law firms expand globally, "the people best equipped to maximize the opportunities presented in any market are invariably those who are nationals of that market, qualified in it and culturally in tune with it" (Brayne n.d.). Liberalization will have a positive effect on small start-up law firms. Foreign law firms will see them as "acquisition targets," and in fact many small firms are setting themselves up as such. Most Indian lawyers who support liberalization do so in hushed voices. They are often apprehensive about coming out openly in support of foreign law firms because of the clout of large patriarchal law firms and the SILF.

E. *Litigating Lawyers and Local Bar Associations*

As mentioned earlier, lawyers across the country protested when the law minister, in 1999, spoke in favor of the liberalization of legal services. As Jayanth Krishnan documents, after Ram Jethmalani unveiled his proposal to (1) amend the Civil Procedure Code ("CPC") to curtail appeals and adjournments and (2) allow foreign law firms, large protest rallies were organized, including the one on February 24, 2000, when approximately forty thousand lawyers gathered in New Delhi and nationwide an estimated five hundred thousand lawyers struck, shutting down the courts throughout the country (Krishnan 2010a, 72). However, much of the protest was a result of the proposed amendments to the CPC because lawyers felt they would significantly reduce their work.

Most important, the government can, by engaging with local bar associations and district lawyers, allay their concerns. The litigating bar – especially the bulk of lawyers who argue in district courts in the vernacular – should be the most unlikely group of opponents. After all, foreign firms have time and again stated that they are not interested in litigation and wish to restrict themselves to transactional corporate law work (Brayne n.d.). Contrary to their expectations, litigating lawyers are likely to gain from liberalization because foreign law firms will rely on them for the litigation side of transactions and engage them for appearance and arguments before courts. Therefore, litigating lawyers have little to fear from legal market liberalization, and the government and Bar Council of India must inform them of the relevant facts in this debate.

But is the practicing bar opposed to the entry of foreign firms only because they are ill informed? It is possible that practicing lawyers deeply dislike the transformation of law from a profession that was primarily oriented around appearing on behalf of clients in courts to a business that dispenses legal advice and pursues big profits. Foreign firms are a unique source of pressure on traditional legal culture. Big Indian firms have been exerting pressure on it for decades now, but the entry of foreign firms would still contribute significantly to the disintegration of traditional legal culture, and therefore practicing lawyers oppose it.

F. *Foreign Law Firms*

Foreign law firms are the flag bearers of the proliberalization lobby. Global law firms are consistently looking to extend their operations overseas, and India has, together with Brazil and China, been on the top of their agenda. However, foreign firms have not had much success in getting government representatives and bar associations to effectively lobby the Indian government. For example, the UK government and many dignitaries and world leaders have lobbied hard to convince India to liberalize its legal market to little avail, and US President Barack Obama dropped liberalization from his agenda during his India visit last year (Ganz 2011f).

In any case, it seems that foreign law firms' interest in the Indian market is often exaggerated. No more than twenty global firms plan to open offices in India as soon as liberalization takes place. Most firms are happy with the present arrangements in which they work for foreign clients on India-related transactions indirectly. In the long term, however, these firms are likely to get more ambitious and do what they have done in other countries: open full-fledged offices and advise both Indian and foreign clients.

G. *Law Students*

Most law students at elite Indian schools are in favor of admission of foreign law firms. They believe that it will increase competition and lead to higher salaries and more jobs. To start with, foreign firms are likely to restrict recruitment from Indian law schools since a majority of them fail to meet basic academic standards. Speaking at the National Consultation for Second Generation Reforms in Legal Education, the former prime minister of India, Dr. Manmohan Singh, recognized this problem and pointed out that Indian legal education is characterized by a few "islands of excellence amidst a sea of institutionalized mediocrity" (Gingerich and Singh 2010). However, gradually Indian law students will generally benefit from admission of foreign law firms. This is particularly true for students at major elite Indian law schools. As a recent graduate of a national law school in India, I had the opportunity of discussing this issue with my peers at the National Academy of Legal Studies and Research (NALSAR) and other law schools. Most ambitious Indian law students are dissatisfied with the way in which Indian law firms function.

Compensation has improved but continues to be low when compared with associate compensation at international levels. Interestingly, this is not true for partner compensation. The path to partnership is uncertain in family-dominated law firms, and Indian firms lack structured training and mentorship programs for incoming associates. As a result, several students have accepted offers from prestigious UK law firms. Clifford Chance, Linklaters, Slaughter & May, Allen & Overy, and Herbert Smith, among others, have also responded by showing keen interest in Indian law graduates from the top schools (Ganz 2008; Bar and Bench 2010). In these firms, Indian students find better training and compensation and work in a more professional environment, which opens up greater opportunities for professional development. But there is a problem – most students join these firms with the aim of gaining international exposure for a few years before returning to India. Admission of foreign law firms will benefit such students, as many would prefer to stay if they can work in India without moving to a foreign country (Krishnan 2010a, 72).

IV. THE JUDICIAL STANCE: ASSESSING THE LEGAL ARGUMENTS ON FOREIGN ENTRY

A. Lawyers Collective – *Interpreting "Practice of Law"*

Between 1993 and 1995, three foreign law firms – Chadbourne & Parke, White & Case, and Ashurst Morris Crisp – applied to the Reserve Bank of India (RBI) to open liaison offices in India.[10] The RBI granted permission and issued licenses to these firms to open their respective liaison offices. In 1995, Lawyers Collective, a public interest organization, challenged the legality of these licenses before the Bombay High Court. It alleged that these firms had brought in foreign lawyers who were advising on transactions involving Indian law and using their liaison offices as fronts for legal practice in India.

In an interim order in 1995, the Bombay High Court held that rendering legal assistance and executing documents amounted to practice of law and ordered an RBI investigation to examine the compliance of foreign firms with the restrictions under Indian law (Vena 2011, 197). The law firms appealed this decision to the Supreme Court, but the court declined to decide any substantive issues and sent the case back to the Bombay High Court. After thirteen years, the Bombay High Court finally declared its final judgment on December 16, 2009. In *Lawyers Collective v. Bar Council of India Chadbourne, Ashurst, White & Case, and Others*, the Bombay High Court was ruling on whether the Advocates Act restricts the "practice of law" to only Indian citizens (Bombay High Court 2009).

1. Legal Questions

The court held that the RBI's permission to foreign firms to open liaison offices was illegal. The court considered alternative interpretations of sections 29 and 33. Section 29 states that "subject to the provisions of this Act and any rules made there under, there shall, as from the appointed day, be only one class of persons entitled to practise the profession of law, namely, advocates." Section 33 states that "except as otherwise provided in this Act or in any other law for the time being in force, no person shall, on or after the appointed day, be entitled to practise in any Court or before any authority or person unless he is enrolled as an advocate under this Act." The court considered American (*Reel v. New York County Lawyers Ass'n*, 3 N.Y.2d 224), Australian (*Legal Practice Board v. Wilhelmus Van Der Zwaan* WASC 133 [2002]), and Indian precedent (*Ex Capt. Harish Uppal v. Union of India* 2 SCC 45 [2003]) to interpret the expression "practice of law."[11] The law firms had argued that section 29 is merely declaratory in nature, but the court disagreed with this view and held that a person necessarily has to be enrolled under this section in order to be able to practice law. It added that by virtue of section 33, in order to practice law before a court, a person needs to be enrolled as an advocate (Shankar and Kak 2010, 308). The court emphasized that every person enrolled as an advocate under section 29 need not avail of the right under section 33 and practice before a court. Hence, the court concluded that section 33 does not exclude the application of the Advocates Act to nonlitigious practice, and therefore section 29 applies to such practice, too (ibid., 309). The court's interpretation is unsatisfactory when we see the Advocates Act as a whole, together with its purpose. The Advocates Act was promulgated to consolidate the different groups of legal practitioners in India. Therefore section 29 reads like a provision that sought to institute a single class of legal practitioners and merely declares an entitlement. Section 33, on the other hand, defines the scope of this entitlement of advocates enrolled under section 29 as "practise in any court or before any authority." Therefore, the right to practice is the genus of which the right to practice before a court or authority may be a specie (*Pravin Shah v. K. A. Mohd. Ali*, 8 SCC 650, para. 16 [2001]).

Section 35, which provides for punishment of advocates for misconduct, was also at issue. Specifically, the court was looking at section 35(4), which says that an advocate suspended from practice shall, during the period of suspension, be debarred from "practicing before any court or before any authority in India." This provision does not make any reference to suspension from nonlitigious practice. However, the court said that lawyers in nonlitigious practice could not be unregulated and included this group of lawyers under the scope of section 35(4). This approach of the court runs contra to the well-established principle of statutory interpretation that a penalty provision needs to be strictly construed (*Iqbal Singh Marwah v. Meenakshi Marwah*, AIR 2005 SC 2119, 2131), and in case a reasonable interpretation leads to avoidance of penalty, such a construction should be adopted (*Tuck & Sons v. Priester* 19 QBD 629, 638 [1887]; *Tolaram v. State of Bombay*, AIR 1954 SC 496 [1954]).

2. Policy Questions

Law firms had also argued that the act does not contain any penal provisions for breaches committed by a person practicing in nonlitigious matter and therefore the act did not apply to such persons (Bombay High Court 2009, 51). However, the court rejected this argument and pointed out that if this argument were accepted, then an advocate who is found guilty of misconduct while practicing in nonlitigious matters would go unpunished (ibid., 57). This, the court said, was an unacceptable interpretation, which would defeat the object of the Advocates Act (ibid.). The court decided that nonlitigious or transactional lawyers cannot be left unregulated.

Therefore, to ensure that transactional lawyers are included in the Advocates Act, the court expansively interpreted the expression "practice of law." This seems like a strange approach. As a matter of policy, why should a court expansively interpret a term merely for the sake of regulating a group of lawyers? When the Advocates Act was enacted, in 1961, Indian lawyers did not have an active nonlitigious or transactional practice. And expectedly, this act does not have effective enforcement or penalty provisions for transactional lawyers. Contrary to what the court suggests, there would be no anomaly if a transactional lawyer found guilty of misconduct were to go unpunished under the act. From a policy perspective, forced inclusion of a group of lawyers that the Advocates Act was not meant to regulate serves no purpose. Instead, exclusion may pave the way for a legislation that will, in fact, be able to regulate this group effectively (Ganz 2009; Shankar and Kak 2010, 311).

3. Practical Impact and Government's Stance

Two crucial points of discussion emerge from the legal discussion that has transpired before the courts – first, the practical impact on the current arrangements between foreign and Indian law firms and second, the government's stance during the proceedings before the Bombay High Court.

What is the impact of this decision on existing arrangements between Indian and foreign law firms? Almost none. Of course, the three firms that were directly involved in this case have all closed their India liaison offices: US-based White & Case and Chadbourne & Parke after the 1995 interim order and UK-based Ashurst after the December 2009 decision (Shamdasani 2010, 29; Ring 2010). However, the Bombay High Court did not deal with any of the indirect methods through which foreign law firms are working on India-based transactions. This means that referral arrangements and the numerous "best friends" agreements between foreign and Indian firms are unaffected by this judgment. Within a few months of this decision, Ashurst entered into a "best friends" agreement with a Delhi-based Indian law firm (Lawyer 2011). This reflects the trend in arrangements between foreign and Indian law firms. Lawyers – especially those who have made "best friends" in recent times – are certain that this decision does not affect their "strategic partnerships."[12] Therefore, the decision simply reiterated the status quo and had little impact on foreign law firms that have found an indirect way of engaging in India-related transactional work (Natrajan 2009).

This case, however, significantly gives us an insight into the government's legal stance on the question of the scope of the Advocates Act and the interpretation of the term *law practice*. The Counsel for Union of India informed the court that the government was in the process of consulting all stakeholders and any decision would be taken only after considering all competing views. More importantly, he argued that for drafting legal documents or giving opinions on aspects of foreign or international law, one need not be on the roll of the

Bar Council. The government's official legal stance before the Bombay High Court was that the Advocates Act does not govern persons practicing in nonlitigious matters (Bombay High Court 2009, 20). Therefore, the legal position of the Indian government – that is, its interpretation of practice of law in the Advocates Act – seems to be in favor of legal market liberalization. However, the decision on whether to allow foreign firms is one in which political and economic considerations are far important than legal interpretation of existing rules.

B. A. K. *Balaji Petition: What Lies Ahead?*

Global law firms are very keen in entering the Indian market, however liberalization opponents have taken the fight to big international players. In March 2010, just as all the "best friends" were feeling relieved at how the *Lawyers Collective* case decision had ignored their arrangements, A. K. Balaji, a lawyer from Tamil Nadu, filed a writ petition before the Madras High Court against thirty-one foreign law firms and a LPO company for illegally practicing law in India (Balaji 2010; Lin 2010). The writ makes the following arguments: (1) there is no reciprocity between India, the United Kingdom, and the United States because Indian lawyers have to go through a more complex process in the United States and United Kingdom compared with their lawyers in India; (2) foreign lawyers are violating India's income tax and immigration laws and causing loss of revenue by "entering India through [a] visitor's visa when the actual intention is to indirectly market and earn money out of clients from India by way of seminars"; (3) international law firms have offices in India, but they are fashioning themselves as LPOs; (4) it is important to ensure proper safeguards and mutual arrangements for Indian lawyers before allowing foreign firms and therefore, the Court should prohibit the law firms and the LPO from having "... any legal practice either on the litigation side or in the field of non-litigation and commercial transactions in any manner within the territory of India ..." (Balaji 2010).

On February 21, 2012, the Madras High Court held in the A. K. Balaji case that there is no a prohibition under the Advocates Act 1961 or the Bar Counsel of India rules that prevent foreign lawyers from visiting India on a temporary, "fly in fly out" basis to advise clients on foreign law and international legal issues. The Court made clear, however, that foreign lawyers remain prohibited from practicing Indian law without qualifications accepted by Indian authorities and the requisite level of reciprocity from the foreign country in question. The Court also noted that activities performed by BPOs and LPOs do not constitute practice of law and hence do not conflict with the Act. Since the

Madras High Court's decision, the case has been taken up by the Supreme Court of India, where it is currently pending.

V. COMPARATIVE LESSONS: HOW ARE GLOBAL LAW FIRMS EXPANDING ELSEWHERE?

A. *Brazil*

Brazil has great opportunities for sure – but you can't let the guy who wasn't invited to the party come in and steal all the sweets.

– Francisco Müssnich, Senior Partner, Barbosa Müssnich Aragão, São Paulo (*Economist* 2011)

In Brazil, Law 8906/1994 governs the practice of law and entitles only attorneys enrolled with the Brazilian Bar Association (*Ordem dos Advogados do Brasil*, or OAB) to practice law in Brazil. There are two ways in which foreign-trained lawyers may be allowed to practice law in Brazil. First, they may appear for the OAB bar examination and have their foreign law degree validated by a Brazilian law school. Alternatively, they may register as foreign law consultants without having to validate their law degrees in Brazil or pass the OAB bar examination.[13] Importantly, foreign law consultants are barred from advising clients on Brazilian law. While they are allowed to incorporate a legal entity such as a foreign law consultancy firm to advise clients on foreign and international law, they cannot engage in local law practice (Machado and Pisaneschi 2010). Moreover, local Brazilian lawyers and foreign law consultants are not allowed to merge – that is, a Brazilian law firm can only have lawyers regularly licensed by OAB who are allowed to practice Brazilian law. On the other hand, only foreign law consultants may establish a foreign law consultancy firm. A lawyer licensed to practice law by OAB (also a holder of a law degree abroad) may not obtain a license to act as a foreign law consultant before having "suspended" his or her license as an attorney in Brazil. This means that Brazilian and foreign firms cannot, for example, share the same letterheads, so Brazilian firms practicing Brazilian law cannot sport the logo of an international firm (McEwan 2011).

In the past decade, about twenty law firms have opened offices in Brazil to operate as foreign law consultants (Baxter 2010). As is clear from Müssnich's quote, entry of foreign law firms in Brazil in this form has indeed led to some controversy. In February 2011 the São Paulo chapter of Brazil's national bar association (*Ordem dos Advogados do Brasil – Seçao de São Paulo*) rendered an advisory opinion, reiterating a view first issued in 2010, that it is improper for Brazilian lawyers to create any kind of formal alliance with foreign legal consultants (Aldridge 2010). The federal bar association in Brazil is now considering the matter, and if it agrees, all formal local-foreign legal alliances may have to be dissolved (Economist 2011). Since such consultants are not lawyers under Brazilian rules, alliances with them violate Brazil's ban on multidisciplinary practice. In spite of the uncertainty on this matter, large law firms have continuously shown interest in the Brazilian legal market with big names including Davis Polk, Cleary Gottlieb, and K&L Gates establishing offices in São Paolo to function as foreign legal consultants.

B. *China*

As the world's fastest-growing emerging economy, China hosts many foreign law firms but strictly regulates the scope of business of these firms (Godwin 2009, 133). The Provisional Rules of 1992 were China's first foray into allowing foreign law firms to practice law in China. These rules were similar to the ones in Brazil – foreign lawyers could advise only on international treaties, international commercial law, and the laws of the country in which the foreign lawyers are permitted to practice (article 15), but they could not represent clients in Chinese legal matters (article 16). During the World Trade Organization (WTO) negotiations and after the passing of the Administrative Regulations of 2002, there was some confusion on the permissible scope of business of foreign firms (Liu 2008, 771). Again, as in Brazil, there has been disagreement on the manner in which foreign firms operate. In 2006 the Shanghai Bar Association (SBA) accused foreign law firms of violating the Administrative Regulations by practicing Chinese law (Shanghai Bar Association 2005; Asialaw Profiles 2006; Shanghai Lawyers Association 2006).

The Chinese context reveals a gap between strict regulations and the almost deliberate lax enforcement. Regulators in China are aware of the important contribution of foreign law firms and have not strictly enforced these restrictions. As a result, there has been "de facto liberalization" in China, and it is widely acknowledged that foreign law firms are today advising clients on Chinese law. Of course, local law firms have protested, but the benefits of having foreign law firms to Chinese businesses, at least according to the regulators, far outweigh the costs to domestic lawyers. Given the overall approach of the Chinese government on this issue, China will likely permit foreign firms to hire local lawyers and build domestic practices or allow complete liberalization by letting foreign and local law firms enter into partnerships (Godwin 2009, 162).

C. *European Union*

The European Union (EU) has a liberal regulatory regime for legal services for member states (Gromek-Broc 2002, 109; Worth 2003–04, 7). Lawyers who are community nationals and are admitted to practice in a member state are entitled to practice in other member states. Since 1977, several directives have made it easier for lawyers in the region to practice in other EU countries by providing for mutual recognition of professional qualifications.[14] For lawyers qualified in other countries, this liberalization has had little impact. Firms based outside the EU that wish to set up offices in the EU have to acquire rights to practice on a state-by-state basis (Garth and Silver 2002, 932). Therefore, a firm intending to establish an office in Paris or anywhere else in the EU cannot do so on the basis of its London office.

How the EU's legal regime has liberalized and its impact can be better understood by looking at the German example. Legal liberalization in Germany began in 1987, when the German Constitutional Court held that the federal Bundesrechtsanwaltsordnung (BRAO) statute regulating German legal practice conflicted with the EC Services Directive (Martin 2007, 182). Soon after this decision, the European Court of Justice held that the German regulation requiring German lawyers to appear in court together with a foreign lawyer also violated the EC Directive (Case 427/85, *Commission v. Germany*, 1988 E.C.R. 1123). In spite of opposition from the German Bar Association, the German Supreme Court, or Bundesgerichtshof (BGH), held in a September 1989 decision (*Überörtliche Sozietäten*) that mergers between foreign and German law firms were permissible, thereby liberalizing the German legal services market (*International Financial Law Review* 1989a, 4; 1989b, 3). In response, like large law firms in the United States and United Kingdom, many German law firms started growing, and during the 1990s more German firms merged than anywhere else in the world (Ferguson 1999, 36). The German legal profession has expanded significantly over the past two decades, and it continues to be "a locus for lawyers without frontiers" (Henssler and Terry 2001, 308).

D. *Japan*

During the 1980s, as Japan was liberalizing its economy, it relaxed its rules regarding the legal market. Before this, the Japan Federation of Bar

Associations (*Nichibenren*) had successfully convinced the Ministry of Justice to exclude foreign law firms (Struble 2009, 118). In 1986, however, the Japanese government enacted the Foreign Lawyers Special Law after negotiations with the US government. This law allowed foreign lawyers to practice their home jurisdiction's law in Japan if they had five years of experience in their home jurisdictions and if there was reciprocity. However, to protect domestic lawyers, foreign lawyers were not allowed to practice under a foreign firm's name and could not hire local Japanese lawyers (*bengoshi*) (ibid., 121). Some firms showed interest in spite of these restrictions, but the real growth of foreign law firms in Japan began in 1994, when amendments were introduced to the 1986 law. Foreign lawyers (*gaiben*) were allowed to use their firm names in Japan (Chan 2005, 56).

In recent years, foreign firms have rapidly expanded in Japan. The latest amendment in the law, introduced in 2003 and implemented in April 2005, has contributed to this significant increase in interest (Keleman and Sibbitt 2002, 269). By permitting *gaiben* and *bengoshi* lawyers to form specific joint enterprises as well as permitting full mergers, Japan has encouraged American, British, and Australian law firms to target its legal market (Kim 2006, 199).

E. *Singapore*

Singapore has liberalized its legal market in a phased manner. It is a good example to other countries that are looking to allow foreign law firms – by learning from the shortcomings of regulation, Singapore has made changes in its policy toward liberalization of legal services. For a long time, Singapore allowed entry to foreign law firms but restricted them from practicing Singapore law. After dialogue with foreign law firms and the local bar, in the late 1990s the Singapore government allowed foreign law firms to establish "joint law ventures" (JLVs) (Krishnan 2010b, 433). From 2000 to 2009, eleven JLVs were created between foreign and local law firms. These JLVs never operated as one entity, and there was little or no integration. For instance, the foreign and local law firms in these JLVs maintained separate accounts and the foreign firm was under no obligation to bring onto its payroll any of the Singaporean JLV lawyers (ibid., 446). To protect local law firms and lawyers, foreign firms that entered JLVs were prohibited from creating a separate practice of their own or setting up a Singapore office, but local firms in JLVs could have a distinct practice. Moreover, foreign firms could not engage in litigation work in Singaporean courts or practice real estate law.

This lack of integration had a direct impact on the way JLVs operated. Within the first five years, six JLVs disbanded, including global law firms such as White & Case, Shearman & Sterling, Freshfields Bruckhaus Deringer, Clifford Chance, and Allen & Overy (ibid., 452). From the foreign firms' perspective, the JLV model did not meet their expectations: the return on their investment was small. Because of restrictions on the areas of practice, they could not capture the Singapore legal market as they had hoped. Local Singapore lawyers, on the other hand, resented being treated as second-grade citizens (ibid., 446). They were not paid as well as their foreign counterparts in the JLV (ibid., 454). Contrary to their expectations, they felt that foreign lawyers were not keen to mentor them to transfer best practices. The JLVs that managed to survive this were the ones where both foreign and domestic lawyers had a clear understanding of how work was to be divided between them (ibid., 450).

Aware of this discontent, the Singapore government in 2006 asked Justice V. K. Rajah of the Singaporean Court of Appeal to examine the benefits and shortcomings of the JLV model (ibid., 456). In December 2007 the Rajah Committee Report presented its findings to the government. Some of the key findings that led to major policy changes are as follows: First, in its effort to enhance the JLV model, the committee permitted foreign law firms within the JLV to directly "hire Singapore-qualified lawyers to advise on Singapore law" (Rajah Committee 2007, 7.44–7.52). Second, even while retaining the restriction on litigation, the Rajah Committee allowed foreign lawyers to practice international commercial arbitration in Singapore (ibid., 7.40–7.43). This is consistent with Singapore's aim of becoming a global hub for international arbitration. Finally, Singapore introduced the Qualified Foreign Law Firm (QFLF) program, which permitted foreign law firms to enter the Singapore legal market to "practice Singapore law in commercial matters" through the direct hiring of Singapore-qualified lawyers. To secure a five-year QFLF license, firms have to go through a competitive selection process where they are expected to provide revenue projections, among other information (ibid., 7.44c). In early 2009 six foreign law firms – Allen & Overy, Clifford Chance, Herbert Smith, Latham & Watkins, Norton Rose, and White & Case – were granted QFLF licenses (Hoare 2008; Asian Legal Business 2009). By now, Singapore is again expected to review the functioning of these six firms and also decide on how it can further liberalize its legal market (Asian Legal Business 2009; *People's Daily* 2011).

Singapore has had its share of problems while liberalizing its legal market. The jury is still out on the implementation of the Rajah Committee recommendations. However, the Singaporean government, supported by its bar, has constantly engaged with relevant stakeholders and tried to improve its regulatory framework.

VI. HOW CAN GLOBAL LAW FIRMS OPERATE IN INDIA?

I would rather fight someone openly than have to deal with surrogate outfits. You can give it any sort of euphemism, but foreign firms are already here.
– Somasekhar Sundaresan, Partner, J. Sagar Associates (in Vasani 2007)

While the Indian legal market is formally closed to foreign law firms, global players continue to service clients on India-related transactions in various indirect forms. The extent of their India practice is clear from the fact that major law firm rankings, including Legal500 and RSG India Consulting, now have a separate Foreign Firms category. Even league tables on capital markets and mergers and acquisitions work being handled by law firms regularly feature numerous foreign firms (Ganz 2011c; Ganz 2011e). This section discusses the various modes through which foreign law firms are currently doing India-related legal work and how direct entry can be facilitated if and when the Indian government permits entry. The table on page ____ lists the top ten highest-grossing law firms in the world in 2011 (as per *American Lawyer Daily*) and provides information on whether the firm has an India practice group, the number of lawyers in such group, and tie-ups with Indian firms.

A. *Present Position*

1. India Desks or Groups in Foreign Offices

Most major global law firms today work on India-related transactions from their London, New York, Singapore, Hong Kong, or Washington offices (Russell 2010, 35). Large international players, including Skadden, Arps, Slate, Meagher, & Flom; Linklaters; Clifford Chance; White & Case; Davis, Polk & Wardwell; Allen & Overy; and Herbert Smith, have very active groups that are usually headed by a senior partner who is related to India (the head of White & Case's India practice based in New York City is Nandan Nelivigi) and staff dozens of associates, many of whom are directly recruited from Indian law schools. Lawyers in these India groups work on the international and foreign elements of transactions for their clients doing business in India or with Indian businesses. Having an Indian desk is advantageous as a precursor to establishing an Indian office. Indian graduates working in such groups hope to return to their firm's India office postliberalization. However, India desks may have a disadvantage because the costs of hiring and training Indian graduates for such groups are significantly higher than hiring an Indian law firm to do work on that part of the transaction that involves Indian law (Vena 2011, 211).

2. "Best Friends" Agreements and Referral Arrangements

In addition to India practice groups, top foreign law firms have entered into "best friends" or exclusive referral agreements and arrangements with Indian law firms. This is not just with British and American firms (where most of these arrangements come from). Indian law firms have also entered into such arrangements with French, Uruguayan, and Singaporean law firms. Under "best friends" agreements, both firms will exclusively refer work to each other when dealing with cases involving Indian parties and vice versa. (For a fuller discussion of these agreements, see Chapters 3 and 10 of this volume.) Moreover, the arrangements also reflect the view that the foreign firms will eventually merge with the India "best friend" in the event of liberalization (Kanekal 2011).

In recent times, "best friends" relationships have faced serious challenges. Clifford Chance (CC), one of the world's largest law firms, and AZB & Partners, one of India's largest law firms, entered into a "best friends" agreement in January 2009, and CC had even sent a senior partner on a secondment to the AZB Bombay office (Byrne 2009). In January 2011, however, both firms decided to end their relationship. The general difficulties that arise with "best friends" and exclusive referral arrangements reflect the reasons for this high-profile breakup.

First, firms want greater freedom to work with other firms. Both local and international law firms gain little by being tied down to one foreign counterpart, as there is a possibility of missing out on referrals from other firms. In the AZB-CC arrangement, CC missed out on some referrals from AZB. In Bharti Airtel's $10.7 billion takeover bid of the African business of Zain, AZB acted for Bharti Airtel, but Linklaters, Herbert Smith, and Herbert Smith's Benelux alliance partner Stibbe, CC's competitors, worked on the international side of the deal (RSG India Law Centre 2010). AZB also gained little from this arrangement because foreign firms, with which it had previously close relationships, began referring work to AZB's competitor Indian firms (Ganz 2011g). Even the greatest critic of any foreign affiliation, Lalit Bhasin, has said: "It makes sense for an Indian firm to work with different global players instead of tying up with one exclusively as that gives better exposure in terms of the number of clients" (Chatterjee 2010). Second, when these agreements were signed, there was a feeling that legal market liberalization would happen sooner rather than later; but several years later, uncertainty has only increased. Pratap Amin, the head of the India practice of Freshfields Bruckhaus Deringer, sums up the feeling among foreign law firms: "The market's been opening up 'next year' for the past ten to fifteen years" (Harris 2011). Third, there have been fewer joint mandates and inbound referrals than expected, and foreign firms would have reputational concerns because of the flightiness of Indian law firms (Ganz 2011a).

Two months after AZB and CC ended their relationship, UK-based Clyde & Company and Indian firm ALMT Legal had a messy breakup. Similar to the AZB-CC situation, Clyde & Company's Indian counterparts were disappointed with the results of the agreement. According to one of ALMT Legal's senior partners, Aliff Fazehlboy, there was a significant drop in referrals from other international law firms. This even led to a split of ALMT Legal, with five partners leaving to create a new firm – Clasis Law, Clyde & Company's new "best friend" in India (Ganz 2011d).

More recently, law firms Allen & Overy (A&O) and Trilegal ended their five-year referral arrangement (Allen & Overy 2012). For these firms, too, the lack of liberalization progress and the inability to explore broader options for collaboration were the primary causes (Ganz 2012). Anand Prasad, cofounder and partner of Trilegal, noted in an interview at the time that "the decision to tie up with A&O was taken in the expectation that the Indian legal services market would open up in next six months to a year. However, that has not happened" (Kachhwaha 2013).

Firms can learn many lessons from the AZB-CC and ALMT-Clyde failures. Most importantly, foreign firms and their Indian counterparts have to realize that mere token partnerships are unlikely to add value to practices. It is important to have aligned interests and client bases; for example, clients may prefer if foreign firms looking to partner with Indian firms were to consult them prior to establishing arrangements. Similarly, even if firms have similar structures and ideology, it may be worthwhile to have "interpractice" referrals as opposed to "interfirm" referrals. This would mean that firm X in New York with Indian clients looking for mergers & acquisition (M&A) work would partner with an Indian firm with a strong M&A practice but align with another Indian firm when dealing with an international arbitration dispute.

3. Fly in, Fly Out

Those against liberalization often argue that foreign law firms send their lawyers to advise Indian clients out of five-star hotels and business centers. In fact, the A. K. Balaji petition before the Madras High Court alleges that these lawyers practice law in India under the guise of LPO units and seminars and conferences (Balaji 2010). As expected, no information is available on the extent to which foreign lawyers attending seminars in India advise clients from their hotel lobbies. Suffice it to say that given the possibility of referral

TABLE 1. *AmLaw 2011 Global 100: Most revenue and India*

Name of firm	India group/desk	Indian "best friend"
Baker & McKenzie	Yes. More than 200 lawyers with head of India group in Sydney.	–
Skadden, Arps, Slate, Meagher & Flom	Yes. More than 10 partners based in 9 offices.	–
DLA Piper	Yes. Around 150 lawyers across offices.	–
Latham & Watkins	Yes. More than 50 lawyers primarily based in Singapore and London.	–
Clifford Chance	Yes. Around 200 lawyers based in 9 offices.	AZB & Partners from January 2009 to January 2011
Linklaters	Yes. Around 120 lawyers with head of India group in London.	Talware Thakore & Associates since December 2006 and an antitrust "best friends" agreement with Dhall Law Chambers
Freshfields Bruckhaus Deringer	Yes. 35 lawyers with head of India group in London.	–
Allen & Overy	Yes. More than 60 lawyers based in London, Singapore, and Hong Kong.	Trilegal from February 2008 to September 2012
Hogan Lovells	Yes. More than 10 partners based in 6 offices.	–
Kirkland & Ellis	Yes.	–

arrangements and India practice groups and improvement in technology and communications, it is unlikely that foreign law firms are too excited about this mode of engagement in India.

B. *Future Possibilities*

Going by the way in which emerging economies have permitted foreign law firms to directly enter their legal space and how India has previously admitted multinational accountancy firms (MAFs), India is likely to admit foreign law firms directly into its legal market in two ways.

1. Direct Entry: "The India Office"

If India liberalizes, foreign law firms may be allowed to set up independent offices in the different cities in India. This could again take various forms.

First, the government could allow foreign law firms to set up offices that are entitled to do transactional and litigation work in India. It is highly unlikely that entry in this form will be allowed in the near future. The litigating bar in India is surely going to rise in protest, thereby making this a politically unviable option. But more importantly, foreign firms are not interested in litigation work in India because (1) much of the litigation in lower courts is in the vernacular; (2) foreign firms are wary of the legendary delays in the court system; and (3) foreign firms have already made it clear that going by comparative experiences, they are not interested in creating a new client base for litigation in India and want to focus on areas that are being globalized, i.e., corporate transactional work and international commercial arbitration.

The second option would be to allow foreign firms to set up independent offices but only to practice international law or the law of their home jurisdictions. This would be similar to the Brazilian position and also the Singaporean law before JLVs were allowed. Indian lawyers against liberalization would likely protest this as well because of the prevalent belief that foreign firms will enter the Indian market in a limited sense but gradually capture all the clients and the talent.

Third, foreign firms could be permitted to establish an office where they practice Indian and foreign law but no litigation. Like the previous option, the antiliberalization lobby is likely to oppose this form of entry. Foreign firms, however, would want to work on both the Indian as well as the international side of corporate transactional matters. This would also allow foreign firms to hire Indian qualified lawyers to work on Indian law. As I explain in the conclusion, this mode of entry is the most desirable.

2. Joint Venture – Affiliate Offices

The other option for the government is to allow foreign firms to enter into joint ventures with local firms, like the enhanced Singapore JLV model. Even if the government allowed joint venture and affiliate offices, it would have to address the complex issues that arise with allowing independent offices. For example, would the Indian JLV be allowed to practice Indian law or only foreign law? Would it be able to engage in litigation? And would the local firm in the JLV be allowed to maintain a separate entity? But beyond these regulatory issues, the firms looking to partner will have to deal with economic and practical considerations. As discussed earlier, the initial JLV model adopted in Singapore engendered conflicts over profit sharing and compensation, sharing of best practices and training by foreign counterparts, and cultural differences where local lawyers feel belittled by foreign lawyers. In

India, some elements of these challenges appear in the failures of "best friends" agreements and referral arrangements (for example, the AZB-CC failure). In spite of the shortcomings, Indian policy makers as well as other stakeholders should seriously consider this mode of entry. In a debate that is more political than legal or economic and where a fight to find a middle ground is elusive, this may indeed be a good bargaining chip for foreign lawyers in negotiations. As Rajiv Luthra, the managing partner of Luthra & Luthra, has noted, this model is in the interest of local Indian firms and is likely to face less opposition (Luthra 2007).

VII. CONCLUSION: WHERE DO WE GO FROM HERE?

Globalization is not only redrawing boundaries, it is also profoundly changing the landscape of the legal profession. Today, legal professionals across the globe find themselves working in a world that is undergoing a radical transformation (Terry 2008). As discussed in this paper, the changing nature of law practice exemplifies the challenges and opportunities of globalization. The legal profession has much to gain from this – growing businesses need lawyers capable of facilitating mergers just as they need lawyers to protect intellectual property (Moore 2007, 37). At the same time, the initial failure of the JLV model in Singapore due to cultural differences and indeed the furious debate around legal market liberalization in Brazil, Japan, and India reflect the challenges to a globalizing legal profession.

But how can Indian policy makers best respond to globalization of the legal profession? And what can Indian lawyers expect from foreign law firms coming into the Indian legal market? In my view, India's policy of protectionism in the legal market is not consistent with its aim of playing an important role in the global economic arena. Indian lawyers have been exposed to cutting-edge legal work and have grown into technically competent and knowledgeable professionals, capable of competing with foreign lawyers. In fact, they have been constantly working on international transactions together with their foreign counterparts. As I have highlighted in this paper, entry of foreign firms will not only directly benefit clients and law students by providing more options and better opportunities but also contribute to the growth of the Indian legal profession because foreign firms will offer better knowledge management techniques and other best practices.

To settle this political debate, any change in the current position will require an amendment to the Advocates Act, and the government has to build consensus among political parties. Indeed, protest is inevitable, and lawyers constitute a strong political force. Therefore, the government and proliberalization lobby need to engage in dialogue with opponents and incorporate dissenting views in the proposal for reform. I believe that the complete opening up of the market is neither politically acceptable nor suitable to the interests of the Indian legal profession. Allowing firms to set up independent offices in India and permitting them to hire Indian lawyers, but restricting their area of practice to nonlitigious practice, is the best way forward. Foreign firms want to be able to serve the needs of their clients doing business in India and are therefore primarily interested in transactional work. They neither have the inclination nor the expertise to engage in litigation in Indian courts. Similarly, a majority of the Indian legal profession still focuses on litigation and would not be affected by such form of entry. Instead of following the Singapore JLV model, which forces partnerships down the throats of both local and foreign firms and has thus led to integration difficulties, Indian policy makers should consider the independent "India office" option with restrictions on scope of practice.

What is perhaps most disappointing in the discussion on legal market liberalization in India is the indecisiveness of decision makers – the government and Bar Council of India – in this debate. In July 2009, in response to a question in the Rajya Sabha (the Upper House in the Indian Parliament), Law Minister Veerappa Moily pointed out that the "issue of allowing foreign law firms to establish their offices to give legal advice and assistance on foreign law is being discussed with all the stakeholders including the Bar Council of India."[15] In December 2009 the Bombay High Court in the *Lawyers Collective* case made the following observation: "Counsel for the Union of India had argued that the Central Government is actively considering the issue relating to the foreign law firms practicing the profession of law in India. Since the said issue is pending before the Central Government for more than 15 years, we direct the Central Government to take appropriate decision in the matter as expeditiously as possible" (Bombay High Court 2009, 159). Following this decision, in March 2010 the law minister yet again responded by saying that the government was studying the implications of the *Lawyers Collective* judgment in consultation with the Bar Council of India and other stakeholders.[16]

Since neither the government nor the Bar Council of India had paid any heed to the observation of the Supreme Court of India to decide this matter expeditiously, in July 2011 I filed an application under the Right to Information Act, 2005, asking the government to provide information on the decision-making process. What was the current viewpoint of the government? Who are the stakeholders involved in this process? And what is their view? Unfortunately, on August 10, 2011, I received a response that a decision on the issue of entry of foreign law firms will be taken after receiving comments from stakeholders, "which are still awaited."[17]

This indecision has led to great uncertainty and is bound to damage India's reputation on the global scene. Periodically, international and domestic media reports have indicated that a decision on foreign law firms' admission to India is expected soon (Koppel 2011; Press Trust of India 2011). Irrespective of the choice they make, Indian policy makers must make a decision and end the uncertainty. Even a draft proposal from the government on how to address the situation will usher in debate and go a long way toward building consensus among the various stakeholders.

Notes

1 As Galanter argues, this was due to low business activity. Clients were individuals, societies, and even corporations who approached lawyers for dispute resolution in courts. With economic globalization, the nature of legal services has expanded in its scope and lawyers' orientations have evolved accordingly (Galanter 1968–1969, 201; Galanter 1989, 282).

2 Proviso to section 24(1)(a) and section 47 deal with reciprocity. These provisions state that if any country prevents citizens of India from practicing the profession of law or subjects them to unfair discrimination in that country, no citizen of that country would be entitled to practice the profession of law in India. The Bar Council of India is empowered to prescribe conditions subject to which foreign qualifications in law obtained by persons other than citizens of India shall be recognized for the purpose of admission as an advocate under the Advocates Act.

3 The Legal Services Act, 2007 established the Legal Services Board in the United Kingdom. It came into being on January 1, 2009, and became fully operational on January 1, 2010.

4 Lalit Bhasin, the president of the Society of Indian Law Firms (SILF), argues that there is "no logic or reason or rationale as to why a new entity is created which anyways will superimpose itself on the Bar Councils which have been set up at the state level and the national level" (Dalal 2010). M. P. Bharucha points out that the Legal Services Board takes the position that competition is good and if foreign lawyers have a right to entry, then opponents will have to "toe the line" (ibid.).

5 The bill has a very broad definition of "legal professional," which covers all advocates as defined by the Advocates Act, including qualified lawyers engaged in legal practice in their chamber, drafting and conveyancing, and all other professional services where legal issues are involved (see clause 2(d) of the Legal Practitioners Bill, 2010).

6 Cyril Shroff, managing partner of India's largest law firm Amarchand & Mangaldas & Suresh A. Shroff & Company, points out that domestic law firms, which are not strong enough to face competition, will collapse and will be bought out for "ridiculously low values." What does that mean? The main assets of firms are their lawyers, who can leave. Of course, firms have goodwill, but in law, a lot or all of the goodwill is tied to the lawyers. It is therefore not clear why firms would be worth much aside from the value of their lawyers. Lawyers would not leave unless they would rather work somewhere else, so what would a buyout of a law firm for a "low value" be?

7 Chinese walls are a way of preventing conflict of interests. A lawyer or a team of lawyers representing a party on a deal or litigation is separated from another party with contrary interests or with confidential information from an adverse party.

8 Rule 36 of the Bar Council of India Rules states that an advocate "shall not solicit work or advertise either directly or indirectly whether by way of circulars, advertisements, touts, personal communications, interviews not warranted by personal relations, furnishing or inspiring newspaper comments or producing his photograph to be published in connection with the cases he has been engaged with or concerned."

9 Ganz notes, "Many of the younger generation of Indian corporate lawyers working in law firms are often privately in favor of allowing foreign firms into India, because many of them secretly hope to get poached by foreign firms wanting to set up their own local offices" (Ganz 2011g).

10 These "liaison offices" were not allowed to practice law or advise clients. They could not receive any commission, fee, or other remuneration for the liaison activities. They were, however, permitted a range of activities including (1) coordinating and communicating between the foreign office and Indian lawyers advising the same clients; (2) collecting information and data on clients and prospective clients and furnishing it to the head office and other foreign offices; (3) establishing business contacts and acting as "listening posts" between the head office and Indian entities; (4) providing information regarding the firm to clients and other interested parties; and (5) providing administrative and secretarial services to visiting lawyers from foreign offices (*Collective v. Anand Niketan*, MANU MH 0846 [1995]).

11 In the case of India, the Bombay High Court relied on *Ex Capt. Harish Uppal v. Union of India* 2 SCC 45 (2003), where the Indian Supreme Court has made the following observation: "The right of the advocate to practise envelopes a lot of acts to be performed by him in discharge of his professional duties. Apart from appearing in the courts he can be consulted by his clients, he can give his legal opinion whenever sought for, he can draft instruments, pleadings, affidavits or any other documents, he can participate in any conference involving legal discussions, he can work in any office or firm as a legal officer, he can appear for clients before an arbitrator or arbitrators etc... The right to practise, no doubt, is the genus of which the right to appear and conduct cases in the court may be a specie."

12 Zia Mody, a named partner of one of India's biggest law firm, AZB & Partners, says that this "judgment will have no impact on our 'best friends' agreement with Clifford Chance as they are not practicing here. Neither do they have any liaison office in the country" (Meherally 2009). Shobhan Thakore, a named partner in Linklater's Indian "best friend" Talwar Thakore & Associates, underscores his view that "apart from the fact that 'best friends' relationships were not in issue, the judgment does not in any way affect them" (Ganz 2009).

13 The foreign legal consultants have to simply comply with the specific requirements established in OAB Ordinance 91/2000. These requirements include holding a permanent visa in Brazil; being licensed to practice law by a bar association or equivalent body abroad; and providing evidence of good conduct and reputation, of never having been punished for a disciplinary violation, of never having been convicted in a criminal lawsuit, and that their country or state of origin offers

reciprocal treatment to Brazilian attorneys. License to such foreign law consultants is valid for three years and is renewable for successive three-year terms.

14 Prior to the 2005 directive, several regulations liberalized the legal services in the European market. These include the Legal Services Directive 77/249/EC, adopted in 1977; the Legal Services Directive 89/48/EC, adopted in 1988, and Directive 98/5/EC of the European Parliament and of the Council of 16, February 1988.

15 Ministry of Law and Justice, Government of India, Unstarred Question No. 2484, *Entry of Foreign Law Firms*, answered on July 27, 2009.

16 Ministry of Law and Justice, Government of India, Unstarred Question No. 1904, *Entry of Foreign Law Firms*, answered on March 15, 2010.

17 Reply to Right to Information Petition filed by author, Ministry of Law and Justice, Department of Legal Affairs – Implementation Cell, August 10, 2011.

References

Aldridge, Alex. 2010. "Brazil Bar Rules Against Associations with Foreign Law Firms." *Legal Week*, September 24. www.legalweek.com/legal-week/news/1735286/brazilian-bar-rules-foreign-law-firm-associations.

Allen & Overy. 2012. "Allen & Overy and Trilegal to End Referral Arrangement," news release, September 27. www.allenovery.com/news/en-gb/articles/Pages/Allen–Overy-and-Trilegal-to-end-referral-agreement.aspx.

Arackal, Peter. 2010. "Legal Eagles Eye $479m Fee Pie of India Inc." *The Times of India*, March 17. www.articles.timesofindia.indiatimes.com/2010–03–17/india-business/28116434_1_legal-eagles-legal-sector-law-firms.

Asialaw Profiles. 2006. "Foreign Law Firms in China: Breaking the Law?" September 1. www.asialawprofiles.com/Article/651700/Article.html.

Asian Legal Business. 2009. "Singapore's New QFLP Licencees," February 13. www.asia.legalbusinessonline.com/site-search/singapores-new-qflp-licencees/33707.

Balaji, A. K. 2010. Writ Petition No. 5614. High Court of Judicature at Madras. www.legallyindia.com/images/stories/docs/Balaji-writ-petition.txt.

Bar and Bench. 2010. "Career Paths of NLSIU, NALSAR and NUJS Graduates," June 28. www.barandbench.com/brief/9/809/377-choose-law-firms-209-choose-in-house-and-98-choose-lit-career-paths-of-nlsiu-nalsar-and-nujs-graduates.

Baxter, Brian. 2010. "Brazil Bar Concludes Foreign Law Firm Associations Break Rules." *AmLaw Daily*, September 27. www.amlawdaily.typepad.com/amlawdaily/2010/09/brazilforeignfirms.html.

Bhasin, Lalit. 2009. "Indian Legal Profession Not for Sale." *Economic Times*, April 2. www.articles.economictimes.indiatimes.com/2009–04–02/news/27642259_1_foreign-lawyers-indian-lawyers-advocates-act.

Bombay High Court. 2009. Writ Petition No. 1526 of 1995, December 16. www.bombayhighcourt.nic.in/data/judgements/2009/OSWP8152695.pdf.

Brayne, Jonathan. n.d. "Will India Benefit or Suffer from the Presence of Foreign Law Firms on Indian Soil?" On file with author.

Byrne, Matt. 2009. "CC Sends Ambassador to Indian Ally AZB." *Lawyer*, June 8. www.thelawyer.com/cc-sends-ambassador-to-indian-ally-azb/1000974.article.

Chan, Kay-Wah. 2005. "Foreign Law Firms: Implications for Professional Legal Education in Japan." *Journal of Japanese Law* 10 (20): 56–79.

Chatterjee, Paramita. 2010. "Law Firms Shy Away from Global Tie-Ups." *Economic Times*, September 6. www.articles.economictimes.indiatimes.com/2010–09–06/news/27585230_1_indian-law-firms-client-referral-arrangements-talwar-thakore-associates.

Dalal, Isha. 2010. "Does India Need a Legal Super-Regulator?" *The Firm: Corporate Law in India*. CNBC TV-18. www.moneycontrol.com/news/management/does-india-needlegal-super-regulator_500328.html.

Deccan Herald. 2010. "Centre to Move SC Over Entry of Foreign Law Firms," July 19. www.deccanherald.com/content/82369/centre-move-sc-over-entry.html.

The Economist. 2011. "Keep Out: Brazilian Lawyers Don't Want Pesky Foreigners Poaching Their Clients," June 23. www.economist.com/node/18867851.

Express News Service. 2008. "Advocates Can Now Advertise." *Indian Express*, July 29. www.indianexpress.com/news/advocates-can-now-advertise/341616/.

Ferguson, Nick. 1999. "Merger Fever Grips German Market." *International Financial Law Review*, September: 26 (9): 35–50.

The Firm: Corporate Law in India, CNBC TV-18. 2009. "No Foreigners Please!" December 26. www.moneycontrol.com/news/management/no-foreigners-please_432690.html.

Frumin, Ben. 2007. "Lowering the Bar." *India Business Legal Journal*, November: 12–20. www.indilaw.com/pdfs/Is%20India%20ready%20for%20foreign%20lawyers.pdf.

Galanter, Marc. 1968–1969. "Study of the Indian Legal Profession." *Law and Society Review* 3 (2/3): 201–217.

1989. *Law and Society in Modern America*. Oxford, England: Oxford University Press.

Ganz, Kian. 2008. "Clifford Chance Eyes India Market with Amarchand Hire." *Lawyer*, August 19. www.barandbench.com/brief/9/809/377-choose-law-firms-209-choose-in-house-and-98-choose-lit-career-paths-of-nlsiu-nalsar-and-nujs-graduates.

2009. "Advocates Act Unfit for Purpose After Lawyers Collective Judgment." *Legally India*, December 18. www.legallyindia.com/20091218353/Analysis/advocates-act-unfit-for-purpose-after-lawyers-collective-hc-judgment.

2010. "Note on Legal Market Liberalisation and the Entry of Foreign Law Firms," September 2. On file with author.

2011a. "Referral Drought Puts Paid to CC-AZB Best Friend Status." *Lawyer*, January 24. www.thelawyer.com/referral-drought-puts-paid-to-cc-azb-best-friend-status/1006719.article.

2011b. "New Lawyer Ethics Guidelines to Be Delayed by a Year: Subramanium." *Legally India*, February 7. www.legallyindia.com/201102071773/News/new-lawyer-ethics-guidelines-to-be-delayed-by-a-year-subramanium.

2011c. "2010–11 IPO Rankings." *Legally India*, April 15. www.legallyindia.com/201104152029/Capital-Markets/–201011-ipo-rankings-luthra-azb-chip-at-amarchand-dominance-dla-debuts-big-time.

2011d. "Referral-Drop Scuppered ALMT-Clydes Marriage: New Offices Planned." *Legally India*, April 29. www.legallyindia.com/201104292054/Law-firms/referral-drop-scuppered-almt-clydes-marriage-new-offices-planned.

2011e. "M&A H1 League Table." *Legally India*, July 8. www.legallyindia.com/201107082198/Corporate-/-MA/maa-h1–2011-league-table-azb-with-most-but-fewer-chunky-deals-desai-a-diwanji-rules-volume-tta-links-strong-duo.

2011f. "Liberalisation Talks Ditched for Jobs in Obama's Visit with DLA, Edwards Angell Partners." *Legally India*, November 10. www.legallyindia.com/201011101482/Law-firms/liberalisation-talks-ditched-for-jobs-in-obamas-visit-with-dla-edwards-angell-partners.

2011g. "Corporate Law 2011: The Year That Was." *Live Mint*, December 23. www.livemint.com/2011/12/22214808/Corporate-Law-2011-The-year-t.html.

2012. "Best Friends Trilegal and Allen & Overy Break Up, Citing Lack of Liberalisation Progress." *Legally India*, September 27. www.legallyindia.com/201209273146/Law-firms/breaking-best-friends-trilegal-and-allen-a-overy-break-up-citing-liberalisation.

Ganz, Kian and Neha Chauhan. 2010. "Write Petition Versus Foreign Firms Unlikely to Hit SC as Raft of US, UK, Oz Firms Grab Dua, Kachwaha and Counsel." *Legally India*, August 5. www.legallyindia.com/201008051174/Law-firms/writ-petition-v-foreign-firms-unlikely-to-hit-sc-as-raft-of-us-uk-oz-firms-grab-dua-kachwaha-and-senior-counsels.

Garth, Bryant and Carole Silver. 2002. "The MDP Challenge in the Context of Globalization." *Case Western Reserve Law Review* 52 (4): 903–942.

Gingerich, Jonathan and Aditya Singh, 2010. "Envisioning Legal Education Reform." *CriticalTwenties*, November 10. www.criticaltwenties.in/lawthejudiciary/envisioning-legal-education-reform.

Godwin, Andrew. 2009. "The Professional 'Tug of War': The Regulation of Foreign Lawyers in China, Business Scope Issues and Some Suggestions for Reform." *Melbourne University Law Review* 33 (1): 132–162.

Gromek-Broc, Katarzyna. 2002. "The Legal Profession in the European Union – A Comparative Analysis of Four Member States." *Liverpool Law Review* 24 (2): 109–130.

Harris, Joanne. 2011. "UK-Indian Firms' Relationships in Stasis as Liberalisation Remains a Pipe Dream." *Lawyer*, January 31. www.thelawyer.com/uk-indian-firms%E2%80%99-relationships-in-stasis-as-liberalisation-remains-a-pipe-dream/1006793.article.

Henssler, Martin and Laurel Terry. 2001. "Lawyers without Frontiers – A View from Germany." *Dickinson Journal of International Law* 19 (2): 269–308.

Hoare, Steve. 2008. "UK and UK Firms Win Singapore Licenses." *Lawyer*, December 5. www.thelawyer.com/uk-and-us-firms-win-singapore-licences/135977.article.

International Financial Law Review. 1989a. "The Plot Thickens in Germany," August: 4.

International Financial Law Review. 1989b. "German Lawyers Win Through," November: 3.

Kachhwaha, Richa. 2013. "Talking Law: Anand Prasad, Co-founder and Partner, Trilegal, New Delhi." Live Law, August 13. www.livelaw.in/talking-law-anand-prasad-co-founder-and-partner-trilegal-new-delhi/.

Kanekal, Nikhil. 2011. "Foreign Law Firms' Entry Still Deadlocked." *Live Mint*, September 28. www.livemint.com/2011/09/28230524/Foreign-law-firms8217-entry.html.

Keleman, R. Daniel and Eric C. Sibbitt. 2002. "The Americanization of Japanese Law." *University of Pennsylvania Journal of International Economic Law* 23 (2): 269–323.

Kim, Hyung Tae. 2006. "Legal Market Liberalization in South Korea: Preparations for Change." *Pacific Rim Law and Policy Journal* 15 (1): 199–231.

Koppel, Nathan. 2011. "India Considers Opening Its Doors to U.K. Law Firms." *Wall Street Journal* (law blog), September 27. www.blogs.wsj.com/law/2011/09/27/india-considers-opening-its-doors-to-u-k-law-firms/.

Krishnan, Jayanth K. 2010a. "Globetrotting Law Firms." *Georgetown Journal of Legal Ethics* 23 (1): 57–102

2010b. "The Joint Law Venture: A Pilot Study." *Berkeley Journal of International Law* 28 (2): 431–461.

Lawyer. 2011. "Ashurst Seals Best-Friends Deal with India Law Partners," July 15. www.thelawyer.com/ashurst-seals-best-friends-deal-with-india-law-partners/1008640.article.

Lin, Anthony. 2010. "Indian Lawyers Group Seeks to Prohibit Activities of Foreign Law Firms." *American Lawyer Daily*, March 24. www.amlawdaily.typepad.com/amlawdaily/2010/03/madras.html.

Liu, Sida. 2008. "Globalization as Boundary-Blurring: International and Local Law Firms in China's Corporate Law Market." *Law and Society Review* 42 (4): 771–804.

Luthra, Rajiv. 2007. "Level the Playing Field." In "Lowering the Bar." Ben Frumin. *India Business Legal Journal*: 17–18. www.indilaw.com/pdfs/Is%20India%20ready%20for%20foreign%20lawyers.pdf.

Globalizing Legal Education in India: Issues and Perspectives (on file on record).

Machado, José Maurício and Renata Almeida Pisaneschi. 2010. "Foreign Law Firms' Operation in Brazil." Law.com. www.law.com/jsp/law/LawArticleFriendly.jsp?id=1202473434702.

Martin, Eric L. 2007. "Liberalization and Cravathism: How Liberalization Triggered the Reorganization of the Legal Profession in Germany and Japan." *Stanford Journal of International Law* 43 (1): 169–199.

McEwan, Dale. 2011. "Bumpy Road to Rio." *Lawyer*, October 10. www.thelawyer.com/bumpy-road-to-rio/1009682.article.

Meherally, Almas. 2009. "Foreign Law Firms Barred from Country." *Economic Times*, December 17. www.articles.economictimes.indiatimes.com/2009–12–17/news/27646066_1_foreign-law-firms-liaison-offices-clifford-chance.

Moore, James C. 2007. "Economic Globalization and Its Impact Upon the Legal Profession." *New York State Bar Journal* 79 (1): 35–39.

Nath, Shloka. 2010. "Unbinding Indian Law." *Forbes India*, August 27. www.forbesindia.com/article/what-if/unbinding-indian-law/16352/1?id=16352&pg=1#ixzz1dRX2FuZQ.

Natrajan, Vinaya. 2009. "Looking Past the Hype: Lawyers Collective v. Chadbourne, Ashurst and White & Case." Bar and Bench, December 17. www.barandbench.com/brief/3/402/looking-past-the-hype-lawyers-collective-v-chadbourne-ashurst-and-white-case.

People's Daily. 2011. "Singapore May Ease Rules on Foreign Law Firms," March 10. www.english.peopledaily.com.cn/90001/90777/90851/7314336.html.

Press Trust of India. 2011. "Government Indicates It Will 'Fast Track' Decision on Foreign Law Firms." *Economic Times*, September 26. www.articles.economictimes.indiatimes.com/2011–09–26/news/30204552_1_foreign-law-firms-legal-firms-indian-legal-fraternity.

Rajah Committee. 2007. "Report of the Committee to Develop the Singapore Legal Sector, 7.44–7.52, September 27.

Ring, Suzi. 2010. "Ashurst Shuts India Liaison Office as Court Rules Against Foreign Firms." *Legal Week*. www.legalweek.com/legal-week/news/1592834/ashurst-shuts-india-liaison-office-court-rules-foreign-firms.

RSG Consulting. 2010. "Top 40 Indian Law Firms." www.rsg-india.com/rankings.

Russell, George W. 2010. "The New Legal Architects." *India Business Law Journal*, June: 35. www.indilaw.com/pdfs/Top%20foreign%20law%20firms.pdf.

Shamdasani, Ajay. 2010. "What Now for Foreign Law Firms?" *India Business Law Journal*, February: 29.

Shanghai Bar Association. 2005. "Notification of Legal Services Risks, No. 1." (on file with author).

Shanghai Lawyers Association. 2006. "The Situation of Illegal Business Activities Practiced by the Foreign Law Firms in Shanghai Is Severe: The Foreign Law Services Market Needs Regulating" (news brief no. 9/150), April 17.

Shankar, Gitanjali and Amba Uttara Kak. 2010. "Litigation Versus Non-Litigation: 'Practice of Law' under the Advocates Act." *NUJS Law Review* 3 (3): 300–308.

Shroff, Cyril. 2007. "Deregulating India's Legal Market." *Business Standard*, November 1. www.business-standard.com/india/news/cyril-shroff-deregulating-india%60s-legal-market/302899/.

Singh, Aditya. 2011. Reply to Right to Information Petition filed by author, Ministry of Law and Justice, Department of Legal Affairs – Implementation Cell, August 10.

Struble, Erich. 2009. "Gaiben & Bengoshi LLP: Cross-Border Legal Practice in Japan." *Journal of the Professional Lawyer* 9: 111–118.

Terry, Laurel S. 2008. "The Legal World Is Flat: Globalization and Its Effect on Lawyers Practicing in Non-Global Law Firms." *Northwestern Journal of International Law and Business* 28 (3): 527–560.

Vena, Chris. 2011. "More Than Best Friends: Expansion of Global Law Firms into the Indian Legal Market." *Northwestern Journal of International Law and Business* 31 (1): 195–223.

Vasani, Bharat. 2007. Time To Open Up: Indian Bar Associations And Law Firms Are Fighting Over Deregulation, But Everyone, Local And International Firms Alike, Can Benefit." *International Financial Law Review*, 26 (5): 14–17.

Worth, S. M. 2004. "The Transnational Practice of Law: Staggering Growth in Spite of Economic and Regulatory Barriers to Entry." *Gonzaga Journal of International Law* 7 (1): 1–36.

12

Festina Lente or Disguised Protectionism: Monopoly and Competition in the Indian Legal Profession

Rahul Singh

I. INTRODUCTION

India has come a long way since its leading lawyers pioneered independence from British colonialism in 1947. Compared with their role in the struggle for political freedom, lawyers played a limited role in the 1991 economic reforms, which initiated the dismantling of the Indian brand of socialism (Das 2002). The 1991 reforms are sometimes regarded as India's second independence leading to economic freedom. Perhaps owing to the lawyers' limited role in India's second independence, the legal profession has largely remained insulated from the process of deregulation initiated post-1991.

In spite of this insularity, the impact of globalization on the Indian legal profession, nevertheless, is inevitable. Globalization portends challenges as well as opportunities for the legal profession. While India seeks accelerated economic growth to lift millions above poverty, legal institutions strive toward the delivery of just, fair, and efficient dispute resolution. This paper will focus on the regulation of the Indian legal profession and its implications upon the entry of foreign law firms. The paper posits that although the Indian legal profession is ostensibly protectionist, owing to multifarious "push" (external) and "pull" (internal) factors, it has been taking baby steps toward liberalization, such as with the entry of foreign law firms.

Since the current debate on the entry of foreign law firms has unnecessarily generated more heat than light, this paper critically surveys the relevant legislations. A closer scrutiny of the Advocates Act of 1961 – the fundamental legislation governing the Indian legal profession – indicates little regulatory barriers for the entry of foreign law firms on a reciprocal basis.

Further, the paper analyzes the legislative provisions and the precedents emanating from the Supreme Court of India and the high courts. The paper takes into account certain international instances, such as that of the

South African Competition Commission's decision regarding advertising by lawyers.

To be sure, the legal profession's lethargy toward liberalization has costs associated with it. This paper, however, considers it beyond its scope to undertake a cost-benefit analysis or to analyze the pros and cons of the entry of foreign law firms.

Structurally, the paper is divided into several parts. Part II deals with the advent of the Advocates Act and the Indian legal profession's diffident approach toward liberalization. It enumerates the position of the Bar Council of India, state bar councils, Society of Indian Law Firms, and Bombay High Court. Part III builds upon part II and catalogues the multifarious "push" and "pull" factors in the liberalization. Both international and domestic factors have been accounted for. Part IV analyzes the baby steps toward the liberalization of the Indian legal profession. Toward this endeavor, the inception of the common market for legal professionals, the Bar Council of India's monopoly, the initiation of a pan-India bar examination, the creation of limited liability partnerships, the regulation of advertisements, and the infusion of a modicum of competition through a Madras High Court judgment have been assessed. Part V summarizes the concluding observations.

II. THE LEGAL PROFESSION'S INCIPIENT DIFFIDENCE AND THE BUMPY ROAD TO LIBERALIZATION

Perhaps the most germane framework to appreciate the contradictory interpretations of the Advocates Act is to recognize the underlying incongruence in philosophy. The Advocates Act is of 1961 vintage, and the underlying philosophy of the legislation is perhaps far removed from the idea of globalization.

A. *The Advent of the Advocates Act*

At the dawn of Independence, the overriding concerns of the freedom fighters were to preserve the "idea of India" and engender unity among Indians.[1] The inarticulate major premise was that the lack of unity was responsible for the loss of freedom. Similar concerns about fostering unity among the legal profession led to the formation of the All-India Bar Committee in 1953. Taking into account the recommendations of the All-India Bar Committee and the Law Commission of India report on the reform of judicial administration, the purpose of the Advocates Act was stated to be:

- The establishment of an All-India Bar Council and a common roll of advocates, and advocates on the common roll having a right to practice in any part of the country and in any court, including the Supreme Court

- The integration of the bar into a single class of legal practitioners known as advocates
- The prescription of a uniform qualification for the admission of persons to be advocates
- The division of advocates into senior advocates and other advocates based on merit
- The creation of autonomous bar councils, one for the whole of India and one for each state

Thus, the overarching objectives of the Advocates Act were democracy, meritocracy, unification/integration, and uniformity (Advocates Act, 1961, §4(1), §16(1), §16(2)). Interestingly, in its zeal for the infusion of uniformity, the Advocates Act appeared to be quite concerned about the varying terms for legal professionals and sought to unify the profession under the single title of "advocates."[2] The concern about the multifarious names is perhaps redolent of the notions of unity/disunity at the dawn of Independence.

In accordance with these objectives, the Advocates Act repealed the colonial Indian Bar Councils Act, 1926 (1926 Act). Contrary to the Advocates Act, the 1926 Act was understood to have promoted stratification (§3(1)) and nonuniformity (§8(2)) among the legal profession.

This zeal for the integration of the legal profession masked the organized profession's incipient diffidence emanating from the colonial history. Of course, this diffidence was contrary to Mahatma Gandhi's statement: "I do not want to stay in a house with all its windows and doors shut. I want a house with all its windows and doors open, where the cultural breezes of all lands and nations blow through my house. But I refuse to be blown off my feet by any."

In spite of the passage of half a century since the advent of the Advocates Act, the remnants of the xenophobia, however, continue in the form of opposition to the entry of foreign law firms. Is this xenophobia an attempt toward *festina lente* (Latin for "hastening slowly"), or is it a disguised form of protectionism? To explore this query, a survey of the various stakeholders of the legal profession and their respective responses to the question of the entry of foreign law firms is set out below.

1. The Bar Council of India

Although the Bar Council of India has seldom articulated the rationale behind its opposition to the entry of foreign law firms, it has been consistent in its opposition. For instance, the affidavit filed by the Bar Council of India in *A. K. Balaji v. The Government of India* (2010), represented by its Secretary to Government, Law Department (A. K. Balaji), categorically stated that foreign lawyers not enrolled as advocates under the Advocates Act are not entitled to practice law (including foreign law) in India (A. K. Balaji 2010). Similarly, in the 1995 case of *Lawyers Collective v. Bar Council of India*, the Bar Council of India had opposed the entry of foreign law firms (Lawyers Collective 1995).

2. State Bar Councils

Similar to the Bar Council of India, the state bar councils, too, haven't really explained their opposition to the entry of foreign law firms in spite of its consistency. For instance, in a joint resolution passed with the Bar Council of India at Kochi on November 17–18, 2007, the unanimous resolution stated:

> This joint consultative conference of the Bar Council of India and the Chairmen, Vice-Chairmen and Chairmen, Executive Committee of all State Bar Councils in India hereby unanimously resolve to support and affirm the resolution of the Bar Council of India No. 17/2006 dated 12.02.2006 and further resolve to request the Government of India not *to open up Indian legal profession to foreign lawyers or foreign law firms at this juncture* and not to permit the entry of foreign lawyers or foreign law firms into India for function or practice in any form in India as advocates, lawyers or solicitors.
>
> (emphasis added)

Such positions of the Bar Council of India and the state bar councils have done little to explain the philosophy behind the stand they have taken. What is the real reason behind the opposition by the Bar Council of India and the state bar councils? For instance, do the Bar Council of India and state bar councils agree with the stand adopted by the Society of Indian Law Firms?

3. The Society of Indian Law Firms

The Society of Indian Law Firms (SILF) is a club of Big Law and is quite articulately opposed to the entry of foreign law firms. The rent-seeking behavior of the SILF is based on the calculation that the longer it delays the inevitable, the more profitable it will be. To be sure, the SILF takes a mutually contradictory stance on the entry of foreign law firms with arguments ranging from the entry being barred by law to the relative unpreparedness of domestic law firms to compete with their foreign counterparts (Bhasin 2011). At times, powerful members such as Amarchand & Mangaldas have suggested the China model with a bar on foreign law firms to hire Indian lawyers.

4. *The* Lawyers Collective *Court*

The Indian judiciary has also been opposed to the entry of foreign law firms. The *Lawyers Collective* case, although initiated back in 1995, was left to linger for about fifteen years without any clarity on either the decision or the interim order. Indeed, one of the parties in the *Lawyers Collective* case – White & Case – was forced to approach the Supreme Court of India to seek clarity on the nature of the interim order.

In late 2009 the Bombay High Court, in the *Lawyers Collective* case (1995), decided to expansively interpret the recurring phrase "practice the profession of law" under the Advocates Act.[3] The *Lawyers Collective* case also held that both litigious (within the courtroom) and nonlitigious (without the courtroom) work will constitute the practice of the profession of law (Lawyers Collective 1995, 60). The dichotomy between litigious and nonlitigious was as follows: "while rendering of legal assistance by acting, appearing, and pleading on behalf of the client before a court or authority is litigious, rendering of legal assistance through drafting documents, advising clients, and formulation of opinions was considered nonlitigious" (Lawyers Collective 1995, 3).

The *Lawyers Collective* court was concerned about a fact-situation where foreign law firms, such as White & Case, Chadbourne, and Ashurst, had set up non-fee-earning liaison offices in India to coordinate with clients within India and abroad. One of the questions before the Bombay High Court was whether the permission granted by India's Federal Reserve – the Reserve Bank of India, entrusted with the task of managing foreign exchange – to set up a liaison office was legally valid under the applicable foreign exchange laws.

The court answered this question in the negative on the grounds that the Reserve Bank of India, under the applicable foreign exchange laws, had the jurisdiction to permit the establishment of a branch office for carrying on "trading, commercial, or industrial" activities but not "professional" activities (Lawyers Collective 1995, 42). The court relied on a past Supreme Court precedent (*M.P. Electricity Board v. Shiv Narayan* 2005) to draw an artificial dichotomy between "business" and "professional" work and concluded that since the latter lacks "commercial" character, the Reserve Bank of India did not have the jurisdiction to grant permission for setting up the liaison office. The *Lawyers Collective* court, in the interest of judicial economy, could have stopped at this analysis and chosen not to address other issues.

However, the court expanded the scope of its inquiry and dealt with the question of whether liaison activities will constitute nonlitigious practice of the profession of law. The court answered this in the affirmative on the basis of the logic that the nature of activity carried on by a liaison office was the same as those of its head office, i.e., the practice of the profession of law. Accordingly, the *Lawyers Collective* court characterized the activities of the liaison offices as the nonlitigious limb of the practice of the profession of law. And since the liaison offices carried nonlitigious activities, they ought to have been subject to the regulatory framework of the Advocates Act. As the court wrote, " . . . it is evident that the liaison activities were nothing but practicing the profession of law in nonlitigious matters."

The approach of the *Lawyers Collective* court is political. Under the garb of interpreting the term "practice the profession of law," the court draws an artificial dichotomy first between litigious and nonlitigious practice, and second, between business and profession. Interestingly, the dichotomy is inconsistent, messy, patchy, and at times inchoate. For instance, the court characterizes the legal profession loftily as a "noble" profession but fails to address how liaison offices (which were run on a no-fee, no-profit basis) either were less than noble or were nonlitigious practice of the profession of law. As paragraph 2 of the *Lawyers Collective* case states:

> The Parliament has enacted the Advocates Act, 1961 to regulate the persons practicing the profession of law. To ensure the dignity and purity of the noble profession of law, the Act provides for establishment of the State Bar Councils and the Bar Council of India. The Bar Councils have been created at the state level and also at the central level not only to protect the rights, interests and privileges of its members but also to protect the interest of the general public by ensuring them that the professionals rendering the legal services maintain high and noble traditions of the profession."
>
> (Lawyers Collective 1995, 2; emphasis added)

Further, the reliance upon the Supreme Court precedent in the *M.P. Electricity Board* case to draw the distinction between business and profession is disingenuous. The *M.P. Electricity Board* was concerned about whether a lawyer running his office is liable to pay a commercial tariff for the usage of electricity or if he can continue to take advantage of the cheaper domestic tariff. Although the Supreme Court generally stated that there is a distinction between professional and commercial activity, it desisted from passing any final order due to a contrary precedent and merely referred the matter to a large bench for final decision making.

Such a political, inchoate approach of the *Lawyers Collective* court also glosses over other anomalies. First, the artificial dichotomy between litigious and nonlitigious does not address the problem of law professors acting as consultants to federal and state governments. Since the Bar Council of India's rules prohibit a person in full-time employment from being enrolled as an advocate, full-time law professors, while advising government, will be understood to be violating the Advocates Act. This problem is exacerbated because the law professors do not intend to enroll as an advocate, but they are barred by the Bar Council of India from doing so! Similar issues will arise for in-house counsels as well since they are required to suspend their license to practice.

To be sure, the *Lawyers Collective* court manages to skirt these issues as they were not raised by counsels. However, the counsel for the government of India did raise the issue about bureaucrats advising government. Curiously, the court addressed the anomaly through a dubious suggestion that the bureaucrat advising the government is answerable to his superiors (Lawyers Collective 1995, 55). If supervision were an issue, it is unclear why liaison offices of foreign firms being under the supervision of their head offices abroad were not considered adequate.

Furthermore, the *Lawyers Collective* court not only managed to skirt logical problems with the holding but also ignored significant committee reports. For instance, it is unclear why the court chose to ignore the report of a committee set up under the stewardship of Justice B. P. Jeevan Reddy, former judge of the Supreme Court, in 1999, which had suggested that the nonlitigious matters shall be carved out from the framework of the Advocates Act. Interestingly, in an ironic twist to the tale, the *Lawyers Collective* court chastised the government of India for being a sitting duck for "more than fifteen years" on the issue of the entry of foreign law firms but chose to keep quiet about its own delay (Lawyers Collective 1995, 59).

In spite of the role played by the Bombay High Court in installing a modicum of the presence of foreign law firms in India, there have been several "push" and "pull" factors responsible for the baby steps toward the liberalization of the legal profession.

III. THE "PUSH" AND "PULL" FACTORS

The "push" and "pull" factors impacting the Indian legal profession are external as well as internal. While international factors are largely working toward attaining liberalization of the legal professions, certain domestic stakeholders, particularly government departments (without seeking any coordination with bar councils), are assisting the international stakeholders. The shortsighted approach of the government, however, has sometimes created more problems than solutions.

A. *International Factors*

The most notable international factor that has provided fillip to the liberalization of the legal profession is the World Trade Organization (WTO). Interestingly, India has been among the founding members of both the General Agreement on Tariffs and Trade (GATT) in 1947 as well as the WTO in 1995. The focus of the GATT and the WTO – trade in goods – instantiates the insignificance of trade in services at the time of the negotiation of the GATT/WTO framework.[4]

While neither the GATT nor the WTO initially had legal services within their ambit, the increasing significance of the legal profession in a globalized world is evident from the ambitious agenda of the General Agreement on Trade in Services (GATS). The WTO envisages a "single package" offer for the GATT, the Trade-Related Aspects of Intellectual Property Rights (TRIPS), and the Dispute Settlement Body (DSB). Under this single-package approach it is not possible for member countries to choose à la carte. However, the GATS is not a part of the single-package offer, and it is possible for member countries to pick and choose. For instance, India has not yet signed an agreement on public procurement. Under the GATT, legal services are one of the areas of discussion, but at the WTO, India has, until now, kept its cards too close to its chest. As discussed below, domestically the Ministry of Commerce and other stakeholders have been pushing for the liberalization of the legal profession.

B. *Domestic Factors*

There are several domestic stakeholders – government and private players – who have been at the forefront of the push for the liberalization of the legal profession.

1. Ministries and Departments of Government

While ostensibly reluctant during the WTO negotiations, domestically the Ministry of Commerce – the administrative ministry responsible for international trade – has been pushing for the liberalization of the legal profession. To provide structure to such a liberalization program, the Ministry of Commerce has created bilateral joint committees with law firm representatives from the United States and the United Kingdom. The Indian representatives consist of the Bar Council of India and the law firms.[5] The Bar Council of India has, however, consistently demanded a larger share in representation through nominees of the state bar councils.

The Ministry of Commerce has shown little enthusiasm for nominating members from the state bar councils. The snail's progress on the Bar Council of India's demands and, at times, the hostile attitude toward the Bar Council of India has ensured that the Ministry of Commerce has not been able to get the Bar Council of India onboard.

In addition, the Ministry of Law and Justice has made several attempts to rein in the Bar Council of India. Initially, the Ministry of Law and Justice sought to bring the Bar Council of India under its administrative control.[6] When the ministry's efforts at mollycoddling the Bar Council of India failed, it launched a sustained campaign to emasculate the powers of the Bar Council of India.[7] Such proposals emanating from the Ministry of Commerce and the Ministry of Law and Justice have engendered distrust in the minds of the Bar Council of India.

Indeed, the Bar Council of India's opposition to the liberalization of the legal profession is most likely not because of any ideological difference of opinion but because of the vitriolic approach of the government ministries against the Bar Council of India. The Bar Council of India's reservations against the liberalization of the profession have been accentuated due to the hostile attitude of the Ministry of Human Resources Development – the ministry responsible for education – in taking away the power of regulation of legal education through the National Commission for Higher Education and Research Bill, 2010.[8] The government's proposal to exclude the Medical Council of India from the ambit of the bill has added fuel to the fire of the Bar Council of India's suspicion of the government's motives.

2. Private Players

Two significant stakeholders from the private sector have added to the "push" for the liberalization of the legal profession. First, the rising LPO companies have raised the income level of law graduates from tier two and tier three law schools who previously did not have access to the same opportunities as the premier national law school graduates. Second, since early 2000 UK-based law firms have recruited graduates from the National Law School, Bangalore (and later, other law schools) at relatively high salaries (compared to the salary level then prevalent in India). The beneficiaries of such newfound opportunities have been vocal on the Internet to permit liberalization of the legal profession.[9]

Perhaps owing to the push from these private players, coupled with the Bar Council of India's lack of overarching, ideology-based opposition, India has been taking baby steps toward the liberalization of the legal profession. The baby steps can be traced back to the creation of the common market for legal professionals envisaged through the Advocates Act way back in 1961 but achieved only recently.

IV. THE BABY STEPS

India's penchant for taking baby steps toward the liberalization of the legal profession is not new. As discussed further, in spite of the constitutional and legal mandate for a common market for legal professionals, the idea of a pan-India legal professional market has taken shape only recently. Concomitantly, other significant reforms such as the introduction of a pan-India bar examination and liberalization of law firm partnership have also taken place.

A. *Inception of the "Common Market"*

The Constitution of India came into force on January 26, 1950. Besides engendering the idea of a secular, democratic, and rule of law–based India, it promised to usher in the right of lawyers to move throughout the territory of India and to practice any profession.

The constitutional promise of the right to reside in any part of India and practice one's profession was especially critical for the legal profession. The Indian Bar Councils Act, 1926 had provided for a fragmented market for lawyers. The constitutional promise of the "common market" was carried out through the Advocates Act, which repealed the Indian Bar Councils Act, 1926. §30 of the Advocates Act mandates,

> Subject to the provisions of this Act, every Advocate whose name is entered in the State roll shall be entitled as of right to practice throughout the territories to which this Act extends: (i) in all courts including the Supreme Court; (ii) before any tribunal or person legally authorized to take evidence; and (iii) before any other authority or person before whom such advocate is by or under any law for the time being in force entitled to practice"
>
> (Advocates Act, 1961, §30; emphasis added).

The mandate for the creation of a common market under the Advocates Act was, however, thwarted by the executive by its refusal to notify §30, which entitles legal professionals to practice in any court throughout the territory of India.[10]

The Advocates Act received the president's assent on May 19, 1961. Twenty-seven years later, in the case of *Aeltemesh Rein*, the Supreme Court of India was approached for the enforcement of §30 mandating common market (Aeltemesh Rein, *Advocate Supreme Court of India v. Union of India* 1988). The

Supreme Court was evidently perturbed about the absence of common market through the nonenforcement of §30. The court stated:

> ... We have travelled a long distance from the days when it was considered that the appearance of a lawyer on one side would adversely affect the interests of the parties on the other side. The Legal Aid and Advice Boards, which are functioning in different States, can now be approached by people belonging to weaker sections, such as Scheduled Castes, Scheduled Tribes, women, laborers etc. for legal assistance and for providing the services of competent lawyers to appear on their behalf before the courts and tribunals in which they have cases. In these circumstances prima facie there appears to be now no justification for not bringing into force Section 30 of the [Advocates] Act.
>
> (Aeltemesh Rein 1988, 30; emphasis supplied)

Nevertheless, the *Aeltemesh Rein* court consisted of two judges and was bound by the decision of the Constitution Bench (five judges) in *A. K. Roy v. Union of India* (A. K. Roy 1982). In *A. K. Roy*, the petitioner – A. K. Roy – was a communist leader and was detained under preventive detention laws. The *A. K. Roy* court was concerned about the reforms in preventive detention laws that were passed by Parliament but not notified by the executive. The court, however, relied upon the doctrine of "separation of powers" and refused to issue the writ of mandamus.

Interestingly, the *Aeltemesh Rein* court, even though it was bound by the holding in the *A. K. Roy* case, chose to distinguish the *A. K. Roy* case and suggested that it is not barred from issuing a writ of mandamus to the central government to "consider" whether enforcement of §30 will be appropriate. The court fixed a deadline of six months for the federal government.

Notwithstanding the grandstanding of the Supreme Court, there was little action from the central government in spite of the writ of mandamus issued in the *Aeltemesh Rein* case. Indeed, an advocate approached the Allahabad High Court in 2010 citing government's inaction on the holding in the *Aeltemesh Rein* case as Rein was being prohibited from practicing in courts in Uttar Pradesh despite his enrollment in Delhi (*Rahul Singh v. Union of India* 2010). The Allahabad High Court decided to exercise judicial economy and suggested that an alternative efficacious remedy in the form of contempt of court petition may be filed at the Supreme Court.

It is interesting to note that though the central government paid little heed to the six-month deadline fixed in the *Aeltemesh Rein* case, in the midst of the fracas with the Bar Council of India, it suddenly decided to notify §30 in June 2011. However, the trust deficit between the Bar Council of India and the ministry has ensured that the dream of common market under §30 is back to square one. The Bar Council of India continues to require advocates to file an application for transfer, increasing the transaction costs for legal professionals to practice within the territory of India.

B. *The Bar Council of India's Monopoly*

The Bar Council of India's monopoly right over regulation of advocates and consequent monopoly of the advocates to practice the profession of law in India stems from the historic reality of the stratification of the Indian legal profession. The edifice of this monopoly is based upon the statutory mandate contained in the triumvirate of §29, §2(1)(a), and §33 of the Advocates Act. §29 ensures that no one but advocates can practice the profession of law. §2(1)(a) defines the term *advocate* to mean a person whose name is found in the rolls maintained by the state bar councils. §33 embellishes the mandate contained in §29 read with §2(1)(a) by imposing an embargo on the practice of the profession of law without enrollment.

In spite of the triumvirate of §29, §2(1)(a), and §33, it will be a tremendous leap in logic to conclude that there is any regulatory barrier to the entry of foreign law firms within the paradigm of the Advocates Act. Indeed, the qualification for enrollment of a person as an advocate on the rolls of the State Bar Council envisages the possibility of enrollment of foreign nationals on the basis of the principle of reciprocity. The principle of reciprocity involves a "tit for tat" approach and envisages that citizens of those countries will be barred from being advocates where Indian legal professionals are not permitted to practice the profession of law.

The Bar Council of India, nevertheless, has a specific legislative mandate to permit foreign nationals to practice the profession of law in India. The Advocates Act states, "Subject to the provisions of sub-section (1), the Bar Council of India may prescribe the conditions, if any, subject to which foreign qualifications in law obtained by persons other than citizens of India shall be recognized for the purpose of admission as an advocate under this Act" (Advocate Act 1961, §49(2)). Besides the broad legislative mandate, there are specific rule-making powers of the Bar Council of India for recognizing foreign nationals as advocates.

The legislative scheme of the Advocates Act suggests cooperation between the central government and the Bar Council of India for the purpose of recognizing foreign nationals as advocates. Indeed, the second proviso to §49(1) states that the Bar Council of India's rule-making powers for foreign national advocates is subject to approval of the central government. Contrary to the statutory scheme, there has been no such cooperation between the central government and the Bar Council of India to enable the entry of foreign law firms or lawyers. It seems that the central government's endeavors of emasculating its powers has ensured the Bar Council of India's inertia on foreign nationals as advocates.

Interestingly, although the Bar Council of India has conveniently ignored its legislative mandate and specific rule-making powers to admit foreign advocates, it has chosen to initiate a pan-India bar examination even in the absence of a legislative mandate or rule-making powers. This duality in the Bar Council of India's approach reflects the politics involved in the liberalization of the legal profession.

C. *The Advent of the Pan-India Bar Examination*

The Bar Council of India's role in the initiation of a pan-India bar examination is fascinating not in the least because it was done in the absence of a legislative mandate or specific rule-making powers. The pan-India bar examination was introduced in spite of a trenchant opposition from the state bar councils.

The official justification of the Bar Council of India has been based on the Supreme Court's order in *Bar Council of India v. Bonnie Foi Law College* (2008). A close scrutiny of the *Bonnie Foi* case, however, indicates that reliance upon the Supreme Court order was a smokescreen. First, the order does not categorically mandate the Bar Council of India to initiate the pan-India bar examination. It merely notes that the Solicitor General of India has voluntarily undertaken to conceptualize a pan-India bar examination. Secondly, the *Bonnie Foi* court consisted of two judges and faced a coordinate bench's decision in *V. Sudeer v. Bar Council of India* (1999), which had held against a bar examination. If the *Bonnie Foi* case disagreed with the *V. Sudeer* case, it ought to have referred the matter to a higher bench.

Although the introduction of a pan-India bar examination may have been highly desirable, the manner in which the Bar Council of India went about achieving its aim is of dubious legal validity (Nariman 2010). The absence of legal validity may be better understood based upon a deeper analysis of the *V. Sudeer case*, which deals with the fact situation of an earlier attempt by the Bar Council of India to introduce a qualifying bar examination.

The *V. Sudeer* case notes that the Bar Council of India and state bar councils, at the early stages of implementation of the Advocates Act, used to have the mandate of a qualifying bar examination (V. Sudeer 1999, 8). Such authority of the Bar Council of India emanated from a legislative mandate, specific rule-making powers, and a concomitant power of the central government to exempt certain candidates from the requirement of the bar examination.

The *V. Sudeer* court notes that the earlier-referenced powers of the Bar Council of India and state bar councils were repealed through an amendment of the Advocates Act in 1973 (V. Sudeer 1999, 10). Indeed, the deletion of the requirement for the bar examination was carried at the request of the Bar Council of India due to the introduction of a three-year graduate program (ibid.). Presumably, due to an inadvertent legislative oversight, vestigial remains of the legislative mandate for a bar examination are on the statute in the form of central government's power to exempt a category of persons from undergoing the examination (Advocates Act, 1961, §49A (2)).

The Bar Council of India's powers to conduct an examination were categorically taken away by Parliament through an amendment. Interestingly, this was carried out at the specific request of the Bar Council of India. Through a disingenuous distinction of the *V. Sudeer* case on facts as being confined to only "preenrollment" examination and not "postenrollment" examination, the Bar Council of India has reintroduced the idea of a bar examination through the back door. Such an attempt by the Bar Council of India also suffers from a democracy/legitimacy deficit: unlike the central government's rules, the rules formulated by the Bar Council of India are not mandated to be placed before Parliament for ex-post-approval, per §49A(5) of the Advocates Act.

This democratic deficit could have been easily avoided if the Bar Council of India, for the purpose of the introduction of the bar examination, had worked with central government. Since central government had publicly supported the idea of a bar examination, there was little likelihood of central government's noncooperation. The rationale behind the Bar Council of India's reluctance in taking the central government onboard remains unclear.

In any event, the Bar Council of India's reliance upon the *Bonnie Foi* case (while distinguishing the *V. Sudeer* case on facts) for its mandate to conduct the bar examination is inappropriate. The *Bonnie Foi* court did not analyze the *V. Sudeer* case, and hence the *Bonnie Foi* case is per incuriam and lacks any binding value. This lack of binding value of the *Bonnie Foi* case, however, hasn't come in the way of the Supreme Court's general approval of the bar examination, and other benches of the court have unequivocally refused to interfere with the conduct of the bar examination (Chauhan 2010).

Although the idea of a pan-India bar examination may have been introduced to score brownie points over the central government, an unintended consequence has been leveling the playing field between Indian advocates and foreign lawyers.[11] From this perspective, the introduction of the bar examination may be understood as a baby step toward leveling the playing field for the reciprocity envisaged under the Advocates Act. An endeavor toward leveling the playing field is also evident from other steps taken by the central government – reforms of law firm partnerships and a modicum of progress on advertisements.

D. *The Limited Liability Partnership Act, 2008*

One of the arguments made by Indian Big Law against the liberalization of the legal profession has been based on the argument of the non-level-playing field. The argument goes thus: unlike foreign law firms, Indian law firms are constrained at both ends – in raising capital, due to a ceiling of twenty partners and an unlimited personal liability – envisaged under the [Indian] Partnership Act, 1932 (Economist 2010).

As a response to this contention, the central government has notified the Limited Liability Partnership (LLP) Act, 2008 on March 31, 2009. Unlike the Indian Partnership Act, 1932, the LLP Act does not place any fetters on raising capital (through the number of partners) and has done away with the concept of unlimited personal liability.

Since its inception, very few law firms have utilized the LLP Act. Interestingly, most Big Law have shied away from converting to the LLP form. In addition, some who have tried to convert to the LLP structure have faced dubious letters from the State Bar Council of Delhi questioning whether law firms are permitted to convert to the LLP structure, such as with Khaitain & Co. (Ganz 2011).The letter from the State Bar Council of Delhi, incidentally, appears to be mischievous as the Bar Council of India has, until now, remained neutral and neither supported nor opposed the LLP Act (Ganz 2010).

E. *Regulating Advertisements*

Another complaint related to domestic constraints leading to non-level-playing is the bar on advertisement (Economist 2010). The rationale behind this prohibition is the dubious dichotomy between "business" and "profession" – while the former is understood as part of trade and commerce, the latter is expected to uphold lofty ideals. Indian lawyers advertising themselves is perceived to be against the profession's dignity.

Some of the prohibition is changing. First, law firms have been permitted to maintain a website with basic, minimal contents. Second, many Indian law firms do heavily advertise in journals that predominantly cater to the overseas market (Ganz 2013). Some have devised ingenious ways to beat the regulation by focusing on the creation of knowledge-based research contents, such as the law firm Nishith Desai Associates. In theory, the Bar Council of India may haul up the law firms for crossing the (murky) lines. In practice, the Bar Council of India lacks the wherewithal to regulate all advertisements and determine which ones cross the limits and which ones don't. As expected, there are no clear rules on the regulation of advertising.

As regulations on advertisements get lax, other questions are bound to crop up. Will relaxation of advertisement mean that merely the well-heeled lawyers will be able to take advantage? The answer is maybe, but the well-heeled ones boast a wide network anyway. Establishing the bright line rules on acceptable advertising is not going to be an easy task.

In addition, there is yet another significant development of note. India has adopted a new competition law – the Competition Act, 2002 – replacing the older Monopolies and Restrictive Trade Practices Act, 1969. Though the Competition Act received presidential assent on January 13, 2003, it was notified to be partially enforced from May 20, 2009. The nascent Competition Commission of India (CCI) is on a steep learning curve working against cartels, bid riggers, and abusers of dominance.

At this stage of its development, the CCI usually looks at precedents from other jurisdictions such as (mostly) the United States, the European Union, and (sometimes) Australia and South Africa. Interestingly, in a recent case on lawyers' advertising, the South African Competition Commission has held that restricting lawyers' advertising is against "consumer interest" (Lawyers Weekly 2011).

Similarly, to the South African competition law, there is no exception for lawyers under the [Indian] Competition Act. Further, the CCI has a sweepingly broad mandate to deal with not only contentious and noncontentious matters but also to advise the government on the formulation of competition policy, as laid down in §49(3) of the Competition Act. In addition, for the promotion of competition policy, the central government has also announced the formulation of a national competition policy. It is likely that the restriction on lawyers' advertising will attract the attention of competition policy enforcement.

F. *The* A. K. Balaji *case's Judgment and Infusion of Competition*

We have seen that the Bombay High Court in the *Lawyers Collective* judgment played a spoiler in the liberalization of the Indian legal profession. The Madras High Court in the *A. K. Balaji* case has, however, attempted to salvage the damage inflicted upon the liberalization of the legal profession and infused the much-needed dose of competition in the sector.

Interestingly, the Madras High Court in the *A. K. Balaji* case took note of the holding in the *Lawyers Collective* case and distinguished it on facts. Steering clear of the dubious dichotomy between "litigious" and "nonlitigious" practice, on the one hand, and between "business" and "profession" on the other, the *A. K. Balaji* court formulated the question narrowly: whether the "fly in and fly out" practice of the profession of (foreign) law by foreign nationals will be subject to the regulatory framework of the Advocates Act:

> However, the issue for consideration before this Court is as to whether a foreign law firm, without establishing any liaison office in India visiting India for the purpose of offering legal advice to their clients in India on foreign law, is prohibited under the provisions of the Advocates Act. In other words, the issue here is, whether a foreign lawyer visiting India for a temporary period to advise his client on foreign law can be barred under the provisions of the Advocates Act. This issue was neither raised nor answered by the Bombay High Court in the [*Lawyers Collective*] judgment.
>
> (Advocates Act, 1961, 45)

The *A. K. Balaji* case answered this in the negative, i.e., such practice would be outside the regulatory domain of the Advocates Act (A. K. Balaji 2010). It is noteworthy that the A. K. Balaji court shied away from formulating the legal question in terms of reciprocity, i.e., when Indian advocates are permitted to carry on "fly in and fly out" practice, on what grounds could one discriminate against the foreign lawyers?

Perhaps the reason behind the pragmatic approach of the refusal to characterize the legal question in terms of reciprocity is the political nature of the problem. This did not deter the *A. K. Balaji* court from basing its reasoning upon policy analysis of the promotion of international commercial arbitration in India: ". . . to advocate a proposition that foreign lawyers or foreign law firms cannot come to India to advise their clients on foreign law would be a far-fetched and dangerous proposition and in our opinion, would be a step backward, when India is becoming a preferred seat for arbitration in International Commercial Arbitrations" (A. K. Balaji 2010, 57). For such reasoning based on policy, the *A. K. Balaji* court took shelter under the *Vodafone* decision delivered by the Supreme Court.

The *A. K. Balaji* court is pragmatic but leaves several critical questions unanswered. For instance, if by merely opening a liaison office, foreign law firms breach the Advocates Act mandate of the practice of the profession of law, what would be the status of websites exclusively catering to Indian markets? After all, it's nobody's case that in the increasingly globalized world one needs a physical office address to engage in a profession. Would permitting online liaison activities be permitted in spite of the holding in the *Lawyers Collective* case? Further, what will be the status of the "best friendship" arrangement several global law firms have in India? Will they be saved under the rubric of "fly in and fly out" practice, or will they open up a liaison office through the back door?

Fortunately, the A. K. *Balaji* court does not miss the opportunity to realign the terms of the debate toward the statutory framework under the Advocates Act, which permits the practice of the profession of law by foreign law firms. It relies upon the principle of reciprocity embodied under the triumvirate of §24(1)(a), §47(1), and §47(2), which have been explained earlier in this paper. Curiously, the court misses the opportunity to deal with §49(1)(e).

In addition, the court stops short of analyzing why the principle of reciprocity has been truncated to cover merely "fly in and fly out" practice. A critical analysis of the statutory framework would have been helpful at the Supreme Court stage. At the very least, the A. K. *Balaji* court has been successful in thwarting the interpretation that under the paradigm of the Advocates Act, it is impermissible for foreign law firms to practice foreign law in India. The A. K. *Balaji* case states: ". . . if an interpretation is given to prohibit practice of foreign law by foreign law firms within India, it would result in a manifestly absurd situation wherein only Indian citizens with Indian law degrees who are enrolled as an advocate under the Advocates Act could practice foreign law, when the fact remains that foreign laws are not taught at [the] graduate level in India law schools, except comparative law degree courses at the Master's level" (A. K. Balaji 2010, 60).

The government of India has, in the past, been criticized for failing to appeal the Bombay High Court's *Lawyers Collective* judgment in the Supreme Court. The relatively pragmatic outcome in the A. K. *Balaji* case has, however, faced an appeal in the Supreme Court as both Clifford Chance and the Bar Council of India have appealed the Madras High Court decision (Kanekal and Ganz 2012). This may be a useful opportunity for parties to deal with arguments comprehensively, and the apex will be forced to adjudicate on the matter. The conflict between the *Lawyers Collective* and A. K. *Balaji* cases will require the Supreme Court's intervention.

It would be naive to think that the deep-seated difference of opinion about the practice of the profession of law by foreign law firms could be settled by court judgments. Nevertheless, pragmatic decisions such as the Madras High Court in the A. K. *Balaji* case do contribute to the baby steps toward the liberalization of the Indian legal profession. Ultimately, such decisions of wide ramifications will always be subject to broader public scrutiny.

V. CONCLUSION

There seems to be the belief, at least among the Indian elite, that India's democracy is a drag. There appears to be a general distaste for the slow process emanating from India's noisy democracy. The Bar Council of India and the state bar councils are the epitome of India's boisterous democracy. The political tussle with the government departments indicates that the unelected yet indubitably powerful bureaucracy doesn't have any love lost for the democratically elected bar counselors.

Nevertheless, if the history of the liberalization of the legal profession is any indication, most liberalization has been a result of governmental efforts and not that of bar counselors. On the liberalization of the legal profession at the WTO level, India seems to be holding its cards too close to its chest. Crystal-ball gazing is made difficult because of India's penchant for taking baby steps toward the liberalization of the legal profession.

Two recent instances indicate contradictory signaling. On a positive note there are signs that with the change in federal government, there are green shoots of a movement toward the liberalization of the legal profession (Basu 2015). Such a move, if at all successful, would indicate that India has finally achieved the denouement of the baby steps toward a confident liberalization process.

Even so, contrary to the earlier narrative of the newfound confidence exhibited by the government, there appears to be indications of fragmentation of the common market mandate of the Advocates Act. In Chhattisgarh, an Indian province where the indigenous population is engaged in a legal tussle over myriad human rights abuse issues, there seems to be a move to ensure that only local lawyers represent the victims. Worryingly, the High Court of Chhattisgarh seems to be hand in glove in a move that is being enforced through some of the bar associations (which incidentally are not recognized by the Advocates Act). The statutorily recognized State Bar Council has maintained a conspicuous silence.

While the crusaders merely interested in the entry of foreign law firms may not notice, the regressive movement afoot at Chhattisgarh to limit the normative promise of the "common market" in terms of the Advocates Act will also have a bearing upon the liberalization of the legal profession.

It would be foolhardy to hope that the Supreme Court of India, while dealing with the A. K. *Balaji* appeal, would be in a position to settle the debate. The aspects of monopoly and competition in the Indian legal profession, as delineated in this paper, remain as much a political issue as a legal issue. And the Supreme Court could notoriously take years to hear an appeal and rule.

Perhaps history will be a better judge of whether India's seemingly slothful (and undoubtedly costly) baby steps toward liberalization of the legal profession were the result of a well-designed, deliberate attempt at *festina lente* or disguised protectionism.

This paper critically surveyed the applicable legislation and found little regulatory barrier for the liberalization of the Indian legal profession. Of course, players in the Indian legal market erect artificial barriers. This paper analyzed the legislative framework and precedents emanating from the judiciary and found that although the Indian legal profession is ostensibly protectionist, the multifarious "push" and "pull" factors do ensure baby steps toward liberalization.

Notes

1 This is the reason behind the Constitution of India's emphasis on a strong federal government.

2 For instance, §2(i) of the Advocates Act recognizes the substitutable terms of *advocate, vakil, pleader, muktar,* and *revenue agent* as the terms used to denote a legal practitioner (Advocates Act, 1961, §2(i)).

3 For instance, section 29 of the Advocates Act states, "Subject to the provisions of this Act and any rules made thereunder, there shall, as from the appointed day, be only one class of persons entitled to practice the profession of law, namely, advocates." (emphasis added)

4 The GATT, in 1947, was incidentally supposed to lead to the International Trade Organization (ITO), which was much wider in scope and dealt with barriers to trade created by private entities in addition to the government.

5 Pallavi Shroff of Amarchand & Mangaldas and Rajiv Luthra of Luthra & Luthra Law Offices are representatives of Indian law firms.

6 The logic behind such a move was the relationship between other statutory bodies such as the Medical Council of India and their administrative ministry, the Ministry of Health.

7 For instance, the Draft Legal Practitioners (Regulation and Maintenance of Standards in Profession, Protecting the Interests of Clients and Promoting the Rule of Law) Bill, 2010, contains several provisions that conflict with the Advocates Act.

8 Despite this, there appears to be a truce between the Ministry of Human Resources Development and the Bar Council of India (Nanda and Kanekal 2012).

9 A survey of the online portals such as www.legallyindia.com and www.barandbench.com indicates a very high level of interest among law students for liberalization of the legal profession.

10 In terms of Indian law, legislation is required to be notified by the executive for its enforcement.

11 For instance, the argument in the A. K. Balaji case stated that "... the procedure for Indian lawyers to practice in foreign countries is far more cumbersome and very costly, and there are also very many restrictions like qualifying tests, prior experience, work permits, etc., but no such procedures are contemplated in the Advocates Act, 1961 in respect of foreign lawyers who intend to practice law in India ..." (A. K. Balaji 2010, 2[a])

References

Advocates Act, 1961. www.barcouncilofindia.org/wp-content/uploads/2010/05/Advocates-Act1961.pdf.

Aeltemesh Rein v. Union of India 1988 4 SCC 54.

A. K. *Balaji v. The Government of India* 2010 WP No. 5614.

A. K. *Roy v. Union of India* 1982 1 SCC 271.

Basu, Nayanima. 2015. "Government Mulls Legal Services' Liberalisation." *Business Standard*. www.business-standard.com/article/economy-policy/government-mulls-legal-services-liberalisation-115062900875_1.html.

Bhasin, Lalit. 2011. Speech (Globalization, Lawyers and Emerging Economies conference, New Delhi, October 9).

Bar Council of India v. Bonnie Foi Law College, Petition for Special Leave to Appeal (Civil) no(s). 22337/2008 WP no. 13698/2007.

Chauhan, Neha. 2010. "Supreme Court Doesn't Want to Hear Bar Exam Cases, to Move into Delhi HC." *Legally India*. www.legallyindia.com/201008021165/Law-schools/supreme-court-doesnt-want-to-hear-bar-exam-cases-to-move-into-delhi-hc.

Das, Gurcharan. 2002. *India Unbound: The Social and Economic Revolution from Independence to the Global Information Age*. New York: Anchor Books.

The Economist. 2010. "Law and Globalisation: Not Entirely Free, Your Honour." www.economist.com/node/16693882?story_id=16693882&CFID=134992265&CFTOKEN=66996759.

Ganz, Kian. 2010. "Law Firms Can't Agree on LLP Conversion as Trilegal Waits for BCI Clarification." *Legally India*. www.legallyindia.com/201008061179/Law-firms/law-firms-cant-agree-on-llp-conversion-as-trilegal-waits-for-bci-clarification.

2011. "Law Firm Scraps LLP After Illegal Threats from Delhi Bar Council Chairman." *Legally India*. www.legallyindia.com/201112092439/Law-firms/law-firm-scraps-llp-after-illegal-threats-from-delhi-bar-council-chairman.

2013. "Of Paid News, 'Leading Players' and 'Editorial Content': How Indian Law Firms Advertise." *Legally India*. www.legallyindia.com/201308223927/Legal-opinions/of-paid-news-leading-players-and-editorial-content-how-indian-law-firms-advertise.

Kanekal, Nikhil and Kian Ganz. 2012. *Live Mint*. "Bar Council May Appeal HC ruling." www.livemint.com/2012/02/24002628/Bar-Council-may-appeal-HC-ruli.html.
Lawyers Collective v. Bar Council of India 1995 WP no. 1526.
Lawyers Weekly. 2011. "Commission Says Law Firms Should Be Able to Advertise." www.lawyersweekly.com.au/news/7877-commission-says-law-firms-should-be-able-to-advert.
M.P. Electricity Board v. Shiv Narayan 2005 7 SCC 283.
Nanda, Prashant K. and Nikhil Kanekal. 2012. "BCI Retains Sway Over Legal Education. *Live Mint*. www.livemint.com/Politics/JRTIKumDKOhE72OAkdlqyI/BCI-retains-sway-over-legal-education.html.
Nariman, Fali. 2010. *Before Memory Fades: An Autobiography*. New Delhi: Hay House India.
Rahul Singh v. Union of India 2010 Wri C. no. 36296.
V. Sudeer v. Bar Council of India 1999 3 SCC 176: AIR 1999 SC 1167.

SECTION V

OLD LAWYERS, NEW LAWYERS, AND TRANSFORMING ROLES

13

The Evolving Global Supply Chain for Legal Services: India's Role as a Critical Link

Vikramaditya S. Khanna

I. INTRODUCTION

The legal profession has been undergoing substantial change over the last two decades. With increasing globalization, better information and communication technologies, a weaker economy, and more cost-conscious clients, the US legal profession is often described as being at a turning point (Wilkins and Gulati 1998; Susskind 2008; Coates et al. 2011). One development that seems to reflect all these considerations is the rise of legal process outsourcing (LPO) to India (Wharton 2008; Kazmin 2009). Moreover, because it involves dividing legal work into smaller tasks and sending it across the globe for completion, the advent of LPO to India can be viewed as an important step in the evolution of a global supply chain for legal services. However, what does this evolution mean for the legal profession? Will we witness the kinds of profound changes seen in other sectors where global supply chains have become ubiquitous, such as manufacturing, medicine, and financial services (Monarch et al. 2013; Cohen 2014)? For example, what impact might these developments have on the employment prospects of US attorneys, the structure of law practice, the type and amount of work that can be outsourced, ethical standards, and legal education, among others?

These questions are important and merit closer examination (something I am pursuing in other projects), but this chapter narrows its focus to one key question: what are the likely employment effects of LPO on US attorneys? This question has attracted a great deal of discussion with some commentators voicing concern about a "hollowing out" of the profession (as junior and midlevel positions might be replaced by less expensive workers overseas), others suggesting that little legal work is likely to be outsourced at all, and yet others concerned about the impact on quality, ethical standards, and confidentiality (Cotts and Kufchock 2007; Daly and Silver 2007; Timmons 2011; Spellman and Varrichio 2012). In spite of this, there remain few theoretical or empirical studies exploring this question and little available data that might be useful in addressing it.[1] This chapter engages this question with the goal of laying out the conceptual groundwork for a more careful and nuanced inquiry into it. Indeed, one of the modest contributions of this chapter is to systematically address some of the theoretical and conceptual concerns and issues that seem to have developed around the employment effects question.

Assessing employment effects is challenging for a number of reasons. First, as this chapter argues, these effects are more ambiguous than might appear at first blush. This is largely due to outsourcing having partially offsetting effects – in particular, outsourcing might not only reduce US attorney employment by sending some work overseas (i.e., a substitution effect) but also increase US legal work because it reduces the price for legal services, making it more likely that more of that work will be demanded (i.e., an increasing demand effect). Which effect prevails depends on many factors and is likely to vary across areas of law and the seniority of attorneys affected (e.g., junior attorneys in mergers and acquisitions practices most likely face negative consequences, while attorneys working in the public interest and representing underserved groups face more-positive consequences). Second, limited data is available to test the predicted effects in legal services markets, and studies in other sectors where outsourcing is more common provide mixed employment effects (suggesting similar outcomes are likely for law). Third, even when effects might be discernible, we have complicated questions about what their normative implications might be. This all suggests that employment effects are likely to vary substantially, be modest in magnitude, be difficult to estimate with precision, and provide us with relatively difficult-to-parse policy guidance. The overall message is that caution and context are advisable in assessing these effects.

Of course, employment effects are not the only effects of LPO. Thus, this chapter briefly lays out some other important potential effects (e.g., on the structure of law practice) that are likely to be longer lasting and could form the basis of future research – some of which is already under way.

Part II begins with a general overview of LPO by focusing on LPO to India (where the primary providers of LPO services are located). This provides the background against which one can examine the potential effects of LPO to India. Moreover, because the LPO sector is evolving rapidly and there is limited data on it, this part relies on information obtained through a series of detailed interviews with more than thirty key industry participants from across the globe. Through this it becomes clear that LPO is more global than commonly perceived (involving more than two dozen countries) and that it is growing into many areas of law and levels of legal work. Moreover, its growth prospects depend in part on further technological innovations and the willingness of key purchasers to "try" it. In particular, if insurance firms (or the government) decide to encourage, or use, more outsourcing, that could have seismic effects given their large roles in the markets for paying for (or purchasing) legal services. Efforts appear to be under way to persuade these large purchasers to consider LPO.

Part III explores the likely effects of LPO on the employment prospects of US attorneys (section A) and the potential normative consequences that may follow (section B). Given the small scale of the LPO sector (relative to the US legal profession) and limited data, this part utilizes a "thought experiment" to explore these effects – if LPO to India were to become a significant player in the US legal services market, what key factors are likely to influence its impact on US attorney employment? The focus is on these key factors in order to obtain conceptual clarity, which enables more careful and nuanced analyses.

Section A argues that LPO has cross cutting effects. LPO is likely to result in a reduced price for some legal services (because costs are dropping), which should increase demand for these legal services. However, at the same time, LPO shifts some work overseas, which is likely to put downward pressure on US employment and salaries. The overall effect is thus somewhat muddy in the abstract and is likely to depend on many factors, including how much more legal work is purchased due to the price drop associated with LPO. This in turn depends on the amount of savings generated by outsourcing relative to the expected net gain of the activity, the underlying population of potential litigants in an area of law, and to what extent job losses or salary reductions might be mitigated by alternative employment opportunities, such as LPO firms opening up offices in the United States or the United Kingdom (a practice commonly called "onshoring" or "reshoring") (Timmons 2011). These factors, however, likely vary by area of law and the seniority of the attorneys – for example, the effects are probably quite different across mergers and acquisitions, compliance, employment discrimination, and the public interest. In light of these cross cutting effects, and evidence from nonlegal sectors showing mixed employment outcomes from outsourcing, one suspects the employment impact on US attorneys is likely to be small and quite contingent (Bhagwati et al. 2004; Grossman and Rossi-Hansberg 2008, 2010; Benz and Kohler 2010; Feenstra 2010; Monarch et al. 2013).

However, even if we ascertained the likely employment effects, the policy or normative conclusions are not straightforward. Section B argues that the impact on US attorneys is not the only socially relevant criterion. For example, if the cost reductions accompanying LPO result in more suits then our normative analysis would depend partly on what kinds of additional suits are being brought (e.g., are the new suits meritorious ones that were previously not initiated, perhaps because of high legal costs, or are they frivolous suits?). Indeed, LPO to India might also impact a host of other policy matters that have received scant attention in the literature, such as effects on settlement, precedent formation, and maintenance of ethical standards. For example, if global supply chains became more common, what, if anything, might happen if some of the suppliers were in countries with different ethical rules than those in the United States (e.g., a country where third-party financing or multidisciplinary practice were permitted)? Should the response be to regulate in some manner or permit competition in ethical rules or something else? The impact on policy is thus much less clear and more complex.

Indeed, this discussion underscores how focusing on the potential employment effects might provide a rather impoverished and narrow view of the effects of LPO. LPO to India could also impact the structure of how legal services are provided, which in turn has important implications for the structure of the legal profession and the practice of law. In many respects these effects may dwarf those associated with potential employment outcomes.

Part IV begins an exploration of two of these longer-lasting effects, leaving more fulsome inquiry for future work. Section A examines the possibility for the "atomization" of the legal services market. Given an enhanced ability to disaggregate legal work into smaller pieces, one might imagine that legal work would then be split into many pieces and sent out to many different providers (located all over the world) – in short, the atomization of the legal services market. However, it appears we are seeing only a limited amount of atomization – that is, we might have the capability to split legal work into many parts (say twenty), but we tend to contract with only five or six different providers. This is indeed the trend in other sectors where global supply chains are common, suggesting some deeper forces at work (Feenstra 2010; Regan and Heenan 2010; Coates et al. 2011; Teixeira 2014)[2]. Probing into this question suggests that it is not simply the coordination costs of dealing with multiple suppliers driving this outcome, but also the likely advantages of dealing with a smaller set of consistent suppliers who reduce the complexity, and assuage the uncertainty, associated with doing business in an increasingly global world.

Section B examines the potential for LPO to further restructure features of the legal services markets. In particular, this section discusses how LPO may impact the size of law firms and change the competition between legal service providers. On the first issue, LPO may reduce the size of law firms by potentially reducing the need to hire as many junior associates (especially if the increasing demand effects noted earlier are weak) and by also making it less necessary for partners and senior lawyers to stay with a large law firm for back office support. This latter point is already happening with smaller law firms arising that rely on outsourcing to compete with larger firms. The second issue is even more open because the presence of LPO impacts the number of competitors in the legal services market. Thus, if a client is willing to go outside of its in-house department to purchase legal services, that client can choose between an LPO, a large law firm, a smaller law firm supported by LPO, and so forth. What drives this choice? What are the key differentiators among these providers? One can imagine many – the type of work performed, the skills of the people working at the provider (e.g., litigation, project management), the internal incentive and accountability structures at each provider, and so forth. Do these translate into different areas of legal work where each provider has an advantage? Does the ability of smaller law firms to use LPO to compete with larger law firms influence a client's choice among law firms, and if so, how? These questions merit much greater inquiry, as do recent claims that legal service providers focused on process (such as LPO firms) may be able to provide better compliance services to major banks (after the enactment of Dodd-Frank) than top law firms (Global Legal Post 2013; Moore and Harris 2014).

Part V concludes and reiterates that we are in many respects just at the beginning of a series of changes to the legal profession that warrant closer scrutiny. Indeed, one eagerly anticipates the changes the future holds for the legal profession as technological innovations continue to develop and globalization grows.

II. OVERVIEW OF LEGAL PROCESS OUTSOURCING

This part provides a general overview of LPO by focusing on LPO to India – the country that remains the largest provider of LPO services. LPO to India generally involves an entity in the United States, United Kingdom, or European Union (e.g., law firm, corporate client, legal practitioner) sending law-related work or tasks to a non-law-firm entity in India for completion (Krishnan 2009; Mathew and Thomas 2009; Ballakrishnen and Wilkins 2012). This work is completed primarily by attorneys (or employees with some relevant training) in India (or elsewhere) who are supervised by US-, UK-, or Indian qualified attorneys based in India (or elsewhere). Although outsourcing often involves the use of technology in communicating legal work, developing software to assist in completing the work, and so forth, LPO still expects that the client is represented by an attorney. This distinguishes it from "unbundled legal services," often involving only technological options with no attorney representation, which is discussed more often in the context of attempting to enhance access to justice.[3] Thus, typical examples of work outsourced to India include patent application/prosecution, e-discovery work, contract management, and some brief writing, among others.

Although this may appear novel, it is not – US law firms have used contract attorneys (i.e., attorneys outside the firm) for years (Roberts 2010). However, the growth of LPO to India is fascinating because it represents a substantially more organized method of outsourcing, a more process-oriented method of providing legal services, and a greater reliance on sending legal work overseas (Pollak 2006).[4]

The description of LPO to India that follows is based primarily on a series of more than thirty semistructured interviews conducted with key LPO providers, law firms, corporate clients, and individuals working in, or with, the LPO industry.[5] It is supplemented by reference to preexisting materials. Reliance on participant interviews in this sector is critical because there is limited, if any, reliable data on LPO to India and the sector is evolving quite quickly. For organizational clarity, the discussion of LPO to India is divided into six sections describing: (i) why someone might outsource legal work, (ii) what kinds of services (or work) are outsourced, (iii) what countries are touched by outsourcing, (iv) what the key drivers of outsourcing growth are, (v) whether outsourcing meets ethical requirements in the United States, and (vi) the organizational structure of LPO firms.

A. *Why Outsource?*

Generally speaking, a firm is likely to engage in LPO when the net benefits of using LPO (i.e., the benefits minus the costs) exceed those of alternative sourcing options (e.g., in-house, law firm) (Sako 2009).[6] Respondents indicated that compared with alternative options, LPO's benefits include the cost savings from lower salaries in India, enhanced flexibility in staffing, and potentially better service for some types of legal work (Wharton 2008; Borsand and Gupta 2009; Mathew and Thomas 2009; Neil 2009; Davies 2014; interviews 1–17, 19, 21, and 28–31, 2014–2015). LPO does, however, come with additional costs, such as enhanced monitoring costs (to ensure work sent far away is still being done as per expectations and at an acceptable quality), coordinating costs (to first divide and then reintegrate work sent overseas), and other costs (e.g., ensuring that firm assets, such as intellectual property rights, are not expropriated in the process) (Grossman and Rossi-Hansberg 2008; Benz and

Kohler 2010; Feenstra 2010). This also includes concerns with maintaining client confidentiality, although respondents appeared comfortable with the steps taken by LPOs (Hadfield 2000; Wharton 2008; Mathew and Thomas 2009; Neil 2009).

Perhaps the most surprising item on this list is the idea that LPO firms may provide better service for some kinds of legal work. This is because one might think that longstanding legal service providers (e.g., well-regarded law firms) were more likely to have a higher quality than LPOs. The sense of better LPO quality reflects a perception that some LPO firms have brought better management and process operations to the provision of certain legal services (Interviews 1, 2, 4–9, 1–14, 19, 21, and 30, 2014–2015).

Indeed, some LPOs have teams devoted to particular kinds of legal work to develop a high level of efficiency and specialization with that work. Further, these teams work closely with clients to learn their needs and understand where the LPO can add value (Gardner 2014).[7] This is critical for a number of reasons. First, these relationships provide LPO firms with the kind of access to multiple clients that helps transform idiosyncratic work done for these clients into routine, or more outsourceable, work (Maskell et al. 2006; Sako 2006; Burke Robertson 2011). Second, the things learned through these interactions enable LPOs to provide customers with protean measures of quality (often more than law firms provide). Interviews suggest that such metrics involved setting targets, measuring achievement of those targets, running practice drills, and using regular iterative feedback loops with clients to better understand clients' needs (Interviews 2, 5, 6, 11, 18, 22, 24, 25, and 27, 2014–2015).[8] These measures were important in persuading clients to try LPO to India given that LPOs were new (and had little accumulated reputation) and most clients were not in India to monitor the LPO firm. Overall, these steps appear to have helped LPOs enhance the perceived quality of some of their services. Of course, not all LPO services (or providers) are considered high quality (some respondents indicated having disappointing experiences), but, as many respondents noted, even law firms and in-house departments do not always perform at a superior-quality level (Interviews 1, 2, 4–9, 12, 13, and 19, 2014–2015).

Although this might appear somewhat surprising, these kinds of arguments mirror those made nearly three or four decades ago, when corporate clients started taking some work from law firms and bringing it in-house (Rosen 1989). The arguments then were that in-house lawyers would cost less than outside law firms, as LPOs probably would now, and provide better services on some fronts (due to their greater familiarity with the client), as might LPOs for the reasons noted here (Rosen 1989; Chapter 4 of this volume).[9]

TABLE 1. *Types of offshoring to India*[10]

Type of work	Description
Document support and back office work	Formatting and editing briefs and memos, transcription, and similar paralegal work
Compliance-related work[11]	Statutory and regulatory compliance work, implementing court orders
Litigation and transaction support	Document review, e-discovery, document coding, due diligence, and other "junior associate" type work
Intellectual property (IP) related work	Patent drafting and prosecution, prior art searches, IP asset management
Legal research and writing	Researching and writing appellate briefs (circuit court and Supreme Court level), memos on statutes and case law
Negotiation and drafting of contracts	Drafting, reviewing, and negotiating contracts (e.g., nondisclosure agreements)

B. *The Kinds of Work Being Outsourced*

The variety and types of legal work being outsourced to India is growing and morphing, but some general contours can be discerned. Table 1 provides a brief overview.

This is a fairly broad range of work. Indeed, as a general matter, work that can be broken down into a process and replicated can be outsourced (Geis 2010). Sometimes the work is so commonly desired that it essentially becomes commoditized, while at other times it remains more specialized. What is particularly intriguing is that customers in the United States appear to have started outsourcing some work that would normally be considered more-skilled work requiring judgment, less easily replicable, and hence less likely to be outsourced (e.g., appellate brief writing and drafting contracts) (Neil 2007; Economist 2010; Global Legal Post 2013). It appears that work such as contract drafting is more likely to be outsourced if the LPO has cultivated a medium- to longer-term relationship with customers (Interviews 1, 2, 4, 6–8, 12, 13, and 30, 2014–2015). Indeed, one imagines that contract drafting often requires some degree of familiarity with the business involved (Pollak 2006; Sako 2006; Schultz 2010).

Having said that, one should not overestimate the presence of this type of work. The bulk of outsourcing work is still in process-driven areas such as document support, litigation support, and intellectual property. Indeed, interviews indicated that these other more complex practice areas had some, albeit quite moderate and idiosyncratic, growth (Interviews 1, 2, 4, 6, 13, 19, and 30, 2014–2015).

Another area exhibiting moderate growth appears to be what is called "process reengineering," which involves work that may fit in multiple categories in table 1. This involves combining technology, legal work, and process knowledge to provide a different kind of legal service to what is traditionally provided at law firms or in general counsel's offices.[12] This particular development may be an area where LPO firms can bring some value add and display unique skills.

In light of the growing breadth of work that might be outsourced, it may help to provide some context by discussing how a typical outsourcing assignment occurs. This description is not representative of every LPO assignment but captures points that were frequently repeated in the interviews.

First, let us assume that we are dealing with more-specialized services that are not usually purchased, such as commodities.[13] For these more specialized services, LPO firms and potential clients usually enter discussions to understand the client's needs and the LPO firm's offerings as well as to obtain assurances on quality and confidentiality (Interviews 1, 2, 4–7, 9, 12–15, and 19, 2014–2015).[14] This most likely requires interaction with the client (more interaction if the client's needs are somewhat *sui generis*) as well as some understanding of how legal work is completed.[15]

Once the process has been set up, performance targets are often set and monitoring of workflow and feedback begins (Schultz 2010; interviews 2–6, 9, 14, 21, 26, and 29, 2014–2015). Some LPO firms provide ongoing reports to clients, but that varies with client requirements (and budgets) and LPO capabilities. Confidentiality is often maintained via encrypted technologies. Some respondents expressed admiration for the level of encryption, which they thought appeared to exceed the level experienced with some law firms (Interviews 1, 4, 6, 8, 12, 21, and 29, 2014–2015).

The work is supervised by someone who is a US, UK, or EU qualified attorney. This particular element seemed one on which respondents had different, and at times strong, views. Some indicated that supervision quality was quite good, whereas others had substantial concerns ranging from a sheer absence of real supervision to suspecting only sporadic supervision (Schultz 2010; interviews 1, 2, 4, 6, 8, 12, 14, and 29, 2014–2015). Indeed, some respondents were not thrilled with the final work product and had considered going elsewhere (Interviews 1, 6, 8, 12, and 29, 2014–2015). Of course, clients are not always pleased with law firm work, too. In spite of these concerns, it appears LPO to India has been growing steadily.

C. *How Global is LPO?*

India has been the primary geographic choice for most firms outsourcing legal work because of cost savings; India's general experience with outsourcing; the presence of many English-speaking attorneys; being considered part of the common law family; and the time difference between the United States and India, allowing for a 24-hour workday (Pollak 2006; Mathew and Thomas 2009). Other reasons also most likely contributed to India obtaining the lion's share of global outsourcing work (e.g., institutional conditions in India leading to strong project management skills) (Kochhar et al. 2006; Kuruvilla and Ranganathan 2008).

Although this combination of reasons directs much business toward India, it has become increasingly clear that India is not the only provider of LPO services. Respondents consistently indicated that LPO customers were recently approached by an LPO from another country (e.g., South Africa, Latin America, the Philippines) or had thought about going there, while Indian LPO firms had often considered opening up offices in countries beyond India (Romagnino 2011; Kriegler 2013; Interviews 2, 4–6, 13, and 29, 2014–2015). In addition, we are witnessing more "onshoring" or "reshoring," with Indian LPOs opening offices in the United States (near some of their clients) and large English law firms setting up exclusive LPOs in Northern Ireland (Herbert Smith Freehills 2010; Allen & Overy 2011; Panagea3 2011; Timmons 2011).

Some of the primary reasons for this appeared to be (i) cost increases in India, (ii) proximity to the customer's base of operations, which was considered useful for some types of work, (iii) the growth of good project managements skills elsewhere, (iv) data privacy laws in some jurisdictions (e.g., the European Union), leading firms not wanting to send their data overseas, and (v) cementing the customer-provider relationship by being geographically closer and perhaps setting up an exclusive arrangement between the LPO firm and the customer (Economist 2010).

Similarly, the perceived uniformity of customer countries (i.e., only common law countries) is changing. Most LPO firms indicated that they either had or were developing customers in the European Union and Australia (Interviews 2–4, 6, 7, 9, 13, and 29, 2014–2015).[16] This development is somewhat surprising given that Indian lawyers are trained in common law rather than civil law. One explanation is that it is not only familiarity with the actual substantive law or legal system that may be important, but also the ability to take legal work (from any jurisdiction) and put it into a process that generates more consistent, less expensive, and efficient results. In other words, the "process" in LPO may be quite attractive for a number of customers. We witness this in recent reports that German firms are thinking of increasing their reliance on LPO to India (as more Indian attorneys appear to speak German and work on arbitration and export cases) (Research and Markets 2011). Recent reports also suggest that firms in Japan are likely clients as are firms in South Korea, China, Malaysia, and Australia (Schultz 2010; Vee LPO 2014; Vyas 2014).

D. *LPO Industry – Drivers of Growth*

The LPO industry's growth has been impressive (starting in 1995 and ratcheting up after 2004) with well over one hundred LPO providers now (Prism Legal 2005; *Global Legal Post* 2013), but it faces important challenges. Respondents indicated that the two biggest challenges were changes in technology and the willingness of key purchasers to actually use outsourcing (Interviews 1–9, 13–17, 20, and 29–30, 2014–2015).[17]

Changes in technology are a two-edged sword – some changes make it more likely that LPO to India will grow (e.g., better communications technology), but other changes may lead clients to rely more heavily on technologically enabled legal services (e.g., IBM Watson) rather than outsourcing (Interviews 1–7, 9, 13, 14, 20, 29, and 30, 2014–2015). An example is e-discovery software developed in the United States that might reduce the need to rely on legal services provided overseas.[18]

The second factor is the willingness of key purchasers to use outsourcing. These purchasers are in-house departments, law firms, individual attorneys, and insurance programs (private and public) that pay for legal services (in full or in part). All of these players want some way to assess the quality of the services provided. However, there are few, if any, measures of quality (except the LPO industry's own protean measures) and few credible independent certifiers of LPO quality as one might see in the manufacturing space.[19] This makes it more challenging to assess quality and might constrain the growth of LPO. Having said that, some law firms and in-house departments seem to have become more comfortable with outsourcing as their experience with it has increased (Interviews 4–6, 12, 21, and 29, 2015).

Moreover, LPO firms have been trying to provide assurances to clients by requiring "admissions" tests of sorts for their employees and expecting employees to pursue ongoing and on-the-job training (Interviews 2–6, 9, 14, and 30, 2014–2015).[20] How "assuring" these steps have been is open to question. Indeed, some respondents wondered what level of training was truly provided given the inconsistent work quality they witnessed (Interviews 1, 6, 8, 12, and 29, 2014–2015).

Perhaps the most intriguing prospect may be the interest of insurance providers and government-funded legal services to consider outsourcing, given how much legal services they purchase. Respondents suggested that if large liability insurers (or government) were willing to provide premium discounts to firms using LPO (or otherwise encourage firms), one might anticipate increasing demand for LPO services (Interviews 4, 6, 7, 12, and 29, 2015). Larger LPOs are clearly exploring this option and ways to bring insurers "on board." Moreover, entities like the Legal Services Corporation (LSC) have been considering ways in which technology and perhaps outsourcing may enable them to leverage their resources more effectively (Interviews 27 and 28, 2015).[21]

Two critical issues are designing ways to assure insurers that the quality produced at LPOs is acceptable and finding a way to price the possibility of greater liability for the risk of negligence as more players work in the supply chain. If these concerns were adequately addressed, some liability insurers might start charging their clients a lower premium (to reflect the cheaper legal costs) and that might induce more parties to try outsourcing. This has also been at play in other professions impacted by globalization and supply chains – in particular, the medical profession (Cohen 2014). What impact this may have is difficult to gauge at this stage, but if liability insurers started providing discounts to those using technology and outsourcing, that would most likely generate an increase in demand.[22]

E. *Is LPO the "Unauthorized Practice of Law"?*

An important question is whether LPO to India amounts to the "unauthorized practice of law" because it involves Indian attorneys or engineers, who have not usually passed any US bar, providing legal services to US clients. In August 2008 the American Bar Association issued an opinion holding that LPO to India did not amount to the unauthorized practice of law if a US qualified attorney is supervising the outsourced activities (American Bar Association 2008).[23] Supervision in this context means making some evaluation about, among other things, whether (i) the foreign legal education system is comparable to the United States, (ii) the foreign professional regulatory system has similar core ethical principles, (iii) the enforcement systems are effective, (iv) the laws of the country to which work is being outsourced are comparable (e.g., on rights to personal property and judicial seizure), and (v) the judicial system of that country functions appropriately (ibid.). The required rigor of these evaluations is not specified. Other relevant matters are attending to security risks and perhaps even personal visits to the work site(s) of the LPO (ibid.).

The American Bar Association's opinion is consistent with rulings from several state and city bar associations, as well as some state court decisions.[24] Typically, the outsourcing entity (e.g., a US lawyer) had to take steps to ensure client confidentiality, disclose that LPO services were being used, and charge reasonable fees for their administration/supervision work. If these requirements are met, it appears LPO to India faces little concern of being tagged as the unauthorized practice of law.

F. *How are LPOs Structured?*

Although LPO firms come in a variety of forms and adopt a variety of business methods, there do appear to be a few commonalities. First, virtually all LPO firms are structured as corporate entities (interviews 1–23 and 28–31, 2014–2015). This allows LPOs advantages over law firms in terms of raising financing (i.e., they are not limited to attorneys as equity owners), greater stability than the typical partnership, and the use of more-powerful incentive alignment devices (e.g., stock options) (Ribstein 2004, 2010; Burke Robertson 2014; Morley 2015). However, these advantages may be short-lived because recently the United Kingdom and Australia have allowed law firms to raise capital from nonlawyers, and the American Bar Association seems willing to consider the issue (Lattman 2007a; Flood 2012).

Second, LPO firms have been more willing to be flexible in coming up with billing options. Their fees can range from flat fees to hourly charges as well as different payment options ranging from upfront payment, payment for services as performed, or payments based on meeting performance targets (interviews 1–15, 19–23, and 29–31, 2014–2015).

Finally, there appear to be a number of business models for LPO that are in use in India. Of course, more could be said about each of these models, but the goal in this section is to simply provide an overview of what the LPO industry looks like (table 2).

This taxonomy, however, understates the variety of structures adopted by providers of legal services that are not law firms (sometimes called "alternative law"). One of the better-known entities in this space is Axiom Law. Axiom bills itself as a different kind of legal service provider. It appears to combine being (i) a temp agency for lawyers, (ii) an outsourcing provider/organizer, (iii) a place where corporate clients can hire lawyers to work within their firm for six months to one year ("embedded" lawyers), and (iv) a place where clients can obtain Axiom's project management skills to help them find their optimal

TABLE 2. *LPO business models in India*[25]

Business model	Description
"Pure play"	LPO firm focuses only on providing LPO services.
Division in broader outsourcing firm	LPO is just one service offered by a firm providing a variety of general and business outsourcing services.
Arm of Indian law firm	LPO services are provided by Indian law firm to clients (especially foreign clients).
Arm of foreign law firm	LPO is owned by a foreign entity and provides LPO services to anyone (e.g., Smith Dehn Dern).
Captive of foreign entity	LPO is owned by a foreign entity and provides services only to that entity (e.g., GE, Clifford Chance).
Joint venture	Foreign firm teams up with Indian firm to provide LPO services.

arrangements for sourcing legal services. Axiom has made substantial waves in the legal services market with its mélange of services (Lattman 2007b; Fisher 2011).

III. EFFECTS ON EMPLOYMENT OF LAWYERS IN THE UNITED STATES AND NORMATIVE CONCERNS

This part explores the potential effects on US attorney employment from LPO. Section A discusses the likely employment effects on US lawyers, assuming, as a thought experiment, that LPO to India grows to become a significant player in the US legal services market. Section B explores some normative issues arising from section A.

A. *Potential Effects on US Attorney Employment*[26]

Estimating the impact of LPO to India on US attorneys' employment prospects is difficult because it involves examining a number of effects – which often cut in opposite directions – with limited data available on them. Indeed, most of the theoretical and empirical work on outsourcing has not focused on the legal services markets but rather on other sectors (e.g., manufacturing) (Grossman and Rossi-Hansberg 2008, 2010; Benz and Kohler 2010; Feenstra 2010; Monarch et al. 2013). In light of that, the discussion in this part builds upon the work in these other sectors (particularly Grossman and Rossi-Hansberg 2008, 2010 and Feenstra 2010) while bringing additional insights where appropriate to reflect some of the more unusual attributes of the legal services market.

To add some context, let us begin with a relatively simple example. Assume that law firms, in-house departments, and other providers of legal services complete legal work through the combination of two types of attorneys: those with high skill or experience (e.g., partners, general counsels) and those with less skill or experience (e.g., junior associates). Currently, there is only a modest amount of outsourcing (e.g., contract attorneys). Due to some technological innovations (e.g., the Internet, e-discovery, encryption) and business innovations (e.g., greater skills in project management), the cost of sending legal work commonly done by US junior associates to India has dropped and many firms are exploring options for outsourcing. This would not necessarily lead to all junior associate work being sent to India, as some might need to be conducted in the United States for a variety of reasons.[27] These assumptions provide a useful starting point for analyzing the likely effects in a methodological and careful manner.

1. Effects on the Amount of Legal Work Done in the United States

First, if outsourcing reduces the cost (and price) of certain legal services in the United States, we would expect demand for these legal services to increase.[28] An increase in demand should have a positive effect on the amount of legal work where junior associates are involved.[29] Specifically, as the amount of legal work increases (e.g., more plaintiffs file securities fraud suits or employment discrimination suits), that should lead to more work for some US qualified (and resident) attorneys as they are increasingly approached to represent clients in the United States. Further, the increasing work effect need not be limited to litigation because a drop in legal costs might induce the purchase of more transactional services, too.

Second, LPO firms in India will need to hire additional US qualified attorneys to supervise their employees, thereby leading to more work for US qualified attorneys (although this may or may not be in the United States). This is both to help assure US clients of quality as well as to avoid being categorized as the "unauthorized practice of law" as discussed earlier.

Third, offshoring legal work to India has the effect of increasing the supply of people doing junior associate work because now both the current set of junior associates in the United States and the employees of LPO in India are providing such work. This has a deleterious effect on US junior associates even though more of their work is being demanded because that demand can be met (or substituted) in part by overseas workers (Grossman and Rossi-Hansberg 2008, 2010; Feenstra 2010).[30] However, to the extent that junior associates are given other work at their current firms or obtain work at another employer (e.g., law firm, in-house, a reshoring outfit of an LPO, non-law-firm entities such as Axiom Law), these negative effects would be mitigated (ibid.). These three effects cut in opposite directions, and thus the net effect is not obvious in the abstract (ibid.). However, more can be said to elicit which factors drive the overall outcome. In order to do this, let us start with some basics.

People usually purchase legal services (e.g., initiate litigation, transactional work) when their expected private benefits exceed their expected private costs (including legal costs) of doing so. Outsourcing may reduce legal costs and lead some people to purchase more legal services than before. How much more depends on the price elasticity of legal work or more generally the amount of inframarginal purchases (i.e., those purchases that did not occur before outsourcing but would now occur due to the drop in costs arising from outsourcing). This probably varies across areas of law because the expected benefits and costs of legal services vary across areas (and purchasers). For example, if in a particular area of law there were very few (many) new purchases of legal services, attributable to the savings from outsourcing, the increasing demand effect would be quite small (large). This could then be balanced against the negative employment effects of outsourcing noted earlier.[31]

However, there is little general information about the likely inframarginal purchasers (or purchases) or the underlying population of likely purchases in most areas of law. In light of this, we need to rely on more basic indicia or perhaps proxies, such as (i) whether outsourcing saves a substantial amount of costs and (ii) how the savings from outsourcing compare to the overall expected benefits and costs of purchasing the legal service or engaging in the activity. These considerations may serve as useful proxies for thinking about the likely inframarginal purchases.

As a general matter, if the amount of savings generated by outsourcing were small, it would be unlikely to result in many more purchases of legal services. An exception to this might arise if the underlying population of potential litigants was comprised of many people whose expected benefits and costs of purchasing legal services were very close in magnitude such that a small change in costs could generate a large response to purchase services. Although such a situation is possible, it seems fairly unlikely to occur often.[32] Indeed, one suspects there are generally more inframarginal purchases if the cost savings are substantial than if they are small.

Second, because the actual savings must be compared to the expected net gain from purchasing legal services or engaging in the activity, one must also pay attention to what comprises these expected net gains. In particular, if the expected benefits are very large, it is less likely that even a sizable savings in outsourcing will have much impact. For example, if the outsourcing savings are

$100 and the expected benefits are $5,000, these savings will influence behavior only if there are many purchasers whose expected costs (before outsourcing) are between $5,000 and $5,100, because these are the purchasers who did not buy legal services before but would after the cost reduction. Although it is possible that many purchasers might be in this narrow band, it seems less likely compared to a situation where the expected benefits are not so large relative to the savings. Analogous comments apply if one were looking at expected costs (e.g., if the savings from outsourcing are large relative to expected costs, it is more likely the savings will have an impact on inframarginal purchases than when the savings are small relative to expected costs).

Let us then use these indicia to get a sense of the likely inframarginal purchases in different areas of practice. For example, research suggests that pro bono litigation, immigration, legal aid, and employment litigation are often underprovided due in part to the costs of litigation, and thus one might expect a reduction in litigation costs to be important (Greiner et al. 2013; Sandefur and Clarke 2015). Here a 20 percent decrease in legal costs could spur a substantial amount of new litigation. Indeed, conversations with people and entities operating in these areas indicate that they are actively exploring (and implementing) methods to incorporate outsourcing and technology in the provision of legal services to leverage their resources. However, one should note that outsourcing (which envisions a US attorney using outsourcing while representing a client) is different than pure reliance on technology (which may result in the client receiving some online information about a legal issue without the representation of an US attorney). Nonetheless, they are sometimes mentioned together as they involve exploring the impact of cost-reducing mechanisms.

As examples, consider that commodification and process management were topics for debate at a recent Pro Bono Institute conference, that immigration attorneys have been exploring how technology and outsourcing might be useful to them in deferred action programs, and that officials at the Legal Services Corporation have indicated a willingness to explore how technology and perhaps outsourcing can help them leverage resources (Pro Bono Wire 2015; Interviews 26, 27 and 28, 2015). Similar arguments also apply for underprovided transactional work (e.g., legal work related to public parks, some trusts, and wills) (Interviews 22 and 23, 2015). Thus, it is plausible that the increasing demand effect could be quite large here.

At the other extreme might be mergers and acquisitions (M&A) work. In this arena it seems highly unlikely that a reduction in legal costs would lead to business people engaging in new mergers.[33] This is because legal costs make up a fairly small portion of the expected costs of engaging in a merger and the expected benefits of a merger are likely to be quite a bit larger than legal costs. Simply put, the gap between a merger's expected benefits and costs is probably larger than the savings associated with outsourcing. Here one expects little increasing demand effects, suggesting that the employment effects are more likely to be negative in this area.[34]

Of course, pro bono and M&A are not the only kinds of legal services of interest – there is a wide continuum between them. For example, in private securities class action litigation, the legal costs might be a large portion of the plaintiff's costs and hence a decline in them may lead to more of these suits being filed. Similarly, if government enforcement agencies considered legal costs an important part of their total costs, a reduction in those costs might result in more enforcement actions as well. If one prefers to look at more transactional work, a reduction in the costs of drafting commercial contracts might make them more attractive. Further, in the area of compliance (e.g., compliance with requirements of banking, securities, and environmental laws), the primary costs are likely to be legal costs as well as the value of employee time. A substantial reduction in legal costs might make it more desirable for firms to purchase more legal services related to compliance.[35]

2. Distribution of Work Among Senior and Junior People

The analysis so far has focused on the amount of legal work in the United States, but not how it is distributed among senior and junior people. Generally LPO would lead to more work for senior attorneys and either more or less work for junior attorneys depending on the strength of the increasing demand effect. To obtain a sense of how this may play out, it is useful to consider an example.

Let us assume that, prior to LPO, one legal project requires ten senior people (e.g., partners, senior associates) and fifty junior associates to complete. This might represent an employment discrimination lawsuit or a particular type of transaction (e.g., project finance). Let us also assume that each year ten such legal projects arise. Thus, there are one hundred senior people and five hundred junior people working on these ten projects in the United States.

Now, let us assume the presence of LPO results in cost savings such that half the US junior associates working on a project are longer necessary (as their work is outsourced), but one additional senior person is needed to supervise the outsourced work. This leaves us with one project requiring eleven senior people and twenty-five junior people in the United States with additional people in LPOs in India. If there were only 10 projects, then there are 110 senior and 275 junior attorneys employed in the United States, which looks particularly bad for US junior associates.

This, however, assumes no increasing demand effect, but if we change that assumption, our results change rather quickly. For example, assume that the cost reductions occasioned by LPO lead to twenty projects a year (a doubling of projects from the current ten). This leads to 220 senior and 500 junior attorneys employed in the United States (i.e., eleven senior and twenty-five junior people per each of the twenty projects) and more in India. This looks good for both junior and senior US attorneys. Thus, senior attorneys (whose work is not outsourced) benefit from LPO regardless of the increasing demand effect, while the potential effect on junior attorneys (whose work is partially outsourced) depends on the increasing demand effect.

3. Potential Effects on Salaries of US Attorneys

In addition to the effects on the amount of work and its distribution, one might also be interested in the effects on salaries. Here too the magnitude of the increasing demand effect is critical. Outsourcing means US junior associates need less time to complete a task (because some of the work is being completed overseas), which results in US junior associates either working fewer hours, being paid a smaller salary, or being dismissed. However, if the cost reduction generates a substantial amount of new purchases of legal services, the demand for US junior associates will rise (because, as assumed, outsourcing only reduces, not eliminates, the need for US junior associates on a particular project). This may raise salaries back up (or increase hours worked) if the desired numbers of junior associates are not available in a short time frame. It is thus plausible that the rise in demand will be sufficient to lead to an increase in total payments to junior associates in the shorter term.[36] Of course, if the rise in demand is not great, it is more likely that US junior associates will suffer a reduction in salary even if the amount of legal work purchased has increased. Thus, again, the overall effect depends on the magnitude of the increase in demand as compared to the negative employment effects on junior associates.[37]

4. Empirical Evidence to Date

The foregoing analysis suggests cross cutting effects that vary across areas of legal practice – which means empirical examination of employment effects may be useful. Although studies have examined the impact of outsourcing on other sectors of the economy (with mixed results), there is little examination of the impact of outsourcing in legal services. A key reason for this is that many client firms (and individuals) do not provide detailed data on their spending on legal services and many providers of legal services – such as law firms – are not publicly traded, so obtaining data on their activity is not easy.[38] Even when some data on these providers might be available (e.g., from the US Business Census, which occurs every five years), the kind of data one would need to assess employment effects (e.g., how much junior associate work/outsourceable work goes into providing a legal service, the price elasticity for specific legal services) is not generally available. Although this suggests that it might be difficult to empirically assess employment effects on US attorneys, one suspects the net effect may be quite modest in either direction. A key reason for this is that studies on the net employment effect in other sectors (where outsourcing is more common) suggest fairly mixed results (Grossman and Rossi-Hansberg 2008, 2010; Benz and Kohler 2010; Feenstra 2010; Monarch et al. 2013). Another important reason is that the short-run effects may look quite different to the longer-run effects (which allows for prices across an economy to adjust more fully) (Feenstra 2010). The evidence thus far from outsourcing in other sectors is that the effects tend to change over time (Grossman and Rossi-Hansberg 2008, 2010; Benz and Kohler 2010; Feenstra 2010; Monarch et al. 2013). All of this underscores how difficult it is to come to conclusions about the employment and salary effects of LPO to India in both the short run and the longer run.

B. *Normative Concerns and Policy Interventions*

However, even if we had convincing estimates about the employment effects on US attorneys, that would not necessarily tell us whether there were significant normative concerns at play (or which direction those concerns might cut). The key reason for this is that the employment effects on US attorneys are not the only issues of normative significance.

In particular, even if many more legal services were purchased, we cannot say whether that is desirable without knowing whether the new suits or legal services purchased are socially desirable or not (Shavell 1997). Thus, if plaintiffs are likely to bring new frivolous suits, then LPO to India is increasing the amount of undesirable frivolous litigation. However, if the new suits brought are likely to be socially desirable, then LPO to India increases desirable litigation.[39] Which is more likely is probably going to vary with the area of law.

As an example, let us consider private securities fraud litigation and assume that LPO to India reduces litigation costs for both plaintiff and defendant. If we assume that the bulk of the plaintiff's total costs in bringing a suit are the legal costs, then the drop in costs from LPO may well induce more new suits

(Alexander 1991; Pritchard et al. 2007). Now let us look at the defense side. It seems unlikely that defense costs in this area are primarily associated with the attorney's fees for defending the case – one might expect the primary costs to be distraction of executives' time and bad publicity for the defendant firm (ibid.). In light of this, we might not expect the drop in legal costs to have much effect on defense behavior. If so, then the drop in costs primarily leads to more plaintiff suits. If these suits are likely to be frivolous, this seems socially undesirable. Of course, other areas of law may exhibit the opposite tendencies, and that would lead to more-desirable suits (e.g., suits involving matters where access to legal services is underprovided).This analysis, however, provides only a slight window into the complexity of the normative issues. For example, the distributional impact of LPO to India on senior and junior attorneys is a topic that may generate its own normative issues (e.g., training of the next generation of senior attorneys). Another important effect may be what greater LPO does to the likelihood of settlement and the development of precedent (Fiss 1984; Prescott and Spier 2016). To the extent that the reduction in legal costs makes litigation relatively more attractive to settlement than before, we might see more suits going to judgment, which may lead to more decisions establishing precedent.

These broader social effects are important, but there are yet other issues that directly affect the regulation of the legal profession, such as the impact the emergence of a global supply chain might have on ethical standards. For example, let us assume that a US law firm running a large products liability suit decides to outsource a substantial amount of legal work to an LPO in India that is: (i) a corporation, (ii) receives third-party (nonlawyer) financing, (iii) is a division within a larger entity providing accounting, finance, and information technology services (i.e., a multidisciplinary practice), and (iv) allows attorneys to freely advertise. These practices may run afoul of ethical standards in the United States, but perhaps not elsewhere. If so, should the US or state bars then attempt to prevent this? As a normative matter, might it be desirable to encourage some degree of competition among ethics regulators (as some might argue in other contexts, such as corporate governance and medical tourism)?[40] These kinds of issues have important implications meriting further inquiry and should not be eclipsed by the potential employment effects. It is to some of these broader issues that I now turn.

IV. GOING BEYOND EMPLOYMENT EFFECTS

LPO to India is likely to have effects beyond those on US attorney employment. To highlight these, I discuss two potential effects: the possibility of increasing atomization of the legal services market and the potential to restructure legal services markets, thereby impacting their competitive terrain.

A. *Atomization*

As firms break legal work into smaller and smaller tasks, an issue arises about whether we may see greater atomization of the legal services market – that is, firms contracting with more and more suppliers (e.g., law firms, LPO firms) for completing the smaller tasks associated with one legal project. This is not the same as the question of how many tasks a legal project can be decomposed into (e.g., twenty tasks), but rather whether we see the sourcing of these tasks from twenty different providers or from just a handful of providers (e.g., five to six).

Respondents indicated that it was not common to source through twenty different providers in "spot market-like" transactions (interviews 2, 4–7, 9, 10, 11, 14, 19, and 29, 2014–2015). Rather, customers hire either one LPO firm or a small number of LPO firms (e.g., five to six) when it is clear that there could be greater atomization (Sako et al. 2013; interviews 2, 4–7, 9, 10, 11, 14, 19, and 29, 2014–2015). This seems somewhat surprising because atomization has benefits – for example, greater supplier portfolio flexibility makes the firm less reliant on particular suppliers, resulting in the smoother provision of services, and the greater competition from having so many suppliers is likely to lead to lower costs (Arroyo and Bitran 2007; Wei and Møller 2009; Teixeira 2014). Yet we see little movement in this direction.

One explanation is that breaking up supply chains into so many different providers raises coordination and contracting costs (Sako et al. 2013). Of course, there was coordination even prior to LPO, but that happened at the outside law firm (i.e., deciding how to divide up work among associates and partners) and at the client's in-house department. However, in both cases the coordination is occurring within an organization, which very likely results in lower coordination costs than using twenty different outside suppliers (Coase 1937; Williamson 1981). This is a familiar result from Coase's seminal 1937 paper on transaction costs explaining the choice of whether to engage in production within the firm or to buy from the market.

Although clearly a plausible explanation, there are ways to reduce coordination costs, such as hiring an intermediary to coordinate (e.g., a wedding planner or project manager). Indeed, the recent appearance of entities operating as project managers (of sorts) for legal work (e.g., Axiom Law) suggests that coordinating costs may not be a terribly large impediment to atomization. Moreover, as technology improves, coordination costs are likely to decline (Arroyo and Bitran 2007; Dakshinamoorthy and Gordon 2010).[41]

Another supplementary explanation is that clients value the closer and ongoing relationships obtained by having only five or so LPO providers. Of course, closer relationships can be obtained by keeping the work in-house, too, so for a "five to six outside LPO supplier" strategy to make sense, the client needs to desire both (i) a closer relationship with suppliers and (ii) the expertise and skills associated with outside legal service providers. When might this combination be desirable?

One possible area is when a client is increasingly global in its operations. First, global business is more complex and uncertain than operating in just one market (Sako et al. 2013). There are different rules, norms, and ways of doing business across countries, and there is greater uncertainty because more things may change when you are active in twenty countries than when you are active in just one. Consequently, we might expect clients to hew closely to a smaller set of providers who provide multiple services or products to the client and are thus more likely to invest in developing a deeper understanding of their client's businesses than a firm that just supplies one thing to the client (Bhagat et al. 2004; Roe (1994).

Second, global firms may need to rely on more than just their in-house departments to obtain legal services, because in-house departments probably do not attempt to keep track of all the different areas of law across countries with a high level of expertise (on both substantive law and process matters) and still meet the client's daily legal needs. This can be addressed by working with some outside legal service providers. These features of global business suggest clients are likely to have larger in-house departments (which has happened) (ibid.) as well as a smaller set of outside providers to obtain both the closer relationships and greater range of expertise. This explanation – in combination with coordinating costs and other matters (e.g., being able to obtain extra legal services or legal capacity from their preferred providers should that be necessary – Coates et al. 2011) – appears to provide a more complete explanation for the limited atomization of the legal services market.

Finally, it is noteworthy that this pattern of purchasing LPO services also bears substantial similarities to how larger US corporate clients, which tend to be more global, purchase legal services from outside law firms (Coates et al. 2011). The use of a small number of multiple providers is common, but the providers often have relationships built on longer-term contact with the clients. Simply put, legal services are purchased in similar ways whether one is dealing with an outside law firm or an LPO as the supplier. This is not altogether surprising given that their clients are often similar and their concerns about purchasing legal services are likely to be somewhat similar. Indeed, the small number of outside providers with closer relationships with the firm also seems common in other sectors with global supply chains (Sako et al. 2013; Teixeira 2014).

B. *Restructuring of Legal Services Markets?*

The emergence of a global supply chain appears primed to reshape the legal services markets. Although there may be many areas in which this restructuring may occur, I focus on two in this section: first, changes to the size of legal service providers, and second, changes to how providers compete for work.

A global supply chain may aid not only in disaggregating legal work but also in disaggregating law firms and legal service providers, thereby reducing their size. This might happen in at least two ways: (i) there may be less need to hire as many junior associates (because some of their work is completed by LPOs), unless there is a substantial increase in demand effect, and (ii) some partners might choose to leave the firm and branch out on their own, relying on LPO to help them scale up when necessary.

This latter effect may be more likely if the primary reason that some partners were in the law firm was because of back office support. If that back office can be obtained now through outsourcing, there is less need for these partners to stay within the firm. Indeed, respondents indicated that they have witnessed an increasing number of younger partners and senior associates leaving well-known law firms to set up their own practice while openly acknowledging their reliance on outsourcing (often on their websites) as a way for them to provide comparable service to that found in larger firms (interviews 12 and 21, 2015). Although one of the key reasons for this change is the compensation/equity structure at large firms for younger partners and increasingly individualized partner reputations, the emergence of outsourcing has made the decision to leave the larger firm that much easier (interviews 21, 22, and 29, 2015).

Of course, other forces impact the size of law firms (some pushing toward larger firms), so definitive conclusions would be premature at this stage. However, there is little research examining these issues in spite of their significance and their likelihood for having a large impact on the practice of law. This would be a fruitful area for further research.

In addition to this effect, the rise of LPO adds another player into the legal services marketplace that is likely to affect its competitive structure. This is on at least two fronts – first, LPOs and large law firms might become both competitors as well as collaborators. Because LPOs and large law firms are both outside legal service providers, they are at least partial competitors (for work that both can provide) and collaborators (for work they do together in the supply chain that neither provides by itself) (Burke Robertson 2011; Gardner 2014). Second, when an LPO provides support to a small law firm (perhaps composed of former partners of larger law firms), that small law firm is more able to compete with the larger law firms. Thus, if a client is now willing to send work out of its in-house department, it is likely faced with a choice between a large law firm, an LPO, or a provider offering to utilize both in combination (e.g., a smaller law firm relying on LPO).[42]

These choices raise issues about how the interaction between these players should be conceptualized. For a sliver of how such an analysis might proceed, consider that each of these providers may have comparative advantages over one another. Although final answers are difficult to provide at this early stage, some of the key factors can be identified.

First, LPOs and law firms probably deliver different kinds of work (and may have different types of employees). For example, LPO firms likely provide process- and technology-driven outcomes, and large law firms usually provide subject matter expertise. This creates some sense of division. Thus, when a client needs "high-end" subject matter expertise (akin to artisanal work), it may go to a large law firm, and when it needs a process-driven outcome, it might go to an LPO firm. Although plausible, this account is too simplistic because it assumes that subject matter expertise and process outcomes do not overlap (which they might), but it also ignores the presence of the small law firm with LPO support, which should be able to provide the artisanal features as well as the process in some measure.

Second, the provider types might vary in their internal incentive structures and accountability mechanisms, and that may have an impact on their skills. For example, promotion at large law firms is often modeled on a tournament structure in which skill in a particular area of law and ability to recruit new business are thought to be important (Galanter and Palay 1991). Promotion at LPO firms appears to depend in part on the ability to recruit new business but also on the ability to staff teams and meet targets for fairly narrow areas of business (Interviews 2–4, 6, 7, 9, and 19, 2014–2015). Small law firms working with LPO firms may have a different set of structures. Moreover, accountability mechanisms are likely to vary, too – reporting lines in LPOs probably look quite different to those in large law firms. Compounding this is the likelihood that those who are considering careers in these organizations may self-select into them (assuming they are aware of their relative strengths, weaknesses, and preferences) and that the organizations may adopt different ongoing training or "skilling" regimes.

Here also the interaction between these players is little researched and provides multiple areas for future research. Although there are many further wrinkles one might discuss, the object of this section is simply to highlight that the rise of LPO opens up a number of very significant questions that might have long-lasting effects. Indeed, in many ways, this is just the beginning of an important inquiry into the likely restructuring of the legal services markets.

V. CONCLUSION

The evolving global supply chain for legal services portends significant changes to the legal services markets. This essay explores some of these changes by focusing on the offshoring of legal services to India, providing an analytical framework for exploring its effects on questions of substantial interest and highlighting some fruitful future avenues of inquiry.

The key findings are that LPO to India is available for a wider range of legal services than is commonly thought, is growing and morphing rapidly, and touches many more countries than just the United States and India – making it a truly global phenomenon. Second, its likely effects on employment of US attorneys are quite complex and nuanced. In particular, its effects cut in multiple directions – some increasing employment and salaries of US attorneys and others decreasing them. The net impact is thus ambiguous in the abstract, depends on a number of factors, and is likely to vary with the area of law and the seniority of the attorney. For example, the employment effects on junior attorneys working in mergers and acquisitions is likely to be different (and probably more negative) than those working in underserved areas of legal practice (where the effects are likely to be positive). However, even if we were to identify likely employment effects across all areas of practice, it is not clear what, if any, normative or policy prescriptions might follow. This all serves to underscore one of the core messages of this paper – how difficult it is to divine definitive across-the-board answers to these questions and the value of careful, nuanced, and contextual scholarship in this area. Third, the potential effect on the employment of US attorneys is only one of the effects of LPO to India and perhaps not the most long-lasting. Other effects include potential changes to the structure and operation of law practice. Indeed, these changes may be the ones that have the truly seismic effects on the legal profession.

However, one can imagine many other questions of great significance, too, such as how ethics regulators might respond to the impending competition on ethics rules, how law firms might respond to a growing demand for LPO-type services (e.g., creating captive LPO firms), how law schools and legal educators might respond, and how junior attorneys might be trained in the future. These questions arise from the emergence of a global supply chain for legal services and are provided as small teasers for the kinds of issues that may be addressed in more fulsome analyses in future research.

Notes

1 Some empirically oriented LPO papers (though not focusing on the effects noted in the text) include Wharton (2008), Sako (2006, 2009, 2010), Krishnan (2009), Mathew and Thomas (2009), Ballakrishnen and Wilkins (2012), and Sako et al. (2013).

2 Recent scholarship has also examined outsourcing from the perspective of modularity (Blair et al. 2011). For a more broad discussion of modularity, see Smith (2012).

3 For an early discussion of "unbundling," see Mosten (1994). For an excellent recent discussion, see Greiner et al. (2013).

4 One might call overseas outsourcing *offshoring*, but I use the terms interchangeably.

5 Thirty-one individuals were interviewed and were promised confidentiality. Thus, they are referred to as "Interview X."

6 There are other types of legal service providers as well (e.g., "new law" or "alternative law"), but I do not discuss those here. For a general discussion on the value of business lawyers, see Gilson (1984).

7 LPO providers seem to have been successful (thus far) at maintaining low attrition rates and providing a team of people with experience who possess the subtle knowledge that comes from working with the same set of people on similar tasks (Kazmin 2009).

8 This bears some similarity to performance measures being designed at some firms in the United States for assessing in-house counsel and law firms (Johnson 2013).

9 That raises an interesting matter – as in-house departments grew, so did law firms. This did not seem to result in a reduction in legal work.

10 For more, see Krishnan (2009), Mathew and Thomas (2009), and interviews 1–21 and 29–31, 2014–2015.

11 In India, the lion's share of the compliance-oriented work was conducted by company secretaries and other functionaries, not lawyers. Some Indian firms specialize in providing just these services, and many of their customers are technology-related firms (both of Indian and foreign origin). These firms are not considered LPOs in India (Interviews 2–6, 8, 9, and 13, 2014–2015). It is noteworthy that some of the work listed above (e.g., compliance work) may be conducted in the United States not only by law firms but also by accounting or consulting firms and corporate secretaries.

12 For example, in a standard merger scenario three to four areas of law are often implicated (e.g., corporate law, competition law, tax), and many law firms provide services along these lines – in a sense, a vertical division of labor. However, a few LPOs are trying to describe some legal services as being more horizontal. Thus, some LPOs offer processing that cuts across competition and corporate law such that it is not "legal area" expertise per se, but rather expertise in processing of parts of a merger (Interviews 1, 4, 6, 14, and 29, 2014–2015).

13 Commoditized services compete on price and quality as any other commodity (e.g., pens) might. For an example in the context of LPO, see some of the services offered at BraMoh law, www.bramohlaw.com/ (accessed October 9, 2015).

14 If a specialized service, developed to meet the requirements of one client, were to be valuable to other customers, the LPO firm could use its first encounter to standardize a product for other clients. This is similar to how some technology consulting firms offer new services and how some investment banks produce new financial products (Blair et al. 2011).

15 LPO firms offering appellate brief writing appear to follow a model whereby they undertake the tasks that would be assigned to junior and midlevel associates in the United States and then give their work product to the senior US person in charge (Interviews 2, 4–6, 15, and 21, 2014–2015).

16 This is also consistent with anecdotal evidence gleaned from programs targeted in part to EU audiences where LPO was an important agenda item (Mendonca 2014; Panagea3 2011).

17 These two factors also contribute to the continued growth of disaggregation of legal services.

18 Of course, if Indian firms developed the software, that would increase their business.

19 For a discussion in the context of manufacturing, see Blair et al. (2011).

20 For an example of such training services, see www.lawwave.com and Mathew and Thomas (2009).

21 LSC also has a Technology Initiative Grant program (www.lsc.gov/grants-grantee-resources/our-grant-programs/tig) to encourage further thought and research on this issue.

22 Some respondents indicated a concern that technology-enabled legal services, not accompanied by representation by a qualified attorney, may not result in better services (Interviews 22–25, 2015), but I do not address that question in this paper because outsourcing generally assumes that the client is still being represented by an attorney.

23 This was later followed by part of the ABA's 20/20 Ethics Report, which proposed changes to the Comments to the Model Rules of Professional Conduct (consistent with the 2008 opinion) to spell out what attorneys are expected to do when they outsource (ABA 2012).

24 See Florida Bar, Opinion 2007–2 (2008); North Carolina State Bar Association, Formal Opinion 12 (2007); Association of Bar of City of New York 2006–3 (2006); Los Angeles County Bar Association, Opinion 518 (2006); San Diego City Bar Association, Opinion 2007–1 (2007); The Supreme Court of Ohio, Opinion 2009–6; and Board of Commissioners on Grievances and Discipline, August 14, 2009. Available at www.supremecourt.ohio.gov/PIO/news/2009/BOCadvisoryOp_082409.asp.

25 For more, see Mathew and Thomas (2009) and Global Legal Post (2013).

26 It is noteworthy that LPO to India has been happening since at least 2001 (and picking up steam in 2004), yet the employment situation for lawyers in the United States did not appear to suffer at that time. The primary job losses (or deferments) arose in 2008–2009 due to the global economic crisis rather than outsourcing. (Ribstein 2010; Gunderman and Mutz 2014; Morley 2015).

27 Also, for now, one can assume that the cost savings (and other efficiencies) from LPO to India apply across the board to all US legal services.

28 See Grossman and Rossi-Hansberg (2008) for the general argument, albeit not in the context of legal service outsourcing. Susskind (2008) hints at this when he refers to "latent" demand.

29 If no junior associates were involved, there would be no cost savings from outsourcing.

30 The economic literature identifies one further effect: the "relative price effect" (Grossman and Rossi-Hansberg 2008; Feenstra 2010). However, I do not discuss this in greater depth because LPO is available across the world (not just in the United States), making interpreting this effect more ambiguous, and even if LPO grew to be a large part of the US legal market, it would still be small in global trade terms and, one suspects, likely to have a very small relative price effect.

31 Although not discussed in this paper, it is plausible that other matters could be important as well (e.g., outsourcing costs might change as the amount used increases) (Feenstra 2010).

32 For example, if the expected costs of litigation before outsourcing were $100 and outsourcing reduced those by $2, the number of new purchasers depends heavily on whether many people have expected benefits of litigation between $98 and $100 because these are the only people who will now purchase legal services, but did not before (i.e., those with more than $100 expected benefits would have purchased before and after and those with less than $98 would not have purchased before and after). However, if outsourcing reduced costs by $20, the potential cache of new purchases are those with expected benefits of litigation between $80 and $100, which seems larger.

33 An alternative would be to focus on whether business clients might respond to outsourcing by asking law firms to do more work on the existing number of mergers (i.e., work them more intensively). That is possible, but one suspects there may not be much more work available to be done – most business clients probably instruct law firms, for M&A, to spend what is necessary to make the deal happen, which leaves little room for more-plausible expenditures.

34 How much might depend on the incentives of the senior partners at law firms. One doubts that the clients will push hard to save money on big M&A deals (the legal costs are probably too small relative to the merger), but the law firm partners may find it profitable to outsource. If the law firm is charging flat fees, they have an incentive to outsource to India to make larger profits. However, if they are charging on an hourly basis, they may be less inclined to outsource unless it helps attract deals to their law firm or they consider the quality better.

35 Such purchases will be split across the various providers of compliance services (e.g., law firms, consulting firms, accounting firms, compliance officers, corporate secretaries, LPO firms). One should note, however, that a large driver of compliance work is new regulation, which it seems safe to assume LPO providers have little control over.

36 This can be seen if one takes the example in the text and additionally assumes that each senior person devotes one hundred hours to the project, charging $1,000 per hour, and each junior person devotes eighty hours, charging $250 per hour (prior to outsourcing). This means ten projects require ten thousand hours of senior attorney

time and forty thousand hours of junior attorney time (i.e., four thousand hours of junior associate time per project) for a total cost of $20 million (i.e., 10[(10 × 100 × $1,000) + (50 × 80 × $250)]). When outsourcing becomes available, the need for junior associate time on each project drops to half of what it was before (i.e., before it was four thousand per project, so now it is two thousand per project), and there is also an increase in demand for the projects. Let us assume that demand now rises to twenty-two projects per year, which means there is a need for forty-four thousand hours of junior associates time in the United States (plus more senior attorney time and of course the costs of outsourcing to India). If this increased need for US junior associate time is not met by an increased supply of US junior associates, then US junior associates' salaries may rise to reflect the increased total demand and limited supply of their services. Of course, if the increasing demand effect is smaller, the salary effect may disappear, but conceptually it is possible (Grossman and Rossi-Hansberg 2008).

37 This is largely consistent with the trade literature on the effects of outsourcing low-skilled tasks on those engaged in high-skilled work (Grossman and Rossi-Hansberg 2008, 2010).

38 There is data on trade in services at the global level, but it does not break out legal services separate from other services. See the US Census Bureau's website, www.census.gov/foreign-trade/Press-Release/current_press_release/index.html.

39 See Greiner et al. (2013) for an excellent discussion of access to justice and the use of evidence-based research (e.g., randomized controlled trials) to assess questions of importance in this area. See also Sandefur and Clarke (2015) for an overview of some of the key issues. Note that if LPO leads to an increase in desirable litigation, that may enhance the deterrent effect of the law and reduce the number of wrongs that occur as well (e.g., related to compliance matters). There are likely to be other effects of increased litigation activity that I do not discuss in this paper for expositional brevity.

40 For a discussion of regulatory competition in corporate law, see Bebchuk (1992) and Romano (1993) and in the context of medical tourism, see COHEN (2014).

41 Indeed, one of the advantages of Alibaba (or any business-to-business connector) is its ability to help reduce these costs for business-to-business transactions.

42 I have not included in-house departments as competitors to LPO and outside law firms both for expositional brevity and because keeping work in-house is a decision to "make" rather than "buy," but of course, in a choice among alternative ways to obtain legal services, in-house would be an important alternative.

References

Alexander, Janet Cooper. 1991. "Do the Merits Matter? A Study of Settlement in Securities Class Actions." *Stanford Law Review* 43 (3): 497–598.

Allen & Overy. 2011. "Allen & Overy Launches Office in Belfast." www.allenovery.com/news/en-gb/articles/Pages/Allen-and-Overy-launches-office-in-Belfast.aspx.

American Bar Association. 2008. "ABA Commission on Ethics and Professional Responsibility." *Formal Opinion* 08–451. www.americanbar.org/groups/professional_responsibility/publications/ethics_opinions/aba_formal_ethics_opinions_index_by_issue_dates.html.

2012. "ABA Commission on Ethics 20/20, Resolution 105C." www.americanbar.org/content/dam/aba/administrative/ethics_2020/20121112_ethics_20_20_overarching_report_final_with_disclaimer.authcheckdam.pdf.

Arroyo, Pilar Ester and Gabriel R. Bitran. 2007. "Coordination of Supply Chain Networks and the Emergence of Mini-Maestros (research paper no. 4674–08, December 1, MIT Sloan School of Management, Cambridge). www.ssrn.com/abstract=1082440).

Ballakrishnen, Swethaa and David B. Wilkins. 2012. "Putting "India" Back into the Study of the Indian LPO Industry." Draft on file with author.

Bebchuk, Lucian A. 1992. "Federalism and the Corporation: The Desirable Limits on State Competition in Corporate Law." *Harvard Law Review* 105 (7): 1435–1510.

Benz, Sebastian and Wilhelm Kohler. 2010. "Managerial versus Production Wages: Offshoring, Country Size and Endowments." CESifo Working Paper Series no. 3292. www.ssrn.com/abstract=1738172.

Bhagat, Sanjai, Bernard S. Black, and Margaret Blair. 2004. "Relational Investing and Firm Performance." *Journal of Financial Research* 27: 1–30.

Bhagwati, Jagdish, Arvind Panagariya, and T. N. Srinivasan. 2004. "The Muddles Over Outsourcing." *Journal of Economic Perspectives* 18 (4): 93–114.

Blair, Margaret, Cynthia A. Williams, and Li-Wen Lin. 2011. "The Roles of Standardization, Certification, and Assurance Services in Global Commerce." In *Corporate Social Responsibility and Corporate Governance: The Contribution of Economic Theory and Related Disciplines*. International Economic Association Series, Conference, vol. 149, edited by Lorenzo Sacconi et al. London: Palgrave Macmillan.

Blair, Margaret, Erin O'Hara O'Connor, and Gregg Kirchhoefer. 2011. "Outsourcing, Modularity, and the Theory of the Firm." *Brigham Young University Law Review* 2011 (2): 263–314.

Borsand, Sasha and Amar Gupta. 2009. "Public and Private Sector Legal Process Outsourcing: Moving toward a Global Model of Legal Expertise Deliverance." *Pace International Law Review Online Companion* 1 (1): 1–21.

Burke Robertson, Cassandra. 2011. "A Collaborative Model of Offshore Legal Outsourcing." *Arizona State Law Journal* 43 (1): 125–179.

2014. "Private Ordering in the Market for Professional Services." *Boston University Law Review* 94 (3): 179–234.

Coase, R. H. 1937. "The Nature of the Firm." *Economica* 4 (16): 386–405.

Coates, John C., Michele DeStefano, David B. Wilkins, and Ashish Nanda. 2011. "Hiring Teams, Firms and Lawyer: Evidence of the Evolving Relationships in the Corporate Legal Market." *Law and Social Inquiry* 36 (4): 999–1031.

Cohen, I. Glenn. 2014. *Patients with Passports: Medical Tourism, Law and Ethics*. New York: Oxford University Press.

Cotts, Cynthia and Liane Kufchock. 2007. "US Firms Outsource Legal Services to India." *New York Times*, August 21. www.nytimes.com/2007/08/21/business/worldbusiness/21iht-law.4.7199252.html.

Dakshinamoorthy, Vijay and Michael D. Gordon. 2010. "Wealth Creation through Coordination and Efficiency in the Rural Procurement Supply Chain: An Examination of Mechanisms, Structures and Costs." www.ssrn.com/abstract=1550194.

Daly, Mary C. and Carole Silver. 2007. "Flattening the World of Legal Services? The Ethical and Liability Minefields of Offshoring Legal and Law-Related Services." *Georgetown Journal of International Law* 38 (3): 401–447.

Davies, Robert. 2014. "SA Growing as Legal Outsourcing Host." *IOL*. October 12. www.sbeta.iol.co.za/business/opinion/columnists/sa-growing-as-legal-outsourcing-host-1763835.

Economist. 2010. "The Growth of Legal Outsourcing, Passage to India: Companies and Law Firms Are Turning to India for Cut-Price Legal Services." June 24. www.economist.com/node/16439006.

Feenstra, Robert C. 2010. *Offshoring in the Global Economy: Microeconomic Structure and Macroeconomic Implications*. Cambridge: MIT Press.

Fisher, Daniel. 2011. "New Precedent for Law Firms." *Forbes*, June 8. www.forbes.com/forbes/2011/0627/entrepreneurs-mark-harris-axiom-law-moving-target.html.

Fiss, Owen M. 1984. "Against Settlement." *Yale Law Journal* 93 (6): 1073–1090.

Flood, John. 2012. "Will There Be Fallout from Clementi? The Repercussions for the Legal Profession After Legal Services Act 2007." *Michigan State Law Review* 2012 (2): 537–565.

Galanter, Marc S. and Thomas Palay. 1991. *Tournament of Lawyers: The Transformation of the Big Law Firms*. Chicago: University of Chicago Press.

Gardner, Heidi K. 2014. "The Collaboration Imperative for Today's Law Firms: Leading High-Performance Teamwork for Maximum Benefit" (research paper no. 2014–23, Harvard Law School Center on the Legal Profession, Cambridge). www.ssrn.com/abstract=2517314.

Geis, George S. 2010. "An Empirical Examination of Business Outsourcing Transactions." *Virginia Law Review* 96 (2): 241–300.

Gilson, Ronald J. 1984. "Value Creation by Business Lawyers: Legal Skills and Asset Pricing." *Yale Law Journal* 94 (2): 239–313.

Global Legal Post. 2013. *Legal Outsourcing Guide 2013/2014*. www.s3-eu-west-1.amazonaws.com/www.globallegalpost.com/lpo/lpo-handbook-2013–14.pdf.

Greiner, D. James, Cassandra Wolos Pattanayak, and Jonathan Hennessy. 2013. "Limits of Unbundled Legal Assistance: A Randomized Study in a Massachusetts District Court and Prospects for the Future." *Harvard Law Review* 126 (4): 904–989.

Grossman, Gene M. and Esteban Rossi-Hansberg. 2008. "Trading Tasks: A Simple Theory of Offshoring." *American Economic Review* 98 (5): 1978–1997.

2010. "External Economies and International Trade Redux." *Quarterly Journal of Economics* 125 (2): 829–858.

Gunderman, Richard and Mark Mutz. 2014. "The Collapse of Big Law: A Cautionary Tale for Big Med." *Atlantic*, February 11. www.theatlantic.com/business/archive/2014/02/the-collapse-of-big-law-a-cautionary-tale-for-big-med/283736/.

Hadfield, Gillian K. 2000. "The Price of Law: How the Market for Lawyers Distorts the Justice System." *Michigan Law Review* 98 (4): 953–1006.

Herbert Smith Freehills. 2010. "Herbert Smith Opens Dispute Operation in Belfast." November. www.herbertsmithfreehills.com/news/news20101124-hs-opens-disputes-operation-in-belfast.

Interview 1. New Jersey, 2014.

Interview 2. Mumbai, India, 2014.

Interview 3. New Delhi, 2014.

Interview 4. Hyderabad, 2015.
Interview 5. Bangalore, 2015.
Interview 6. New Jersey, 2015.
Interview 7. New Jersey, 2015.
Interview 8. Mumbai, 2015.
Interview 9. Hyderabad, 2015.
Interview 10. Georgia, 2015.
Interview 11. New York, 2015.
Interview 12. Florida, 2015.
Interview 13. New York, 2015.
Interview 14. Bangalore, 2015.
Interview 15. Kolkata, 2015.
Interview 16. New Jersey, 2015.
Interview 17. New Delhi, 2015.
Interview 18. New York, 2015.
Interview 19. Michigan, 2015.
Interview 20. New York, 2015.
Interview 21. New York, 2015.
Interview 22. Florida, 2015.
Interview 23. Georgia, 2015.
Interview 24. Michigan, 2015.
Interview 25. Michigan, 2015.
Interview 26. Michigan, 2015.
Interview 27. Illinois, 2015.
Interview 28. Washington DC, 2015.
Interview 29. Boston, 2015.
Interview 30. New Delhi, 2015.
Interview 31. Mumbai, 2015.

Johnson, Patrick. 2013. "Top Ten Metrics That Your Legal Department Should Be Tracking." Association of Corporate Counsel. www.acc.com/legalresources/publications/topten/ttmtyldsbt.cfm.

Kazmin, Amy. 2009. "Outsourcing: Law Firms Fuel the Demand for Offshore Services." *Financial Times*, January 30. www.ft.com/cms/s/0/6012adeo-ecdd-11dd-a534–0000779fd2ac.html.

Kochhar, Kalpana, Utsav Kumar, Raghuram Rajan, Arvind Subramanian, and Ioannis Tokatlidis. 2006. "India's Pattern of Development: What Happened, What Follows?" (working paper WP/06/22, International Monetary Fund, Washington, DC). www.imf.org/external/pubs/ft/wp/2006/wp0622.pdf.

Kriegler, Yun. 2013. "LPO provider CPA Global Expands into Mainland China and the US." *Lawyer*, February 28. www.thelawyer.com/lpo-provider-cpa-global-expands-into-mainland-china-and-the-us/.

Krishnan, Jayanth. 2009. "Outsourcing and the Globalizing Legal Profession." *William and Mary Law Review* 48: 2189–2246.

Kuruvilla, Sarosh and Aruna Ranganathan. 2008. "Economic Development Strategies and Macro- and Micro- Level Human Resource Policies: The Case of India's 'Outsourcing' Industry." *Industrial and Labour Relations Review* 62: 39–72.

Lattman, Peter. 2007a. "Slater & Gordon: The World's First Publicly Traded Law Firm." *Wall Street Journal*, May 22. www.blogs.wsj.com/law/2007/05/22/slater-gordon-the-worlds-first-publicly-traded-law-firm/.

2007b. "Axiom: A Different Kind of Legal Practice." *Wall Street Journal*, November 27. www.blogs.wsj.com/law/2007/11/27/axiom-makes-temping-look-tempting-but-is-it/.

Maskell, Peter, Torben Pedersen, Bent Petersen, and Jens Dick-Nielsen. 2006. "Learning Paths to Offshore Outsourcing: From Cost Reduction to Knowledge Seeking." www.ssrn.com/abstract=982122.

Mathew, Shaun and Vikram Thomas. 2009. "Legal Process Outsourcing: An Examination of Its Structure, Viability, Limits and Potential." Draft (on file with author).

Mendonca, Jochelle. 2014. "Legal Process Outsourcing Firms See New Opportunities in Europe." *Economic Times*, June 27.

Monarch, Ryan, Jooyoun Park, and Jagadeesh Sivadasan. 2013. "Gains from Offshoring? Evidence from New US Microdata." Draft. www.ssrn.com/abstract=2211571.

Moore, Geoffrey A. and Mark Harris. 2014. "Bigger Fines Against Wall St. Should Not Result in More Lawyers." *New York Times*, September 4.

Morley, John D. 2015. "Why Law Firms Collapse." Draft on file with author.

Mosten, Forrest S. 1994. "Unbundling of Legal Services and the Family Lawyer." *Family Law Quarterly* 28 (3): 421–449.

Neil, Martha. 2007. "Hollywood Outsourcing Higher-End Legal Work to India." *ABA Journal*, November 12. www.abajournal.com/news/article/hollywood_outsourcing_higher_end_legal_work_to_india/.

2009. "As Rio Tinto Saves Millions, Other Corps. Will Outsource, Too, Counsel Says."*ABA Journal*, July 27.

Pangea3. 2011. "Legal Outsourcing Leader Launches London Office." www.pangea3.com/legal-outsourcing-leader-pangea3-launches-london-office.html.

2011. "Panagea3 Opens Major US Location." June 3. www.pangea3.com/Press-Releases/2011/pangea3-opens-major-us-location.html.

Pollak, Darya V. 2006. "'I'm Calling My Lawyer . . . in India!': Ethical Issues in International Legal Outsourcing." *UCLA Journal of International Law and Foreign Affairs* 11 (1): 99–160.

Prescott, J. J. and Kathryn E. Spier. 2016. "A Comprehensive Theory of Civil Settlement." *NYU Law Review* (forthcoming). www.ssrn.com/abstract=2632612.

Prism Legal. 2005. "Outsourced Legal Services." www.prismlegal.com/outsourced-legal-services/#List.

Pritchard, Adam C., Karen K. Nelson, and Marilyn F. Johnson. 2007. "Do the Merits Matter More? The Impact of the Private Securities Litigation Reform Act." *Journal of Law, Economics and Organization* 23 (3): 627–652.

Pro Bono Wire. 2015. "Letter from Esther: Reengineering Pro Bono." www.pbi.informz.net/admin31/content/template.asp?sid=41982&brandid=4063&uid=1000974576&mi=4590646&mfqid=18951829&ptid=0&ps=41982.

Regan, Milton C., Jr., Bruce MacEwen, and Larry E. Ribstein. 2007. "Law Firms, Ethics, and Equity Capital: A Conversation." *Georgetown Journal of Legal Ethics* 21 (1): 61–94.

Regan, Milton C., Jr. and Palmer T. Heenan. 2010. "Supply Chains and Porous Boundaries: The Disaggregation of Legal Services." *Fordham Law Review* 78 (5): 2137–2191.

Research and Markets. 2011. "Indian Legal Process Outsourcing Market: Public Sector Use of LPO Is the Largest New Source of Growth in 2011." Business Wire, October 7. www.mobile.reuters.com/article/2011/10/07/idUS87702+07-Oct-2011+BW20111007.

Ribstein, Larry E. 2004. "Lawyers as Lawmakers: A Theory of Lawyer Licensing." *Missouri Law Review* 69 (2): 299–364.

2010. "The Death of Big Law." *Wisconsin Law Review* 2010 (3): 749–816.

Roberts, Brandon. 2010. "The Firm Is Flat: Ethical Implications of Legal Offshoring." *Georgetown Journal of Legal Ethics* 23 (3): 799–812.

Roe, Mark J. 1994. *Strong Managers, Weak Owners: The Political Roots of American Corporate Finance*. Princeton, NJ: Princeton University Press.

Romagnino, Kara D. 2011. "Nearshore Alternative: Latin America's Potential in the Offshore Legal Process Outsourcing Marketplace." *University of Miami Inter-American Law Review* 42 (2): 367–413.

Romano, Roberta. 1993. *The Genius of American Corporate Law*. New York: American Enterprise Institute.

Rosen, Robert Eli. 1989. "The Inside Counsel Movement, Professional Judgment and Organizational Representation." *Indiana Law Journal* 64 (3): 479–553.

Sako, Mari. 2006. "Outsourcing and Offshoring: Implications for Productivity of Business Services." *Oxford Review of Economic Policy* 22 (4): 499–512.

2009. "Global Strategies in the Legal Services Market: Institutional Impacts on Value Chain Dynamics" (working paper, Novak Druce Centre for Professional Service Firms, University of Oxford, Oxford, England). www.eureka.bodleian.ox.ac.uk/4562/.

2010. "Make-or Buy Decisions in Legal Services: A Strategic Perspective" (working paper, Novak Druce Centre for Professional Service Firms, University of Oxford, Oxford, England). www.eureka.bodleian.ox.ac.uk/4561/.

Sako, Mari, George Chondrakis, and Paul M. Vaaler. 2013. "How Do Firms Make-and-Buy? The Case of Legal Services Sourcing by Fortune 500 Companies" (working paper, Oxford Saïd Business School, Oxford, England). www.sbs.eprints.org/4791/.

Sandefur, Rebecca L., and Thomas M. Clarke. 2015. "Increasing Access to Justice through Expanded 'Roles Beyond Lawyers': Preliminary Evaluation and Classification Frameworks." American Bar Foundation. Discussion Draft.

Schultz, Courtney I. 2010. "Legal Offshoring: A Cost Benefit Analysis." *Journal of Corporation Law* 35 (3): 639–661.

Shavell, Steven. 1997. "The Fundamental Divergence between the Private and the Social Motive to Use the Legal System." *Journal of Legal Studies* 26 (4): 575–612.

Smith, Henry E. 2012. "Property as the Law of Things." *Harvard Law Review* 125 (7): 1691–1726.

Spellman, Jennifer and Jeannea Varrichio. 2012. "Bad Reputation? The Potential Negative Impact of Outsourcing on the Legal Profession." *Hofstra Labour and Employment Law Journal* 29 (2): 575–608.

Susskind, Richard. 2008. *The End of Lawyers*. Oxford, England: Oxford University Press.

Teixeira, Joao C. A. 2014. "Outsourcing with Long Term Contracts: Capital Structure and Product Market Competition." *Review of Quantitative Finance and Accounting* 42 (2): 327–356.

Timmons, Heather. 2011. "Legal Outsourcing Firms Creating Jobs for American Lawyers." *New York Times*, June 2. www.nytimes.com/2011/06/03/business/03reverse.html.

Vee LPO. 2014. "About Us." www.veelpo.com/about-us.htm.

Vyas, Priyanka. 2014. "East Asia a Market for Legal Outsourcing." LegalEase Solutions. www.legaleasesolutions.com/newspage/east_asia_legal.htm.

Wei, Wei and Charles Møller. 2009. "Supply Chain Flexibility: Review and Future Directions." www.ssrn.com/abstract=1463066.

Weiss, Debra Cassens. 2008. "Indian Lawyers Handling Outsourced Work Do More Than Document Review." *ABA Journal*, May 12. www.abajournal.com/news/article/indian_lawyers_handling_outsourced_work_do_more_than_document_review/.

Wharton. 2008. "Why the Downturn May Not Leave Outsourcing Firms Down and Out." Knowledge@Wharton, December 11. www.knowledge.wharton.upenn.edu/india/article.cfm?articleid=4340.

Wilkins, David B. 2001. "Law Firms." In *International Encyclopedia of the Social and Behavioral Sciences*. Edited by Neil J. Smelser and Paul B. Baltes. Oxford, England: Pergamon.

Wilkins, David B. and G. Mitu Gulati. 1998. "Reconceiving the Tournament of Lawyers: Tracking, Seeding, and Information Control in the Internal Labor Markets of Elite Law Firms." *Virginia Law Review* 84 (8): 1581–1681.

Williamson, Oliver E. 1981. "The Economics of Organization: The Transaction Cost Approach." *American Journal of Sociology* 87 (3): 548–577.

14

Grand Advocates: The Traditional Elite Lawyers

Marc Galanter and Nick Robinson

I. INTRODUCTION

An observer of the legal scene in contemporary India quickly becomes aware of the presence of a stratum of legal superstars – advocates based at the Supreme Court and some of the High Courts who are very much in demand and widely known. These "Grand Advocates," as we call them, are the most visible and renowned legal professionals in present-day India. Stories abound of their strategic acumen, their preternatural articulateness (speaking for hours and days without notes), their esoteric quirks and outsized incomes, and their contributions to the "rule of law." This elite handful of lawyers is involved in almost every high-profile case in what is one of the most active and powerful higher judiciaries in the world (Robinson 2009; Rajamani and Sengupta 2010). Their clients include India's new überrich, major multinational corporations, and the country's political class.

We argue that grand advocates have not only survived but flourished in the age of globalization – benefiting from, while resisting absorption by, the rising law firm sector. A series of structural features of litigation and the judiciary in India have played a dominating role in perpetuating this unique set of lawyers and the culture they inhabit. Litigation in India tends to be less about money (as there are fewer deep pockets, judges rarely grant large monetary compensation, and it is difficult to collect an award) and more about control. Given the backlogged courts, cases may drag on for years, so it is necessary to secure beneficial interim orders as they relate to the ownership of property, command over an organization, or the validity of government regulation. To achieve these ends, Grand Advocates use the extensive human capital they have developed within the court system and their nuanced knowledge of both formal and informal judicial procedure. These assets are in many ways positional goods – particularly their reputational capital before certain judges –

that are difficult to share with juniors or partners. They are also assets that can be used in a wide range of cases, thus lessening the pressure to specialize among this select group of lawyers, who are still largely generalists.

We know of no close parallels to grand advocates among lawyers in other countries, at least outside South Asia. Unlike the venerated French or Brazilian jurists, who flourish in a system where judicial precedent is less decisive, the grand advocates are not based in or linked to academic institutions, nor do they produce books or concepts (Sweet 1992, 30–35). They are not "authorities" whose intellectual products are considered authoritative like the eminent British barristers who furnish "opinion of counsel" memoranda (Niles 1963, 86). Like the increasingly exclusive US Supreme Court bar, whose lawyers' name recognition increases the chance that their clients' cases are granted certiorari, grand advocates in India are known for securing hearings for their clients (Sundquist 2010). However, the US Supreme Court bar handles far fewer cases than the grand advocates and does not wield the same dominating influence in their relationship with judges.

The grand advocates' relative uniqueness when compared with their potential peers elsewhere is worth noting, as one of the central debates in comparative law is the degree to which legal systems around the world are converging. For example, scholars have examined whether and to what extent constitutions are converging (Tushnet 2009; Posner and Dixon 2010), or whether convergence is occurring between civil law and common law traditions (Merryman 1987; Mattei and Pes 2009). Meanwhile, few systematic comparative studies of the legal profession have been undertaken, and much less attention has been paid to the question of whether the structure of the legal profession is converging (Dias et al. 1981; Abel and Lewis 1988; Burrage 2006; Dezalay and Garth 2010; Halliday and Karpik 2011).If globalization is creating increasingly similar laws, regulations, and adjudicatory proceedings, one might expect the legal profession to also become more alike across countries as lawyers adapt to increasingly analogous contexts.

Answering this larger question about whether the structure of the legal profession is converging across countries is beyond the scope of this chapter. Instead, we provide a counterexample to the convergence thesis and, by detailing how grand advocates shape and are shaped by distinct features of the legal system in which they operate, show how unique forms of legal practice may be perpetuated even in the face of potentially homogenizing forces.

We begin our study, which is based on interviews with more than fifty legal professionals in Delhi, Mumbai, and Madras, by analyzing the structure of the legal system and the Indian bar in which grand advocates flourish.[1] We then turn to examine the type of work grand advocates do, the arc of their careers, and the impact they have on the legal system. Although the structure of this section of the bar has witnessed notable continuity, we conclude by finding that a new set of demands from clients, judges, and other lawyers may in the future fundamentally alter the space grand advocates currently occupy. This will likely not erase the distinctiveness of the grand advocates but will certainly shape their evolution.

II. BACKGROUND

Pre-British India had learned specialists in law, but nothing that corresponded to the legal professions of the modern world, which are made up of qualified practitioners who earn a living by representing clients before courts and tribunals and designing transactions that are affected by legal rules (Calkins 1968–1969; Rocher 1968–1969). Today's Indian legal profession is a product of the complex of British-style legal institutions imposed on India in the eighteenth and nineteenth centuries, but lawyers in India developed along different lines than their counterparts in Britain or elsewhere in the common law world (Setalvad 1960).[2]

The professional pattern as it crystallized in the late nineteenth century was a composite, drawing upon two main streams: (1) the royal courts in the Presidency towns (Bombay, Madras, and Calcutta), which were ruled by the British Crown and where English law was administered by British judges and there was a dual profession, with barristers briefed by solicitors, and (2) the East India Company, which until 1857 ruled most of India (i.e., the mofussil or interior) and operated courts staffed by civil servants that licensed indigenous *vakils* (a Persian word that once referred generally to an agent or emissary) to represent clients in those courts. The two systems of courts were merged when the British government displaced the East India Company after the 1857 rebellion (Derrett 1963).

Recruitment to the profession was through multiple sources: British barristers arrived from the United Kingdom to enjoy the higher fees that could be earned in India; elite Indians went to the Inns of Court in London to secure qualification; others acquired on-the-job training at the Indian courts and (after the establishment of universities in India starting in 1857) were joined by those who had attended law courses in India (Galanter 1968–1969; Gandhi 1988).

There was not a single hierarchy of courts in British India. Instead, there was a hierarchy within each province, culminating in a high court (or in a few cases, a court of the Judicial Commissioner). Appeal from these courts lay to the Privy Council in London and was expensive and rare. In 1935, under the Government of India Act, a federal court was established with a narrow jurisdiction over all of British India (Gadbois 1963, 19). After Independence in 1947, the constitution (1950) brought unification into a single hierarchical system of courts, headed by a supreme court with an expansive jurisdiction and wide powers of judicial review.

With the passage of the Advocates Act (1961), all the old grades of practitioners (vakils, barristers, pleaders of several grades, and mukhtars) were abolished and consolidated into a single body of advocates who enjoy the right to practice in courts throughout India. The only *formal* distinctions that remain within this body of advocates are:

1. Lawyers can be designated as senior advocates by the Supreme Court or any of the twenty-one High Courts. This is an elite stratum along the lines of the British Queen's Counsel (QCs). But the Indian distinction is far more selective: QCs make up almost 10 percent of British barristers, while senior advocates are less than 1 percent of Indian lawyers (The Bar Council 2013). Senior advocates enjoy priority of audience; they cannot appear without a separate "briefing" advocate (or, in the Supreme Court, an Advocate on Record [AOR]). Seniors are foreclosed from doing pleadings, drafting, and conveyances (Bar Council of India Rules 2009, Part 6, Chapter 1). We estimate that there are about a thousand senior advocates, including some four hundred designated by the Supreme Court (Supreme Court of India). A senior advocate designated by one court is recognized as a senior in other courts as well. Senior advocates may be attached to firms not as partners or employees but on retainers or fee arrangements. Few of the most prominent are so attached.
2. The requirement that an advocate on the Original Side of the Bombay and Calcutta High Courts be briefed by a solicitor was abolished in 1976, but it is still possible to qualify as a solicitor. This requires an extended apprenticeship as an articled clerk and passing an examination. Of those who seek this qualification, only a small portion (5–10 percent) pass the examination. For example, in 2010 in Bombay, only 11 of the 171 candidates (and none of the 30 first-time takers) passed (Ganz 2010). Some elite advocates in Bombay still insist on being briefed by a solicitor, but this is a mandate of custom rather than law (Interview 32, 2012).
3. Early on, the Supreme Court enacted rules requiring that all matters at the Supreme Court be filed by an AOR. AORs can argue matters, but frequently they serve in a solicitor-like role, briefing advocates. In all cases they perform the various formalities of registration and scheduling

TABLE 1. *Number of practitioners enrolled with the state bar councils*

Year	Number
1952	72,425
1985	290,676
1999	626,603
2011	1,273,289

Source: Report of the All-India Bar Committee (1953); Institute of Developing Economies (2001, 72); Ganz (2013)

of the case. One becomes an AOR by passing an examination administered by the Supreme Court.[3] In 2011 there were some 1,872 AORs. Estimates of the number actively engaged in practice range from 400 or 500 to 1,000 (Shrivastava 2012).

The number of persons admitted to practice law in India has increased from about 70,000 at the time of independence in 1947 to some 1.2 million today. No one knows how many of these are actually engaged in the practice of law. Our guess is that at least one-third and possibly one-half are *not* practicing law.

Less than 1 percent of these advocates are admitted to practice at the Supreme Court. As of 2013 the Supreme Court Bar Association lists 6,806 active resident members, 908 active nonresident members, and 2,701 temporary members.[4] The fraction of those with a substantial practice at the Supreme Court is not known.

III. THE BASIC STRUCTURE OF THE INDIAN LEGAL PROFESSION

Most of the old categories and grades of practitioners have been abolished, but new forms of diversity among lawyers have emerged. Lawyers may be found in firms, as in-house counsel, and in LPO (Weiss 2008; Wilkins 2012). All of these have proliferated in the past twenty years, but the great bulk of India's lawyers remain attached to the dominant model of professional life – the freestanding advocate who practices mainly, if not exclusively, at a single court. This model, formed in colonial times, was firmly institutionalized by the early twentieth century. In spite of the vast political and social change India has undergone, if we were to observe lawyers in India in 2013, we would find a set of distinctive and characteristic features of professional life that are surprisingly similar to what we would have found in 1913.

We might think of these features as the basic structure of the Indian legal profession. A schematic portrait of the model organization of legal services in India, then or now, would include:

- Lawyers practice by themselves, usually assisted by clerks, and sometimes by juniors in a casual and temporary apprenticeship arrangement. There are few firms or other enduring units for coordination and sharing among lawyers. Firms are proliferating but still involve only a tiny fraction of practicing lawyers – perhaps 2–3 percent – and the larger firms are rarely focused on litigation.
- Lawyers are oriented to courts (and other court-like forums) to the virtual exclusion of other legal settings. The orientation to courts is displayed spatially: lawyers spend much of their working day at a particular court. They typically see clients in home offices or in chambers near or attached to the court, or simply at the verandah or a corridor of the court. The identification of the lawyer with a particular court goes back to the earliest days of British rule (Sahay 1931, 24, 26, 33).
- The performance of the lawyer is overwhelmingly oral rather than written. With occasional exceptions, advocates focus on courtroom advocacy rather than advising, negotiating, or planning. That is, they are de facto barristers who operate in a setting in which the "solicitor" functions of advising are far less developed. Judges frequently cite oral argument in their judgments, and advocates feel little constraint in making arguments that were only partially developed in the written submissions, or not mentioned at all. The dominance of the barrister model is displayed in, and reinforced by, the structure of remuneration. Lawyers are typically paid by the "appearance" – that is, for court work in a particular case on a given day (Moog 1992, 26).
- Lawyers are relatively unspecialized. Although some advocates have a special expertise in tax or criminal matters, few lawyers limit themselves to one area of law.

One significant consequence of the thick and continuous interaction of lawyers at the court premises is that the lawyers at each court form a guild with a capacity for collective action. This was displayed dramatically in the resolute and persistent actions of the Pakistani lawyers – who occupy a social world similar to that of their Indian counterparts – who struck and demonstrated when judges of the Pakistan Supreme Court were removed by President Musharraf in November 2007 (Ghias 2010). The Indian examples of lawyers' strikes and boycotts are generally less inspiring. The first such assertion of lawyer muscle at the Supreme Court took place in 1982, when the Supreme Court Bar

Association staged a strike in response to a judicial memorandum that suggested eliminating oral argument in certain categories of cases (Dhavan 1986, 55–56). The strike action was called off when the judges reassured the lawyers that the suggested changes, which would have undercut a major source of income for lawyers, were merely proposals (Hindustan Times 1982). In 2012 the district court in Delhi was brought to a halt by lawyers protesting a rule that placed a monetary limit on cases that could be heard by the district courts (IBNLive 2012). In the same year lawyers in Karnataka boycotted courts across the state after a police attack on lawyers at the civil courts complex in Bangalore, where lawyers had attacked journalists covering a politically important trial, claiming that the journalists had portrayed them poorly in connection with earlier encounters (Daily News and Analysis 2012).

While grand advocates frequently hold bar offices, they are removed from involvement in such direct action. They typically disapprove of exercises of lawyers' street power, although as we will see, the bar's militant opposition to reform helps to preserve many features of the setting in which the grand advocates flourish.

IV. STEEP HIERARCHY

The preeminence of the grand advocates is a contemporary expression of a long-standing and pervasive pattern of steep hierarchy at the bar. At every level, the provision of legal services was (and is) dominated by a small number of lawyers with outsized reputations, who have the lion's share of clients, income, prestige, standing, and influence.

The pre-eminence of the Grand Advocates is a contemporary expression of a long-standing and pervasive pattern of steep hierarchy at the bar. At every level, the provision of legal services was (and is) dominated by a small number of lawyers with outsized reputations, who have the lion's share of clients, income, prestige, standing and influence.

This pattern has been noted by a number of observers of the Indian legal scene over the last half century. For example, in his late-1960s study of a district bar of about a hundred lawyers in Haryana, Charles Morrison identified "five or six" who are "recognized as 'leading lawyers'" (Morrison 1968–1969, 261). In his late-1970s study of a district court in Punjab, J. S. Gandhi reports that the twelve "specialist" lawyers (in a bar of more than two hundred) "handled among themselves at least 50 percent or more of the total practice" (Gandhi 1982, 79). Robert Moog in his mid-1980s account of the Varanasi bar describes how, of the more than three thousand advocates in Varanasi, "[a]pproximately two dozen senior advocates . . . dominate the civil practice . . . . It is not unusual for members of this elite group to have as many as twenty-five matters scheduled in court on one day" (Moog 1997, 73–74). In his 1991 study of lawyers in a Haryana district, Hans Nagpaul found that 10 percent of the three hundred lawyers enjoyed some 75 percent of the legal business (Nagpaul 1994, 59).

Upon the establishment of the Supreme Court of India in Delhi, in 1950, lawyers were drawn to the new court from cities where there were existing High Courts. At first these lawyers commuted to Delhi to argue their cases. Later many shifted to the capital, as prominent lawyers at the High Courts have continued to do. Before long, the Supreme Court had its own steep hierarchy of practitioners headed by an entourage of "leading lawyers," much along the lines familiar in High Courts and district courts throughout the country.

We estimate that the number of preeminent seniors – those we are calling "Grand Advocates" – at the Supreme Court today is something on the order of forty to fifty. If we add those of comparable status at the High Courts, there are at most a hundred that make up what one observer refers to as the "giants and legends of the litigation system" (e-mail from Nikhil Chandra 2012). This shape – very steep hierarchy, with a concentration of prestige, authority, and prosperity in a narrow group of senior lawyers – has been a constant feature of law practice in India in colonial times and after Independence, in the highest courts and in local courts, both when the bar was flourishing and when it went through difficult times.

In 1983 T. K. Oommen, a leading sociologist, provided a shrewd assessment of the profound consequences of the steep and pervasive professional hierarchy in the Indian bar (Oommen 1983). The concentration of business in a few hands, he observed, underlies a culture of postponement in the judiciary. Judges give postponements to eminent lawyers, who are constantly juggling more courtroom obligations than they can possibly attend, meaning that cases are dealt with in disconnected bits over a long period of time. As one young lawyer observed – this was almost thirty years later – "There is a cartelization of litigation by the senior counsel. They take on more cases than they can deal with. This leads to delays in the courts because the seniors don't make it for appearances . . . As a result, the quality of litigation suffers overall and it gets more expensive" (Interview 18, 2012).

Oommen concluded his study by remarking that "most importantly, the leading lawyers rather than the judges emerge as norm-setters and value-givers in the Court system (Oommen 1983, 24). Interpreted meanings provided by the lawyers in support of their clients rather than interpretations by judges assume importance in the application of law." Oommen made these observations about the dominant position of the top lawyers compared to the judges in the 1980s, before liberalization. But this sense of the dominance of the top lawyers is, if anything, more pronounced today. One leading lawyer observed: "The judges are almost irrelevant. We all know some man has to do it. It's good if they are good, but [it is] not expected. The counsel have learned to treat them with kid gloves. To guide them, I think the judges have a deep-rooted inferiority complex" (Interview 23, 2012). As this suggests, at least some grand advocates perceive themselves as positioned further up in the hierarchy than most judges. This sense of superiority may be reinforced by the social backgrounds of many of the grand advocates and judges. While grand advocates are almost always from a cosmopolitan background and well versed in English, judges come from a variety of settings, with many raised in non-English-speaking households in more-provincial settings.

We might think of the dominance of the lawyers as an instance of regulatory capture, in which the agenda and decisions of an agency (the courts in this instance), established to regulate an industry (here, litigation) in the light of external standards, instead reflect the perspective of the industry they are supposed to regulate (especially in relation to courtroom management) (Bernstein 1977). This is especially likely where, as here, the agency decision makers are recruited from among the regulated.

But the capture metaphor may lead us to overlook a more fundamental point. Thomas Reed Powell (1880–1955), a Harvard law professor, is credited with the observation that "if you think you can think about a thing that is inextricably attached to something else without thinking of the thing which it is attached to, then you have a legal mind" (Simpleman 1986, 545). In this spirit we can appreciate the artificiality of thinking about the institution of the grand advocates without thinking of the judicial setting in which they flourish. Indeed, we might imagine the grand advocates and India's higher courts as the inextricably attached parts of the same creature. In a setting where oral presentation overshadows written submission and where the judges have insufficient time and resources for independent research, the grand advocates enjoy the esteem of the judges, who give them more "face time" to argue and who rely on their accounts of the law and the facts. The grand advocates play an oversized role, and their presence thus helps to maintain the acephalous system in which similar legal questions are decided in slightly different ways by multiple small benches of judges of the Supreme Court and High Courts.

As far back as 1977, Rajeev Dhavan observed the phenomenon of "different judges deciding the same point of law as part of differently constituted Benches [of the Supreme Court] reach[ing] different results" (Dhavan 1977, 415). Since then, departure from uniformity has been aggravated by the multiplication of judges and benches and the reduction in the number of larger benches

(Robinson 2013a, 173). When the Supreme Court was established in 1950, there were just eight judges. In the 1950s they sat on five-judge (or larger) benches for 13 percent of published decisions; otherwise they regularly sat on three-judge benches. By the first decade of the 2000s the designated strength of the court had grown to twenty-six justices, increasing to thirty-one in 2008. Some forty thousand admission matters are now heard on admission days (nowadays Mondays and Fridays) by more than a dozen division benches that typically consist of just two judges each. Similarly, the fifty-five hundred or so regular hearing cases (heard on Tuesdays, Wednesdays, or Thursdays) are decided by these smaller division benches (Robinson 2011, 28; Robinson 2013b).

The presence of so many benches, and the resulting pervasive (though mild) indeterminacy of precedent, increases the chances that representation by a GA may make a difference in outcome. At least it is perceived to possibly make a difference by significant numbers of clients with deep pockets engaged in controversies where the stakes make the size of legal fees irrelevant. The standing of grand advocates with the judges is a positional good in limited supply – there can only be so many top lawyers familiar to the judges, so lawyers with reputations of being top lawyers have enhanced value to many clients (Hirsch 1976). We might think of litigation in India as a kind of fabulous beast guided by modest and quickly replaced judicial forelegs and driven by powerful GA hind legs. The outcomes are, as Dhavan observed, "technically unpredictable" and invite investment in high-end advocacy to further destabilize the results (Dhavan 1977, 461).

V. THE SENIORITY FACTOR

Seniority is a major theme that surfaces at many points in our scan of the profession. Seniority works differently for judges than for lawyers. On the bench, adherence to seniority in promotion (senior judges of the High Courts are generally elevated to the Supreme Court) is combined with a rigid and early retirement age: sixty-five on the Supreme Court, sixty-two on the High Courts, and sixty on the lower courts. Seniority makes retirement and promotion predictable and means that most judges will not serve on the Supreme Court for more than five years (Chandrachud 2012).[5]

Some distinguished advocates decline to ascend to the bench, many because of the money, but others because compulsory early retirement diminishes the attraction. One GA told us that he turned down a judicial appointment because he could predict that he would eventually be Chief Justice of India for one year (Interview 32, 2012). For those on the bench, seniority is a wasting asset that affords standing, influence, and a privileged lifestyle but then suddenly disappears. The forcibly retired judge is then dependent on political figures who can bestow appointments to commissions, tribunals, etc., or on private parties – including at times grand advocates – who can then engage the former judge for lucrative arbitration assignments. It is difficult for retired judges to serve, even as volunteers, with their former courts, for it is not clear how they are to be placed on the all-important seniority ladder.

For the grand advocates, on the other hand, seniority brings with it not only enhanced standing but also an enlarged fund of human capital in the form of contacts, experience, and reputation. Often Supreme Court judges are not only younger than the senior advocates who argue before them but may have looked up to these advocates when they themselves were young lawyers. The judge almost undoubtedly has had his post for less time than the GA has been practicing in the Court, meaning that the GA may feel more at home in the institution than the judge.

By tradition, senior advocates enjoy a right of preaudience according to seniority, defined by the date they became senior – that is, they are entitled to be heard before those junior to them. If two advocates are briefed on a matter and they must meet for a conference, tradition dictates the junior lawyer should go to the senior lawyer's office. Punctiliousness about seniority may limit collaboration. In a famous instance, in Indira Gandhi's 1975 election case, "she wanted [famed advocate Nani] Palkhiwala to come to Allahabad to represent her," but Satish Chand Khare, her senior counsel, objected. "He said that Palkhiwala was junior to him and he would withdraw from the case if Palkhiwala was brought in. Since Khare had been involved from the very beginning and was familiar with all the facts, Gandhi did not want to run the risk of his withdrawing and dropped the idea of bringing Palkhiwala to Allahabad" (Bhushan 2008, 131). After she lost at the High Court in Allahabad, Palkhiwala did represent her on appeal to the Supreme Court.

VI. GRAND ADVOCATES' CLIENTS

Jawaharlal Nehru's father, Motilal Nehru, became one of the wealthiest men in Allahabad litigating the disputes of the zamindars (wealthy aristocratic landowners).[6] After Independence, the zamindars disappeared with land reform, but other clients, such as industrialists and banks, multiplied. Compensation remained high for top advocates, but given the sluggish pace of national growth and the government's large hand in the economy, fee increases remained tempered. In fact, law was seen as one of the least attractive career choices for promising young students, who instead flocked to more-desirable professions such as medicine, engineering, or the civil service.[7] However, this changed as liberalization opened up abundant new revenue streams for lawyers – multinational corporations began to eye India as a prime global site for investment, India minted thousands of new millionaires and billionaires, and law firms rose to prominence to cater to the businesses that were helping drive the country to the 7–9 percent growth rates it witnessed in the first decade of the 2000s.

As a result, today's top counsels' fees are exceptionally high. As of 2012, leading advocates not infrequently charged 500,000–600,000 rupees per appearance ($10,000–$12,000) at the Supreme Court. In the Supreme Court's hallways, grand advocates can be seen moving briskly from courtroom to courtroom with a flock of juniors, clerks, and clients in tow as they proceed from argument to argument. This is a business plan in action. On admission days at the Supreme Court, sometimes referred to among top lawyers as "harvest days," an advocate is often able to appear in as many as five to eight arguments. Many of these arguments may last just a few minutes, allowing the advocate to reap substantial monetary rewards in the course of just a few hours. On regular hearing days, advocates usually have far fewer matters, which they argue at greater length and more substantively, although counterintuitively they charge about the same for these matters as for the shorter admission hearings. To prepare for admission and regular hearing arguments, lawyers hold conferences with their clients for which they charge an hourly fee. Otherwise, all preparation costs are incorporated into the appearance fee. It should be emphasized that the earnings of these advocates do not derive from their ownership interest in a business (i.e., a law firm) with salaried workers, but are payment for services rendered by them personally. Unlike the partners in law firms they do not collect payments for leasing their reputational capital to subordinates who can then command enhanced fees (Galanter and Palay 1991).Instead, they pay their juniors, clerks, and other staff out of their own pockets for the marginal contribution of the latter to the bundle of services delivered to clients by the senior advocate.

Top advocates in India enjoy incomes that rival the most highly remunerated lawyers anywhere in the world (Sahgal and Bamzai 2010). Abhishek Manu Singhvi, who along with being a top litigator is also a member of the Rajya Sabha, reported his annual income at 50 crore (about $10 million) in 2010–2011. Ram Jethmalani, another leading lawyer who is a member of the Rajya Sabha, reported his income at 8.4 crore ($1.7 million) (Dhawan 2011). Shanti Bhushan, a leading advocate who was on a public committee to design a new anticorruption agency, disclosed an annual income of 18 crore ($3.6 million) (The Hindu 2011). Both Jethmalani and Bhushan are well over eighty and no longer litigate as much as they once did. One advocate estimated that top Supreme Court lawyers are generally earning between 10 and 50 crore a year (i.e., $2–10 million annually) (Interview 25, 2012). Leading lawyers appear before the Bombay and Delhi High Courts have comparable fees, while those elsewhere in the country usually charge considerably less.

Despite their high rates, client demand for these select lawyers is robust. Most of the leading advocates we interviewed conceded that their fees were exorbitant, but justified continuously raising fees as a mechanism to keep their workload manageable. As one Supreme Court lawyer explained, "Lawyers like me charge the sky. It is a way of filtering clients" (Interview 14, 2012).

Risk aversion often brings cases to senior counsel, especially those with big names. As one lawyer who worked at a distinguished law firm stated, "The head of legal at a large corporation wants to ward off blame. They first hire a large firm like Amarchand so they can say 'Amarchand told me.' The firm doesn't want the responsibility, so they then hire a Grand Advocate so that they can say they had the best. Everyone just keeps passing on risk" (Interview 24, 2012). On a similar note, explaining why 10 percent of the lawyers got 90 percent of the work, a top Supreme Court lawyer noted, "When the stakes are high, you get the best surgeon. It's the same in law" (Interview 9, 2012).[8]

Under the Advocates Act, senior counsel are not permitted to have their own clients. Instead, they must be approached by a briefing counsel who is retained by the client and who actually files the case. Briefing counsel are often solo practitioners who argue smaller matters themselves, but for larger cases enlist a senior counsel. Other times briefing counsel are attached to law firms. Senior counsel are traditionally not attached to law firms, and some senior counsel interpret the law as barring them from being a part of a law firm.[9] One prominent lawyer at the Indian Supreme Court estimated that about 70 percent of his work came through individual advocates, while about 30 percent came from law firms (Interview 10, 2012). Most large law firms in India do not have extensive litigation practices, perhaps in part because they anticipate senior counsel would take up too much of the firm's profit margins.

Clients who have had positive experiences with certain seniors commonly request their briefing counsel to hire those seniors. At the Supreme Court, clients from particular regions of the country often seek out top advocates from their region. Other times, clients request a top advocate who is from the same region as the judge hearing the case or is otherwise perceived to have a particularly good rapport with the judge. Some leading advocates seem to cultivate relationships directly with clients, although under the Advocates Act and Bar Council Rules (Part VI, Chapter 1), they cannot deal with clients directly. As one top Bombay lawyer suggested, "If a senior has a good client – say Reliance [a major Indian corporation] – they aren't going to let them go away, so they will keep a junior as an AOR for that client" (Interview 21, 2012). In-house counsel frequently demand that their briefing counsel ensure that certain senior advocates argue their cases, and more generally work with these senior advocates on their matter. As a leading lawyer noted, "The growth of in-house counsel has been positive. Often the associate of the law firm is clueless and you get your real briefing from the general counsel" (Interview 10, 2012).

Firms and briefing counsel often have a strong role in guiding clients toward their favorite seniors. As a partner in a leading solicitor firm in Bombay explained, "There are seven or eight top arguing counsel in Bombay that I would trust a brief with. At the Supreme Court, to be honest, it is only five or six. In the Delhi High Court, it is larger. I judge a good counsel on (1) competence level, (2) how much times we can get with the senior, and (3) their face value, particularly for [admission matters] in the Supreme Court where at most you will have ten to fifteen minutes in front of the judge" (Interview 20, 2012). One well-known high court lawyer estimated 75 percent of his work came from twenty to twenty-five law firms and briefing counsel, who kept returning to him for work. He described how "each senior counsel has favorite briefing firms. Particular law firms use 'x' or 'y' as senior counsel" (Interview 8, 2012).

Top senior counsel are notoriously inaccessible, and this is one of the largest complaints from briefing counsel and clients. As a lawyer at a solicitor's firm in Bombay lamented, "Half my job is chasing senior counsel" (Interview 19, 2012). Some firms are known to designate young lawyers to follow seniors while they argue matters in court so that the firm can keep track of where the senior is and remind him to attend their client's hearing.

Indeed, seniors will frequently miss hearings because they are arguing another case in a different courtroom. This results in part from the unpredictability of a chronically backlogged and poorly managed judicial system. In this context, judges will often allow advocates (or their juniors) to reschedule matters, requesting a "passover" if the senior is either not available or inadequately prepared. As a top senior in Bombay explained, "It's fair when clients complain that we aren't there for hearings, but I think we make reasonable estimates about what matters the judges will and will not reach" (Interview 21, 2012). Another argued, "When I have five or six matters on a day, I think only one or two will go forward meaningfully. The system allows this. There is no penalty from the court or client if I miss a hearing. There isn't good scheduling, so there is the possibility to have a lot of flexibility" (Interview 23,

2012). Other seniors countered that their colleagues booked too many matters, and even charged for hearings that they actually missed. A handful of leading advocates have a reputation for taking fewer cases, despite the loss in income, because they feel taking too many matters would be unfair to the interests of their clients.

Since at least the 1980s, litigants with deep pockets have used "blocking" or "negative retainers" to disqualify the major top advocates from being engaged by opponents (Interview 10, 2012). Back in 1986 a distinguished academic reported that "resourceful clients, especially big corporations and universities, make it a practice to offer a retainer to expert lawyers, not so much with a view that they will act in the case but with the view that their services do not become available to the other side . . . . Wholesale buying of legal services in this way is now a standard strategy for corporate clients" (Baxi 1986, 459). These litigants identify the top lawyers in the court who would be ideal for their case and then "block" them, usually by paying them for a conference to discuss the case. Since the advocate has been retained by one party, he can then not appear for the other side, limiting the talent the opposition has to choose from. This practice is controversial, and some lawyers will back out if they feel they are being used for blocking or will require that they be given the first chance to argue. Others view it as an acceptable form of business and will accept a negative retainer without even holding a conference or insisting that they argue part of the matter. In a major case, it is not uncommon for a litigant to block, or attempt to block, five or six lawyers.

For large matters, litigants frequently retain more than one senior, not only to "block" the other side but because there is no assurance that their counsel will actually be available for the hearing, given lawyers' propensity to overbook and the unpredictability of the court's scheduling (Interview 12, 2012).[10] Some sought-after lawyers are even rumored to charge a double rate to guarantee their appearance. One Supreme Court lawyer recalled a joke told about Ashok Sen (a very prominent Supreme Court advocate and onetime law minister who practiced up until his death in 1996) that Sen required a triple fee – "one for the case, one for the promise to appear, and the third to keep the promise" (Interview 27, 2012).

One of the largest sources of litigation work is the government. Top Supreme Court lawyers will often serve as an additional solicitor general, solicitor general, or attorney general at some point in their careers, taking a sharp cut in their income to do so. A handful of top lawyers are also closely related to political parties. For example, Ram Jethmalani and Shanti Bhushan were law ministers, Abhishek Manu Singhvi is a Rajya Sabha member, Arun

Jaitley is the leader of the opposition in the Rajya Sabha, Kapil Sibal is minister of communications and technology, and P. Chidambaram is finance minister.[11] Some leading advocates also engage in lobbying work, but most official lobbying is done by law firms.

VII. GRAND ADVOCATES' WORK

Advocates at the Supreme Court have strikingly wide-ranging practices. As one quipped, "We are all generalists here" (Interview 12, 2012). Almost all grand advocates have a portfolio that includes a substantial amount of corporate work but usually also some combination of tax, constitutional law, intellectual property, government employment law, property, and criminal law. Leading lawyers tend to be focused in the Supreme Court or one High Court but will travel to other cities to argue in another court for their client, charging a much higher rate to do so. Work before tribunals – such as the securities appellate tribunal, the competition appellate tribunal, the national green tribunal, the income tax appellate tribunal, the central administrative tribunal, and the electricity appellate tribunal – has made up a growing portion of these lawyers' work as these forums have multiplied and gained prominence postliberalization. Some top advocates we interviewed also reported that they now spend 5–15 percent of their time on arbitration. Indian Supreme Court and high court judges often serve on tribunals or as arbitrators postretirement, so it is not surprising that litigants seek out grand advocates, who have established reputations before these judges, to represent them.

Most of the grand advocates' work at court is dominated by more procedural aspects of law. For example, one leading Supreme Court lawyer speculated that 70 percent of his work came from admission day (Interview 10, 2012). Pleading for stays and interim relief accounts form a substantial part of these advocates' work in court. During these shorter hearings, top lawyers' face value is at a premium. One lawyer explained, "Face value matters in matters like SLPs [i.e., admission hearings] at the Supreme Court, where a decision is made in a minute. A man who regularly appears will matter to that judge. That lawyer will know what that judge considers worth hearing" (Interview 16, 2012). For the actual full hearing, clients will frequently enlist another, less expensive lawyer who will go into the details of the case. A top advocate's chief asset in many ways is the time and sustained attention he can obtain for the client before a congested and otherwise impatient court.

In Delhi and Madras, lawyers typically operate out of offices in their homes or in chambers near the High Court or Supreme Court. In Bombay, lawyers tend to have their offices outside their homes. These offices, which usually have a conference room, an extensive law library, and a large, wide desk at which the senior sits, bustle with juniors, clerks, briefing counsel, and clients. Clients (and their briefing counsel) typically come to the lawyer's office because as one top lawyer explained, one "shouldn't go to a client's office" as that indicated a degree of eagerness to please the client that denigrated the profession (Interview 9, 2012).[12]

A top advocate might have anywhere from three to twenty juniors. A junior may work on one type of matter more than others, but explicit specialization is rare, although not unheard of. In Bombay, juniors are traditionally not paid and instead use their senior's chambers to become known among briefing counsel by giving noteworthy comments during conferences with clients. They use the infrastructure of their senior's chamber for their own work in their first years. In Delhi and Madras, juniors generally do receive a salary, although they also take on their own work. Some seniors pay their juniors just a token salary, while others pay the equivalent of salaries of junior associates at law firms. Historically in Madras, pay for juniors has been higher on average even though seniors themselves are generally paid somewhat less there.

Briefing counsel draft the initial brief, or at least set out the facts of the case. The senior then examines the draft, revising it with the help of juniors and the briefing counsel. In general the brief is given limited attention by the senior since the argument in court often deviates from it; instead he generally focuses on preparing his own notes for oral argument.

As already noted, multiple senior lawyers will often be hired by a client to argue a case together. They may coordinate strategy in advance on the telephone. However, this coordination is frequently minimal and sometimes nonexistent. As one Supreme Court lawyer explained, "I find there is a bizarre situation where sometimes you don't even know which lawyers are on your side . . . The solicitor often won't tell the senior who is on their side. Maybe it's because they feel the lawyer won't study as much if they know another big gun is coming" (Interview 12, 2012).

Many seniors and other lawyers we interviewed commented on the lack of professionalism in litigation, which they felt meant that the quality of the work often suffered. As one rising lawyer surmised, "The expectations for work here are different [than in the West]. There doesn't need to be a high level of refinement. When you reach 85 percent, you are good to go. The judges aren't great lawyers. The opposition lawyer will not be well prepared. It's not worth putting in the extra 15 percent, which takes 50 percent of the time. It's not that the lawyers couldn't perform, but there is no incentive" (Interview 23, 2012).

VIII. ENTRY AND ASCENT

Young lawyers often complain about how difficult it is for them to break into the elite world of litigation. Some of these barriers to entry are obvious. For example, grand advocates operate in an English-speaking world, where fluency is a necessity and British diction lauded. Only a minority of lawyers in India grew up in English-speaking households. Others struggled to gain the necessary command over language to become a GA. However, language is not the only filter restricting entry into this high-end world.

Family connections, or being part of a certain social stratum, have clear benefits for a young litigator. As one leading Bombay advocate recounted, "My father was a lawyer so (A) you get familiar with terms; and (B) socially you meet successful lawyers and judges. It demystifies everything. Many of the big names were my dad's close friends. The Original Side of the Bombay High Court is like one big family. Everyone knows everyone professionally and socially. Being part of that makes it easier" (Interview 17, 2012). With a family member in the profession, clients and briefing advocates become aware of a lawyer more quickly and the lawyer can use the office space and library of one's family member. All this helps in the early years of litigation, when paying briefs are rare and income negligible. Indeed, being able to make it through the early bare-bones years as a litigator is perhaps the most formidable screening mechanism for the profession, favoring the survival of those who come with wealth and connections.

Being part of the same social milieu also helps in arranging to junior with a leading senior. Most of today's prominent seniors had themselves juniored for a prominent senior, and older seniors we interviewed spoke proudly of their "alumni" who had gone on to become successful lawyers themselves. There is a feeling that if you don't have an actual father in the profession, you at least need a "godfather" (i.e., a prominent senior that you junior with) who can help guide you in the early years and raise your profile, bringing you critical early cases. However, most seniors said they accepted juniors on the request of friends, retired justices, or colleagues – there was no formal selection process. Thus it is beneficial, if not essential, to be located in this social stratum in order to elicit the needed referral to a senior.

The powerful role of social networks in acquiring clients and setting up a practice helps perpetuate the disproportionate presence of certain ethnic and religious groups in the profession. For example, in Madras, elite Brahmins dominate the upper ranks of the bar because of their tight networks and long-standing proficiency in English. In Bombay, the Parsis, Gujaratis, and Bohra Muslims were early first movers in the profession and continue to dominate its upper reaches.[13] In the Delhi High Court, postpartition refugees, particularly Sikhs from the Lahore High Court, had an advantage, and their descendants continue to be disproportionately represented in the top ranks of the bar. The Supreme Court bar tends to be an amalgam of these privileged groups from around the country. Despite repeated inquiries we could not identify any Scheduled Caste, Scheduled Tribe, or Other Backward Class advocates who were regarded as part of the elite stratum of lawyers.[14]

Women also have had a difficult time breaking into the small group of grand advocates and into the upper ranks of litigation more generally. Of the eighty-one senior advocates designated by the Bombay High Court in the twenty-year period, 1991–2010, only three were women. No women have been designated since 2006 (Menon 2011). Historically, women have faced discrimination from colleagues, judges, and clients, even if there are signs such barriers may be lessening. As one seasoned woman lawyer explained, "Women lawyers before me were not married. Clients didn't take you seriously then. If you did get married, then you moved with your husband so that you couldn't set up a practice.... Some judges treated us well. Others were patronizing. [The discrimination]... isn't as bad now, but it hasn't totally vanished. I find if a woman raises her voice, they don't like it, even though a male could do the same thing" (Interview 5, 2012). In 2012, after a woman lawyer was slapped by a male colleague in the Delhi High Court, sixty-three women lawyers successfully petitioned the Supreme Court to set up a committee to hear complaints of sexual harassment at the Supreme Court and in the lower courts (Times of India 2012). More women are entering litigation, but clearly discrimination and obstacles still remain.

Many leading lawyers we interviewed bemoaned the deficiency of their own formal schooling, although it frequently did provide them with future networking resources. For example, many Bombay High Court lawyers are graduates of the Government Law College, while many Delhi High Court lawyers are graduates of Delhi University. During the 1990s, as law became a more fashionable field of study because liberalization provided increasing opportunities for graduates, the National Law Schools achieved prominence in legal education. These schools were originally created to produce high-quality publicly minded litigators to strengthen the "public interest" salient of the bar (Menon 2009).However, graduates of the National Law Schools were in marked demand by law firms and corporations flourishing in the postliberalization economy, and many entered practice as in-house counsel or with firms in India and abroad. Some though have entered litigation and are becoming an increasingly prominent network in the courts.

In earlier generations, aspiring lawyers like Motilal Nehru, Mohandas Gandhi, and Mohammed Ali Jinnah pursued a university education abroad (almost always in Britain) and enrolled at the Inns of Court to qualify as barristers. But few of today's top advocates were educated in other countries, perhaps in part because in the decades after Independence, there were severe restrictions on foreign exchange and law had lost its standing as a path for ambition. In recent years, far more rising lawyers have gone abroad for education, particularly to obtain an LLM in the United States or United Kingdom, perhaps signaling that foreign credentials are returning in importance.

Several top advocates used government positions to further their careers. In their early years, being a panel lawyer or standing counsel for a state government or public sector undertaking could bring assured income and visibility. Later, being assistant solicitor general, solicitor general, or attorney general often cemented an already prominent reputation and brought advocates into the elite heights of the profession. One lawyer discussed how he "used these government jobs to work my way up" (Interview 8, 2012). Many lawyers claimed they were simply asked one day to take on such government appointments, although others suggested securing such appointments required significant networking. One well-known lawyer even cast aspersions on those taking political appointments, saying, "For a political appointment you have to hob-nob with industrialists and politicians. It's crony legalism" (Interview 9, 2012).

Another, less frequently taken path to the upper ranks of the profession is to become known for one's academic work, usually by writing a treatise in an area of law.[15] As one lawyer who took this route explained, "When my first book came out, my income went up four times" (Interview 9, 2012). No full-time academic is known as a leading lawyer, likely in part because academics are prohibited from practicing law in India (although practitioners can and do hold appointments to teach) (Bar Council of India Rules, Part VI, Chapter II, Section VII).

Public interest litigation (PIL), although only a tiny fraction of what the higher courts do, plays an important role in the public image of the judiciary and in the self-perception of the bar. Of the small set of lawyers who have a practice focused on public interest cases, variously defined, there is a tiny subset who are regarded as peers of the grand advocates. Such lawyers may be supported by a NGO or may be able to fund their operations from their personal wealth. A few other grand advocates combine extensive PIL with a commercial practice, while a large number of the top lawyers engage in occasional pro bono work that may include PIL or a prominent constitutional law or environmental matter. This pro bono work can help to establish an advocate's reputation in high-profile matters and later helps maintain public

TABLE 2. *Public visibility of various sectors of the legal profession: Number of articles in the Times of India from 2009 to 2012 referencing*

Judges		Top advocates		Prominent law firms/partners	
Justice Sathasivam	524	Prashant Bhushan	638	Amarchand Mangaldas	27
Chief Justice Kapadia	491	G. E. Vahanvati	568	J. Sagar	16
Justice Aftab Alam	408	Ram Jethmalani	499	AZB	10
Justice Singhvi	369	Harish Salve	385	Zia Mody	9
Justice Kabir	265	Gopal Subramaniam	368	Trilegal	5
Justice DK Jain	213	Shanti Bhushan	233	Cyril Shroff	2
Justice Dattu	147	Mukul Rohtagi	147		
Justice Lodha	147	KK Venugopal	145		
		Abhishek Manu Singhvi	139		
		Darius Khambata	133		
		Colin Gonsalves	88		
		P. P. Rao	83		
		Indira Jaising	81		
		Soli Sorabjee	70		
		Fali Nariman	43		

Source: Factiva

visibility while supporting a cause lawyers are passionate about.[16] Relying too much on engaging in pro bono type work though has potential pitfalls for an aspiring senior lawyer. Advocates are designated senior advocates by the bench. This means that lawyers who are perceived to be too far outside the mainstream may be overlooked for this designation by the judges.

For many grand advocates, the media offers an important means to gain and maintain visibility. Advocates can be found regularly giving interviews on the news channels, which have multiplied since liberalization. This practice is controversial among some grand advocates who prefer to keep a low and, they argue, more dignified profile. They view interviews as a form of advertisement, which is banned for lawyers in India. Yet, such publicity, through either direct interviews or simply newspaper reports about their cases, has assured that many advocates have become familiar presences in middle-class households. For example, Ram Jethmalani, a well-known criminal lawyer, had his name referenced in 499 articles between 2009 and 2012 in the *Times of India*, a leading English daily that also sets story trends for many local language papers. This was a comparable amount of reporting to the most covered judges on the court and far more coverage than prominent law firms or law firm partners receive.

A few grand advocates contribute op-ed articles to the English-language newspapers. Lawyers and judges in the upper reaches of the system are avid readers of these papers, whose contents become generally known in these circles. Other lawyers have used professional associations as part of their rise or as a signal of their clout. Many leading advocates are or were presidents of their respective High Court Bar Associations, the Supreme Court Bar Association, or the Bar Association of India.

IV. THE IMPACT OF GRAND ADVOCATES

The flourishing of grand advocates is intertwined with other features of the Indian legal system, such as congested courts, insular social networks, overwhelmed and underresourced judges, and the centrality of the judiciary to Indian political life. And their outsized presence has numerous consequences for the legal system itself.

Many younger lawyers and briefing counsel resent grand advocates. One rising advocate repeated a common refrain that many of the top lawyers are unnecessarily idealized by clients and judges, noting that, "We have given up maharajas on elephants, but we still have this" (Interview 6, 2012).

Lawyers whom we interviewed at law firms and in other practice settings often reported that at the outset of their careers, they had considered litigation but thought the field would be too difficult to break into given the social connections that were perceived to be a prerequisite. They viewed workplaces like firms as providing a more professional and meritocratic environment. Even as globalization has channeled more money into the legal profession, the top rungs of litigation are still seen as an old boys' network where social connections among a select community, and face value with judges, are put at a premium. Indeed, these networks may be getting further entrenched instead of swept away (Dezalay and Garth 2010).

An older lawyer lamented what he saw as the decline of the profession led by the grand advocates: "There is a lack of competence and discipline among the lawyers. They no longer tell clients they have a frivolous case. They don't try to figure out the best remedy based on cost-benefit analysis. Now it's just about familiarity of faces in the Supreme Court and who can speak best" (Interview 7, 2012). As one senior commented, "In the old days our role models were people like Seervai and Gupte,[17] who didn't have massive work or the most earnings. Now the role model is the lawyer who is earning most" (Interview 27, 2012). A younger top leading lawyer described his generation as more "client and service oriented while the older seniors are more classical. We are more aggressive in my generation, less moral, and not as much about the jurisprudence" (Interview 14, 2012).

Because their attention is spread so thinly among so many cases, some view the grand advocates as hurting the quality of jurisprudence as they do not spend as much time as they should developing their oral and written arguments, resulting in poorly briefed judges (Interview 33, 2012). Further, since grand advocates often have multiple matters scheduled on the same day, they frequently have conflicts requiring judges to reschedule matters, contributing to delays in the judicial system overall. grand advocates also price out many clients, meaning only those who can afford these lawyers benefit from the distinct advantage they bring in receiving either admission for their matter or more-favorable orders (Galanter 1974).

Despite these complaints, senior counsel frequently noted their positive impact on the judicial system, upholding the rule of law. They commended themselves as a check on overstepping or unaccountable judges. The grand advocates prize their independence from firms and other corporate and government interests, which they view as giving them the ability to speak out more readily if they see problems in the justice system.

Their generalist knowledge and prominent stature also enable grand advocates to more actively push novel lines of argument in court, pushing jurisprudence in new directions. Perhaps the best known example of this is the celebrated role senior advocate Nanabhoy Palkhivala had in shaping the basic structure doctrine in the landmark Supreme Court case *Kesavananda Bharati v. Union of India*, AIR 1973 SC 1461 (Andhyarujina 2010, 19). In that case the court held that there was a certain "basic structure" to the Indian constitution that could not be amended, including its democratic, federal, and secular nature. Arguably having a preeminent lawyer advocating for a controversial position allows judges more intellectual and reputational cover to take a new jurisprudential initiative, particularly if the judges do not feel confident in their own standing.

V. CONCLUSION

If Motilal Nehru or Muhammad Ali Jinnah[18] visited the Supreme Court today, they would find a court not altogether different than the Allahabad or Bombay High Courts in which they argued in the early years of the twentieth century. The multiple courtrooms, the buzz of lawyers and clients in the hallways, and the structure of the bar would all seem quite familiar. Independence, liberalization, and globalization may have changed some of the clients, key provisions of law, and office technology – briefs are now neatly typed on a computer – but many elements of the culture of the justice system have remained surprisingly constant. In particular, the steeply hierarchical structure of the bar has endured, suggesting that it is an expression of more deeply entrenched features of Indian social life, or at least of Indian legal institutions. The reputational capital of the GA remains one of his primary assets in a court system marked by overwhelmed judges with little assistance, the multiplicity and blurriness of precedent, and the centrality of oral presentation. In such a context, being known and trusted by judges is a positional good of which there can only be so much, placing those who have it in both a potentially lucrative and commanding position in relation to the rest of the bar.

Yet there are signs that larger structural shifts are afoot that may affect the grand advocates' privileged position in this system. Law firms are increasingly looking for ways to bypass senior advocates. As one top firm partner indicated, "We have taken the step of encouraging our own in-house lawyers to argue. There are two reasons. First, arguing counsel are hugely expensive and really unreliable. . . . Second, it adds value for money" (Interview 20, 2012). As more firms develop more of their own competent lawyers to argue for them, this may undercut some of the business of grand advocates. Eventually, senior lawyers may even be brought into law firms where they can be given more-extensive infrastructure for research and case management. Currently, there is little incentive for grand advocates to agree to such an arrangement because they would then lose the clients who come to them through other law firms or briefing counsel, and their reputational capital is not shareable in the same way as a law firm partner's.

Meanwhile, the courts themselves are becoming less the exclusive site for litigation, affecting the business model of the grand advocates. The development of tribunals for tax, competition, telecom, airports, and other areas means that advocacy is becoming increasingly specialized. It is more difficult for a GA to visit all these venues compared with going from courtroom to courtroom in a High Court or the Supreme Court. These tribunals are developing specialized bars, and although some tribunal judges are former High Court or Supreme Court judges, many of the other judges on the tribunal are not even legally trained, meaning they are not well acquainted with the reputations of the top lawyers, thus depriving them of much of their face value. Arbitration is also increasingly attracting lawyers' time as companies try to avoid the delays and unpredictability of the courts. Harish Salve, a prominent Indian senior advocate, joined Blackstone Chambers in London in 2013 in a move designed to allow foreign companies to more easily approach him to represent them in international arbitration or to consult him regarding the Indian market (Ganz 2013a).[19] Later the same year Gopal Subramanium, another well-known senior advocate, joined 3 Verulam Buildings in London as an associate member and arbitrator for seemingly similar reasons (Ganz 2013b).

The proliferation of forums and the attendant specialization in the law is inducing more lawyers to become experts in certain areas of law. Generalist advocates may increasingly be relegated to procedural matters and points of natural justice, while more-substantive arguments about intellectual property or competition law gravitate to specialists. Meanwhile, some grand advocates may voluntarily turn away from litigation and spend less time in the courtroom, acting more as advisors or consultants to a client. As one leading advocate explained, "Today, where law ends is not clear. It is becoming a mesh of consultancy and law. It's about policy" (Interview 10, 2012).

In addition, there are new pressures on grand advocates to increase the quality of their work. As one lawyer noted, "It might not be specialization that brings the leading lawyers down, but professionalization, which requires more time on each case – briefing, preparing argument, and the court limiting its time so it's more content, less fluff" (Interview 13, 2012). Such professionalization might be prompted by the entry of foreign law firms. These firms would likely not litigate directly themselves, and instead the effect of their arrival would likely be an initial upsurge in demand for the service of the grand advocates. But over the long run, as increasingly important customers of top advocates, they might demand higher standards and more emphasis on reliability, leading to a narrowing of grand advocates' famously sweeping portfolios.

A demand by clients for enhanced professional performance of grand advocates would be more likely if it was also demanded, or at least rewarded, by judges. For example, if judges admitted cases more selectively, punished lawyers for failing to appear at hearings, and placed more reliance on written arguments (and less on often repetitious oral advocacy), this might push grand advocates to fine-tune their briefs and schedules. Yet, given the pay disparities between the bar and the bench, it is unlikely in the near term that a widespread improvement in the quality of judges will occur that might push for more professionalization among grand advocates.

The increasing number of talented students entering legal education means that there is a larger group of high-quality young lawyers graduating each year. This group of rising lawyers may eventually help professionalize standards in litigation. More broadly, since so many of these top law graduates are now entering firms rather than litigation, the balance of power within the profession may eventually shift away from litigators and toward law firms and other forms of legal practice.

Studying the continuing vitality of segments of the bar like grand advocates allows us to better understand how the law is actually practiced, applied, and produced in India today. While some aspects of the legal profession may seem to be outwardly "converging" in a country like India – such as the increasing presence of domestic law firms that look like those found elsewhere in the world – the comparative uniqueness of grand advocates demonstrates how certain structural features of a nation's legal system can also generate and support a markedly divergent pattern of legal practice.

Notes

1 Interviewees are kept anonymous in this article. Many of the interviewees would themselves be considered grand advocates. We also interviewed younger litigators, advocates-on-record, law firm partners, general counsel, and other legal professionals with knowledge of these advocates.

2 The reference to India here is inclusive of all of British India. To a considerable extent our observations about Indian lawyers apply to Pakistan and Bangladesh, whose legal institutions also derive from those of colonial India.

3 An AOR must practice as an advocate for four years, train with a senior AOR for one year, then appear for an examination conducted by the Supreme Court. An AOR must maintain a registered office within sixteen kilometers of the Supreme Court building. Supreme Court of India Rules, Order IV (2010).

4 Supreme Court Bar Association Members Directory, www.scbaindia.org/Web/aspx/directory.aspx.

5 Although it is a matter of custom rather than law, the power of the seniority norm was enhanced by the "supercession" of three more senior Supreme Court judges in 1973. A succinct account is found in Lee 2010. During the Emergency (1975–1977), Indira Gandhi superseded Justice H. R. Khanna, who was next in line to become chief justice, after he dissented in *ADM Jabalpur v. Shukla*, AIR 1976 SC 1207, which held that because of the Emergency, citizens did not have a right to petition the courts for their habeas corpus rights. When he was not made chief justice, Khanna resigned in protest. With the end of the Emergency, Gandhi and many of her policies, including her political manipulation of the judiciary, fell into disrepute. Since then the government has adhered faithfully to the seniority norm.

6 Advocates in India have long been paid at high rates. Indeed, part of the appeal for British barristers to come from England to India was the higher rate of compensation (Schmitthener 1968–1969, 346).

7 As Schmitthener noted in the late 1960s, "The legal profession no longer offers the most honored and profitable work that can be attained in India. It no longer draws the best students, and it no longer dominates the social and political life of the country. The monopoly it had on the leadership of the country for over a century is now gone. In a way the rest of society has caught up with the profession" (Schmitthener 1968–1969, 47).

8 In the US context, Frank and Cook have commented that top lawyers receive salaries far higher than their social value would justify because everyone wants the "best" lawyer, particularly for high-stakes litigation (Frank and Cook 1996, 16).

9 There is no specific prohibition of a partnership between a firm and a senior counsel, except many senior counsel argue that if a firm they were part of met with a client, it would be perceived as them meeting with a client, thus violating provisions under the Advocates Act barring seniors from meeting directly with clients.

10 The interviewee went on, "Here you have to engage at least two seniors to make sure you'll have one. This is because in the Supreme Court everyone keeps papers

as you never know when the case will reach. It can be about to reach for three months. The system accommodates you if you have a conflict" (Interview 12, 2012).

11 Note that Jaitley, Sibal, and Chidambaram cannot currently practice before the court because of their political positions.

12 Compare the observation of Theron Strong, who traced the transformation of the legal profession in early-twentieth-century New York. Relations with clients, he reports, had "undergone a complete and marvelous change..... The lawyer no longer receives the obsequious client hat in hand, but is subject to the beck and nod of the great financial magnate, who, whenever he desires to see his lawyer, 'sends for him.' It would never do for the lawyer who values his practice to insist that his client should call upon him, instead of he calling upon the client" (Strong 1914, 378).

13 Marathi speakers dominate the bar of the less prestigious appellate side of the Bombay High Court.

14 Scheduled Caste (SC) is the official term for the groups formerly referred to as "untouchables" or "Depressed Classes" and more recently as "Dalits"; Scheduled Tribe (ST) is the official term for the many aboriginal peoples of India; the "Other Backward Classes" are a set of groups officially determined to be underprivileged and, like the SC and ST, entitled to be beneficiaries of government "affirmative action" programs, typically in the form of "reservations" (i.e., quotas) in educational institutions and government jobs. These groups comprise somewhere between one-half and two-thirds of the entire population of India (Galanter 1984; Deshpande 2011; and Verma 2012).

15 Such treatises, typically organized around the annotation of a statute, are the mainstay of the working library of most Indian lawyers. Many of the classics of the genre were produced by practitioners.

16 As a side effect PIL cases provide work for other lawyers representing concerned clients. As one prominent PIL lawyer recounted, "The big commercial lawyers are happy with me because I bring them business. They have told me this several times. They must have earned crores from me" (Interview 12, 2012).

17 H. M. Seervai (1906–1996) was a distinguished Bombay lawyer and constitutional scholar whose highly respected commentary on the Indian constitution was first published in 1967. S. V. Gupte was a distinguished Bombay lawyer who served as attorney general of India during the 1977–1979 Janata government and was the author of a leading commentary in the field of Hindu law.

18 Muhammed Ali Jinnah (1876–1948) was a prominent lawyer in Bombay, a founder of the movement to partition British India and create Pakistan, and that country's first governor-general.

19 Salve continues to maintain a flourishing Delhi practice where he is well known for representing and advising Indian and multinational corporate clients.

References

Abel, Richard and Philip Lewis. 1988. *Lawyers in Society: The Common Law World*. Berkeley: University of California Press.

Andhyarujina, T. R. 2010. "A Genius in Advocacy." In *Nani Palkhivala: A Role Model*. Edited by Nilendra Kumar. New Delhi: Universal Law Publishing.

Baxi, Upendra. 1986. "The Pathology of the Indian Legal Professions." *Indian Bar Review* 13 (3/4): 455–484.

Bernstein, Marver. 1977. *Regulating Business by Independent Commissions*. Ann Arbor, MI: Greenwood Publishing Group.

Bhushan, Shanti. 2008. *Courting Destiny: A Memoir*. New Delhi: Penguin India.

Burrage, Michael. 2006. *Revolution and the Making of the Contemporary Legal Profession: England, France, and the United States*. Oxford: Oxford University Press.

Calkins, Philip B. 1968–1969. "A Note on Lawyers in Muslim India." *Law and Society Review* 3 (2/3): 403–406.

Chandrachud, Abhinav. 2012. "Supreme Court's Seniority Norm." *Economic and Political Weekly* 47 (8): 26–30.

2012. "The Need to Have a Uniform Retirement Age for Judges." *Economic and Political Weekly* 47 (46): 24–27.

Daily News and Analysis. 2012. "Bangalore Clash: Karnataka Lawyers to Boycott Courts on Monday." March 4. www.dnaindia.com/india/report-bangalore-clash-karnataka-lawyers-to-boycott-courts-on-monday-1658448.

Derrett, James. 1963. *An Introduction to Modern Hindu Law*. Oxford: Oxford University Press.

Deshpande, Ashwini. 2011. *The Grammar of Caste: Economic Discrimination in Contemporary India*. New Delhi: Oxford University Press.

Dezalay, Yves and Bryant Garth. 2010. *Asian Legal Revivals: Lawyers in the Shadow of Empire*. Chicago: University of Chicago Press.

Dhavan, Rajeev. 1977. *The Supreme Court of India: A Socio-Legal Critique of Its Juristic Techniques*. New Delhi: India Law Institute.

1986. *Litigation Explosion in India*. New Delhi: India Law Institute.

Dhawan, Himanshi. 2011. "Abhishek Manu Singhvi, Vijay Mallya Are Top Earners in Rajya Sabha." *Times of India*, November 18. www.timesofindia.indiatimes.com/india/Abhishek-Manu-Singhvi-Vijay-Mallya-are-top-earners-in-Rajya-Sabha/articleshow/10773614.cms.

Dias, Clarence, Robin Luckham, Dennis Lynch, and James Paul. 1981. *Lawyers in the Third World*. Uppsala: Uppsala Offset Center.

Frank, Robert and Robert Cook. 1996. *The Winner-Take-All Society*. New York: Penguin Books.

Gadbois, George H. 1963. "Evolution of the Federal Court of India: An Historical Footnote." *Journal of the Indian Law Institute* 5: 19–46.

Galanter, Marc. 1968–1969. "Introduction: The Study of the Indian Legal Profession." *Law and Society Review* 3 (2/3): 201–218.

1974. "Why the 'Haves' Come Out Ahead: Speculations on the Scope and Limits of Legal Change." *Law and Society Review* 9 (2): 95–160.

1984. *Competing Equalities: Law and the Backward Classes in India*. Berkeley: University of California.

Galanter, Marc and Thomas M. Palay. 1991. *Tournament of Lawyers: The Transformation of the Big Law Firm*. Chicago: University of Chicago Press.

Gandhi, J. S. 1982. *Lawyers and Touts: A Study in the Sociology of the Legal Profession*. New Delhi: Hindustan Publishing.

1988. "Past and Present: A Sociological Portrait of the Indian Legal Profession." In *Lawyers in Society: Volume 1, The Common Law World*, edited by R. Abel. Berkeley: University of California Press.

Ganz, Kian. 2010. "No First Timers Pass Latest Bombay Solicitors Exam…" *Legally India*, June 21. www.legallyindia.com/201006201000/Law-firms/no-first-timers-pass-latest-bombay-solicitors-exam-could-you-download-the-test-paper.

2013. "RTI Reveals: 1.3 Million Advocates." *Legally India*, February 18. www.legallyindia.com/201302183448/Bar-Bench-Litigation/rti-reveals-number-of-lawyers-india.

2013a. "Harish Salve, Fast-Tracked to English Bar." *Legally India*, July 19. www.legallyindia.com/201307193853/Interviews/harish-salve-liberalisation-english-bar.

2013b. "Gopal Subramanium Joins English Barristers Set 3 Verulam as an Arbitrator." *Legally India*, November 1. www.legallyindia.com/201311014083/Bar-Bench-Litigation/gopal-subramanium-joins-english-barristers-set-3-verulam-as-an-arbitrator.

Shoaib A. Ghias, Shoaib. (2010). "Miscarriage of *Chief* Justice: Judicial Power and the Legal Complex in Pakistan under Musharraf." *Law and Society Review* 35 (4): 985–1022.

Halliday, Terrence and Lucien Karpik, eds. 2011. *Fates of Political Freedom: The Legal Complex in the British Post-Colony*. Cambridge: Cambridge University Press.

Hindustan Times. 1982. "Bar Association on the Warpath." May 6.

Hirsch, Fred. 1976. *Social Limits to Growth*. London: Routledge.

IBNLive. 2012. "Lawyers Strike Disrupts 2G Scam Case Hearing." August 11. www.ibnlive.com/news/india/lawyers-strike-disrupts-2g-scam-case-hearing-391423.html.

Institute of Developing Economies. 2001. *Judicial System and Reforms in Asian Countries: The Case of India*. New Delhi: India Law Institute.

Interview 5, 2012.

Interview 6, 2012.

Interview 7, 2012.

Interview 8, 2012.

Interview 9, 2012.

Interview 10, 2012.

Interview 12, 2012.

Interview 13, 2012.

Interview 14, 2012.

Interview 16, 2012.

Interview 17, 2012.

Interview 18, 2012.

Interview 19, 2012.

Interview 20, 2012.

Interview 21, 2012.

Interview 23, 2012.

Interview 24, 2012.

Interview 25, 2012.

Interview 27, 2012.
Interview 32, 2012.
Interview 33, 2012.
Mattei, Ugo and Luca Pes. 2009. "Civil Law and Common Law: Toward Convergence?" In *The Oxford Handbook of Law and Politics*. Edited by Gregory A. Caldeira, R. Daniel Kelemen, and Keith E. Whittington. Oxford: Oxford University Press.
Menon, Madhava. 2009. *Turning Point: The Story of a Law Teacher*. New Delhi: Universal Law Publishing.
Menon, Meena. 2011. "Women as Senior Advocates, Any Takers?" *The Hindu*, September 25. www.thehindu.com/news/national/women-as-senior-advocates-any-takers/article2482763.ece.
Merryman, J. H. 1987. "On the Convergence (and the Divergence) of the Civil Law and the Common Law." *Stanford Journal of International Law* 17 (2): 357–388.
Moog, Robert. 1992. "Delays in the Indian Courts: Why the Judges Don't Take Control." *Justice System Journal* 16 (1): 19–36.
1997. *Whose Interests Are Supreme? Organizational Politics in the Civil Courts in India*. Ann Arbor: Association for Asian Studies.
Morrison, Charles. 1968–1969. "Social Organization at the District Courts: Colleague Relationships among Indian Lawyers." *Law and Society Review* 3 (2/3): 251–267.
Nagpaul, Hans. 1994. "The Legal Profession in Indian Society: A Case Study of Lawyers at a Local Level in North India." *International Journal of the Sociology of Law* 22 (1): 59–76.
Niles, Russell. 1963. "Ethical Prerequisites to Certification of Special Proficiency." *American Bar Association Journal* 49 (1): 83–89.
Oommen, T. K. 1983. "The Legal Profession in India: Some Sociological Perspectives." *Indian Bar Review* 10 (1): 1–46.
Posner, Eric, and Rosalind Dixon. 2010. "The Limits of Constitutional Convergence." *Chicago Journal of International Law* 11 (2): 399–423.
Rajamani, Lavanya and Arghya Sengupta. 2010. "The Supreme Court of India: Power, Promise, and Overreach." In *The Oxford Companion to Politics in India*. Edited by Niraja Gopal Jayal and Pratap Bhanu Mehta. New Delhi: Oxford University Press.
Robinson, Nick. 2009. "Expanding Judiciaries: India and the Rise of the Good Governance Court." *Washington University Global Studies Law Review* 8 (1): 1–70.
2013a. "Structure Matters: The Impact of Court Structure on the Indian and US Supreme Courts." *American Journal of Comparative Law* 61 (1): 173–208.
2013b. "A Quantitative Analysis of the Indian Supreme Court's Workload." *Journal of Empirical Legal Studies* 10 (3): 570–601.
Robinson, Nick, et al. 2011. "Interpreting the Constitution: Supreme Court Constitution Benches Since Independence." *Economic and Political Weekly* 56 (9): 28–31.
Rocher, Ludo. 1968–1969. "Lawyers in Classic Hindu Law." *Law and Society Review* 3 (2): 383–402.
Sahay, Nawal Kishor. 1931. *A Short History of the Indian Bar*.
Schmitthener, Samuel. 1968–1969. "A Sketch of the Development of the Legal Profession in India." *Law and Society Review* 3 (2/3): 337–382.
Setalvad, Motilal C. 1960. *The Common Law in India*. London: Stevens and Sons.

Shrivastava, Prachi. 2012. "PXV's Mohit Abraham on the Record: How to Top the Advocates-on-Record (AOR) Exam & Other Secrets." *Legally India*, January 25. www.legallyindia.com/201201252519/Interviews/pxvs-mohit-abraham-on-the-record-how-to-top-the-advocates-on-record-aor-exam-a-other-secrets.

Simpleman Jr., A. 1986. "Sentimental Metaphors." *UCLA Law Review* 34: 537–576.

Sundquist, Matthew Lee. 2010. "Learned in Litigation: Former Solicitors General in the Supreme Court Bar." *Charleston Law Review* 5 (1): 59–97.

Supreme Court of India, Senior Advocates of the Supreme Court. 2011. www.supremecourtofindia.nic.in/circular/senioradvocates.pdf.

Sweet, Alec Stone. 1992. *The Birth of Constitutional Politics in France: The Constitutional Council in Comparative Perspective*. Oxford: Oxford University Press.

Strong, Theon. 1914. *Landmarks of a Lawyer's Lifetime*. New York: Dodd, Mead and Company.

The Bar Council, Statistics. Accessed August 4, 2013. www.barcouncil.org.uk/about-the-bar/facts-and-figures/statistics/.

The Hindu. 2011. "Anna Hazare, Others Declare Assets," April 16. www.thehindu.com/news/anna-hazare-others-declare-assets/article1699994.ece.

Times of India. 2011. "Himanshi Dhawan, Abhishek Manu Singhvi, Vijay Mallya Are Top Earners in Rajya Sabha," November 18. www.timesofindia.indiatimes.com/india/Abhishek-Manu-Singhvi-Vijay-Mallya-are-top-earners-in-Rajya-Sabha/articleshow/10773614.cms.

2012. "Panel to Look into Sexual Harassment Cases within SC Premises Created," October 10. www.timesofindia.indiatimes.com/india/Panel-to-look-into-sexual-harassment-cases-within-SC-premises-created/articleshow/16745218.cms.

Tushnet, Mark. 2009. "The Inevitable Globalization of Constitutional Law." *Virginia Journal of International Law*. 49 (1): 985–1006.

Verma, Vidhu. 2012. *Non-Discrimination and Equality in India: Contesting Boundaries of Social Justice*. London: Routledge.

Weiss, Debra Cassens. 2008. "Indian Lawyers Handling Outsourced Work Do More Than Document Review." *ABA Law Journal*, May 12. www.abajournal.com/news/article/indian_lawyers_handling_outsourced_work_do_more_than_document_review/.

Wilkins, David. 2012. "Is the In-House Counsel Movement Going Global? A Preliminary Assessment of the Role of Internal Counsel in Emerging Economies." *Wisconsin Law Review* 2 (4): 251–304.

15

Aggregation of Land for a Growing and Globalizing Economy: The Role of Small-Town Lawyers in India

Pavan Mamidi

I. INTRODUCTION

The rapid infrastructure development and industrialization that accompany globalization in developing countries depend on the availability of a prime asset – land. The essence of a capitalist economy lies in resources being allocated to their best use. This often involves transfers of land from small landholders to private infrastructure developers and industrialists who can undertake large projects and leverage economies of scale.

Due to systematic land reforms in post-Independence India that broke up large holdings of land into smaller units, it is now difficult to find the large pieces of land needed for setting up factories, special economic zones (SEZs), and technology parks in the globalized economy. This shortfall is somewhat similar to the problem with the anticommons that occurs as a result of overpropertization (Heller 1998). The transaction costs of aggregating disparately owned property rights are high and prevent the coordination required for production of goods and services. Heller and Eisenberg (1998) theorize that when the problem of the anticommons occurs in the field of biotechnology patents (that is, there are too many patent holders with proprietary interest over small elements of knowledge), the high transaction costs of contractually bringing multiple, complementary pieces of knowledge together, coupled with the possibility of holdouts, retard innovation (ibid. 1998).

Until January 2014, when sweeping regulatory changes kicked in, traditionally small landholdings were aggregated in two ways to meet the growing demands of infrastructure and multinational corporations in India:

1. The government acquired small holdings of land from farmers by an exercise of eminent domain and transferred the aggregated and

contiguous pieces of land to private infrastructure firms and multinational corporations under the Land Acquisition Act of 1894. Price was based on market prices of other pieces of land sold in the vicinity, but consent of the existing landowners was unimportant (Ghatak and Ghosh 2011). However, the Land Acquisition and Rehabilitation and Resettlement (LARR) bill came into effect in January 2014 (LARR 2013 Act) and tried changing this dramatically. According to this new set of laws, price was to be set at a markup of four times the market price. Furthermore, private parties could acquire land only if they obtained the consent of 80 percent of the small landowners (and the consent of 70 percent of the landowners if the project was a public–private partnership [PPP]). This was based on the consent clause of the LARR 2013 Act. Almost as soon as this new set of regulations kicked in, India witnessed another attempt to change land acquisition laws. In December 2014 the new NDA government, led by the recently elected Narendra Modi, brought in an ordinance to amend the LARR 2013 Act. This set of amendments seeks to do away with the consent clauses for industrial corridors, PPP projects, rural infrastructure, affordable housing, and defense projects. It also seeks to bring procedures of land acquisitions back to what they were in the past – procedures that employ state coercion with little need for consent from small landholders.[1]

2. Infrastructure and multinational corporations employ the services of local intermediary real estate aggregator partnerships and firms, consisting of small-town, newly turned transactional lawyers, to negotiate and mediate long-standing title disputes between farmers and arrange for purchases on behalf of a single entity.

The first method, which involves the use of eminent domain by the government, usually produces resentment from the original owners. Political backlash is a likely outcome of the coercive nature integral to this method (especially from the leftists and Maoists), even though there is some compensation for the takings. Human rights activists often protest the displacement of small farmers and argue that the "just" compensation given by the government is not really just. The problem of price discovery in the exercise of eminent domain by the government is also compounded by allegations of corruption and insinuations that the government subsidizes land purchases by big industrial groups at the expense of marginal farmers. Skeptical activists are also likely to question whether there is ever a public interest that is served by the exercise of eminent domain when the ultimate transferees of the property are private corporations, especially multinational corporations. A notable example of these outcomes is the public outcry after the taking and transfer of land to Tata Motors to build their Nano car project in West Bengal. The Tatas had to withdraw in the face of this opposition. A second example is the opposition to the South Korean steel company POSCO, which wanted to set up a steel plant in Odisha (Mandal 2012), possibly displacing hundreds of thousands of farmers.

Courts that have not yet bought into the merits of globalization or capitalism sometimes question the use of eminent domain by governments in globalizing democracies. While governments may try to invoke eminent domain to solve the problem of holdouts in the aggregation of land, courts that are not yet persuaded by the public-interest arguments are likely to delay aggregation by giving interim injunctions against government takings.

The second method of land aggregation is very different. Acquisition managers and in-house legal departments of big companies that wish to acquire large pieces of land use intermediary aggregators comprising small-town lawyers and real estate brokers who have contacts in rural areas to negotiate deals for them and purchase land from farmers. Because firms find it hard to approach, negotiate, and strike deals with the farmers directly, corporations outsource these tasks to secret intermediary aggregators.

There are several reasons that corporations and their in-house lawyers find it hard to deal with small landowners and farmers. First, corporations face higher reservation prices because landowners tend to feel an exaggerated value of their holdings when approached by corporations (Ghatak and Ghosh 2011). Second, there are often disputes involving multiple claims on small pieces of land due to complicated family and inheritance laws. Third, holdout problems accompany the process of aggregating contiguous tracts of land. Corporations and their in-house lawyers do not routinely specialize in the skills needed to solve these problems. Typically, small-town lawyers who are involved in fighting these disputes in lower courts are already familiar with the nitty-gritty details of the disputants and their disputes, their real interests and their exit options, and the laws that are pertinent to these disputes. They are also thoroughly familiar with the social norms and the local political positions that affect such disputes.

The second method is an increasingly popular method that is being used in aggregating lands in suburban towns and villages that abut cities like Bangalore, Hyderabad, Delhi, and Chennai, where there is a growing demand for land from infrastructure companies that want to build large projects (housing, logistics parks, office spaces, airports, parks, shopping malls, and so forth) and from offshore services companies that require space for their expanding pool of personnel. Notable examples of infrastructure developers and private companies that use the intermediary method of purchases at negotiated prices include Poddar Developers, Jindal Group, DLF, and Satyam Computer Services (Srivastava 2013).

When big infrastructure firms or corporations offer landowners prices that are far above the market prices prevailing in the absence of aggregation or greater expected benefits of settling these land cases (which can take a lifetime to get resolved) in court, many things happen. First, the small-town lawyers, who until now were only small-time litigators in lower courts, turn into skilled transactional lawyers by exploiting their social skills and offer integrative solutions to the disputing farmers. Second, the lawyers are able to offer farmers a larger slice of the pie. They persuade farmers to settle their disputes outside court in order to sell their claims at much higher prices than what they could ever hope to make in their lifetimes. Given long-standing rivalries, feuds, and strong attachments to ancestral properties, a mediator is absolutely essential for getting multiple landowners to accept an offer even when it is very attractive financially. Finally, even if one farmer holds out, it is possible that the aggregated land is not a contiguous piece and the corporation will not buy it. In the event there are holdout problems, small-town lawyers operating as members of intermediary aggregation partnerships are able to use their social networks to galvanize other cooperative owners in the community to exert social pressures to make the unyielding owners sell.

Overall, the method by which land acquisition and aggregation are undertaken via the purchase of many small landholdings at revealed negotiated prices promises to be a better method than the eminent domain method.[2] The intermediary method reduces discontent among small landowners who are "displaced." The government is not involved, and small landowners displace themselves "voluntarily" by selling their land. No one, at least from outside their community, displaces them forcibly in the name of globalization or progress. A relatively greater sense of control and choice is preserved for them. This is in stark contrast to the experience of farmers who lose property to eminent domain for questionably "just" compensation.

In what follows, I describe the intermediary method of negotiated land aggregation that contrasts with the government method involving forcible ejection of small property owners from their land. In describing these methods, I also identify the reasons that small-town lawyers are particularly adept at using the intermediary method. In section II, I briefly describe my data sources. Section III outlines the aggregation landscape and then introduces a model of negotiation in section IV. Section V discusses holdout problems and their solutions. Section VI examines new roles for small-town layers and section VII concludes.

II. DATA SOURCES

Preliminary data was obtained from semistructured interviews conducted in Hyderabad and three districts of Andhra Pradesh – Ranga Reddy, Mahabubnagar, and Medak. Field interviews were conducted in January 2012, and telephonic interviews were conducted in February and March 2012. The sample included the following respondents:

1. Fifteen landowners whose lands were taken by the government exercising eminent domain
2. Ten landowners whose lands were purchased by intermediary land aggregators
3. Four small-town lawyers who are currently fighting against land acquisitions by the government
4. Fifteen small-town lawyers who were partners in intermediary land aggregation partnerships
5. Three in-house lawyers of three big corporations who employed intermediary aggregators to aggregate land for them
6. Three political activists who resisted land acquisition by the government
7. Twenty local land dealers and real estate brokers who engage in aggregation

Several of the interviews were conducted in an adversarial focus-group setting, but no focus group included a mix between the first, third, and sixth types in the list with any of the other types. Many interviews were also conducted one-on-one in person and by telephone.

A unique opportunity to interview both landowners whose lands were taken by eminent domain, as well as their proximate neighbors whose lands were not taken by eminent domain, was afforded in an SEZ site in the Mahabubnagar district. Similarly, there was also an opportunity to interview landowners in the Ibrahimpatnam area close to Hyderabad whose lands were bought by intermediary aggregators, as well as their neighbors whose lands were not bought by intermediary aggregators. This part of the data will be useful in a future study dedicated to undertaking a difference-in-difference analysis in a qualitative setting.

Most of the respondents were found by a "snowballing" technique in Hyderabad and surrounding districts; therefore some of the mechanisms found in this study may not have external validity outside this geographic zone.

III. BACKGROUND ON LAND AGGREGATION

Land aggregators typically form two types of informal partnerships that operate in the real estate landscape (I will refer to these partnerships in general as "aggregators"). First, there are partnerships of local businessmen that aggregate land for their own local purposes (I will refer to these partnerships as "local business aggregators"). Real estate brokers and property developers who want to build housing projects, apartment complexes, shopping malls, and gated communities usually form this group. Their land requirements vary between five and fifty acres. They sometimes have small-town lawyers involved as partners. Second, there are partnerships of local individuals who aggregate land not for themselves but for corporations (I will refer to these partnerships as "intermediary aggregators"). They usually consist of both real estate brokers and small-town lawyers. The land requirements of corporations that use intermediary aggregators vary anywhere from ten to a few hundred acres.

Field interviews suggest that intermediary-based methods involve a process in which all aggregators enter into "agreements of sale" with small landowners by giving them a token amount of money (usually 10 percent of the total sale amount) and a time frame by which the purchase is to be completed. Typically, there are two stages in the sale-purchase of land. The first stage is when the owners and buyers enter into an agreement of sale. The second stage, called "registration," is when the actual sale happens and the sale documents are registered at a land registrar's office. During the early stages, aggregators present themselves as individual persons, not as aggregating partnerships. They do not reveal to landowners that they are engaged in aggregation. They say only that they are buying the land for their own individual purposes.

Agreements of sale are not the same as sale deeds. They specify the terms and conditions of a sale but do not actually transfer possession or title. Full payments for the land are not made either. Technically speaking, agreements of sale must be binding and lead to an executed sale deed by way of registration with the land registration office, but in reality they serve as contingent contracts for prospective purchasers. The advantage of using agreements of sale versus outright purchases is that with agreements of sale, the only risk for aggregators is the loss of the token amount they have given, which is a fraction of the cost of the outright purchase.

An aggregator, especially with small-town lawyers as partners, knows that it can breach agreements of sale at a low cost. Even if it reneges on these agreements by not completing the purchase in the specified period of time, small landowners do not have the needed incentives or resources to fight protracted legal cases seeking specific performance. They would rather wait out the expiration period of the agreements and live their lives without the hassles of legal disputes (the marginal cost of fighting these disputes for the small-town lawyers by comparison is small). The aggregator would, of course, lose the token amount, but it is small compared with the total amount of the outright purchase. Further, the aggregator can hold a potential reneging owner to specific performance if the sale does not happen within the stipulated period of time of the agreement of sale. The aggregator partnership may bring a court injunction preventing the continued use of the said property, potentially inflicting huge costs on the small landowner. In other words, the agreement of sale can act as a contingent contract in favor of aggregators due to an in-built asymmetry in the strengths and costs of the two parties. The asymmetry of strengths is higher when aggregators have small-town lawyers as partners because small-town lawyers can bring injunctions preventing the use of lands at little cost.

As noted earlier, the intermediary-based method involves secrecy of the intent of aggregation, the identity of the aggregators' partnerships, and the identity of the ultimate corporate purchasers (if there are any) in the initial phases of the aggregation. But information leaks occur at some stage in the sequence of negotiations causing holdouts. Aggregators leverage social norms and social pressure, and sometimes extralegal coercion, to solve any holdout problems. Partners of aggregators also engage in extensive dispute resolution in cases where titles to the small holdings are in question in the court.

Although the intermediary-based method described here is a dominant method in land aggregation in Andhra Pradesh, field data shows that a new innovation has been recently added to this method. It appears that upwardly mobile, entrepreneurial small-town lawyers who are able to go beyond their own local areas of operation can partner with other small-town lawyers and negotiate with individuals owning large tracts of land in rival. In this modified version, when small-town lawyers negotiate with landowners in a rival location for a different contiguous piece of land, they create a competitive rivalry and get small landowners in their own local area to lay extra pressure on members of their group who attempt to hold out for a better offer. In other words, they are able to create conditions of competitive auctions between different sets of landowners owning parcels in different contiguous tracts of land and increase their own outside options in the event that negotiations with one set of landowners in a given location fail. This method has been used in land aggregation efforts in the United States and is called a combinatorial auction (Kressin 2011).

IV. SEQUENTIAL MARKET NEGOTIATIONS: WHY SMALL-TOWN LAWYERS ARE BETTER THAN OTHERS

In this section, I outline a simple model that describes negotiations between aggregators and owners of small parcels of land and the way in which these negotiations change as more and more owners progressively enter into agreements of sale. I also try to explain why small-town lawyers enjoy certain advantages compared with their nonlawyer colleagues when faced with sequential negotiations that risk exposure to escalating sunk costs.

I employ the standard ideas of "zone of possible agreement" (ZOPA) and "best alternative to the negotiated agreement" (BATNA) that are common in negotiation literature (Raiffa 2003; Fisher and Ury 2011). A ZOPA exists when there is an overlap in the reservation prices of the aggregator and the owner and there is some likelihood of a deal being struck. There is a distinction to be made between the BATNAs of the two parties and their reservation prices. For instance, the BATNA of a farmer who is unable to sell his parcel of land may be continued use of his piece of land for farming or grazing purposes, from which he stands to receive utility. In making a negotiation decision, he will compare this utility with the utility he stands to enjoy by selling his land at his reservation price.

As one might expect, the reservation price of the aggregator is determined by a prior consideration of the total project cost and the considerations of how much to spend on land. In the case of an intermediary aggregator operating on behalf of a corporation, the reservation price is a function of the deal that it has struck with the corporation. If the intermediary aggregator and the ultimate purchaser have entered a fixed-price contract for the large tract of land, the intermediary aggregator will work backward and determine the maximum amount of money it is willing to pay each farmer, after deducting a minimum margin it wishes to keep for itself from the total amount it will receive from the corporation.

Every negotiation is attended by what is classically called the "negotiation dance," where almost always both the parties start off with first offers that fall outside the ZOPA and slowly start converging within the ZOPA to a single price point that is mutually acceptable. There is likely to be a marked difference between first offers made to corporate purchasers who engage in land purchases directly and local individual partners acting secretly on behalf of an intermediary aggregator (which in turn is acting secretly on behalf of a corporation) in the negotiation. When corporations enter the field directly and start negotiating, small landowners tend to jack up their first offers significantly.

But the surprising thing is that landowners also tend to have higher reservation prices when they negotiate with corporate purchasers versus individual purchasers. In other words, small landowners not only show a tendency to bargain from a higher starting point but also have a higher walkaway price when negotiating with corporations. This is surprising from a purely economic point of view. One expects that the price should not be affected by the identities of the players in a market. Even if it appears that the purchaser is a big player with deep pockets, it should affect the initial offers, but ultimately it should not influence the seller's reservation prices – especially if the bargain is seen as part of a one-off sale that is unrelated to a hidden attribute that is fungible and enticing to other businesses and corporations as well.

I reason that small landholders experience a heightened sense of value for their property when approached by a big corporation that leads them to bargain hard even if it means risking the negotiation. When approached by a corporation, small landowners are likely to infer that there is something special about their land. They develop an inkling that there is some attribute of their holding that the corporation is aware of, but they themselves are not yet fully aware of, such as an upcoming project nearby (a bigger public road, or railway line, or market). They believe that this attribute will be attractive to other potential big players as well and that they have reason to be intransigent about a higher bargain price.

Next, there is also some evidence to show that the local and nonlocal identities of the purchasers are likely to affect reservation prices of small landowners. Reservation prices of landowners in the case of nonlocal purchasers tend to be higher than with local purchasers. This can be due to a variety of reasons, but two explanations stand out prominently. First, it is conceivable that small landowners do not wish to come across as hard bargainers within the local community, where considerations of social capital and networks prevail. But when faced with nonlocal purchasers, this is not an issue for the landowners. There are fewer network connections to bother about. But it is also conceivable that with nonlocal purchasers, small landowners jack up their reservation prices, again because they feel that there is something special about their land, making it attractive to a nonlocal purchaser. In much the same way that a corporate purchaser can cause small landowners to evaluate their lands at higher prices as compared to local individuals, prospective nonlocal purchasers, even if they are individuals, signal to the small landowners that there might be an unexamined potential in the land for a higher price. Again, small-town lawyers and individuals who operate in areas where land is being acquired satisfy the condition of being from the local area. This is hard for nonlocal real estate brokers, individual nonlocal lawyers, and corporations to emulate.

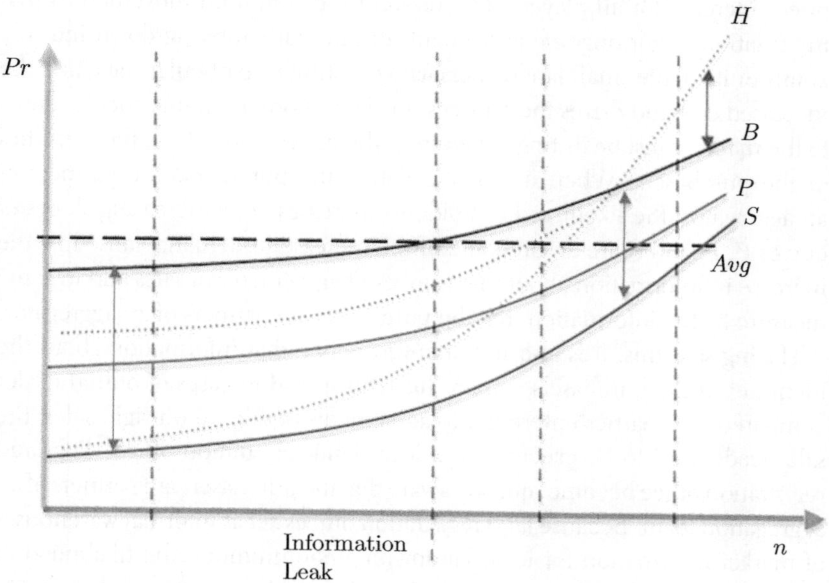

FIGURE 1 Curves showing the progression of prices

During a negotiation, individual partners in an aggregating partnership can appear as a small individual with a routine use of the purchased land, thereby camouflaging the identity of both the aggregator partnership as well as the corporation behind it. Most local real estate brokers, small-town lawyers, and businessmen can provide this camouflage. But as we shall soon see, small-town lawyers have an advantage over others in this regard.

Let me now consider how reservation prices of small landowners in negotiations may change – initially when purchasers are seen as individuals, and then when information spreads that they are partners in an intermediary aggregator. In order to do this, I include here an illustration of curves showing the progression of prices (Figure 1).

Curve *S* represents the movement of reservation prices of small landowners with an increase in the number of agreements of sale in a given location and the purchaser is a partner of an intermediary aggregator making secret purchases. Similarly, curve *B* represents the movement of reservation prices of the intermediary aggregator. Curve *P* is the final negotiated price curve. As an alternative possibility to *S*, curve *H* represents the reservation prices of landowners that cross curve *B*, indicating that there is no ZOPA, meaning that holdouts occur. The model also shows that curves *B*, *P*, and *S* slope upward, indicating that with more agreements of sale struck, the reservation prices increase for all players. The reason for this upward movement is that information about ongoing agreements of sale starts filtering down into the community of the small landowners who constitute a particular tract, and the increased demand drives these prices up. The information that trickles down to the market must be distinguished from the information about the identities of the purchasers. When it is realized that the purchasers are partners of an aggregator, the likelihood of holdouts increases. The increasing slopes of curves *B*, *P*, and *S* are an outcome of the increase in demand caused by the increase in information about the number of agreements of sales and in some measure by the information that the purchasers are partners of an aggregator.

Having said this, it is also important to notice that information about the identities of the purchasers is more likely to spread in cases of outright sales compared with parties entering into agreements of sale. In outright sales, the sale deeds need to be executed at a local land registration office. The land registration office becomes quickly aware that the purchasers are partners of an aggregation team. Because land registration offices act as informal warehouses of market information for local landowning communities, the likelihood of this information spreading quickly and causing holdouts increases. In order to shield against this happening, aggregators commonly use multiple subagents. However, this can increase transaction costs and has a marginally ameliorative effect.

The vertical intercepts represent the relative positions of the reservation prices of the aggregators and landowners for any aggregator-owner pair in the temporal sequence in which they go to negotiation. The whole sequence of negotiations itself starts with the first pair and, hopefully for the aggregator, culminates in purchases of all the bits without a single unsuccessful negotiation caused by a holdout.

A couple of preliminary observations need to be made about this model. The area under curve *B* (i.e., the buyer's reservation price curve) represents the total budget outlay of the aggregator – in other words, it is the reservation budget for the entire aggregated piece of land. But we know that curve *B* is a function of the amount of information of aggregation activity in the market, which itself is a function of the number of landowners who have already entered into a contingent contract (i.e., the agreement of sale).

Although aggregators know that the purchase price of each negotiation is likely to progressively increase, they make their decisions by a rule of thumb – i.e., assess the average price (P_{avg}) of the entire transaction. Partners of aggregators, who are brokers and real estate agents by profession and not lawyers, tend to be anchored at the P_{avg} (Kahneman and Tversky 1979). In contrast, when small-town lawyers encounter each additional owner after crossing the P_{avg}, they are likely to calculate the viability of the purchase on the basis of estimating the balance amount they expect to spend on the entire aggregated land transaction by calculating the increment X as an average of the difference between what they have spent so far and their reservation budget. Nonlawyer partners tend to defiantly stick to the average of the prices that they have sold up to that point and not budge. This is because they are not only scared that they may overshoot their budget but also are more willing than lawyers to resort to extralegal measures in support of their anchoring points.

Small-town lawyers seem to manage this progressive uncertainty about likely prices rather well. Perhaps they are more used to guarding against behavioral anchoring points than others. Perhaps they are also better informed about the costs of taking up extralegal measures and more risk-averse than nonlawyer aggregator teams. Also, as I will discuss later, they certainly are more able than others to form coalitions of owners with unsold landholdings, for a single predictable increment above the average, thereby reducing the purchasers' uncertainty in the negotiations. In other words, small-town lawyers are better able to pursue a process of aggregation beyond the point where other types of partners in aggregator partnerships are likely to feel trapped, complete the purchase of all the subunits of land that comprise the large tract, and still come out with a handsome profit.

One more thing to notice about the curves is that the rate at which curve S increases is likely to be higher than the rate at which curve *B* increases. This is because curve *B* is constrained by a looming budget constraint of which aggregators are constantly conscious. The different rates of increase between curves S and *B* lead to a convergence between the two curves, which has a net effect of progressively reducing the size of the ZOPAs between negotiating parties. When ZOPAs become smaller and smaller, the likelihood of failures in negotiations increases. A failure in agreements even when positive ZOPAs exists is often caused by information asymmetries and behavioral biases. This is a fairly well-explained phenomenon in negotiations literature (Bazerman 2006). Whenever first-round negotiations start failing at some stage in the process of aggregation, aggregators start pushing sellers of these cases into a common pool of failed negotiations that they will approach at a later time.

V. HOLDOUTS AND SOLUTIONS: SOCIAL NORMS, LEGAL AND EXTRALEGAL MEASURES

A. *Holdouts*

As shown earlier, the price and reservation price curves slope upwards as the number of agreements of sale increases. They slope upwards for two reasons: (1) an increase in information about the number of agreements of sale happening in the community of owners in the location of the aggregation; and (2) greater information of the involvement of a single aggregator, engaged in a concerted attempt to acquire a large tract of land, entering the market. But the information about the involvement of a single aggregator causes holdouts. Holdouts are represented by curve *H*, which shows the reservation prices of landowners when aggregators do not use their normal tactics to push it down to curve S.

The most obvious reasons for holdouts are strategic in nature. Several small landowners, who have the advantage of prior exposure to trading in land and business, are likely to hold out temporarily when they know that an aggregator has sunk a substantial amount of money. Although the sunk cost to the aggregator of entering into agreements of sale is only a fraction of the cost it would have incurred had there been outright purchases, it can still add up to a significant amount for the aggregator to lose. Temporary holdouts are risky strategies because they can often lead to irreconcilable and permanent deadlocks.

An important question that comes up is how strategic owners decide what their reservation prices are. Unless they have concrete exit options, they know that they do not want the negotiations to break down, and they only want to stall the process of aggregation temporarily with the hope that the aggregator will come back. So how do they locate the separating point between when the aggregator will come back and when the aggregator will not come back? They have some information about how much the aggregators have invested in the agreements of sale, but they do not know the outer boundaries of what the aggregators can spend on total land. The difference between landowners who engage in strategic holdouts and regular landowners who bargain hard to get a larger share of the pie that ZOPA constitutes is that those who engage in strategic holdouts are aware of the involvement of an aggregator and its sunk costs, whereas the regular landowners are not. In other words, strategic owners are aware of an aggregator's lowered BATNA due to the aggregator's sunk costs.

One thing that strategic owners can do is try to form coalitions among other owners who have not entered into agreements of sale yet and demand a price that will not make the aggregators let its sunk cost go to waste. They expect, and rightly so, that aggregators will adjust their prices in order to recover the value of their sunk costs.[3] A respondent says, "How will those fellows who have put in so much money now go away? In the least they will have to spend the amount they have already spent on rescuing what they have spent" (Interview 12, 2012).[4]

This reasoning gives the strategic owners an idea of one part of the puzzle, i.e., of where to pitch their bargain prices. But this reasoning still does not give them a complete picture. It cannot still be entirely clear what the upper budget for the aggregator is at this stage. Of course, strategic sellers do distinguish between local business aggregators from intermediary aggregators working for ultimate corporate purchasers. This is because they have a better idea of what local business aggregators want the land for but have absolutely no clue what corporate entities want to do with the land and what their reservation budgets are. Local business aggregators are typically involved in small housing projects, and strategic owners are informed enough to predict sales and profits of these types of projects. As a result, they are also likely to know the spending capacities of local business aggregators.

The reason strategic owners try to form coalitions with other strategic owners is that it reduces the uncertainty about making predictions about the reservation prices of aggregators. When strategic owners act individually, there is greater uncertainty for the aggregator about how much it has to spend on the entire aggregation project. This in turn introduces uncertainty in the negotiations and might force the aggregator to retreat. This is an outcome that strategic owners wish to avoid. Their aim is only to take advantage of an aggregator's lowered BATNA and not break down the negotiations permanently.

Similarly, it is also in the interest of the aggregators to encourage coalition formation among strategic sellers so that they can make better predictions about how much more money they need to spend on completing the project. Of course, there are likely to be other problems when strategic owners form coalitions, but counting for all the tradeoffs, aggregators would much rather deal with a single coalition than have to deal with multiple strategic sellers disparately.

An aggregator says, "It is profitable for us when those who want to demand crazy amounts of money come together. Otherwise, if they start demanding crazy amounts of money individually, there is no way for us to manage the uncertainty (and keep within the budget)."[5]

Not all holdouts are caused by strategic owners. There are also inadvertent holdouts in the aggregation landscape that are caused for reasons other than extracting more money from the aggregators. For instance, landowners who have title disputes with third parties can cause inadvertent holdouts. Small-town lawyers estimate that at least 10–15 percent of lands in Andhra Pradesh are under litigation. The absence of clear titles due to the existence of multiple claims on a single piece of land prevents successful transfers to aggregators. So, even if one of the two parties to a dispute in a title wants to sell his land, it is possible that the other may want to hold out to get a larger share of a settlement price. Disputants are usually not on talking terms with each other and therefore Coasean solutions are not feasible. Aggregators that wish to buy disputed lands give the promise of breaking impasses. But as we shall soon see, aggregators have to go to extra lengths to resolve such problems.

Holdouts may also be caused by landowners due to family reasons or emotional attachment with the land, leading to a reluctance to part with their lands for any amount of money. A significant proportion of rural land is inherited, and such land is often accompanied by an emotional component of "personhood" that is not easy to price in a market (see Radin 1982). Owners often use their lands to bury their ancestors and may treat their landholdings as extensions of their families. Owners may also practice certain types of rituals meant to appease dead ancestors, involving the continued preservation of lands and tending to them in special ways. Ritualistic sentiments are often intertwined with views that cashing in on family inheritances is sacrilegious and shows disrespect for elders and ancestors. Several elderly owners highlight the temporality of money and, in contrast, emphasize the enduring value of land.

An aging respondent says with emphasis, "Money comes and goes, but this 'motherland' will remain with us as long as the sun and moon exist" (Interview 3, 2012).[6]

It is not surprising that this sentiment is somewhat less prevalent among younger respondents who grew up in a postliberalized India. Their elders, who grew up in more uncertain times, consider land a form of insurance against hunger and poverty provided by their ancestors.

A related type of holdout is caused by the consideration of the losses in social capital that are attached to owning pieces of land in a neighborhood. Being owners of small holdings of land in a village makes people a part of an invisible community. Landholdings are usually segregated along caste lines, where neighbors are related. Selling landholdings can mean a displacement from these communities, which are important sources of social insurance and social capital. People can be inclined to cling to the community and refuse to migrate to urban areas where they risk anonymity and a loss in this social capital. This is particularly true of elders who grew up in a preliberalized era in India.

There are also holdouts caused by political reasons. If an aggregation is being undertaken by a local business aggregator with a strong political affiliation to one of the two or three dominant political parties (Congress, Telugu Desam, or Communist), landowners who are affiliated with a rival party are likely to see the aggregation as a route to greater wealth among the aggregators, which can significantly impact the political balance in the area. More money means greater ability to spend on elections, and greater chances of political success. Political affiliations are often linked to the sellers' ethnic and caste identities. Given that partnerships in aggregation are often struck along caste lines (i.e., Reddy MLA, a Reddy small-town lawyer, and a Reddy real estate broker could be an aggregation team), sellers who do not belong to the caste of aggregators may feel polarized, making them reluctant to sell their lands.[7] Preexisting political groupings can naturally lead to coalitions against sale of lands, leading to holdouts. However, aggregators solve this problem by taking partners from different dominant political parties.

Finally, sellers may display a behavioral bias that makes them subject to loss aversion (Kahneman and Tversky 1979). Landholdings among farmers are seen as sources of livelihood, and farmers are more likely to compare income streams from a use of lands that make up their livelihoods, with potential income streams from cashing out on sale of the lands. One expects that they can see value in depositing cash from land sales in banks and collecting interest, or in investing the cash from sales in alternative businesses that can produce higher rates of return than income streams from their lands. However, the idea of using banks and collecting interest is still a relatively unknown phenomena among poor landowners. Information about making the right types of deposits that can generate optimal interest rates is scarce among many landowners. Investing in alternative businesses is also perceived to be risky and unfamiliar. As a result, landowners are more likely to prefer having a certain income from using their existing lands than getting an uncertain income from alternative revenue-generating activities employing their cash from sales, even if the expected benefits from the alternative revenue-generating activities is higher than the sure income they get from owning and using their lands. This is the classic problem of loss aversion that has been discussed in behavioral economics (ibid. 1979).

B. *Holdout Solutions*

So how do aggregators solve these various types of holdout problems? As mentioned earlier, the first step that is common to all the methods is an attempt to preserve the secrecy of the involvement of a single individual or entity that tries to aggregate the landholdings. In the case of corporate entities that use intermediary aggregators, not only do the intermediary aggregators try to keep the involvement of the corporation a secret, they also try to keep their own involvement as a partnership a secret. Similarly, local business aggregators also try to keep their activities of aggregation under wraps. Efforts at entering into agreements of sale are divided among partners of an aggregator.

Sometimes partners cheat – an aggregating partner may strike a private deal with a landowner informing him about an impending aggregation process so that the spoils from the higher price charged by the owner are split between the owner and himself. The loss incurred by the aggregating partnership is divided between more than two partners, leaving more for the cheating partner than for others in the partnership. Ugly and violent fights erupt when such behavior is detected, and cheaters are thrown out without any continued interest in the aggregation project. Trust is a precondition to the formation of aggregating partnerships that must operate in conditions of secrecy much like extralegal and underground organizations (Gambetta 2010; Mamidi 2011).

At some point during the negotiations, landowners develop an inkling that there is an aggregation effort afoot, but they are still not clear about the specific details of the aggregator's identity. At this stage, intermediary aggregators acting on behalf of corporations are likely to admit more openly that there are aggregation efforts under way, but they still try to maintain that they are doing it on their own as local business ventures, not as deals for a corporate entity hidden in the background. This is clearly because there is a difference in perception among landowners about the reservation prices of local business aggregators and corporations. So, by preserving the secrecy of the corporation even when the aggregation attempt has been detected, the intermediary aggregator tries to keep the prices of landholdings down.

Field data shows that different nonlawyer players such as real estate dealers, local businessmen, and politicians are equally capable of maintaining the secrecy of aggregation or the involvement of a background corporate entity. However, small-town lawyers have an advantage over the nonlawyer players. When regular real estate dealers or local businessmen enter into several agreements of sale in a given area, cues of a concerted aggregation activity are more revealing than when small-town lawyers do the same. It is not uncommon for small-town lawyers to pick up interests in small pieces of land in their regular course of business when they provide services to people in the community. Frequently they receive small landholdings as fees from landowners for fighting their cases in courts, settling disputes with third parties, or helping them regularize their titles by doing their paperwork in the revenue or *mandal* offices. So, when small-town lawyers enter into agreements of sale for aggregation purposes, they can easily disguise their acquisitions in the aggregation activity as proceeds from rendering their legal services in the regular course of their professional business.

When it becomes amply clear that there is aggregation activity in the market, several landowners who enter agreements of sale (the first stage of the sale process, i.e., the contingent contract) realize that there is some chance that the final sales will not be completed and that the chances of the aggregators completing the sales will depend on whether they are able to get everyone who owns pieces of land in the large tract to sell. They keep in close contact with the partners in aggregating partnerships, who in turn are likely to give them optimistic reports on the chances of completing the aggregation process and realizing the benefits of completed sales. In the back of their minds these landowners may feel that they have lost nothing in the process of entering the agreements of sale. In fact, they are happy that they have made a bit of money from the initial token amounts they have taken from the aggregators. In the worst-case scenario, the sales may not go through, but at least they get to keep their lands and the token amounts they know they do not need to return.

The main strategy of aggregators at this stage is to initiate coalition formations among landowners who have already entered into agreements of sale, with the hope that they will contribute to the pressure on the noncooperative owners who refuse to sell. This is an informal process that involves organizing parties, functions, and social gatherings. What until now was kept a closely guarded secret becomes an open cause for celebration. Partners in aggregators and owners who entered the agreements of sale become new "best friends forever," with wealth to spend and a shared optimism that the full aggregation process will go through.

With the token amounts they have received from the initial contingent contracts, those who agreed to sell kick-start a new lifestyle and become members of a new moneyed class jointly with the aggregator partners. Reciprocity and status signaling become important in this new group. New aspirations come into existence. Weddings become ostentatious, cradle ceremonies become glitzy, religious festivals become garish, and shopping trips to Dubai and Singapore become common.

Feasts and public functions become opportunities for the neo-rich to flaunt their newfound wealth. Those who did not own vehicles now own new scooters and motorcycles, and those who owned two-wheelers now have fancy new cars. Some buy costly signals of affluence, including air-conditioned cars and jewelry. They now drink only Johnnie Walker Red Label and Teacher's Highland scotch whisky, not Indian whisky. Conversations at parties are frequently about holidays overseas and family connections in New Jersey and Texas, and kitty parties replace the more traditional pastimes for women. Bigger TVs in the front drawing rooms of landowners who agree to sell signal the onset of a new lifestyle (Veblen 1899).

The sudden creation of a new moneyed class, even if it is based on money earned from precariously positioned contingent contracts, has a rather powerful impact on many noncooperative owners who hold out. The social pressure of exclusion from the shared lifestyles of the cooperative members in the owners' community is felt in many telling ways. Marriage alliances get struck between families of cooperative sellers while noncooperative members fall out of the marriage market. Daughters get "exported" to "IT sons-in-law" in San Jose, and sons get visas to pursue IT careers overseas because they can now show bank balances in their visa applications. Cooperative owners who agreed to sell can also now send their kids to better schools in big cities or for higher education overseas. Their poorer, noncooperative counterparts who hold on to their properties can only hope that their kids will become farmers like themselves. New power positions emerge as new nodes of social capital develop in networks.

The resulting pressure from such exclusion forces the hitherto unyielding elders who refused to sell due to emotional and ancestral reasons to change their minds. They do not want to sacrifice the interests of their own families for outdated reasons that they cannot justify to anyone, including their own selves. They too want to get on the bandwagon of selling out and buying an apartment in the city. Slowly but surely, a nontrivial percentage of the noncooperative sellers come back to the negotiation table.

It is important to note that the festivity and exuberance of the cooperative landowners is tinged by the worry that they will not realize the full benefits of the sale of their lands unless the noncooperative members sell, too. The partners of aggregators waste no time in reminding the cooperative owners that they will miss the opportunity of their lifetimes unless the noncooperative owners alter their position. They warn about possibilities of downturns in the market and that the community of landowners risks becoming great losers if the noncooperative landowners do not reconsider their stand.

Meanwhile, during the process of coalition formation, there still remain several noncooperative landowners who question the authenticity and good-faith intentions of partners of aggregators. They are usually the landowners who hold out for strategic reasons. They raise doubts about the longevity of sudden prosperity. They ask for reasons that they should believe in the warnings and exhortations of the aggregators, especially if it is clear that the aggregators have vested interests in the matter. In response to accusations of conflict of interests, aggregators try not to deny that they make large profits from the aggregation efforts. They openly admit that they will benefit hugely from the aggregation efforts, and for that matter, by a much larger magnitude than the owners. But they remind the landowners that it is not rational to compare how much they will make with what others make. They ask them not to begrudge someone else's happiness but only be bothered about their own benefits and see whether their benefits are in excess of what they are likely to get from an open market without any aggregation. They also try to link their own higher earnings to the effort that they have to put into the task of aggregation. In effect, they try to educate the landowners and help them overcome their biases of inequity aversion that noncooperative owners may invoke (Kahneman and Tversky 1979).

C. *Advantage of Small-Town Lawyers*

The first advantage that small-town lawyers have over other types of players in coalition formation is that they come across as people who are interested in the welfare of everyone in the community, not just their own. Their voice of reason is better heard by landowners than the voices of other types of aggregating partners, including the land brokers and politicians. They are seen as people with the least conflict of interest. They do not carry the stereotypical image of rapacious, self-serving mercenaries that their corporate or western counterparts seem to carry. They are also considered more trustworthy than other players who engage in aggregation. Furthermore, they are more articulate than other types of aggregating partners in explaining the future of land markets to the landowners and the accompanying difficulties associated with holding lands in a changing regulatory scenario. They can couch their arguments in a technical language, talk about uncertainties in property titles under law, and scare the noncooperators. Other types of aggregating partners cannot accomplish some of these tasks as easily as small-town lawyers.

The formation of coalitions of cooperative landowners also has a huge impact in ways other than creating pressures of exclusion. The cooperative owners who entered into agreements of sale now better understand that their own happiness, beyond the little they received from the initial token amounts from the contingent contracts, depends on whether the noncooperative owners will sell. They have bought into the benefits of affluence with the little amount they received from the initial agreements of sale, and now they want to sustain it. Their reactions toward the noncooperative owners range from expressing indignation and irritation, to attempting to rationally and calmly explain the benefits of cashing out at prices higher than the prevailing market prices. Some of them become violent, and others become persuasive advocates of the communal cause. Some of them talk about why they should not be held hostage by a bunch of irrational fools, yet others plan punishments and boycotts in the event that the noncooperative owners do not yield at some point. On the whole, the community of cooperative owners progressively gets galvanized into a proactive force against the unyielding noncooperative owners.

When coalitions of cooperators proactively engage in actions against noncooperators, there are likely to be legal ramifications. Should the cooperative owners become violent, they are ably helped by the aggregators, especially the partners who are small-town lawyers. The marginal costs for small-town lawyers of protecting cooperative sellers from criminal sanctions is next to nothing. When cooperative owners rationally explain the benefits of selling versus holding out, the small-town lawyers are better able to complement the discussions with a professional voice of reason.

Small-town lawyers enjoy several other advantages. They have much better information about the titles of noncooperative owners. This can be of critical importance in bargaining with noncooperative owners who wish to hold out for strategic reasons. Given the complexities of land laws, noncooperative owners often overestimate their strength in bargaining. They may be sitting on titles that are not clearly established and subject to further inquiry by courts, and that have remained with the noncooperative owners simply because they have not been brought up for questioning.

A good example of a questionable title is one that has been transferred to a current holder by a previous owner in violation of family inheritance laws, especially with regard to female children. Many people give out cash as a dowry when their daughters are married off and leave their land to their sons with an implicit agreement of the division. Leaving all the land to sons may be problematic, and there may be continued legal interests of daughters in the land by way of formal inheritance laws. So, when the land is subsequently transferred by the sons to noncooperative owners, it may be possible to question the titles in the hands of the noncooperative owners by bringing back a potential female claimant from the past. These problems in title are even more severe in the case of properties that were once held by Muslims, whose family laws are considered to be more complicated than those of Hindu families by a mostly Hindu judiciary. Finally, even if there are no kinks in the lineage of titles to properties, small-town lawyers are easily capable of fabricating them purely for extortionary purposes.

As noted, property rights in India tend to be imperfect due to the complexities of inheritance laws. The problems that arise out of these complexities are further exacerbated by the sheer length of time it takes for any rights to be established by the courts. Because property rights are inherently imperfect due to delays and transaction costs of dealing with inefficient institutions, the ability of any current property owner to sufficiently insulate his rights against extortionary threats of litigation advanced by lawyers are almost nonexistent. Further, there are no formal institutional costs to lawyers who initiate such extortionary litigation.

Clearly, not all cases that small-town lawyers threaten to bring against noncooperative owners have defendable legal substance. But they believe that as long as they can work the system by initiating frivolous cases against the noncooperators at zero marginal costs, they can gain an upper hand in bargaining with the noncooperators. As for the noncooperators, going to a court can be a nightmare because cases can take forever to be resolved. They are likely to suffer irreparable damage in the interim if the small-town lawyers bring injunctions against the use of the properties in consideration. It is rather paradoxical and ironic that the formal legal system is used as a threat rather than a predictable and just system in such dealings. Small-town lawyers justify their use of such tactics by arguing that the end outcomes increase the happiness of the many and that resorting to such practices is an inevitable by-product of the inefficiencies of the system.

Small-town lawyers can cause extortionary pressure on noncooperative owners in other related ways. For instance, they can create easement problems. They can block out convenient road access to pieces of the property of noncooperative owners and give them highly inconvenient road access that reduces the value of their properties. Here again, the noncooperative owners know that getting the courts to protect their rights to reasonable easements is a costly and time-consuming process. Noncooperative owners want to avoid being in situations where the value of their properties is lowered below existing market prices.

Do small-town lawyers use this extortionary power in their daily course of business to make a living? After all, courts and bar associations barely play a role in regulating the behavior of lawyers. So why don't we see a higher incidence of extortionary behavior by lawyers in contexts other than aggregation projects? The answer lies in that small-town lawyers, and lawyers in general, are prevented from an indiscriminate use of their extortionary power by widely prevalent social norms that operate within local communities. When small-town lawyers start making their living by indiscriminate extortion, people react negatively and inflict punishment. Punishments can vary between reputational damage and violence against them. Small-town lawyers can function only as long as they have social support for their behavior or are not punished for their behavior.

On the flip side, when small-town lawyers threaten to file frivolous cases against unyielding landowners in aggregation projects that can potentially benefit a majority of landowners, they will not be stopped by the community. In fact, the community will support them. The interest of the community is larger than the interests of individuals and their individual property rights. Property rights at an individual level are not seen as absolute. Social norms deem that the case for the protection of someone's property (here, the right not to be forced to sell, as recognized by the state) that entails losses to an entire community by way of unrealized sales on several others' property is weak. Property rights cannot work individually. Every person's property is inextricably linked to everyone else's property. Accordingly, the role of small-town lawyers is socially evaluated to see whether they are supporting the larger interests of the community.

As noted earlier, not all legal cases that small-town lawyers threaten to bring against noncooperative owners have defendable legal substance. Some of them are fabricated. But small-town lawyers know they can work the system by initiating frivolous cases with nuisance value against the noncooperative owners at zero marginal costs, and they use these threats to gain an upper hand in bargaining. Noncooperative owners know that going to court is a nightmare because cases can take forever to be resolved. They can also suffer irreparable damage if these small-town lawyers bring injunctions against the use of their properties in consideration. When reminded of these possibilities in subsequent negotiations, even the strategic noncooperative owners are likely to reconsider their hard-line positions of not selling within the ZOPA.

In most cases, it is rather paradoxical and indeed ironic that lawyers use the inefficiencies of the formal legal system as a threat to produce outcomes desired by the community rather than using the formal legal system as a predictable system to produce just outcomes. But small-town lawyers justify their tactics by arguing that the end outcomes increase the happiness of the many, and that resorting to such practices is an inevitable means to accomplish socially acceptable outcomes.

Small-town lawyers are able to achieve solutions with noncooperative owners in another important way that other players are unable to. They are more capable than others in understanding the real interests of owners who hold out. This is important because it allows small-town lawyers to strike integrative deals in their negotiations. They have a better idea of the real interests of owners than other aggregating partners simply because they have repeat interactions with many more members of the community. Although politicians interact with many people on a day-to-day basis, too, I propose that small-town lawyers interact with more people in dispute settlements and transactional contexts than anyone else.

There is also some evidence to conjecture that small-town lawyers exhibit lesser zero-sum biases than do other types of aggregating partners. Land brokers and real estate agents usually engage in one-off trades in the land business, and they tend to work with a single issue – price. They view transactions as processes in which there is a fixed pie to share and that a gain to one party will mean a necessary loss to the other. In contrast, small-town lawyers deal with multi-issue problems on a daily basis and are likely to have expertise in making optimal intrasubjective tradeoffs needed for optimization and joint problem solving more so than the land brokers and real estate agents, who focus only on price.

Consider an example. Small-town lawyers in the Medak district in the new state of Telangana, working on a particular aggregation project, came up with an innovative way to satisfy intransigent landowners by finding them equivalent pieces of land in alternative locations. They discovered that the real interests of the farmers who were holding out were not strategic but only a preservation of livelihood through farming. These particular farmers did not have any skills other than farming and would have faced high switching costs were they to sell their lands and attempt a different economic activity. When the small-town lawyers understood this, they started buying out alternative pieces of land in a different location outside the boundaries of the land they wished to aggregate and exchanged them with the parcels of the landowners in the area of interest. They even sweetened these deals by throwing in small add-ons like free two-room tenements, borewells, water pump sets, and minor monetary adjustments needed to make the exchanges fair and enticing.

Other aggregators in the landscape were quick to adopt this method. Many aggregators now go to negotiations already prepared with alternative pieces of land to exchange in case they discover noncooperative owners who are only interested in preserving their livelihood. There are also instances in which aggregators with small-town lawyers offered alternative pieces of land (or apartments) to entire communities of people who preferred to remain together as neighbors. This was a way of enticing owners with the option of preserving their communities when they move to a new location.

The differential value between the specific pieces of land held by owners in an area under aggregation and the pieces of land held elsewhere is the key to the arbitrage generated by these relocation strategies. The specific pieces of land that constitute an area under aggregation acquire their high value to an aggregator because they make the area under aggregation contiguous. An equivalent piece in a different location, that can give exactly the same utility to an owner of a piece in the area under aggregation, costs far less to an aggregator. The potential for an integrative transaction arises from this difference.

In other cases, aggregators with small-town lawyers also help otherwise non-cooperative landowners with services unrelated to land transactions: getting kids admissions into engineering colleges or jobs, opening bank accounts, settling marriage alliances, and providing soft loans. Offers of these services unrelated to land transactions also presuppose a superior understanding of the real interests of the noncooperative owners. Small-town lawyers are vastly better than other types of players in this regard.

Small-town lawyers have another notable innovation in aggregation efforts that distinguishes them from other types of aggregating partners. Due to their work in the local district courts, they know small-town lawyers from locations other than the ones where they normally operate. As a result, they are able to form partnerships with them and set up aggregation efforts in rival locations in the event that the aggregation efforts in their own normal areas of operation run into problems. So, for example, small-town lawyers from Medak, with an ongoing aggregation effort there, are now able to initiate aggregation efforts in Zahirabad (another district in Telangana) with the cooperation of small-town lawyers in Zahirabad.

When they do this, they tell the community of landowners in Medak about it. When landowners in Medak realize that an aggregation effort in a rival location can materialize, they feel the pressure of coercing sales in their own location. As a result, small-town lawyers in Medak now have a competitive outside option. They feel a greater pressure in ensuring that aggregation in their own location happens quickly and as smoothly as possible. There is now a competition between owners in one location of aggregation and another area of aggregation, which pushes prices down closer to market prices in the absence of any aggregation (Subramanian 2010).

Strategically oriented owners in the first location realize that aggregators who engage in opening this type of an auction must incur higher initial fixed costs because aggregators have to invest in initial token amounts now in two locations, not just one. However, they also recognize that holding on too hard to their own positions is likely to push the aggregators to the second location because it may still be worthwhile to the aggregators to pursue this option even after discounting for the losses in token amounts in the location where the aggregation did not succeed. They are also likely to be unaware that small-town lawyers have a growing proximity with in-house counsels of multiple corporations and that they may continue pursuing the first option without losing anything in the end. But small-town lawyers know that their proximity with multiple corporations can provide insurance against losing token amounts given out in the first location. Finally, there is also the possibility that intermediary aggregators comprised of small-town lawyers who are in demand by multiple corporations can now start bargaining for lower token amounts at multiple locations of aggregation activities.

It is important to recognize that small-town lawyers gain their distinct advantages over other types of players because of their networks with other small-town lawyers. It is conceivable that real estate brokers too can start networking with real estate brokers in rival locations and start creating auction markets, but they are inherently local players, with local jurisdictions of trust. They do not have the professional networks that small-town lawyers have. Small-town lawyers are able to go past locational boundaries better than other types of players because of their profession.

VI. NEW ROLES FOR SMALL-TOWN LAWYERS

The role of small-town lawyers does not stop with activities involving the aggregation of land for corporations. There is a strong trend of these lawyers finding jobs in in-house departments of corporations and being assimilated into a wider set of corporate activities. As land aggregators, even if their tasks are one-off for any single corporation, given their unique set of negotiation and social skills that are applicable in multiple contexts, they make attractive employees for in-house departments in corporations.

There is some evidence to show that the skills required to engage in sequential negotiations with multiple parties, with an all-or-none structure of success built into the negotiation process, make small-town lawyers especially useful to corporations on a repetitive basis. Corporations often have to deal with government agencies and departments, and need their various compliance-related documentation and applications for permissions to pass through multiple nodes and levels of hierarchy in a government office. Getting these things done in a sequential order in a government office is very similar to the sequential negotiations these lawyers engage in when they aggregate land and buy bits of land from landowners. Any single failure in a negotiation in the sequence undermines the value of the entire process and costs the lawyers the resources already sunk into the process. The costs can be in terms of either time spent at each level of bureaucratic authority or even bribes given to government officers.

Corrupt government hierarchies are especially prone to holdouts. When all officers occupying positions of power in a hierarchy collude, the problem of holdouts is minimized. One only needs to liaison with a single individual in an office hierarchy to strike a bargain and get things done. The rent (or the bribe) is automatically divided between members who occupy these hierarchies according to a prefixed ratio. However, when government offices are not already organized in such a manner, the possibility of holdouts is high. In such situations, one needs to have the requisite skills to negotiate with multiple officers to get one's "file passed" to a successful outcome. Small-town lawyers who join corporate in-house jobs are masters of this trade. They are able to use techniques similar to the ones used in aggregation of land.

For instance, they are able to strike contingent agreements (much like they do with landowners) with the officers wherein the officers are paid a small fraction of a bribe payment in advance of a job being done – say, passing a file from his or her desk – and the entire amount when the file passes all the desks in the office. But agreements of payments of money to government officers in exchange for favors are illegal. These agreements cannot be formally protected by the law and can be upheld only by informal norms and trust. Small-town lawyers are better able to build relationships of trust with government officers than anyone else in an in-house legal department because small-town lawyers have the most experience in building relationships in environments of institutional vacuum. They are used to dealings that depend on repeat interactions with people and form relationships based on trust. As a result, whenever multiple people need to be managed in a sequence, involving transactions based on trust, in-house lawyers with backgrounds as small-town lawyers are able to better manage the uncertainties of corporate "spending" and minimize loss and exposure to sunk costs than their colleagues in the same in-house departments.

Finally, in-house lawyers with experiences as small-town lawyers are likely to be from socioeconomic backgrounds that are very different from the backgrounds of their colleagues. They usually come from semiurban and rural backgrounds, have not attended the English medium schools their colleagues in the in-house departments have, and are often from lower- to middle-rung castes. Their social experiences make them especially adept at understanding grass-root politics, including mediating political and social conflicts. Corporations in India do not operate in a social vacuum. They constantly face demands from politicians, ranging from campaign funds to substantial returns for the favors that are rendered to them.

Typically these politicians themselves share a common socioeconomic background with small-town lawyers. In fact, several small-town lawyers end up becoming politicians themselves. The relationships between the corporate world and the political world are extremely delicate and require to be negotiated on a continuous basis. The boundaries between the corporate world and the political world separate two very different types of behaviors and expectations. Globalizing corporations expect predictable, professional behavior, with transactions and terms of exchange set ex-ante, whereas behavior in the political world is continuously in a state of flux and attended by uncertainties. Small-town lawyers who initially engage in land aggregation projects for corporations and thereupon shift to corporations can straddle these boundaries between the two worlds with great dexterity. They understand the excellences of predictability and efficiency, and standardization of transactions on the one hand, and at the same time recognize that the world outside a corporation has its own logic.

It is believed that in the early 2000s small-town lawyers who joined in-house departments of corporations were not treated on par with their "posher" colleagues who came from the burgeoning National Law Schools of India. They were treated as second-class country sods who did "shady" odd jobs outside the walls of the corporation. They were considered inarticulate, unable to draft contracts in English without making spelling or grammatical errors, and the kind who drank cheap rum and watched bawdy films in their local language for entertainment. They did not mix too well with their more confident National Law School counterparts who ate in fancy restaurants, were not shy of talking to their female colleagues, and could pronounce the word "champagne" correctly. In turn, small-town lawyers considered their posh colleagues *study bacchas*, i.e., the "kids who studied books" or those who fit the description "Ramu is a good boy" ("Ramu" being a common name in South India). It is also likely that there was a caste division between these two types of lawyers occupying the same office floor in a corporation, with small-town lawyers typically hailing from relatively lower caste backgrounds, and the rest of their colleagues from a relatively higher caste background.

However, over the years this subtle caste system between the two types of in-house lawyers has evaporated. In-house lawyers with backgrounds as small-town lawyers have become aware of their value to corporations. They seem to now have a voice in meetings and are respected for their understanding of the chaotic world outside. They drive big cars, live in expensive houses, pick up best-sellers in airport bookstores, and want to send their kids to National Law Schools. They too have arrived.

VII. CONCLUSION

This research finds that there is a growing demand for large, contiguous pieces of land in the face of economic growth and globalization. Companies need land to set up factories and large facilities where services are produced.

Two dominant methods of aggregation are found – the first method involves the intervention of government in exercising eminent domain and taking over land from small landowners and transferring the whole to a private entity that pays the equivalent of just compensation, which the government gives the small owners. The price of land in this method is ostensibly equivalent to market price, but a market price discovered ex-post by taking into account prevailing prices of land around the acquired lots. As a result, for the companies that acquire land by this method, land costs less in the short run. Importantly, this method also solves holdout problems for the acquiring companies. But it has been found that this method produces great resentment in owners and elicits protests from activists and political movements.

The second method of aggregation does not involve the intervention of the government. Companies and private entities use the services of intermediary aggregators. Intermediary aggregators are usually partnerships of real estate brokers, local businessmen, and small-town lawyers. They purchase small landholdings without initially revealing the fact that they are aggregators because they want to minimize the reservation prices of sellers and the possibilities of holdouts. Several holdouts in this process are strategic, but many are inadvertently caused due to social reasons, including behavioral biases of loss aversion among small landowners, who prefer the certainty of an income from the usage of their lands rather than an uncertain but higher expected income from postsale cash flows. It is found that intermediary aggregating partnerships that involve small-town lawyers have a greater advantage in solving these holdout problems. Small-town lawyers bring special attributes in leveraging contingent contracts and social norms in resolving disputes and producing trust among landowners. They are better able to solve holdout problems than any other type of player in the landscape. Small-town lawyers have also found innovative, integrative solutions in solving these problems, including creating competitive auction markets between rival aggregation sites, which places downward pressure on reservation prices of landowners.

This research was conducted in and around the city of Hyderabad, where there has been a huge real estate boom over the last decade. Respondents for this study include small-town lawyers, real estate brokers, aggregating businessmen, activists, and corporate in-house counsel. Potential sample biases may arise due to the fact that I reached my respondents by a snowball method. There was no way that I could obtain a superset of respondents from any public database and randomize a sample for this study. Second, the sample is representative of land aggregation in and around Hyderabad, and therefore several findings may not extend to other parts of India.

There are likely to be huge policy implications – as I was writing this paper, the LARR Bill was being debated in India. The LARR Bill seeks to rationalize the process of land acquisition in India. There is a debate about a mixed method of land aggregation – a provision states that a private aggregating entity should aggregate a minimum of 70 percent of land directly through the market and only then be eligible for involving the government in acquiring the balance of 30 percent by eminent domain. This paper makes the case that there should be an effort to collect more quantitative data on the possibilities of aggregation without the need of government intervention before any blanket rule is proposed.

The government should also be encouraged to investigate the role of small-town lawyers in land aggregation efforts at the grassroots level. There is some evidence to show that small-town lawyers rely on extralegal means to pressurize noncooperative landowners to sell. However, it is well worth realizing that this behavior is an outcome of a systemic failure of formal institutions rather than the moral turpitude of a profession.

Notes

1 While there is some evidence to suggest that these amendments have met with severe resistance from opposition parties, it is still early in the political process to determine where these regulations will ultimately settle. The debate around land acquisition is still unfolding as I write this chapter.

2 Ghatak and Ghosh posit that owners may have incentives for exaggerated claims in negotiations. However, as we shall later see in this chapter, such a risk is mitigated by the concealment of the identity of the ultimate corporate purchaser by the intermediaries (Ghatak and Ghosh 2011b).

3 For more on this, see "escalation bias" (Bazerman 2006).

4 This quotation is the author's translation from a local language.

5 This quotation is the author's translation from a local language.

6 This quotation is the author's translation from a local language.

7 Reddy is a caste in Andhra Pradesh.

References

Bazerman, Max. 2006. *Judgment in Managerial Decision Making*. New York: Wiley.

Benson, Bruce. 2005. "The Mythology of Holdout as a Justification for Eminent Domain and Public Provision of Roads." *Independent Review* 10 (2): 165–194.

Bernstein, Lisa. 1992. "Opting Out of the Legal System: Extralegal Contractual Relations in the Diamond Industry." *Journal of Legal Studies* 21 (1): 115–157.

Ellickson, Robert. 1985. "Of Coase and Cattle: Dispute Resolution among Neighbors in Shasta County." *Stanford Law Review* 38 (3): 623–687.

1991. *Order without Law: How Neighbors Settle Disputes*. Cambridge: Harvard University Press.

1998. "Law and Economics Discovers Social Norms." *Journal of Legal Studies* 27 (2): 537–552.

Elster, Jon. 1989. *The Cement of Society*. Cambridge: Cambridge University Press.

Fisher, Roger and William Ury. 2011. *Getting to Yes: Negotiating Agreement without Giving In*. New York: Penguin Books.

Gambetta, Diego. 2010. *Codes of the Underworld: How Criminals Communicate*. Princeton: Princeton University Press.

Ghatak, Maitreesh and Parikshit Ghosh. 2011. "The Land Acquisition Bill: A Critique and a Proposal." *Economic and Political Weekly* 46 (41): 65–72.

Heller, Michael. 1998. "The Tragedy of the Anticommons: Property in the Transition from Marx to Markets." *Harvard Law Review* 111 (3): 621–688.
Heller, Michael and Rebecca Eisenberg. 1998. "Can Patents Deter Innovation? The Anticommons in Biomedical Research." *Science* 280 (5364): 698–701.
Interview 3, 2012.
Interview 12, 2012.
Kahneman, Daniel and Amos Tversky. 1979. "Prospect Theory: An Analysis of Decision under Risk." *Econometrica* XL (VII): 263–291.
Kressin, Brandon. 2011. "The Holdout Myth Underlying the Current Takings Doctrine." *New York Journal of Law and Liberty*. www.nyufedsoc.blogspot.com/2011/10/holdout-myth-underlying-current-takings.html.
Mamidi, Pavan. 2011. "Signaling and Screening for Recruitment among the Maoists in India" (doctoral dissertation, University of Oxford).
Mandal, Piyali. 2012. "Posco's mega project remains stuck." *Business Standard*, February 1. www.business-standard.com/article/companies/posco-s-mega-project-remains-stuck-112020100046_1.html.
McAdams, Richard. 1994. "Cooperation and Conflict: The Economics of Group Status Production and Race Discrimination." *Harvard Law Review* 108 (4): 1003–1084.
1997. "The Origin, Development, and Regulation of Norms." *Michigan Law Review* 96 (2): 338–384.
Pildes, Richard. 1998. "Why Rights Are Not Trumps: Social Meanings, Expressive Harms, and Constitutionalism." *Journal of Legal Studies* 27 (2): 725–763.
Posner, Eric. 1996. "The Regulation of Groups: The Influence of Legal and Nonlegal Sanctions on Collective Action." *University of Chicago Law Review* 63 (1): 133–197.
Raiffa, Howard. 2003. *The Art and Science of Negotiation*. Cambridge: Belknap Press.
Radin, Margaret Jane. 1982. "Property and Personhood." *Stanford Law Review* 34 (5): 957–1015.
Singh, Ram. 2012. "Inefficiency and Abuse of Compulsory Land Acquisition: An Enquiry into the Way Forward" (working paper no. 209, Centre for Development Economics, Department of Economics, Delhi School of Economics).
Srivastava, Vikas. 2013. *Project and Infrastructure Finance*. New Delhi: McGraw Hill Education.
Subramanian, Guhan. 2010. *Negotiauctions: New Dealmaking Strategies for a Competitive Marketplace*. New York: W.W. Norton & Company.
Sunstein, Cass. 1996. "Social Norms and Social Roles." *Columbia Law Review* 96 (4): 903–968.
Veblen, Thorstein. 1899. *The Theory of the Leisure Class: An Economic Study of Institutions*. New York: Macmillan.
Wahi, Namita. 2011. "Equity of Land Acquisitions." *New Indian Express*, November 11. www.newindianexpress.com/columns/article250235.ece.

SECTION VI

LEGAL EDUCATION

16

Responding to the Market: The Impact of the Rise of Corporate Law Firms on Elite Legal Education in India

Jonathan Gingerich and Nick Robinson

I. INTRODUCTION

Corporate law firms have emerged in the past twenty years as a small but economically important and growing part of the Indian legal sector (Chapter 3 of this volume). Their growth has been driven by corporate clients who demand the legal services necessary to operate in the increasingly deregulated, privatized, and globalized Indian economy, including transactional legal services related to foreign direct investment, mergers and acquisitions, project finance, and other complex legal needs. To provide the services that their clients require to do business in a liberalized India, corporate law firms have sought lawyers with a different skill set than typical (elite) lawyers had before liberalization. While elite lawyers in India have traditionally tended to be skilled oral advocates who had established "face value" with judges that enabled them to effectively advance their clients' positions in court (Chapter 14 of this volume on grand advocates), Indian corporate law firms have employed lawyers who can effectively conduct rigorous legal research, write clear legal documents and memos, interact with corporate clients, work on teams with other attorneys, meet deadlines, and speak and write polished English (Gingerich et al. 2014).[1]

To find lawyers with appropriate skills to meet client demand, law firms have generally not turned to lawyers from the practicing bar, but instead have hired newly minted law school graduates. Corporate firms offer high salaries even at the entry level, genteel work that avoids the rough and tumble of the courtroom, and the promise of relatively meritocratic recruitment and promotion. To many law students these incentives have helped make jobs at these new types of law firms more attractive than jobs available in the legal sector before liberalization. Yet, because law firms and the corporate legal sector more broadly were seeking a different type of lawyer than had traditionally practiced in India, the existing models of legal education in the country were not well prepared to meet this new development in the market.

In this chapter we explore three impacts on legal education in India caused by the growing demand for corporate lawyers. First, we argue that the prospect of high-paying prestigious corporate work has changed who applies to law school, how these prospective students pick the law schools they attend, and how much they are willing to pay for their education. Second, dividing elite law schools in India into three categories ("national law schools," "legacy schools," and "private law schools"), we find that these institutions have each changed the educational experience they offer as they have adapted to an increasingly corporate-oriented legal environment. Third, we claim that inside the institutional context of elite law schools, students have emphasized and shaped parts of their legal education they believe will be appealing to corporate firms. Together these three impacts have fundamentally altered the educational experience at elite law schools in the country.

To be clear, we are not arguing that all law students at elite law schools in India want to become corporate lawyers (although many do) or that those who enter corporate law upon graduation will spend their entire career there. Students and graduates have diverse goals, and many students seek to attend schools where they have a greater possibility of being offered a corporate law job not because they aim to work in a law firm, but because they wish to have a well-respected fallback option that offers secure employment if their other goals, such as working in government, going into litigation, or starting a business, do not succeed. Additionally, many students who pursue corporate legal positions do so not because they wish to spend their entire career in this work, but because they believe that working for a large firm for a few years before heading off on a different path will provide valuable legal experience, professional connections, or credentials. The corporate legal employment market therefore functions more as a background force that shapes how all, or almost all, students experience law school rather than as an ambition that all law students at elite schools aim for.

Although there has been considerable writing on legal education in India, much of this work has been historical (Krishnan 2004; Gupta 2006; Ballakrishnen 2008; Menon 2009) or prescriptive in nature – focusing on proposed reforms to improve teacher quality, curriculum design, infrastructure, or other aspects of the legal academy (Agrawala 1973; Avasthi 2004; Schukoske 2009). This chapter is instead largely descriptive, focusing on how the rise of law firms in India has affected the educational experience at the elite tier of law schools. It is important to emphasize that although these schools – perhaps fifteen or so – are prominent within the legal academy, they represent only a small fraction of the 1,390 law colleges recognized by the Bar Council of India as of 2013.[2] These other law schools produce the vast majority of lawyers in the country and deserve considerably more scholarly attention. While sixty thousand to seventy thousand law students graduate annually in India, the available entry-level corporate positions number only in the hundreds in a given year.[3]

Law schools in India offer either a five-year (BA/LLB) or three-year (LLB) program for the study of law. These schools are regulated by a number of bodies including the Bar Council of India, the University Grants Commission, the Law Ministry, their respective state legislatures, and the Indian Supreme Court. Law colleges or law departments that are part of a university also have to comply with the rules of the larger university. The requirements of these different bodies have sometimes led to significant regulatory rigidity. Notably, the Bar Council of India prescribes twenty-six mandatory law courses for all law graduates, limiting the flexibility schools have over the curriculum they may offer to students (Bar Council of India).[4] The Bar Council also limits teaching at law schools by practitioners and caps the number of students who may sit in any class to sixty, creating hurdles for both clinical teaching and a disincentive for a school to institute a mixture of larger and smaller class sizes (Bar Council of India).

In 2010 the Bar Council introduced the All India Bar Examination. The exam is meant to screen out underperforming graduates from entering the profession and so may eventually lessen the perceived need for direct Bar Council supervision of the educational experience itself, shifting the regulatory focus from the educational process to educational outcomes. Students and lawyers upset about the introduction of the bar exam have challenged the legality of the Bar Council to require it, casting doubt on its continued existence (Ganz 2012). The Bar Council has also been criticized for poor administration of the exam and a corruption scandal that has led to the arrest of Bar Council members for accepting bribes to accredit a law school (Venkatesan 2011), both of which have weakened the credibility of the Council's claims that it can act as a competent authority to regulate entry into the profession.

II. PROSPECTIVE LAW STUDENTS

In response to the growing demand for corporate legal talent, Indian students have attempted to develop the skills and credentials that law firms want in order to secure highly remunerative positions as associates in corporate law firms. In this section, we discuss how *prospective* law students have responded to and been impacted by the emerging demand for junior associates prepared to work in law firms.

A. *Changing Student Demographics*

In the 1980s law was not regarded as a particularly prestigious profession in India. Students who could gain admission to a medical school, an Indian Institute of Technology, or an Indian Institute of Management were unlikely to enroll in a law school, even a highly regarded school like Delhi Law Faculty or Government Law College–Bombay, unless they had family connections to law (Interview 6, 2012).

When the legal jobs available to lawyers graduating from elite law schools consisted largely of positions as junior advocates that paid little or nothing, law was a highly unattractive profession for students who did not have families that could support them financially for a long period of time while they developed the skills and reputation necessary to practice by themselves (Galanter and Robinson 2016). Law school had a reputation for being a last-resort option for middle-class students who did not have the grades to get into other, more prestigious fields of study. But with high remuneration available for entry-level associates at law firms, law has become a much more alluring profession for bright students, particularly from English-speaking backgrounds (Interview 10, 2012). Additionally, the growing esteem of law as a profession, due in part to the emergence of corporate firms, has made prestige-conscious students who want to obtain jobs in fields that are highly regarded in Indian society more likely to attend law school (Interviews 5, 6, 7, 9, 10, 2012).

A 2010 survey of seventy-two students from the National Law School of India University (NLSIU)–Bangalore – a school whose graduates are heavily recruited by law firms – found that almost all had been instructed in English in their secondary schooling and only 3 percent had received their twelfth standard education in a rural area (IDIA Law Survey 2010). Students were drawn from across geographic regions of India and were predominantly the children of government employees or businessmen (only 7 percent were the children of lawyers). Most students came from a middle-class or wealthy background. Forty-four percent of students reported their family incomes as between 300,000 and 1,000,000 rupees a year ($6,000–$20,000), 15 percent between 1,000,000 and 1,500,000 rupees ($20,000–$30,000), 21 percent more than 1,500,000 rupees, and fewer than 3 percent less than 50,000 rupees

($1,000). The average annual income in India in 2010 was slightly less than 50,000 rupees. Although there are reservations at NLSIU for traditionally marginalized castes (15 percent of the class), tribal groups (7.5 percent), and persons with disabilities (3 percent), there are no reservations for Muslims. The same 2010 survey found only 1.4 percent of the class were Muslim (although Muslims make up 13.4 percent of the Indian population).

A comparison of this 2010 survey of National Law School–Bangalore students to a survey of 383 Delhi Law Faculty students in 1968–1969 is telling even if there are obvious difficulties in comparing data across two very different, if elite, institutions (the history of both of these schools will be discussed in greater detail later in this chapter). Yet, some insights can still be gleamed about how the student bodies at elite law schools in India have changed over these forty years. The 1968–1969 survey found that only 38 percent of Delhi Law Faculty students were educated in English in secondary school and more than half came from Delhi, with most of the others being from a small number of states in northern India around Delhi. Tellingly, only about a third of students in the 1968–1969 study claimed they even wanted to be a lawyer, with the rest saying they were planning on taking a civil service exam, entering business, or just hoping the degree might improve their employment possibilities. Contrast this with NLSIU, where more than 90 percent of the class will generally enter a job in the legal field after graduation. Notably, while today NLSIU, and the national law schools more broadly, has near gender parity in their student body (Agrawal 2013), in 1968–1969 the Delhi Law Faculty survey found that only 6.5 percent of students were women.

Although it is difficult to draw any firm conclusions from such a limited data set, these two surveys do seem to support the idea, also supported by anecdotal evidence, that students at an elite law school like National Law School–Bangalore today are more female, educated, legal career focused, and geographically diverse than their peers from an elite law school like Delhi Law Faculty would have been forty years ago. While the rise in the number of women attending law school tracks is increasing female presence across higher education in India, the prospect of being able to be employed in corporate desk jobs rather than competing as a solo practitioner in the more male-dominated and entrepreneurial litigation world is one of many factors that has likely contributed to the growing presence of women in law schools.[5] Additionally, the students at today's national law schools are likely to come from significantly wealthier backgrounds than were their counterparts at Delhi Law Faculty forty years ago, reflecting the increased prestige and desirability of law as a profession.[6]

TABLE 1. *Common law admission test takers by year*[7]

Year	CLAT takers
2008	10,773
2009	12,270
2010	16,350
2011	21,353
2012	23,881
2013	27,627

B. *Changing Demand for Elite Schools*

As firms have begun to offer high-paying, prestigious entry-level jobs to the graduates of a handful of law schools, students interested in corporate legal work have scrambled to gain admission to one of the small number of schools from which law firms hire associates. While there are almost 1,400 law schools in India, large and medium-sized corporate law firms in the country generally hire students from an elite cluster consisting of no more than twenty-five law schools, with most of the associates hired by corporate law firms coming from a group of about a dozen schools (Gingerich et al. 2014). Students are aware of which law schools corporate firms are likely to hire from and work to get into this small group that feeds into firms.

The Common Law Admission Test (CLAT) was implemented by the national law schools in India beginning in 2008 as a common admissions test for students seeking to attend a national law school, and it is now used as an admissions test by almost all national law schools. Since 2008 the number of CLAT test takers has dramatically increased.

To some extent, the growing number of CLAT takers reflects that the test is now needed for admission to a larger number of schools than in 2008 as new national law schools have opened, but it also likely reflects a growing student demand for positions in the law programs at the small number of national law schools that dominate hiring by law firms. Additionally, prospective law students from wealthy and middle-class families have recently shown a willingness to pay considerable fees for CLAT coaching, which many companies now offer, to help improve their scores on the CLAT (and get into higher-ranked law schools). In a 2010 survey of NLSIU students, more than 80 percent of students stated that they had paid for formal CLAT coaching to prepare for the exam (IDIA Law Survey 2010).

TABLE 2. *India Today's rankings for the past five years for select schools*

Law school/year	2009	2010	2011	2012	2013
NLSIU–Bangalore	1	1	2	1	2
NALSAR–Hyderabad	2	2	1	3	1
Campus Law Centre, Delhi University	3	4	4	2	3
NLIU–Bhopal	4	3	3	5	5
Symbiosis–Pune	6	5	5	4	7
NUJS–Calcutta	8	6	6	7	4
ILS–Pune	5	7	7	10	9
NLU–Jodhpur	7	8	10	6	8
Gujarat National Law University	–	9	12	9	6
Amity Law School–Delhi	9	10	9	12	12
Government Law College–Mumbai	10	–	16	11	14

In the past decade a market for law school rankings has also developed as aspiring students attempt to pick schools in what has increasingly become a national, and hierarchical, legal education market. Since 2003, India Today has published rankings of Indian law schools. *Outlook* began publishing rankings in 2009, as did Mint. The Week published rankings in 2010 and 2011. Law schools that routinely place their graduates into jobs in corporate law firms have dominated the top ten spots on these lists. While the rankings have not been uncontroversial, with questions raised over their methodology and accusations of school administrators unduly influencing the ranking process (Ganz 2010), there continues to be demand for rankings to help prospective students decide where to go to school, in part by indicating which schools are likely to help them secure the jobs that they desire.

C. *Greater Willingness to Pay for Law School*

Prospective law students and their families have also shown a greater willingness to pay larger amounts in fees to attend a law school that they believe will provide them with a good chance at securing a job as an associate in a law firm. To some extent, growing law school fees predated the emergence of the corporate legal sector in India, with NLSIU charging higher tuition than other public law schools beginning in the late 1980s (Interview 12, 2012). While tuition and other fees at the Delhi University LLB program remains at about 5,500 rupees ($89) per year and has changed little for years, tuition at elite national law schools and private law schools is now many times higher than

TABLE 3. *Annual fees by law school for undergraduate Indian students admitted in the general category to a five-year BA/LLB program entering in 2013*

Law school	Total fees in Indian rupees per year[8]*	Total fees in US dollars per year**
Delhi Law Faculty	5,500	$89
GLC–Bombay	5,520	$89
Amity, –Delhi	66,200	$1,068
GNLU	101,000	$1,629
NLU–Delhi	110,500	$1,782
NALSAR	115,000	$1,855
NLSIU	119,000	$1,919
NLU–Jodhpur	135,100	$2,179
NUJS	140,000	$2,258
NLIU–Bhopal	142,500	$2,294
Symbiosis Law School–Pune	146,000	$2,354
Jindal Global Law School	525,000	$8,468

* Indian rupees per year, excluding hostel and mess fees, refundable deposits, and onetime fee. **Exchange rate of rupees 62:$1

the tuition that elite law schools charged before the rise of corporate firms. While student loans remain uncommon, some law schools now offer to help secure student loans for their students.

With the possibility of much higher starting salaries than they could have earned working as juniors to senior advocates or in the government, prospective law students (and their parents) are willing to pay more to attend law schools that they believe will give them a better chance at securing remunerative legal jobs. While litigating advocates are sometimes able to run very lucrative practices later in their careers (Chapter 14 of this volume), the payoff from working in law firms comes much sooner and is more certain than the financial payoff from working in litigation, making a substantial investment in law school tuition a less risky calculation.

III. INSTITUTIONAL CHANGE

Although law firms and corporate counsel have been significant beneficiaries of reform and changes in the law school model in India, they have generally been only an indirect instigator. The corporate sector has provided funding to some schools, but this has generally been limited and corporations have rarely become directly involved in reforms in the regulation of legal education or the direction of particular schools. Instead, changes in the model of legal education have been initiated more often by reformers within the academy, government, and bar council–led initiatives, and the demands of students looking for a legal education that will best situate them for high-prestige postgraduation opportunities. The impact of the corporate sector on elite legal education in India has become increasingly apparent as more and more graduates enter law firms and the administration and faculty of law schools navigate how they wish to situate themselves and their students in relation to this lucrative section of the legal market.

We examine the impact of the rising corporate legal sector through the prism of three elite law schools, each representing different types of legal education available in India today. We begin with National Law School of India University (NLSIU)–Bangalore, the first of the national law schools. It is considered by many to be the top law school in the country, while several other national law schools are also seen in this highest tier. Out of all the law schools in India, these schools send the largest percentage of their graduates into the corporate law firm sector. We then look in detail at Delhi Law Faculty as an example of a legacy school, one of several law departments in historically prestigious universities, such as Government Law College–Bombay, ILS–Pune, and Aligarh Muslim University Department of Law. These academic institutions have storied traditions and continue to produce sought-after graduates despite often facing significant institutional rigidity and financial constraints, as well as new competitors like the national law schools. Finally, we turn to Jindal Global Law School as one of the latest and most prominent examples of a privately funded law school, joining others in this more recent private law school movement, including institutions like Symbiosis Law School, Amity Law School, and the School of Law at Christ University. The impact of these relatively new private players is yet to be fully seen, but they have already made their presence known in the elite tier of Indian law schools, and their institutional goals clearly include producing graduates for the corporate legal world.

A. *National Law School of India University–Bangalore and the Rise of the National Law Schools*

The National Law School of India University (NLSIU)–Bangalore is today widely recognized as the most prestigious law school in India. It is frequently ranked as the number one law school in the country; in its twenty graduating classes, it has produced twenty-four Rhodes scholars as of 2013; and its students are much sought after by law firms both domestically and abroad (E-mail from

Rhodes Committee in India, 2013). In 2012 the BA/LLB class had sixty-five graduates out of which forty-six went to law firms or major corporations (most of the others went into the civil service, studied abroad, or became litigators) (Gingerich et al. 2014). Yet, when NLSIU opened its doors to its first class in 1987, providing highly skilled graduates for the corporate legal sector was not the goal, nor did it even seem a significant possibility.

By the 1980s the low quality of legal education in India was a common lament. A large number of law schools had been founded in the decades after independence, helping increase access to the profession, but standards had suffered in the resulting explosion of law school students. Given this environment, the Bar Council of India convinced Madhava Menon (then a professor at Delhi Law Faculty) to found a "model" law school, which was envisioned as a "Harvard of the East" (Menon 2009, 40). Helping pioneer a newly minted five-year model of legal education, the National Law School recruited its relatively small class directly out of high school from across the country on the basis of a competitive exam and provided them a multidisciplinary education. Following the success of the specialized Indian Institutes of Technology for engineering and Indian Institutes of Management for business, the National Law School was to provide a similar high-quality education in law to a select and relatively small group of students.

The learning environment at NLSIU was a departure from traditional Indian law schools in more ways than its five-year model, multidisciplinarity, or consciously all-Indian student body. In each class students were required to write a lengthy research paper, as well as pass a final. Oral presentations by the students were incorporated into student assessments. All this was a departure from classes in other law schools where lectures, rote memorization, and only a final at the end of the term were the norm. The school also broke new ground by requiring students to undertake internships during their breaks where they were exposed to litigators, judges, nongovernmental organizations, government offices, law firms, and companies.

This unique learning environment explains much of the school's early success. Students were not only introduced to many different learning contexts, but the internship program showcased the students to potential employers, particularly in the suddenly booming law firm sector of the early 1990s (Interview 12, 2012). More early accolades and publicity were brought to the school and its graduates when a group of NLS students won the Philip C. Jessup moot in 1999, a major international mooting competition.

To pay for this new type of education, the school raised its fees in its early days from 2,500 rupees a year to 25,000 rupees – a tuition increase that seemed monumental at the time compared to that of other public law schools, yet was largely accepted by parents of the students as a cost for increased quality (Menon 2009, 51). Today, tuition is about 80,000 rupees a year with total costs (including living expenses), coming to 159,000 rupees a year (or about $2,565).[9] Importantly, the school received a large early grant from the Ford Foundation that allowed it to move from a cramped facility in the city of Bangalore to an eighteen-acre campus just on the edge of town in 1990 (Krishnan 2004, 492).

Although NLSIU was envisioned to be an elite law school, since its founding there has always been debate about what it should be elite at, leaving the school in seemingly perpetual uncertainty over its identity. The Bar Council had been primarily interested in creating NLSIU to increase the quality of lawyers becoming litigators and judges (the traditional career path of the overwhelming number of active lawyers in India) (Interviews 10 and 12, 2012). However, NLSIU's graduates soon began flocking to the law firm and corporate sector of the newly liberalized India, leading many in the legal profession, and even some of the school's professors, to lament that the school was not fulfilling its mission even as it gained international fame.

The school's unease with its relationship to the law firm sector is perhaps best typified by how law firm recruitment occurs. When firms first wanted to recruit on campus in the 1990s, they were refused space by the administration, who pointed to the bar's mandate for NLSIU of producing litigators, not corporate lawyers (Interview 12, 2012). The students instead organized recruitment themselves off campus, a tradition that continues today and is explained in detail in the next chapter of this volume (Gingerich et al. 2014).

An early professor at the school who supported firm recruitment and has since gone on to be a vice chancellor at another national law school expressed his frustration over the Indian bar's (and some faculty's) insistence that NLSIU and the other national law schools produce only litigators: "Whenever I go anywhere, I get this comment about the national law schools not producing litigators . . . . I don't understand why students have to go into litigation. Don't most top litigators appear for corporations? So why not work at a firm? This is hypocrisy . . . . [W]hy should any of the students join the bar? Is there any system in place by the government or the bar to hire these students?" (Interview 10, 2012).

Meanwhile, many of the founders of the school had envisioned a broader mission than preparing either litigators or lawyers for law firms – instead, wanting to use new teaching methods to create more well-rounded graduates. As one of the founders of NLSIU explained, "We didn't want to just produce litigating lawyers. We wanted to prepare a person to engage in policy or governance. We taught social science subjects – political science, sociology, history, economics, and psychology . . . . It was an exciting period. Something novel was attempted. We did cooperative teaching, where you would have an economics and a contracts teacher in the same classroom together. The idea was to combine theory and practice. This was not comparable to the case method or the Socratic method. It was something different" (Interview 12, 2012).

As the prestige of NLSIU rose, it led to replication. Six years after NLSIU's first class graduated, the National Academy of Legal Studies and Research (NALSAR) in Hyderabad and the National Law Institute University (NLIU) in Bhopal opened in 1998. The National University of Juridical Sciences (NUJS) in Calcutta was founded the following year. Today there are seventeen so-called national law schools, with one now planned for each state. Although their quality varies, and there is some structural variation, they are all founded on a similar model to the original National Law School of India University in Bangalore.

Almost all of these national law schools use the same entrance exam, the Common Law Admission Test (CLAT).[10] In 2013 there were 27,627 CLAT takers. Out of the fifty-nine highest scorers in the general (for example, unreserved) category, fifty-five chose to go to NLSIU (meaning the school's acceptance rate was about 0.21 percent). NALSAR was the next most-sought-after school by students followed by NUJS, NLIU–Bhopal, and NLU–Jodhpur (Common Law Admission Test Revised Provisional Allotment List-1 for Under-Graduate Programme, 2013).

These schools attract many students lured by the prospect of high law firm salaries upon graduation. As one of the former vice chancellors of a top national law school said, "The national law schools are very firm oriented." As he explained, the faculty and students often push for "marketability" in the education offered (Interview 5, 2012). In 2012, NLSIU, NALSAR, NUJS, and NLU–Jodhpur each placed over half their class in corporate positions upon graduation, with graduating class sizes ranging from sixty-five to one hundred (Gingerich et al. 2014).

As time has gone on, NLSIU has arguably become more welcoming of the corporate sector that courts many of its graduates. Unlike many other law schools, NLSIU's curriculum requires students to take *two* corporate law classes, as well as classes in international trade law, intellectual property, banking law, and insurance law. Of the fifteen endowed faculty positions at NLSIU, two law firms have endowed chairs – Allen & Overy (a large British law firm) has a chair in international financial law, while Singhania & Company (an Indian law firm) has endowed a chair in alternative dispute resolution. A major Indian company, Reliance, has endowed a chair in corporate law and governance, while Hindustan Aeronautics Limited, a major state-owned defense company, has a chair in business law, as does ICICI Bank.[11] Meanwhile, the law school's library, the most modern and impressive of the buildings on the school's well-equipped but understated campus, was made possible by a donation from the chairperson of Infosys, who named the building after her father (NLSIU, 2013).

NLSIU offers twenty-five slots each year in its two-year LLM program for business law (and offers an additional twenty-five slots in an LLM that specializes in human rights law). NLSIU's correspondence classes have multiplied in number over the years. Although hardly visible as a presence on campus, perhaps the largest revenue-raising operation for NLSIU is its master of business law. The master's (which does not qualify one to practice law) requires ten courses over two years, with an examination twice a year in Bangalore.[12] Students are often midcareer public service employees looking to add further credentials, commerce majors, or practicing lawyers wanting to fine-tune their skills (Interview 13, 2012).

At national law schools today, prestigious law firms support moot courts or send partners to teach compressed classes, while companies send representatives to lecture in areas of business law (Interview 5, 2012). Perhaps most importantly, alumni from national law schools who are now in the corporate legal sector communicate with current students about how to best position themselves for recruitment, adding to an overall firm-oriented culture at the schools.

Despite their obvious strengths, NLSIU and other national law schools have struggled to recruit and retain top law faculty. Not only are there a limited number of talented law school professors available in India, the schools are often very hierarchically organized, avenues of promotion can be unclear, and the schools are often overwhelmingly controlled by the vice chancellor, leading to sometimes dramatic unpredictability with the arrival of new leadership. Despite many of NLSIU's students going off to do further study abroad, in 2013 out of forty-two listed law faculty on the school's website, only two had pursued some type of higher-education degree abroad (while ten indicated some type of fellowship experience abroad).

B. *Delhi Law Faculty and the Legacy Schools*

The Delhi Law Faculty has long occupied a privileged place in the history of Indian legal education. Founded in 1924, as part of Delhi University (one of the marquee institutions in Indian higher education), the school has produced a disproportionate share of prominent litigators and judges, from the district courts to the Supreme Court (University of Delhi 2015). Its alumni include law ministers, solicitor generals, members of parliament, and chief ministers, as well as several prominent law firm partners. Many of the country's best-known legal academics have taught or been educated at Delhi Law Faculty. Today, it is consistently ranked among the top five Indian law schools in the country.

Yet Delhi Law Faculty's structure and the education it offers is markedly different than a school like NLSIU and, partly as a result, law firms rarely actively recruit out of its graduating class in any structured manner. While five-year BA/LLB degrees have come to dominate elite legal education in India, Delhi Law Faculty offers only a three-year LLB degree that students apply to after completing a degree from another college and taking the school's entrance exam (13,400 students took the exam in 2013 to fill about 2,400 seats).[13] The Delhi Law Faculty is actually comprised of three schools, each with its own faculty – the Campus Law Centre, Law Centre I, and Law Centre II. The Campus Law Centre, situated in North Delhi, holds its classes in the morning, is considered the most prestigious of the three, and has about eight hundred students in each class. Law Centre I, which is adjacent to the Campus Law Centre, offers afternoon and evening classes with a class size of about one thousand, while Law Centre II offers only evening classes (often catering to those who have full-time jobs) and is located on a South Delhi campus, with a class of about six hundred students a year.

The administration likes to make a point of the school's low costs, which are subsidized by the government (with tuition and fees at 5,500 rupees, about $90, a year), and inclusiveness. As the dean of the Faculty of Law states in a prospectus to potential students: "The normal strength of a national law school is at best six hundred students compared to over seven thousand students we have. We do it consciously to cater to the large masses and deprived sections. I am confident that about 30 percent of our students outclass the best in comparison to national law schools with just about one-tenth of budget allocations and fee" (Delhi Bulletin 2013, 2).

If inclusiveness has been a strength of the institution, it has also been a challenge. Some students at Delhi Law Faculty are graduates of prestigious Indian colleges like St. Stephens or Lady Shri Ram, while others come from more peripheral schools and frequently have difficulty communicating fluently in written and even spoken English. This diversity has added to the intellectual and political ethos of the campus (where political rallies and campaigns are a common sight compared to the generally more apolitical environment of the national law schools). While the school may be alive with debates over identity and social upliftment, the academic environment at the school does not always provide the academic support that students need, particularly those from less privileged backgrounds. Writing and research is rarely stressed in classes, meaning there are few opportunities to improve these skills. The syllabus for classes is identically set across the law centers by a joint meeting of the faculty, and the faculty similarly standardizes exams and their grading. While this process is undertaken in part to increase perceived fairness, as a result faculty have less room to innovate in their curriculum to meet the different needs of their class, as well as tailor courses to their own interests or specialties. Hiring of new faculty can be a drawn-out process, meaning the school often misses out on recruiting desirable law professors. Nor has the faculty had that much exposure to foreign educational or professional models. In 2013, out of fifty-three listed law faculty on the school's website, only four had pursued some type of higher-education degree abroad (although sixteen did indicate having undertaken some type of foreign fellowship abroad).

Given Delhi Law Faculty's extensive alumni network and location in the capital, the school is still seen as a gateway to a successful litigation career and has become a powerhouse in producing students who take the judicial exam to become lower court judges across the country. However, it has fared less well positioning itself in the law firm market. Courses involving corporate law are mostly optional, reflecting the school's focus on litigation (Interviews 2 and 5, 2012).[14] As one professor at Delhi Law Faculty described the challenges of the recruitment process: "The law firms never really touch us. They categorize us as a grade C law school. I used to get into arguments with them. Luthra [a managing partner at a top firm] is one of us. Sagar [the same] is an alumnus. I said, 'You are all from here. Why don't you recruit?' I think it's because they think our students are not good enough in researching and writing. I told them you need street smarts" (Interview 2, 2012).

Following the experience of NLSIU and other schools, during the last decade outside internships have become an accepted norm at Delhi Law Faculty. This change has occurred despite the Delhi Law Faculty's calendar not incentivizing internships as the school's break is during the court's break, meaning many students who want to intern with a judge or litigator must do so during classes.

Despite today having a reputation for institutional rigidity, Delhi Law Faculty's history is one of being a leading innovator in legal education. In 1966, Dean P. K. Tripathi transitioned the school from a two-year LLB to a three-year model, which was soon replicated widely. Faculty from Harvard, Yale, Columbia, and Michigan law schools frequently came to Delhi to share ideas and pedagogy throughout the 1960s and 1970s, producing an exciting period of collaboration and exchange (Krishnan 2004; Menon 2009, 34).[15] The development of the Socratic method, as opposed to pure lecturing, was pioneered in India at Delhi Law Faculty, and a number of professors were involved in developing cases and materials for teaching law that are still used widely to this day (Menon 2009, 28).

Notwithstanding its inability to vigorously compete in the law firm recruitment market, Delhi Law Faculty has maintained its prestige far better than other schools that were once considered highly respected, like University of Calcutta or University of Madras, but are no longer regularly spoken of as in the top rung of Indian law schools at the national level. Some other legacy schools have also continued to maintain their reputations. Government Law College in Mumbai (founded in 1855), Aligarh Muslim University Department of Law (1891), and ILS Law College in Pune (1924) are all considered top Indian law schools, albeit each with distinct models of education. Government Law College, for example, has classes early in the morning so that students may spend most of their day in externships at law firms, litigation offices, and other employment venues around Mumbai, where much of their legal education occurs. However, like at Delhi Law Faculty there are laments at each of these legacy schools about antiquated instruction, the rigidity of having tests that are graded centrally, inadequate language and writing preparation, and poor infrastructure. At ILS–Pune, to bypass some of this institutional rigidity, diploma classes are now offered on campus in corporate law, medical jurisprudence, cyberlaw, and human rights, since it has proven too difficult to revise the universitywide curriculum to include these subjects (Interview 7, 2012). Importantly, these legacy schools also pride themselves on, and try to distinguish themselves from the national law schools by, their graduates' robust contribution to the litigating bar and bench and the arguably broader social and economic diversity of India represented in their student bodies.

C. *Jindal Global Law School and the Private Law School Movement*

O.P. Jindal Global University rises out of the agricultural fields north of Delhi like a sleek office complex. An Indian flag on one of the largest flagpoles in Asia towers over its sixty-acre campus. Opening its doors in 2009, Jindal Global Law School (JGLS) was the first of four professional schools created as part of O.P. Jindal Global University (a business school opened the next year, an international affairs school the year after, and a public policy school the subsequent year, while a school of liberal arts and humanities is slated to open in 2014). Naveen Jindal, who is chairman and owner of one of the largest steel companies in India, has so far given at least $60 million to the university, which is named after his late father (and sits in the constituency for which Naveen Jindal is a member of parliament) (Indian Express, 2009). Jindal also presides as the chancellor of the university, which is a nonprofit educational institution unaffiliated with his company.

The university is the product of the entrepreneurial efforts of C. Raj Kumar, a former Rhodes scholar and Delhi Law Faculty graduate who returned to India to found the university after teaching law at the University of Hong Kong. As the name suggests JGLS has emphasized its global orientation from the beginning, with an international board of advisors, available online, that includes faculty from prominent law schools in the United States and United Kingdom. JGLS's own faculty, as represented on its website, is very much a creation of many of these same foreign education institutions. In 2013, out of sixty listed law faculty on the school's website, thirteen had received all of their higher education abroad (and many were foreign citizens) and thirty-nine had pursued some type of higher-education degree abroad (usually a master's or doctorate), while just eight had received all of their higher education in India (Jindal Global Law School). The law school consciously envisions its faculty as knowledge producers with clear expectations that they should publish and contribute to public debate.

Since its founding, the law school has undertaken numerous joint efforts with foreign universities. For example, it created a joint Centre on Global Corporate and Financial Law and Policy with the University of Michigan Law School. It also offers a double degree with the University of Arizona Law School where students can gain both an Indian LLB and an American JD in one year less than it would take to do them separately. An Oxford-Jindal summer school program has been created at Oxford for JGLS students. In its short history, JGLS has also held several joint conferences with visiting faculty, who have taught at well-known law schools in the United States, United Kingdom, Canada, and Australia (Jindal Global Law School).

The school uses a specially designed Indian LSAT for admissions, although it also allows CLAT scores to be used as a substitute. Its first class in the BA/LLB program was about ninety students. By 2013 its incoming class size was about three hundred. The school also offers a three-year LLB program that attracts about fifteen to twenty-five students a year.

To support this globally oriented education, students pay the highest fee of any Indian law school. Tuition in 2013 was 525,000 rupees and accommodation an additional 125,000 rupees (or about $10,500 a year total). The Jindal family provides scholarships to several students each year, while the law firm Khaitan pays for one scholarship. The school also has tie-ups with a number of banks to provide loans to students to attend, but many potential students, even from a middle-class background, still find these fees prohibitive, limiting the school's applicant pool.

JGLS has been aggressive in promoting internships and postgraduate employment opportunities for students, creating an active Career Development and Placement Division. The school has an agreement with the international law firm White & Case for a set number of students to intern with them and to pursue joint conferences and continuing legal education programs together (White & Case 2011). It also has a Memorandum of Understanding with a host of leading Indian law firms to facilitate internships while students are at JGLS (Jindal Global Law School). The first BA/LLB class has yet to graduate, and it will likely take a number of years after this first class to see how the law firm market responds to JGLS's graduates, but the school is clearly positioning itself as a conduit into these high-end jobs.

JGLS is not alone in carving out this niche but is instead part of a larger movement toward elite private law schools that has witnessed a noteworthy rise in the last fifteen years. Symbiosis Law School was founded in 1977 as part of the University of Pune and then broke off in 2002 to become a private law school to gain more control over its curriculum and become more internationally focus (it opened a second campus outside of Delhi in 2010) (Interview 8, 2012). Amity Law School in Delhi was founded in 1999, while the School of Law at Christ University in Bangalore opened in 2006. While JGLS is the best funded, each of these other schools also positions itself as an institution with a global outlook that is producing graduates capable of meeting the demands of the corporate legal sector. These new private law schools claim to be more flexible and innovative than schools affiliated with the government, as well as being more in tune with India's liberalized and more open economy.

However, private law schools like JGLS must also submit to considerable regulatory oversight. For instance, in order to be established as a new university and law school, JGLS not only needed to secure regulatory approval from the Bar Council of India and the University Grants Commission but also required approval by an act of the Haryana Legislative Assembly passed in accordance with the Haryana Private Universities Act, 2006.[16] Private universities seeking approval under the Haryana Private Universities Act, 2006 must submit to significant regulatory oversight and satisfy a wide range of requirements, including setting aside a large percentage of seats for admission for students from Haryana (Haryana Private Universities Act, 2006 § 35). This act also requires that significant decisions about academic policy made by private universities' governing bodies must be submitted to the Haryana state government for approval and requires that the governor of Haryana serve as the "visitor" of private universities established under the act, giving the governor a wide range of discretionary oversight powers (Haryana Private Universities Act, 2006 §§ 15, 33). While private law schools seek to be more flexible than public schools, they must navigate a complex regulatory environment in which they often face struggles to maintain their autonomy.

Although they attempt to offer a globally competitive education, private law schools have often had difficulty recruiting some of the best-known faculty in the country. As one well-respected former vice chancellor said, "There is still a lot of suspicion among faculty about private universities in India" (Interview 5, 2012). Similarly, many prospective students and their parents are wary of private law schools in a country where the majority of prestigious institutions of higher education are government affiliated and there are a large number of disreputable private institutions of higher learning. For faculty there also may be concern that there is less job security in private institutions than at public universities, where it is exceedingly difficult to be removed once one becomes permanent faculty. JGLS's connection with Jindal Steel has also complicated its image, as the steel company has been involved in controversial mining operations in the eastern part of the country that have led to conflicts with local community members.

III. LAW STUDENTS AT LAW SCHOOL

For students the quest for a good job with a corporate law firm does not end with matriculation at the right type of law school. Outside of the three or four of the most prestigious national law schools, only some of the students of the class of an elite law school who want to will secure a "desk job" with a law firm or an in-house counsel's office upon graduation (Gingerich et al. 2014). Even at a school like NLSIU, where almost all students who want a job with a law firm or corporate employer will be able to secure one, only some students will be able to secure jobs as associates with the largest, most prestigious, and highest-paying law firms (Gingerich et al. 2014). Unlike the legal market in the United States, where large law firms typically offer identical entry-level salaries, in India the best-paying entry-level jobs with law firms pay in the neighborhood of 100,000 rupees ($1,610) per month, but jobs with second- or third-tier firms pay as little as 25,000 rupees ($403) per month (Interview 10, 2012). Furthermore, in recent years, several London-based "Magic Circle" law firms have hired an extremely small number of Indian law students (typically one or two per firm per year) for jobs as trainee attorneys in London that pay internationally competitive salaries and offer the prestige of association with a large international law firm (Gingerich et al. 2014).

Because students attracted to the legal work, employment environment, prestige, and salary of law firm jobs are often drawn to the most prestigious and best-paying jobs, and because many students want to recoup the costs of law school with the most lucrative job they can secure, students understand that the race to secure a spot at an excellent law firm is not over once they get to law school. Students interested in corporate legal employment therefore work during their time in law school to position themselves as attractive recruits for law firms.

Although grades are an important factor in firms' recruitment decisions, they are often not the decisive – or even the most important – factor when firms decide whom to hire as junior associates. For many firms, when selecting among the students at any given law school, students' work experience, extracurricular activities, interpersonal skills, and academic achievements not represented in grades are more significant than class rank (Interview 8, 2012). Aware of the factors that matter to firms in making recruitment decisions, law students have attempted to signal their suitability for a firm by building résumés that demonstrate writing, communication, and legal research skills; some expertise in areas of law practiced by corporate law firms; and an interest in corporate legal work. They do this along such set patterns that as a result students from prestigious law schools seeking jobs in law firms often have nearly identical CVs (Interview 3, 2012). In this section, we discuss several of the ways in which the law school learning experience has changed as law students have responded to the demand for junior associates.

A. *Course Selection and Effort*

While the curriculum in Indian law schools is highly regulated by the Bar Council of India, how students who aspire to positions with corporate law firms experience the curriculum in action has changed significantly in the past twenty years. First, within the regulatory constraints imposed by the mandatory curriculum, students who aspire to work for corporate law firms have gravitated toward electives that they think are likely to prove attractive to recruiters from law firms and have pushed their law schools to offer more such electives. The head of an elite law school articulates a representative view when he reports that when students have an opportunity to choose electives, "eighty percent will take Mergers and Acquisitions over International Humanitarian Law," because students and their parents think that completing course work on corporate subjects will make it easier to secure placement into a corporate desk job (Interview 6, 2012).

Aside from choosing electives that seem more likely to draw the attention of law firms, students also make strategic decisions about how to allocate time and effort among their electives and compulsory courses. Students at elite national and private law schools face many academic and extracurricular demands on their time. For instance, at many national law schools, students are required to take five or six courses per semester and to write a five-thousand- or six-thousand-word research paper for each course in addition to taking exams (Gingerich and Singh 2010, 12–15). On top of this, students complete internships, compete in moot courts, run academic journals and conferences, play sports, and have social lives. When students have to make trade-offs between commitments, students will often decide to put less effort into courses that they think are less important to potential law firm employers, like Family Law, and more effort into classes like Company Law or Taxation in the hope that good results in classes about areas of law that corporate law firms practice will help them to land jobs or internships (Interview 14, 2012).

When students face pressure to develop CVs that look as impressive as all of the other CVs that firms receive and also maintain very good grades, law students may resort to plagiarism, which is widespread in many top Indian law schools. Students surveyed at several national law schools claimed they made strategic decisions to plagiarize papers for some of their classes, particularly for classes in which they believed the teacher was unlikely to read their paper anyway or for classes where they thought the teacher had a poor grasp of the law (Gingerich and Singh 2010).

When students think that their law school does not offer adequate course work to prepare them for a job as an associate in a corporate law firm, they will sometimes seek training and credentials from outside of their law school. For instance, of the students at ILS-Pune seeking placements with firms in the 2012–2013 placement season, the three students with the highest grades all listed "specialized courses" that they had taken outside of ILS–Pune on their CVs. Two of the three had taken courses to be certified as company secretaries; two had completed nondegree courses for certificates offered by the Asian School of Cyber Laws–Pune, a school that offers nondegree law courses on topics like mergers and acquisitions, corporate finance, and cyberlaw; and one had completed a diploma course at Symbiosis Law School–Pune (ILS Law College Pune Placements Booklet, 2013).

B. *Extracurricular*

Students who aspire to desk jobs in law firms want to get good grades in law school, but they also believe that their grades poorly reflect their potential as lawyers in firms and understand that firms do not decide whom to hire exclusively on that basis (Gingerich and Singh 2010). Part of how students attempt to signal to law firms that they have skills that would make them successful in corporate practice is by participating in extracurricular activities, like moot courts, journals, and conferences. Moot court competitions are particularly popular among students in India, where doing legal research, writing, and speaking provides an opportunity to gain more realistic legal experience than is provided by courses. Additionally, success at mooting provides a basis for potential employers to evaluate a law student's talent relative to students from other law schools (and, in the case of international moots, like the William C. Vis International Commercial Arbitration Moot and the Phillip C. Jessup International Law Moot, students from other countries). Such opportunities may be especially important for students from less well known law schools who hope to break into corporate legal practice.

Additionally, many students seeking to enter firms participate in extracurricular activities that provide an opportunity to develop their legal writing skills and demonstrate these skills to potential employers. While many law students are required to complete written assignments for their courses, these assignments often require students to only state legal standards rather than engage in legal analysis (Gingerich and Singh 2010). To show that they have more sophisticated legal writing and research skills, many students attempt to publish articles in academic journals or at least to present papers at academic conferences. Students interested in corporate legal work may be particularly likely to publish and present papers on topics of potential interest to employers, like finance or taxation, to demonstrate either an interest in the subject matter or some level of expertise (ILS Law College Pune Placements Booklet, 2013).

C. *Internships and Externships*

Students who want to work for corporate law firms after they graduate frequently try to secure placements as interns or externs (lasting from one or two weeks to several months) with law firms, but also with banks, public-sector undertakings, legal nonprofits, international organizations, practicing advocates, judges, and large private corporations. As employers have moved toward making permanent job offers to interns, rather than running wholly independent hiring processes for interns and associates, it has become more and more attractive for law students to secure positions as interns during their time in law school (Gingerich et al. 2014). However, law students seek out internships not just as a promising path to permanent jobs but also to get experience that will better position them to get a good entry-level job, signal to employers their interest in corporate legal practice, and expand professional networks that may help them secure jobs (or clients) in the future. As a result of students' desires for internships, students are likely to spend more time away from their law school than in the past, leaving to take up short-term positions in different parts of the country during every break between terms. Some law schools not only encourage but mandate internships during breaks. Notably, they generally require students to intern with nonprofits, judges, and government offices during the students' first years in law school, while during their later years, closer to hiring decisions for employment, they are mandated to intern at law firms and corporate offices.

IV. CONCLUSION

The influence of corporate firms on the education of lawyers, of course, does not end with graduation from law school. Law firms arrange significant further training for their own lawyers, usually in house. While the Bar Council has no continuing legal education requirement, lawyers themselves are often interested in pursuing further professional development. Since the beginning of the 2000s some students have pursued clerkships with supreme court or high court judges after graduation for further training. Although these clerkship opportunities have multiplied in recent years, they are not seen as a gateway into a law firm job and instead are pursued more often by students trying to build their résumé for a LLM program abroad or those particularly interested in the judicial process (Chandrachud 2014).

Postgraduate training programs for lawyers have also multiplied. Law schools such as NLSIU, NALSAR–Hyderabad, and JGLS offer legal education or executive education courses for a fee. Companies like Rainmaker provide supplementary or continuing online legal education in subjects like drafting, reviewing commercial contracts, and mergers and acquisitions. These programs are in their early stages and, although often well subscribed among law students, are not yet widely popular among those actively engaged in work at corporate law firms.

Many recent graduates of elite law schools decide to pursue a LLM abroad, often after working at a law firm for a few years before. International LLMs, particularly those from top schools in the United States or United Kingdom, had traditionally been seen as a positive market signal and a way to secure a job at a leading domestic law firm. With the rise of national law schools and other screening devices, an international LLM has become a less important signal for the domestic market, although it can still act as a useful stepping-stone for those interested in jobs at international law firms, other opportunities abroad, or as a way to transition to other types of work within India (such as policy making, a position with a different type of corporate employer, or employment at an international NGO). Students who received an education at an elite law school rarely pursue LLM degrees offered within India at these same top law schools. Instead, those who graduated from less elite schools more often pursue these degrees to gain further training and as a prestige marker. Graduates of these domestic LLM programs tend not to go to elite corporate law firms in India, but often an assortment of other corporate jobs, including at banks, public corporations, and smaller, more traditional law firms. However, Indian LLMs may become more appealing to Indian law students in the years to come as the Bar Council has allowed schools to offer the degree through a one-year program, rather than two years, as of 2013.

The rise of corporate law firms in India has clearly shifted the landscape of elite legal education. This shift has engendered debate over what the future of Indian legal education at elite law schools should look like. On the one hand, practitioners at corporate law firms and some faculty lament that legal education, even at the most reputed schools, still does not adequately prepare law school graduates with the legal skills they need for corporate work (Interview 8, 2012). They call for deeper partnerships between law schools and the corporate world and for faculty to be more responsive to the needs of corporate employers. On the other hand, some faculty and administrators express reservations that students and law schools had become too fixated on the priorities of corporate firms rather than trying to create more well-rounded or public-minded law graduates. They fear that a single-minded focus on corporate employment would limit the avenues graduates would or could explore later in their lives and have a larger negative impact on society overall. Still others are concerned that law schools are simply unclear about their core values. Charismatic leaders may come to head a school and leave their imprint, but these critics fear that many elite Indian law schools lack a long-standing institutional mission. As a result, their actions in relation to the new market created by corporate law firms are not based on values, but are often reactive and ad hoc (Interview 5, 2012). Some blame the perceived instability of these school's missions in part on limited alumni involvement in shaping and guarding their institutional goals.

The rise of domestic law firms has certainly not been the only driver of change in elite legal education in India in the past twenty-five years. The legal employment market has seen other notable shifts that have provided new opportunities to graduates and in the process impacted who enters law school and the education they receive there. For example, law graduates may now take the judicial service exam to become a judge in the subordinate judiciary immediately upon graduation (previously, one had to practice for several years before taking the exam). Starting in the 2000s students at top and mid-tier law schools have been actively recruited by an expanding legal process outsourcing (LPO) sector that services mostly corporate and law firm clients based in the United States and United Kingdom. Although still a small sliver of the market, there are now more entry-level positions at public-interest-oriented organizations and human rights and environmental government agencies as these institutions have both multiplied and formalized employment opportunities. Even the famously traditional litigation world has seen shifts, such as the creation of new specialized tribunals, which have created new markets for litigators, more women entering litigation, and broader structural changes that have helped lower barriers to entry to litigation (see Chapter 14 of this volume). Importantly, with the rise in the prestige of the BA/LLB model, some students use their time at law school to receive a more general education that teaches critical thinking skills and then immediately or shortly after graduation choose nonlegal career paths. This route, although still considered untraditional, may gain more adherents in the future given the paucity of quality liberal arts programs in the country.

Beyond these broader shifts in the employment market for law graduates that have affected legal education, there have been important reforms in pedagogy and to specific institutions of legal education by the government, law school administrators, and legal academics, while exposure to foreign models of legal education has continued to have significant impact. Yet the demand of law firms for law graduates has perhaps been the most profound driver of change over this period. While law firms have done little to directly change legal education themselves, the market these firms have created for graduates has sent ripples throughout elite legal education, leaving it fundamentally altered and reoriented.

Notes

1 It is important to avoid overstating the transformations that have taken place in the market. Before liberalization, there were a number of old, prestigious solicitors' firms in Bombay and Calcutta that performed primarily transactional work, although these firms were not as large as today's corporate firms and did not perform legal work of comparable complexity to the work that large firms in India now complete.

2 Recently there has been explosion of law schools in India. Of the 1,390 recognized law colleges in 2013, 246 had been founded since 2010 and 859 had been founded since 2000. Only 158 were founded before 1970 and just 23 before 1940. Bar Council of India, List of Law Colleges having approval of affiliation of the Bar Council of India on January 1, 2013.

3 Although the Bar Council of India claims there are approximately 1.2 million lawyers in India, in fact this number is likely considerably lower. The Bar Council tallies this number by compiling the number of lawyers provided by each state bar council. However, since there are no annual fees, the lists in many states include many lawyers who are retired, have stopped practicing, or have died. About

thirty thousand to forty thousand law students take the bar exam each year, and approximately 70% pass.

4 The story of the regulation of the syllabus of law schools by the Bar Council of India seems to be of mandating ever-more required classes. In 1975 the Bar Council of India required ten courses (including contracts, torts, property, criminal law, and constitutional law), as well as four more courses that were chosen from a list of nineteen subjects. By 1986 the Bar Council had mandated twelve courses and required six more from a list of twenty-three alternatives. The latest Bar Council Rules, published in 2008, mandate twenty courses as well as six more chosen from a list of one hundred subjects. Between 1975 and 2008 courses on topics such as administrative law, company law, public international law, taxation, environmental law, and labor and service law were all added to the required curriculum, while Indian legal history was removed. Many law schools mandate their students take other courses beyond those required by the Bar Council, meaning students have little discretion over which classes they take during their legal education.

5 Today, Delhi Law Faculty's student body is still majority male, but the school now has a much larger percentage of female students. For example, out of 718 students who took the fourth-term LLB exam at Campus Law Centre in 2013, 300, or about 42%, were women (Campus Law Centre Fourth Term Examination 2013). Delhi Law Faculty may lag slightly behind the national law schools in gender equity because, unlike the five-year national law schools, the three-year Delhi Law Faculty degree is completed later in life after completing an undergraduate degree at another college at which point there are more pressures on women in India to consider marrying and starting a family. Also, many more of Delhi Law Faculty's graduates enter litigation, which continues to be male dominated, while NLSIU's graduates are much more likely to enter corporate law firms, which have much closer gender parity not only at recruitment but also at the partner level (Chapter 7 of this volume).

6 In the 1968–1969 survey, about 16.5% of Delhi Law Faculty students stated that their parents made less than 3,000 rupees a year (about 58,000 rupees adjusted for inflation to 2010). The comparable cohort at NLS in 2010 was about 3% of the student body. In 1968–1969 only 3% of students at Delhi Law Faculty reported their parents made more than 50,000 rupees a year (about 1,000,000 rupees adjusted for inflation). At NLS this cohort in 2010 was about 36% of the student body. It is important to note that the nation also became significantly wealthier over this forty-year period between the two surveys. Anecdotally it seems that today Delhi Law Faculty students continue to come from generally poorer backgrounds than their NLS–Bangalore peers.

7 CLAT Results 2008, CLAT Consolidated Merit List 2009, CLAT 2010 UG Provisional Merit List, CLAT Consolidated Merit List 2011, CLAT 2012 Consolidated Merit List of Candidates for Undergraduate Programs, and CLAT 2013 All-India Merit List for Under-Graduate Programme.

8 Fees were compiled from online and print sources, including law school websites and CLAT materials.

9 More information about the National Law School of India University fees for 2013–2014 is available at www.nls.ac.in/resources/UGSTUDENTS/FeeNotif1to2yr2013.pdf.

10 National Law University–Delhi, which uses its own admissions test, is a notable exception.

11 Of the rest, five are endowed by different government ministries or commissions (for example, the Ministry of Commerce has a chair in international trade law). The Ford Foundation, the International Bar Association, and the United Nations High Commissioner for Refugees have each endowed a chair as have two private individuals (relating to constitutional law and public governance). More information can be found on the NLSIU Endowment Chairs website available at www.nls.ac.in/index.php?option=com_content&view=article&id=58&Itemid=31.

12 The master in business law generated 49,709,624 rupees in revenue for the year ending in March 2012. This is more than the tuition the school collected from BA, LLB, LLM, and PhD students combined for the same year. More information can be found at the Distance Education Programmes website, available at www.ded.nls.ac.in/courses_available#mbl

13 More information can be found on the University of Delhi LLB Entrance Exam is available at www.du.ac.in/fileadmin/DU/students/Pdf/admissions/2013/PG/21062013LLBRSLT.pdf.

14 The school does offer optional courses on corporate law, intellectual property, international trade law, banking law, or insurance law (which are all mandatory at NLS). Some students supplement their course work at the India Law Institute in Delhi, which offers short courses in topics like cyberlaw that are popular among students aspiring to corporate opportunities after graduation.

15 Madhava Menon, who was an eyewitness to this period and traveled from Delhi Law Faculty to Columbia Law School for a year himself, writes: "The few changes that have come about in Indian legal education can largely be attributed to the role played by dozens of American educated law teachers . . . " (Menon 2009).

16 Jindal Global University was ultimately established by the Haryana Private Universities (Second Amendment) Act, 2009.

References

"A Survey of Law Students of the Faculty of Law, University of Delhi, 1968–69." 1972. *Delhi Law Review* 1 (1): 150–154.

Agrawal, Anuj. 2013. "National Law Universities – Bringing Gender Equality in the Indian Legal Profession?" *Bar and Bench*. July 20. www.barandbench.com/national-law-universities-bringing-gender-equality-indian-legal-profession/.

Agrawala, S. K., ed. 1973. *Legal Education in India: Problems and Perspectives*. Bombay, India: N. M. Tripathi Private Ltd.

Avasthi, A. K. 2004. "Powerlessness of the BCI to Improve Standards of Legal Education." *Journal of the Indian Law Institute* 46 (1): 55–78.

Ballakrishnen, Swethaa. 2008. "Where Did We Come From? Where Did We Go?" LLM long paper, Harvard Law School, Cambridge, MA.

Bar Council of India. www.barcouncilofindia.org/.

Chandrachud, Abhinav. 2014. "From Hyderabad to Harvard: How U.S. Law Schools Make Clerking on India's Supreme Court Worthwhile" Working Paper on file with the Harvard Law School Center on the Legal Profession.

Common Law Admission Test Revised Provisional Allotment List-1 for Under-Graduate Programme. 2013. www.nlujodhpur.ac.in/downloads/Over_All_Allotment.pdf.

Delhi Faculty of Law. 2013. *Bulletin of Information*. www.lawfaculty.du.ac.in/Faculty_of_law.pdf.

Ganz, Kian. 2010. "NUJS-ers Threaten Outlook & India Today Law School Rankings with Press Council Complaint." *Legally India*, August 20. www.legallyindia.com/201008201213/Law-schools/nujs-ers-threaten-outlook-a-india-today-law-school-rankings-with-press-council-complaint.

2012. "The India Bar Exam: A Regulator's Rocky Road." *Mint*, December 27. www.livemint.com/Politics/Z9HH7jg4q8Any5PILN9FfP/The-India-bar-exam-a-regulators-rocky-road.html.

Gingerich, Jonathan and Aditya Singh. 2010. "Writing Requirements, Student Assessment, and Plagiarism in Indian Law Schools." *India Law News* (Fall 2010): 12–15.

Gupta, Sushma. 2006. *History of Legal Education*. New Delhi: Deep and Deep Publications Pvt Ltd.

Haryana Private Universities Act. 2006. www.higheredularhry.com/DownloadSection/o/Private_Uni_Act.pdf.

Indian Express. 2009. "Jindal Invests 300 Crore to Set up a Law School." January 9. www.archive.indianexpress.com/news/jindals-invest-rs-300-cr-to-set-up-global-law-school/408610/.

IDIA Law Survey. 2010. "Increasing Diversity by Increasing Access 2010." idialaw.com/research/.

ILS Law College Pune. 2013. "Placement Booklet."

Interview 2, 2012.

Interview 3, 2012.

Interview 5, 2012.

Interview 6, 2012.

Interview 7, 2012.

Interview 8, 2012.

Interview 9, 2012.

Interview 10, 2012.

Interview 12, 2012.

Interview 13, 2012.

Interview 14, 2012.

Interview 16, 2012.

Jindal Global University. www.jgls.edu.in.

Krishnan, Jayanth. 2004. "Professor Kingsfield Goes to Delhi: American Academics, the Ford Foundation, and the Development of Legal Education in India." *American Journal of Legal History* 46 (4): 447–499.

Menon, Madhava. 2009. *Turning Point: The Story of a Law Teacher (Memoirs of Padmashree Prof. N. R. Madhava Menon)*. New Delhi: Universal Law Publishing.

NLSIU. 2013. *A Brief History*. www.nls.ac.in/index.php?option=com_content&view=article&id=16&Itemid=15.

Sathe, S. P. 1989. "Access to Legal Education and the Legal Profession in India." In Access to Legal Education. Edited by Rajeev Dhavan et al. London: Buttersworth.

Schukoske, Jane. 2009. "Legal Education Reform in India: Dialogue Among Indian Law Teachers." *Jindal Global Law Review* 1(1): 251–279.

Sunshine, Russell B., and Arthur L. Berney. 1970. "Basic Legal Education in India: An Empirical Study of the Student Perspective at Three Law Colleges." *Journal of the Indian Law Institute* 12: 39–118.

University of Delhi. 2015. *Law Bulletin*. www.du.ac.in/du/uploads/Admissions/2015/PG/29062015_Law_InfoBulletien.pdf.

University Grants Commission. 1979. *Towards a Socially Relevant Legal Education: A Consolidated Report of the University Grants Commission's Workshop on Modernization of Legal Education*. Delhi, India: Central Electric Press.

White & Case. 2011. *White & Case Teams Up with Jindal Global Law School in India*. www.whitecase.com/press-05232011/#.Ug4nVFPgLX8.

Venkatesan, J. 2011. "Former BCI Vice-Chief Gets Bail in Corruption Case." *The Hindu*, April 20. www.thehindu.com/news/national/former-bci-vicechief-gets-bail-in-corruption-case/article1712785.ece.

Von Mehren, Arthur Taylor. 1963. "Aspects of Legal Scholarship and Education in India: Confidential Report."

17

The Anatomy of Legal Recruitment in India: Tracing the Tracks of Globalization

Jonathan Gingerich, Vikramaditya S. Khanna, and Aditya Singh

I. INTRODUCTION

Globalization is changing the Indian legal profession through, among other things, its effects on the corporate legal sector and legal education. Over the past two decades the Indian corporate legal sector has grown so quickly that now the majority of India's elite law school graduates take positions in the corporate sector rather than, as in the past, in litigation or government. In addition, Indian legal education has changed, with more course offerings focusing on corporate, business, and international matters. Despite the considerable discussion this has generated,[1] relatively little is known about one of the critical channels through which these developments are occurring – the legal recruitment processes in India. Understanding recruitment, however, is important because it not only influences the profession's membership but also serves as a bridge between the profession and legal education. Indeed, many of the effects of globalization can be traced through the recruitment process. We explore this topic through a detailed description and analysis of recruitment in the corporate legal sector in India, as well as through in-depth interviews of those involved in it. Our analysis provides insights into India's recruitment process, how it has changed over time, and how globalization has affected it.

This is an opportune moment to explore recruitment at elite Indian law schools because seismic changes to recruitment have occurred since India became increasingly globalized. Indeed, since 1991 recruitment has gone from an ad hoc model (geared toward placement in litigation) to a more structured but student-facilitated process (targeted at the corporate legal sector) to an emerging and somewhat more mixed model where corporate legal sector employers rely on student-facilitated processes as well as internships, professional recruitment services, and in-service training.

These changes led us to explore the important role of student-formed and -run entities, which act as intermediaries, in the recruitment process. These entities are the result of the collective action by students at each school (with little support or direct compensation) and perform a variety of tasks including those performed by career service offices in the United States (such offices are rare in India). We explore in greater depth the formation, structure, norms, and functioning of these student-run entities as well as *why* this recruitment structure developed in India,[2] considering that the recruitment models in other countries are quite different.[3]

We also examine the factors that are most likely driving these changes in recruitment. In particular, we explore how increasing globalization and market growth in India are putting pressure on recruitment processes. For example, if the demand for law firm services continues to increase, we might see Indian law firms growing larger and becoming more willing to invest resources in recruitment. Further, as the complexity of law firm work increases (e.g., due to increasing cross-border work or greater reregulation in India), law firms may want their new hires to be more informed about these matters, putting greater pressure on recruitment systems to assess complex legal skills and on legal education to provide them (whether in law school or later at work). This interaction provides us with a window into the impact of recruitment on legal education and allows us to explore (1) the evolving relationships between law firms and law schools and (2) how changes in that relationship may impact recruitment practices.

Part II describes our research strategy and methodology. Part III describes the dominant model of recruitment in the corporate legal sector in India. Part IV explains why this model was developed. Part V identifies the pressures that the current model of recruitment faces and highlights several important changes that the recruitment function is likely to undergo in the near future. Part VI analyzes how globalization and market pressures might lead to changes in the broader relationship between law firms and law schools. Part VII concludes.

II. DATA AND METHODOLOGY

We obtained information on recruitment processes largely by conducting semistructured interviews of the primary employers and employees in the Indian corporate legal sector. For employers we interviewed people involved in recruitment of entry-level lawyers at thirty-eight corporate law firms, LPO firms, in-house counsels' offices, and legal nonprofits in Kolkata, Delhi, Gurgaon, Hyderabad, Bangalore, and Mumbai in July and August 2011.[4] We selected law firms to approach for interviews based on their presence in Legal 500, Chambers and Partners, and PLC Which Lawyer?, because the larger law firms are likely to have a more pronounced impact on legal recruitment. For employees we interviewed students involved in the recruitment processes at the more elite law schools in Delhi, Mumbai, Bangalore, Hyderabad, and Jodhpur.[5] Although there are more than nine hundred Indian law schools and colleges, the graduates of the elite law schools largely populate the employee bases of corporate law firms and larger in-house departments in India (Bar Council of India 2010).[6]

Our research strategy may be biased by our exclusion of less selective schools and noncorporate legal-sector employers (which is where most Indian law graduates work), but this enables us to concentrate on changes in the corporate legal sector, which is the sector where we see the greatest recruitment changes and can trace the impact of globalization most clearly (Bar Council of India 2014; interview 2 with recruitment agency executive, 2011). Having said that, it is important to note that although the corporate legal sector in India has been growing rapidly and is paying fairly high salaries,[7] its scale (and the scale of the more elite law schools) is still quite modest relative to other countries, especially the United States, as noted in "Pro Bono and Corporate Legal Sector in India," by Arpita Gupta (this volume). This suggests that our research strategy is likely to cover many of the most significant current players. However, the recruitment system in India is also likely to be somewhat different from those in countries with a larger corporate legal sector. Simply put, the scale of the corporate legal sector is likely to affect its recruitment system because the structure of recruitment depends in part on how many people firms wish to hire. Although we discuss the differences in recruitment in India, the United States, and the United Kingdom, there are important similarities, too.

Finally, in addition to the interviews, we use data reported in *Legally India*, a website dedicated to discussions on the legal sector in India. This data is self-reported by student-run recruitment coordination committees (RCCs) and may be biased because RCCs wish to present their schools in a good light, indicating that they were highly successful in placing their students. On the other hand, the relatively large size of RCCs and the ease with which law students pass information to one another suggest that egregious misrepresentation of law student placements in self-reported data would be corrected through leaks from dissatisfied law students from any school whose RCC engaged in misrepresentation. Moreover, based on the interviews that we conducted with legal employers, the self-reported placement data from RCCs appears to be fairly accurate.

III. THE LANDSCAPE OF LEGAL RECRUITMENT IN INDIA

The process of recruitment for Indian law graduates has changed substantially in the past two decades. Prior to 1991 and the liberalization of the Indian economy, most graduates from leading law universities pursued a career in litigation where the process for recruitment was relatively informal (Galanter 1968; Galanter and Robinson, 2017, this volume). You might start your own practice (with all its challenges and uncertainties) or seek to be a "junior" (working as an apprentice, often for very little or no pay, in an established advocate's chambers). The selection process was largely ad hoc and depended on what the established advocate considered important. Although this might seem unappealing, starting a successful litigation practice in India was often considered very difficult to do without strong personal or business connections (ibid.). In addition, at this time, law firms were few in number, small in size, had informal hiring processes, and did not do the majority of hiring at elite Indian law schools.[8] In light of this, there were no recruitment or placement services at Indian law schools and little formal selection processes or criteria for the vast majority of law school graduates.

Liberalization in 1991 and increasing globalization brought more opportunities for the growth of corporate legal work (Chapter 3 of this volume). Law firms began expanding and became more important employers. Additionally, the National Law Schools were being established in this time frame. (The first national law school, National Law School of India University (NLSIU)–Bangalore, was founded in 1987 and others in the late 1990s.) These highly selective institutions produced a large number of the more recent employees at India's larger law firms.[9] Indeed, NLSIU–Bangalore first organized campus placements around 1995, coinciding with the growth of the Indian economy and the corresponding emergence and growth of Indian corporate law firms (Interview with Umakanth Varottil, 2012). The confluence of economic liberalization and the development of the National Law Schools satisfied some of the large and increasing demand for corporate lawyers. In the remainder of this section we discuss the factors that were important in recruitment and the recruitment processes that took root in the National Law Schools starting in the mid-1990s and early 2000s.

A. *Important Factors in Recruiting Decisions*

A key consideration in recruitment was which law school a student attended. Large law firms in India generally made entry-level hires from a small number of elite Indian law schools – often just the top five National Law Schools

TABLE 1. *Number of distinct mentions in thirty-eight interviews with corporate legal employers*[11]

School	Number of mentions
NLSIU–Bangalore	19
NALSAR–Hyderabad	18
NUJS–Kolkata	16
NLU–Jodhpur	11
Delhi University	9
ILS–Pune	9
NLIU–Bhopal	9
Symbiosis–Pune	9
GLC–Mumbai	8
GNLU–Gandhinagar	8
HNLU–New Raipur	8
Amity Law School–Delhi	5
NUALS–Kochi	5
Christ University–Bangalore	4
ULC–Bangalore	3
Army Institute of Law–Mohali	2
CMR Law School–Bangalore	1
CNLU–Patna	1
Jindal Global Law School	1
NALSAR LLM program	1
NLSIU LLM program	1
RMNLU–Lucknow	1
School of Excellence in Law Chennai	1

(Interview 11 with law firm managing partner in Kolkata, 2011; Interview 14 with law firm founding partner in Mumbai, 2011; Interview 22 with senior law firm partner in Delhi, 2011; Interview 24 with law firm head of strategy and HR executive in Delhi, 2011; Interview 26 with law firm partner in Hyderabad, 2011). Although some law firms did look outside this cluster, they rarely recruited junior associates outside of roughly twenty-five law schools (Table 1).[10] The perception is that there is a high variance in quality at most Indian law schools and that the National Law Schools and the other schools listed in the chart tended to have better students.

Another important consideration was the grades students receive while at law school. Law firms would have access to three or four years of students' grades because recruitment usually begins in the fourth year of legal studies (out of five) at the National Law Schools. Out of the thirty-eight legal employers we interviewed, eighteen believed that grades were important or very important factors, including at least three employers who have explicit cumulative grade point average (CGPA) cutoffs, while only four stated that grades were unimportant or irrelevant. In addition to grades, law firms desire students who participate in national and international moot court competitions, present papers at conferences, work on a law review, and possibly do research with a professor.[12]

Thus far, the factors considered to be important are substantially similar to what we might see in the United States (i.e., which law school you attended and how you performed) (Ginsburg and Wolf 2004). Scholars in the United States have noted that US law firms hire on the basis of limited information about the candidate (e.g., often with only first-year law school grades to consider). In India there is more information on grades in that students have completed more courses by the middle of their fourth year of legal studies. However, those courses rarely include corporate or commercial courses (which are more common in the fourth and fifth year of legal studies), so a corporate legal employer may not get a good sense of a student's aptitude or ability in these key areas.

B. *The Recruitment Process in India*

In this section we briefly describe the recruitment processes for graduates from elite law schools in the United States and the United Kingdom looking to enter corporate law practice. We then describe the processes that corporate legal employers use to recruit law students from India's elite law schools. There are, as we shall see, significant differences.

1. Recruitment Processes in the United States

Tom Ginsburg and Jeffrey Wolf provide a detailed discussion of law firm recruitment in the United States (Ginsburg and Wolf 2004). Recruitment is run by professionally staffed law school career services offices that coordinate interactions between law firms and students (Ginsburg and Wolf 2004). These offices have a nationwide professional organization, the National Association for Law Placement (NALP), whose members include "virtually every American Bar Association–approved law school in the United States, Canadian law schools, and hundreds of legal employers from both the public and private sectors" (NALP 2012). The NALP has adopted detailed guidelines regulating the behavior of law schools, students seeking jobs, and legal employers seeking to hire students (NALP 2010). Law firms typically conduct interviews on campus at the beginning of law students' second year of law school or during the summer after their first year of law school. On the basis of students' grades, résumés, recommendations, and performance in on-campus interviews, firms invite the students to interview at the law firm's office (ibid.). After conducting these interviews, firms will offer paid summer internships to the students they wish to hire for the summer between their second and third year of law school. Large firms in the United States primarily make permanent job offers, for positions starting after students complete their third and final year of legal studies, to those students who were selected as summer associates. Indeed, these firms make job offers to a very high percentage of the summer associates. Over the years there has been a drift toward recruiting students even earlier in their law school careers, perhaps as a way to hire the best students before there is too much competition for them (Ginsburg and Wolf 2004).

2. Recruitment in England and Wales[13]

In England and Wales, the process at leading universities does not involve an active career placement office. Instead, students are introduced to various law firms at career fairs generally during the first year of university (with their likelihood of success depending somewhat on the size and prestige of their college).[14] By the end of the first year students may apply for a "vacation scheme" or "vacation placement" for the summer after the second year of university. Vacation schemes are two-week programs that are similar to summer associate programs in American firms. Getting a vacation scheme depends on a mix of grades and interview performance. Generally, at the end of the vacation scheme, students can interview for a permanent position – a two-year training contract that may or may not result in an associate position at the end of the two-year period.[15] A training contract is often contingent on passing the legal practice course (a one-year course students have to take following completion of a law degree and before joining a firm) and on earning certain grades in their third (and final) year exams. This process is for students who choose to work as solicitors in law firms, as opposed to qualifying as barristers by pursuing a pupilage at one of the chambers.

3. India

The path from law school to law firm takes a different course in India. There are two ways to secure a permanent job offer from a law firm in India. The first is through "campus recruitment" – students interview with a law firm on campus and, on the basis of their interview, résumé, grades, and other materials, the law firm decides whether to offer them a permanent postgraduation job. These interviews now occur in the fourth year of law studies (out of five) at the National Law Schools in India.[16]

The second is through "preplacement offers" (PPOs) – students intern with a law firm while in law school and, on the basis of their performance as an intern, the firm may offer them a permanent postgraduation job. These internships often take place in the third year of law studies at the National Law Schools. The likelihood of obtaining an offer for a permanent position after an internship is not as high as the chances of obtaining a permanent position after being a summer associate at a law firm in the United States. Indeed, it is not uncommon for law students in India to intern at multiple firms before obtaining an offer for a permanent position. Moreover, the internships in India are, in general, fairly low-paying, and students are expected to cultivate an active, busy schedule ("wining and dining" or "courting" is less common than in the United States or United Kingdom).

The direct campus recruitment path is the most common way to be offered a permanent position, although PPOs are becoming more popular.[17] In addition, these two processes are significantly similar – students frequently obtain internships through an on-campus selection process, which strongly resembles the campus recruitment process. They may also obtain positions by directly approaching law firms, relying on private recruitment agencies, or using connections and contacts from friends and family. We first discuss campus recruitment and internships (the most common methods of recruitment) and then briefly discuss other methods.

a. CAMPUS RECRUITMENT AND RECRUITMENT COORDINATION COMMITTEES Indian law schools do not have professional career services offices. Instead, students coordinate the recruitment process for securing a "desk job." Law students interested in finding jobs through campus recruitment set up an administrative apparatus that they usually call the "campus recruitment committee," "recruitment coordination committee," or "recruitment coordination cell (RCC)." Students who use an RCC pay a small fee to cover the administrative costs of the cell (such as taxi costs for law firm representatives to get to campus from the airport and a brochure containing the members CVs) and elect several members of the organization, who are usually not actively seeking employment that year, to form an executive committee to manage the recruitment process.[18] Every year these student-formed RCCs write their own rules for interactions between law students and law firms. Prior RCC rules typically serve only as a starting point and can vary considerably from year to year (and among schools).

RCCs perform several functions. First, they sort and vet candidates. Students send their CVs (or résumés) to the RCC, which checks every line of the CV, as well as provide the committee with certificates or witnesses to prove that they interned with the people they claimed they did (NALSAR RCC 2011, 2014; NLSIU RCC 2014). The committee also checks students' CGPAs and then ranks them by CGPA for law firms (interview 42 with two RCC members, 2011; interview 41 with RCC member, 2011).

Second, RCCs serve as intermediaries between students and employers. RCCs will decide which firms to invite to campus recruitment. One RCC member told us, "We decide when firms will be invited to recruitment based on the name of the firm, reputation, pay scale, and whether they hire a large number of people" (interview 41 with RCC member). Generally, international law firms and Indian firms paying the highest salaries and hiring the largest number of students receive the earliest time slots for campus recruitment. All communications between students and the firms go through the RCC's executive committee – students are usually strictly prohibited from communicating personally with employers participating in the RCC process, and RCCs may impose severe penalties for violations of these rules (e.g., being barred from using the RCC process and sometimes paying monetary fines) (NALSAR RCC 2011).

Third, RCCs impose rules on their members regulating how they can interview with legal employers and what they must do when they receive job offers. Some RCCs have rules requiring members to respond to job offers from large firms within two days of receiving the offer. RCCs also require that students disclose job offers that they receive through preplacement offers or other method (NALSAR RCC 2011). More substantively, some RCCs have imposed "no hold" policies, prohibiting students from holding open job offers or turning down job offers (Ganz 2011a). For instance, an RCC at a well-established national law school imposed a no-hold policy recently under which any student utilizing the RCC's services who received a job offer with total annual compensation of 500,000 rupees or more was automatically withdrawn from the RCC and therefore debarred from sitting for further RCC-arranged interviews, whether or not he or she accepted the job offer (E-mail from NALSAR RCC to members, 2011).

The presence of no-hold policies and functional equivalents to "exploding offers" is fascinating given the rarity of such measures in the more formal US recruitment process (Ginsburg and Wolf 2004). This may reflect both the Indian students' interest in maximizing the number of students getting desk jobs and the law firms' interest in being able to staff their firms quickly (without having to get into a bidding war for individual students). It may well be that as India's corporate legal sector continues to expand and the "war for talent" becomes more intense, it will become difficult to maintain such no-hold policies.[19]

Finally, faculty are not normally actively involved in recruitment at the elite law schools (interview 41 with RCC member, 2011). Recruitment is largely student driven, and only the newer law schools attempt to involve faculty.[20] Indeed, one might view faculty efforts at these newer schools as steps to get greater recognition for newer entrants in legal education by increasing the placement prospects for their students.[21]

b. INTERNSHIPS LEADING TO PREPLACEMENT OFFERS An important alternative (and in some cases supplement) to the RCC model described earlier is the increasing use of internships, which may then lead to preplacement offers (PPOs). Internships in India are programs where law students spend somewhere between two to eight weeks during one of their term breaks (or over the summer) working at an Indian law firm. Law firms may then choose to make a PPO to that student. Internships can be obtained through an RCC or an internship coordination committee set up with procedures similar to those for RCCs (interview 42 with two RCC members, 2011). Many students obtain internships through less formal processes without going through an RCC or internship coordination committee (Interview 19 with person in charge for recruitment of freshers at a law firm in Delhi, 2011; Interview 32 with law firm cofounding partner in Mumbai, 2011; Interview 36 with law firm director of human resources and senior associate in Mumbai, 2011; Interview 37 with general counsel in Mumbai, 2011; Interview 38 with law firm founding partner and partner in Bangalore, 2011).

Additionally, many corporate legal employers review applications for internships from a larger pool of schools than they are willing to consider when making permanent hires.[22] This is in part due to the low pay and reasonably high work (and hour) expectations for interns, suggesting law firms face little risk in hiring them. Further, firms will also sometimes make PPOs to students from schools they do not normally recruit from if the students perform well during their internships (Interview 24 with law firm head of strategy and HR executive in Delhi, 2011; Interview 29 with law firm founding partner in Mumbai, 2011). From our interviews it appears that many law firms (of all sizes) and in-house departments have started using internships. Indeed, many employers, especially smaller law firms and in-house departments, increasingly hire students permanently through their internship programs, and some larger law firms are beginning to hire significant numbers of junior associates via internships.[23]

c. "FREE AGENTS" Although most large corporate legal employers prefer to go through RCCs or internships, a significant number will at least look at CVs and application materials sent from students outside of formal recruitment processes, particularly those at schools where the firm or corporation does not do campus recruitment (Interview 40 with general counsel in Bangalore, 2011).[24] Some smaller corporate legal employers prefer to receive applications from individual law students because they either think individual applicants are more likely to really be interested in their firm or they suspect that by the time they interview students through an RCC, the best students at a school will already have been hired by other (usually larger and perhaps higher-paying) employers (Interview 34 with law firm founding partner in Bangalore, 2011; Interview 30 with law firm partner responsible for human resources and hiring in Mumbai, 2011). Additionally, some very small corporate law firms do not hire on an annual basis or do not have the resources necessary to participate in campus recruitment, and these firms tend to hire "freshers" (first-year junior associates) exclusively through internship programs or through applications that they receive from individual students (Interview 4 with law firm partner in Delhi, 2011; Interview 5 with law firm founding partner in Delhi, 2011.)[25]

d. PRIVATE RECRUITMENT AGENCIES Some private headhunting and recruitment agencies have emerged in the past several years that try to match lawyers to firms. These agencies tend to focus their efforts on senior associates and partners, although occasionally law students will go through these firms to obtain entry-level jobs with corporate legal employers (interview 2 with recruitment agency executive, 2011). Nonetheless, this path is not a common one for obtaining entry-level positions.[26]

e. RECRUITMENT THROUGH FRIENDS AND FAMILY Some students may be able to obtain internships and permanent jobs through their own contacts (e.g., family members or friends). As this process is more informal and idiosyncratic, we did not study it carefully. Most legal employers report that family ties and friendships do not play any role in permanent hiring decisions, but can be important in awarding internships (which may then lead to permanent jobs) (Interview 20 with law firm named partner in Delhi, 2011; Interview 21 with law firm lead partner in Gurgaon, 2011; Interview 16 with law firm managing partner in Mumbai, 2011; Interview 37 with general counsel in Mumbai, 2011).

Although these five different mechanisms operate to some extent at a large number of corporate legal employers, it is clear that the dominant method for recruiting new lawyers at corporate law firms and in-house offices is campus recruitment through RCCs, while the role of internship programs has grown significantly in the past several years.[27]

IV. THE DEVELOPMENT OF THE INDIAN MODEL OF LEGAL RECRUITMENT

Our description raises a natural question: Why did this model develop in India? Indeed, given that recruitment is considerably important to law firms in India, it is somewhat surprising that they are willing to rely on a student-facilitated recruitment structure. Of course, law firms do interview candidates before making final offers, but the firms appear to accept student-run organizations taking on a very active intermediary (and screening) role. Correlatively, it is not immediately obvious why students are willing, without receiving any direct compensation, to invest the time and effort necessary to run and manage RCCs not just for themselves but for other students who are usually one year junior to them.

At the same time, one wonders why Indian law schools do not take a more active role given that student placement is an important factor in school rankings as well as where students choose to enroll. Further, given the less active role of law schools in recruitment, one wonders why Indian law firms weight grades so heavily. Indeed, for many law firms, law school grades are critical despite little evidence that grades achieved by one's fourth year correlate with success in a corporate law job.

In this part, we explore how the motivations and incentives of law schools, students, and legal employers led to the development of the student-run RCC model. We also note some similarities and differences to the US recruitment model. Following that, we explore how recent changes are putting mounting pressure on this recruitment model.

A. *Indian Law Schools*

The first national law school, NLSIU, initially set up interviews with students and law firms upon the request of law firms, but once it became clear that law firm positions were becoming the dominant job for graduates, the NLSIU administration, led by founding director Professor N. R. Madhava Menon, began moving away from facilitating such interviews and the RCC model emerged (Interview with Umakanth Varottil, 2012). This model was in turn adapted with some modifications by other National Law Schools.

Why did the administration pull away from taking a more active role in recruitment efforts by law firms? One likely explanation was that NLSIU was not initially set up to train and educate corporate lawyers, but rather to train the best and the brightest for areas of public interest law (see Chapter 16 of this volume). One might speculate that some law teachers and administrators were hesitant to assist law firms in recruiting so many students because of concerns that law firms might undermine student interest in public interest law (Interview with founder of a national law school, 2013). In addition, the elite law schools in India were (and are) by and large state-run and their interests may not have included a high degree of focus on corporate law firms. Further, most law professors were not working in the areas of commercial and corporate law and were perhaps unlikely to think of career services for the law firm sector as part of what legal education is, or perhaps should be, about.

Even so, one might have thought schools would display greater interest in placement matters to compete for better students and to enhance their rankings. Here a number of factors are likely to be at play. First, in the mid-1990s (when NLSIU began to pull back from assisting in recruitment), there was little pressure from prospective students for more professionalized recruitment for corporate law work because the corporate legal sector – although growing fast – was still small, most students went into litigation, and most other elite schools did not have active faculty or administration involvement in recruitment. Second, once demand for graduates by corporate law firms increased, law schools probably thought it was not necessary to invest in recruitment because students were obtaining corporate law positions quite quickly. This reflected the high growth in demand for these students by corporate legal employers and the small number of elite law school graduates (even after more National Law Schools were formed), which meant they were likely to find positions with little investment of resources by the schools.

In this context schools had little impetus to invest in recruitment unless new entrants in legal education thought offering recruitment services would be a differentiator. Indeed, at present, the law schools with the most faculty involvement in recruitment are the newer ones (which are often private).

B. *Indian Law Students*

Students appear concerned with ensuring that everyone in their class gets a job at a law firm if they want one, both to reduce the uncertainty of obtaining positions for themselves (and other students they are concerned about) as well as to enhance the importance of their alumni network in the future (Ganz 2011a). The National Law Schools in India are tight-knit social environments and some, such as NLSIU, have developed and maintained strong alumni networks.[28] Students aware of the benefits of such networks are likely to find value in trying to ensure that their classmates are also well placed. Students can increase the likelihood that everyone who wants a corporate job offer gets one by forming a group that coordinates and imposes rules, such as no-hold policies, that they think will increase the odds that all students, or as many students as possible, get offers from firms.

This then raises another question: Why would students be willing to work and serve on the RCC executive committee gratis when the committee members themselves could not directly and immediately benefit from it (i.e., they were not looking to obtain positions) and the benefits would go to the students one year junior to them? One potential explanation is that RCC executive members build valuable contacts with firms they coordinate with (even though they are not typically interviewing with them) who may be valuable later on in their professional lives. Serving as an RCC executive might also signal a willingness to work with a team and contribute to building institutions, which might be attractive traits to potential employers. Finally, RCC executives gain information about how the recruitment process works, which might enhance their own ability to make lateral moves later on in their careers.

Another likely motivator is social esteem. Law school student bodies in India, as noted earlier, are tight-knit social groups. In the National Law Schools fewer than one hundred people are in a class and they are living together on fairly remote campuses for five years. Through this close interaction they get to know one another very well. Serving on an RCC provides social esteem from their classmates (McAdams 1997).

However, there are issues with having RCCs intermediate with law firm hiring. Students and the RCC's executive committee are in a principal-agent relationship, as the students' welfare somewhat depends on how well the executives perform their job, but the executives may have different interests from the students (Hansmann and Kraakman 2004). For example, students might worry that RCC executive committee members could tilt the playing field by making use of the RCC's resources to present their friends (or perhaps themselves) more favorably to law firms. Further, students may worry about RCC executives' shirking their broader responsibilities, especially if students serve on the executive committee just to list the RCC on their CVs.

These agency problems appear to be addressed with several monitoring and bonding strategies.[29] Generally, RCC executive committee members are prohibited from interviewing with employers with whom they are responsible for communications, and executive committees are large enough that it would be difficult for a member to break any conflict-of-interest rules without other committee members noticing (interview 42 with two RCC members, 2011).[30]

Students are also more likely to vote for executives who are perceived as uninterested in securing a placement through campus recruitment, because they either plan to purse an LLM abroad or have already secured a PPO (Interviews 44–47 with former national law school RCC executive, 2011–2012).[31] Incompetent RCC executives might be removed by a vote of the RCC's members and would likely also suffer social sanctions from other students, resulting in reputational damage (NALSAR RCC 2011). Indeed, monitoring executives' behavior may not be that costly for students because they may be able to assess this through normal social interactions and as participants in the campus recruitment process.[32] Finally, some schools have a faculty member as an advisor to the RCC, which may also serve to police or deter tilting the field by RCC executives (interview 41 with RCC member, 2011; interview 42 with two RCC members, 2011).

Although RCCs may have ways to address agency problems, students with stronger academic records still have an incentive to either not be part of the RCC process or defect from it and approach law firms individually (e.g., as free agents). This does not often happen for several reasons. First, applying for jobs through RCCs may dramatically cut search costs for applicants relative to applying to firms individually (Ginsburg and Wolf 2004). Second, successful students might do almost as well, and perhaps better, going through an RCC than approaching firms as a free agent (Interview 24 with law firm head of strategy and HR executive in Delhi, 2011).[33] One LPO firm told us that while they accept applications outside of the RCC, they would offer a student who applied directly a salary of 100,000 to 200,000 rupees lower, holding all else equal.[34] Third, successful students might lose the esteem of their colleagues in very tightly knit student bodies if they were to go outside of the RCC to seek corporate law jobs, making defection less likely (Alchian and Demsetz 1972). Thus, the potential gains from defecting for students with strong CVs might not be enough to outweigh the increased costs of conducting an independent job search without the resources of the RCC and taking whatever attendant risks that may entail.[35]

C. *Indian Law Firms*

There are several reasons why law firms may desire a largely student-run recruitment process. First, many small and midsize Indian law firms lack the scale necessary to make dedicated human resources (HR) personnel worthwhile, and larger firms have smaller and less professionalized HR departments than British or American firms of comparable size. Further, many lawyers do not think that building human resources is as important as building a professional practice (i.e., business and client development). Indeed, some firms may not think having their better or more senior attorneys spend time on recruitment, as opposed to business development or corporate legal work, is wise given the extremely high demand and low supply of corporate legal talent at the senior associate level and above. Thus, one might expect law firms to economize on recruitment costs by having outside entities undertake some of it. Relying on RCCs to vet CVs, prepare rank lists of students, and schedule campus interviews helps firms trim the number of likely candidates to a smaller number on which firms can then focus their own (costly) recruitment efforts. Moreover, this screening is being done at essentially no cost to the law firms, which is attractive.

One might still wonder why firms would trust student-run RCCs to vet applicant CVs given that RCCs want to make their members look as good as possible. One suspects the reputational costs of gaming the system would be high to the executive committee. RCCs and law schools are in a repeat-play scenario with law firms (each year they will have new graduates looking for positions at law firms) and have incentives to ensure that law firms are pleased with the services provided by the RCC – otherwise law firms may choose to go to the next closest competitor school for hiring. Further, one of the benefits of being on an RCC is the goodwill and contacts developed, so RCC executives do not wish to be cavalier about how law firms perceive their efforts. Indeed, given the relatively small size of India's corporate legal sector, such concerns may weigh heavily on RCC behavior and would likely deter RCC members from performing poorly.[36] In addition, because students have friendships that span across years at law schools, some of the social prestige pressures that help ensure that RCC executives perform their duties may also encourage them to be aware of how their behavior in one year could impact future recruitment by corporate employers at their school.

Although this account explains the emergence of the RCC model of recruitment, one wonders why law firms seem to have little interest in consulting with faculty on hiring or in bringing the law school administration more actively into the mix. Part of the explanation appears to be that most law faculty do not espouse much interest in commercial law matters and consequently may not be able to provide helpful insights about students to law firms (Chapter 16, this volume). Further, our interviews indicated both law firms and law students seem to share a fairly low opinion of the administrative competence of law schools. Indeed, some students said that students do a far better job running the recruitment process than their schools could (Interview 41 with two RCC members, 2011). Finally, firms might think that students are more likely to be trustworthy than law school faculty or administrators, because most RCC executives are entering legal practice and might face more severe reputational costs for misleading employers than would administrators or teachers at a law school.

V. PRESSURE ON THE INDIAN MODEL OF RECRUITMENT

As we have seen, there are plausible explanations for how the current model of recruitment has developed. But why are we starting to see movement away from this model toward a model that relies more on hiring through internship programs?

A. *Pressure From Newer Law Schools and Students*

Less elite or established schools are beginning to involve faculty more in placement as well as professionalizing their processes to enhance their students' chances for obtaining "desk jobs." For instance, Christ University has had strong faculty involvement in developing connections between students and law firms, and Jindal Global Law School has signed memoranda of understanding with a variety of Indian and foreign law firms (Interview 40 with general counsel in Bangalore, 2011; Interview 33 with law firm senior partner in Mumbai, 2011; Interview 12 with law firm managing partner in Mumbai, 2011; Interview 12 with law firm managing partner in Mumbai, 2011). It is not surprising that newer entrants to legal education are attempting to restructure recruitment, because new schools may have greater difficulty finding desk jobs for their students if they are unable to disrupt currently dominant practices. If they are unable to make progress on this, they are likely to have trouble attracting qualified students willing to pay their tuition.

Further, even if firms have some skepticism about the value of faculty involvement in recruitment at the National Law Schools (where student quality is very high, there is little faculty interest in commercial law matters, and administrative support is weak), they might still value faculty involvement where there is greater variation in student quality and better administrative support (e.g., the newer law schools). This would aid firms in identifying generally talented students at these less elite schools.[37]

The students from these less elite law schools may also be putting pressure on the traditional system of recruitment by applying directly for internships or permanent positions with law firms that do not typically recruit at the law school the student is attending. If law firms think that they can find better candidates by looking at independent applications from students at the top of the class at a less famous law school, rather than applications from the middle of the class at a more prestigious law school, firms might have an incentive to move away from the current structure.

B. *Pressure from Legal Employers*

Firms have been developing more-sophisticated techniques for evaluating job applicants including using in-depth, in-person job interviews, written exams, and what some firms call "psychometric testing" (i.e., some sort of behavioral testing or personality profiling) (Interview 24 with three lawyers and HR executives at large law firm in Delhi, 2011). Although law firms of all sizes are beginning to make greater use of internships to recruit new lawyers, the reasons are different for small and midsize firms and for large firms.

1. Small and Midsize Legal Employers

Small and midsize firms (i.e., those with fewer than 50 lawyers) appear concerned with their inability to influence campus RCC recruitment because they cannot offer to place as many students as the larger firms. These firms do not get the early slots for on-campus interviews and hence suffer a disadvantage in attracting talent relative to the larger firms, who interview earlier and make offers that students must accept or reject before interviewing with other employers. These smaller firms thus think they can do a better job of finding good talent through internships (Interview 21 with lead partner at a small law firm in Delhi, 2011; Interview 30 with law firm partner responsible for human resources and recruitment in Mumbai, 2011; Interview 38 with law firm founding partner and partner in Bangalore, 2011). In addition, some smaller employers, like boutique law firms with very competent lawyers, are highly attractive to talented students who may prefer to work for them than the larger firms.[38] If these kinds of smaller and midsize employers continue to increase their use of internship programs and PPOs for recruitment, then the traditional campus recruitment model could be considerably eroded.

2. Large Legal Employers

Larger law firms are also moving toward greater use of internal tests and internships. There could be a number of reasons for this. First, as larger law firms engage in more-sophisticated corporate legal work (often related to increasing globalization), they are keen to hire students with the talent for this kind of work.[39] Moreover, firms cannot easily screen for this when they hire through the RCC process because grades may not reflect this skill. However, internships – which provide a longer window over which to view a student's skills – allow firms to assess a candidate's skills for complicated transactional work (Interview 32 with law firm cofounding partner in Mumbai, 2011). Second, since many firms are willing to give internships to students from a broader range of law schools than they normally consider for recruitment, the internship provides students from less prestigious schools and less well known employers the opportunity to get to know one another and assess whether their needs and skills match. Finally, as firms grow, they are likely to find it attractive to develop more professional human resources processes and hire human resources specialists, who may be better placed to implement mechanisms like written and oral tests to sort applicants for internships and permanent positions. In a larger firm with continual hiring needs, there may be significant economies of scale such that firms will become willing to invest the resources necessary to run recruitment through their own systems (or obtain such resources, like proprietary tests, through best friends arrangements with foreign law firms), rather than systems designed and run by RCCs (Interview 30 law firm partner responsible for human resources and recruitment in Mumbai, 2011)

C. *Pressure From Other Sources*

Several other factors, while less frequently cited by our interviewees, may play some role in changes in the recruitment system.

1. Pressure From Private Recruitment Firms

Several private recruitment agencies now exist that specialize in legal jobs. While law firms generally rely only on private recruitment firms to identify talent at the middle to senior associate level, some agencies aspire to provide credentials that better reflect the skills that law students need to succeed as attorneys. So far, none of these agencies appears to have developed any successful credentialing service for junior associates, but if a private recruitment agency were to succeed in developing such a service, it could disrupt the existing RCC model. Such a credentialing service might, however, have more impact on LPO than on corporate law firms given the relative novelty of LPO and the fact that many LPO customers are from outside of India, where the credentialing may have additional benefits.

2. Pressure from Hiring Date Competition

Over the past several years, large legal employers have moved the dates on which they hire during campus recruitment earlier and earlier as they compete with one another to lock up the most talented students. As employers face pressure to hire earlier and earlier in the recruitment process, the process might become less valuable to them (Interview 40 with general counsel in Bangalore, 2011). Particularly if hiring talented students requires that employers hire so far in advance that they cannot adequately assess the candidate or anticipate their staffing needs, they may conclude that they would be better off foregoing the RCC process. The movement of the hiring date has analogs in US experience, too (Ginsburg and Wolf 2004).

D. *Recruitment and Globalization*

One of the questions raised by these rapid changes in recruitment is what is causing them? We suggest that globalization has a major role to play in these unfurling developments.

Prior to liberalization, the primary employment Indian law graduates targeted was litigation, particularly noncommercial (see Chapter 2 of this volume). Given the tight state controls on the economy and the rather slow pace of adjudication in Indian courts, most business matters might not have been adjudicated in courts but rather in government agencies or through private dispute resolution fora (or through social or family networks). Against this background, there was little need for a highly structured recruitment process into law firms.

However, as globalization and liberalization began to influence the Indian economy, we witnessed rapid growth leading to more contracts, more acquisitions, and more business generally. This also led to more commercial disputes, a different kind of client (corporate clients versus individuals or government), and a greater need for specialized legal talent in the corporate space. The advent of the National Law Schools around the same time that law firms needed to recruit many corporate lawyers provided a supply of talented, freshly minted attorneys.

RCCs might be seen as a response to this increased demand against a background of limited human capital and the relatively small size of Indian law firms. Consider the following constraints (some surely short term) law firm recruitment in India might face: the administrative structure of law schools was not directed to recruitment issues (and especially not recruitment at law firms), law faculties' attentions were focused on other important issues, and law firms simply did not have the time for their better attorneys to spend on recruitment as opposed to business development and corporate legal work. Law firms were also fairly small and may not have found it worthwhile to invest in large recruitment or HR departments.

In this context, one potential solution might be to rely on a group of people who (1) had knowledge of the legal education system and its participants, (2) could effectively vet student CVs, coordinate communications between firms and applicants, and structure the campus recruitment process, and (3) had conflicts of interest that could be managed. Final-year law students who had already secured employment appear to meet these conditions and would have done so at extremely little cost to law firms. Moreover, their incentives (likely based on goodwill, connections with future employers, and social esteem) to perform a screening and verification function might have been sufficient to provide law firms with the basics they needed to conduct their work – which at the beginning of globalization may not have been particularly complicated corporate work.

The changes to recruitment we are now witnessing may reflect the increasing number of players who need corporate legal services (including midsize firms and in-house departments) and the increasingly complex nature of their work (which is driven in part by globalization and the rising complexities of domestic and cross-border legal work). With this need for added quality, services are developing that allow employers to assess a candidate's knowledge as well as ability to perform the tasks at hand (e.g., internships). Globalization has a major impact here as well because as business continues to grow and as India becomes a destination for those selling products, as well as a place to source and produce goods, we are likely to see growing demand for increasingly complex corporate legal work.

V. THE RELATIONSHIP BETWEEN LAW SCHOOLS AND LAW FIRMS

At present, Indian law firms have minimal involvement with law schools beyond recruitment, but there appears to be a desire for change. A number of the employers we interviewed indicated they wanted stronger involvement in Indian law schools, especially to identify and recruit strong legal talent (in particular, because the highest value transactions appear to require better education and more-sophisticated attorneys).[40] This might include greater offerings on subjects that interest them (e.g., project financing). Further, some of the schools outside of the elite cadre are expanding their efforts at placing their students and increasing course offerings, which may begin to put pressure on elite schools to become more active in providing recruitment and educational services.[41]

In addition to these developments, foreign law firms (which sometimes hire graduates of elite law schools) have run short courses at Indian law schools (Venkatesan 2011; Indian Universities Support Initiative, Herbert Smith

Freehills). This is in part because they want to develop good relations with members of the Indian corporate legal sector in case, or for when, the legal market opens up to the broader presence of foreign law firms, but also because they want to identify talented students they can recruit to work in their London or Singapore offices (Chaturvedi 2013). Their increasing presence is also likely to affect the pressures on legal education in India.

VI. CONCLUSION

In this paper we have presented several important findings. Law students and legal employers organize recruitment through student-run recruitment coordination committees (RCCs) at highly selective law schools in India. For students, RCCs represent a way of coordinating activity with a view to maximizing placements for themselves, while for law firms they save scarce time and resources that can be used on business development rather than recruitment. The RCCs are also fascinating for how the students developed detailed internal systems to address the most likely problems RCCs may face. While the RCC-run campus recruitment process remains the dominant model of recruitment of new associates in the Indian legal market, legal employers are moving toward hiring through internships, and there are some concerns with the RCC-run campus recruitment process from small and midsize firms and in-house law offices. At the same time, less prestigious and less established law schools are developing more-professionalized career services in the hopes of disrupting the current model of legal recruitment.

The changes just described have been influenced by globalization's impact on India. The student-run recruitment model can be seen as a response to changes wrought by liberalization and globalization in India against a backdrop of limited human capital and the size and incentives of Indian law schools, law firms, and law students. As India's interactions with globalization increase and as India's domestic laws and business become more complex, one can anticipate further changes to the model of recruitment. More complex (and often cross-border) work and the presence of even larger, and growing, law firms may lead to greater incentives for law firms to invest in recruitment and a desire by law firms and students to demand more from law schools in terms of available educational offerings. This is complemented or supplemented by increasing reliance on internships, which help firms identify those students with greater knowledge and sophistication about the issues relevant to globally oriented business.

Although India's model of corporate legal sector recruitment has many interesting and perhaps somewhat unusual features, it still shares a number of similarities with recruitment systems from elsewhere (e.g., such as the United States). For example, Ginsburg and Wolf (2004) note that the US system of recruitment tends to rely on limited information about students and is quite decentralized (in contrast to other professional services markets such as medical residencies) and provide explanations for why this might be (Ginsberg and Wolf, 2004). We see some similar features in India's recruitment model (decentralization, limited information), but some differences as well (e.g., no-hold policies). We discuss some of these differences and likely explanations for them in this paper. Indeed, exploring recruitment systems across countries in a comparative manner may also be a fruitful avenue of inquiry. We leave that for future research.

Notes

1 Scholarship examining the impact of globalization on the legal profession is a fast-growing area, including Dezalay and Garth (2002), Ribstein (2010), Silver (2011), Terry et al. (2012), Li and Liu (2012), Garoupa (2014), Wilkins and Papa (2015), and other chapters in this book. Two websites are dedicated to legal issues in India: Legally India (www.legallyindia.com) and Bar and Bench (www.barandbench.com).

2 These entities are examples of private ordering and thus connect to a vast literature, including Ellickson (1991), McAdams (1997), Posner (2000), and McAdams and Rasmusen (2004). There are also potentially interesting comparisons to the judicial clerkship system in the United States, for example Avery et al. (2007) and the operation of US law reviews.

3 For discussion of US recruitment, see Ginsburg and Wolf (2004).

4 We have numbered the interviews that we conducted, and they are referenced in the following format: interview with [code number of interview] [brief description of position of person interviewed] [year]. Interviews numbered 1–43 were conducted in July and August 2011; interviews numbered 44–47 were conducted by e-mail in February and March 2014.

5 The incoming class sizes of these elite law schools are smaller than at many US law schools. For example, the top fifteen Indian law schools probably average fewer than one hundred students enrolling each year, and many of these top fifteen schools did not exist even ten years ago (interview 2 with recruitment agency executive, 2011).

6 Some students also secure nonlegal jobs with large international firms as management consultants or investment bankers (Chaturvedi 2013). In 2011, at the five most selective "National Law Schools" in India, 69% of graduating students took "desk jobs," which are jobs involving some sort of corporate legal work, and half took jobs with corporate law firms, international or domestic (Ganz 2011, relying on figures that are self-reported by the student-run campus recruitment committees). The five most selective law schools in India among the schools that use the Common Law Admission Test (CLAT) are National Law School of India University (NLSIU)–Bangalore, National Academy of Legal Studies and Research (NALSAR)–Hyderabad, West Bengal National University of Juridical Sciences (NUJS)–Kolkata,

National Law Institute University (NLIU)–Bhopal, and National Law University (NLU)–Jodhpur (Ganz 2011). Almost all of the National Law Schools use the Common Law Admissions Test.

7 The starting salaries at the larger Indian law firms have been increasing quite quickly over the past twenty years (Ganz 2011; Legally India 2013).

8 One important exception to this is Government Law College–Mumbai, which has a long record of placing graduates into articleships in solicitors' firms in Bombay (Sayta 2011a; Gingerich and Robinson 2017. this volume; Interview 32 with law firm partner in Bombay, 2011).

9 In 2013 there were an estimated thirty thousand CLAT test takers competing for about fifteen hundred seats (Ganz 2013; Information Brochure, Common Law Admission Test, 2013).

10 However, one large firm reported that they avoid hiring graduates of National Law Schools: "First, NLS–Bangalore has a very strong network, and I am worried about confidentiality . . . Friends tell other friends about what is happening at the firm . . . These NLS grads also seem overconcerned with money and promotion, and even as they are bright, I do not know if they are competent. . . . They have no sense of ownership toward the place" (Interview 16 with law firm managing partner in Mumbai, 2011). It may well be likely that several recently founded law schools, including National Law University–Delhi and Jindal Global Law School, will join this list once students start graduating from their five-year BA/LLB programs.

11 This table may understate the degree to which law firms hope to hire from the most selective National Law Schools, because some employers told us that they recruit from the "top eight" or "top ten" law schools without specifying which schools they consider these to be.

12 Graduates from the top five most selective law schools may be able to obtain positions even with more lackluster grades. For example, in 2011 all of the students at NLSIU, NALSAR, and NUJS who sought "desk jobs" in law firms or in-house offices managed to secure them (Ganz 2011a, 2011b; Sayta 2011b).

13 Sandie Ferrans, Jennifer MacLeod, and James Woolrich provided background information on the legal recruitment process in England and Wales (DATE). Some law firms in the United Kingdom appear to recruit students out of high school.

14 In England and Wales, a student need not study law in university to secure a training contract with a law firm. Students who study a different subject complete a one-year "conversion course" after law school to obtain legal training.

15 It is also possible, though not very likely, to secure a training contract without having completed a vacation scheme at a firm.

16 Some other elite schools allow for three-year LLBs after completion of a bachelor's degree in another subject. For this latter category the interviews are usually in the second year of law studies.

17 More information can be found in stories published by *Legally India* at www.legallyindia.com/tag/campus-recruitment.

18 At some law schools, such as NALSAR, students who do not pay the RCC fees or participate in campus recruitment nonetheless participate in elections of RCC executives (NALSAR Recruitment Coordination Committee (RCC) Rules 2011 and 2014; NLSIU Recruitment Coordination Committee (RCC) Rules 2014).

19 There may be some movement on this already in that some RCCs recently have allowed students to sit for interviews with domestic and international law firms and hold one of the offers for at least some period of time (NALSAR RCC 2011).

20 The legal employers we spoke with rarely noted interacting with faculty members when dealing with RCCs (Interview 40 with general counsel in Bangalore, 2011; Interview 43 with faculty member at an elite non-national law school, 2011). For more on this, see "Placement Details," Jindal Global Law School, www.jgls.edu.in/content/placement-details (accessed February 27, 2014). This strategy seems to be enjoying at least some success (Ganz and Shrivastava, 2013).

21 Twenty of the legal employers we interviewed reported that they are never, or only rarely, contacted by faculty for students.

22 Eighteen of the corporate legal employers we spoke with reported that they consider applicants from a broader range of schools for their internship programs than when hiring for permanent positions.

23 Five employers in our sample reported that their internship programs have become a more important part of their recruitment strategy within the past year or two (Interview 32 with law firm cofounding partner in Mumbai, 2011; Interview 33 with law firm senior partner in Mumbai, 2011; Interview 35 with law firm founding partner in Bangalore, 2011; Interview 36 with law firm human resources director and senior associate in Mumbai, 2011; Interview 40 with general counsel in Bangalore, 2011). Others report that PPOs are a very important part of their recruitment strategy, with one reporting that they now recruit exclusively through their internship program (Interview 14 with law firm founding partner in Mumbai, 2011; Interview 19 with law firm person in charge for recruitment in Delhi, 2011; Interview 22 with law firm senior partner responsible for hiring decisions in Delhi, 2011; Interview 29 with law firm founding partner in Mumbai, 2011; Interview 38 with law firm founding partner in Bangalore, 2011). No employers reported that internships are becoming a *less* important part of their recruitment strategy.

24 At least twelve of the legal employers with whom we spoke entertain applications received from individual students outside of RCCs.

25 Some recently formed small firms, including one firm in Mumbai with fewer than five lawyers, reported going through campus recruitment for their limited hiring needs (Interview 15 with law firm founding partner in Mumbai, 2011).

26 None of the legal employers whom we interviewed reported relying on private recruitment agencies for hiring entry-level associates.

27 Twenty of the employers we spoke with report that they hired freshers through campus recruitment, but this included all of the corporate legal employers with one hundred or more lawyers whom we interviewed. Many of the largest corporate legal employers reported hiring freshers exclusively, or almost exclusively, through campus recruitment.

28 National Law Schools appear more likely to have socially tight-knit student bodies than do traditional law schools because their student bodies are relatively small (there are typically fewer than one hundred students in a graduating BA/LLB class), they are stand-alone institutions rather than part of larger universities, and some, such as NALSAR and NLUJ, are geographically isolated, making it more likely that students will form social bonds with one another (Ballakrishnen 2009). Also see "For the Kind Attention of Alumni Students," National Law School of

India University–Bangalore www.nls.ac.in/resources/oldsiteresources/alumni.html (accessed February 27, 2014).

29 The agency problem might also be reduced by selling RCC executives a residual claim to the income that RCC members will earn after they have secured employment with law firms, causing executives to internalize the cost and value of their management decisions. However, because successful RCC members will secure jobs with salaries that depend on effort and skill rather than easily alienable resources, such a strategy is problematic (Fama and Jensen 1983).

30 For more, see Fama and Jensen describing how professional partnerships resolve agency problems in part by delivering services through "small group[s] of professionals who interact and monitor one another intensively" (Fama and Jenson 1983).

31 Other factors influencing elections include possessing contacts in law firms, friendships with students voting in the RCC election, gender, and CGPA. At some schools, voters tend to prefer candidates who seem likely to contest general student body elections in their final year in law school, as it is assumed that such students will try to do a good job running the RCC to secure votes in general elections (Interview 45 with former national law school RCC executive, 2012).

32 Moreover, students at each elite law school are small-enough groups (usually fewer than eighty in a year) that there may be real individual welfare benefits from monitoring RCC executives.

33 Many firms state that while they will consider applications sent by individuals, they prefer applications submitted through RCCs.

34 One might speculate as to why an employer may pay less in this context. It is conceivable that it reflects the additional verification costs the employer may expend to check the applicant's details (which are done gratis by the RCC) or perhaps a perception that the candidate (by going outside of the RCC) was signaling something negative about himself or herself (e.g., less of a "team player" or less loyal) (Ginsburg and Wolf 2004).

35 Finally, we might still wonder why law students do not hire a recruitment agency or headhunting firm to run campus recruitment on their behalf, rather than doing it themselves. One reason is that hiring an outside agency does not eliminate monitoring costs for the students – they must still monitor the outside agency and it may be more difficult to assess the agency's efforts because students do not know (or live close to) the people running the agency. The RCC has the distinct advantage of being relatively low cost to monitor for students (Alchian and Demsetz 1972). Ultimately, the RCC presently survives as an organizational form because it delivers the product demanded (recruitment coordination) at lower costs than other organizational forms that are available (e.g., external agencies) (Fama and Jensen 1983).

36 One also suspects law firms are not taking much of a risk when hiring from the top National Law Schools, given the high admissions standards (Menon 2009).

37 It may also be that if law school incoming class sizes increase and law firms continue to hire actively, then law schools may find the investment in placement offices to be more worthwhile.

38 Talented students may prefer such firms both because of the nature of work and work culture and because chances of becoming an equity partner might be brighter here than at the larger corporate law firms.

39 That law school grades are not highly informative is a criticism that is often leveled at law school grades in the United States, and they may be even less so in India because of high rates of academic misconduct and faculty often put little or no effort into grading accurately (Ginsburg and Wolf, 2004; Gingerich and Singh 2010).

40 Twenty-one of the legal employers whom we interviewed desired greater collaboration with law schools.

41 There are, of course, countervailing pressures: some stakeholders in law schools are upset that National Law Schools do not do more to serve the practicing profession or to serve the human rights community, for instance (Interview 23 with head of a legal services organization in Delhi, 2011).

References

Alchian, Armen A. and Harold Demsetz. 1972. "Production, Information Costs, and Economic Organization." *American Economics Review* 62 (5): 777–795.

Avery, Christopher, Christine Jolls, Richard A. Posner and Alvin E. Roth. 2007. "The New Market for Federal Judicial Law Clerks." *University of Chicago Law Review* 74 (2): 447–486

Ballakrishnen, Swethaa. 2009. "Where Did We Come From? Where Do We Go? An Inquiry into the Students and Systems of Legal Education in India." *Journal of Commonwealth Law and Legal Education* 7 (2): 133–156.

Bar Council of India. 2010. "List of Law Colleges Maintained by Bar Council of India with Addresses in All the States as on 10.04.2010." www.subharti.org/Documents/approvedlawcolleges.pdf.

Vision Statement 2011–2013. www.barcouncilofindia.org/about/about-the-bar-council-of-india/vision-statement-2011–13/.

Chaturvedi, Anumesha. 2013. "Recruitments Pick Up Steam at Country's Top Law Schools NLSIU, Nalsar, NUJS." *Economic Times*, November 5. www.articles.economictimes.indiatimes.com/2013–11–05/news/43695049_1_law-students-nlsiu-placements.

Common Law Admission Test. 2013. "Information Brochure."

Dezalay, Yves and Bryant G. Garth. 2002. *The Internationalization of Global Palace War: Lawyers, Economists, and the Contest to Transform Latin American States*. Chicago: University of Chicago Press.

The Economist. 2010. "Not Entirely Free, Your Honour." July 29. www.economist.com/node/16693882.

Ellickson, Robert C. 1991. *Order without Law: How Neighbors Settle Disputes*. Cambridge, MA: Harvard University Press.

E-mail from NALSAR RCC to members, on file with the authors, 2011

Fama, Eugene F. and Michael C. Jensen. 1983. "Agency Problems and Residual Claims." *Journal of Law and Economics* 26 (2): 327–349.

Galanter, Marc. 1968–1969. "Introduction: the Study of the Indian Legal Profession." *Law and Society Review* 3 (2/3): 201–217.

Galanter, Marc and Thomas M. Palay. 1990. "Why the Big Get Bigger: The Promotion-to-Partner Tournament and the Growth of Large Law Firms." *Virginia Law Review* 76 (4): 747–811.

1991. *Tournament of Lawyers: The Transformation of the Big Law Firm*. Chicago: University of Chicago Press.

Galanter, Marc and V. S. Rekhi. 1996. "The Impending Transformation of Indian Legal Profession" (unpublished manuscript on file with authors).

Galanter, Marc and Nick Robinson. 2017. "Grand Advocates: The Traditional Elite Lawyers." In *The Indian Legal Profession in the Age of Globalization*. Edited by David B. Wilkins, Vikramaditya S. Khanna, and David M. Trubek. Cambridge: Cambridge University Press.

Ganz, Kian. 2010. "Amarchand Turnover Near $40m, Law Firms Bill $350m, Says Report." *Legally India*, March 19. www.legallyindia.com/20100319599/Law-firms/amarchand-turnover-near-40m-law-firms-bill-350m-says-report.

Ganz, Kian. 2011a. "Nalsar 2011: 59 Desk Jobs, 8 LLMs with In-House Filling Up 100% RCC Quota." *Legally India*, April 16. www.legallyindia.com/201104162030/Law-schools/nalsar-2011–59-desk-jobs-8-llms-with-in-house-filling-up-100-rcc-quota.

2011b. "Result for All 75 NUJS Grads into Desk Jobs; Plus 3 Foreign Firms, 5 LLMs, 2 Start-Ups." *Legally India*, June 8. www.legallyindia.com/201106082149/Law-schools/result-for-all-75-nujs-grads-into-desk-jobs-plus-3-foreign-firms-5-llms-2-start-ups.

2011c. "Old-School CLAT Prefs Wobble as NUJS Gains on Nalsar; NLIU, NLU-J Locked Dead-Heat." *Legally India*, June 16. www.legallyindia.com/201106162164/Pre-law-student/old-school-clat-preferences-wobble-as-nujs-gains-on-nalsar-nliu-nlu-j-locked-dead-heat.

2011d. "Indian Graduates See Salaries Double." *The Lawyer*, December 5. www.thelawyer.com/indian-graduates-see-salaries-double/1010532.article.

Ganz, Kian. 2013. "CLAT 2013: 29,500 Law Aspirants Apply, 15% More Than Last Year." *Legally India*, April 3. www.legallyindia.com/201304023561/Pre-law-student/clat-2013-many-apply.

Ganz, Kian and Prachi Shrivastava. 2013. "Day Zeros: NLU Delhi RCC Confirms 12 Jobs, 3 Vac Schemes; Jindal on 8 and 2 White & Case." *Legally India*, May 16. www.legallyindia.com/201305163677/Law-schools/day-zeros-nlu-delhi-rcc-confirms-12-jobs-3-vac-schemes-jindal-on-8-and-2-white-case.

Garoupa, Nuno. 2014. "Globalization and Deregulation of Legal Services." *International Review of Law and Economics* 38 (S): 77–86.

Gilson, Ronald J. and Robert H. Mnookin. 1988. "Coming of Age in a Corporate Law Firm: The Economics of Associate Career Patterns." *Stanford Law Review* 41 (3): 567–595.

Gingerich, Jonathan and Aditya Singh. 2010. "Writing Requirements, Student Assessment, and Plagiarism in Indian Law Schools." *India Law News* (Fall): 12–15.

Gingrich, Jonathan and Nick Robinson. 2017. "Responding to the Market: The Impact of the Rise of Corporate Law Firms on Elite Legal Education in India." In *The Indian Legal Profession in the Age of Globalization*. Edited by David B. Wilkins, Vikramaditya S. Khanna, and David M. Trubek. Cambridge: Cambridge University Press.

Ginsburg, Tom and Jeffrey Wolf. 2004. "The Market for Elite Law Firm Associates." *Florida State University Law Review* 31 (4): 909–963.

Hansmann, Henry and Reinier Kraakman. 2004. "Agency Problems and Legal Strategies. In *The Anatomy of Corporate Law: A Comparative and Functional Approach*. 2nd. ed. Edited by Reinier Kraakman et al. Oxford: Oxford University Press.
Common Law Admission Test. 2013. *Information Brochure*. www.polymathedu.com/polymathadmin/upload/PMEA_524050a903edc.pdf.
Interview with Umakanth Varottil, 2012.
Interview 2 with recruitment agency executive, 2011.
Interview 4 with law firm partner in Delhi, 2011.
Interview 5 with law firm founding partner in Delhi, 2011.
Interview 11 with law firm managing partner in Kolkata, 2011.
Interview 12 with law firm managing partner in Mumbai, 2011.
Interview 14 with law firm founding partner in Mumbai, 2011.
Interview 15 with law firm founding partner in Mumbai, 2011.
Interview 16 with law firm managing partner in Mumbai, 2011.
Interview 19 with person in charge for recruitment of freshers at a law firm in Delhi, 2011.
Interview 20 with law firm named partner in Delhi, 2011.
Interview 21 with law firm lead partner in Gurgaon, 2011.
Interview 22 with senior law firm partner in Delhi, 2011.
Interview 23 with head of a legal services organization in Delhi, 2011.
Interview 24 with law firm head of strategy and HR executive in Delhi, 2011.
Interview 26 with law firm partner in Hyderabad, 2011.
Interview 29 with law firm founding partner in Mumbai, 2011.
Interview 30 with law firm partner responsible for human resources and hiring in Mumbai, 2011.
Interview 32 with law firm cofounding partner in Mumbai, 2011.
Interview 33 with law firm senior partner in Mumbai, 2011.
Interview 34 with law firm founding partner in Bangalore, 2011.
Interview 35 with law firm founding partner in Bangalore, 2011.
Interview 36 with law firm director of human resources and senior associate in Mumbai, 2011.
Interview 37 with general counsel in Mumbai, 2011.
Interview 38 with law firm founding partner and partner in Bangalore, 2011.
Interview 40 with general counsel in Bangalore, 2011.
Interview 41 with RCC member, 2011.
Interview 42 with two RCC members, 2011.
Interview 43 with faculty member at an elite non-national law school, 2011.
Interviews 44–47 with former national law school RCC executive, 2011–2012.
Interview 45 with former national law school RCC executive, 2012.
Krishnan, Jayanth K. 2010. "Globetrotting Law Firms." *Georgetown Journal of Legal Ethics* 23 (1): 57–103.
Li, Xueyao and Sida Liu. 2012. "The Learning Process of Globalization: How Chinese Law Firms Survived the Financial Crisis." *Fordham Legal Review* 80 (6): 2847–2866.
McAdams, Richard H. 1997. "The Origin, Development and Regulation of Norms." *Michigan Law Review* 96 (2): 338–433.

McAdams, Richard H. and Eric B. Rasmusen. 2004. "Norms and the Law." In *Handbook of Law and Economics* 2, edited by A. Mitchell Polinsky and Steven Shavell, 1573.

Menon, N. R. Madhava. 2009. *Reflections on Legal and Judicial Education*. New Delhi: Universal Law Publishing Ltd.

NALP. 2012. What Is NALP?" www.nalp.org/whatisnalp.

NALP. 2010. "Principles and Standards for Law Placement and Recruitment Activities." www.nalp.org/fulltextofnalpprinciplesandstandards.

Posner, Eric A. 2002. *Law and Social Norms*. Cambridge: Harvard University Press.

Ribstein, Larry E. 2010. "The Death of Big Law." *Wisconsin Law Review* 2010 (3): 749–815.

RSG Consulting. 2013. "Top 40 Indian Law Firms." www.rsgconsulting.com/rsg-india.

Sayta, Jay. 2011a. "Easy Money for NLS Bangalore: 100% Jobs, Strong Domestic, Int'l Firm Interest." *Legally India*, June 2. www.legallyindia.com/201106022128/Law-schools/easy-money-for-nls-bangalore-100-jobs-strong-domestic-intl-firm-interest.

2011b. "Classical Recruitment Mix at GLC Mumbai with Bar, Solicitors, LLMs, 50 Desk Jobs." *Legally India*, June 7. www.legallyindia.com/201106072148/Law-schools/classical-recruitment-mix-at-glc-mumbai-with-bar-solicitors-llms-50-desk-jobs.

Schmitthener, A. Samuel. 1968–69. "A Sketch of the Development of the Legal Profession in India." *Law and Society Review* 3: 337.

Silver, Carole. 2011. "The Variable Value of U.S. Legal Education in the Global Legal Services Market." *Georgetown Journal of Legal Ethics* 24 (1): 1–57.

Terry, Laurel S., Steve Mark, and Tahlia Gordon. 2012. "Trends and Challenges in Lawyer Regulation: The Impact of Globalization and Technology." *Fordham Law Review* 80 (6): 2661–2684.

Venkatesan, J. 2011. "Jindal Law School Signs MoU with US Firm." *Hindu*, May 24. www.thehindu.com/todays-paper/tp-national/jindal-law-school-signs-mou-with-us-firm/article2043887.ece.

Wilkins, David B. and Mihaela Papa. 2015. "Globalization, Lawyers, and India: Toward a Theoretical Synthesis of Globalization Studies and the Sociology of the Legal Profession." *International Journal of the Legal Profession*. 18 (3):175–209.

Wilkins, David B. and G. Mitu Gulati. 1998. "Reconceiving the Tournament of Lawyers: Tracking, Seeding, and Information Control in the Internal Labor Markets of Elite Law Firms." *Virginia Law Review* 84 (8): 1581–1681.

18

The Making of Legal Elites and the IDIA of Justice

Shamnad Basheer, K. V. Krishnaprasad, Sree Mitra, and Prajna Mohapatra

I. INTRODUCTION

In his book *The Idea of Justice*, Amartya Sen acknowledges the futility of searching for a perfectly just world. However, he argues that, as human beings, we are often moved to remedy immediate injustices wherever we find them:

> It is fair to assume that the Parisians would not have stormed the Bastille, Gandhi would not have challenged the empire on which the sun used not to set, Martin Luther King would not have fought white supremacy in the "land of the free and the home of the brave," without their sense of manifest injustices that could be overcome. They were not trying to achieve a perfectly just world, but they did want to remove clear injustices to the extent that they could.
>
> (Sen 2009, vii)

The National Law Universities (NLUs), often perceived as premier institutions of legal education in India, routinely teach lofty ideals such as social justice and equality, yet have a serious issue of manifest injustice staring them right in the face.[1] The current student composition at many of these elite institutions is bereft of meaningful diversity, comprising students primarily from privileged backgrounds (Ballakrishnen 2009, 149). The numbers from low-income backgrounds, rural areas, small towns, and areas such as the North East and Kashmir are deplorably low.

A variety of factors have contributed to this phenomenon, including the extremely high fees charged by these institutions, a lamentable lack of awareness among low-income students about law as a career option, and a rigorous entrance examination (the Common Law Admission Test, or CLAT), for which expensive coaching has all but become a prerequisite.

It is imperative that all stakeholders in the legal ecosystem come together to foster access to legal education and enhance student diversity at the leading NLUs. The reasons are obvious enough. First, increasing access to legal education in favor of the underprivileged will empower such communities and the "capabilities" of such people (Sen 2009, 231). This will in turn foster social justice, one of the principal aims of most legal systems (Russell 2002, 1827).

Second, diversity is an important end in itself in that it enhances the educational experience of mainstream students and improves the quality of education overall (Orfield and Whitla 2001, 172). As Neil Rudenstine, former president of Harvard University, noted in the 1995 President's Report,

> [T]he range of undergraduate "interests, talents, backgrounds and career goals affects importantly the educational experience of our students" because "a diverse student body is an educational resource of coordinate importance with our faculty and our library, laboratory and housing arrangements.
> (Rudenstine 1996, 1357)

A diversity deficit effectively translates to an underrepresented legal system that excludes a large number of people and communities, particularly minority communities, whose interest it is purportedly meant to serve (Anderson 2009, 1016–1017). We posit that the diversity deficit at the NLUs will soon translate to a lack of diversity at the premier law firms, now the largest recruiters of NLU graduates.[2] Almost all these firms engage with corporate commercial transactions and have benefited significantly from globalization (Thacker 2011, 2).

The reputation of the NLUs has grown significantly due to the liberalization reforms of the 1990s and the subsequent need for high-quality corporate attorneys (Wilkins 2011). According to Wilkins, emerging economies such as India, China, and Brazil liberalized their economies in the 1990s, which led to the development of a "vibrant corporate sector" that in turn fueled the growth of a "vibrant corporate legal sector" (Wilkins 2011, 2). NLU graduates went on to fill this gap and became the top picks for leading law firms. The lack of student diversity at NLUs essentially means that a vast majority of underprivileged students will be denied access to premier law firms and the benefits of globalization.

This paper proposes ways of addressing this diversity deficit and fostering what is now coming to be labeled as "inclusive growth," a term that is used interchangeably with "broad-based growth," "pro-poor growth," and "shared growth" (Ianchovichina and Lundstrom 2009). This is a particularly important area of study for the Globalization, Lawyers, and Emerging Economies

(GLEE) project within the overall globalization and legal education framework, as many scholars criticize globalization for having had an exclusionary effect (Sainath 2004, 533; Goldberg and Pavcnik 2007, 52).

Part II of the paper reflects on the process of globalization and its ramifications on equitable access to resources, particularly in relation to legal education and the legal profession. In many ways, this part sets the tone for the rest of the paper. Part III discusses the issue of diversity and the need to enhance access to education in favor of marginalized communities. It then empirically establishes the lack of meaningful diversity (particularly income and geographical diversity) at the leading NLUs and explores the underlying reasons for that. Part III also examines the recruitment data from leading NLUs to determine if any student groups are consistently unable to gain access to the premier law firms. Part IV advocates solutions for fostering a more inclusive model of legal education and discusses one project – Increasing Diversity by Increasing Access (IDIA) – that is aimed at enhancing access. Part V reflects on earlier chapters and draws some broad conclusions.

Since this paper is part of the GLEE project to study globalization and the legal profession, our reflections on access and diversity concerns will be largely confined to this framework.

II. GLOBALIZATION AND EQUITABLE ACCESS

The term "globalization" subsumes within its fold several sets of distinct yet inextricably interconnected processes (Cole 2003, 325). For the large part, it involves a perceived "flattening of the world" and a consequential spread of human culture, artefacts, institutions, information, knowledge, and patterns of living across borders (Bagchi 1999, 3219; Friedman 2007, 6). Some argue that this has invariably led to a preference for certain kinds of institutions, modes of business, information, knowledge, and cultures over others (Bagchi 1999, 3219).

This conundrum has triggered a spirited debate about the inclusive nature of globalization and its impact on marginalized peoples and their access to resources (World Commission on the Social Dimensions of Globalization, 2004). While many scholars argue that a global market inherently increases the availability of resources to a large part of the world, several others point to the fact that the distribution of resources so engendered is inequitable, leading to a severe lack of access for a number of marginalized communities (Deacon 2000; Mandelson 2007).

Scholars also argue that globalization has not only increased the income gap between the global north and south but also contributed significantly toward accentuating income inequalities in even the most developed countries (Sala-i-Martin 2002; Mahler 2004, 1027). As Sen puts it:

> The central issue of contention is not globalization itself, nor is it the use of the market as an institution, but the inequity in the overall balance of institutional arrangements, which produces very unequal sharing of the benefits of globalization. The question is not just whether the poor, too, gain something from globalization, but whether they get a fair share and a fair opportunity. There is an urgent need for reforming institutional arrangements – in addition to national ones – in order to overcome both the errors of omission and those of commission that tend to give the poor across the world such limited opportunities. Globalization deserves a reasoned defense, but it also needs reform."
>
> (Sen 2002)

As one strives to resolve the complex conflicts posed by globalization, it is clear that the world is witnessing a far greater interconnectedness than known before. With a rapid escalation in the porosity of borders, activities in one part of the world have a far greater probability of impacting another. Therefore, any inequitable sharing of resources and consequent marginalization of communities is likely to have deleterious effects far beyond national borders housing these communities. Sen states, "The very existence of potentially large benefits makes the question of fairness in sharing the benefits of globalization so critically important" (Sen 2002).It is, therefore, critical that globalization work toward inclusive growth and an enhancement of overall being, rather than limiting the pie to a small set of beneficiaries.

Debates on globalization are also inextricably interwoven with concerns of diversity. While some argue that globalization poses no immediate threat to diversity and may even legitimately be expected to promote this value in the long run, others argue that globalization effectively leads to more uniformity in the world in that it endorses certain ways of living, cultures, and practices, and even of organizing and governing a profession (Kellner 2013; Guillén 2000, 17).

Against this backdrop, this paper seeks to critically analyze the implications of a "global market paradigm" on legal education and its effect on the development of India's corporate legal sector, and to advocate solutions to redress the various "access" issues that emerge (Cornia 2003, 1). As indicated in prior chapters, India's corporate legal sector has benefited significantly from a liberalized economy. Given that the elite national law schools constitute the main base for recruitment by elite law firms, the nature and composition of students at these law schools determines the nature of new entrants to elite law firms.

Unfortunately, the composition of students at the elite law schools suffers from a significant diversity deficit; the benefits of a globalized Indian law practice will therefore be limited to a miniscule proportion of India's highly diverse population.

In the next part of this paper, we discuss the need for inclusive education and diversity and then specifically highlight the various diversity deficits at the premier NLUs.

III. INDIAN LEGAL EDUCATION: ACCESS AND DIVERSITY CONCERNS

Law is often characterized as an instrument of power, with leading lawyers constituting an enviable ensemble of elites, relishing significantly high incomes and social standing (Erlanger 1980, 884; Garth 1987, 183–184). Those who gain entry to the upper echelons of the profession are able to access this powerful social and political corridor.

Given that the elite law schools operate as gatekeepers to the elite layers of the legal profession, enhanced educational opportunities in favor of the marginalized translates to inclusive growth and empowerment (Alvi et al. 1992, 176). Such access also advances equity, fairness, and social justice, lofty ideals routinely taught in law schools (Pratt 2006–2007, 78). As Pratt states, "Enhanced power sharing with people from subordinated groups helps to ensure that the power of the majority does not operate, even unintentionally, to effectuate tyranny upon those in a subordinate group" (ibid.).

In *Grutter v. Bollinger* (539 US 306, 332–33 [2003]), the US Supreme Court, while rejecting the challenge to the constitutional validity of the University of Michigan Law School's race-based affirmative action program, categorically noted that "access to legal education (and, thus, the legal profession) must be inclusive of talented and qualified individuals of every race and ethnicity, so that all members of our heterogeneous society may participate in the educational institutions that provide the training and education necessary to succeed in America."

The reasoning in *Grutter v. Bollinger* can be extrapolated to India as well, where access to legal education is likely to enhance the upward social mobility of those who are marginalized and underprivileged (Twining 1987, 202).[3] Whether one emphasizes individual opportunity or social equality or group representation or general welfare, increasing access is also desirable in that it rests on the notion that the disadvantaged are in no way inferior (ibid.).

Further, such access also fosters a well-rounded and positive "learning environment" (ibid.). In *Grutter v. Bollinger*, the court noted the significant "educational benefits" flowing from having a diverse student body: "[t]hese benefits are important and laudable, because classroom discussion is livelier, more spirited, and simply more enlightening and interesting when the students have the greatest possible variety of backgrounds" (*Grutter v. Bollinger* 2003, 331).

This advantage has been empirically borne out as well, where a survey at two major US law schools revealed that students exposed to diverse learning environments found their learning considerably enhanced (Orfield and Whitla 2001, 159). One expects a similar logic to apply to India, a country known for its wide range of diverse communities. India ranks as one of the most diverse democracies racially, culturally, linguistically, ethnically, and religiously (Swenden 2010).

A diverse student body has positive implications at an individual, societal, and institutional level. The individual benefits include "enhanced openness to diversity and challenge" and "enhanced critical thinking ability" (Milem and Hakuta 2000, 33). At a societal level, a diverse educational ecosystem leads to the development of an "educated and involved citizenry" and one of the main aims of higher education is the production of good citizens (Bowen and Bok 1998; Milem and Hakuta 2000, 20–23). At an institutional level, the benefits of diversity include the cultivation of a workforce with a higher level of "cross-cultural" competence, as well as the ability to widen the net and attract the best possible talent pool (Milem and Hakuta 2000, 33).

A diverse student body is one that is representative of a variety of different markers including socioeconomic status, race, caste, ethnicity, sexual orientation, religion, disability, etc. (Johnson 2011, 1566). Such representation ensures that the law school broadly reflects the composition of society at large (Twining 1987, 171). For want of time and space, our focus in this paper is limited to two significant markers for diversity, namely income level and caste.

A. *Diversity at the National Law Universities (NLUs)*

As with many other countries, the quality and reputation of an Indian law school has a significant bearing on one's employability at a leading law firm.[4] For some years, the NLUs have been hailed as sites of premier legal education in India. These autonomous institutions were largely conceptualized to offer a significant face-lift to law and legal education, until then one of the lowest-ranked preferences within the professional education basket.[5] The model essentially comprises an integrated five-year BA/LLB course, with students picked fresh out of high school through a highly competitive entrance examination and subjected to a rigorous academic schedule replete with long teaching hours, frequent exams, and innumerable writing assignments.

It was first piloted through the National Law School of India University (NLSIU)–Bangalore, an institution created under the National Law School of India University Act but purportedly "national" in character (The Times of India, 2011). The relative autonomy enjoyed as a result of its deemed university status, a rigorous examination filter similar to the Law School Admission Test (LSAT) – the standardized test designed to be an integral part of the law school admission process in the United States – and a committed teaching faculty ensured that it garnered success and reputation in no time.

But what prompted its meteoric rise in terms of public perception was the absorption of its new graduates into high-paying corporate jobs at law firms, which were rapidly proliferating in a newly globalized India.

Naturally, the model began to be replicated in other states, albeit with suitable adaptations. Thus, the National Academy of Legal Studies and Research (NALSAR)–Hyderabad, while retaining its national character, also provided for state-based reservations (domiciliary reservations); NLU–Jodhpur went beyond the traditional integrated social science and law degree (BA/LLB) by offering alternatives such as a science and law degree (BSc/LLB) and even a management and law degree (BBA/LLB).

Currently, there are eighteen national law schools, with sixteen being bound by a common entrance examination (called the CLAT). While one of them (NLU–Delhi) refuses to join the pack and conducts its own entrance examination (AILET), presumably due to the various legal skirmishes associated with the CLAT and its alleged misconduct year after year, the other (NLU–Mumbai) was established only this year and it may take a year or so before it joins the pack (Maharashtra National Law University 2015; Basheer 2015).

While the NLUs are critiqued frequently on various grounds, including their inability to generate quality research and scholarship, they continue to be widely perceived as the leading sites of legal learning. Indeed, around five years ago, the prime minister of India spoke of them in glowing terms as "a small number of dynamic and outstanding law schools," which "remain islands of excellence amidst a sea of institutionalized mediocrity" (Sunderajan 2010; Basheer 2012).

While there are other law schools that are of equal, if not better, quality than the NLUs, we restrict our analysis to the NLUs, given that it provides for a more focused set of premier institutions bound by their apparent "national" character, autonomous statuses, and a common entrance exam, namely the CLAT. Indeed, Professor Venkata Rao, the current vice chancellor of NLS–Bangalore, is known to quip that with the increasing pressure for statewide domiciliary reservations, the law schools should no longer be treated as "national" law schools but as "notional" law schools.

Unfortunately, these "islands of excellence" suffer from a severe lack of representation, particularly from low-income students and those from rural India (Han 2007, 206–207).[6] The result is that the current student composition at many of the leading NLUs lacks meaningful diversity, comprising students primarily from middle-class or upper-middle-class families. The numbers from low-income backgrounds and from areas of India such as the North East are deplorably low.

For example, only 4–5 percent of the candidates who were admitted to the West Bengal National University of Juridical Sciences (NUJS) in 2013 hailed from lower-middle-class families, i.e., families with an income of less than INR 1 lakhs (US$1,930) per annum (IDIA 2014). Contrast this with the fact that 50 percent of the students in that batch belonged to upper-middle-class families or higher, i.e., families with an income of more than INR 10 lakhs (US$19,300) per annum (IDIA 2014, 34). Apart from this, the composition also suffers from a severe lack of representation from marginalized parts of India such as the North East and Kashmir.[7]

We present here a summary of the surveys conducted at nine of the leading law schools (NLSIU–Bangalore, NALSAR–Hyderabad, NUJS–Kolkata, NLU–Delhi, NLU–Jodhpur, Dr. Ram Manohar Lohia National Law University–Lucknow, Chanakya National Law University–Patna, NLU–Odisha, and National University of Advanced Legal Studies–Kochi) in 2014 to highlight this diversity deficit.

- **Medium of instruction:** A vast majority of incoming students at the leading NLUs had studied in English medium schools, i.e., where the primary mode of instruction is in English. A mere 2.5 percent of students studied in vernacular medium schools prior to gaining admission to the NLUs (IDIA 2014, 46). India has twenty-eight states with around 1,652 spoken languages (Mallikarjun 2002). An English medium education suggests wealth and social status in India – often those studying in such schools are from richer families compared with those from vernacular medium schools (Faust and Nagar 2001; The Hindu, 2004).
- **Rural versus urban:** A mere 1–3 percent of students in the incoming batches did their schooling in rural areas (IDIA 2014, 50–86).
- **Geographical diversity:** The lack of geographical diversity is evident when one considers the domicile of incoming students. For example, while 8.22 percent of the students of the incoming batch of NLSIU (2013) belonged to the state of Karnataka, there was only one student each from Jammu, Kashmir, and Nagaland, and no students at all from Arunachal Pradesh, Assam, Manipur, Meghalaya, Mizoram, Sikkim, and Tripura

(IDIA 2014, 14–15).[8] The numbers are broadly similar for all other law schools.[9]

- **Family income:** The majority of students at the various NLUs hailed from upper-middle-class families (Saxena 2010).[10] Those from low-income families constituted a significantly low percentage. Only around 7 percent of NLU students surveyed hail from families with an annual income lower than INR$100,000 (US$1,628) per annum (IDIA 2014, 90).
- **Training for the CLAT:** As a clear indication that expensive training has become a prerequisite for doing well in the CLAT, more than 80 percent of all incoming students opted for CLAT coaching (IDIA 2014, 120). The main institutes engaged in CLAT training such as LST and IMS charge approximately INR$85,000 (US$1,300) per year of training. It bears noting that the average per capita income of an Indian is around INR$3,000 (US$46) per month (The Economic Times 2009).

We argue that the shocking diversity deficit at the NLUs will inevitably translate to a lack of diversity at the premier law firms, now the largest recruiters of NLU students. As discussed earlier, many of these law firms engage with corporate commercial lawyering and have benefited significantly from globalization (Thacker 2011).

B. *Recruitment Data at the NLUs*

In order to explore whether students belonging to marginalized communities were on the recruitment margins, we studied data pertaining to recruitment at some of the leading law firms in India: Amarchand & Mangaldas & Suresh A. Shroff & Company, AZB & Partners, Luthra & Luthra, Trilegal, and Khaitan & Company[11] We analyzed recruitment data for three batches (2010–12) at each of the three premier law schools under investigation (NLSIU, NALSAR, and NUJS). Here is a summary of our findings (IDIA 2013).

- The income factor did not play a significant role in recruitment. In other words, there was no significant difference between the proportion of recruited students hailing from higher-income groups (upper middle class) and those from lower-income groups (middle class to lower middle class). However, this could be because the current outgoing batches at the NLUs are far more diverse in income than the incoming batches.[12]
- The caste factor appears to bear an important nexus with recruitments. In each of the law schools that we studied, the percentage of students recruited from within the Scheduled Caste/Scheduled Tribe (hereafter

> SC/ST) community was significantly lower than the percentage of students recruited from the general category.[13] Illustratively, in the year 2010, of the ninety-two outgoing students from NUJS for whom we had data, none of the fourteen SC/ST candidates were recruited by the top law firms. Contrast this with the fact that of the remaining seventy-eight general candidates, a good 32 percent (twenty-five out of a total batch of ninety-two) were recruited (IDIA 2014).

Recruitment data for NLS students in 2010 reveals similar results. While eleven students out of sixty-two general students were recruited by top law firms, only one was recruited from among eighteen SC/ST students. In other words, while 17 percent of the students belonging to the general category were recruited, only 5.55 percent of the SC/ST students were recruited (ibid.).

Our empirical investigation did not extend to asking SC/ST candidates at the various law schools if corporate jobs at the top law firms were their first career choice. However, given that roughly three-fourths of graduating batches from NLUs typically prefer law firm jobs, we assumed that a large percentage of SC/ST candidates would have expressed this preference as well.

It would be wrong to infer from the data here that this low proportion of recruitment from within the SC/ST community reflects a hiring bias on the part of law firms. The more plausible explanation could be that academic performance measured in terms of cumulative grade point average (CGPA) plays a strong role in recruitments, with reserved categories tending to not perform as well as general category candidates.[14] The data from the 2012 outgoing batch of NUJS makes this clear:

- The average CGPA of students recruited from the 2012 batch of NUJS was 5.3 (out of a possible 7).
- The average CGPA of the entire batch was 4.35.
- The average CGPA of the fourteen SC/ST students who constituted the batch was 3.49.
- The average CGPA of the rest of the batch (excluding SC/STs) was 4.504.

The data here reveals that there is a difference of 1.014 (approximately one grade) between the average CGPA of the SC/ST students and the average CGPA of the rest of the class.[15]

A comparison of the income distribution shows that SC/ST candidates hail from a more modest economic background than their general category counterparts. For example, 85.7 percent of the SC/ST students in the 2011 batch of NUJS fell within the INR 1–5 lakhs (US$1,630–$8,140) income bracket (IDIA 2013). Contrast this with the fact that only 47 percent of the students from the general category fell within this income bracket (INR 1–5 lakhs) (ibid.).

C. *Conclusions From Data*

Our data suggests that students from reserved categories are not recruited as frequently as others. This may not relate to hiring policies but could stem from the students' relatively poor academic performance. We, therefore, argue that it is imperative that such underprivileged sections are provided additional support within law schools to help them blossom to their full academic potential. Indeed, in *Avinash Singh Bagri & Ors. v. Registrar IIT*, the Supreme Court espoused the need to provide additional support to students admitted via reservation. The Court wrote, "[t]hese socially and economically backward categories are to be taken care of at every stage even in the specialized institutions like IITs. They must take all endeavours by providing additional coaching and bring them up at par with general category students" (*Avinash Singh Bagri & Ors. v. Registrar IIT* 2009).

Although the data does not suggest any disadvantage experienced by those from low-income families, we argue that this could be attributed to the fact that the earlier batches comprised students with wider income diversity than the newer batches. We also suggest some caution in relying upon the income figures of the older batches, as it is plausible that some of the income declarations may have been deliberately lowered in a bid to inter alia attract available scholarships and lower fee slabs at the NLUs.[16]

Since the incoming batches at NLUs appear to be leaning more toward the higher-income brackets, it can be expected that over time, the entrants to the premier law firms will also comprise this limited percentage of the Indian population, resulting in an exclusion of a vast majority of India's poorer sections.

We, therefore, argue that it is imperative that steps be taken to diversify the student intake at the NLUs and thereby foster a more plural representation at the law firms. We reiterate that the data does not appropriately capture actual career choices but assumes that a vast majority of students are likely to prefer jobs at elite law firms.

Lastly, a note of caution: our analysis should not be taken to suggest an implied preference for jobs at elite law firms but to acknowledge that the underprivileged have as much of a right to access premier law firms as the rest of India does (Wilkins 1993, 1981; Wilkins 1998, 1).

V. THE BUSINESS CASE FOR DIVERSITY?

Given the causal interconnection between elite law schools and elite law firms, with the schools effectively acting as labor pools for these firms, it is only a matter of time before the deplorable diversity deficit at law schools spills over to the premier law firms (Shin et al. 2014).

While advocacy for enhanced diversity and access are essentially driven by ideals of social justice such as inclusion and fairness, some argue that there is an equally persuasive "business" case for diversity within law firms (Herring 2009, 208; United Kingdom Government Equalities Office 2013.). This view is predicated on several purported advantages, many of them having found resonance in judicial decisions and court filings. A significant example is Justice Powell's opinion in *Regents of the University of California v. Bakke*, a case involving a constitutional challenge to the University of California Medical School's "special admissions program," where sixteen out of one hundred seats in a class were reserved for "disadvantaged minority students" (*Regents of the University of California v. Bakke* 438 US 265 [1978]). The key issue was whether or not the classification under challenge was necessary to further a legitimate state interest. Relying on Justice Brennan's opinion in *Keyishian v. Board of Regents*, Justice Powell remarked:

> Our Nation is deeply committed to safeguarding academic freedom which is of transcendent value to all of us and not merely to the teachers concerned. That freedom is therefore a special concern of the First Amendment.... *The Nation's future depends upon* leaders trained through wide exposure to that robust exchange of ideas which discovers truth "out of a multitude of tongues, [rather] than through any kind of authoritative selection."
>
> (*Keyishian v. Board of Regents* 385 US 589; emphasis added)

The court went on to hold that medical professionals cater to the needs of a heterogeneous population and that diversity (ethnic, geographic, and cultural) was essential to "equip [the defendants] graduates to render with understanding their vital service to humanity." This reasoning is equally applicable to lawyers and legal education.

More than half a century later, Justice Powell's reasoning formed the cornerstone of an amicus brief filed by sixty-five leading American business corporations before the US Supreme Court in *Grutter v. Bollinger*. This brief essentially affirmed the "business case for diversity," noting:

> The existence of racial and ethnic diversity in institutions of higher education is vital to amici's efforts to hire and maintain a diverse workforce, and to employ individuals of all backgrounds who have been educated and trained

> in a diverse environment. As explained in this brief, such a workforce is important to amici's continued success in the global marketplace."
>
> (Curiae 65 Leading American Businesses in Support of Respondents in *Grutter v. Bollinger* 2003)[17]

The amici buttressed their business case for diversity on four main counts. First, a diverse workforce enabled a multinational business enterprise to develop unique and creative approaches to problem solving. Second, a diverse working culture equipped companies to develop products and services that appealed to a wider cross section of consumers. Third, a racially diverse group of managers was better able to work with business partners, employees, and clientele in the United States and around the world. Finally, individuals educated in a diverse setting were more likely to contribute to a positive work environment by decreasing incidents of discrimination and stereotyping.

In *Grutter v. Bollinger*, General Motors Corporation filed a separate amicus brief that mirrored many of these submissions. Relying on the RAND Report, General Motors suggested that "[c]rosscultural competence is the most important new attribute for future effective performance in a global marketplace" (Bikson and Law 1994). They went to argue that:

> In General Motors' experience, only a well educated, diverse workforce, comprising people who have learned to work productively and creatively with individuals from a multitude of races and ethnic, religious, and cultural backgrounds, can maintain America's competitiveness in the increasingly diverse and interconnected world economy.
>
> (Bikson and Law 1994)

They also note that markers of diversity such as race and ethnicity are powerful factors that may help shape an individual's own unique perspective. This drew support from General Motor's more radical suggestion that the mere fact of being a member of a racial or ethnic minority in this society – standing alone – is itself an experience that creates unique perspectives (Wilkins 2004).

It is not clear if the purported advantages touted here apply on all fours to the "globalized" legal profession in India. That could well be the subject matter of another paper. Further, the business case for diversity is not without its fair share of critique; a study of the relationship between diversity on corporate boards and economic performance of companies failed to reveal any conclusive correlation (Joy et al. 2007; Fairfax 2011, 856).

However, for the purposes of our paper, we do not intend to conclusively establish the business case of diversity. We simply point to it and note that since law and legal education is about social justice, the case for diversity and inclusion is better predicated on these considerations than a business one.

VI. IDIA: A FEASIBLE IDEA FOR BRIDGING THE ACCESS AND DIVERSITY DEFICIT?

As argued earlier, given that Indian corporate law firms have benefited significantly from a globalized economy, it will be a sheer travesty of justice if only a miniscule portion of India is able to participate and partake in the ensuing benefits (Choy 2007, 1). Some of the authors of this paper are involved in a project to enhance access to legal education for the underprivileged. We discuss the broad features of this project and argue that, though currently modest in terms of scale and impact, it might constitute one way to redress the access impasse.

IDIA was conceptualized as a student-run project in early 2010 to empower underprivileged communities through legal education. Specifically, teams of volunteers (mainly law students) spread across the length and breadth of India would reach out to marginalized and underrepresented groups, sensitize them to law as a career option, and help those interested to secure admission to the premier law schools.

IDIA was premised on the notion that access to legal education empowers underprivileged communities by granting them access to law, a powerful instrument of social change. Further, given the nexus between advocacy and leadership, access to a premier legal education helps create a potent pool of community leaders for the future (Rhode 2010, 413; Sturm 2013, 49). Indian history bears out this sentiment rather well, with a significant number of freedom fighters such as M. K. Gandhi and Jawaharlal Nehru qualifying as lawyers and using their advocacy skills to battle the British. More importantly, B. R. Ambedkar, born into a very poor Dalit family, went on to study at the prestigious Columbia law school and played a critical role in the drafting of India's Constitution, widely acknowledged as one of the most progressive constitutions around the world (Maitra 2012, 301–20).

In its statement of objectives, IDIA notes on its public website that "it is hoped that access to legal education would go some way towards empowering the marginalized and underprivileged students and the communities that they represent... (and) ... ensure that these communities can directly deploy this instrument of power called 'law' to improve their lot and contribute towards the creation of a more just and fair society. Secondly, a diverse student population would make for a more optimal mix of views and perspectives at such law schools, thereby enriching the process of education itself." The statement of objectives also notes that enhanced diversity would, in the long run, translate to diversity within the upper echelons of the legal profession as well.

In order to avoid the various bureaucratic bottlenecks associated with NLUs, IDIA was modeled as a voluntary student-run movement, with law students from across the country constituting the backbone of the project. The idea was also to help sensitize privileged sections of Indian law students (who constituted the large majority of the student population at the NLUs) to the glaring social inequities plaguing Indian society and to encourage them to play some role in helping to bridge it through IDIA.

The project has now been institutionally moored as a trust, with an advisory board comprising an eclectic array of legal luminaries.[18] The project was first piloted in Pelling, a tiny town in the Himalayan state of Sikkim, where the following steps were taken:

- **Sensitization:** Students (along with their parents and teachers) were sensitized to the prospects of a premier legal education and a career in law. Typically, from a mere two students who expressed some interest in law out of a class of one hundred, the number rose to fifty at the end of the sensitization program.
- **Aptitude test:** A test was conducted to select students with some aptitude for the study of law. The test was a simplified version of the CLAT and aimed at largely testing one's logical reasoning prowess.
- **Selection:** The most promising candidates were selected, based on their aptitude for the study of law, their underprivileged status (the key identifier being that of income), and a round of interviews with their schoolteachers and parents to ensure that they would support this career choice.[19]
- **Internet access:** Free Internet access was provided to selected students (IDIA scholars) through an arrangement with local cybercafes to foster online CLAT training. Scholars with IT proficiency were encouraged to train other scholars. The most dynamic scholar in the group was selected as the group leader to keep the group motivated and to liaise with the IDIA training team. The attempt was to foster a self-organized learning environment (Mitra 2013).[20]
- **Training:** The scholars were then trained on a regular basis for the CLAT and All India Law Entrance Test (AILET) by IDIA student volunteers as well as two of the leading CLAT training centers, LST and IMS, which agreed to provide materials and train IDIA scholars free of cost.[21] The CLAT is currently one of the biggest "access" bottlenecks, given that it requires a high level of proficiency in the English language. Typically, the brightest students from underprivileged backgrounds have relatively weak English language skills compared with their more privileged counterparts

in the urban areas. Therefore, an intensive English training session was provided to the scholars.

This pilot was then replicated in twenty Indian states including Karnataka, Rajasthan, Gujarat, Kerala, Mizoram, Bihar, Jammu, and Kashmir. Within five years of its inception, IDIA volunteers visited more than 250 schools, spoke on the wonders of the legal profession to more than 15,000 students, and picked about 200 students who demonstrated some aptitude for the study of law. These students were then put through a rigorous training program after which they wrote the leading law entrance exams, namely the CLAT and the AILET. Of these students, fifty-four gained admission to the NLUs and twenty-five to various other law schools.

These scholars hailed from low-income families, with parental professions ranging from stone quarry workers and farmers to clerks and daily wage laborers. Apart from economic disadvantage, many were less privileged in other respects, too. Nineteen scholars were differently able (visually impaired), sixteen were women ("girl children"), thirteen were from the Scheduled Caste category, and nine were from the Scheduled Tribe category (Heyer and Jayal 2009, 4).[22] There was significant geographical diversity as well, with scholars hailing from places such as the Sundarbans in West Bengal; Gudemaranahalli in Karnataka; Machhilipatnam, Kurnool, and Nellore in Andhra Pradesh; Raebareli in Uttar Pradesh; Phagwara in Punjab; Barmer in Rajasthan; Pitij in Jharkhand; Chhinga Veng in Mizoram; Kollam in Kerala; and L. Gamnom in Manipur.

Given that the ultimate end was to create outstanding lawyers and community leaders, once the IDIA scholar gained admission to an NLU, the following additional steps were taken:

- **Scholarships and financing:** As a first step, IDIA appealed to the various NLUs to grant scholarships and/or fee waivers or reductions to the IDIA scholars who gained admission. Some law schools (NLSIU, NUJS, and NLU–Delhi) agreed to a full fee waiver, and others to a partial waiver (NLU–Orissa). But a vast majority of NLUs simply refused to offer any financial assistance. IDIA began raising funds from individual and institutional donors. Some of the contributing donors include partners at premier law firms around the country including AZB, Luthra & Luthra, Jyoti Sagar Associates, Khaitan & Company, Wadia Ghandy & Company, and Trilegal.
- **Mentorship:** IDIA scholars were allotted multiple mentors comprising at least one senior law school student, one lawyer, and one faculty member. The school and faculty mentors ensured that the scholars were able to

navigate law school life both academically and socially. Given that the present-day compositions of the law schools consist mainly of the urban rich, students from a different background often face "fitting in" problems. The mentors from within the legal profession would, apart from counseling the scholars from time to time, also help them access a wide array of internships to maximize the scholars' chances of employment upon graduation. In late 2012, IDIA entered into a collaborative arrangement with the legal team at General Electric (India), wherein several members of the legal team have begun to act as mentors for the various IDIA scholars.[23]

- **Soft skills/resilience:** Given their vastly different backgrounds, IDIA scholars often face social isolation and some level of discrimination at NLU campuses. In a telling incident, when the IDIA movement was gaining a fair amount of momentum within the law schools, one student attempted to dissuade another from joining the IDIA team by stating that "*yeh dehati logon ko laake law school ka standard kharab kar denge*." This derogatory remark translates to "Such villagers, if allowed to enter law school, would degrade our fine standards."

Instances of social isolation and discrimination have been captured in the diversity surveys undertaken by the IDIA Research and Policy (RAP) wing year after year. According to a survey conducted by IDIA in 2014, among 768 students of incoming batches across nine NLUs (including NLSIU, NALSAR, and NUJS), nearly 30 percent of the students faced a "fitting in" problem in law school owing to, as some of the student respondents admit, their social, cultural, or economic background (IDIA 2014). Further, 12.85 percent of the students found it difficult to communicate effectively with their peers, while 12.76 percent faced harassment and ridicule on account of their background (IDIA 2014, 187–89, 197). Such accounts of marginalization within NLUs and subtle discrimination impact the confidence of these students and their ability to participate meaningfully in university activities and blossom to their full potential.

The mentorship program detailed here aims at addressing this issue to some extent. IDIA now plans to impart strategically designed training programs to enhance the soft skills (well-spoken English) and resilience of its scholars so that they can, to some extent, withstand a hostile, isolationist, and discriminatory outside environment.

- **Leadership skills:** IDIA's overarching goal is to facilitate the evolution of leaders from within marginalized sections of society. Indeed, as noted earlier, the nexus between legal training and leadership is a significant one with a number of political leaders and thinkers having trained in the law. To this end, special leadership training programs and techniques would be imparted to IDIA scholars from time to time. More significantly, during the course of their law studies, the scholars, along with other interested law students, faculty, and legal professionals, would visit the locales of the scholars, identify specific problems faced by their communities, and examine the extent to which law could help resolve some of those issues. Apart from imparting valuable skills training to IDIA scholars, such an approach sensitizes them to the power of the law in redressing a wide range of issues and trains them to assume leadership positions. IDIA does not, at any stage, interfere with their career choices (other than facilitating them through career counseling to make the most appropriate choice) but continually impresses upon them that whatever career path they choose, they must have an eye toward the well-being of their community in some way. As an example, consider the case of B. R. Ambedkar, a young man from an extremely poor Dalit (a designation for a group of people traditionally regarded as untouchables) family in rural Gujarat, who was picked up by a Jesuit priest, who trained him and facilitated his admission to NLSIU–Bangalore many years ago (Webster 1999; Heyer and Jayal 2009). Ambedkar went on to earn his master's degree in law (LLM) at the prestigious Columbia University and is now a solicitor with a leading London firm. Recently, he began building a crematorium for the lower-caste community (Dalits) in his little village, as the upper-caste communities (Patels) refused to let them use the main crematorium in the locality. One should note that his experience is not a one-off incident. Recently, a group of Dalits staged a public protest because upper-caste Hindus were preventing them from cremating their bodies anywhere in the village (The Hindu 2014).

Scholars will not be forced to assume community leadership roles or engage with their community if they do not wish to do this with their future. IDIA will counsel and guide scholars in making this decision while formulating programs and processes that would effectively "nudge" them toward more of a community engagement and possibly a leadership role. In the context of IDIA, it is expected that by fostering community development programs involving IDIA scholars in a central role, they would be persuaded to take community leadership roles.[24]

- **Internships:** Internships are extremely valuable for law students, not just for skills training but also for maximizing employment opportunities. IDIA therefore seeks to facilitate a wide range of good internships for

IDIA scholars through their tenure at law schools. To this end, IDIA has entered into informal arrangements with a number of law firms, corporate outfits, policy think tanks, and NGOs that have promised to accommodate IDIA scholars in their internship programs, wherever feasible. Law firms including AZB & Partners, J. Sagar Associates, Wadia Ghandy & Company, and Tatva Legal (which provide considerable legal assistance to the IDIA trust), and corporations such as General Electric (India) and DuPont, have agreed to offer internship opportunities to IDIA scholars.

- **Diversity-friendly ecosystem:** Since its inception, IDIA has advocated for a more diversity-friendly ecosystem. This is the most challenging task, particularly in relation to candidates with disabilities. A significant amount of advocacy work in this regard is undertaken through IDIA's RAP team. This team has inter alia helped challenge arbitrary eligibility criteria at the NLUs and advocated for a fairer testing framework through CLAT – one that does not disadvantage socially and economically disadvantaged sections of society (Basheer et al. n.d.).[25] RAP has also advocated for a disabled-friendly entrance examination and made representations before the CLAT Committee highlighting the disadvantages faced by students with disability (Shrivastava 2013; Basheer 2010).
- Without the measures mentioned here, the mere entry of underprivileged sections to the law schools would have come to naught. As the data on recruitment demonstrates, candidates from SC/ST backgrounds may require additional academic and other support (such as training to enhance proficiency in English, IT, and soft skills) in order to enhance their academic performance and future job prospects. The Supreme Court weighed on this issue several years ago and severely castigated the Indian Institutes of Technology (IITs) for deploying affirmative action at the entry level but not doing much thereafter to ensure that candidates from the reserved classes received appropriate academic support (*Avinash Singh Bagri & Ors. v. Registrar IIT* 2009). The IITs are premier institutes of technical and scientific education in India that provide admission to students through a competitive joint entrance examination, i.e., the IIT-JEE.

One swallow of an IDIA project does not an "access" summer make. To achieve a significant enhancement in access and diversity, the measures described in this paper need to be replicated on a much larger scale and for a significantly longer term. As noted earlier, IDIA trains around forty to fifty underprivileged students each year, and approximately fifteen make it to the law schools annually. Although this is a small number from a quantitative perspective, it is fairly significant from a qualitative perspective, i.e., in terms of the potential for each of these students entering the club of legal elites to make a future impact on their communities and the wider ecosystem. However, these numbers need to be scaled up.

To this end, IDIA recently began expanding its reach beyond the NLUs (i.e., there are more than one thousand institutions imparting legal education in the form of universities, government colleges, and private colleges). IDIA scholars who did not make it to the NLUs were encouraged to apply to the traditional universities (such as Calcutta University and GLC), where the quality of teaching and infrastructure were relatively poor compared with the leading NLUs. IDIA supported them by supplementing their teaching and training (i.e., scholars were tutored and mentored by IDIA volunteers and high-quality legal learning materials were made available to them). Further, IDIA is committed to arranging good internships for them that maximize their clinical learning and job opportunities when they graduate. In the near future, IDIA plans to create a wider impact and reach out to a far greater number of underprivileged students by leveraging the SOLE framework that relies on greater technology deployment and less human intervention (Mitra et al. 2004).

VII. CONCLUSION

Given that the premier legal institutions (mainly comprising the leading NLUs) suffer from a severe access and diversity deficit, it is imperative that measures be taken to promote access to marginalized students.

Apart from empowering underprivileged communities, such access also promotes diversity, an important end in itself in that it enhances the educational experience of mainstream students and the quality of education overall.

We posit that the sheer lack of student diversity in the current batches of the NLUs will soon translate to a lack of diversity within the premier law firms, many of which engage with corporate commercial lawyering and have benefited significantly from globalization. Unless we mend the composition at the law schools, a similar homogeneity will pervade elite law firms as well, with the result that only a minute percentage of India's diverse population will benefit from a globalized legal profession.

The current recruitment data from the leading NLUs suggests that underprivileged students from reserved categories (SC/ST) are able to access only a miniscule portion of the recruitment pie. However, this appears to stem more from their low academic grades than any hiring bias. Therefore, it is incumbent on law schools to immediately create support programs to cater to students on the fringes and help them cope with the curriculum and blossom to their full potential.

We outline a project, IDIA, which seeks to redress the inclusion impasse in a modest manner by helping underprivileged children gain admission to the leading law schools. Law school admission is merely the first step; the more challenging work is to guide and mentor these underprivileged students and create a new cadre of outstanding lawyers and social leaders.

The intake of more underprivileged scholars will translate to greater diversity at the elite law schools and later at the premier law firms, promoting social justice in the long run. However, in terms of its current scale of operations, IDIA leaves much to be desired. If we are serious about making the elite law schools and the elite legal profession more representative and just, one project is hardly enough; much more needs to be done by all stakeholders, including the legal profession, the law schools, and the government.

Notes

1 Beginning with the creation of the National Law School of India University in Bangalore in 1988, the country boasts around eighteen NLUs today in various states of India. These deemed universities, which focus only on law, were created to offer a face-lift to legal education and make it a more attractive professional course.

2 Recent recruitment trends in the top five NLUs indicate that almost 70% of the graduates opt for corporate jobs in national/international law firms and legal departments of corporate houses (Bar and Bench 2011).

3 In a more recent case involving race-based admissions at the University of Texas, Austin, the Supreme Court was called upon to effectively re-examine the ruling in *Grutter v. Bollinger*. The court directed that the case involving summary judgment in favor of the university be sent back to the Fifth Circuit US Court of Appeals for reconsideration to assess whether the university provided sufficient evidence to prove that its admissions policies are narrowly tailored to obtain the educational benefits of diversity (*Fisher v. University of Texas* 2012).

4 The case might, however, be different for those opting to become litigators. Our interviews with leading litigators reveal that there is no significant hiring preference in favor of national law school graduates. In fact, some remarked that NLU graduates might turn out to be a liability, given that they have been "spoilt" by high salaries offered by law firms and often expect red carpet treatment. Further, and more importantly, the number of students from the NLUs entering litigation is abysmally low (Bar and Bench 2011).

5 The "authorship" of the national law school model remains contested, with several legal luminaries, past and present, asserting their prime role in its creation. It would perhaps be fair to suggest that it was a joint effort, where a number of legal luminaries, including institutions such as the Bar Council of India (BCI), helped conceptualize and implement the idea. The broad genesis of the idea could be traced back to the Gajendragadkar Committee, which noted: [I]t would perhaps

be a good idea if three or four model National Law Schools are instituted in our country....These National Law Schools... would be able to attract eminent law teachers who believe in the significance and importance of reorienting legal education in India and who would be prepared to dedicate themselves to that task.... [Also,] these National Law Schools would enjoy more freedom of action in trying newer and newer experiments in improving legal education."

6 The tuition fees alone at most of the NLUs are between 1.5 and 2.5 lakhs a year (US$2,419–$4,032). Adding the other costs, including living expenses, books, travel, etc., the average cost per year for a law student works out to approximately INR 3–3.5 lakhs (US$4,839–$5,364) a year; or INR 15–17.5 lakhs (US$22,989–$26,820) for a five-year law education (Shrivastava 2015).

7 The eight states that comprise North East India are Arunachal Pradesh, Assam, Manipur, Meghalaya, Mizoram, Nagaland, Sikkim, and Tripura. These eight states and Kashmir had no representation among the eighty-two students who joined NUJS in 2013 and participated in this survey (IDIA 2014).

8 While one might argue that the large number of students from Karnataka may be explained by the fact that the college itself is based in Karnataka (and a larger number of Karnataka's students preferring NLSIU over other law schools), it bears noting that since NLSIU–Bangalore is widely acknowledged to be the top law school in the country and rates as the top CLAT preference for the vast majority of students appearing for the CLAT, the competition for seats is pan-Indian, and there is no university admission preference for state students.

9 In the nine NLUs surveyed, out of the 768 students admitted in 2013 who participated in the survey, only 3 were from Jammu and Kashmir, 4 from Assam, 1 each from Meghalaya and Nagaland, and none from Arunachal Pradesh, Manipur, Mizoram, Sikkim, and Tripura (IDIA 2014, 28–31).

10 Much in line with what appears to be a widely accepted notion, we define "upper middle class" as having an earning capacity of INR 5–10 lakhs (US$6,140–$16,280) (Ram-Prasad 2007; Live Mint 2011).

11 These law firms were selected because they qualify as some of the largest recruiters of NLU graduates in recent years. In the 2010–2011 financial year, Amarchand Mangaldas, Luthra & Luthra, Khaitan & Company, and Trilegal together hired at least 144 students across national law schools, which is more than the next largest 22 firms put together, which hired fewer than 100 students across 14 colleges (Ganz 2012).

12 According to IDIA surveys in the three outgoing batches of NLSIU (2010, 2011, and 2012), 76.83% of the students belonged to the INR 1–10 lakhs (US$1,630–$16,280) income bracket. The figure was 69.35% for NALSAR and 82.47% for NUJS. Furthermore, the majority of the students on average belonged to the INR 1–5 lakhs (US$1,630–$8,140) income bracket (46.76% for NLSIU, 43.77% for NALSAR, and 56.37% for NUJS). Contrast this with the figures for the incoming batch of 2011 where, according to the data available, the maximum number of students in NLSIU and NUJS, on average, belonged to the INR 15 lakhs (US$24,420) per annum income bracket.

13 "Scheduled Caste" is the official term for a group of people widely considered to be the lowest in caste system hierarchy in India, with a history of having been treated as "untouchables." "Scheduled Tribe" is the official term for tribal populations, widely

considered to have been outside mainstream society in India for a long time. Under Article 15(4) of the Constitution of India, special provision for the advancement of SC/STs and any other socially and educationally backward classes may be made. Further, Article 16(4) permits the granting of reservation for appointments or posts to any backward class of citizens that, in the opinion of the state, is not adequately represented in the services under the state. The "general" category is used in university/college admissions to denote students who do not fall within any of the reserved categories such as Scheduled Caste and Scheduled Tribe.

14 CGPA stands for cumulative grade point average. It is calculated by assigning a particular number to the grade scored by a student in a certain course and then calculating the average of all the scores of the student in all courses throughout the BA/LLB (Hons.) program. CGPA is calculated out of a total of 7 at NLSIU and NUJS, while it is calculated out of 8 at NALSAR.

15 At the time of recruitment, the average CGPA of those who were recruited was 5.2976 (out of a possible 7). Therefore, there was a difference of 1.8076 grade points between the average CGPAs of the group of students recruited by the top firms and the SC/ST students in the batch (IDIA 2013).

16 Some of the law schools that based tuition fees on income levels discontinued this practice and have begun charging a uniform fee for all students.

17 For a critique of this position, see Sung Hui Kim's "The Diversity Double Standard" (Kim 2011). Labeling it as a "double diversity standard," she points out that the amici effectively draw a distinction between "corporate diversity" and "educational diversity." In so far as the former is concerned, they advocate diversity only to the extent that it helps them and their bottom line (self-interest). However, in the context of educational diversity, which was the central concern in *Grutter v. Bollinger*, diversity is advocated regardless of whether or not that attitude is in the interests of the educational institution in question.

18 A list of trustees and advisors can be found on the IDIA website.

19 In large parts of India, particularly in small towns and villages, the legal profession suffers a severe perception issue, with lawyers being seen as unscrupulous agents out to make a fast buck. A number of Bollywood flicks have only added to this distasteful imagery. Therefore, for a number of parents and teachers, law is often relegated as the last possible choice in the career arsenal of a student. To this day, parents and teachers in various parts of India harbor an undue bias in favor of engineering and medicine degrees. Although law and legal education have benefited from a significant face-lift in the last two decades or so, the perception issue still plagues large parts of India, particularly villages, small towns, and underprivileged communities (Basheer 2011).

20 "SOLE" is a term coined by Professor Sugata Mitra, who conducted a "hole in the wall" experiment to demonstrate that children without any prior knowledge of computers could teach themselves the basics of how to use one through their own experimentation (Mitra et al. 2004; Mitra 2013).

21 The AILET is the entrance exam conducted by NLU–Delhi for admission to its BA/LLB (Hons.), LLM, and PhD degree programs. This exam is separate and distinct from the CLAT.

22 In various parts of India, particularly rural areas and small towns, girl children are severely disadvantaged and even discriminated against (Patel 2007, 149).

23 Shrivastava notes that the GE team assists in strategizing sensitization programs and mentoring scholars. Members from GE's legal team have accompanied IDIA volunteers for outreach activities such as sensitization programs (Shrivastava 2013).

24 "Nudge," a term credited to Richard Thaler and Cass Sunstein, is defined by them as "any aspect of the choice architecture that alters people's behavior in a predictable way without forbidding any options or significantly changing their economic incentives" (Thaler and Sunstein 2008, 6).

25 In 2012, Donnie Ashok, an IDIA scholar, was denied admission to Gujarat National Law University (GNLU) based on an alleged eligibility condition in the university brochure stipulating that candidates who failed to clear their Class 12 examination in the first shot would be denied admission, despite making the cut on the CLAT score. The RAP wing of IDIA assisted Ashok in filing a writ petition before the Gujarat High Court alleging that this brochure condition contravened GNLU's own charter and was also arbitrary and violated the equality clause in the Constitution of India. The writ petition was disposed off after Ashok was given admission through an amicable settlement with GNLU.

References

Alvi, Tariq, Rose Boyko, Lilian Ma, Wade MacLauchlan, Trish Monture, Yvonne Peters, and Joanne St. Lewis. 1992. "Equality in Legal Education: Sharing a Vision, Creating the Pathways." *Queen's Law Journal* 17 (1): 176–214.

Anderson, Michelle J. 2009. "Legal Education Reforms, Diversity and Access to Justice." *Rutgers Law Review* 61 (4): 1016–1017.

Avinash Singh Bagri & Ors. v. Registrar IIT. 2009. Delhi, 8 SCC 220.

Bagchi, Amiya Kumar. 1999. "Globalisation, Liberation and Vulnerability: India and Third World." *Economic and Political Weekly* 34: 3219.

Ballakrishnen, Swethaa. 2009. "Where did we come from? Where do we go?: An enquiry into the students and systems of legal education in India." *Journal Of Commonwealth Law And Legal Education* 7 (2): 133–154.

Basheer, Shamnad. 2010. "Raising the Bar." *The Indian Express*, April 28. www.indianexpress.com/news/raising-the-bar/612296/.

2011. "The Lure of the Law." *India Today*, December 28. indiatoday.intoday.in/story/career-law-advocacy-skills-national-law-school-of-india-university/1/166227.html.

2012. "Set the Bar Higher." *The Indian Express*, May 10. www.indianexpress.com/news/set-the-bar-higher/947349/0.

2015. "An Extra-Legal League of Extraordinary Gentlemen." *The Wire*, June 25. www.thewire.in/2015/06/25/an-extra-legal-league-of-extraordinary-gentlemen-4758.

Basheer, Shamnad, Shambo Nandy, and Debanshu Khettry. n.d. "CLAT Policy Note: A Proposal by IDIA." Accessed August 20, 2015. www.idialaw.com/wp-content/uploads/2013/09/CLAT-Policy-Note.docx.

Bikson, T. K. and S. A. Law. 1994. *Rand Report on Global Preparedness and Human Resources: College and Corporate Perspectives*.www.rand.org/content/dam/rand/pubs/monograph_reports/2005/RAND_MR326.pdf.

Bowen, W. G. and D. Bok. 1998. *The Shape of the River: Long-Term Consequences of Considering Race in College and University Admissions*. Princeton: Princeton University Press.

Brief for Amici Curiae 65 Leading American Businesses in Support of Respondents in *Grutter v. Bollinger.* 2003. www.vpcomm.umich.edu/admissions/legal/gru_amicus-ussc/um/Fortune500-both.pdf.

Choy, William K. W. 2007. "Globalisation and Workforce Diversity: HRM Implications for Multinational Corporations in Singapore." *Singapore Management Review* 29 (2): 1–19.

Cole, Ken. 2003. "Globalisation: Understanding Complexity." *Progress in Development Studies* 3 (4): 323–338.

Cornia, Giovanni Andrea. 2003. "The Impact of Liberalisation and Globalisation on Income Inequality in Developing and Transitional Economies." CESIFO Working Paper no. 843, January. www.papers.ssrn.com/sol3/papers.cfm?abstract_id=380347.

"Dalits Prevented from Cremating Body in Mandya." 2014. *The Hindu,* February 14. www.thehindu.com/news/national/karnataka/dalits-prevented-from-cremating-body/article5685846.ece.

Deacon, Bob. 2000. "Globalization and Social Policy: The Threat to Equitable Welfare" (occasional paper no. 5, United Nations Research Institute for Social Development, Geneva).

The Economic Times. 2009. "Monthly Income of Average Indian Crosses Rs 3,000: CSO." May 29. www.articles.economictimes.indiatimes.com/2009–05–29/news/28401681_1_capita-income-monthly-income-national-income.

Erlanger, Howard S. 1980. "The Allocation of Status within Occupations: The Case of the Legal Profession." *Social Forces* 58 (3): 882–903.

Fairfax, Lisa M. 2011. "Board Diversity Revisited: New Rationale, Same Old Story." *North Carolina Law Review* 89 (3): 853–886.

Faust, David, and Richa Nagar. 2001. "English-Medium Education and Social Fracturing." *Economic and Political Weekly* 36 (30): 2878–2883.

Fisher v. University of Texas, Austin. 2012. No. 11–345.

Friedman, Thomas L. 2007. *The World Is Flat: A Brief History of the Twenty First Century, Release* 3.0. New York: Picador.

Freitas, Kripa. 2006. "The Indian Caste System as a Means of Contract Enforcement." November 9. www.stanford.edu/~avner/Greif_228_2007/Freitas,%20Kripa.%202006.%20The%20Indian%20Caste%20System.pdf.

Ganz, Kian. 2012. "From the Frontlines: Of Law School Pay Packages, the Economy and Campus Recruitment Wars." *Legally India,* July 27. www.legallyindia.com/201207272978/Analysis/from-the-frontlines-of-law-school-pay-packages-the-economy-and-campus-recruitment-wars.

Garth, Bryant G. 1987. "Independent Professional Power and the Search for a Legal Ideology with a Progressive Bite." *Indiana Law Journal* 62 (2): 183–214.

Goldberg, Pinelopi Koujianou and Nina Pavcnik. 2007. "Distributional Effects of Globalization in Developing Countries" (working paper 12885, National Bureau of Economic Research Working Paper). www.nber.org/papers/w12885.pdf?new_window=1.

Grutter v. Bollinger. 2003. 539 US 306.

Guillén, Mauro F. 2000. "Diversity in Globalization." www.sss.ias.edu/files/papers/papersix.pdf.

The Hindu. 2004."English-Medium Education Deepening Rich-Poor Divide." August 30. www.hindu.com/2004/08/30/stories/2004083006960400.htm.

Ianchovichina, Elena and Susanna Lundstrom. 2009. "What Is Inclusive Growth?" *World Bank*, February 10. www.siteresources.worldbank.org/INTDEBTDEPT/Resources/468980–1218567884549/WhatIsInclusiveGrowth20081230.pdf.

Han, Tan Cheng. 2007. "Change and Yet Continuity – What Next After Fifty Years of Legal Education in Singapore?" *Singapore Journal of Legal Studies* 2007 (2): 201–215.

Herring, Cedric. 2009. "Does Diversity Pay? Race, Gender, and the Business Case for Diversity." *American Sociological Review* 74 (2): 208–224.

Heyer, Judith and Niraja Gopal Jayal. 2009. "The Challenge of Positive Discrimination in India" (working paper no. 55, CRISE, Oxford). www.r4d.dfid.gov.uk/PDF/Outputs/Inequality/wpr55.pdf.

IDIA. 2013. "Recruitment Data for 3 NLU's." www.idialaw.com/wp-content/uploads/2013/09/Recruitment-Data.docx.

IDIA. 2014. Diversity Survey. www.idialaw.com/wp-content/uploads/2015/02/NUJS.pdf.

IDIA. 2015. "Fees Charged by National Law Universities for the 2014–15 and 2015–16 entrants." www.drive.google.com/a/idialaw.com/file/d/0B8yEFEOSUAkYWTl5Q3NtTHM4cVE/view?pli=1

Johnson, Kevin R. 2011. "The Importance of Student and Faculty Diversity in Law Schools: One Dean's Perspective." *Iowa Law Review* 96 (5): 1549–1577

Joy, Lois, Nancy M. Carter, Harvey M. Wagner, and Sriram Nirayanan. 2007. "The Bottom Line: Corporate Performance and Women's Representation on Boards." *The Catalyst*. www.catalyst.org/system/files/The_Bottom_Line_Corporate_Performance_and_Womens_Representation_on_Boards.pdf.

Kellner, Douglas. 2013. "The Conflicts of Globalization and Restructuring of Education." Working Paper. www.pages.gseis.ucla.edu/faculty/kellner/essays/conflictsofglobrestructureed.pdf.

Keyishian v. Board of Regents. 1966. 385 US 589.

Kim, Sing Hui. 2011. "The Diversity Double Standard." *North Carolina Law Review* 89 (3): 946–1002.

Live Mint 2011. "Demystifying the Middle Class." July 31. www.livemint.com/2011/07/31211906/Demystifying-the-middle-class.html.

Mahler, Vincent A. 2004. "Economic Globalization, Domestic Politics, and Income Inequality in the Developed Countries: A Cross-National Study." *Comparative Political Studies* 37 (9): 1025–1053.

"Maharashtra National Law University MUMBAI Admission Test-2015 (MNLUAT)." 2015. Maharashtra National Law University, Mumbai. www.nlumumbai.edu.in/minutes/admission/Admission-announcement-test.pdf.

Maitra, Keya. 2012. "Ambedkar and the Constitution of India: A Deweyan Experiment." *Contemporary Pragmatism* 9 (2): 301–320.

Mallikarjun, B. 2002. "Mother Tongues of India." *Language in India*. www.languageinindia.com/aug2002/indianmothertongues1961aug2002.html.

Mandelson, Peter. 2007. "Can Globalization Be a Level Playing Field?" Speech at the MEDEF Summer University, Paris. www.trade.ec.europa.eu/doclib/docs/2007/august/tradoc_135740.pdf.

Milem, J. and K. Hakuta. 2000. "The Benefits of Racial and Ethnic Diversity in Higher Education." In *Minorities in Higher Education*. Edited by J. D. Wilds. Washington, DC: American Council on Education.

Mitra, Sugata. 2013."SOLE – How to Bring Self-Organized Learning Environments to Your Community." www.ted.com/pages/835#public.

Mitra, Sugata, et al. 2004. "Investigating the Effects of Unsupervised Computer Use on Educationally Disadvantaged Children's Knowledge and Understanding of Computers." Proceedings of CATaC Conference, Karlstad, Sweden.

Orfield, Gary and Dean Whitla. 2001. "Diversity and Legal Education: Student Experiences in Leading Law Schools." In *Diversity Challenged: Evidence on the Impact of Affirmative Action*. Edited by Gary Orfield and Michael Kurlaender. Cambridge: Harvard Education Publishing Group.

Patel, Tulsi, ed. 2007. "A Son Meaning Space under the Sun." *Sex-Selective Abortion in India: Gender, Society and New Reproductive Technologies*. New Delhi: Sage Publications.

Pratt, Carla D. 2006–07. "Taking Diversity Seriously: Affirmative Action and the Democratic Role of Law Schools: A Response to Professor Brown." *Houston Law Review* 43 (1): 55–79.

Ram-Prasad, Chakravarthi. 2007. "India's Middle Class Failure." *Prospect*, September 30. www.prospectmagazine.co.uk/magazine/indias-middle-class-failure/.

Regents of the University of California v. Bakke. 1978. 438 US 265

Rhode, Deborah L. 2010. "Lawyers as Leaders." *Michigan State Law Review* 2010 (2): 413–422.

Rudenstine, Neil L. 1996. "The President's Report 1993–1995: Diversity and Learning." Cited in "Note: An Evidentiary Framework for Diversity as a Compelling Interest in Higher Education." *Harvard Law Review* 109 (6): 1357–1374.

Russell, Margaret. 2002. "McLaurin's Seat: The Need for Racial Inclusion in Legal Education," *Fordham Law Review* 70 (5): 1825–1829.

Sainath, Palagummi. 2004. "The Globalization of Inequality." *India Seminar*. www.india-seminar.com/2004/533/533%20p.%20sainath.htm.

Sala-i-Martin, Xavier. 2002. "The Disturbing 'Rise' of Global Income Inequality" (working paper no. 8904, April, NBER). www.nber.org/papers/w8904.pdf?new_window=1.

Saxena, Rachna. 2010. "The Middle Class in India." *Deutsche Bank Research*, February 15. www.dbresearch.de/PROD/DBR_INTERNET_DE-PROD/PROD0000000000253735.pdf.

Sen, Amartya. 2002. "How to Judge Globalism." The American Prospect Winter 2002: A2-A6.

Sen, Amartya. 2009. *The Idea of Justice*. Cambridge,: Belknap Press.

Shin, Patrick, Devon Carbado, and Mitu Gulati. 2014. "The Diversity Feedback Loop" Research Paper no. 13–38, UCLA School of Law, www.papers.ssrn.com/sol3/papers.cfm?abstract_id=2348420.

Shrivastava, Prachi. 2013. "The IDIA of Clat Diversity Faces Challenges and Funding Woes, Continues to Book Successes." *Legally India*, May 31. www.legallyindia.com/201305313713/Pre-law-student/the-idia-of-clat-diversity-faces-challenges-and-funding-woes-continues-to-book-successes.

Shrivastava, Prachi. 2015. "Cost of Legal Education Shoots Up as Younger Colleges Struggle." Live *Mint*, July 28. www.livemint.com/Politics/Fl8PoH4CjdAbBAtLNrhecN/Cost-of-legal-education-shoots-up-as-younger-colleges-strugg.html.

Sturm, Susan. 2013. "Law Schools, Leadership and Change." *Harvard Law Review Forum* 127 (1): 49–53.

Sunderajan, P. 2010. "Manmohan Calls for Overhaul of Legal Education System." *The Hindu*, May 1. www.thehindu.com/news/national/article419060.ece.

Swenden, Wilfried. 2010. "Managing Diversity in India: From Integration to Accommodation." Conference paper. www.psa.ac.uk/journals/pdf/5/2010/849_702.pdf.

Thacker, Shardul. 2011. "Indian Financial Regulation Developments." www.yumpu.com/en/document/view/22530985/2012-iflr1000.

Thaler, Richard and Cass Sunstein. 2008. *Nudge: Improving Decisions about Health, Wealth, and Happiness*. New York: Penguin Books.

The Times of India. 2011."NLSIU to Double Intake from 2012." June 11. www.articles.timesofindia.indiatimes.com/2011–06–11/bangalore/29647122_1_nlsiu-r-venkata-rao-intake.

"The Business Case for Equality and Diversity." 2013. United Kingdom Government Equalities Office. www.gov.uk/government/uploads/system/uploads/attachment_data/file/49638/the_business_case_for_equality_and_diversity.pdf.

"Top Five NLU Recruitment Tracker." 2011. Bar and Bench, October 11. www.barandbench.com/brief//1776/top-5-nlu-recruitment-tracker-50-opt-for-law-firms-and-17-opt-for-companies-8-for-higher-studies-and-less-than-7-opt-for-litigation.

Twining, William. 1987. "Access to Legal Education and the Legal Profession: A Commonwealth Perspective." *Windsor Yearbook of Access to Justice* 7 (1): 157–208.

Webster, John. 1999. *Untouchable, Dalits in Modern India*. Boulder: Lynne Rienner Publishers.

Wilkins, David B. 1993. "Two Paths to the Mountaintop? The Role of Legal Education in Shaping the Values of Black Corporate Lawyers." *Stanford Law Review* 45 (6): 1981–2026.

1998. "Doing Well by Doing Good? The Role of Public Service in the Careers of Black Corporate Lawyers." *Houston Law Review* 41 (1): 1–91.

2004. "From 'Separate Is Inherently Unequal' to 'Diversity Is Good for Business': The Rise of Market-Based Diversity Arguments and the Fate of the Black Corporate Bar." *Harvard Law Review* 117 (5): 1548–1615.

2011. "Globalization, Lawyers and the Rule of Law: Private Practice and Public Values in the Global Market for Corporate Legal Services" (lecture presented at the World Justice Forum, Barcelona, June 21).

World Commission on the Social Dimensions of Globalisation. 2004. "A Fair Globalisation: Creating Opportunities for All." www.ilo.org/public/english/wcsdg/docs/report.pdf.

19

Experiments in Legal Education in India: Jindal Global Law School and Private Nonprofit Legal Education

C. Raj Kumar

I. INTRODUCTION[1]

Globalization has changed the dynamics of polity and society. These changes have, in turn, put a premium on creating people and institutions capable of operating in an increasingly complex and interdependent global environment. This is particularly true for emerging economies such as India, which have to develop new institutions and practices to deal with the host of new challenges globalization presents for its domestic society, and train individuals in both the private and public sectors who can operate in these new institutions, as well as mediate between India and the broad array of foreign entities and institutions of global governance with which India's state and civil society increasingly interact. As a result, virtually every emerging economy is striving to create world-class institutions of higher learning that can help prepare them for the knowledge economy of the twenty-first century.

Unfortunately, in India, this largely remains an unmet challenge. The Times Higher Education World University Rankings 2015–16 found that India did not have a single university that ranked in the top two hundred universities of the world (Times Higher Education World University Rankings 2015–16). This contrasts sharply with other Asian countries, including China, Taiwan, Hong Kong, Japan, Singapore, and the Republic of Korea, which all boast universities that feature prominently on this list.

If anything, the situation of legal education is extremely dire. As indicated elsewhere in Chapter 16, until the late 1980s the general quality of the Indian legal profession was exceedingly poor, mirroring the poor esteem that the legal profession was held in by most Indians, other than the country's founders, such as Nehru and Gandhi, virtually all of whom were trained abroad.

In 1987 the Indian government sought to reverse this trend by establishing the National Law Schools, beginning with the National Law School University of India– Bangalore. As documented in Chapter 16 of this volume, these law schools have played a significant role in producing highly skilled lawyers working in various aspects of the legal sector, including in institutions fostered by globalization, such as corporate law firms, in-house legal counsel, and nongovernmental organizations (NGOs).

Nevertheless, even champions of the National Law School system readily admit that as fine as these institutions are, they alone have not – and indeed could not – eliminate the gap between India's critical need for lawyers capable of transforming India into a society where both private markets and public institutions are governed by the rule of law. Specifically, the National Law School system suffers from two problems that are likely to continue to inhibit India's development of the kind of legal profession it will require to meet its domestic and international needs. The first is simply one of scale. Although there are now eighteen National Law Schools across the country, including the latest in Mumbai, which welcomed its first class of students in 2015, these schools remain a tiny fraction of the more than twelve hundred higher-education institutions offering legal education in India. Given the expansion of law schools in the country, there has been a major challenge with regard to quality and excellence that was hitherto pursued vigorously in the early years of the institution-building initiatives at the National Law Schools. In 2010 the former prime minister of India, Dr. Manmohan Singh, stated:

> Over half a century ago, the then-president of India, Dr. Radhakrishnan – and he himself was a great teacher – lamented that "our colleges of law do not hold a place of high esteem either at home or abroad, nor has law become an area of profound scholarship and enlightened research." It's no doubt we have traveled a long distance since that time. But we must admit and have to ask honestly ourselves whether we have significantly altered the landscape of our legal education system. We do have a small number of dynamic and outstanding law schools, but I am afraid they remain islands of excellence amidst a sea of institutionalized mediocrity. We are not marginally nearer to profound scholarship and enlightened research in law. As we introspect honestly, we must sadly accept that Dr. Radhakrishnan's powerful yet poignant words may not be amenable to any radical restatement even today.
>
> (Dayal 2010)

But even if one confines their view to the best Indian law schools – which in 2010 were generally considered the National Law Schools – the prime minister's remarks underscore that there is still a shortage of "profound scholarship and enlightened research in law" in even these great institutions. Legal education in India was never envisaged to be a framework for seeking fundamental reforms in improving the quality of justice-delivery mechanisms. Nor was it seen to be a tool for promoting access to justice. Globalization and the changing dimensions of the Indian economy and polity have accentuated these shortcomings in traditional Indian legal education by producing new governance challenges in both the private and public sectors. Establishing the rule of law in all its dimensions, therefore, remains the single most important challenge the country is facing. Law schools must play a critical role in developing lawyers who are rational thinkers and social engineers, and who can foster the development of a knowledge economy in India (Bloch and Prasad 2006; Ulen 2009; Kosuri 2012). This can be done only if the law schools are able to attract some of the best and the brightest lawyers to make a lifelong commitment to teaching, learning, and research so that they are able to inspire generations of students to work toward establishing a rule of law society in India.

The rest of this chapter will focus on the challenges India faces in creating a rule of law society in a globalized era and its implications for legal education in India. It does so by using the Jindal Global Law School (JGLS) as an example of a new kind of law school that seeks to fill the important gap between Indian legal education and the complex global problems that India now confronts. JGLS is one of several law schools in India and around the world founded on the express premise that there is a critical need to develop "global" lawyers capable of operating in today's new interdependent global reality. Part II describes JGLS and how it has attempted to meet this challenge. Part III examines the challenges that law schools like JGLS face as they seek to bring truly global – but effective – legal education to India and other emerging economies. Part IV discusses how changes in the Indian market for legal services are likely to increase the demand for global law schools such as JGLS but will also create challenges for legal education and for the legal profession itself.

Before proceeding, a note of disclosure is necessary. I am the founding vice chancellor of O.P. Jindal Global University and dean of JGLS. As I indicate, my purpose in describing the goals and activities of the school is not to debate the merits of our approach, although, as I am sure this shall also be clear, I am very proud of what we have achieved in our short history. Instead, I aim to provide one model of what a "global" law school can look like in the Indian context as a predicate for the challenges and opportunities that any such school will face in the coming years.

II. THE JINDAL STORY

O.P. Jindal Global University (JGU) was founded on September 30, 2009. It was established through the philanthropic initiative of the founding

Chancellor, Mr. Naveen Jindal. Mr. Jindal contributed substantial financial resources besides, committing to academic freedom, functional autonomy, and not-for-profit governance. The first school of JGU, the Jindal Global Law School (JGLS), began its academic programs in 2009 with a five-year BA/LLB program and a three-year LLB program. In 2013 JGLS launched a one-year LLM program. As of 2015 more than thirteen hundred students are enrolled at JGLS in some combination of these three programs.

From its founding, the goal of JGLS has been clear: to create an institution of global excellence. While the effort was to develop a global curriculum, a global course structure, and a global program framework, the most important aspects of JGLS's global orientation was to create a globally recognized selection process for the students who would attend JGLS, create a globally fluent faculty (including important connections to leading faculties around the world), and develop a global research agenda with a commitment to doing cutting-edge research that would meet international standards. This vision was significantly influenced by many aspects of the outstanding legal education that I personally experienced during my time at Oxford, Harvard, and the City University of Hong Kong, most notably the recognition of the critical role that research and scholarship through faculty publications plays in creating world-class legal education. The next three sections briefly describe how we have tried to achieve these objectives.

A. *Student Selection*

As a new law school, JGLS was faced with the challenge of attracting high-quality students. Given our mission, however, the challenge was even more daunting, since it was important that we attracted students who understood and were committed to achieving the school's global ambitions. To facilitate this match and to ensure that the students who were admitted would be able to compete on a global level, JGLS decided to use the Law School Admission Test (LSAT), which is taken by students applying for admission to law school in the United States, even though the Common Law Admission Test (CLAT) was required by the National Law Universities.

Not surprisingly, this was a controversial decision. In 2009 the LSAT was not even administered in India. It was only after an elaborate set of discussions that the Law School Admissions Council that administers the test agreed to conduct the LSAT-India examination for students in India who were aspiring to join Jindal. But getting the LSAT administered and certified in India was only the beginning. It was then necessary to convince students to take the test and to explain to them and the Indian legal education community why it was important for students at JGLS to meet this international standard. Although the CLAT clearly does a good job of selecting highly qualified students for India's National Law Schools, many of its questions are almost completely focused on India. The very mission of JGLS, however, was to transcend this national focus. We therefore wanted students who could pass an international examination, one that transcends jurisdictional barriers and tests students on their analytical and logical reasoning, as well as reading comprehension, at the level they will need to compete in a global context.

Although the process of demonstrating the importance that students seeking to attend JGLS have this global qualification has not always been smooth, the school has been able to institutionalize the LSAT as the only examination for admission to JGLS. In so doing, the school has played a key role in making the LSAT an important test in India. In just six years, the number of LSAT takers has increased twenty-fold, from a little more than 150 in 2009, when JGLS first negotiated to have the test administered in India, to more than 4,000 in 2015.

B. *Recruiting and Developing Faculty*

Hiring top-quality faculty is a challenge for every law school, but particularly in India. Generally, the financial incentives the private sector offers are far more attractive than those available in the public sector, including law schools, for good lawyers to make a commitment to academia (Grove 2012). This gap has traditionally been particularly acute in India, where academic salaries are especially low. Once again, JGLS was at an even greater disadvantage, since the school was attempting to build a world-class faculty from scratch, without any of the history or pedigree of the National Law Schools that were competing for the same pool of talent. Yet, without a world-class and globally fluent faculty, the school would never be able to achieve its ambitions of creating a world-class and globally fluent educational environment for its students.

JGLS has adopted a three-pronged strategy to address this critical issue. First, the school made a serious commitment to highlight the need for broad educational reform within India, including better compensation for those who go into academia. By hosting conferences, writing articles, and giving speeches about the critical need to develop a new generation of top-quality Indian legal academics, I and other administrators and faculty associated with JGLS have attempted to get policymakers to focus on the importance of this issue.

Second, from the outset the school has sought to turn one of the biggest challenges that globalization has posed for the India's institutions of higher learning into an important advantage. For years, Indian scholars and policymakers have lamented the significant "brain drain" that has occurred in the years since liberalization as many leading and potential scholars have left India for teaching positions and other related careers in other parts of the world. Although this process certainly has had its downside, it has also meant that issues relating to the Indian legal system are now taught and researched not only in India but also in many other parts of the world – often by scholars and lawyers who are part of the Indian diaspora. In part by reaching out to these scholars – and their students, many who are also Indian – JGLS has been able to create an international faculty interested in doing research in India and contributing to its growth story. Eighty-two percent of Jindal Global University's faculty members possess education qualifications from international universities. Our faculty members have been recruited from around the world, and 20 percent of professors at JGU are from abroad. Importantly, 46 percent of faculty members at JGU, and more than 50 percent of faculty at the law school, are women, reflecting a strong commitment to promoting gender diversity. This is particularly significant given the serious gender-balance issues confronting the judiciary and other institutions in India, and the long-standing gender inequality within the academy in India.

Third, to complement this strategy of recruiting faculty from abroad, JGLS has also developed strong international collaborations with leading institutions around the world, particularly with law schools in the United States. Since 2009, Jindal Global University and JGLS have established substantive relationships with more than one hundred institutions in thirty-five different countries. These relationships have led to the implementation of ten different types of programs that have immensely benefited the faculty members and students of JGLS. The ten forms of international collaborations are structured around faculty exchanges, student exchanges, joint teaching, joint research, joint conferences, joint publications, dual degrees, summer and winter exchange schools, study abroad programs, and joint executive education programs. These initiatives have played a key role in attracting and retaining faculty as well as extending our ability to provide a globally focused education beyond our existing resources.

C. *Creating a True Research Law School*

The most important – and in the Indian context, the most unique – aspect of JGLS's model has been the school's strong commitment to faculty and research. As indicated here, not a single university in India is ranked in the top two hundred in the world. Jindal Global University is striving to break this long-standing drought, in part by hiring faculty members who have studied at the best universities around the world. The vast majority of faculty members at JGU have received their educational qualifications from the top two hundred universities in the world, with 45 percent graduating from the top fifty universities in the world, per the Times Higher Education World University Rankings 2014–15.

Recruiting faculty from top institutions, however, is only the first step in creating an Indian university that can achieve similar distinction. These talented professors must also be given the opportunity to create and disseminate world-class research. Although much of the emphasis in Indian institutions of higher learning has understandably been on teaching, it is a commitment to producing cutting-edge scholarship that continues to distinguish the best universities in the world. To underscore its commitment to research, JGLS launched the first issue of *Jindal Global Law Review* in August 2009 before the arrival of its faculty and first class of students. Since then the school's law review has been published continuously, producing influential articles on matters of significant importance to India by an impressive collection of scholars from JGLS, other top Indian law schools, and leading institutions around the world. In recognition of this record of scholarly accomplishment, in 2015 Springer, a globally reputed publishing company began publishing the school's flagship journal.

This culture of scholarship and intellectual engagement is reinforced by JGLS's location within an increasingly broad and interdisciplinary educational environment. JGLS is now one of the five schools at JGU, which also includes a business school, a public policy school, an international affairs school and a school of liberal arts & humanities. In 2014, JGU launched a liberal arts and humanities college. Such an interdisciplinary approach to law brings thematic, empirical, and applied research to the key issues concerning law and justice, which is key to helping promote good governance and enables a thorough examination of the role of law and justice in the Indian society (Barry et al. 2012; Brooks 2012).

D. *Making a Global Law School*

As this brief description demonstrates, JGLS has made considerable progress in achieving its goal of creating a truly global law school. By "global" we of course do not simply mean that we aspire to create a law school that exclusively studies "globalization." Instead, JGLS tries to recognize that globalization has impacted every aspect of society and therefore calls for a new understanding of how law schools and universities can play a critical role in preparing students, and Indian society in general, to respond to this complex phenomenon in all its manifestations. We have thus made a consistent and conscious effort to create an ecosystem that has always looked to the world as a part of a collective institutional imagination within Jindal.

The results to date have exceeded even my own high expectations for the project. JGLS's students have excelled in top national- and international-level moot court competitions in the past years, winning the international rounds of the Oxford Media Law Moot and the Nani Palkhivala Tax Law Moot, and reaching the finals of the Henry Dunant Memorial Moot. Graduates have started their legal careers in a diverse set of workplaces in the leading law firms of India and the world, such as Cyril Amarchand Mangaldas, AZB & Partners, Khaitan & Company, Trilegal, J Sagar Associates, Lakshmikumaran & Sridharan, Anand & Anand, S&R Associates, Economic Law Practice, Nishith Desai Associates, and the coveted international law firm, White & Case. They have also worked in the chambers of eminent senior counsels and judges in the Supreme Court, various high courts, and trial courts. Others have made contributions across various industries, including in corporate houses like PriceWaterhouseCoopers, Tata Sons, Cognizant, Ersnt & Young and Star India Private Limited. Meanwhile, some of our students have also taken up careers at NGOs and advocacy groups, making an invaluable contribution to nation building, such as CRY International, Teach for India, Software Freedom Law Centre, and the Human Rights Law Network. The year 2015 was very special as four JGLS students were selected to pursue judicial clerkships at the Supreme Court of Hawaii in the US.

Finally, and perhaps most importantly given the critical shortage of Indians pursuing careers in the academy, a large number of JGLS graduates have opted for higher studies in universities abroad, including the Oxford, Cambridge, Georgetown University, Cornell University, and many others. To be sure, not all these graduates will become academics. However, the fact that so many JGLS graduates are studying in prestigious universities abroad will significantly increase the pool of qualified candidates from which JGLS and any other Indian law school interested in pursuing a similar global mission will be able to recruit.

Not surprisingly, we are very proud of this record of accomplishment. We are also aware, however, that many challenges remain to building JGLS into a world-class global law school and, more generally, to creating a world-class legal profession in India that is capable of competing effectively in today's increasingly competitive global environment. Some of these challenges are common to all Indian law schools. Thus, JGLS and law schools across India must continue to work to develop a greater interest among Indian high school graduates in studying law as a discipline. Others, such as keeping legal education affordable, are particularly acute for JGLS as a private institution. Legal education of high repute and good standing is expensive everywhere in the world. This is particularly true for private institutions like JGLS, which are not subsidized by the state and are committed to recruiting outstanding faculty and providing them with adequate compensation and opportunities for career development. JGU and JGLS were fortunate in having a benefactor in Chancellor Naveen Jindal, whose philanthropic effort in establishing the institution was not only revolutionary but also transformative. As a result, JGLS has been able to provide substantial scholarships, fellowships, and other opportunities for students to improve access and create affordability. Despite this considerable advantage, the school finds it difficult to provide adequate access to students who may not be able to afford tuition and other costs.

But the greatest challenges facing JGLS and legal education in India in general are those that are inherent in the complex and often contradictory possibilities created by globalization itself. The next section outlines four dichotomies that are likely to shape India's approach to global legal education in the coming years.

III. REFORMING LEGAL EDUCATION IN INDIA

Globalization has posed multiple challenges to the future of legal education in India, but as the experience of JGLS has shown, it has provided an opportunity to challenge the status quo, which is an essential condition for seeking any reform. This section outlines four choices in higher education that are being remade in India as a result of globalization: (1) public versus private; (2) teaching versus research; (3) regulation versus autonomy; and (4) national versus international. These choices are typically framed as all-or-nothing, in which institutions and policymakers must make either-or decisions. In fact, although real tradeoffs are involved, I will argue that it is better to conceive of these issues as presenting points on a continuum in which the best solutions incorporate elements of "both-and" (Minow 1991). This kind of thinking will only become more critical as India further liberalizes its markets, including the market for legal services.

A. *Public and Private – But Not for-Profit*

India needs to overcome its biases and prejudices about whether a university is private or public (Kumar 2012a). Many of the top universities in the world are private – for example, Harvard, Yale, Stanford, and MIT – while some of the oldest and most reputed universities continue to be public, such as Oxford, Cambridge, and the University of London. Universities should be assessed on the basis of objective standards relating to the quality of teaching, faculty, research, and capacity building rather than the school being public or private.

The future of higher education in India will be highly dependent on the role of the private sector and to what extent the regulatory policies in higher education favor the role of this sector (Jayanthi 2012). Governments in developing countries like India are not in a position to wholly support the significant financial commitment needed to establish and sustain reputed higher-education institutions (Ganz 2012). The stellar reputation of the Indian School of Business in Hyderabad, which became one of the top twenty business schools in the world within a decade, is an inspiring example of how a private initiative can promote a world-class institution of higher learning (Kaul 2006).

However, while private higher-education institutions should be encouraged, it is important that they be truly nonprofit, philanthropic, and committed to promoting academic freedom and institutional excellence. Promoting private initiatives in higher education should also go hand in hand with other equally committed efforts to strengthen and develop our public universities, which are suffering from problems relating to lack of faculty, poor infrastructure, inadequate funding, and lack of autonomy in curriculum development and course administration (National Knowledge Commission 2009; Sunder 2011).

In the recent book *What Money Can't Buy: The Moral Limits of Markets*, Michael J. Sandel, a professor of political philosophy at Harvard, observed, "At a time of rising inequality, the marketization of everything means that people of affluence and people of modest means lead increasingly separate lives . . . Democracy does not require perfect equality, but it does require that citizens share in a common life . . . the question of markets is really a question about how we want to live together. Do we want a society where everything is up for sale? Or are there certain moral and civic goods that markets not honor and money cannot buy?" (Sandel 2012).

Available and affordable good-quality higher education that promotes equity and efficiency is an essential public good, which needs to be promoted both by the public and by nonprofit private-sector initiatives (Kumar 2012b). Judged by this standard, the Planning Commission's 2011 proposal in the draft 12th Five Year Plan to promote for-profit initiatives in higher education is a retrograde step in our efforts to raise the quality of higher education and research in India (Government of India 2011, 102). The ostensible reason for promoting such an idea is to address the growing concerns relating to a lack of good faculty, infrastructure, and resources, and the Commission has observed that the objective is to "bridge the demand-supply gap in higher education."

The critical aspect of "non-profit" framework is that the additional income generated by the institution over and above the expenditures incurred in running it is retained and used for the development of the institution, such as research initiatives, scholarships and fellowships for students, and infrastructure development. Ideally, the management or the private donors who created the institution should not take the additional income back for themselves. This is how an endowment can be created and the financial viability and sustenance of the institution can be protected and promoted for posterity.

As we aspire to increase the quantity and raise the quality of higher-education institutions, we need to draw from experiences around the world. There is a reason that there is not a single world-class university that is run on a for-profit basis. Promoting for-profit institutions in India will expand and expedite the pace of mediocrity that is already deeply entrenched in the Indian higher-education system. The success of a corporation and the continuous assessment of its output can be measured through accepted frameworks of evaluation. In this context, profitability is measurable. However, universities by their nature are institutions that are designed with larger social goals and purposes (Krishnan 2004). The yardsticks that are available to measure growth and development, including profits and losses, in corporations are not suitable to measure the contribution of universities.

Finally, successful nonprofit private universities require philanthropy, which is still rare in India in general, and in education in particular. The National Knowledge Commission report noted with regard to philanthropic contributions: "It is clear that we have not exploited this potential. In fact the proportion of such contributions in total expenditure on higher education has declined from more than 12 per cent [*sic*] in the 1950s to less than three per cent [*sic*] in [the] 1990s . . ." (National Knowledge Commission 2009). There is an urgent need for encouraging philanthropic initiatives in promoting excellence in legal education and research in the country (Sunder 2011). Such philanthropy is more likely where private schools are not seeking profit, but instead the furthering of the public good.

B. *Creating a Mutually Reinforcing Environment for Teaching and Research*

As indicated, until recently the importance of legal education for establishing a rule of law society did not receive any serious priority or attention in traditional university law departments in India, although due to the sheer motivation of students themselves, the departments successfully produced many of the brightest lawyers and some of the best academics in the country. There has not been adequate progress in academic standards within these law departments, with little scope for innovation in the design of courses, development of appropriate teaching modules, planning or conducting research, or even promotion of advocacy in lawyering. These traditional departments also suffered from a lack of independence and institutional autonomy as they were within a university system where the priorities of senior administrators did not always match what was best for the law school. As a result, the ability to attract serious students with a passionate commitment to study law in all its ramifications has been dramatically reduced, culminating in institutionalized mediocrity in a large number of law faculties across the country.

There is no doubt that the establishment of the National Law Schools successfully challenged this institutionalized mediocrity and succeeded in attracting serious students to the study of law. In fact, the study of law has received more attention among India's high school graduates with the introduction of five-year integrated programs. Nevertheless, these schools face significant challenges in attracting faculty members who are top researchers in the field of law and can combine sound teaching methods with established track records of research.

Universities are institutions where research needs to be the priority. Research does inform teaching, and teaching should contribute to research. Understanding and nurturing this critical link is essential to attracting and retaining top faculty. As indicated, at present, faculty members across disciplines have little or no motivation to work in Indian universities. Many prefer to work in think tanks, research institutions, scientific and professional organizations, intergovernmental and nongovernmental organizations, and corporations. In the process, Indian universities have lost some brilliant minds. Our record in attracting Indian academics back to India after their higher studies and work abroad is poor compared with China, Singapore, Hong Kong, Taipei, and South Korea. We need to create a conducive and enabling environment for research with a strong commitment to producing knowledge through research and publications (Kumar 2012c).

Globalization and the transformation of the Indian economy have created huge opportunities for Indian graduates to seek careers in a range of sectors in India and abroad. Unless and until dramatic efforts are taken to identify and inspire the best graduating students across the Indian universities to consider taking up academic positions in India and to encourage the Indians who are studying abroad to return to India to take up faculty positions, we will not be able to address the central challenge of faculty recruitment in Indian universities. We also need to recognize that the democratization of knowledge creation means that faculty members should have mobility to work in India regardless of their nationality. We have to attract the intellectual talent from around the world to India, and that is possible only if we are able to re-examine our faculty-recruitment policies, including visa regulations and compensation (Kumar 2012c).

Time and again, we have recognized that lack of rigorous research and absence of academic scholarship leading to publications has been the bane of Indian universities. There are little or no incentives whatsoever for the faculty in most, if not all, Indian universities to undertake research (Kumar 2012c). The ecosystem of our universities does not promote such an effort. To the contrary, most Indian law schools and universities specifically discourage faculty research through an overemphasis on teaching large classes; lack of career development and financial incentives for research; lack of recognition and appreciation among the academic peer group in India; and lack of financial support in the form of research grants for faculty to undertake research. All this has created a situation where there are no policies, programs, initiatives, or incentives that encourage research in Indian universities.

There is no doubt that poor financial incentives discourage many young and brilliant lawyers from considering a career in academia (National Knowledge Commission 2009). It is important to address this issue as well. But improvements and changes are feasible in other areas, such as career development opportunities within the law schools; development of research infrastructure including the resources to organize and participate in national and international conferences and the undertaking of serious research; a harmonious environment that fosters mutual respect; transparent governance of the law schools; and, above all, faith in the leadership of the institution that not only will excellence be promoted as a general policy, but affirmative efforts will be taken to encourage and support excellence (National Knowledge Commission 2009, 81).

Publication and citation of research by other scholars and policymakers around the world is one of the most effective ways by which a university gains international recognition and global reputation (Kumar 2012c). It also fulfills the central goal of most universities, which is to contribute to the world of ideas and hopefully help solve the pressing problems of society in all fields.

Research and scholarship ought to become a priority in law schools in India so that creation of knowledge becomes the fundamental objective of higher education (Thakur and Patel 2010). The creation, development, and dissemination of knowledge need to be democratized. This can take place only if both the state and private sectors make efforts to develop many global universities that will meet the governance challenges of India and the world at large (Terry et al. 2012). Otherwise put, India needs a number of excellent global universities – and global law schools – imparting world-class education and promoting cutting-edge research across disciplines that can shape the development of our youth to assume a leadership role in nation building.

In a globalized world, not only should research be aimed at India's interrelationship with the other countries, but teaching should too (Griggs 2005). A few decades back, law schools in India could do well as long as their curriculum was focused on Indian law and issues relating to the country's legal system. While there was some limited impetus to the study of international and comparative law, the larger focus was primarily on issues relating to the Indian legal system.[2] This was, of course, necessary and proper at the time given India's circumstances. Indeed, even today there is still great need for improvement in promoting excellence in teaching and research relating to Indian law and to addressing the challenges facing the legal system, including the need for establishing a society that respects the rule of law and meets the challenges of globalization. However, new and emerging law schools cannot afford to limit their focus to teaching and research on issues relating to Indian law. In fact, the appetite of Indian law students for understanding international and comparative law has significantly increased over the years, given their participation in international moot competitions that range from maritime law to humanitarian law to dispute resolution.[3] The most challenging task is to strike a proper balance to ensure that students are given a fair mix of courses that give them knowledge and training in Indian law, but at the same time prepare them for facing the challenges of globalization, whereby domestic legal mechanisms interact with both international and foreign legal systems (Varghese 2010).

C. *Regulating the Space for Autonomy*

If Indian universities need to improve their academic standards, research contribution, and capacity-building efforts, they need to be given more autonomy and greater freedom to accomplish these goals. But all freedom comes with responsibility and accountability. The existing legal framework for the governance of Indian universities is based upon a lack of trust and confidence by policymakers that our institutions of higher learning will be able to do the right thing. This approach reinforces the belief that tight regulatory control over universities is the only way to ensure quality and maintain high academic standards. But if there is one thing we should learn from past attempts to regulate universities, it is that the more we try to regulate, the more avenues it creates for corruption, nepotism, abuse of powers, and other forms of vested interests (Kumar 2012a).

To be sure, laws and regulations that are transparently enforced with proper procedure and process are needed to determine the status of a university. But once a university is established, it should be governed independently with academic freedom and institutional autonomy so that it is able to make all decisions in a transparent and democratic manner within the institution. The practice of seeking permission from regulatory bodies and government departments for every aspect of the internal governance of the university needs to be changed so that our universities can function more effectively.

Given the challenges of privatization and globalization, there is an urgent need to emphasize academic freedom as a core component of ensuring higher academic standards and to develop curriculum that will meet the needs of the future (Kumar 2007; Schauer 2012). Resistance from academics can actually serve as a check on the different branches of the government to ensure that rights are duly protected and that there is a greater sense of transparency and accountability in governance (Chaput 2006). This is particularly true for law schools, which, as I have argued here, have a special role to play in ensuring the rule of law – a role that is especially crucial as India increasingly interfaces with the global economy and the institutions of global governance.

There needs to be a public debate on the inherently difficult issue of how academic freedom in Indian universities can be balanced with the equally important value of ensuring transparency and accountability within public and private institutions (Jonathan 2006). The question of accountability becomes critical in the context of growing commercialization of education, which has also undermined academic freedom (Glazer and Tuteur 2012). Promoting greater understanding of academic freedom has a significant bearing on the purpose of higher education (Macintyre 2010).It will also have an impact on determining all policies relating to higher education, including curriculum development, program administration, recruitment of faculty members, teaching pedagogy, assessment regimes, and professional engagement of educational institutions (Todd 2007; Harden 2012).

While the legal and institutional framework for protecting the freedom of speech and expression in India is sound, backed up by an independent judiciary that is ready and able to enforce this fundamental right, certain aspects of political culture, religious intolerance, and cultural dogmatism pose challenges to the protection of academic freedom (Greenawalt 2009; Ramachandran 2011; Harden 2012). Once again, this is particularly dangerous with respect to law schools that are charged with training those who will ultimately have responsibility for protecting these freedoms.

In the end, protecting academic freedom must be part of the social responsibility of every individual and institution (Rapoport 2010). But the culture in which this is likely to happen will flourish only if regulators give universities – particularly law schools – the space to exercise these freedoms in a way that encourages their independence. At the same time, Indian law schools must recognize their responsibility to use those freedoms to promote justice and equality for all Indians. It is only by encouraging a greater degree of mutual respect and understanding that India will be able to create the kind of rule of law society the country will need to achieve its true potential on the global stage.

D. *A National Strategy for India as an International Power*

Time and again, it has been asserted that we need to focus our higher-education agenda on dealing with the problems of India. While India's universities and law schools must focus on the country's pressing problems, many countries in the world, including most parts of the developing world, are looking to India for leadership, inspiration, and institution building. Globalization has affected every aspect of life, including higher education. Indian universities have to provide opportunities for students in India, but also in South Asia, Africa, the Middle East, and even Latin America. The outlook needs to be international. India and Indian universities cannot continue to have parochial views, outdated perspectives, and a myopic vision that does not take contemporary global realities into account.

Indian universities have grappled with these challenges for far too long. It is time for us to work toward a radical change. Given the extraordinary intellectual capital that we as a nation have and the passion and desire of the young people of India to contribute to the nation-building agenda, it is indeed possible for us make our universities – and our law schools – inspiring, and the learning experiences truly transformative, for students.

Universities worldwide are preparing themselves to face the challenges of globalization. Some of the most reputed universities in the world are gearing up for galvanizing their efforts to promote internationalization in education (Bradney 1995).

Speaking at Jawaharlal Nehru University in 2005, the president of Yale Richard Levin said:

> The globalization of the university is in part an evolutionary development... But creating the global university is also a revolutionary development – signaling distinct changes in the substance of teaching and research, the demographic characteristics of students and scholars, the scope and breadth of external collaborations, and the engagement of the university with new audiences. When I speak of becoming a global university, I envision

> a curriculum and a research agenda permeated by awareness that political, economic, social, and cultural phenomena in any part of the world can no longer be fully understood in isolation . . .
>
> (Levin 2005).

India's law schools must take a similar view. It will be possible to tackle the country's pressing domestic legal, political, social, and economic needs only by understanding the complex ways globalization is reshaping India. This orientation will become only more critical as India continues the inevitable process of integrating into the global economy – including the global market for legal services.

E. *An Opening Legal Profession*

The commerce secretary of India, Rajeev Kher, recently announced that the government shall, in phases, open India's nonlitigious services and international arbitration legal services to foreign law firms. This is a significant development. Kher observed, "The Bar Council of India, which regulates the legal fraternity, and the Society of Indian Law Firms, which represents the interests of large law firms, have, in principle, agreed to the proposal" (Mehra 2015). Never before in recent times has the opening up of legal services to international law firms received such broad consensus within the legal profession in India, particularly with the Bar Council of India (BCI).

India's law schools have to respond to this development. More than fifty thousand law students graduate each year, and they have a variety of career aspirations. While many of them may join the litigating bar and others may pursue higher education and academia, a substantial number seek opportunities in commercial law firms. The existing Indian law firms are not able to absorb the overwhelming majority of these graduates. As a result, Indian law students stand to benefit from the entry of international law firms. Currently, a small proportion of Indian students will work in an international environment as part of law firms in New York, London, Singapore, or Hong Kong. With international law firms opening offices in India, law school graduates will have more opportunities for growth, better training, and international exposure.

Greater training and employment opportunities for India's law school graduates, however, are not the only benefit that the entry of foreign law firms will have on Indian legal education. A unique aspect of legal education in the United States, and some other more-developed countries, is the deep and pervasive engagement that law schools in these countries have with law firms, corporations, nongovernmental organizations, legal aid centers, think tanks, government agencies, and intergovernmental organizations. Unfortunately, in India the legal academy and the legal profession are almost completely separated with little interaction, let alone collaboration. While lawyers almost always lament that legal education doesn't prepare law graduates to engage in legal practice, most practitioners make little or no contribution to producing the kind of teaching, training, capacity building, and mentoring of law students that might help remedy this situation. Allowing international law firms to open offices in India will help reverse the brain drain and retain legal talent in India. The collaboration between domestic and international law firms and the law schools in India can lead to funding of research centers and endowments for chair professorships, faculty and student exchanges, executive and continuing legal education, and knowledge development initiatives, all of which would go a long way toward bridging the gap between theory and practice in Indian law schools.

Another area where the entry of foreign law firms could improve Indian legal education is pro bono services. Many international firms have well-organized pro bono practices, with a number of lawyers dedicated to coordinating the pro bono efforts of their firm. When global law firms enter India, they will help create a culture of pro bono in legal services among India's commercial law firms, as they have in other countries. To date, India's large commercial law firms have been largely indifferent to engaging in public interest legal work. The entry of international law firms could help change this reality. Indeed, the extraordinary contribution to different facets of social responsibility by some of the world's leading international law firms such as White & Case is not just confined to the pro bono work of its lawyers. These firms have also worked to provide knowledge and access to legal education in the developing world, research and analysis on important issues of human rights and justice, and legal support and scholarships to those seeking legal education. Once again, if these firms bring these practices with them to the Indian market, it could help spur similar actions by Indian corporate firms, thereby changing both legal education, and the culture of corporate legal practice in general.

Nor should we be afraid that these benefits will come only at the price of undermining India's traditional litigating bar or the independence of Indian law or the courts. International law firms have no interest in practicing Indian law or appearing before the Indian courts. The opening up of the Indian legal services market should therefore not be seen as an opportunity for international law firms to appear before the courts of India or for that matter engage in the practice of Indian law. Instead, with Indian business increasingly expanding overseas, the international law firms can advise Indian businesses on foreign and international law in international commercial transactions and arbitrations. International firms that come into India will be led and staffed by Indian lawyers. With more than twelve hundred law schools in India, including eighteen National Law Schools, it is important to keep in mind the need for creating a diversified set of career opportunities for Indian law graduates.

India can democratize the legal profession so that Indian lawyers can tap the resources that are available around the world. While it is important for Indian lawyers to develop global lawyering capabilities, including the professionalization of legal services, such liberalization also needs to be accompanied by appropriate regulation (Krishnan 2013). The body best placed to regulate the liberalization of the Indian legal profession is the BCI. The BCI has taken a lead in important historical developments in relation to legal education and the legal profession. In so doing, the BCI has kept in mind the best interests of legal education and the legal profession. In this same vein, the BCI should embrace the new changes taking place in the legal profession and create a framework that will help fulfill the aspirations of the new generations of students and lawyers in India.

IV. CONCLUSION

The impending liberalization of the Indian legal services market and the likely entry of at least some foreign law firms is only a small example of how globalization is likely to reshape the Indian legal profession in the future. Nor is India alone. As documented in the preface to this volume, the forces that are transforming Indian lawyers – the globalization of economic activity and the increasing shift in that activity from the traditional powers of the Global North to the newly emerging economies of the Global South, the explosion in the size and sophistication of information technology, and the blurring of the boundaries between traditional categories of organization and thought – are transforming every part of the world's economic, political, and social order, bringing dramatic changes to the legal profession as well. These changes are likely to intensify in the coming years, putting further pressure on legal education to respond, in part by creating more opportunities for training students to meet the challenges of this new and increasingly complex global environment.

JGLS offers one potential model for trying to meet these new challenges. It joins a number of other law schools in both developing and developed legal markets – for example, the Peking University School of Transnational Law in China, Fundação Getulio Vargas in Brazil, Bucerius Law School in Germany, and New York University's Global Network in the United States, to name only a few – that are seeking to bring a global perspective to legal education while continuing to train lawyers who must also master local law and legal institutions (Chesterman 2015). As the previous discussion underscores, creating a new "global" law school from the ground up offers important avenues for developing innovative practices that can then be adopted by more-established law schools. But this virtuous circle will occur only if academics, policymakers, and practitioners move away from the kind of "either-or" thinking that has typically dominated the debate over education reform in India and other countries and embrace the idea that training lawyers for the twenty-first century will require a mix of solutions that incorporate public and private entities, respect teaching and scholarship, regulate Indian legal education in a way that protects both standards and academic freedom, and prepares Indian lawyers to operate in both a national and an international domain. Needless to say, achieving this kind of synthesis will not be easy. But in the end it is the only way to produce lawyers with the broader framework and vision to contribute to society through public service.

Notes

1 Parts of this article have been drawn from previous articles published in the Hindu, the Hindustan Times, the Indian Express, and the New Indian Express, as well as other magazines published in India. Another version of this article is being published by the *Indiana Journal of Global Legal Studies*.

2 For example, the Bar Council of India has established a Curriculum Development Committee. For more information, visit www.barcouncilofindia.org/about/legal-education/curriculum-development-committee.

3 For example, NALSAR University of Law–Hyderabad won the 2012 world rounds of the Monroe E. Price International Media Law Moot Court Competition conducted by Oxford.

References

Barry, Margaret Martin; Rachel Karn, Margaret E. Johnson, Catherine F. Klein, and Lisa Vollendorf Martin. 2010. "Teaching Social Justice Lawyering: Systematically Including Community Legal Education in Law School Clinics." *Clinical Law Review* 18 (2): 401–457.

Bloch, Frank and M. R. K. Prasad. 2006. "Institutionalizing a Social Justice Mission for Clinical Legal Education: Cross-National Currents from India and the United States." *Clinical Law Review* 13 (2): 165–212

Bradney, Anthony. 1995. "Raising the Drawbridge: Defending University Law Schools." *Web Journal of Current Legal Issues*. www.webjcli.ncl.ac.uk/articles1/bradney1.html.

Brooks, Susan L. 2012. "Meeting the Professional Identity Challenge in Legal Education through a Relationship-Centered Experiential Curriculum." *University of Baltimore Law Review* 41 (2): 395–440.

Chambliss, Elizabeth. 2012. "Two Questions for Law Schools about the Future Boundaries of the Legal Profession." *Journal of the Legal Profession* 36: 329–352

Chaput, Catherine. 2006. "Academic Freedom, Professional Transparency, and Intellectualism in the Era of Globalization." *Journal of Compositional Theory* 26 (1): 326–335.

Chesterman, Simon. 2015. "The Fall and Rise of Legal Education in Asia: Inhibition, Imitation, Innovation" (presentation at the Legal Education in Asia: From Imitation to Innovation conference, November 21).

Daniel, Philip T. K. and Scott Greytak. 2012. "Requiem for Affirmative Action in Higher Education: Case Analysis Leading to *Fisher v. University of Texas at Austin*." *Education Law Reporter* 279 (2): 539–570.

Dayal, Keshav. 2010. *Famous Lawyers of Freedom Struggle and Trials of Freedom Fighters*. Delhi: Universal Law Publishing.

Galanter, Marc and Jayanth K. Krishnan. 2004. "'Bread for the Poor': Access to Justice and the Rights of the Needy in India." *Hastings Law Journal* 55 (3): 789–834.

Ganz, Kian. 2012. "Funding Crunch Looms Over Indian Law Schools." *Live Mint*, April 26. www.livemint.com/2012/04/26202957/Funding-crunch-looms-over-Indi .html.

Glazer, Julia B. and Michael J. Tuteur. 2012. "Tenure Decisions and Academic Freedom." Massachusetts Continuing Legal Education. www.mcle.org/product/ catalog/code/2122367WCH.

Government of India, Planning Commission. 2011. "Faster, Sustainable and More Inclusive Growth: An Approach to the 12th Five Year Plan (2012–17)."

Griggs, Lynden. 2005. "Comment: The Integration of Teaching and Research in Higher Education." *Herdsa News* 25. www.herdsa.org.au/wpcontent/uploads/ 2007/06/3_herdsa_news_december_2005.pdf.

Greenawalt, Kent. 2009. "Religious Law Schools: Tension between Conscience and Academic Freedom." *Journal of Legal Education* 59 (1): 131–135

Grove, Jack. 2012. "Academic Salaries No Longer Attract Top Talent, Survey Finds." *Times Higher Education*, March 22. www.timeshighereducation.co.uk/story.asp? storycode=419399.

Harden, Nathan. 2012. "Academic Freedom Requires Political Freedom." *International Business Times*, April 4. www.ibtimes.com/articles/324107/20120404/ nypd-muslim-surveillance-spying-education-students.htm.

Jayanthi, C. 2012. "Private Sector Needed in Higher Education." *The Hindu*, February 23. www.thehindubusinessline.com/opinion/private-sector-needed-in-higher-education/article2924685.ece.

Jonathan, Ruth. 2006. *Academic Freedom, Institutional Autonomy and Public Accountability in Higher Education: A Framework for Analysis of the 'State-Sector' Relationship in a Democratic South Africa*. Council of Higher Education South Africa. www.che.ac.za/media_and_publications/frameworks-criteria/ academic-freedom-institutional-autonomy-and-public.

Kaul, Sanat. 2006. "Higher Education in India: Seizing the Opportunity" (working paper no. 179). www.icrier.org/pdf/WP_179.pdf.

Kosuri, Praveen. 2012. "Losing My Religion: The Place of Social Justice in Clinical Legal Education." *Boston College Journal of Law and Social Justice* 32 (2): 331–344.

Krishnan, Jayanth K. 2004 "Professor Kingsfield Goes to Delhi: American Academics, the Ford Foundation, and the Development of Legal Education in India" *American Journal of Legal History* 46 (XLVI):447–499.
Krishnan, Jayanth K. 2013. "Peel-Off Lawyers: Legal Professionals in India's Corporate Law Firm Sector." *Socio-Legal Review* 9 (1): 1–59.
Kumar, C. Raj. 2007. "Academic Freedom and Higher Education." *The Hindu*, November 13. www.thehindu.com/todays-paper/tp-opinion/academic-freedom-and-higher-education/article1947069.ece.
Kumar, C. Raj. 2009. "Building Nation through Legal Education." *The Pioneer*, March 26. www.dailypioneer.com/165034/Building-nation-through-legal-education.html.
Kumar, C. Raj. 2012a. "Indian Universities Need an International Outlook." *The New Indian Express*, October 7. www.newindianexpress.com/opinion/article1288575.ece.
Kumar, C. Raj. 2012b. "Profit and Loss in a Knowledge Society." *The Indian Express*, November 30. www.indianexpress.com/news/profit-and-loss-in-a-knowledge-society/1038205/.
Kumar, C. Raj. 2012c. "A Study in Mediocrity." *Hindustan Times*, September 25. www.hindustantimes.com/News-Feed/Editorials/A-study-in-mediocrity/Article1–935619.aspx.
Levin, Richard C. 2005. "The Global University: Inauguration of the Fox International Fellowships" (speech delivered by the president of Yale University at Jawarharlal Nehru University, January 3).
MacIintyre, Stuart. 2010. *The Poor Relation: A History of Social Sciences in Australia*. Melbourne: Melbourne University Publishing.
Mehra, Puja. 2015. "Foreign Law Firms Will Soon Carry Out Arbitration in India." *The Hindu*, June 30. www.thehindu.com/news/national/bci-agrees-to-centres-propsal-to-open-up-arbitration-legal-services-to-foreign-law-firms/article7368041.ece.
Minow, Martha. 1991. *Making All the Difference*. Ithaca, NY: Cornell University Press.
National Knowledge Commission. 2009. "Report to the Nation 2006–09." www.knowledgecommission.gov.in/downloads/report2009/eng/report09.pdf.
Noorani, A. G. 2007. "Academic Freedom in Kashmir and Elsewhere." *Economic and Political Weekly* 42 (36): 3600–3602.
Ramachandran, Sudha. 2011. "Ramayana Row Divides India." *Asia Times*, November 10. www.atimes.com/atimes/South_Asia/MK10Df01.html.
Rapoport, Nancy B. 2010. "Academic Freedom and Academic Responsibility." *Green Bag 2d* 13 (2): 189–201.
Sandel, Michael. 2012. *What Money Can't Buy: The Moral Limits of Markets*. New York: Farrar, Straus and Giroux.
Schauer, Frederick. 2012. "The Permutations of Academic Freedom." *Arkansas Law Review* 65 (2): 193–202.
Sunder, Shyam. 2011. "Higher Education Reforms in India" (Yale SOM working paper, December 7). www.ssrn.com/abstract=1975844.
Terry, Laurel S., Steve Mark, and Tahlia Gordon. 2012. "Trends and Challenges in Lawyer Regulation: The Impact of Globalization and Technology." *Fordham Law Review* 80 (6): 2661–2684.

Thakur, Anil Kumar and Mohan Patel. 2010. *Challenges of Education in the 21st Century*. Delhi: Deep and Deep Publications.

Times Higher Education World University Rankings 2012–2013. www.timeshighereducation.co.uk/world-university-rankings/2012–13/world-ranking.html.

Titus, Jordan J. 2011. "Pedagogy on Trial: When Academic Freedom and Education Consumerism Collide." *Journal of College and University Law* 38 (1): 107–166.

Todd, Jeff. 2007. "State Universities v. State Government: Applying Academic Freedom to Curriculum, Pedagogy, & Assessment." *Journal of College and University Law* 33 (2): 387–428.

Ulen, Thomas S. 2009. "The Impending Train Wreck in Current Legal Education: How We Might Teach Law as the Scientific Study of Social Governance." *University of St. Thomas Law Journal* 6 (2): 302–336.

Varghese, John. 2010. "Global Legal Education and India – A Blueprint for Raising Indian Legal Education to Global Standards" (working paper, Government Law College, December 10). www.papers.ssrn.com/sol3/papers.cfm?abstract_id=1728451.

SECTION VII

CAPACITY BUILDING

20

Equalizing Access to the WTO: How Indian Trade Lawyers Build State Capacity

Gregory Shaffer, James Nedumpara, Aseema Sinha, and Amrita Bahri

I. INTRODUCTION

The law of the World Trade Organization (WTO) is not autonomous. It shapes and is shaped. It not only affects countries' trade and tariff policies but also shapes their laws, regulations, and institutions. In particular, it creates new accountability mechanisms with particular normative frames and opens markets, creating new demand for professional expertise such as legal expertise. The WTO institutionalizes capitalism and thus provides opportunities directly and indirectly for business lawyers. Yet it does not do so in a uniform manner. Rather, nation states, working with private constituents, negotiate the terms of WTO law and shape its meaning, whether directly through engagement or indirectly through lack of engagement.

The WTO should not be viewed as static and deterministic, autonomously affecting states. Rather, the WTO legal order is shaped by those who negotiate its terms and who participate in their interpretation, affecting how WTO law is understood and applied. The negotiation and interpretation of WTO law, in turn, affects countries' policy space for social and developmental initiatives, as well as their ability to challenge foreign countries' trade restrictions affecting their exports. The scope of the WTO legal order entails not only formal disputes, which are of great interest and generate reams of scholarship, but also the shadow effects of law on claims that are settled and never known and on domestic regulatory policy initiatives that are advanced, not considered, or shelved (Shaffer 2015).

Participating in the construction and interpretation of WTO law, however, is not free – not for governments or for private parties. Its interpretation has become highly complex and evolving, with its jurisprudence exceeding ninety thousand pages of panel and Appellate Body decisions issued through

April 2014.[1] Not all are in the position to participate in shaping the WTO legal order and its effects. Thus a rule-based system such as that of the WTO can favor those members that have significant legal capacity (such as the United States and the European Union) over those that do not (such as most developing countries).

For India, the negotiation and interpretation of WTO law affects multiple policy issues, from the contours of intellectual property (IP) law and its implications, to the right to health, to the export of generic drugs, to the development of industrial policy, to the regulation of labor and the environment, to restrictions on imports and exports. All of these issues have been directly or indirectly the subject of WTO disputes, and all of them involve disputes in which India has been a party. Formal WTO disputes, however, only begin to reflect the implications of WTO law.

This chapter examines the growing role of Indian lawyers in the transformation of Indian trade policy through the development of trade-related legal capacity. By trade-related legal capacity, we mean, broadly, the ability of a country to use law to engage proactively in the development and defense of international and domestic policy. Such capacity is critical for the drafting and interpretation of international legal agreements, the adaptation of domestic regulation within those agreements' constraints, the monitoring of foreign commitments, and the development of legal arguments in formal international litigation and informal dispute settlement. Through developing legal capacity, public and private actors work together to open export opportunities abroad and defend domestic policy measures at home. While others have written about the legalization of international trade through the increased role of the WTO Legal Secretariat and the emergence of the WTO Appellate Body in international dispute settlement, this chapter addresses the growing role of lawyers in the development of trade policy at home in one of the world's rising emerging economies, India (Weiler 2002).

The chapter builds from years of field research in India and Geneva, involving more than 150 semistructured interviews with Indian officials and stakeholders.[2] The interviewees included former ambassadors and members of the WTO Mission in Geneva, members of the Indian bureaucracy in Delhi, private lawyers, private trade association and industry representatives, officials of international organizations, researchers in think tanks, academics, representatives of nongovernmental organizations (NGOs), and news reporters. We complemented these interviews with participant observation in Geneva and New Delhi and reviewed our findings against primary and secondary documents.

II. TERRAIN OF THE DEBATE AND THEORETICAL CONTEXT

Our arguments and findings resonate with and contribute to three interrelated literatures and debates that implicate the role of law and lawyers in emerging economies. They are: the creation of transnational legal orders, the rise of the new developmental state, and the building of legal capacity to engage with and shape such transnational legal orders and their implications for the developmental state.

First, this study documents the increasing role of transnational legal ordering and its implications for law and lawyers in nation states (Shaffer 2013; Halliday and Shaffer 2015). The study of transnational legal ordering places the relationship between international, transnational, and domestic legal processes in tension that gives rise to the potential institutionalization of legal norms, and in particular within nation states. Transnational legal ordering involves both top-down and bottom-up processes that operate recursively and dynamically, shaping the meaning of legal norms. This chapter addresses how India has engaged lawyers to enhance its ability to participate and shape the WTO legal order – and in the process also changed, in part, itself. It examines the reciprocal transformations entailed in the WTO legal order about how a country transforms itself in order to engage with the WTO and, in turn, shape it, giving rise to transnational legal ordering.

Second, our findings contribute to an emergent revisionist argument about the developmental state across regions and issue areas (Stubbs 2011; Trubek 2013). We find that the Indian state has not withdrawn from global and transnational influences (as per the developmental state model of the 1950s) but rather been transformed and enhanced. The WTO catalyzes the building of new state capacity, including legal and regulatory capacity, even though its **raison d'être** is to free markets and liberalize trade among nations. As Aseema Sinha writes, the "globalization of trade rules . . . creates pressures to strengthen national state agencies and trade policy processes" (Sinha 2007, 1184. We find that the WTO and WTO law have spurred, and should continue to spur, the Indian developmental state to enhance its legal capacity in relation to both international economic law and the law's implications for domestic law reform and policy by expanding coordinated linkages with the private sector.

Third, because of the implications of transnational legal ordering for the developmental state, states invest in the building of legal capacity so as to engage in the shaping of global rules and assess alternatives for their implementation in order to protect policy space (Shaffer et al. 2008; Shaffer and Melendez 2010; Santos 2012). This study contributes to our understanding of how developing countries build legal capacity so as to better participate in the construction of the WTO legal order and its implications for the developmental state. India is pressed to adapt to WTO legal norms and at times uses them to facilitate policy reforms. But it also seeks to shape and modify the understanding of the rules for its own ends. To do so, it aims to build legal capacity, in particular through opening the state bureaucracy to engage with the private sector and private lawyers, facilitated through the building of a specialized bar comprising industry- and government-hired private lawyers.

III. INDIA AND THE GATT YEARS: LITTLE ROLE FOR LAW AND LAWYERS

As indicated in the overview, before the creation of the WTO, India was a closed economy, built on a socialist model of five-year plans, wary of international economic commitments in light of its colonial heritage, erecting a centralized bureaucracy and administering what was known as the "License Raj." The Indian bureaucratic system was viewed as sclerotic in that decision making could be time- and resource-consuming, slowing entrepreneurial endeavor, although it also demanded a certain nimbleness for businesses to navigate (Sinha 2005). Firms were preoccupied with obtaining licenses to import, and subsidies to export, as part of complicated government policies to manage Indian balance of payments, for which they had little need for lawyers. The result was considerable rent seeking by Indian businesses. Their primary market was domestic. They felt unable to compete internationally. As the development economist Ian M. D. Little wrote in a widely read text in the early 1980s, "Developing countries never expected to be able to export manufacturers to the developed countries" (Little 1982).

The political and economic climate that prevailed in India before 1975 (the time of the "Emergency" declared by Indira Gandhi) had a significant impact on the policies that India followed for the next two decades. The Indian economy, which grew at a rate of 4.1 percent from 1951 to 1965, declined to a rate of 2.3 percent from 1965 to 1975, while at the same time the population rate also grew at 2.3 percent per annum – a net impact of zero percent per capita growth for that decade. This performance gave rise to the popular expression "Hindu rate of growth," a growth rate that totaled just 3.5 percent per year between 1960 and 1985, leaving a significant percentage of Indians in extreme poverty. The phrase captured a sense of inevitability, of predestination, a mix of sober acceptance and incapacitating despair.[3]

The socialist-oriented government engaged in four forms of policy that left little room for law, and thus for business and trade lawyers. First, it heavily regulated the private sector in terms of technology choices, location, and prices, while relying on the state-funded public sector for investment in capital goods.

Second, it promoted small businesses with policies that were biased against capital development and investment. Third, it created an import licensing system where government approval was needed to trade. And finally, it adopted high tariffs and quantitative restrictions to segregate its internal market from international competition. Arvind Panagariya notes that by the mid-1970s, India's trade regime had become so repressive that the share of nonoil and noncereal imports to the GDP fell from the already low level of 7 percent from 1957 to 1958 to 3 percent from 1975 to 1976 (Panagariya 2004).

In 1951, India adopted the Industries (Development and Regulation) Act (IDRA), which ensured that companies were formed and expanded only through obtaining a license. The government wielded discretionary power over the approval of any proposed change in capacity, location, expansion of production facility, or obtaining foreign exchange for the import of plant and machinery. In 1967 the government introduced a small-scale industry (SSI) reservation policy, creating a list of items that could be manufactured only by small-scale units. The regulations defined small-scale units as those with an investment of no more than INR$750,000 (as of early 2017, approximately US$11,00) in plant and machinery. The SSI reserved list included clothing, shoes, leather products, sports goods, stationery, office products, and furniture. As late as 1991, the SSI reservation applied to 830 goods as classified under the international harmonized customs system (Panagariya 2008, 65).[4] Economic policies at this time had a dual-pronged structure: public-sector investment led by the state, and labor-intensive employment encouraged in diverse ways through reservation policies for small-scale producers. In addition, the government reserved production of coal, power, telecommunications, insurance, mining, and oil to the public sector. As a result, India had one of the most controlled investment regimes in the world. Such policies gave rise to inefficiency, a lack of technical innovation, and low productivity.

In conjunction with tight import licensing procedures, India applied import controls and high levels of tariff protection. It introduced import controls in the 1940s to conserve foreign exchange. It introduced high tariffs in Nehru's second Five-Year Plan in 1956 as part of an import substitution policy and out of balance-of-payments concerns (Bhagwati and Srinivasan 1975). The substantial foreign exchange balances that India built during the Second World War had eroded by 1956, resulting in a substantial real appreciation of the rupee in relation to the British pound sterling and the US dollar. Regulation of balance of payments became the central concern of India's economic policy, giving rise to comprehensive and tight import controls (Bhagwati and Srinivasan 1975; Pursell et al. 2007). In the 1970s the government liberalized slightly by creating an open general licensing (OGL) list, but this list was also subject to bureaucratic control. Essentially, India was a small inward-oriented economy incapable of affecting international trade and largely uninterested in shaping international trading rules and their application.

The tight import licensing conditions, combined with an overvalued Indian exchange rate, created significant differences between domestic prices and lower international ones. This difference, in turn, created a bias against Indian exports. In order to offset that bias, the government provided export subsidies (Srinivasan 2000; Interview 26, 2010). Many Indian businesses were not so much interested in obtaining the subsidies to gain market share in international markets than to use the funds to obtain price advantages in the more important, but profit-squeezed, domestic market (Interview 26, 2010).

As a result, neither the government nor the private sector had much of a focus on international trade, so India paid little attention to the General Agreement on Tariffs and Trade (GATT), the predecessor to the WTO, and made few legal commitments under it. At the time that the Uruguay Round negotiations were in full swing from 1990 to 1991, India's maximum tariff rate was 355 percent and its simple average applied tariff rate was 125 percent. Only 6 percent of Indian tariff lines were bound, meaning that India could raise tariff rates for 94 percent of its tariff lines at any time. India complemented the tariff regime with different types of quantitative restrictions. These restrictions took various complicated forms, such as those administered through nonautomatic licenses, canalized agencies, and special import licenses, and those that were subject to different conditions.[5] They were imposed on the grounds that India had to monitor continually its unfavorable balance-of-payments situation (Mehta 2000, 1667).

The administrative system for import restrictions required a bureaucracy, creating delays, uncertainty, and opportunities for corruption. The bureaucracy was insular and nontransparent, and the private sector that engaged with it did so to obtain quota rents from the licensing system. As an example of such nontransparency, a former India Ministry of Commerce official told us that the first shredder provided to a service within the Ministry of Commerce went to the trade division handling the GATT (Interview 26, 2010). In such a closed, nontransparent system, law and trade lawyers had little role to play.

IV. CATALYSTS OF BUILDING INDIAN CAPACITY IN TRADE LAW

The Indian development model changed in the 1990s. With the fall of the Berlin Wall in 1989 and the socialist model discredited, Indian officials eyed with envy the rise of East Asian economies with their export-oriented growth models. While East Asia grew, India in 1991 was struck by a severe economic crisis from the Gulf War oil shock and India's dependence on petroleum imports. The government went to the International Monetary Fund (IMF) for emergency credits of US$2.3 billion and, to its shame, even exported gold to the vaults of Great Britain as the value of the rupee plunged and the country could not meet its debts.[6] As a condition to the IMF financing (a *conditionality*, in the IMF's terms), the IMF called for reforms of the Indian system, including an opening to foreign trade. Under duress, the Indian government of Prime Minister Narasimha Rao and Finance Minister Manmohan Singh responded. They later spun these reforms as homegrown, calling them the "1991 reforms," which is how the reforms are conventionally discussed within India to this day (Singh 1991). Yet, as a former high-level member of the Indian Administrative Service (IAS) confirmed to us, "the IMF and international institutions helped to provide an excuse to do what otherwise was more difficult to do politically, as change was otherwise very difficult to obtain" (Interview 1, 2012). The reforms had a significant impact, as India engaged with a globalizing economy. The proportion of trade (imports and exports) to India's GDP was 8 percent in 1970, but expanded sevenfold to 53 percent by 2013.[7]

The United States and European Union dominated the Uruguay Round negotiations, and India was pressed to respond to US and EU initiatives. Although the Indian government consulted with the private sector and civil society, civil society activists roundly critiqued the government for insufficient consultations. The most controversial issues for civil society activists were agriculture and pharmaceutical patents, although much of the industrial sector was also concerned about the implications of the agreements for their competitiveness.

The Uruguay Round negotiations and the resulting WTO agreements that became effective on January 1, 1995, were broad in their coverage, encompassing nineteen distinct multilateral agreements, affecting market access in manufacturing, agriculture and textiles, intellectual property, services, and trade-related investment measures. Joining the WTO meant that India had to implement these WTO commitments, opening its economy to competition and, in the process, providing new opportunities for business lawyers, directly and indirectly.

Under the WTO, India bound almost 65 percent of its tariff lines (World Trade Organization 1998). It significantly reduced import duties. In practice, India lowered its applied tariff rates much beyond its actual WTO commitments to an average of around 12 percent by 2010 (World Trade

Organization 2011). India also joined the new Information Technology Agreement in 1996, which a subset of WTO members finalized at the WTO Ministerial Conference in Singapore, which binds tariff rates at zero percent on information technology products. India, in addition, made market access commitments regarding services for the first time under the General Agreement on Trade in Services (GATS) involving thirty-three services sectors. Pursuant to the transparency provisions of the WTO's Technical Barriers to Trade (TBT) Agreement and Sanitary and Phytosanitary Measures (SPS) Agreement, India also created new administrative enquiry points for all technical regulation and sanitary and phytosanitary protection measures and committed to new publicity, transparency, and due process requirements.

However, the Indian government and businesses did not engage in legal capacity building immediately in response to the WTO's creation. Rather, they responded to the WTO law in action, and in particular to politically sensitive complaints brought against India by the United States. What spurred India's development of legal capacity, as in the case of Brazil and China, was being placed on the defensive (Shaffer and Melendez 2010). The United States and European Union brought a series of critical cases against India in the WTO's first years that pressed the Indian bureaucracy to develop new partnerships with the private sector and private lawyers. The key disputes were *India-Patents* involving a US and EU challenge to India's implementation of the TRIPS Agreement; *India-QR* involving a US challenge against India's use of quantitative restrictions on balance-of-payments grounds; and *India-Autos* involving a US challenge of Indian measures to favor the development of a domestic auto sector.[8] The United States itself worked through public-private partnerships involving government and private US lawyers, a model that India would soon take into account (Shaffer 2003).

In *India-Patents*, the United States and European Union challenged India's implementation of its commitment under the TRIPS Agreement to create a transitional "mail-box system" where patent applications could be filed to establish priority and obtain exclusive marketing rights on a transitional basis until India provided patent protection for pharmaceuticals and chemical products used in agriculture, such as fertilizers and pesticides. In defense, India contended that it had fulfilled its commitments through administrative instructions, but it was unsuccessful before the panel and Appellate Body. Within India, the case was called a "shot over the bow of a Hobbesian essence of sovereignty" (Camen and Norchi 2002, 167, 184). The case nonetheless triggered significant legal debate regarding how India could ultimately comply with the TRIPS Agreement in a way that would make use of the flexibilities provided in the agreement in light of India's development and social policy objectives (Kapczynski 2009; Gopakumar 2010).[9]

The most broad-reaching case affecting Indian industry and agriculture was the *India-QR* decision, which implicated the reform of India's import licensing regime. India had experienced a major balance-of-payments crisis from 1990 to 1991, and it had to go to the IMF to receive US$2.3 billion in credit. As a condition to the credit, India agreed to a series of reforms, including the removal of quantitative restrictions and import licensing on most goods (Panagariya 2004). India nonetheless maintained import licensing and quantitative restrictions on consumer goods that accounted for 2,714 tariff lines, nearly 30 percent of its total number. In *India-QR*, the United States challenged India's invocation of quantitative restrictions on balance-of-payments grounds for these remaining tariff lines. The case was a wake-up call for India, given its systemic importance for India's import controls. India had wished to keep the measures in effect until at least 2006 and invoked its status as a developing country in defense. But India did not prevail. Rather, an IMF representative reported that India no longer faced a balance-of-payments crisis, and the panel and Appellate Body cited the IMF report as critical support of their decision against India.

The case exhibited the role of judicialization of WTO dispute settlement in comparison with that under the GATT. Under the GATT, disputes over balance of payments had been addressed politically within the GATT committee system (Eglin 1987). India contended that preexisting practice under GATT precluded the dispute settlement panel from hearing the case, but it again failed in this defense.

The WTO decision spurred fears in India that foreign products would flood the Indian market, particularly marine and dairy products, confectionary items, and fruits and vegetables (Muralidharan 2001). The Ministry of Commerce promised to establish a "war room" to keep a vigil on some three hundred sensitive products, and it constantly assured stakeholders that it had put adequate monitoring mechanisms in place (Interview 11, 2010).[10] The government appointed a committee headed by the Ministry of Commerce secretary and the secretaries of Agriculture and of Small Scale Industries to identify any safeguards required and to forewarn industries and trade bodies if any action was needed.

Shortly later, the United States challenged India's policy to support the development of a national auto sector in *India-Autos*, which involved India's use of local content, foreign exchange, and trade balancing requirements as conditions for imports and investment in the auto sector. The *India-Autos* dispute was in part a "mopping up" operation to eliminate the remaining vestiges of the import-licensing regime that India was required to modify in the *India-QR* decision (Bagwell and Sykes 2004). In addition, however, the Memorandum of Understanding ("MoU") that the government required from auto companies included commitments both to meet local content requirements in their manufacturing operations and to ensure that the value of their exports balanced the value of their imports. India lost this case as well but, in practice, was able to use the dispute settlement system to continue its requirements for a number of years to help develop local manufacturing know-how and enhance competitiveness. Government officials contend that the policy was successful, as India now exports autos to the Middle East, South Asia, and Central Asia, creating a new hub in competition with Thailand and Indonesia in the region (Interview 24, 2010).

In each case, India had to defend its system in a losing case but in the process learned the importance of developing legal capacity, including adapting its domestic measures to protect development objectives. The Indian media covered these politically sensitive cases against India in the WTO's early days, raising awareness about the implications of the WTO dispute settlement system for India. As Atul Kaushik, the lawyer in the government who handled WTO dispute settlement in Geneva from 2003 to 2006, states, "These disputes were of high visibility for India. The government felt it needed to build capacity regarding WTO law" (Interview with Atul Kaushik, 2010).

With the launch of the Doha Round in 2001, government and business realized that they needed to invest more resources in trade law-related capacity. As a representative of the Indian chamber of commerce, FICCI, states, FICCI realized that it was "imperative" that business become more involved "because of our sense of failure to do so in the Uruguay Round" (Interview 3, 2010). Although the Doha Round collapsed, India engaged in a growing number of bilateral and plurilateral trade negotiations for which private-sector collaboration was needed and continued to engage in periodic multilateral trade negotiation initiatives. By late 2006, advocates of a "new India" saw the country as part of a global shift of economic power away from the United States and European Union and toward larger developing countries, namely the BRIC (Brazil, Russia, India, and China). Yet to be a global leader, India needed to continue to enhance its legal capacity in the public and private sectors, giving rise to public-private partnerships. As a lawyer who worked with economists in think tanks noted, while economists traditionally have been most important for Indian policy-making analysis within and outside of the government, and they continue to be so today, the bureaucratic establishment and economists were pressed to gradually recognize the importance of law and lawyering (Interview 41, 2010). Since legal capacity was not built into the traditional Indian government service, new methods were needed that could work with India's bureaucratic context.

V. REFORMING THE STATE AND THE CREATION OF PUBLIC-PRIVATE PARTNERSHIPS FOR TRADE LAW AND POLICY

India responded to the challenges of the WTO by significantly investing in greater expertise in the Indian bureaucracy that, in turn, became an interlocutor with the private sector and private legal counsel. The government reformed the state, investing in state capacity within the Ministry of Commerce and Industry (MoCI) as a node of trade law and policy, opening the state bureaucracy to build and tap into legal capacity in the private sector, and creating a government think tank, the Centre for WTO Studies, to engage in policy-relevant research and act as a liaison between the Ministry of Commerce, the private sector, and private lawyers and consultants.

The government designated MoCI as the nodal ministry for WTO negotiations and policy, and the ministry grew in prominence within the Indian bureaucracy (Sinha 2007). Within MoCI, the government created three new specialized agencies to handle matters implicated by WTO law: the Department of Industrial Policy and Promotion (DIPP), which manages, among other matters, intellectual property rights administration; a new Tariff Commission; and a reorganized Directorate General of Antidumping and Allied Duties (DGAD). In 1996, K. M. Chandrasekhar became joint secretary at the Department of Commerce and reconstituted the Trade Policy Division (TPD) to enhance government competence on trade matters and support the India mission to the WTO in Geneva.[11] The ministry increased staff strength from nine to forty officials within a few years (Sinha 2007). The status of trade positions, moreover, increased within the Indian bureaucracy so that officials increasingly sought them. This trend complementarily increased the qualitative capacity of Commerce ministry officials in trade law and policy.[12]

The government concurrently more than doubled the size of its mission in Geneva for WTO matters and enhanced coordination between the Geneva mission and the Ministry of Commerce in New Delhi. In 1995, when the WTO started, the Indian mission in Geneva had one ambassador and three officers. By 2010, the mission had six to eight officers, including one dispute settlement specialist (Interview 11, 2010; Interview 2, 2012). As a former ambassador of India to the WTO noted, "In the old days, the Geneva mission received no meaningful inputs from the capital," a situation unlike today (Interview 1, 2012).

Despite these developments and the relative growth in the capacity of trade officials at the Ministry of Commerce in Delhi and Geneva, the government still faced challenges given the scope of WTO issues. It realized that it needed to spur the development of complementary private-sector capacity building and to open itself to greater private-sector and civil-society input. The government obtained critical external support for domestic capacity building through a capacity-building project led by the United Nations Conference on Trade and Development (UNCTAD) and supported by India's Ministry of Commerce and Britain's Department for International Development (DFID), named Strategies and Preparedness for Trade and Globalisation in India (UNCTAD Capacity Building Project). The UNCTAD Capacity Building Project lasted eight years, from January 2003 to December 2010, and was first led by Veena Jha, an Indian trade economist whose husband, Harsha Singh, was one of the four deputy director generals at the WTO (Interview with Abhijit Das, 2010).[13] Aiming to strengthen human and institutional capacity for responding to trade issues, the project organized a series of broad-based and sector-specific stakeholder consultations in India. Through developing a new network of stakeholders, the UNCTAD Capacity Building Project was able to mobilize farmers, fishermen, and small producers to articulate their interests and concerns to inform the government's approach to WTO and new free trade agreement (FTA) negotiations for the first time. The aim was both to assist them with providing input to the government and to enable them to develop better strategies to adapt to economic globalization processes. The UNCTAD project also helped to spur MoCI to work with various state governments to establish WTO cells in order to enhance awareness of the WTO and provide feedback to MoCI from state governments, which govern populations larger than most WTO members.[14]

Given the difficulty of changing the bureaucracy from within, the Ministry of Commerce decided to outsource research and the building of public-private collaboration to government-sponsored think tanks, and, in particular, the Centre for WTO Studies (which directly reports to MoCI) and private lawyers who contract with MoCI or the Centre. MoCI created the Centre for WTO Studies in 1999.[15] The last head of the UNCTAD project, Abhijit Das, son of B. L. Das, former Indian ambassador to the GATT, became the head of the Centre for WTO Studies, which continues the networking initiatives begun in the UNCTAD Capacity Building Project. Das formerly worked in the division of the Ministry of Commerce handling WTO disputes and so understood the need for homegrown legal capacity in light of the implications of WTO law.

The mission of the Centre for WTO Studies is threefold: (1) to conduct research for MoCI; (2) to act as a liaison between MoCI and industry and civil society; and (3) to assist in capacity building and information diffusion by organizing workshops and publishing newsletters and reports (Interview 24, 2010).[16] As of December 2012 the Centre had eight members, one of whom is a lawyer. The Ministry of Commerce refers questions to the Centre relating to international trade negotiations, domestic policy that may be affected by international trade law, and potential claims against trading partners' measures that affect Indian exports. The Centre then outsources some of this work to private contractors, such as private lawyers and academics. One of the authors of this study, James Nedumpara, has served as a consultant.

As it develops, the Centre aims to become a node for trade policy analysis and capacity building in the Asia-Pacific region. In 2011 the WTO awarded the Centre a three-year contract to conduct a WTO regional trade policy course (RTPC) for the Asia-Pacific. The RTPC is a three-month training program that was attended by twenty-five participants from nineteen countries in 2011. In conjunction with the program, visiting experts also offer short-term courses and seminars on WTO issues at Indian universities and other institutions.

As part of its outreach program, the Centre for WTO Studies established regional divisions in different states of India. It appointed officers as the heads of each regional division, which are officially known as "nodal agencies" or "focal points." They are largely responsible for coordinating with the business entities in their respective regional jurisdictions.[17] In order to discharge their functions effectively, these officers receive regular training in international trade and legal aspects at the Centre in New Delhi (Interview with an official representative, Centre for WTO Studies, India Institute of Foreign Trade, 2013). These nodal agencies serve as contact points between the private sector, the advisers at the Centre, and MoCI. In addition, the government's Export Promotion Councils, originally created in the 1960s and 1970s, help coordinate relations between producers and the government.

Over time, the government has felt more freedom to work with the private sector, including skilled private Indian lawyers, regarding WTO legal issues, whether directly or through the Centre, instead of trying to do everything in-house. As a result, today "there is a small industry of [legal] consultants growing around the Department of Commerce that helps to fill the government's needs" (Interview with Atul Kaushik, 2010). As Abhijit Das, head of the Centre for WTO Studies, states, trade policy making became much more "participatory" and was "based on stronger empirical foundations" (Interview with Abhijit Das, 2010). Today, for all major WTO dispute settlement rulings, the Department of Commerce tries to organize a session, with the help of the Centre for WTO Studies, where a private consultant makes a presentation to the Department of Commerce and other ministries (Interview with Amar Sinha, 2013). One of the leading chambers of commerce or federation of industries in India is the lead partner, such as the Federation of Indian Chambers of Commerce and Industry (FICCI), the Confederation of Indian Industry (CII), the Associated Chambers of Commerce and Industry of India (ASSOCHAM), the Federation of Indian Export Organisations (FIEO), or the Federation of Indian Micro and Small and Medium Enterprises (FISME). The lead coordinator decides the date and place of the meeting, in consultation with the TPD, and is responsible for making other administrative and organizational arrangements (Interview with Rajan Sudesh Ratna, 2013). The participants include other chambers of commerce, export promotion councils, trade associations, affected private entities, concerned NGOs, and consumer organizations.

For example, following the *China-Raw Materials* case, the Ministry of Commerce identified twenty affected Indian ministries and invited all of them to hear a presentation of the findings to "raise awareness" (Interview with Amar Sinha, 2013). Similarly, the government organized consultations regarding the EU Reach Regulation in Mumbai, Kolkata, and Ahmadabad.[18] Participants included officials from the TPD; the departments of Pharmaceuticals, Drugs, and Chemicals and Petrochemicals; advisers from the Centre for WTO Studies; officials from the concerned export promotion council; and key exporters (Interview with Rajan Sudesh Ratna, 2013).

The Centre's initiatives exemplify how the WTO has helped to catalyze major changes in government relations with affected stakeholders and with private lawyers, giving rise to a trade law variant of public-private partnerships (Shaffer 2003). The Indian system remains rather top-down, where the private sector plays a much more limited role compared with the United States. Nonetheless, the change constitutes a major one in India, one that appears to be here to stay. As Professor Bipin Kumar of the National Law University–Jodhpur told us, "The new mantra in India is public-private partnerships. The old mentality regarding government is changing" (Interview with Bipin Kumar, 2012).

VI. NEW ROLE FOR ECONOMISTS IN TRADE POLICY NETWORKS

International trade negotiations demand economic expertise, since they have large economic implications. Such expertise must complement legal know-how. Indian officials began to feel the need for enhanced economic expertise as international trade negotiations intensified in the 2000s and became more complex and technical. Although India has many world-class economists, the civil service was traditionally quite insular and relied on "in-house research" through the Indian Economic Service, whose officials were considered much lower in seniority to the generalist officials of the Indian Administrative Service (Sinha 2007). Most of the research conducted within the Indian civil service was poor and not used in a significant way. This began to change after India lost the *India-QR* and *India-Patents* cases in the late 1990s, and the government sought external economic expertise in a more systematic, rigorous, and sustained way.

The government began to consult many external research agencies and institutions while also enhancing the funding of state research institutions, such as the Research and Information System for Developing Countries (RIS), which were asked to expand their mandates to international economic issues. The government allocated a significant budget for economic research to the Centre for WTO Studies. The Indian Ministry of Commerce also extensively consulted with and hired independent research institutes, such as the Indian Council for Research on International Economic Relations (ICRIER), the Madras Institute of Development Studies, the Centre for Management in Agriculture, and the Indian Institutes of Management, among others.[19] From 2002 to 2003 alone, it commissioned eleven new studies at a cost of eight million rupees (ibid.). This funding, in turn, catalyzed new investment in expertise within universities and think tanks, which hired economists to work on the commissioned studies, creating a recursive feedback loop for capacity building across the policy community. Universities and research institutions began to generate a large quantity of research reports, analysis, and commissioned studies, funded by the Indian state. The state's cognitive capacity for international trade negotiations significantly increased.

VII. THE FIELD OF PRIVATE INDIAN TRADE LAWYERS AND THEIR ROLE

Over the past decade, a small group of private Indian lawyers have developed trade law expertise and served the government on a variety of trade law matters. These lawyers perform four types of work. (1) They advise the government on its policies for the purposes of its negotiating positions (negotiating work). (2) They provide input on the drafting of legislation and regulation and the consideration of policy in light of WTO law (internal policy work). (3) They assist the government in evaluating WTO cases for and against it (litigation work). (4) They represent the private sector in import relief cases, such as antidumping, countervailing duties, and safeguard cases (import relief work).

The number of lawyers working on trade law matters is relatively small in light of the primarily intergovernmental nature of the WTO legal system. These highly skilled lawyers have a particular passion for this area of law. They largely work within boutique firms, although such firms can have more than one hundred attorneys overall. The largest elite law firms generally have not developed a major international trade law practice, though Moushami Joshi, a partner in Luthra & Luthra, works on trade matters as part of her portfolio, and R. V. Anuradha, the founder of Clarus Law Associates, a small boutique firm, was formerly a partner at India's largest law firm, Amarchand & Mangaldas & Suresh A. Shroff & Company. A list of the law firms working on international trade law matters, including the type of law firm and the type of trade law work, is included in annex 1.

The private lawyers working in India on trade issues often received some graduate legal education in the United States or Europe. The leading Indian lawyer experienced in WTO cases, Krishnan Venugopal, went to Harvard Law School, where he received an LLM and started an SJD, and practiced with the US law firm Paul Weiss. Suhail Nathani, who started the boutique firm Economic Laws Practice (ELP) based in Mumbai and Delhi, received a BA from Cambridge and an LLM from Duke Law School. Samir Gandhi, who was formerly with ELP, went to the London School of Economics for his LLMRV. Anuradha, who founded Clarus Law Associates, received a master's at SOAS at the University of London and was a global law scholar at NYU Law School. Moushami Joshi, a partner at Luthra & Luthra, received her LLM from George Washington University Law School. As Joshi says regarding her experience in the United States, "I had an interest in international trade, and it just got strengthened when I was in DC. And DC being an international place, you get to attend so many conferences; you are constantly going to all these meetings that think tanks have, which was great because . . . it just opened up my mind to this whole new world of law and legal practice" (Interview with Moushami Joshi, 2010).

The government facilitated the rise of talented, elite lawyers through its investment in the development of highly selective national law schools. Most directly regarding trade law, in 1996, just after the WTO's creation, the government funded a WTO chair at the leading Indian law school, the National Law School of India University (NLSIU) in Bangalore. The government's funding of a specific chair in trade law signaled the government's view of the growing importance of the subject and the hope that the government would indirectly benefit from new talent among young legal professionals (Interview with Atul Kaushik, 2010).[20] As K. M. Chandresekhar, who was instrumental in the chair's creation when he was joint secretary in the Trade Policy Division, informed us, "The idea was to get young lawyers who can follow and provide expertise on WTO matters. The idea was to create new structures within the Indian context" (Interview with K. M. Chandrasekhar, 2012).

Students at these elite law schools have taken a number of independent initiatives that further spurred knowledge building in international trade law in India. For example, NLSIU started one of the first student-edited journals on international trade law, *The Indian Journal of International Economic Law*. The National Law University in Jodhpur followed by creating a specialization in international trade and investment law and publishing a journal founded by a student in 2009 entitled *Trade, Law and Development*. A young generation of academics at Jindal Global Law School organized a concentration on international trade law and trade remedy law for LLM students and run a research center on international trade and economic law (CITEL), where students from leading law schools in India and abroad are offered a paid internship under the Global Research Internship Program (GRIP). In addition, prestigious law schools and law firms in India provide annual awards to students with outstanding academic performance in international economic law and WTO legal studies.

A number of Indian international trade lawyers came out of the national law schools, such as R. V. Anuradha, who graduated from Bangalore National Law School in 1995, and Samir Gandhi and Moushami Joshi, who respectively graduated from there in 1998 and 2001. As Joshi told us, she had three graduates from the national law schools working for her on trade law matters in 2012 (Interview with Moushami Joshi, 2012). Similarly, within the Centre for WTO Studies, Shailaja Singh joined as a legal consultant after receiving a degree from the West Bengal National University of Juridical Sciences–Kolkata, followed by an LLM at Cambridge University (Interview with Shailaja Singh, 2012).

Building from an earlier Brazilian model, MoCI has also created an internship program for law students, which is overseen by the India Institute of Foreign Trade (Shaffer et al. 2008). In parallel, other Indian public and private institutions have run internship programs for students in trade law as well, including the Centre for WTO Studies, Consumer Unity and Trust Society International, and law firms such as Luthra & Luthra, APJ-SLG Law Offices, Dua Associates, Lakshmikumaran & Sridharan, Economic Laws Practice, Seth Dua & Associates, Clarus Law Associates, and Amarchand & Mangaldas & Suresh A. Shroff & Company. Placement in these internships is highly competitive, and law graduates have opted for them even when they have had an opportunity to work full-time in the more lucrative corporate law sector. The internships reflect a radical shift in the previously closed Indian state bureaucracy.

A. *Trade Negotiations Support*

With the launch of the Doha Round in 2001, India adapted in order to play a more engaged role in the WTO system. To do so, the government created new linkages with stakeholders and consulted with them more regularly and transparently. While the trade division was previously known for being remote and nontransparent, now the government began to more proactively and regularly share analysis and documents with the private sector and seek legal opinions from Indian law firms. The government did so because of a sense that it would embarrass itself if the administration did not become more proactive and effective in tapping into and making use of the information and expertise of the private sector and a new generation of professionals engaged with global issues (Interview 26, 2010).

Perhaps most significantly, India worked with Brazil to respond at the 2003 Cancun Ministerial Conference to a joint EU-US proposal on agriculture that failed to reflect the interests of Brazil and India. In practice, Brazil had strong export interests and India protectionist ones (respectively reflecting the situations of the United States and European Union). Indian politicians are particularly concerned about the impact of opening India's market to increased agricultural imports because of the huge percentage of its population still employed in agriculture – about one-half – and the Maoist/Naxalite insurgencies threatening many Indian rural areas. The US-EU proposal, however, managed to account for US and EU interests while alienating both Brazil and India. Brazil and India responded by developing a counterproposal that accommodated their differing interests and by organizing a new group of developing countries known as the G-20, which notably included China, to cosponsor it.[21] The Brazilian and Indian governments worked with think tanks in their respective countries to develop their new modalities for WTO agricultural negotiations. Many consider this proactive developing-country stance on negotiating modalities to be a "defining moment of change for the WTO" and its negotiating system.[22] It was the first time that developing countries had come together to submit an integrated, detailed proposal on modalities that reflected their development concerns (Bhatia 2012). The think tanks' analyses provided the analytic heft for the G-20 in the Doha Round agricultural negotiations. Following this initiative, commentators referred to a new quad as being central for WTO negotiations, one in which India and Brazil joined the United States and European Union as members (Deese 2007).

In order to enhance its capacity, the Indian trade policy-making process became more inclusive (Sinha n.d.). As one senior Indian official observed, the new Trade Policy Division decided to "open its doors" to the private sector and civil society during the Doha Round of negotiations (Interview 1, 2012). The government increasingly invited industry and civil society representatives for consultations. Industry associations such as the FICCI and CII responded. The FICCI established a new WTO, FTA and Foreign Trade Division, and the CII a new Trade Policy Section. They, in turn, conducted their own stakeholder consultations with their members (Interview 3, 2010; Interview 6, 2012). Other industry organizations such as ASSOCHAM and PHD Chamber of Commerce and Industry did as well, conducting industry-wide consultations on trade negotiation matters before and after key events such as ministerial conferences and free trade agreement negotiations. The government shared the cost of these industry consultations and provided technical support, recognizing its ultimate dependence on private-sector support (Interview 7, 2012).

Organizations such as the CII started an India Everywhere campaign with a view to showcasing India to the outside world. Indian business and political leaders became a regular feature at the annual meeting of the World Economic Forum (WEF) in Davos. In November 2012 the WEF organized a session in New Delhi entirely on India. The CII opened an office in Geneva in 2003 to regularly monitor the developments in the WTO negotiations and update the industry of developments.

Although the Doha Round of negotiations stalled in 2008, trade negotiations remained active in bilateral and regional forums, and continued in a less ambitious manner within the WTO itself.[23] Bilateral and regional trade negotiations gave rise to competition among countries to gain market access. These competitive processes have spurred India to enter a slew of bilateral and regional trade negotiations and agreements. India has signed trade agreements with Japan, South Korea, Thailand, Singapore, Malaysia, ASEAN (separately from its members), Sri Lanka, Chile, Afghanistan, Mercosur, South African Customs Union (SACU), Gulf Cooperation Council, and an Agreement on South Asia Free Trade Area (SAFTA) involving Bangladesh, Bhutan, India, Maldives, Nepal, Pakistan, and Sri Lanka. India has also launched negotiations for free trade agreements with the European Union, European Free Trade Association, Canada, Australia, New Zealand, Indonesia, Egypt, Israel, and a Regional Comprehensive Economic Partnership with the countries of Asia. Developments in these bilateral and regional forums potentially could trigger momentum for broader multilateral negotiations.

The government consults a group of trade lawyers regarding the legal texts being negotiated in these trade agreements, as well as other international law agreements implicated by trade law. It also hires private Indian attorneys for specialized assistance in specific legal areas, such as intellectual property, services, standards, import relief, and government procurement. For example, the government hired the Strategic Law Group (now part of the APJ-SLG Law Offices) to help in the preparation of India's proposal for a lesser duty rule under the Rules Negotiations in the Doha Round.[24] For FTA negotiations, firms such as Economic Laws Practice and Lakshmikumaran & Sridharan have also provided the government with advice (Interview 9, 2012). At times, the lawyers work with economists who address the economic implications of particular negotiating positions and modalities, whether for trade in goods or trade in services (Interviews with Indian attorneys, economists in think tanks, and government offices, 2010 and 2012). At times, other government departments have engaged these attorneys for international law-related work that may be indirectly implicated by WTO law, such as the Ministry of Environment and Forests regarding climate change.

Indian business also increasingly recognized the implications of WTO trade negotiations. As Kaushik states, as India opened up its economy to international trade, "there was recognition of industries that they need to get to a higher competitive level vis-à-vis their competitors. Those industries recognized the need for internal capacities to deal with international trade matters" (Interview with Atul Kaushik, 2010). The process started with the creation of WTO cells within Indian trade associations and large companies in the late 1990s and early 2000s. These cells were created across sectors, from auto components to financial services to textiles. They handle different aspects of trade law and policy, including market access issues in trade negotiations, as well as (more broadly) export and import issues, export control matters, trade remedy matters such as antidumping, countervailing duty and safeguard investigations, technical regulations and standards, and other regulatory matters. For example, Tata Iron and Steel Company (TISCO), the largest Indian steel maker, engaged a senior consultant to advise the company and the consortium of Indian steel companies in the Organisation for Economic Co-operation and Development (OECD) steel subsidies negotiations.

B. *WTO Implementation and Policy Space*

The WTO system has significant implications for national law and policy. As an illustration, WTO rules and dispute settlement affected the substance and timing of India's dismantling of its License Raj and system of quantitative restrictions, India's adoption and implementation of a new patent law, and the rise of Indian import relief laws and administrative actions. Yet WTO law and its implementation are also subject to legal interpretation, potentially creating work for lawyers.

The government and businesses have engaged private lawyers to assess government policy options in light of existing trade law. The Department of Commerce receives a large number of questions from other Indian departments on WTO compatibility of legislation and regulation, and at times it outsources such questions to private consultants. Regarding Indian legislation generally, the joint secretary in MoCI informed us that it "gets references about every single day" regarding the WTO implications for proposed legislation, regulation, or policy (Interview with Amar Sinha, 2013).

As other government departments become aware of the implications of WTO agreements, they also have contacted private attorneys for consultations. WTO law affects industrial policy choices, such as the use of subsidies and domestic content requirements, and thus implicates many Indian ministries. For example, the powerful Indian Planning Commission has contacted private attorneys regarding choices over building power infrastructure, including options for increasing or reducing tariffs and applying local content requirements to build domestic manufacturing capacity (Interview with Moushami Joshi, 2012). In the past, we were told, the Planning Commission would never have consulted outside lawyers, much less for international trade law, so this development is a significant one in indicating the broader implications of WTO law for Indian law and policy. The government likewise engaged consultations from private law firms regarding the implications of the GATT and WTO agreements on India's emerging renewable energy policies, including consideration of renewable energy requirements for utilities (Interview with Moushami Joshi, 2012). These government departments have also worked with private attorneys who initially worked with the Department of Commerce on trade law matters and who now also provide consultations regarding Indian legislation in relation to other international law (Interview 31, 2012). The WTO can be seen as a catalyst, and part of a broader trend, for the government becoming aware of the need to integrate outside legal counsel in understanding the international law implications of Indian legislative and administrative policy initiatives.

The WTO cells in private companies and trade associations, addressed here, also provide analysis of trade policy initiatives and regulatory issues. Large Indian companies more generally have hired in-house lawyers to reduce the dependence on law firms, including for work that may require knowledge of WTO law. For example, a Department of Commerce official told us he saw that a "textile fashion designer recruited three lawyers with terms of reference regarding how much WTO law they know" (Interview 26, 2010). Small and medium-sized Indian companies (SMEs), in parallel, have used the services of specialists within industry and trade associations, such as Texprocil, Confederation of Indian Textile Industry (CITI), Automotive Component Manufacturers Association of India (ACMA), Federation of Indian Export Organization (FIEO), Society of Indian Manufacturers (SIAM), Automobile Components Manufacturers Association of India (ACMA), Association of Synthetic Fibre Industry (ASFI), and the National Association of Software and Services Companies (NASSCOM).[25]

WTO law grants countries some flexibility in interpreting its provisions, so India had some leeway in determining how to revise its laws and adapt its institutions. Although international lawyers and international relations scholars tend to focus on the issue of "compliance" as a binary issue, and commentators such as Thomas Friedman refer to the "golden straitjacket" of global markets, countries retain flexibility to engage in hybrid policy making within constraints (Friedman 1999). In implementing, they may invent; in adopting, they may indigenously adapt. Such a mind-set is critical for development (Hausmann and Sabel 2007). India, for example, radically revised its patent law, expanding protection to pharmaceutical and agricultural chemical products pursuant to the TRIPS Agreement. Yet the government did so in an innovative manner after a long internal study and consultations with stakeholders. It created new definitions of what a patent must show in terms of novelty and an inventive step, thus narrowing the scope of patent claims. In parallel, India made it considerably easier to challenge patents under US and EU models by including both pre- and postgrant challenges and permitting these challenges to occur before an administrative body that is more efficient in processing them than a court. Similarly, as we see later, India has indigenized its antidumping law in light of its institutional capacities.

The WTO has created work for lawyers beyond traditional trade law work, as exemplified by intellectual property law. As the World Intellectual Property Organization reports, "From 1997 to 2011, patent filings increased . . . in India by 605 percent" (World Intellectual Property Organization 2013). Major litigation over intellectual property rights is taking place in India in the shadow of the TRIPS Agreement, such as *Novartis v. Union of India* in 2007, *Novartis Ag v. Union of India* in 2013, and *Bayer v. Union of India* in 2010 (Chaudhuri et al. 2010; Hoen 2013). Norms in India have shifted regarding patents. As a former Indian ambassador to the WTO quipped to us, "Now one speaks of patent or perish, whereas before the mantra was no patents or perish" (Interview with former ambassador to the WTO, 2013).[26] These developments reflect the important, but indirect, ways in which the WTO has affected law and lawyering in India in subject-specific areas.

C. *WTO Dispute Settlement*

A small group of Indian lawyers in the private sector has become increasingly important for providing counsel to India on potential and actual WTO trade disputes. The GATT dispute settlement system was slow and weak compared with the WTO's, and India participated little. In GATT's roughly fifty-year history, India was a party in three minor cases, of which only one resulted in a formal GATT report.[27]

With the commitments that India and other countries made in the Uruguay Round, and with the rise of the WTO's legalized and judicialized dispute settlement system, this situation has changed. India has become one of the leading users of the WTO dispute settlement system, along with Brazil and China among non-OECD countries. Through October 2013, India was a complainant in twenty-one disputes and a respondent in twenty-two disputes (World Trade Organization 2013). It was a third party in ninety-one additional ones. A complete list of disputes where India has been involved as a complainant or respondent, together with the lawyers who assisted the government in these disputes, is provided in annexes 2 and 3.

Over the past decade, the government's procedure for the selection of trade lawyers became more systematized. In 2010 the Department of Commerce, in consultation with the Department of Legal Affairs, enlisted seventeen law firms for defending India's interest in WTO disputes (Correspondence with MoCI, 2013). The Ministry of Commerce issues a call of interest to the government-empanelled law firms with expertise in the relevant subject. The law firms that respond to the call are asked to provide information about their team of lawyers and their relevant experience, as well as a legal opinion. The TPD examines their credentials, along with their analytical work, and makes a decision formally approved by the Department of Legal Affairs (ibid.).

India has brought systemically important claims before the WTO system, in addition to those in which it has been a respondent. The *US-Shrimp* dispute is arguably the most referenced WTO case regarding the interpretation of the GATT exception clause, article XX, addressing the interaction of trade rules with environmental protection measures. The *EC-GSP* case is central for understanding legal requirements under the General Systems of Preferences. The *Turkey-Textiles* case establishes the jurisdiction of the WTO dispute settlement body in assessing the legality of measures taken for the formation of regional trade agreements under GATT article XXIV. The *EC-Bed Linen* case was the first to challenge the practice of zeroing used by the European Union and United States, which creates biased calculations of dumping margins against imports (Nedumpara 2012). And in the early case, *US-Shirt and Blouses*, the Appellate Body clarified the burden of proof in WTO cases (WT/DS 33/AB/R, 1997, 16). To bring cases, however, is not enough, given the systemic implications of these decisions. A country's aim is not only to win a case but also to shape the understanding of WTO law in line with its broader economic policy objectives.

After the *India-Patents* case, the government initially outsourced work to foreign lawyers but then increasingly worked with a cadre of Indian lawyers, working sometimes with or sometimes without foreign ones. The government first turned to Frieder Roessler, the former head of the GATT legal secretariat, initially in his private capacity and then as the first executive director of a new Advisory Center on WTO Law (ACWL) in Geneva in 2002. India quickly became the ACWL's most active user. Roessler worked for India in the *India-QR* and *India-Auto* disputes in an individual capacity, and in the *EU-GSP* and the *US-Rules of Origin* disputes as part of the ACWL. The government also periodically works with foreign lawyers in cases involving foreign application of import relief laws against Indian imports, such as with the Brussels-based law firm Vermulst Waer & Verhaeghe in the *EC-Bed Linen* dispute, which had represented the country in the underlying antidumping case in Brussels.

In parallel, however, the government began to work with an Indian attorney, Krishnan Venugopal, on WTO cases, starting with the *India-Patents* case when Venugopal was attached to the attorney general's office of India (from 1996 to 1998). Venugopal would continue to work with the government in future disputes on an ad hoc basis as he established an important Supreme Court practice, following the path of his father, one of India's most renowned lawyers before the Indian Supreme Court. Venugopal worked on the *India-Patents*, *India-QR*, *India-Autos*, *EC-GSP*, and *US-Customs Bond Directive* cases, either alone or jointly with other lawyers. The *US-Customs Bond Directive* case was the first in which Venugopal worked with the government without being assisted by Roessler and the ACWL. This move reflected the government's growing confidence in being able to work with Venugopal individually, and with Indian attorneys more generally (Interviews with Indian attorneys, 2010).

As a new generation of WTO-specialized legal talent developed in India, the government worked with a broader cadre of Indian law firms. The government hired Economics Laws Practice in the *India-Additional Duties* case, in which the Indian attorneys Suhail Nathani and Samir Gandhi worked; Luthra & Luthra Law Offices in the *India-Agricultural Products* case; Lakshmikumaran

& Sridharan in the *US-Steel Plate* case; and Clarus Law Associates, a Delhi-based boutique firm, in the *India-Solar Cells* case. To explore a potential claim, the Department of Commerce also engaged Clarus Law Associates to examine the legal issues behind a WTO challenge against restrictive US visa requirements under the Southwest Border Protection Act and the James L. Zadroga 9/11 Health and Compensation Act. In addition, Indian law firms increasingly provide legal analysis and drafting support for India's third-party submissions in WTO cases (Interview 9, 2012). Third-party submissions are important because decisions in WTO cases involving other countries can have systemic implications for the understanding and future application of WTO law, and India has increasingly asserted third-party rights in WTO cases.

The Indian government's work with the affected private sector in *US-Customs Bond Directive* provides an example of a successful Indian public-private partnership. In this case, India successfully challenged an enhanced bond requirement applied by the United States in an antidumping proceeding involving frozen warm-water shrimp from India and other developing countries. Indian seafood exporters saw their exports decline by almost one-third following the imposition of US antidumping duties in 2004. The government worked with the private sector, which is generally small and unorganized, through the government's Marine Products Exports Development Authority (MPEDA) and the Seafood Exporters Association of India (SEAI). These two public agencies work to enhance foreign market access for Indian seafood products, including in antidumping proceedings abroad. MPEDA and SEAI covered most of the legal fees and expenses in the case (Interview with Sandu Joseph, 2011). SEAI contributed more than 50 percent of the total costs from its internal resources and the rest from member contributions as a function of the value of their respective exports (Battacharyya 2005). Seafood exporters are on MPEDA's management board, which facilitated the cost-sharing agreement.

India and its seafood exporters paid a high price (from an Indian perspective) in the underlying US antidumping investigations, spending nearly US$12 million (around INR$65 crores) from 2003 to 2010 (Interview with Sandu Joseph, 2011). Challenging the measure at the WTO, in contrast, was much less costly, demonstrating the potential benefit of building WTO-related legal capacity. The Indian shrimp exporters also successfully pushed the government to join a group of countries that successfully challenged the US Byrd Amendment (known in the WTO as the US-Offset Act) under which the United States distributed the revenue obtained from US antidumping and countervailing duty proceedings to the petitioning US domestic industry, thereby subsidizing it.

India also worked closely with the private sector in successfully settling its WTO claim against the European Union in the *EC-Drug Seizure* case. India challenged the seizure of Indian generic drugs at various airports in Europe (and, in particular, the Netherlands) when the planes were being refueled before taking the generics to other developing countries, such as Brazil. A number of Indian industry associations, including Pharmaxil and FICCI, worked with the government to assess the facts, legal claims, and negotiating strategies before the government commenced consultations with the European Union. MoCI consulted the Permanent Mission of India to the WTO while it was considering hiring an overseas legal expert in the matter. Concurrently, MoCI compared the credentials and expertise of Indian law firms in intellectual property–related matters. The Department of Commerce short-listed the overseas and Indian legal experts and sought the final approval from the Department of Legal Affairs for the terms of their engagement.[28] The government hired Krishnan Venugopal and US law professor Frederick Abbott to negotiate a favorable settlement in this matter with the European Union. Moushami Joshi at Luthra & Luthra provided an initial opinion regarding the legal viability of launching a formal dispute (Interviews 6, 9, and 16, 2012).

D. *Import Relief Work*

WTO rules cabin the way governments may legally provide economic protection. The WTO creates binding obligations not to increase tariffs above bound rates and not to use quotas and other quantitative restrictions. It further provides that economic protection may be provided (beyond bound tariffs) exclusively through three mechanisms: antidumping, countervailing duties, and safeguard regulations. These rules not only affect national law but spur the creation of entirely new national institutions and new professional specializations, which enhances the role of executive agencies, courts, lawyers, and accountants. Although these rules can be used for purely protectionist purposes, they also offer safety valves that can "provide Indian corporations with the 'breathing space' to become competitive," as Mark Wu shows in his discussion of the Indian telecommunications equipment company M/s Sterlite Industries, which after an antidumping award became one of the ten fastest-growing Indian technology companies and a leading exporter of optical fibers. (For more information, see Chapter 21 of this volume.)

Before the WTO's creation, India had import relief laws on the books but felt no need to use them because of its high tariffs and other import restrictions. Following India's binding and significant reduction of tariffs under the WTO, and the removal of its quantitative restrictions after the *India-QR* case, India updated its trade remedy legislation and practice in a way that requires greater legal analysis both within government and the private sector (Wu 2012). It reorganized the Indian bureaucracy for import controls and reformed the Directorate General of Foreign Trade (DGFT) within the Department of Commerce. In 1998, India reorganized its antidumping agency and established a Directorate General of Anti-Dumping and Allied Duties (DGAD) with greater expertise and autonomy to consider antidumping cases. India, however, did not simply copy the practices of the world's leading users of import relief procedures at the time (the United States and European Union) because it lacked the administrative personnel and experience to engage in their costly and time-consuming procedures. It rather indigenized its antidumping law in the context of WTO rules, just as it did so regarding patent law in light of the WTO TRIPS agreement (Kapczynski 2009).

For these import relief procedures to be used, however, government officials had to reach out to Indian industry. Government officials within the Ministry of Commerce did so through organizing numerous workshops and seminars for Indian corporations and trade associations (ibid.). They also wrote books and brochures. For example, in 1996, R. K. Gupta, who was a customs commissioner and the first director-general of the Directorate General of Specific Safeguards, wrote an extensive book of almost three hundred pages on antidumping and countervailing duty law, which was "the first guide written specifically for Indian corporations on trade remedies" (Wu, Chapter 21 of this volume). The petitions followed these efforts. Although India did not initiate its first antidumping investigation until 1992, which was a fallout of the 1991 economic crisis, it soon became the world's most active user. From 1995 to 2012, India initiated 668 antidumping investigations, more than any other WTO member (Bown 2012).

Such investigations have required increasing legal and accounting expertise, creating work for both government and the private bar. Under WTO antidumping and countervailing duty law, national courts or administrative tribunals are to review executive agency decisions. The agency may retain considerable authority, but judicial authority can be enhanced as a complement. The courts of India have become quite active, and they reference WTO law even though India is a dualist system in which international law formally has no direct effect (Yilmaz 2013). By the end of 2011, it is estimated that lawyers had filed more than 254 appeals before the Customs Excise and Service Tax Appellate Tribunal (CESTAT), a specialized court that hears antidumping matters, as well as fifty-six writs before the state high courts and twenty-five writs before the Supreme Court of India (Jha 2013). The Indian Supreme Court alone issued twelve decisions on antidumping cases between 2000 and 2006, "more than any other Supreme Court in the world," and invalidated a number of Ministry of Commerce practices (Wu, Chapter 21 of this volume). Law gradually and increasingly encroached on administrative discretion.

WTO law and national judicial review advance the role of technocrats within national administrations regarding the criteria for providing protection based on import relief laws. They, in parallel, enhance the role of lawyers in these domains. The laws create demand for legal representation on both sides. Some lawyers specialize in defending respondents, some in representing claimants, and some act for both. They work with accountants to analyze price differentials and sometimes with economists to develop causal arguments regarding injury. Their activation places pressure on investigating authorities to develop legal and factual justifications of agency findings. The government, government officials, and private practitioners respectively write brochures and books to educate industry and attract clients. Expertise pits against expertise in developing the law that becomes ever more demanding, requiring further investment in expertise. Lawyers work within and outside of national administrations. When outside, they work with officials as consultants and against them for private clients. They most frequently work for private parties against other private parties before administrative bodies and courts.

Some government officials see the potential gains to be made from leaving government service and developing their own private practice. In India, many of the leading lawyers came from government service, moving to private practice because it was much more lucrative. For example, the three largest practitioners in the antidumping field – V. Lakshmikumaran, Sharad Bhansali, and A. K. Gupt – all came from government services. More recently, in 2012 Neeraj Varshney left his position as director within the Ministry of Commerce's antidumping directorate to join the accounting firm Ernst & Young to establish trade remedy practice with Tashi Kaul, a former trade economist at White & Case. Varshney earlier published a treatise in 2007 that covered both WTO antidumping rules and Indian antidumping jurisprudence (Varshney 2007).

As a result, a specialized import relief practice has developed and is the most active area of trade law practice in India. The participating law firms range from India's largest, Amarchand Mangaldas, which has around six hundred lawyers, to boutique specialized firms. Pallavi Shroff, the wife of Amarchand Mangaldas's lead senior partner and the niece of renowned trade economist Jagdish Bhagwati, developed Amarchand Mangaldas's practice, which was among the first in India (Wu, chapter 21 of this volume). The firm of Lakshmikumaran & Sridharan was another early leader, soon joined by Economic Laws Practice and others. TPM Consulting, the firm started by Gupta that initiates the largest number of antidumping petitions in India, claims to have handled at least two hundred antidumping investigations in the last ten years. For trade liberals that wish to curtail import relief laws, it should now be more difficult to do so given how the professional stakes of private lawyers and administrative officials have developed. This vibrant legal practice was catalyzed by the WTO's creation and India's commitments under the WTO agreements.

VIII. THE LIMITS OF INTERNATIONAL TRADE LAW WORK

Because of the government's constraints on fees, a WTO law practice is far from lucrative for Indian lawyers. Many large Indian firms thus do not engage in WTO law work. Others, such as Luthra & Luthra, Economic Laws Practice, and Lakshmikumaran & Sridharan, complement their WTO work with a tax, customs, competition, and antidumping law practice. The bulk of trade law practice for most Indian law firms is under India's import relief laws and, in particular, antidumping work. At times, domestic antidumping work can lead to WTO work as well, especially since antidumping measures and other trade remedies have constituted around one-third of WTO dispute settlement cases (Bown and Prusa 2010).[29] Some firms aim to build a complementary competition law practice, which somewhat overlaps with antidumping law-type analysis, such as regarding the definition of an industry, injury from unfair competition, and causation. They include such familiar names in Indian trade law as Krishnan Venugopal, Suhail Nathani, Samir Gandhi, R. V. Anuradha, Moushami Joshi, Sharad Bhansali, S. Seetharaman, and Atul Dua. Those firms that engage in WTO-related legal work often do so for the reputational benefits of representing the country in international dispute settlement, which, in turn, can support their domestic practice.

These practices would be helped if Indian corporations and trade associations were to hire them more frequently for WTO-related work. Although the government has sought to work more closely with the business sector, it has generally had to cover all of the costs for legal analysis and litigation, unlike in other countries such as Brazil (Shaffer et al. 2008). This reliance on government funds reflects, in part, an attitude in the Indian private sector that international trade relations are the government's responsibility. Many in the government, as well as private lawyers, hope that this attitude will change.

IX. CONCLUSION

The WTO may be a rules-based system, but it is not static. It is dynamic, and those that engage it, shape it. Since engaging law is not without costs, a rules-based international system, such as that of the WTO, will tend to favor large and wealthy developed countries unless developing countries build indigenous legal capacity to use and thereby shape the construction and interpretation of international trade law in light of their needs. The building of legal capacity in developing countries has profound normative implications for the fairness of the international trading system. This chapter presented original fieldwork that engages the critical issue of how a developing country may build legal capacity to defend its interests in an international system otherwise characterized by asymmetric power, including the power of financial and legal resources.

The chapter examined India's reciprocal relationship with the global trading system, since countries must often transform themselves to effectively engage the system. On the one side, the chapter assessed India's efforts to build legal capacity for trade negotiations, dispute settlement, and domestic policy in order to defend its interests. On the other side, it showed the impact of the international trade law system on domestic institutions and stakeholders in India.

The WTO privileges the value of legal and economic expertise in national trade and regulatory policy to a much greater extent than before. It catalyzed the development of new legal capacity within the Indian state and pressed the Indian bureaucracy to become more transparent and open to greater input from the private sector and civil society. In the process, trade law-related expertise diffused outside the state's administrative services. The government outsourced work to the Indian private sector to help prepare and defend WTO claims, analyze potential claims, provide the analytic backdrop to assess and develop negotiating positions, tailor the implementation of WTO requirements, and consider new domestic policy initiatives in light of them. The Indian state better positioned itself to participate in the shaping of the international trade legal order by transforming itself within the constraints of its own institutional heritage.

ANNEX 1 – INDIAN LAW FIRMS ENGAGED ON TRADE MATTERS

Among the large law firms in India, only Luthra & Luthra has been involved in WTO dispute settlement. Firms such as Amarchand Mangaldas and J. Sagar Associates handle trade remedy work (mainly antidumping), but they have never been engaged by the government for WTO dispute settlement. We do not list firms engaged in legal practices significantly implicated by WTO law, such as intellectual property law.

WTO Litigation/Consultation

Law firm (WTO dispute settlement)	Number of lawyers	Typology
Luthra & Luthra	>300 lawyers	Elite
Economic Laws Practice	>150 lawyers	Boutique
Lakshmikumaran & Sridharan	~150 lawyers	Boutique
Clarus Law Associates	~10 lawyers	Boutique
Law Offices of Krishnan Venugopal	Senior Advocate, Supreme Court (litigation)	Focused

In addition to WTO work, the above firms also work on trade remedy, export control, and other trade issues, including in relation to bilateral and plurilateral free trade agreements (FTAs) and their negotiation.

The following lists of firms present a sampling of those engaged in the specialized field of trade remedy law, export control, customs, and trade-related consulting practice, which (to our knowledge) have yet to directly engage in WTO litigation or consultation.

Trade Remedy (Antidumping, Countervailing Duty [Antisubsidy], Safeguards) Practice

Law firm	Number of lawyers	Typology
Amarchand Mangaldas	~600 lawyers	Elite
J. Sagar	>200 lawyers	Elite
APJSLG	~50 lawyers	Boutique
Joseph Vellapally	Senior Advocate, Supreme Court (litigation)	Focused

Customs, Customs Valuation, Export Control, FTAs/Trade Agreements, and Trade Remedies

A.K. Gupta	Accounting and consulting firm
Ernst & Young	"Big 4" (accounting and consulting firm)

ANNEX 2 – INDIA AS A COMPLAINANT IN WTO DISPUTES

Title of case	Dispute number	Year of consultation	Panel established	Appellate Body	Status	Sector concerned/ trade association	Lawyers who represented India
Poland-Automobile	19	1995	No	No	Withdrawn, mutually agreed solution	Automobile	
US-Women's and Girls' Wool Coats	32	1996	Yes	No	Withdrawn, mutually agreed solution	Textiles and Clothing (Texprocil)	Frieder Roessler
US-Wool Shirts and Blouses	33	1996	Yes	Yes	US withdrew measures after the DSB and AB report	Textiles and Clothing (Texprocil)	Frieder Roessler
Turkey-Textiles	34	1996	Yes	Yes*	Turkey withdrew measures after the DSB and AB report	Textiles and Clothing (Texprocil)	Frieder Roessler
US-Shrimp	58	1996	Yes	Yes*	Compliance proceedings completed without finding of noncompliance	Fisheries/Marine (SEAI)	Arthur Appleton/ Lalive Lawyers
EC-Rice	134	1998	No	No	Settled during consultations	Agriculture	
EC-Unbleached Cotton Type Bed Linen	140	1998	No	No	Settled during consultations	Textiles and Clothing	Vermulst Waer & Verhaeghe (VWV)
EC-Bed Linen	141	1998	Yes	Yes*	Compliance proceedings completed with finding of noncompliance	Textiles and Clothing (Texprocil)	Vermulst Waer & Verhaeghe (VWV)
South Africa-Pharmaceuticals	168	1999	No	No	Settled during consultations	Pharmaceuticals	
US-Steel Plate	206	2000	Yes	No	Implementation notified by respondent	Steel (SAIL)	Sidley and Austin /Folkert Graafsma
US-Byrd Amendment	217	2001	Yes	Yes**	Authorization to retaliate granted	N/A*** (MPEDA/SEAI)	Willkie Farr & Gallagher (Advised MPEDA/SEAI)
Brazil-Jute Bags	229	2001	No	No	Settled during consultations	Textiles and Clothing (JMDC)	
Argentina-	233	2001	No	No	Settled during	Pharmaceuticals	

Origin					further action required	(Texprocil)	
EC-GSP	246	2002	Yes	Yes	Implementation notified by respondent	Textiles and Clothing (Texprocil)	ACWL/Krishnan Venugopal
EC-Steel Products	313	2004	No	No	Withdrawn, mutually agreed solution	Steel	Squire Sanders
US-Customs Bond Directive	345	2006	Yes	Yes	Implementation notified by respondent	Fisheries/Marine (MPEDA/SEAI)	Krishnan Venugopal/Clarus/ Willkie Farr & Gallagher
EU-Expiry Review of AD/CVD on PET	385	2008	No	No	Settled during consultations	Chemicals and Plastics (Chemplast)	(Consultation stage Krishnan Venu-gopal/ACWL/ Steptoe & Johnson assisted some of the Indian exports
EU-Seizure of Generic Drugs	408	2010	No	No	Settled during consultations	Pharmaceuticals	Consultation stage Krishnan Venu-gopal/Frederick Abbot/Uda Luthra & Luthra (provided initial opinion)
Turkey-Transitional Safeguards	428	2011	No	No	Settled during consultations	Textiles (Texprocil)	Lakshmikumaran & Sridha-ran/Venugopal
US-CVD on Carbon Steel	436	2012	Yes	No	Panel composed	Steel(Companies: Essar Steel, Tata Iron and Steel, Jindal Steel)	Lakshmikumaran & Sridha-ran/Venugopal

Source: Compiled from information on the WTO website

* *Article 21.5 panel established and the findings were appealed to the AB.*

** *Authorization for suspension of concession further to arbitrator's findings.*

*** *Not available. Multiple sector have been affected*

ANNEX 3 – INDIA AS A RESPONDENT IN WTO DISPUTES

Title of the case	Dispute number	Year of consultation	Panel	Appellate Body	Status	Sector concerned/ association	Lawyers who represented India
India-Patents (US)	50	1996	Yes	Yes	Implementation notified by respondent	Pharmaceuticals and Chemicals	Friedler Roessler/Krishnan Venugopal
India-Patents (EU)	79	1996	Yes	No	Implementation notified by respondent	Pharmaceutical and Chemicals	Friedler Roessler/Krishnan Venugopal
India-QRs	90, 91, 92, 93, 94, 95, and 96	1997	Yes	Yes	(DS 90) Implementation notified by respondent (DS 91–96) Withdrawn, mutually agreed solution	Agricultural, Textiles and Industrial Products	Friedler Roessler/Krishnan Venugopal
India-Certain Commodities	120	1998	No	No	Settled during consultations	Agriculture, Leather	
India-Auto (EC)	146, 175	1997	Yes	Yes	(DS 146 and 175) Implementation notified by respondent	Automobile	Friedler Roessler (ACWL)/Krishnan Venugopal
India-Import Restrictions (EC)	149	1998	No	No	Settled during consultations	N/A**	
India-Customs Duties (EC)	150	1998	No	No	Settled during consultations		
India-EXIM Policy (EC)	279	2003	No	No	Settled during consultations	Agriculture and Chemicals	

India-Antidumping on Certain Products (EC)	304	2003	No	No	Settled during consultations	N/A*	
India-Lead Acid Batteries (Bangladesh)	306	2004	No	No	Settled during consultations	Chemicals	
India-Antidumping Measures (Chinese Taipei)	318	2004	No	No	Settled during consultations	N/A*	
India-Import Measures on Wines (EC)	352	2006	No	No	Authority for panel lapsed	Agriculture/Wine and Spirits	Economic Laws Practice/Edwin Vermulst
India-Additional Duties (US)	360	2006	Yes	Yes	Report adopted, no further action required	Agriculture/Wine and Spirits	Economic Laws Practice
India-Taxes on Wine and Spirits	380	2010	No	No	Settled during consultations	Agriculture/Wine and Spirits	Economic Laws Practice
India-Import Measures on Agriculture Products (US)	430	2012	Yes	No	Panel composed	Agriculture	Luthra & Luthra
India-Solar Cells and Solar Modules	456	2013	No	No	In consultation	Renewable Energy	Clarus Law Associates

* *Involved challenges against antidumping actions against various products*

** *Not available. Multiple sector have been affected.*

Source: Compiled from information on the WTO website

Notes

1 Compiled from the WTO Online Bookshop, listing the page count for each annual compilation of dispute settlement reports.

2 We respectively conducted distinct field work on Indian trade law and policy for around a decade, from 2003 to 2014. We identify some sources only by interview number pursuant to their request for confidentiality.

3 Indian economist Raj Krishna coined the term *Hindu rate of growth* in 1978 (Sacchs 2005, 177). According to Jagdish Bhagwati, this expression "suggests predestination and thus captures the sense of despair that we felt about our capacity to reform and improve our performance" (Bhagwati 2003).

4 This was out of around 5,100 goods classifications to the six-digit level.

5 For administrative reasons, products were divided into consumer, capital, and intermediate goods. Most of the capital goods fell into the OGL category, while intermediate goods fell in the banned and restricted OGL list, with the severity of restriction declining in that order. While most of the consumer goods were banned, certain limited items that were judged essential were permitted. The main feature of this import policy was that imports of several items remained the exclusive monopoly of the government through the canalizing agencies. Crude oil and petroleum products were canalized through the Indian Oil Corporation; iron and steel, nonferrous metals, and fertilizers through the Metals and Minerals Trading Corporation; edible oils, natural rubber, newsprint, cement, and sugar through the State Trading Corporation of India; cereals through the Food Corporation of India; and cotton through the Cotton Corporation of India.

6 Joshi and Little state that "[f]or the first time India was nearly forced to the prospect of defaulting on its international financial commitments" (Joshi and Little 1998).

7 Data calculated from World Development Indicators.

8 Appellate Body Report, *India-Patent Protection for Pharmaceuticals and Agricultural Chemical Products*, WT/DS 50/R and WT/DS 50/AB/R (adopted on December 19, 1997) [hereinafter *India-Patents*]; Appellate Body Report, *India-Quantitative Restrictions on Imports of Agricultural, Textile and Industrial Products*, WT/DS/AB/R (adopted September 22, 1999) [hereinafter *India-QR*]; Appellate Body Report, *India-Measures Relating to Trade and Investment in the Motor Vehicle Sector*, WT/DS 175/AB/R (adopted May 15, 2000) [hereinafter *India-Auto*].

9 The Indian Patents Act has limited the scope of patentability by defining patentability criteria on novelty and inventive step and industrial applications, as well as by excluding certain types of inventions.

10 The government set up an interministerial monitoring body consisting of the secretaries for Commerce, Revenue, Agriculture, Small Scale Industries, and Animal Husbandry, and the Directorate General of Foreign Trade to monitor surges on imports of products where QRs were eliminated and potentially take action under India's new import relief laws.

11 A senior official noted, "It was important to get around the system, and it was almost unheard of to have two additional secretaries" in a department, which Chandrasekhar was able to obtain (Interview 13, 2012). Chandrasekhar later became the Indian ambassador to the WTO and eventually the cabinet secretary of India.

12 Traditionally, generalist administrators have been more dominant within the Indian civil service, but this ratio was reversed in MoCI and agencies associated with international trade negotiations.
13 At the time of the interview, Das worked on the UNCTAD project.
14 WTO cells were established at the state level in Kerala, Punjab, Andhra Pradesh, Maharashtra, Rajasthan, Tamil Nadu, Uttar Pradesh, Orissa, Karnataka, West Bengal, Madhya Pradesh, Delhi, Tripura, Nagaland, Haryana, and the Union Territory of Dadra and Nagar Haveli (Jayaram 2006).
15 The Centre is housed in the Indian Institute of Foreign Trade (IIFT), a public management school in Delhi.
16 Details of the outreach and training program provided by the Centre can be found at the Centre for WTO Studies, Indian Institute of Foreign Trade's website.
17 A list of nodal agencies and focal points can be accessed at the website for the Centre for WTO Studies, Indian Institute of Foreign Trade: Nodal Agencies and Focal Points.
18 Details can be found at the Centre for WTO Studies, Indian Institute of Foreign Trade's website.
19 Anwarul Hoda, deputy director general at the WTO from 1995 to 1999, heads ICRIER's WTO initiatives.
20 The endowment for this chair is only roughly $60,000 USD, but it was nonetheless viewed as a coup by Indian trade law officials (Interviews 1 and 13, 2012).
21 JOB (03)/162 (restricted).
22 Shaffer discussed this in an interview with K. M. Chandrasekhar, India's ambassador to the WTO from 2001 to 2004, who was central to the Cancun Ministerial Conference, in Trivandrum, India (Interview with K. M. Chandrasekhar, 2012). In 2004 "the Brazilian and Indian ministers established themselves as co-leaders in the most contentious issue area, agriculture, because they were able to gradually press the US and EC for substantial agricultural reforms they would not offer on their own" (Deese 2007, 155). India's ambassador to the WTO from 2004 to 2010, Ujjal Singh Bhatia, calls this a "watershed moment" in the history of the WTO (Bhatia 2012).
23 Negotiations effectively stopped when the Geneva Ministerial Conference collapsed without agreement on modalities in July 2008 (Cho 2010).
24 Although this proposal did not receive sufficient support among WTO members, it was an innovative proposal under the Rules Negotiations. During his employment at the UNCTAD program in New Delhi, James Nedumpara organized the review process where the proposal was revised and submitted to the WTO negotiating committee.
25 For example, CITI organized a series of awareness programs during the phaseout period of the Multi-Fiber Agreement (1995–2004) and published a newsletter entitled *FocusWTO* to educate its subscribers of the various challenges faced by the India textile industry.
26 For more, see Tricia Olsen and Aseema Sinha, 2013, "Linkage Politics and the Persistence of National Policy Autonomy in Emerging Powers: Patents, Profits, and Patients in the Context of TRIPS Compliance," Business and Politics 15: 3.
27 The first and only case that resulted in a decision was a complaint filed by Pakistan against India for not granting excise rebates goods exported to Pakistan while

providing this benefit for goods destined for other countries in violation of the most-favored-nations clause. The second case was a complaint by India against the United States for imposing countervailing duties on certain dutiable products, which was settled. The third case was a complaint by India regarding certain Japanese restrictions on leather, which also was settled. The three complaints were: *Pakistan-Export Fees on Jute*, Complaint by India, GATT/L/41 (1952) (resulting in GATT report); GATT, *United States Countervailing Duty without Injury Finding*, Complaint by India, BISD, 28th Supplement (1982), p. 113; GATT, *Japanese Import Restrictions on Leather*, Complaint by India under special article XXIII procedure for developing countries, GATT Document L/5653 (1984).

28 This procedure is explained in the written response given by the Trade Policy Division, MoCI, to the RTI application filed by Prashant Reddy T. (advocate), vide document F.No.1/13/2012-TPD, Government of India, Ministry of Commerce and Industry, New Delhi, March 6, 2012. Response can be found at www.docs.google.com/file/d/0Bxi2TzVXul5ZRTF3N3pQbo5RMWktbXFRbUFoMTR3QQ/.

29 From 2001 to 2009, the WTO Dispute Settlement Body spent nearly one-third of its time on cases involving trade remedies.

References

Bagwell, Kyle and Alan Sykes. 2004. "India – Measures Affecting Automotive Sector." In *The American Law Institute Reporters' Guide on WTO Case Law*. Edited by Henrik Horn and Petros C. Mavrioidis. Cambridge: Cambridge University Press.

Battacharyya, B. B. 2005. "The Indian Shrimp Industry Organizes to Fight the Threat of Antidumping Action." In *Managing the Challenges of WTO Participation: 45 Case Studies*. Edited by Peter Gallagher et al. Cambridge: Cambridge University Press.

Bhagwati, Jagdish. 1993. *Indian in Transition: Freeing the Economy*. Oxford: Clarendon Press.

Bhagwati, Jagdish N. and T. N. Srinivasan. 1975. *Foreign Trade Regimes and Economic Development: India*. New York: Columbia University Press.

Bhatia, Ujjal Singh. 2012. "G-20 – Combining Substance with Solidarity and Leadership." In *Reflections from the Frontline: Developing Country Negotiators in the WTO*. Edited by Pradeep S. Mehta. Gurgaon: Academic Publishers.

Bown, Chad. 2012. "Global Antidumping Base." The World Bank. www.econ.worldbank.org/ttbd/gad/.

Bown, Chad P. and Thomas J. Prusa. 2010. "U.S Antidumping: Much Ado About Nothing 1–55." *Policy Research Working Paper* 5352, Trade and Integration Team, The World Bank Development Research Group.

Camen, Ulrich and Charles Norchi. 2002. "Challenging Sovereignty: India, TRIPS and the WTO." In *Sovereignty under Challenge: How Governments Respond*. Edited by John D. Montgomery and Nathan Glazer. New Brunswick: Transaction Publishers.

Chaudhuri, Sudip, Chan Park, and K. M. Gopakumar, eds. 2010. *Five years into the Product Patent Regime: India's Response*. New York: United Nations Development Programme.

Cho, Sungjoon. 2010. "The Demise of Development in the Doha Development Round." *Texas International Law Journal* 45 (3): 573–601.
Correspondence with MoCI, 2013. On file with Author
Deese, David. 2007. *World Trade Politics: Power, Principles and Leadership*. New York: Routledge.
Eglin, Richard. 1987. "Surveillance of Balance-of-Payments Measures in the GATT." *The World Economy* 10 (1): 1–26.
Friedman, Thomas. 1999. *The Lexus and the Olive Tree*. New York: Farrar, Straus and Giroux.
Gopakumar, K. M. 2010. "Product Patents and Access to Medicine in India: A Critical Review of the Implementation of the TRIPS Regime." *Law and Development Review* 3 (2): 326–368.
Halliday, Terrence and Gregory Shaffer. 2015. *Transnational Legal Orders*. Cambridge: Cambridge University Press.
Hausmann, Dani Rodrik and Charles F. Sabel. 2007. "Reconfiguring Industrial Policy: A Framework with an Application to South Africa" Working Paper RWP08–031, Harvard Kennedy School. www.papers.ssrn.com/sol3/papers.cfm?abstract_id=1245702.
Hoen, Ellen. 2013. "A Victory for Global Public Health in the Indian Supreme Court." *Journal of Public Health Policy* 34 (3): 370–374.
Interview 1, 2012.
Interview 2, 2012.
Interview 3, 2010.
Interview 6, 2012.
Interview 7, 2012.
Interview 9, 2012.
Interview 11, 2010.
Interview 12, 2010.
Interview 13, 2012.
Interview 16, 2012.
Interview 24, 2010.
Interview 26, 2010.
Interview 31, 2012.
Interview 41, 2010
Interview with Abhijit Das, 2010.
Interview with Amar Sinha, 2013.
Interview with an official representative, Centre for WTO Studies, 2013.
Interview with Atul Kaushik, 2010
Interview with Bipin Kumar, 2012.
Interview with former ambassador to the WTO, 2013.
Interview with K. M. Chandrasekhar, 2012.
Interview with Moushami Joshi, 2010.
Interview with Moushami Joshi, 2012.
Interview with Rajan Sudesh Ratna, 2013.
Interview with Sandu Joseph, 2011.
Interview with Shailija Singh, 2012.

Jayaram, Suprita. 2006. "Functioning of WTO Cells in India: A Critique" (briefing paper, CUTS International). www.cuts-citee.org/pdf/BP06-DI-9.pdf.

Jha, Madhurendra Nath. 2013. "India: A Three-Tier Judicial Review System." In *Domestic Judicial Review of Trade Remedies: Experiences of the Most Active WTO Members*. Edited by Müslüm Yilmaz. Cambridge: Cambridge University Press.

Joshi, Vijay and Ian M. D. Little. 1998. *India's Economic Reforms 1991*. Oxford: Oxford University Press.

Japczynski, Amy. 2009. "Harmonization and Its Discontents: A Case Study of TRIPS Implementation in India's Pharmaceutical Sector." *California Law Review* 97, no. 6: 1571–1650.

Little, Ian M. D. 1982. *Economic Development: Theory, Policy and International Relations*. New York: Basic Books.

Mehta, Rajesh. 2000. "Removal of QRs and Impact of India's Import." *Economics and Political Weekly* 35 (19): 1667–1671

Muralidharan, Sukumar. 2001. "Opening the Floodgates." *Frontline* 18 (8): 14–27.

Nedumpara, James J. 2012. "Antidumping Proceedings and 'Zeroing' Practices: Have We Entered the Endgame?" *Global Trade and Customs Journal* 7 (1): 15–26.

Olsen, Tricia and Aseema Sinha. 2013. "Linkage Politics and the Persistence of National Policy Autonomy in Emerging Powers: Patents, Profits, and Patients in the Context of TRIPS Compliance." *Business and Politics* 15 (3): 323–356.

Panagariya, Arvind. 2004. "India's Trade Reforms" (working paper, India Policy Forum, Brookings Institution). www.brookings.edu/global/ipf/panagariya.pdf.

2008. *India: The Emerging Giant*. Oxford: Oxford University Press.

Pursell, Garry, Nalin Kishor, and Kanupriya Gupta. 2007. "Manufacturing Protection in India Since Independence" Australia South Asia Research Centre Working Paper. www.econpapers.repec.org/paper/pasasarcc/2007–07.htm.

Sacchs, Jeffrey. 2005. *The End of Poverty*. New York: Basic Books.

Santos, Alvaro. 2012. "Carving Out Policy Autonomy for Developing Countries in the World Trade Organization: The Experience of Brazil and Mexico." *Virginia Journal of International Law* 52 (2): 551–632.

Shaffer, Gregory. 2003. *Defending Interests: Public-Private Partnerships in WTO Litigation*. Washington, DC: Brookings Institution Press.

2015. "How the World Trade Organization Shapes Regulatory Governance." *Regulation and Governance* 9 (1): 1–15.

Shaffer, Gregory and Ricardo Ortiz Melendez. 2010. *Dispute Settlement at the WTO: The Developing Country Experience*. Cambridge: Cambridge University Press.

Shaffer, Gregory, Michelle Ratton Sanchez, and Barbara Rosenberg. 2008. "Winning at the WTO: What Lies Behind Brazil's Success." *Cornell International Law Journal* 41 (2): 383–501.

Shaffer, Gregory, ed. 2013. *Transnational Legal Ordering and State Change*. Cambridge: Cambridge University Press.

2015. "How the WTO Shapes Regulatory Governance." *Regulation and Governance* 9 (1): 1–15.

Sinha, Aseema. n.d. "When David Meets Goliath: How Global Markets and Rules Are Shaping India's Rise to the Power." Working draft on file with authors.

2005. *The Regional Roots of Developmental Politics in India: A Divided Leviathan*. Bloomington: Indiana University Press.
2007. "Global Linkages and Domestic Politics: Trade Reform and Institution Building in India in Comparative Perspective." *Comparative Political Studies* 40 (10): 1183–1210.
Singh, Manmohan. 1991. "Finance Minister, Budget Speech to the Indian Parliament," July 24.
Srinivasan, T. N. 2000. *Eight Lectures on India's Economic Reforms*. Delhi: Oxford University Press India.
Stubbs, Richard. 2011. "The East Asian Developmental State and the Great Recession." *Contemporary Politics* 17 (2): 151–166.
Trubek, David M., ed. 2013. *Law and the New Developmental State: The Brazilian Experience in Latin American Context*. Cambridge: Cambridge University Press.
United States-Measures Affecting Imports of Woven Wool Shirts and Blouses from India. 1997. WT/DS 33/AB/R, April 25, 16.
Varshney, Neeraj. 2007. *Anti-Dumping Measures under the WTO Regime: Law, Practice, and Procedure*. Gurgaon: Partridge Publishing.
Weiler, Joseph. 2002. "The Rule of Lawyers and the Ethos of Diplomats: Reflections on the Internal and External Legitimacy of WTO Dispute Settlement." *American Review of International Arbitration* 13 (1): 177–197.
World Intellectual Property Organization. 2013. Statistical Country Profiles. www.wipo.int/ipstats/en/statistics/country_profile.
World Trade Organization. n.d. Dispute Settlement: Dispute by Country. Accessed November 2 2013. www.wto.org/english/tratop_e/dispu_e/dispu_by_country_e.htm.
1998. "Trade Policy Reviews: India." www.wto.org/english/tratop_e/tpr_e/tp71_e.htm.
2011. "Trade Policy Reviews: India," 43, WT/TPR/S/249, August 10.
Wu, Mark. 2012. "Antidumping in Asia's Emerging Giants." *Harvard International Law Journal* 53 (1): 1–53.
Yilmaz, Müslüm. 2013. *Domestic Judicial Review of Trade Remedies: Experiences of the Most Active WTO Members*. Cambridge: Cambridge University Press.

21

Indian Corporations, the Administrative State, and the Rise of Indian Trade Remedies

Mark Wu

I. INTRODUCTION

Global trade rules permit countries to apply temporary trade remedies to address certain injuries to domestic industries that arise from trade liberalization. Trade remedy cases are complicated legal proceedings, involving administrative investigations, hearings, and judicial review. Domestic firms petition the government, seeking the imposition of a higher tariff rate on a competitor's imports for a fixed period of time. The stakes are often large. The case's outcome may well determine whether a domestic industry survives the onslaught of foreign imports.

For decades, firms in industrialized countries were leaders in petitioning their governments for trade remedies. For example, between 1981 and 1987, advanced economies accounted for more than 97 percent of all antidumping duties applied worldwide.[1] Fast-forward a quarter century, however, and the picture is vastly different. Today, India is the undisputed world leader when it comes to applying trade remedies.

In eleven of the past sixteen years, India has ranked first in the world when it comes to the number of new antidumping cases filed (see table 1). Furthermore, note that in three of the five years in which India was not the top initiator, it ranked second. Nor is this just a story of Indians being litigious in the filing of cases, but the cases then being stuck in a long pipeline. Unlike some other areas of Indian litigation, trade remedy petitions are decided rather expediently through administrative hearings, with judgments rendered in a matter of months. Therefore, even if we shift the metric to the number of actual trade remedies applied, the result is no different. India tops the world's league tables in eleven of the past sixteen years and ranks in the top three every year (see table 2). Indeed, trade remedies are one of the few areas of the global legal profession where India can legitimately claim to be a world leader.

TABLE 1. *India's share of new antidumping investigations initiated worldwide*

Year	Number of new Indian investigations	Ranking among WTO members	Share of worldwide new investigations
2014	38	1st	16.1%
2013	29	3rd	10.1%
2012	21	2nd	10.0%
2011	19	1st	11.5%
2010	41	1st	23.7%
2009	31	1st	14.3%
2008	55	1st	25.2%
2007	47	1st	28.3%
2006	31	2nd	15.3%
2005	28	1st	14.0%
2004	21	5th	9.5%
2003	46	1st	19.7%
2002	81	1st	26.0%
2001	79	1st	21.2%
2000	41	2nd	13.9%
1999	64	1st	17.8%

Source: Author's computation based on statistics reported by the World Trade Organization

Just how did this happen? What set of factors precipitated the rapid change in this facet of the Indian legal regime? Much of the academic discourse to date about India's response to globalization has focused on the external dimension of how India developed legal capacity to assert its interests in international fora, such as in international investment treaty arbitration and dispute settlement before the World Trade Organization (WTO).[2] Yet concomitant with this development is the internal dimension – the question of how actors in the Indian legal regime developed the capacity to utilize global trade rules to assert their interests in domestic administrative fora. To date, this question has received scant attention. Yet India's experience in this dimension is nothing short of extraordinary. This chapter represents an attempt to shed light on this phenomenon.

Methodologically, the chapter draws on a series of semistructured interviews with stakeholders involved in shaping India's trade remedy policy and litigating India's trade remedy cases. The majority of such interviews were conducted in person during five weeks of field research over a two-year period (2012–13) in India and Geneva, with a handful done via telephone. Among

TABLE 2. *India's share of new antidumping measures imposed worldwide*

Year	Number of new Indian AD measures	Ranking among WTO members	Share of worldwide new AD measures
2014	15	3rd	9.6%
2013	12	2nd	7.5%
2012	30	1st	25.6%
2011	26	1st	26.3%
2010	32	1st	23.9%
2009	30	1st	21.1%
2008	31	1st	21.8%
2007	24	1st	22.6%
2006	16	3rd	11.3%
2005	18	2nd	13.0%
2004	29	1st	18.8%
2003	52	1st	23.3%
2002	64	1st	29.4%
2001	38	1st	22.5%
2000	55	1st	23.1%
1999	23	3rd	12.1%

Source: Author's computation based on statistics reported by the World Trade Organization

those interviewed were government officials, lawyers, trade association representatives, business lawyers, think tank researchers, and academics. The chapter also relies on primary source materials on trade remedy cases made available by the Indian government. In addition, it draws on the World Bank's Temporary Trade Barriers Database and India's semiannual submissions to the WTO Committee on Anti-dumping Practices.

This chapter begins with a discussion of why Indians suddenly turned to trade remedy litigation in the late 1990s. Three developments, I suggest, played a key role: the 1991 macroeconomic crisis, the concessions arising out of the Uruguay Round in 1994, and the loss of the India-Quantitative Restrictions case at the WTO in 1999. Collectively, they lowered import barriers, leading Indian firms to seek temporary relief from foreign competitors.

However, in the past quarter century, many other developing countries have also experienced trade shocks. None have embraced trade remedies with the same vigor as India. How is it that, in a country famous for bureaucratic quagmires, the administrative state responded so effectively in this instance?

Scholars examining the response of India and other emerging markets to globalization have emphasized one of two explanations. The first posits that it is the private sector that drives growth and compels the state to adapt (Das 2013). As the authors of this volume have highlighted about other regulatory spheres, often it is India's private sector – working in partnership with India's private law firms – that spurs the government to amend its laws and regulations. The second explanation posits that adaptation results from top-down, government-driven initiative coordinated with other economic policies. Trade law scholars, for example, have applied this narrative to the development of WTO legal capacity in several emerging markets (Ahn 2003; Han and Gao 2010; Shaffer et al. 2010).

This chapter highlights how neither of these narratives accurately accounts for the administrative state's adaptation in this particular instance. While the private sector played a role, it was not the overwhelming driver for change. Nor was change sparked by top-down government directives. Instead, I argue that two groups played the key role: (1) midlevel bureaucrats that function as policy entrepreneurs; and (2) lawyers outside of the top corporate firms. The role of both groups in India's legal transformation – and indeed, in emerging markets generally – has not been well documented in the academic literature. This chapter suggests that their roles may well warrant greater attention.

Whereas policy entrepreneurs are generally conceived of as individuals who labor outside of government to introduce innovations to public practice, many of the specific individuals in this context began their efforts within government before moving out.[3] Yet these individuals did not simply follow the orders of their political bosses. Instead, they displayed strong individual initiative and developed an apparatus within the administrative state to support the emergence of this legal regime. Assisting in this effort was a small set of eclectic lawyers – comprised initially of members of the private bar but joined later by some of the policy entrepreneurs upon leaving government. Rather than simply engaging in outright legal transplantation, these policy entrepreneurs altered borrowed legal procedures to accommodate Indian conditions. This process of legal indigenization, in turn, made trade remedies a much more attractive legal instrument for Indian corporate actors, who grew to embrace them with an enthusiasm unmatched anywhere else in the world. Finally, the success of the Indian experience, I suggest, was also due to strong feedback mechanisms between the key actors within this legal regime.

Beyond simply answering the puzzle of how India was able to scale up so quickly and effectively in this area of law, this chapter aspires to make two other contributions: First, it sheds badly needed light on the trade remedy practices of developing countries, which have received scant attention in the legal academic literature. The few works that have sought to explain this phenomenon have either relied on an outside-in, empirically driven approach using available statistics or a case study analysis limited to one industry.[4] Using a combination of qualitative and quantitative methodologies, this chapter offers important insights into the important role of policy entrepreneurs, the eclectic (and therefore unorganized) nature of the legal bar, and feedback mechanisms, all of which have been previously underemphasized because they cannot be readily teased out of the economic statistics or limited case studies on which prior empirical studies have relied.

Second, this chapter also seeks to enrich our understanding of the processes through which legal transplantation occurs in developing countries. The literature has emphasized the importance of transnational actors who assist with the interaction, interpretation, and internalization of the international norms into domestic legal structures (Koh 1997, 2006; Shaffer 2012). This study suggests that a critical role can also be played in the early stages of the transplantation process by individuals who have limited international interaction and who may not normally be conceived of as genuine transnational actors. What is important is that these individuals, operating mainly on the domestic level, have the capacity to understand the needs of transnational actors and mobilize transnational resources when necessary. India was fortunate to have the right people in the right place at the right time to make the right policy calls, and a flexible bureaucracy and interactive feedback mechanisms allowed the system to further evolve. It is this iterative process that led to the development of Indian trade law professionals and catapulted India to its current position as a world leader in using trade remedies.

II. TRADE SHOCKS AND INDIA'S RAPID EMBRACE OF TRADE REMEDY LITIGATION

The narrative of legal transplantation often presupposes reform-minded agents who introduce foreign legal models, adapt them to fit local conditions, and facilitate their use by local lawyers (Watson 1995). If only in practice, the story proved so simple. India gained exposure to trade remedy law long before its Independence. Britain enacted its antidumping law in 1921, and some Commonwealth countries did so even earlier (Finger 1991, 3–8). By the end of the 1920s, most of the other large economies in the Commonwealth had trade remedy laws in place (Finger 1991, 21). India remained the outlier.

As an original signatory to the General Agreement on Tariffs and Trade (GATT) in 1947, Indian lawyers were once again exposed to trade remedy law. Moreover, the issue featured prominently in GATT negotiations throughout the 1960s and 1970s. Yet, even following the creation of robust international law on trade remedies, India remained indifferent. Indeed, not until 1985 did India bother to enact formal rules for the conduct of trade remedy proceedings.[5] Even so, the laws and regulations languished on the books. As the 1980s came to a close, India had yet to see a single domestic trade remedy case. The idea that India, by the end of the 1990s, would have more trade remedy cases than any other country in the world was unfathomable. Yet, that is exactly what happened.

What drove Indians to reverse their attitude toward trade remedy litigation? Three events played a key role: (1) the macroeconomic crisis of 1991 and its subsequent reforms; (2) the conclusion of the Uruguay Round of trade negotiations in 1994; and (3) the outcome of the India-Quantitative Restrictions case in the WTO. As I will explain, each mandated the opening of portions of the Indian markets. As India's trade restrictions crumbled, many Indian corporations found themselves ill-prepared for global competition. The need for temporary protection increased, and with it, the appeal of trade remedy litigation as a legal means for securing "breathing space."

A. *The 1991 Macroeconomic Crisis*

Why did India ignore trade remedy law for more than half a century? The continued protection of the domestic market through a restrictive trade policy obviated any demand for trade remedies (Debroy and Banik 1999, 51). By 1990, India's import-weighted mean tariff rate was more than five times that of South Korea and Malaysia, and more than double that of Sri Lanka, Thailand, and the Philippines. More than 94 percent of agricultural goods were protected by some form of a quantitative restriction, as were more than 90 percent of manufactured, intermediate, and capital goods. The Indian trade regime was one of the world's most restrictive (Chadha et al. 2003, 15).

This trade policy stance proved unsustainable. As discussed in the Overview chapter, in 1991, India turned to the International Monetary Fund for assistance. In the aftermath of the macroeconomic crisis, India undertook a series of watershed economic reforms. Among these were the elimination of industrial licensing requirements, a phased reduction of its peak customs duties, and a phased reduction of import licensing controls.

Depending on the industry, the net effect varied. Many remained immune to foreign competition, even after the policy reforms. For example, the new Export and Import Policy, which took effect in April 1992, still contained more than twenty pages of categories where imports were restricted and/or licenses required. The policy that it replaced, however, had exceeded two hundred pages (ibid.). Consequently, overall import protection declined following the 1991 crisis, but unevenly across industries.

One industry that experienced a sharp drop in the level of protection was chemicals.[6] As foreign-produced chemicals flowed in, Indian chemical producers discovered what their foreign counterparts had long known – that antidumping cases could prove useful to stem the tide of foreign competition. In 1992 the PVC Resin Manufacturers Association (whose product is used to make thermoplastics) filed the first-ever antidumping petition with the Indian government. The domestic industry accused foreign producers from Argentina, Brazil, Mexico, South Korea, and the United States of "dumping" its product into India at prices that injured Indian manufacturers. The case succeeded in having higher tariffs imposed against manufacturers from four of the accused export markets (Argentina was exempted). A few months later, petitioners also successfully brought an antidumping case against Japanese imports of bisphenol A, a chemical compound commonly used to make plastics. The 1991 crisis and its subsequent reforms had breathed life into India's trade remedy laws. A law that had languished on the books was finally put to use.

However, as table 3 shows, between 1992 and 1994, only a handful of trade remedy cases were filed. The vast majority were by the chemicals industry. Trade remedy cases remained very much a novel legal instrument restricted to a niche segment. It had yet to gain much traction with domestic producers at large. Despite the 1991–93 reforms, much of the Indian domestic market still remained protected.

B. *The Uruguay Round Concessions*

The next shock for some Indian industries occurred in the aftermath of the Uruguay Round trade negotiations in 1994. The negotiations had been ongoing since 1988, and India played an active role in representing both its own interests and those of developing countries at large in the talks. The negotiations resulted in a comprehensive set of agreements, including those for all three major forms of trade remedies: antidumping duties, countervailing duties, and safeguards.

For India, the impact of the Uruguay Round on imports was even greater than that of the immediate reforms following the 1991 crisis. During the negotiations, in exchange for concessions for exporters, India committed to significant tariff reductions.[7] Prior to the Uruguay Round, only 6 percent of India's tariff lines had been "bound," meaning that they were subject to a maximum tariff ceiling. For the remaining 94 percent, India could raise tariffs at will to whatever level it desired. During the Uruguay Round, India agreed to bind

TABLE 3. *Antidumping case initiations, 1992–94*

Date of initiation	Petitioner	Product	Targeted countries
June 10, 1992	PVC Resin Manufacturers Association	PVC resin	Brazil, Mexico, South Korea, and United States
August 12, 1992	M/s Kesar Petroproducts, Ltd.	Bisphenol A	Japan
January 7, 1994	M/s Vinati Organics	Isobutylbenzene	China
August 11, 1994	M/s Alpha Drug India Ltd.	3,4,5-Trimethoxybenzaldehyde	China
August 30, 1994	M/s Bakul Aromatics, M/s Kores India, M/s Suven Pharma	Theophylline and caffeine	China
October 28, 1994	M/s Gujarat Apar Ltd.	Acrylonitrile butadiene rubber	Japan
December 30, 1994	M/s Universal Chemicals and Industries Pvt. Ltd.	Potassium permanganate	China
December 30, 1994	M/s Kesar Petroproducts Ltd.	Bisphenol A	Brazil and Russia

Source: Directorate General of Anti-dumping and Allied Duties, Ministry of Commerce and Industry.

67 percent of its tariff lines, including nearly all of its agricultural products and 60 percent of its industrial goods. India also committed itself to a series of phased reductions of import tariffs over a ten-year period (ibid.).

The average import-weighted tariff on consumer goods, which had been as high as 153 percent prior to the 1991 crisis, had fallen to 86 percent by 1994. But following the Uruguay Round, it plummeted even further, to 48 percent in 1995 and 25 percent by 1998. The same story was true of capital and intermediate goods. Average tariffs on capital goods fell from 97 percent in 1991 to 50 percent by 1994. By 1998, they were cut in half to 24 percent. For intermediate goods, the numbers were even more extreme. From an average rate of 77 percent in 1991, they had fallen to 42 percent by 1994 as a result of the phased reductions following the crisis. Following the Uruguay Round, they were cut further, down to 22 percent by 1996 and 18 percent to 1998 (World Trade Association 1998).

Although the 1991 macroeconomic crisis had breathed life into the antidumping law, it took the Uruguay Round concessions to spark real interest in trade remedies. Following the negotiations, the government passed the Customs Tariff (Amendment) Act, 1995, which updated Indian laws to comply with WTO requirements. In addition, the government put forth a new set of rules governing antidumping investigations, repealing the earlier set of rules established in 1985. Similar updates were made to laws and regulations governing countervailing duties.

The next year (1996), the number of new antidumping initiations jumped suddenly to twenty-one, up from six the previous year. More importantly, the range of sectors filing antidumping petitions broadened beyond the chemicals sector. Two textiles companies – Indian Acrylic Ltd. and Pasupati Acrylon Ltd. – filed petitions alleging dumping of acrylic fiber into India by manufacturers in the United States, Thailand, and Korea. The case gained the support of other domestic producers of acrylic fiber as well as the Forum of Acrylic Fiber Manufacturers. In September 1996 the government decided to proceed with an investigation. Three weeks later, the government announced that it would also investigate an allegation, made by the Indian Graphite Manufacturers Association, of the dumping of graphite electrodes by producers from China, the United States, Germany, Belgium, Austria, France, Spain, and Italy. In December 1996 the government proceeded with investigating a petition filed by the Indian Newsprint Manufacturers Association alleging the dumping of standard newsprint by manufacturers in the United States, Canada, and Russia. Interestingly, that petition was filed after Chinese newsprint manufacturers had filed that country's first antidumping case, which also accused American and Canadian producers of dumping.

Over the next few months, the range of antidumping cases expanded to include vitamin C, metallurgical coke (a key input used to make steel), sewing machine needles, and hot-rolled steel. Two sectors that would later emerge as active users of trade remedies – pharmaceuticals and metals – also filed their first case during this time period. By the end of 1998, the Ministry of Commerce had opened a total of sixty-eight new investigations on the basis of requests from domestic industry. The days of antidumping being a niche legal instrument deployed by only the chemicals industry had disappeared. Others too had discovered that antidumping cases were an effective means to subject imports to higher tariffs and keep competitors at bay.

India's use of trade remedies through this period predominantly took the form of antidumping actions.[8] But the other major legal update to India's trade remedy law occurred in 1997 with the amendment of the Customs Tariff Act, 1975 to implement the WTO's Agreement on Safeguards. The government also implemented the Safeguard Duty Rules, which specified the procedural rules for safeguards investigations. These moves would set the stage for India later to become a global leader in levying safeguard actions against trading partners, just as it was already becoming for antidumping duties.

C. *The India-Quantitative Restrictions Case*

Even as India lowered tariffs in line with its Uruguay Round commitments, not all Indian firms found themselves needing immediately to fend off competition from increased foreign imports. Besides tariffs, the Indian government had relied traditionally on one other instrument to restrict imports and protect its domestic producers: quantitative restrictions (QRs). Narayanan (2006) reports that as of March 31, 1996, out of India's 10,202 tariff lines in place at the time, QRs continued to apply to 4,061 (nearly 40 percent).

Several forms of QRs applied. First, imports of any restricted product listed on the Export-Import Policy required a license from the Directorate General of Foreign Trade (DGFT) within the Ministry of Commerce and Industry. Second, in addition to the general import licensing scheme, certain products were subject to a special import license (SIL) system. SILs were granted in proportion to the applicant's exports or net foreign exchange earnings. The more one exported Indian-made goods, the more one was allowed to import. Third, some products could be imported only through designated government agencies. Only if these agencies did not object could import licenses be issued to other entities. Finally, India also limited the import of certain products to actual users of the products. Intermediary companies, such as private trading companies, could not import the product if they intended to resell, rather than consume, the product. All of these measures effectively limited the number of foreign imports into India, whether directly or indirectly.

As part of its Uruguay Round concessions, India agreed to phase out QRs. During consultations held in November 1994, the GATT Committee on Balance of Payments noted that India's "aim" was to remove them by 1996–97. However, India failed to act on this pledge. The weak United Front coalition government following the 1996 election did not dare to incur the wrath of domestic industries by removing import protections.

Not surprisingly, India's trading partners protested. In July 1997, Australia, Canada, the European Communities, New Zealand, Switzerland, and the United States all filed complaints before the WTO. India subsequently reached bilateral agreements with all parties, except the United States, to phase out QRs over a set timeline. In October 1997 the United States requested that a WTO establish a panel to hear the dispute.

In April 1999 the WTO Panel issued its ruling against India (World Trade Organization 1999b). This was upheld by the WTO Appellate Body in August 1999 (World Trade Organization 1999a). Faced with the threat of WTO-authorized retaliatory trade measures against Indian exports, India finally agreed to dismantle its import licensing regime. In 1999–2000, 894 QRs were lifted. QRs were eliminated on another batch of 714 tariff lines in 2000–2001 and 715 tariff lines in 2001–2002. Most were for textiles, agricultural, and consumer products, but they also included a small number of chemical and petrochemical products (ibid., 1087).

With QRs removed, foreign imports spiked. Over the next five years, imports would more than double, growing from US$49.7 billion to a record US$111.5 billion.[9] The pressure on Indian domestic manufacturers came from all fronts. On the low-cost end, India was now flooded with Chinese goods, particularly after China's WTO accession required India to confer most-favored-nation (MFN) tariff rates. Between 1998–1999 and 2003–1904, Chinese imports increased by more than fivefold.[10] Whereas in 1998–1999, China had ranked thirteenth as the source of imports into India, by 2003–2004, it had overtaken the United States to become the largest. On the opposite end of the spectrum, Indian corporations also faced intense competition from higher-quality goods made by industrialized countries. Imported products from Switzerland more than doubled, those from the United States nearly doubled, and those from the five major European economies increased by more than 50 percent.[11] Korean and Indonesian products also made large inroads, increasingly by nearly threefold.[12]

It was in this aftermath that antidumping cases in India reached their ultimate apex. With the lifting of QRs, many Indian producers found themselves at a competitive disadvantage on account of their poor quality, costly credit, inflexible labor arrangements, and/or technological deficiencies (Rasure 2008, 150–151). Indian corporations and trade associations began to file requests for antidumping duties at an unprecedented rate. In 1999 the Indian government opened sixty-four new antidumping investigations on the basis of new petitions; this was more new cases than the previous three years combined. After a slight dip in 2000, new cases continued at a blistering pace. In 2001, India opened seventy-nine new antidumping investigations. That year represented the first time that India led the world. The following year, 2002, saw India open an additional eighty-one new investigations on the basis of petitions filed by its companies and trade associations. More cases were opened in India in

2002 than in the United States, European Union, Canada, and Australia (i.e., the four traditional dominant users of antidumping) combined.

A few of these cases were filed by repeat players. These firms and/or trade associations sought to counter the effects of trade diversion, as production shifted in response to antidumping duties. Vitamin C producers brought three different sets of litigation against importers from thirteen countries between 1996 and 2000 (Malhotra et al. 2005). Similarly, acrylic fiber producers filed four different sets of petitions against importers from eleven countries between 1996 and 1999.

Many more cases, however, came not from repeat players but instead from firms learning from others in the same industry. For example, the success of the vitamin C cases led to producers for vitamins A and AB2D3K to file a petition. Likewise, the success of the acrylic fiber antidumping petitions led domestic producers of acrylic yarn to file an antidumping petition in July 2001. Similarly, the successful case brought by a firm within steel tycoon Lakshmi Mittal's empire led to cases being filed by other firms in the steel industry. Whereas the intrasector diffusion effect had once been strongest in the chemicals sector, by 2002, it had expanded to also include the textiles, pharmaceutical, metals, steel, and vitamin sectors.

Demand for trade remedy litigation expanded to several new sectors. As QRs were eliminated for consumer goods, not surprisingly Indian manufacturers of consumer goods sought relief through trade remedies. In the early 2000s, producers of sports shoes, toys, batteries, and fluorescent lamps all brought cases; many were targeted against lower-cost Chinese producers. New cases were also triggered by companies in high-tech industries into which India hoped to expand. For example, in July 1999, M/s Sterlite Industries filed a petition alleging dumping by Korean optical fiber producers; it hoped to maintain its share in India's growing telecommunications market and to expand into rapidly growing markets in neighboring countries.

In addition, during this period, the type of trade remedy cases expands beyond just antidumping. From 1998 onward, Indian firms also began to file petitions seeking the use of safeguards as an alternative form of trade remedies. Again, corporations in the chemicals industry led the way. In January 1998 the government began an investigation on acetylene black, a chemical used in the production of batteries, rubber tires, greases, and lubricants. This was followed by three additional new cases in the next month. By the end of 1999, India had enacted safeguards on seven chemical products. Nor was the chemicals industry the only one to seek safeguards. The paper industry also sought safeguards against hard-density fiberboard, but in this instance, its petition failed.

Over the next few years, the same patterns that one sees with antidumping cases also hold true for safeguards, albeit on a much smaller scale. As the safeguards cases on various chemicals succeed, the industry expands the number of products on which it seeks safeguards. In addition, as QRs disappear on agricultural products and consumer goods, the range of industries for which safeguards are sought also expands. By 2002, the Indian government had opened safeguard investigations on edible-grade vegetable oil and industrial sewing machine needles. Not all of these cases will be decided in favor of the domestic industries, but the point is that in the wake of the elimination of QRs, Indian producers learned to avail themselves of a range of trade remedies, including safeguards.

Altogether, a series of trade shocks in the 1990s triggered the rapid onslaught of Indian trade remedy cases. Although Indian lawyers and government officials had known of trade remedy laws for decades and had such laws on their books for decades, they failed to put them to use. By the end of the 1980s, India had not yet seen a single trade remedy case. But the lowering of import tariffs following the 1991 macroeconomic crisis and the Uruguay Round, along with the elimination of most QRs mandated by the WTO's ruling in the India-Quantitative Restrictions case, changed the calculus for domestic corporations. By 2002, India was a global leader in two of the three major forms of trade remedies: antidumping and safeguards.

III. DEVELOPING CAPACITY FOR TRADE REMEDY LITIGATION

While the preceding part details the key developments that made recourse to trade remedy litigation attractive for Indian companies, it did not answer the question of how exactly this became possible. How was it that a country that had absolutely no experience in this area of trade litigation would, over the course of a decade, emerge as a global leader in this field? While a few studies have examined the question for how India developed the capacity to handle external trade litigation in multilateral dispute settlement, none have examined this question for the domestic arena. Yet domestic trade remedy litigation arguably has had as important a role as WTO litigation, if not more, in impacting the competitiveness of India's corporations following India's trade liberalization in the 1990s.

What contributed to this rapid transformation? In this part, I document a confluence of four interconnecting factors that helped to achieve this result: (1) the emergence of a small but important class of policy entrepreneurs who played a key role in diffusing knowledge of trade law to Indian corporations, thus sparking demand for trade remedy litigation; (2) the parallel emergence of an eclectic group of lawyers who developed an array of alternatives to meet the latent demand of those Indian corporations hungry for increased protection; (3) the Indian government's decision to eschew the direct transplantation of existing trade remedy regimes from established foreign jurisdictions such as the United States, European Union, or Canada in favor of developing indigenous processes to handle the procedural elements of trade remedy litigation; (4) the development of a positive feedback cycle within the leading law firms as a result of their willingness to handle cases for both petitioners and respondents, as well as from their close ties with government officials. Collectively, these developments led to a virtuous cycle of coordination between the key actors involved – Indian corporations, lawyers, the administrative state, and the judiciary. This coordination, in turn, allowed India first to build up a trade remedy regime quickly in the face of economic shocks and then to improve the capacity of regime actors over the course of time. The following sections explore each of these elements in turn.

A. *The Key Role of Policy Entrepreneurs*

A policy shift requires both a spark to ignite the shift and a catalyst to sustain it. The external events described in the previous section – the 1991 macroeconomic crisis, the Uruguay Round tariff reductions, and the elimination of quantitative restrictions mandated by the WTO – provided the sparks that kindled interest in seeking trade remedies. One might have thought that the corporations themselves might serve as the catalyst, putting pressure on their government to improve the internal capacity to handle trade remedy cases. However, as mentioned already, very few Indian corporations in the early to mid-1990s were even aware of the concept of trade remedies. Instead, the catalyst came from within the government itself. Individual civil servants discovered that trade remedy laws could play a useful role in assisting Indian corporations facing pressure from India's trade liberalization. They then set out to put this idea into practice. These civil servants functioned as "policy entrepreneurs" – individuals who identify a policy innovation and then invest heavily in getting this adopted by the government (Kingdon 1984; Kelman 1987). This is done through a variety of means, including crafting the problem for the public agenda, shaping public discourse, and building a coalition for the policy innovation (Mintrom 1997).

As is true of many other historical individuals, one can debate whether the rise of these policy entrepreneurs was due to the intrinsic characteristics of the persons themselves or the circumstances in which they found themselves. What is clear is that a series of personnel changes made within the Ministry of Commerce and Industry in the mid-1990s played a key role. At the time, the ministry had only three people allocated to handle antidumping matters within its antidumping department. Because of the dearth of litigation cases, these three individuals were not even expected to devote themselves full-time to antidumping matters.

An initial set of changes began under the watch of R. Parthasarathy, who joined the Ministry of Commerce and Industry in 1993 and became the director of the antidumping division in June 1994. Soon thereafter, the government developed a questionnaire for domestic industry petitioners, thereby making it easier for producers to file a request to initiate a case. It also published a booklet explaining antidumping procedures in order to educate Indian corporations about the process. Parthasarathy notes that his team's efforts were done largely in isolation from others within the government and the private law firms (Interview with R. Parthasarathy, 2013). There was not close coordination on antidumping legal policy between his division and other government ministries, such as the Ministry of Finance and the Ministry of Law. Nor were corporate lawyers or even the general counsels of Indian corporations involved in the process of creating the questionnaire and booklets (ibid.).

Parthasarathy's tenure overseeing the antidumping division was short-lived, as he was reassigned a year later in June 1995. Then, in July 1995, Sharad Bhansali joined the Ministry of Commerce and Industry and was assigned to become the new director of the antidumping department. This was not, he points out, a plum assignment (Interview with Sharad Bhansali, 2012). It involved arcane policy that, at the time, did not seem to matter much to either government officials or the private sector. Antidumping matters, Bhansali points out, were expected only to be a minor policy concern on which he was expected to devote no more than 20 percent of his time (Interview with Sharad Bhansali, 2012).

The Anti-dumping Agreement (ADA) that emerged from the Uruguay Round negotiations in 1994 was full of legal technicalities.[13] This was no surprise; the agreement simply reflected the important role that lawyers had played in crafting such laws in the United States in the 1970s and then embedding their legal concepts within international treaty text. However, Bhansali, at the time he joined in 1995, did not possess a law degree. Instead, he possessed a master's degree in business management from the University of Delhi and a master's degree in economics from Boston University.

However, certain past experiences provided Bhansali with an instinctual awareness that antidumping laws could play a more important role than it had to date. Upon graduating, Bhansali had first joined the Ministry of Finance in 1980 where he was assigned to work on customs matters. As a result, Bhansali was acutely aware of the challenges that some of India's domestic industries could face as its trade barriers were lowered in the early 1990s. He rightly anticipated that many more would find themselves in similar shoes, given the liberalization commitments that India had just made during the Uruguay Round. In addition, his customs work exposed him to the importance of litigation in resolving trade conflicts. Although he did not possess a law degree, Bhansali found himself on teams representing the Indian government before various tribunals. These experiences provided him with an informal exposure to basic concepts in law (Interview with Sharad Bhansali, 2012).

The two other individuals on the team, along with Bhansali, were also nonlawyers, but had similar backgrounds. The deputy director, A. K. Gupta, was trained as an accountant and had worked in the manufacturing sector for three years before joining the government. He therefore was intimately familiar with understanding the books of companies, and though not a lawyer, was adept with the cost-accounting elements of the law (Interview with A. K. Gupta, 2012). The third member, A. K. Kapoor, had a similar background.

Note that at this point, none of the three individuals had been intimately involved with India's trade policy at the international level. Those jobs belonged to others within the Ministry of Commerce and Industry who had been given what were considered to be more plum assignments. None of the individuals participated in the Uruguay Round negotiations, nor were any of them involved in reexamining domestic regulations on trade remedies following the conclusion of the Uruguay Round, in 1994; this process initially was driven largely by government lawyers without consultation from the officials within the antidumping division (Interview with R. Parthasarathy, 2013). None had ever been posted overseas. In short, all three individuals did not fit the typical profile of the transnational actor who plays the key role in spurring legal transplantation and indigenization of international legal principles.

Yet, despite not having any formal legal training, all three individuals were determined for India to utilize antidumping laws in the same manner that developed countries had been for years. However, they faced a major roadblock. At the time, they did not have access to any readily available books that could explain the details of the international treaties governing antidumping laws, nor did they know of any other lawyers within the government or private sector capable of explaining the nuances of the treaties. As Bhansali noted in his interview, "To say that there was any capacity would be an overstatement" (Interview with Sharad Bhansali, 2012). The team therefore had to build up its expertise from scratch. It began by asking the India Mission to the WTO in Geneva to supply it with any materials that could be obtained from the WTO directly and then studied the materials extensively (ibid.).

In the course of doing so, the team realized that the Indian government had been too stringent in its requirements of its domestic industries for filing a petition for an antidumping investigation (Interview with Sharad Bhansali, 2012). WTO law, under article 5.2 of the ADA, requires that any application made for antidumping duties contain evidence of dumping, injury, and causation. Included in the application should be information on prices of the foreign producer alleged to be dumping, provided that information is reasonably available. The prior officials overseeing antidumping investigations within the Ministry of Commerce and Industry had set a high threshold for Indian producers, requiring the domestic petitioner to provide the actual price or cost data of the foreign competitor. This proved difficult, if not impossible, for most firms. Indeed, the nature of an antidumping investigation is for the government itself to request this data of the foreign companies upon receipt of a petition; it ought not to expect petitioners to already possess such data when filing the case.

The new team, upon reexamining the treaty language, noted a caveat. Article 5.2 of the ADA explicitly states that petitioners are not required to submit actual data in instances where it was not "readily available." The team made clear that it would apply this caveat. As long as the domestic petitioner could demonstrate that it could not obtain the actual data, it was not expected to provide it. In other words, petitioners merely had to present a prima facie case based on publicly available information. Once sufficient data was made available so as to justify the initiation of an investigation by the government, it would then fall on the government to gather the data necessary to determine whether the allegation held true. With this change, the new team made it significantly easier for Indian firms to file an antidumping petition.

By itself, this move would have been significant. But Bhansali and his team did not stop there. They also revised India's investigation procedures in a number of other ways. For example, they pressed for authority to do on-site verification of the exporter data submitted by the foreign respondents (Interview with Sharad Bhansali, 2012). Previously, these verification inspections had been handled by officials within the Indian embassy or consulates based in the country who were not appropriately trained to perform such verifications. By taking over this function, the new team ensured a more rigorous inspection of foreign producers' submissions. This also further reinforced the message to domestic and foreign producers alike that the government would take antidumping claims seriously.

Most importantly, these policy entrepreneurs made it their mission to educate Indian producers about antidumping laws. Outside of the chemicals industry, antidumping laws were largely unknown to general counsels within

Indian corporations and trade associations. The team organized a vast number of seminars and workshops for firms where it explained the nuts and bolts of an antidumping case (Interview with A. K. Gupta, 2012). It emphasized that antidumping duties were a possible way to raise tariffs, provided certain legal requirements could be met. The seminars walked corporations through the legal requirements and the procedural rules that governed the proceedings.

In addition to the seminars, these policy entrepreneurs created resource guides that further helped disseminate knowledge about trade remedies. In 1997, R. K. Gupta published a comprehensive book, totaling more than three hundred pages, which provided an in-depth analysis of antidumping duties and countervailing measures.[14] Gupta, like Bhansali, had spent the bulk of his then-career in customs; he had worked on trade policy issues for a brief two years before his book came out. It was the first guide written specifically for Indian corporations on trade remedies. In his preface, Gupta describes his aim as assisting Indian corporations with both domestic claims "needed to protect their industries against dumped imports" and "antidumping and countervailing investigations initiated against Indian exporters" overseas (Gupta 2007, 14). Through his government work, Gupta notes, he found that Indian firms "and other concerned people suffered from an acute dearth of published literature on the subject" and "had little to fall back on by the way of record or precedence to help them build a viable case" (ibid.). His hope was to remedy this shortage. After the safeguard regime was constructed in 1997, Gupta became its director-general. He would play an important role in building out that facet of India's trade remedy regime as well.

Besides Gupta's book, the team at the Ministry of Commerce and Industry produced a shorter manual, authored by Bhansali, titled "Anti-dumping – A Guide" for Indian corporations as a reference. It also issued an annual report that contained a list of past and ongoing cases, as well as contact details for lawyers handling such cases. Indian corporations desirous of protection against imports now could refer to materials to perform an initial check as to whether their foreign competitors' actions could constitute "dumping" and then consult further with legal counsel. These efforts at knowledge diffusion were very successful. Within a few short years, large Indian corporations went from not knowing anything about trade remedies to becoming active participants in filing cases. It would take longer for smaller Indian corporations to become familiar, but the government maintained an active effort at knowledge dissemination through the 2000s.

As noted, the policy entrepreneurs acted largely on their own accord. They were not following orders of senior government officials, nor were their efforts part of a coordinated effort with other parts of the bureaucratic state. Yet they encountered almost no resistance to their efforts to promote policy change (Interview with Sharad Bhansali, 2012; Interview with A. K. Gupta, 2012). Antidumping policy was simply not an area to which more-senior officials in the government paid much attention. Importantly, the prior way of implementing the policy was not linked to any vested interest group. It was simply a bureaucratic procedure that was easy to reverse once the policy entrepreneurs were put in charge of the process.

What motivated these policy entrepreneurs to take action? This question is more difficult to answer. One might speculate that it was the prospect of financial reward; several of the policy entrepreneurs later left government to set up lucrative practices.[15] Yet none of the interviewees mentioned that they had a clear sense at the time that their innovations would position them to benefit financially down the road. In the mid-1990s, it would not have been at all clear that a midlevel bureaucrat in what was then deemed to be a largely insignificant division would find much opportunity for private-sector work. The notion of a revolving door between government and the private sector was more or less nonexistent in the mid-1990s; those who left were largely senior officials and officials in sectors heavily regulated and/or controlled by the state. Trade remedies simply did not fit that profile.

Instead, these individuals were driven to make something of an assignment that had to date been perceived of as a "lemon." From this, they sought to "make lemonade." When asked why his team took actions that differed dramatically from those of his earlier predecessors, Sharad Bhansali replied that they were motivated to "really understand the subject [of trade remedies] because of an inner desire for self-respect" (Interview with Sharad Bhansali, 2012).

Instead of simply following the procedures as they had been done, Bhansali came in and demanded, "Show me where in the law it says that we must do it this way" (ibid.). In instances where an answer was not forthcoming from the lawyers, the team then examined potential alternative approaches and adopted that which they felt best suited Indian interests. Where necessary, they reached out to seek changes in the regulation to provide legal certainty about their new approach.[16] This shift toward a more aggressive approach began under Parthasarathy's brief watch and continued under Bhansali (Interview with A. K. Gupta 2012). A. K. Gupta noted: "Rather than waiting for orders from higher-ups, taking action was our philosophy" (ibid.). In addition, the team sought to professionalize the administrative procedures such that litigants had to make their case through appeals through the law rather than simply lobbying senior officials. Although they lacked law training, their professional backgrounds in cost accounting served them well in understanding how to improve such procedures because the facts of the cases required intensive scrutiny of cost data.

In addition, during the late 1990s, there was a palpable sense that the Indian economy was undergoing an intense transformation. Some of the policy entrepreneurs also possessed a sense of their patriotic duty to assist Indian corporations with this transformation. The way to do so was to strengthen the infrastructure with the administrative state to handle trade remedy litigation and to disseminate knowledge about such litigation among corporations. Yet this should not be equated with a desire to reenable protectionism. The policy entrepreneurs simply wanted to "level the playing field" between foreign and Indian producers. They wanted to equip Indian producers with the same procedures and knowledge that foreign producers had at their disposal in their home markets, but then see to it that the cases were adjudicated as they should be done according to the law (Interview with Abhijit Das, director of the Centre for WTO Studies, 2013; Gupta 2007, 14–15).

By reaching out to the business community at large, the policy entrepreneurs developed a powerful coalition of supporters for their view that India should more actively embrace antidumping measures. Already, India's two main national chambers of commerce – the Federation of Indian Chambers of Commerce and Industry and the Associated Chambers of Commerce and Industry – were clamoring for the government to find ways to moderate India's economic opening and found a sympathetic ear from the then-opposition Bharatiya Janata Party (Kohli 2006, 1363). The new openness shown toward antidumping duties provided the ruling Congress coalition with an example of how it was seeking to address the business community's concerns. And once the Bharatiya Janata Party took power in 1998, the government found itself even more willing politically to use antidumping duties as a safety valve for Indian industries (Wu 2012).

In a few short years, this small team of policy entrepreneurs had managed to create a situation where a policy, on a topic that had received scant attention previously, now became politically costly for either major party to reverse. It is possible that without the efforts of the policy entrepreneurs, Indian corporations might have eventually discovered the utility of trade remedy litigation on their own. But without the push coming from within the government, this transformation would have taken much longer. Furthermore, the policy shift did not emanate from India's policy think tanks or from the leadership ranks of its political parties. It happened because of the entrepreneurial activities of civil servants. But because of their timing – at a moment of political turbulence and mass popular support for renewed economic nationalism – their policies found support across party lines and quickly became ensconced as government policy.

B. *The Emergence of the Trade Remedy Lawyer*

At the start, the policy entrepreneurs faced a limitation. They were not formally trained as lawyers, and the policy that they were emphasizing relied upon litigation. A group of individual lawyers would need to step in to fill this void. Otherwise, the policy would be hampered by a supply constraint that would be unable to meet the burgeoning demand.

Trade remedy litigation is, however, not a particularly lucrative practice. There is a startup cost associated with developing expertise in a legal area that is largely unrelated to other parts of one's practice. As the US experience has shown, the flow of work can be cyclical. And in smaller markets such as India's, there is not the potential promise of a large payout from litigation success that may exist in larger export markets. As one lawyer put it, "You do this type of work because you think it's the right thing to do for your country, not in order to get rich" (Interview with Suhail Nathani, 2012). Among the firms that eventually developed trade remedy practices, many would supplement it with work in more-lucrative areas such as mergers and acquisitions, capital markets, intellectual property, and tax.

Thus, it was not altogether clear that a supply of trade remedy lawyers would develop at a pace necessary to meet the growing demands of corporations for such work. India was fortunate, however, to have an eclectic group of individuals enter into this legal practice. They include three categories of individuals: (1) a few established lawyers; (2) a set of hungry upstarts; and (3) some ex-government officials. Each brought a different set of skills to the emerging legal profession that would service this line of work.

Initially, two main established law firms chose to wade into trade remedies work. Both became interested in this line of work as a result of the background circumstances of key partners. The first firm, Lakshmikumaran & Sridharan (LK&S), had been founded in 1985 by V. Lakshmikumaran. Prior to starting his firm, he was in the Indian Revenue Service and had been a key policymaker in customs and excise legislation. This expertise positioned his firm well to handle the data-intensive trade remedy work. LK&S's preeminent position in this area was further enhanced with the later additions of Parthasarathy, who briefly headed the antidumping division, and S. Seetharaman, who joined after serving as the deputy controller general of accounts in the Ministry of Finance.

The second firm, Amarchand Mangaldas, was one of India's largest and most influential law firms. Its trade remedy practice developed as a result of the efforts of Pallavi Shroff, a lead senior partner and the wife of a managing partner. She was the niece of Jagdish Bhagwati, one of the world's leading trade economists and a longtime advocate of a more-open trade policy. As a result, she was well positioned to understand legal remedies, such as antidumping, that could be applied once India did embark on such a path.

The two established firms did much of the early work on the initial antidumping cases. As demand grew, it was unclear whether the established firms alone would be able to meet demand, nor did all clients want to pay their higher fees. Into the mix entered a set of hungry upstart lawyers ready to capitalize on the opportunities created by India's globalization. Suhail Nathani, for example, was among the early wave of overseas Indian lawyers to return following India's reforms. After obtaining a LLM at Duke Law, he worked for several years as a telecommunications lawyer in the United States. Upon return, however, he found little in the way of such work in Delhi. Instead, through an introduction of an acquaintance who happened to be the son of an industrialist, he was drawn into the first antidumping dispute filed by the metallurgical coke industry in August 1997. As the case progressed, the industry officials found themselves turning to Nathani instead of the more senior litigators who did not devote as much attention to the case. Hungry for work, Nathani threw himself into the case (ibid.). The domestic industry prevailed, winning a judgment imposing antidumping duties against Chinese imports. This led to more work subsequently, eventually leading Nathani to become one of India's most recognized trade lawyers. Today, trade remedy litigation is but a small part of his firm's practice.

Finally, some of the policy entrepreneurs themselves later exited government and ventured into establishing firms to service this burgeoning need. A. K. Gupta left government service in 1999, after having witnessed the transformation of the trade remedy regime during his time in government. Although he did not have a law degree, Gupta teamed with a group of lawyers to form a firm to service domestic industries interested in filing antidumping cases (Interview with A. K. Gupta, interview 2012). While in the civil service, Sharad Bhansali set out to obtain a LLB from Delhi University. In 2001 he left the civil service and joined forces with Nathani at the Strategic Law Group. With their in-depth knowledge of how the regime operated, their services were in high demand. Today, both are widely recognized as being among India's top practitioners for trade remedy disputes, along with other international trade matters.

Having championed a shift in government policy toward trade remedies from within government, these individuals then evolved their careers away from policy entrepreneurship and toward the entrepreneurial pursuit of legal practice. A. K. Gupta, in particular, sought to expand the range of domestic firms and industries that took advantage of antidumping duties. Today, his practice, more so than others, is skewed toward cases for domestic petitioners. He is also assisting Indian companies facing trade remedy cases in the United States, European Union, Egypt, South Korea, Indonesia, Turkey, Brazil, and elsewhere.

However, the policy entrepreneurial spirit that they championed within government survived their departure. For example, in 2002, after Sharad Bhansali and A. K. Gupta had both left, the government continued to hold seminars for domestic industry in conjunction with the major chambers of commerce. And as mentioned, by the time they left, they had built up a solid coalition of business interest groups supportive of their policies such that it would be difficult to undo them following their departure. By moving into private practice, these individuals helped to alleviate any potential supply-constraint problem in the legal sector.

India therefore was fortunate to have an eclectic group of individuals willing to take on trade remedy cases just as demand was booming in the late 1990s. These individuals did not always have much in common. Some came from established law firms; others were upstarts; and still others were ex-civil servants. Some were experienced litigators; others had built the system from within; and still others taught themselves a new area of law from scratch. But they were tied together by a desire to see this area of trade litigation develop within India. Together, they offered a vast array of alternatives to Indian corporations and trade associations interested in pursuing this legal recourse in light of increased foreign competition. As a result, India did not find itself facing a legal capacity constraint that sometimes overwhelms other developing countries. Instead, the supply of legal services for trade remedies grew alongside demand.

C. *Indigenization of the Trade Remedy Regime*

Although economic shocks created latent demand for trade remedies, it was not until a series of policy entrepreneurs and lawyers emerged that this demand could be met. Even so, another potential barrier stood in the way. Recall that trade remedy cases are administrative proceedings handled initially by a government agency and not by a court. The government, therefore, needs to have sufficient resources in place to adjudicate these claims. For India, however, this posed a real problem. As discussed, until 1995, the government devoted few resources as cases were intermittent and limited to chemicals. Following the Uruguay Round, the number of petitions increased gradually, reaching a crescendo in the aftermath of the India-Quantitative Restrictions case. While the authorities opened only six new investigations in 1995, by

1999, the number of new investigations had increased to more than sixty. Yet the civil service staff, while increased, did not grow tenfold.[17] How was the administrative state able to cope with the rapidly growing demand from Indian corporations for antidumping investigations?

The answer lies in the fact that the policy entrepreneurs who implemented the antidumping regime did not attempt to fully transplant the apparatus that industrialized nations were using to investigate the petitions and adjudicate the cases. While they drew from elements of the trade policy regime of developed countries, they did not do so wholesale. Instead, they sought to adapt the apparatus to fit India's unique circumstances. Realizing that India lacked the capacity to replicate the industrialized countries' legal apparatus in full, they instead did what they thought was appropriate given India's capacity constraints, while still staying within the boundaries of India's international treaty obligations.

For example, during an antidumping case, after the domestic firm has filed its petition and it has been accepted, the foreign exporter accused of dumping is then asked to provide information defending itself against the allegations that it is "dumping" in violation of the law. WTO law does not specify a standard for the amount of information required. Article 6.1 of the ADA simply states, "All interested parties in an antidumping investigation shall be given notice of the information which the authorities require and ample opportunity to present in writing all evidence which they consider relevant in respect of the investigation in question."

In deciding what information was necessary, the Indian antidumping authorities looked to the practices of the United States, European Union, and Canada. Yet they quickly realized that their team did not have either the manpower or the capacity to evaluate the depth of information sought by the authorities in developed countries. Nor were they required to do so under the treaty law. The vague language of article 6.1 of the ADA left it to the discretion of the authorities to determine how much information they needed. India's antidumping team created a highly abridged version of the questionnaire given to the foreign exporters. It totals only thirty-five pages. By contrast, just the appendices of the US questionnaire alone total more than thirty-five pages; the main sections, excluding the directions, number more than 130 pages. But the Indian team realized that there was simply no way that it could have copied the US questionnaire wholesale. To do so would have crippled the antidumping investigation process. So instead they adapted the questionnaire so that it would extract what information they needed in order to adjudicate the case. One could say that they look for "shortcuts" to get the job done. But their shortened questionnaire was legal under WTO law.

Nothing stated that other countries needed to mimic the practices of the more established antidumping authorities in industrialized countries.

The fact of the matter is that these forms of legal adaptation was absolutely critical in order to allow India's trade remedy regime to handle the volume of cases coming its way. Without these adaptations, the process would have been slowed down tremendously. Domestic firms would have lost interest, and the policy objectives would have remained unaccomplished.

Nayaranan has highlighted several other ways in which Indian authorities have demonstrated "ingenuity" in adopting antidumping practices to the Indian context (Nayaranan 2006). For example, Indian authorities have decided on several occasions to initiate investigations suo moto, without a petition being received from the domestic industry. This practice is legally permissible under article 5.6 of the ADA but rarely employed in practice. Yet authorities may have chosen to take such an action in instances where the domestic industry could not organize properly and did not have sufficient legal capacity to file properly. In addition, Indian authorities have taken the liberty to find injury on account of the "material retardation to the establishment of domestic industry" in order to impose an antidumping duty. Again, while this move is technically permitted under article of the ADA, few countries have ever employed it. Nevertheless, Indian authorities took advantage of this legal flexibility when ruling on the large stream of cases in the early 2000s.

Commentators have criticized the practices of the Ministry of Commerce and Industry as inadequate. Nayaranan, despite describing several of these practices as ingenious, also acknowledges that they reflect "the protective purposes" of the Indian trade remedy regime. Nevertheless, whatever their faults, the legal adaptations engineered by the administrative state were necessary to get the system in place when it was needed, given the shortcomings that India faced both in terms of the legal capacity of its corporate counsels and within the administrative state. Decisions to indigenize legal practices transplanted from overseas helped to cement domestic support for the newly emergent field of trade remedy law.

D. *Feedback Mechanisms*

Although the regime that was constructed was imperfect, an important factor for India's success in developing its trade remedy regime has been its openness to feedback. This feedback has come from a number of sources including academics, foreign experts, and domestic practitioners. Over time, they have provided a consistent source of knowledge transfer for the government. This, in turn, has allowed the government to evolve its trade remedy regime over time to enhance its effectiveness.

One major force driving the creation of these feedback mechanisms was the growing use of trade remedies against Indian corporations in other countries. Whereas Indian corporations were subject to very few antidumping cases in the early to mid-1990s, this was no longer true by the late 1990s. In 1999 thirteen new investigations were opened against Indian firms, compared with only three in 1995. In seeking to defend themselves in foreign jurisdictions, Indian corporations sought out highly experienced foreign practitioners. This exposure, in turn, created linkages between foreign experts, Indian corporations, and the Indian government.

The case that proved to be the trigger point in improving linkages between Indian practitioners and foreign firms was an antidumping case taken against Indian bed linen exporters in Europe (Abhijit Das, director of the Centre for WTO Studies, interview with the author, December 17, 2012). Concessions made by the European Commission (EC) during the Uruguay Round increased the competitiveness of certain Indian textile products in European markets, including bed linens. European producers accused Indian firms of dumping, and Indian corporations turned to Vermulst Waer & Verhaeghe to defend themselves. The Brussels-based law firm was headed by Edwin Vermulst, a leading expert on antidumping who was the coauthor of a landmark comparative analysis of the world's leading antidumping regimes in 1990 and of a 1997 treatise on EC antidumping law and practice. Although the Indian firms lost their case before the EC, this partnership with Vermulst would prove fruitful for India in the years to come.

After the EC imposed antidumping duties against Indian bed linens, the Indian government decided to challenge the decision before the WTO. The government, like Indian industry before it, turned to Vermulst to make its case. The result was a landmark victory for India in which the WTO Appellate Body first declared the practice of "zeroing" to be illegal. In subsequent years, Vermulst would continue to serve as an important resource and consultant to the Indian government on trade remedy concerns.

Another important force driving the creation of these feedback mechanisms was the launch of the Doha Round in 2001 (ibid.) By then, India had come to recognize the important role that trade remedy rules played in the global trade regime and was determined to play a more active role in the negotiation of such rules. At the time, however, few Indian academics had studied the impact of antidumping duties. As a result, the government had little data on which to rely to determine its negotiating position. Consequently, the Ministry of Commerce and Industry actively encouraged academics and policy think tanks to engage in this research. Aradhna Aggarwal, an economist who has done some of the leading work analyzing India's antidumping regime, was a senior fellow at the Indian Council for Research on International Economic Relations (ICRIER) at the time. She credits this active push from the government with launching her own academic interest in the subject (Interview with Aradhna Aggarwal, 2012). Eventually, her research would culminate in a book examining India's antidumping practices in a comparative light with other developing countries and detailing potential areas of shared concerns among developing countries for reform of WTO trade remedy rules (Aggarwal 2007).

Shaffer, Nedumpara, Sinha, and Bahri, in their chapter in this volume, detail how the government made a concerted effort to build capacity for trade policy analysis. In addition to ICRIER, the government also created its own think tank, the Centre for WTO Studies, organized under the Trade Policy Division of the Ministry of Commerce and Industry. Today, the Centre is headed by Abhijit Das. Because Das was intimately involved in shaping India's negotiating policies on trade remedies during 2000–05, the Centre serves as yet another channel for the government to engage with academic research in trade remedies, should policy questions arise.

As academic research into antidumping practices proliferated, this created yet another feedback mechanism into India's trade remedy regime. Aggarwal (2002) highlighted how a significant number of India's antidumping investigations to date had been driven by protectionist impulses in which foreign imports accounted for a small share of total demand. The study raised awareness of the possibility that while antidumping duties may benefit individual corporations, this might be at the expense of consumers and the economy overall. As a result, the government began placing a greater emphasis on evaluating the impact of antidumping on the public interest overall.

A third conduit for feedback grew out of the business practices of the trade remedy practices at top-tier law firms. Because the number of top-tier legal practitioners was relatively limited, foreign defendants often turned to the same top law firms as the domestic petitioners. Indian law firms developed informal partnerships with top American and European trade remedy practices, as was true in other areas of the law. Not only would the latter provide referral services, but they also served as a valuable source of "knowledge transfer" to Indian firms.

Yet law firms did not self-segregate into primarily petitioner or respondent firms. In this regard, India's experience differs from that of many other countries where such segregation does occur. Law firms continued to represent whoever was willing to hire their services, including domestic corporations. This gave them a certain amount of credibility when providing feedback to government officials based on the knowledge acquired from working with foreign firms. The government did not discount this feedback as simply serving the interests of their foreign clientele, since most firms continued to serve both sides.

Moreover, as the capabilities of Indian law firms grew, they also began representing domestic corporations as respondents in cases overseas. For example, LK&S has handled cases for Indian exporters in the United States, European Union, Thailand, Korea, and South Africa. Its lawyers note that such cases often present opportunities for knowledge transfer. In defending Indian firms abroad, the top-tier law firms gained greater exposure to the trade remedy practices of other countries, which shed further light on what could be done differently back home (Interview with S. Seetharaman and other LK&S lawyers, 2012). Some cases are also done in collaboration with foreign law firms, which also presents opportunities to exchange knowledge with foreign trade remedy lawyers.

A positive feedback loop therefore transpired between practitioners and the government. The government was deeply interested in the feedback of prominent practitioners, some of whom had helped build the regime originally from within. For many practitioners, their interest was intensely personal. Ex-government officials, such as Bhansali and Gupta, knew of the shortcomings that resulted from their initial legal adaptations and were determined to see the system improved. Others, such as Lakshmikumaran, were also present at the creation as lawyers in the earliest cases and felt a duty. In an article titled "The 10 Major Problems with the Anti-dumping Instrument in India," he drew attention to a number of ways in which the Indian regime could be improved (Kumaran 2005). Although not all of the advice was heeded, practitioners knew that their opinions mattered. They contributed thoughtful ideas to the government about ways to further strengthen India's trade remedy regime.

In addition, the feedback mechanism between government and practitioners has continued to operate in both directions. As discussed earlier in this chapter, government bureaucrats played a key role in disseminating knowledge to industry and legal practitioners in the late 1990s and early 2000s. Even as Indian law firms have become more sophisticated in their handling of trade remedy cases, government bureaucrats have continued their time-honored tradition of aggregating and disseminating knowledge acquired through their handling of such cases. For example, Neeraj Varshney, a director within the Ministry of Commerce and Industry's antidumping directorate, wrote a comprehensive treatise on not only the WTO rules under the ADA but also the Indian jurisprudence to date (Varshney 2007). While most of the details would be known to the top-tier practitioners, the book served as a valuable resource to industry officials as well as potential lower-cost attorneys looking to break into this line of work.

Overall, these multiple feedback mechanisms contributed to the continued evolution of India's trade remedy practices. Academics, foreign experts, and domestic practitioners have all played an important role in generating and challenging the government with ideas. The government's receptivity, in turn, has led to gradual improvements over time in India's capacity to handle trade remedies.

IV. CONCLUSION

India's trade remedy regime is a testament to the success of a developing country in adapting the legal instrument of industrialized nations to advance its own interests in the face of the competitive pressures triggered by globalization. Replicating India's success, however, may not be that easy for other developing countries. Just as the need for a stronger trade remedy regime was emerging on account of a set of successive economic shocks, India was fortunate to have several factors line up. It had a set of policy entrepreneurs willing to devote intense energy to transforming government practices. These policy entrepreneurs played an important role in scrutinizing the available legal flexibilities embedded in India's treaty commitments. Through workshops and seminars, they generated awareness of the benefits of trade remedy litigation. India also had an eclectic set of lawyers willing to answer the demands of its domestic business community, even if it was altogether unclear that this line of work would prove lucrative. From the beginning, the government officials made an important call to adapt practices to suit Indian conditions or, put differently, accommodate capacity weaknesses. But they also established an important set of feedback mechanisms that allowed the regime to improve with time. This confluence of factors transformed India from an inactive player in trade remedies into its current status as a global power in this particular area of trade law. What impact this transformation will play in helping India become an overall economic powerhouse still remains to be seen. But however this story ends, India's trade remedy regime will serve as a tribute to the determination of several dedicated citizens, who, at a moment when Indian industries faced peril from imports, used international law, with all its built-in flexibilities for contingent protection, to try to assist their motherland.

Notes

1 Author's computation based on statistics provided in Zanardi (2004).

2 For a comprehensive account of India's development of legal capacity at the WTO, see the Chapter 20 by *Shaffer, Nedumpara, Sinha, and Bahri* in this volume. For examples of other earlier work, see Chimni (2010) and Dhar and Majumdar (2010).

3 Roberts and King offer a classical account of the role played by policy entrepreneurs (Roberts and King 1991).

4 For studies specific to India, see Baruah (2007), Bown and Tovar (2011), and Wu (2012). For case study analysis, see Malhotra et al. (2005) and Malhotra and Malhotra (2008).

5 In 1985, India enacted the Customs Tariff (Identification, Assessment and Collection of Duty or Additional Duty on Dumped Goods and for Determination of Injury) Rules and the Customs Tariff (Identification, Assessment and Collection of Duty or Additional Duty on Bounty-Fed Goods and for Determination of Injury) Rules.

6 Pursell et al. (see table 1) note that the nominal protection coefficient (NPC) for registered chemical manufacturers fell from 1.96 in 1987 to 1.08 in 1993 (Pursell et al. 2007). This decline is even more extreme considering that the NPC had already declined from 3.00 in 1971, when their estimates suggest that it was the most heavily protected Indian manufacturing subsector.

7 An example is the agreement to abolish the Multifibre Agreement (MFA) quotas for textiles. Kathuria et al. noted how the Indian textile and clothing sectors were well positioned to gain from this development (Kathuria et al. 2003). The fact that China's eventual WTO accession would dull the positive impact for Indian exporters was not necessarily apparent in 1994.

8 This is not altogether surprising. Worldwide, only seventeen countervailing duty investigations were initiated in the first two years following the WTO's establishment.

9 Statistics are based on those provided by the Export Import Data Bank maintained by the Department of Commerce within the Ministry of Commerce and Industry.

10 Ibid.

11 Ibid. The five key European economies that import goods into India are Belgium, France, Germany, Italy, and the United Kingdom.

12 Ibid.

13 The ADA is formally known as the Agreement on Implementation of Article VI of the General Agreement on Tariffs and Trade, 1994.

14 Note that R. K. Gupta is not related to A. K. Gupta.

15 Note that this was not the case with all of the early policy entrepreneurs. A. K. Kapoor, for example, did not venture forth into private-sector practice.

16 An example provided in the interviews is the change in the regulation that allowed Indian authorities to treat China as a nonmarket economy, which was the approach followed in other developed countries.

17 Raju notes that the average period of time necessary for carrying out an antidumping investigation is significantly longer in India than for other WTO members. This is likely to be a consequence of the fact that the authorities in charge of the investigations are short-staffed (Raju 2006).

References

Aggarwal, Aradhna. 2002. "Anti-dumping Law and Practice: An Indian Perspective" (working paper 85, Indian Council for Research on Indian Economic Relations, New Delhi).

2007. *The Anti-Dumping Agreement and Developing Countries: An Introduction*. Oxford: Oxford University Press.

Ahn, Dukgeun. 2003. "Korea in the GATT/WTO Dispute Settlement System: Legal Battle for Economic Development." *Journal of International Economic Law* 6 (3): 597–633.

Baruah, Nandana. 2007. "An Analysis of Factors Influencing the Anti-Dumping Behaviour in India." *The World Economy* 30 (7): 1170–1191.

Bown, Chad and Patricia Tovar. 2011. "Trade Liberalization, Antidumping, and Safeguards: Evidence from India's Tariff Reform." *Journal of Development Economics* 96 (1): 115–125.

Chadha, Rajesh, Drusilla K. Brown, Alan Deardorff, and Robert M. Stern. 2003. "Computational Analysis of the Impact on India of the Uruguay Round and the Doha Round of Negotiations." In *India and the WTO: A Strategy for Development*. Edited by Aaditya Mattoo and Robert M. Stern. Washington, DC: The World Bank and Oxford University Press.

Chimni, B. S. 2010. "China, India, and the WTO Dispute Settlement System." In *China, India and the International Economic Order*. Edited by Muthucumaraswamy Sonorajah and Jiangyu Wang. Cambridge: Cambridge University Press.

Das, Gucharan. 2013. *India Grows at Night*. New York: Penguin Books.

Debroy, Bibek and Nilanjan Banik. 1999. "The Anti-Dumping Agreement." In *The WTO Millennium Round: Towards a Negotiating Agenda for India*. Edited by Bibek Debroy. Delhi: Confederation of Indian Industry.

Dhar, Biswajit and Abhik Majumdar. 2010. "Learning from the India-EC GSP Dispute: The Issues and the Process." In *Dispute Settlement at the WTO: The Developing Country Experience*. Edited by Gregory C. Shaffer and Ricardo Meléndez-Ortiz. Cambridge: Cambridge University Press.

Finger, J. Michael. 1991. "The Origins and Evolution of Antidumping Regulation" (working paper 783, World Bank Policy, Research, and External Affairs, Washington, DC).

Gupta, R. K. 1997. *Anti-dumping and Countervailing Measures: The Complete Reference*. New Delhi: Response Books.

Han, Liyu and Henry Gao. 2010. "China's Experience in Utilizing the WTO Dispute Settlement Mechanism." In *Dispute Settlement at the WTO: The Developing Country Experience*. Edited by Gregory C. Shaffer and Ricardo Meléndez-Ortiz. Cambridge: Cambridge University Press.

Interview with Aradhna Aggarwal. December 8, 2012.

Interview with Sharad Bhansali. November 27, 2012.

Interview with Sharad Bhansali. December 18, 2012.

Interview with Abhijit Das, director of the Centre for WTO Studies. December 17, 2012.

Interview with Abhijit Das, director of the Centre for WTO Studies. July 25, 2013.

Interview with A. K. Gupta. December 10, 2012.

Interview with Suhail Nathani. November 21, 2012.

Interview with R. Parthasarathy. November 14, 2013.

Interview with S. Seetharaman and other LK&S lawyers. December 15, 2012.

Kathuria, Sanjay, William J. Martin, and Anjali Bhardwaj. 2003. "Implications for South Asian Countries for Abolishing the Multifibre Arrangement." In *India and the WTO: A Strategy for Development*. Edited by Aaditya Mattoo and Robert M. Stern. Washington, DC: The World Bank and Oxford University Press.

Kelman, Steven. 1987. *Making Public Policy*. New York: Basic Books.

Kingdon, John W. 1984. *Agendas, Alternatives, and Public Policies*. Boston: Little, Brown, and Company.

Koh, Harold Hongju. 1997. "Why Do Nations Obey International Law?" *Yale Law Journal* 106 (8): 2599–2659.

2006. "Why Transnational Law Matters." *Penn State International Law Review* 24: 745–53.

Kohli, Atul. 2006. "Politics of Economic Growth in India, 1980–2005." *Economic and Political Weekly* 41 (13): 1251–1259

Kumaran, Lakshmi. 2005. "The 10 Major Problems with the Anti-dumping Instrument in India." *Journal of World Trade* 39 (1): 115–124.

Malhotra, Nisha and Shaheen Malhotra. 2008. "Liberalization and Protection: Anti-dumping Duties in the Indian Pharmaceutical Industry." *Journal of Economic Policy Reform* 11 (2): 115–122.

Malhotra, Shavin, Sumeet Gulati, and Nisha Malhotra. 2005. "Extent of Protection via Anti-Dumping Law: A Case Study of the Vitamin C Industry in India." *Journal of World Trade* 39 (5): 925–936.

Mintrom, Michael. 1997. "Policy Entrepreneurs and the Diffusion of Innovation." *American Journal of Political Science* 41 (3): 738–770.

Narayanan, Prakash. 2006. "Anti-dumping in India – Present State and Future Prospects." *Journal of World Trade* 40 (6): 1081–1097.

Pursell, Gary, Nalin Kishor, and Kanupriya Gupta. 2007. "Manufacturing Protection in India Since Independence" (working paper 2007/07, Australia South Asia Research Centre).

Raju, K. D. 2006. "Anti-dumping Protectionism in India: A Critical Study." In *Uses and Misuses of Anti-dumping Provisions in World Trade: A Cross-Country Perspective*. Edited by Bibek Debroy and Debashis Chakraborty. New Delhi: Academic Foundation.

Rasure, K. A. 2008. "WTO and Its Impact on Small Scale Industries." In *WTO and India: Challenges and Opportunities*. Edited by Ravishankar Kumar Singh and R. Shashi Kumar. Delhi: Abhijeet Publications.

Roberts, Nancy and Paulette King. 1991. "Policy Entrepreneurs: Their Activity Structure and Function in the Policy Process." *Journal of Public Administration Research Theory* 1 (2): 147–175.

Shaffer, Gregory C. 2012. "Transnational Legal Process and State Change." *Law and Social Inquiry* 37 (2): 22–64.

Shaffer, Gregory C., Michelle Ratton Sanchez Badin, and Barbara Rosenberg. 2010. "Winning at the WTO: The Development of a Trade Policy Community within Brazil." In *Dispute Settlement at the WTO: The Developing Country Experience*. Edited by Gregory C. Shaffer and Ricardo Meléndez-Ortiz. Cambridge: Cambridge University Press.

Tovar, Patricia. 2011. "India: The Use of Temporary Trade Barriers." In *The Great Recession and Import Protection*. Edited by Chad Bown. Washington, DC: Centre for Economic Policy Research and the World Bank.

Varshney, Neeraj. 2007. *Anti-dumping Measures Under the WTO Regime: Law, Practice, and Procedure*. Delhi: Universal Law Publishing.

Watson, Alan. 1995. *Legal Transplants: An Approach to Comparative Law*, 2d. ed. Athens, GA: University of Georgia Press.

World Trade Organization. 1998. Trade Policy Review – India. WT/TPR/S/33.

World Trade Organization. 1999a. Appellate Body Report. *India–Quantitative Restrictions*, WT/DS90/AB/R. August 23.

World Trade Organization. 1999b. Panel Report. *India–Quantitative Restrictions*, WT/DS90/R. April 6.

Wu, Mark. 2012. "Antidumping in Asia's Emerging Giants." *Harvard International Law Journal* 53 (1): 1–84.

Zanardi, Maurizio. 2004. "Anti-dumping: What Are the Numbers to Discuss at Doha?" *World Economy* 27 (3): 403–33.

22

Rising India in Investment Arbitration: Shifts in the Legal Field and Regime Participation

Mihaela Papa and Aditya Sarkar

I. INTRODUCTION: INDIA IN THE INVESTMENT ARBITRATION REGIME

Over the past 60 years, states have negotiated approximately 3,271 international investment agreements (IIAs). These IIAs are comprised of bilateral investment treaties (BITs), which are the bulk of all IIAs, bilateral economic agreements containing provisions or chapters that deal with investment, and other investment-related agreements between two or more states (United Nations Conference on Trade and Development (UNCTAD) 2015, 106). Usually, IIAs include a range of dispute resolution mechanisms, including provisions relating to investor-state (investment) arbitration. Such provisions enable aggrieved investors to sue a host country for damages in case of investment disputes and serve as a constraint on a host country's behavior. Recently, however, the international investment regime has been the subject of increased debate and controversy, particularly with respect to investment arbitration, which has been increasing globally (UNCTAD 2014, Sappideen and He 2015). Both scholars and practitioners have voiced concerns with the system. Investment treaties can significantly constrain domestic policy space, which can be particularly problematic when there is no robust evidence of the link between treaties and investment promotion and concerns with the regime's bias toward foreign investors are proliferating (Neumayer and Spess 2005; Salacuse and Sullivan 2005; UNCTAD 2009; Brower 2009; Sornarajah 2009; Waibel 2010; Van Harten 2011a). At the same time, uncertainties in the regime's evolution harm investors seeking to effectively resolve disputes in tribunals and enforce arbitration awards. Controversies are amplified in rising powers, which are becoming targets of investment to sources of investment, and in the process rethinking their involvement in arbitration policies (Kaushal 2009, 493–496).[1]

India is a relative newcomer in the investment arbitration world given that its first BITs were signed in the mid-1990s, but it has increasingly been the respondent state in a number of disputes with private investors.[2] Since 2011, in fact, India has been embroiled in a large number of high-profile investment disputes, worth up to several billion dollars. The numerous investment treaties combined with broad arbitration provisions and foreign investors' interest in the country makes India a microcosm of broader debates about and within the regime. Yet despite the richness of contemporary investment arbitration debates, our understanding of India's participation in the investment arbitration regime remains limited. Investment arbitration may indeed be one of the most controversial examples of globalization of the legal profession, but how Indian lawyers socialize into this regime, embrace it, and reproduce it remains unclear.

How do lawyers participate in investment arbitration, and what roles do they play? How does investment arbitration affect the Indian legal field, the ensemble of institutions and practices through which law is produced, interpreted, and incorporated into social decision making (Bourdieu 1977; Trubek et al. 1993)? To what extent do developments in this field affect India's participation in the investment arbitration regime?

Answering these questions is important for several reasons. First, doing so enhances our understanding of the processes through which globalization restructures the legal profession. As Trubek and others have argued (1993), the national legal field becomes more "internationalized" as countries use local legal fields as assets in competition for foreign investment: They conduct reforms to provide "modern" laws, "efficient" courts, and "business oriented" legal professions. As a result, the deep-seated practices of lawyers, judges, and academics that constitute the institutions of national legal systems "are being transformed directly, and indirectly, by [these] transnational interactions" and, in turn, are transforming them (Trubek et al. 1993, 412). Investment arbitration is a good example of such restructuring and raises questions about the costs and benefits of sacrificing local legal autonomy. What is more, scholars have been deeply divided on the nature of decision making in investment arbitration and the mechanisms behind regime participation (Van Harten 2011b). Focusing on lawyers offers a new entry point into these debates, captures microprocesses behind regime participation, and illuminates connections among investment arbitration stakeholders. Finally, given India's status as a rising power, this inquiry allows us to examine India's willingness to fully socialize into a more "Western" approach and illuminates the challenges other developing countries may face in their legal fields as they rise.

This chapter analyses the developments in the Indian legal field of investment arbitration by combining deductive and inductive inquiry. Section I situates India's place in the investment arbitration regime and theorizes how investment arbitration is reshaping the legal field in India. Second II of the chapter engages in an open-ended, exploratory process of gathering empirical data on India's regime participation. This includes semi-structured interviews with relevant stakeholders as well as a thorough analysis of significant documents and other sources. The next two sections of chapter examine two core challenges: the legal capacity as India shifts toward a dispute settlement mechanism that operates under different rules and is dependent on different expertise (section III) and the strategizing challenge as India's policy preferences shift from mostly protecting itself to protecting domestic investors engaging in continually larger outward investments (section IV). The final section of the chapter outlines the findings and suggests some areas for future inquiry.

Put together, the study demonstrates how the Indian legal field has dealt with these challenges and explains why full socialization into the regime has not occurred. The Indian government and law firms faced major capacity constraints when dealing with the first investment claim, so mounting an effective response has depended on foreign law firms. However, as claims have proliferated, management challenges have become less pronounced, and local firms have pursued entrepreneurial initiatives to establish their market presence. India's shift from responding to claims made by foreign investors to supporting outbound investors has not been automatic as India has become a source of outward foreign investment. Rather, India has been conditioned and constrained by the large number and controversial nature of claims against it and limited public–private cooperation.

II. INVESTMENT ARBITRATION IN A RISING POWER: REGIME PARTICIPATION AND THE LEGAL FIELD

The emergence of countries such as India, China, and Brazil as drivers of global growth is critically connected to the evolution of the contested investment arbitration regime. These nations may show complete socialization as they integrate into the regime, but they may also use their newfound status to pursue alternative regulatory paths (Narlikar 2010, 5). The nature of these countries' engagement with the regime could undermine or reinforce the legitimacy of existing investment arbitration mechanisms and processes (UNCTAD 2014, 2). As Figure 1 illustrates, rising powers' approaches to investment treaties diverge significantly. India is a particularly interesting case because it strikes a middle ground between China's socialization into the regime and Brazil's rejection of it.

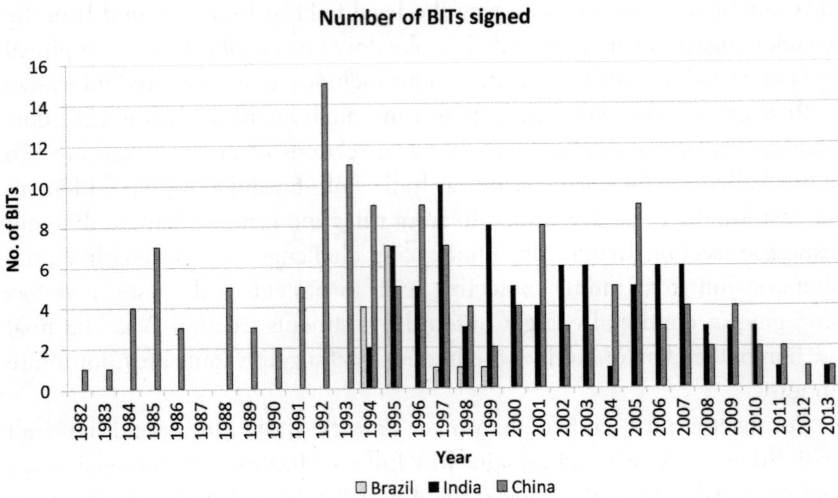

FIGURE 1 Number of BITs signed: India, China, and Brazil
Source: UNCTAD, 2015.

India had a restrictive approach to foreign investment until the early 1990s, when, facing a balance of payments crisis, it undertook economic reforms and progressively opened the economy. Unlike Brazil, which signed 14 BITs in the mid-1990s with none having come into effect, India signed eighty-three BITs – sometimes called bilateral investment promotion and protection agreements or BIPAs – between 1994 and 2014 (UNCTAD 2015, 109, 117).Most of these are in force and generally offer strong guarantees in the post-establishment phase on fair and equitable treatment, national treatment, expropriation, and free transfers as well as direct access to international arbitration.[3] India also engaged in regional investment cooperation, especially more recently. However, unlike China, which joined the World Bank's ICSID, India has refused to join this central institution of investment arbitration governance. On the contrary, India has been at the forefront of resistance to multilateral investment regulation, whether in refusing to join ICSID, opposing the negotiations on a multilateral agreement on investment, or refusing the inclusion of a multilateral framework for investment at the WTO.[4]

India's participation in investment arbitration results from the government's choice to engage with various aspects of the system and the process through which domestic actors embrace and reinforce the process. The mechanisms through which this choice and process play out is contested in contemporary literature, which offers multiple sets of arguments about countries' participation in investment arbitration. These arguments – broadly categorized as institutional, behavioral, and legal – use different entry points into the participation phenomenon and vary in the weight they assign to the role of lawyers and the legal field.

More generally, institutional arguments can generally be thought of in terms of a principal-agent model where participating states (principals) sign investment treaties to enjoy reciprocal benefits from regime participation. They use international dispute settlement bodies as agents: Significant regulatory power is transferred to expert decision makers, who serve the collective goal of promotion and protection of foreign investment (Yackee 2012, 393). This approach can easily explain why states with a large volume of investment want legal protections for their businesses, but incentives for developing countries to constrain their policy space have been more puzzling. An influential theory explaining such self-imposed constraints is that of "credible commitment," which argues that states rationally sacrifice their sovereignty in order to attract and make themselves more competitive for foreign investment – which is itself a finite resource (Guzman 1998, 658–659; Guzman 2002, 1850). This line of argument suggests that, in addition to helping developing countries promote their investments, these types of agreements help strengthen the relationship between developing and developed countries. They also are part of how developing countries are able to liberalize their economies and promote economic growth, encourage domestic entrepreneurs to expand domestic investment, and strengthen the rule of law (Salacuse 2009, 441–445). Further globalization then reinforces delocalization of disputes, strengthens international legal agency, and contributes to further the "legalization" of world politics (Abbott et al. 2000; Goldstein et al. 2000; Romano 2011).[5] Institutional approaches effectively explain China's growing socialization into the investment arbitration regime as its outbound investment grows (Wang 2009, 584; Wang 2011; Wei 2012, 686). However, they fail to explain why Brazil keeps using alternatives to investment arbitration or why India does not follow China's path.

Other approaches question the premise that the investment arbitration regime is a structure of mutual advantage where actors rationally pursue international cooperation gains. Moving into an era of ever-increasing globalization, the willingness to participate in the investment arbitration regime may also suggest that there is another side of the theoretical story – one concerning winners and losers. In this story, the winners – the original enacting coalition of the regime – define rules to the determinate of others (so-called "losers"), who cooperate simply to avoid being left behind (Gruber 2000, 18, 24–25). Scholars of behavioral economics add insight to the "losers" side of the story, arguing that sovereignty is "sacrificed by chance" and that bounded rationality is a better explanation for why developing countries sign treaties (Poulsen 2014).

They suggest that governments of developing countries have systematically overestimated the national economic benefits they would accrue as a consequence of entering into BITs and ignored the attendant risks, dismissing them as low probability until they became "vivid" – that is, until investment treaty claims were filed against these states (Poulsen 2014, 4). Theories of bounded rationality argue that such governments adopt particular forms of investment agreements as a result of a preference for easily adoptable templates, sticking to these until they face investment claims from investors. While some work has been done on the participation challenges of developing countries, such as their limited ability to analyze and litigate a dispute despite potentially high stakes (large damages and the regulation of public services like water, energy and waste disposal), the processes through which the legal sector gets engaged and embraces the system remain unclear, especially in the Indian context (Gottwald 2006, 237).

Argentina offers an interesting example of a country that proactively attempted to build up domestic legal capacity to respond to investment claims. Around 2003, faced with a large number of claims, the Argentine government felt that it was not financially viable to hire outside lawyers, nor would external lawyers "adopt a consistent, unified position on key issues likely to arise in all the arbitration cases arising out of the emergency economic measures" that the country adopted (Gottwald 2006, 264). Consequently, Argentina has invested significant resources in training and building up a large team of government lawyers (based out of the attorney general's office) which now represents it in investment arbitrations (Rosert 2014). Although such investment comes with its own costs and benefits, it represents an example of an active choice by a government to develop domestic legal capacity.

How do lawyers socialize into investment arbitration, and what happens to the legal community during this process? Law and Society-based approaches have focused most directly on the role of lawyers in international dispute settlement, but scholars have primarily examined the WTO dispute settlement and international commercial arbitration. In the case of the WTO, scholars have investigated how the system's legalization has brought about the need for greater legal skills, expertise, and sophistication in institutional engagement and how rising powers have used public–private cooperation to strategically develop legal capacity and win cases (Shaffer et al. 2008). International arbitration scholars have described how a handful of distinguished "grand old men" created a legal field of arbitration, which became dominated by social networks initially centered in the International Chamber of Commerce in Paris and then incorporated large Anglo-American law firms and their arbitrators as new entrants (Dezalay and Garth 1998, 18–29). Given that arbitrators lack independence from those who select them, the lack of transparency is a barrier to learning and entry, and that the field has been dominated by westerners, there have been concerns that arbitration operates as a "mutual admiration club" with a monopoly on expertise (Sornarajah 2009). In both WTO and arbitration cases, lawyers played active roles in advancing countries' participation in international dispute settlement regimes that were originally dominated by westerners. Investment arbitration as a field continues to lag behind WTO and arbitration research, particularly when it comes to India. Yet based on this discussion of the dynamics of the legal fields in other international economic disputes, it is possible to formulate two assumptions that can provide a basis for our inquiry:

1. Investment arbitration is a field of action and discourse that emerges through complex relationships among experts, national elites, and global institutions (Reus-Smit 2004; Dezalay and Garth 2011). Lawyers operate at this interface.
2. Lawyers convert and invest social, economic, intellectual, and political capital into the law and into legal institutions, which strengthens the role of lawyers and the rule of law in this field of practice (Dezalay and Garth 1998).

Drawing on the patterns previously observed in countries' participation in international dispute settlement as they develop, we can anticipate two main ways in which the legal field is evolving, and can therefore structure our inquiry those twin tracks – what we call propositions. The *legal capacity* proposition suggests that India's ability to respond to investment claims is initially limited by the lack of indigenous legal capacity, but the demand and supply of local expertise grows after the first claim. If this is correct, we are likely to observe a shift from a reliance on foreign lawyers in cases against the government and limited indigenous capacity toward a stronger role for domestic law firms and the emergence of multiple intermediaries developing and diffusing investment arbitration expertise. The second proposition concerns India's ability to engage in legal strategizing at the public–private level. As India's outward investment grows, we would expect India's support for domestic investors to increase, which would reinforce pro-investment arbitration policy orientation. If this proposition is correct, we are likely to observe greater interaction between the government and the corporate legal sector in international investment regime-related policy making, especially regarding the representation of corporate interests in primarily importer countries and Indian investors' use of investment arbitration.

The analysis in this chapter is based on data gathered in several ways. First, semi-structured interviews were conducted with thirty-five practicing Indian lawyers, primarily those working in law firms. Other lawyers interviewed include two from the Indian judiciary, one from outside of India who is engaged with Indian investment arbitration, one expert who designs the government's economic agreements, and three Indian academics with expertise in the field. Interviewees are kept anonymous. Lawyers were identified based on their engagement in investment arbitration in India (identified through case records) and law firm engagement with international dispute resolution (identified through the RSG India Law Center database of top law firms).

We used a common template for the interviews and conducted them in October 2011 in person in Delhi and Mumbai, and after that over the phone. Several interviewees helped with access challenges and with clarifying the situation after the major proliferation of claims in 2012. Since the lack of transparency of investment arbitration practice and those involved in it has been a major barrier to research, the chapter uses available public documents to interpret the situation in a more reliable way by capturing contextual developments. Besides the use of legal cases and government documents, legal media and secondary resources were extensively consulted.

III. LEGAL CAPACITY HAS GROWN IN RESPONSE TO CLAIMS

Participation in the investment arbitration regime is complex from the perspective of identifying the relevant actors and their roles. The role of lawyers, in particular, varies through the process. First of all, the government is in charge of negotiating investment treaties. In the case of BITs, the Ministry of Finance acts as the lead agency, but in the case of investment chapters under trade agreements, the Ministry of Commerce acts as the lead agency. It is worth noting that, under the Constitution of India, treaty ratification is done by the executive and the parliament engages only when legislation is required to put a treaty into effect. Consequently, once negotiated, the content of these treaties is not usually debated in the legislature.[6] When the treaty is in effect, lawyers are engaged in investment decisions as they offer legal advice and seek to structure their investments as a way to prevent disputes from occurring. When disputes do take place, lawyers assume center stage in the process: They are engaged on behalf of investors and the government. These lawyers include those from the government (either the attorney general or the solicitor general), those from both domestic and foreign law firms, and international arbitrators, who generally have experience with the ICSID, the United Nations Commission on International Trade Law (UNCITRAL) Arbitration Rules, and the International Chamber of Commerce (ICC). The domestic judiciary is another important sector in the process because it decides on cases and makes and enforces arbitration awards. Legal academics play a key role in advancing the knowledge about investment arbitration as well as interpreting the relevant phenomena in the public sphere.

In order to examine the nature of Indian participation in investment arbitration, this section discusses legal capacity building in the context of major investment disputes and the related changes in the legal field. The first investment treaty dispute that led to claims against India was over the Dabhol power plant. The case was complex, where foreign investors and lenders resorted to investment arbitration to challenge the Indian government's decision to cancel the project and recoup losses, which they were unable to do through commercial arbitration (Kundra 2008; Bettauer 2009). In 2004, the United States called for arbitration against India alleging expropriation of the Dabhol power project. The project's main investors, General Electric and Bechtel, initiated investment arbitrations (claiming 158 million USD together with costs) under the India-Mauritius treaty, since their investments were structured through Mauritian subsidiaries (Capital India Power Mauritius I and Energy Enterprises (Mauritius) Company v. Maharashtra Power Development Corporation, et al., ICC Case No. 12913/MS) although only Bechtel pursued its claim under the tribunal.[7] Seven European banks also filed notices of intent to arbitrate, alleging that the government of India failed to protect their loans and was liable for damages under its BITs with the United Kingdom, Switzerland, Austria, France, and the Netherlands, but they refrained from filing formal requests for arbitration and ultimately settled their claims through negotiation (Peterson 2004).

The Indian government found it challenging to respond to the General Electric/Bechtel claim both in terms of hiring the right lawyers and ensuring that those individuals stayed on the case long enough to defend India at the international tribunal in London (see Papa 2013). The initial legal team, comprised of UK-based DLA Piper and Indian firm Swarup & Co., was changed after a new government came into power and the new attorney general took over. Swarup & Co. was replaced by Fox Mandal, and DLA Piper was replaced by Eversheds, reportedly because the new firms had more experience with international arbitration, the BITs, and public international law (Financial Express 2004, Iyer 2004). Lawyers advising Maharashtra's State Electricity Board and its government were Little & Co. (which subsequently merged with Fox Mandal) and Wadia Ghandy & Co., respectively. Yet the legal team broke down when Eversheds and Fox Mandal were supposed to file their reply against GE/Bechtel in London, and Eversheds resigned fifteen days before the deadline because of a conflict of interest (it was reported that GE had previously worked with the company on some cases and objected to Evershed's appointment). The government urgently interviewed thirty-five US and UK law firms with a significant presence in arbitration in London, and only five did not have a conflict of interest or require a waiver from clients (The Lawyer 2004). With the complete legal team complete, India eventually reached consensus with the US investors regarding compensation and agreed to open the plant for electricity generation (Hansen et al. 2005).

The Dabhol case highlighted two capacity building challenges. First, as one of the Indian lawyers who worked on the case observed, at that time there was limited expertise in investment arbitration in India, so the engagement of foreign lawyers was crucial. The government itself lacked adequate analytical capability to deal with the accumulation of diverse investment provisions in a short time. Yet the incentives for developing legal expertise have also been limited. At the domestic level, commercial arbitration was growing while investment arbitration's growth prospects were modest, so firms were positioning themselves primarily in the commercial arbitration market. At the international level, Indian engagement had been thwarted by the absence of any real Indian constituency that could potentially diffuse expertise. India is not a part of the ICSID, so it cannot designate ICSID arbitrators as other contracting states can. An exception is Fali Nariman's appointment as arbitrator in a number of disputes under the aegis of ICSID.[8] The ICC also has a very small number of Indian arbitrators. With few investment arbitrators with experience in the international fora, as one interviewee with international tribunal expertise observed, Indian legal teams tended to lack the inside knowledge about how to choose the best match for the case and the opponent's arbitrator from among top level arbitrators.

The second capacity-building challenge, as an informant from a Dabhol-engaged law firm suggests, is procedural. The government did not have a formal process through which it would hire assistance – hiring was done through informal networks and established relationships. Therefore, it is not surprising that the government chose Fox Mandal, a well-tested, century-old firm that was a decade ago one of the most experienced and largest in the legal market. However, procedural sensitivities also emerged given that the finance minister P. Chidambaram had previously represented Enron, so it was decided that the law ministry rather than the finance ministry would handle most of the matters related to the Dabhol case (Joseph 2004). Finally, conflict of interest is a common barrier to defending the government, but this was predictable given that the Dabhol case grew in complexity and that large corporations in

India are known for conducting extensive legal work. However, as one of the Mumbai law firm interviewees pointed out, law firms tend to prefer private investors over the government because they pay better and are more likely to generate future business.

The stakes of India's engagement in investment arbitration became apparent again in the White Industries 2011 claim against India regarding the delay in enforcing foreign arbitral awards (UNCITRAL, *White Industries Australia Limited v. Republic of India*). This case was a direct challenge to the autonomy of the Indian judiciary with respect to its procedures for reviewing foreign arbitral awards. Essentially, White Industries spent nine years attempting to enforce an ICC award in India, but had been subjected to prolonged delays – hence its claim under India's BIPA with Australia. The claim successfully relied on India's obligations imported from the Kuwait–India BIPA pursuant to the Most Favored Nation clause in the Australia–India BIPA (Blanshard et al. 2012). The arbitration was held under the UNCITRAL rules in Singapore, and the government hired Fox Mandal Little, Toby Landau, and Salim Moolan of Essex Chambers in London to represent it (Perry 2012). India lost the case, and Coal India paid 9,812,077 Australian dollars to the investor, which included the earlier award under the commercial arbitration together with fees and interest (Ministry of Commerce, 2013).

This decision has since been the subject of great debate among domestic legal circles in India with some lawyers, including those from Fox Mandal Little, voicing their dissatisfaction with existing investment arbitration and suggesting that a state should not face claims because of legislation that was enacted in the interest of economic or social development of that state (Karadelis 2012a). Similar opinions have also been voiced by sitting judges of the Indian Supreme Court, including Justices P. Sathashivam, RM Lodha, and Fali Nariman, who have suggested that some investment arbitration tribunals impinge on the sovereignty of states (Global Arbitration Review 2014). A number of new, albeit unrelated, claims were filed against India after the White Industries case by private foreign investors, which led India to put its investment treaty negotiation program on hold and seek to re-evaluate its approach to the international investment regime (Ranjan 2014, 421).

The year 2012 represents another milestone in the evolution of India's investment arbitration. Several claims were filed against India following the Supreme Court's cancellation of 122 telecom licences in February 2012, and the government received notices of dispute from a number of foreign investors, including Russia's Sistema and Norway's Telenor, as well as Mauritius-based Capital Global, Kaif Investment, and Khaitan Holdings. In a separate telecom-related investment dispute, Cyprus-registered Tenoch Holdings and its Russian owners filed a $400 million claim against India under India's BIPAs with Cyprus and Russia, claiming that India had subjected ByCell to a licensing process that was grossly arbitrary and discriminatory. Two separate investment claims have also been filed against India in relation to claims by Devas Multimedia against the commercial arm of the Indian Space Research Organization. More-recent investment claims against India included ones by Vodafone International Holdings BV, Nokia, and Cairns Energy concerning retroactive tax amendments made by India.

The Indian judiciary has become more active in engaging with the investment arbitration regime, as illustrated by a recent claim involving Kolkata port. Louis Dreyfus Armateurs filed a claim against India in March 2014 under the India–France BIT alleging that the state had prevented the effective implementation of a joint venture operating in Haldia Port in West Bengal. It sought to make the Kolkata Port Trust a respondent to the investor-state arbitration. This was challenged in the Calcutta High Court. The court granted an injunction against Louis Dreyfus Armatures, restraining it from continuing proceedings against Kolkata Port Trust (Satish and Jayasimha, 2015). This decision is perhaps the first by an Indian court on a matter arising out of an investment treaty dispute, and it could have the effect of allowing Indian courts to have jurisdiction (at least for interim measures) over arbitration tribunals with their seats outside India (see, *The Board of Trustees of the Port of Kolkata v. Louis Dreyfus Armatures SAS*, C.S. No. 220 of 2014, September 29, 2014). The Supreme Court has also indirectly influenced (and been influenced by) the investment arbitration regime. In the case of *Bharat Aluminium Co. v. Kaiser Aluminium Technical Services Inc.* ((2002) 4 SCC 105), it overturned a previous decision that allowed intervention by the Indian courts in arbitrations seated outside of India. The White Industries decision was referred to in oral arguments before the court and may have had an impact on the outcome, since the investor-state arbitration in the White Industries case arose out of delays occasioned by challenges to the attendant commercial arbitration in the Indian court system (Herbert Smith Freehills 2012).

Table 1 sets out some claims that have been filed against India since the White Industries decision. The Table illustrates the proliferation of claims in recent years.

Compared with the Dabhol era, the legal field's engagement with investment arbitration has evolved significantly. Now the government is communicating more extensively to find a response to these investment claims, and the law firm market looks very different. The main difference between now and ten years ago, as several interviewees suggested, is that today all top law firms have strong dispute resolution and litigation departments and have developed

TABLE 1. *Proliferation of claims since 2012*

No.	Claims	Description
1.	*Children's India Fund v. India* (withdrawn, December 2014)	Children's Investment Fund petition against Coal India for alleged breach of corporate governance practices under India's BIPAs with the United Kingdom and Cyprus, where the sub funds were domiciled (Bajaj 2012; Times News Network 2012a; Chaturvedi 2014; Crabtree 2014).
2.	Telenor (withdrawn)	Norwegian telecom company Telenor invoked India's Comprehensive Economic Cooperation Agreement with Singapore to protect its investments in India, estimated to be around US$ 260 million). Telenor, however, decided not to proceed with its claim after the Indian government permitted it to set off its losses in the next round of telecom license auctions (Karadelis 2012b; Thomson 2013a; Herbert Smith Freehills 2014).
3.	Sistema (withdrawn)	Sistema JSFC invoked Article 9.1 of the India–Russia Bilateral Investment Treaty to protect its $3.1 billion investment following the cancellation of its 2G licenses by the Supreme Court. Like Telenor, Sistema decided not to proceed with its respective claims against the Indian government. (Times News Network 2012b; Thomson 2013a; Ranjan and Raju 2014).
4.	*Khaitan Holdings (Mauritius) Ltd v. India*	A US $1.4 billion dollar claim was also filed by a Mauritian entity, Khaitan Holdings, over the cancellation of telecom licenses under the India–Mauritius BIPA. In that matter, India nominated Brigitte Stern, a French academic, as its arbitrator on the panel and appears to have engaged the services of the law firm Curtis Mallet-Prevost Colt & Mosle (hereafter, Curtis Mallet) in New York, led by partner George Kahale III (Karadelis 2014). Khaitan holdings has appointed Vinson Elkins to act for it.
5.	*Tenoch Holdings Limited (Cyprus) (2) et al. v. The Republic of India*	ByCell/Tenoch has filed a US $400 million claim against India under the India–Cyprus and India–Russia BITs at the Permanent Court of Arbitration. The claimants have appointed Covington and Burling to represent them (acting through its London office) whereas India has nominated the same arbitrator, Brigitte Stern, and appointed the same legal counsel, Curtis Mallet, as in the Khaitan Holdings case.
6.	*CC/Devas (Mauritius) Ltd et al. v. India*	A claim of US $1.6 billion has been filed under the India–Mauritius BIPA by three entities and concerns the cancellation of a contract for the launch of two

(*cont.*)

TABLE 1. (cont.)

No.	Claims	Description
		space satellites. India has appointed Curtis Mallet along with Khaitan & Co. (through partner Sanjeev Kapoor in New Delhi) to represent it in the UNCITRAL arbitration process and has nominated Justice Anil Dev Singh as its arbitrator on the panel. The claimant has appointed Skadden, Arps, Slate, Meagher, & Flom to act on its behalf (Perry 2013; Spalton, 2013a; Spalton 2013b).
7.	*Capital Global and Kaif Investment v. India*	In connection with the cancellation of their telecom licenses, two Mauritian entities have filed a notice of dispute against the Indian government, relying on the India–Mauritius BIPA (Philip 2012).
8.	*Deutsche Telekom v. India*	A claim has been filed by Deutsche Telekom as a shareholder in Devas Multimedia (see the CC/Devas (Mauritius) Ltd et al. v. India case), and the claimant has appointed Platinum Partners in New Delhi (acting through partner Karam Daulet Singh) to represent it. India (as far as is known) has yet to appoint external counsel in this matter (Thomson 2013b).
9.	*Louis Dreyfus Armateurs v. India*	In its claim, Louis Dreyfus has relied on the 1997 France–India BIT. It is being represented by J Sagar & Associates and Tariq Baloch of 3 Verulam Buildings, whereas the state has yet to appoint external counsel in the matter (Woolley 2014).
10.	*Vodafone International Holdings BV v. India*	Vodafone International Holdings BV has relied on the India Netherlands BIPA alleging retrospective tax claims by the Indian state and has appointed Slaughter and May, Indian firm Dutt Menon Dunmorrsett and Toby Landau QC (Essex Court Chambers) and Harish Salve (Blackstone Chambers) to act for it, whereas India has appointed Curtis Mallet and nominated Justice RC Lahoti (former chief justice of India) to act as arbitrator (Thomson 2014; Spalton 2014).
11.	*Cairn Energy UK v. India*	In a similar claim seeking to block the Indian state from claiming retrospectively notified taxes by Scottish company Cairns Energy under the 1994 India United Kingdom BIT, Shearman and Sterling and Harish Salve are acting for the claimant, whereas India has yet to nominate an arbitrator and external counsel (Thomson 2015a).
12.	*Nokia v. Union of India*	Nokia has notified India of its intention to invoke provisions of the India–Finland BIT to seek an arbitral order preventing India from claiming back taxes of around US $3.5 billion (Spalton 2014).

arbitration expertise. However, this expertise still tends to be concentrated in the sphere of commercial arbitration, which provides the bulk of work for these firms. As a UK-educated Indian arbitration lawyer observed in his interview, it is still rare for top Indian arbitration lawyers to have expertise in investment arbitration and public international law, and most of those who do have such experience are foreign educated. This may change as Indian students are increasingly trained in these fields particularly, through moot court competitions, which often engage investment arbitration cases and where lawyers with such experience are invited to serve as judges. For example, Trilegal as well as Kachwaha and Partners sponsor annual moot courts on the topic of investment arbitration. Law firms have also begun to organize competitions to encourage students to write about the role of arbitration in cross-border dispute settlement and facilitating commerce.[9]

In line with the legal capacity proposition, India's ability to respond to investment claims was indeed initially limited by the lack of indigenous legal capacity, but the politics of developing that domestic capacity has been complex. The government itself has not been proactive in promoting domestic capacity building as we have seen in cases like Argentina. Therefore, despite interest from Indian law firms in developing investment arbitration practices, limited roles and a preference for foreign legal advisers (among claimants and the Indian government) has effectively constrained the government's ability to build up expertise in this field. An issue that four interviewees from Indian law firms mentioned is that expertise aside, foreign lawyers often tend to be "more alert to what is going on" and quicker to identify themselves as interested in the job. The Indian government has also shown a marked preference for a specific legal adviser, Curtis Mallet, which may be due to the firm's experience in acting for other state parties in investment arbitrations. For instance, the firm is known to have acted for Algeria, Kazakhstan, Turkmenistan, Uganda, and Venezuela (Ross and Spalton 2013). After the White Industries decision, the government appears to have instructed an Indian law firm – Khaitan & Co. – only once (the *Devas Multimedia* matter). Where Indian firms were appointed, as they were by the majority of claimants who have filed investment disputes against the Indian government, their role was usually limited to discreet tasks, document management, or, in some cases, litigation assistance in related proceedings before Indian courts or in associated commercial arbitrations.

The Indian case, therefore, illustrates how entrepreneurial law firms can emerge and benefit from strategic positioning in the legal services market. While the provision of legal services related to investment arbitration was initially in the hands of foreign law firms and old colonial–era Fox

Mandal Little, entrepreneurial firms like Luthra & Luthra, Khaitan & Co., and Platinum Partners are accessing and capturing larger parts of the market. For example, the Indian law firm that successfully represented White Industries, Luthra & Luthra, was subsequently hired in other cases, including the Children's Investment Fund petition against Coal India (Karadelis 2012b).[10] Given India's large number of investment treaties, Indian law firms have become more appealing to foreign investors seeking to bring claims against the Indian government.

It is worth noting that there were no Indian arbitrators in either the Dabhol or White Industries arbitrations. However, in the ongoing Vodafone and Cairns Energy claims, the Indian government has nominated a former judge of the Indian Supreme Court as arbitrator. The government has also called on the expertise of international arbitrators, such as Brigitte Stern (in the Tenoch and Khaitan cases), more than once. This is in keeping with the broader, albeit limited, development of capacity in the Indian legal market.

One of the peculiarities of the Indian legal market has been the combination of the demand for investment expertise and the constraint on law firm advertising. Confronted with a lack of awareness of investment legislation, some lawyers have perceived their role to be that of information provider. They have published books on investment and organized conferences to open up discussion on investment arbitration. For example, Som Mandal, the managing partner of Fox Mandal Little, observed when promoting the firm's book on investment, "We at FML would like to think of ourselves as more than just a law firm. Part of our responsibilities as legal professionals of 21st century India is to ensure that we provide true and accurate information, not just to our clients, but also the investors at large" (Bar and Bench News 2011). Nishith Desai Associates has also been at the forefront of efforts to promote public discussion of investment arbitration (for more on the law firm, see chapter 3 of this volume). Not only did the firm organize free online conferences on the topic, it also conducted extensive analytical work on past cases and on the potential for new cases (Nishith Desai Associates 2015). The engagement of law firms as information providers is a win-win situation as it promotes public debate on investment arbitration all the while allowing law firms to market their work, which is otherwise difficulty to do due to bar restrictions on advertising. Finally, there is a larger question of preference for investment arbitration in the Indian legal market. While the practice is gaining more public attention, it remains either a process that investors use in parallel with commercial arbitration or as the very last resort measure when everything else is failing.

IV. HAS LEGAL STRATEGIZING SUPPORTED OUTBOUND INVESTORS?

The second proposition suggests that as India's outward investment grows, we would expect Indian support for domestic investors to increase and pro-investment arbitration attitudes to strengthen. This would require proactive engagement from the Indian government on behalf of outward investors and greater interaction between the private and public sector. However, what we observe instead is a push against investment arbitration and a shift toward more comprehensive agreements rather than investment treaties.

Following the Dabhol experience in the early 2000s, the government became concerned that the reach of investment treaty provisions was too broad and saw a need to reopen all existing agreements, although it was the spate of claims filed against it in 2012 that finally prompted a comprehensive evaluation of its model BIT (Peterson 2003; Singh 2015). Yet it has been difficult to reach consensus among different government departments on future investment policy. The Finance Ministry is in charge of BIPAs, and the Commerce and Industry Ministry negotiates Comprehensive Economic Cooperation Agreements (CECAs). At the same time, however, the Finance Ministry has been adopting investment regulations and strategies independently. For example, the Commerce Ministry's Press Note 2010, which compiled India's domestic regulations on foreign investment in different sectors, does not mention the standards contained in Indian BITs. As a result, some domestic regulations run contrary to India's international obligations contained in BITs (DIPP 2010; Ranjan 2010). Officials from the two ministries also offer competing approaches to investment arbitration fora. To prevent the state from getting drawn into private disputes, the Commerce Ministry has in principle decided not to include such provisions in agreements and to review this particular clause in all the existing investment agreements. The Finance Ministry, meanwhile, believes that BIPAs help Indian companies more than foreign firms and that this clause should not be reviewed (Mishra 2012). India has also developed its own model BIPA, opening it for public comment in early 2015, and has used previous versions of this draft as a touchstone for negotiations, so treaties with various countries differ from it and from each other (Peacock et al. 2015).[11]

An interviewee working with the Commerce ministry on trade agreements argued that the Indian government has turned its attention toward negotiation packages rather than single investment treaties because it seeks to gain from interlinkages amongst goods, services, and investments. The best examples of this are the Compressive Economic Cooperation Agreements (CECA) with

Singapore. The CECA include a free trade agreement in goods, an agreement to facilitate trade in services, a package to promote mutual investment protection, and an agreement for avoiding double taxation (Francis and Kallumal 2013).[12] Such agreements move away from the model BIPA, as it defines investment and investors more precisely, covers the pre-establishment phase, and applies public safeguards clauses more widely Furthermore, the Indian government has also become more careful in negotiating investment treaties, which is perhaps one of the reasons for the sharp slowdown in treaties being signed by India in recent years. Ongoing negotiations also demonstrate India's greater assertiveness in protecting its policy space. The United States–India bilateral investment treaty is on hold. In talks with the European Union, India did not yield under EU pressure to include an investment arbitration clause in the trade agreement and has been cautious about preserving the government's ability to issue regulations to protect public interest. Yet the exact nature of India–EU negotiations as well as investment negotiations more generally remains unclear. Observers complained about the almost total secrecy of the high stakes European Union–India negotiations: Since the agreement would cover many areas besides commodity trade – including intellectual property rights, especially in pharmaceuticals, investment, and trade in services – it would be detrimental to the interest of the vast majority of the poor in India and likely to fuel poverty, inequality, and environmental destruction (Pratyush 2010; Reuters 2015). Yet, as then-Commerce Secretary Rahul Khullar responded to media inquiries about the process, "As a matter of principle, India does not negotiate through the media" (Mishra 2011).

The level of interaction between the government and the legal sector varies at different stages of investment policy making. Corporate lawyers are often asked to sit on government committees that are relevant for investment policy making and advise the government, but they view this engagement differently. While lawyers from top Delhi-based law firms would suggest that this was part of their business and something they mostly do not charge for, Mumbai-based firms were less eager to work for or with the government and more focused on the private sector. For example, the government's pronouncements that it wanted to make India an arbitration hub were less interesting for lawyers in Mumbai, who find it cheaper and more effective to go to Singapore than to Delhi.

The aftermath of the White Industries case and the development of the model BIPA highlight the lack of engagement between the Indian government and the legal sector. In December 2012 leading law firms in India were invited to pitch for two roles: first, to act as counsel for the Indian state during the flurry of new investor-state claims being filed against India, and second, to review the provisions of the model BIPA, which was being drafted then. Although some firms were short-listed and in some cases even instructed by the government for the former role, this work was soon reallocated to Curtis Mallet, ostensibly the Indian government's legal adviser of choice for investment arbitrations (Madhyam 2013; Singh 2015). It is not known which firms (if any) were asked to provide feedback to the Indian government on the model BIPA. In fact, the development of the Indian model BIPA has been shrouded in secrecy with an interministerial committee (led by the Ministry of Finance) reportedly seeking inputs from four international institutions. This contrasts with the process adopted by some of the other BRICS. For example, South Africa held a "multi-stakeholder review" of its bilateral treaty program over a period of three years with a further period of consultation on the resulting legislation (Madhyam 2013).

The growth of India's outward investment has not resulted in a turn toward the use of investment treaty dispute resolution mechanisms by domestic investors, despite the fact that industry organizations actively organize training sessions and conferences on investment arbitration.[13] All of the top-firm lawyers who were interviewed for this project emphasized that there is very little awareness within the business sector on investment treaties and their implications. One of the lawyers based in Bangalore said that the government used the local chamber of commerce to distribute a survey to gain input on investment policy, but that there were very few respondents from businesses and law firms. Some of the lawyers interviewed observed that businesses generally do not have high expectations from the government and try not to rely on any governmental protections but rather exclusively on those provided by the private sector. One of the interviewees suggested that if the Indian government had to protect a sovereign wealth fund, the stakes might be different and it would be more systematically engaged in protecting its investments. Now, it is the lawyers who are trying to convince clients of the importance of considering the treaties when clients approach them with questions about rules and taxes when investing abroad.

However, as Indian investors become more vocal in these issues, there seems to be a shift in thinking with respect to their needs. One of the cases in point is the Indian government's engagement in advancing the Indian business community's interests in Nepal, a major destination for outward investment. India has been pushing for a bilateral agreement with Nepal for a decade in order to protect its investors from continued attacks on investment projects, and the two countries signed such an agreement in October 2011. The Nepalese government was divided on the issue and public interest litigation at the Supreme Court of Nepal demanded the BIPA's immediate annulment because of undue advantages given to the Indian side (Subedi 2013). In its decision, the court directed the government not to implement the treaty without obtaining parliamentary approval under Nepal's interim constitution. It has still not come into effect. Zimbabwe offers another example in which India adopted an assertive attitude regarding the ratification of a BIPA by the Zimbabwean state, suggesting that the delay in ratifying the treaty was directly responsible for Indian investors not making large planned investments in Zimbabwe (Madanha 2014).

Indian investors' engagement with investment arbitration has been limited: There are only two known cases of Indian investors making claims against foreign states. The first originated in 2006 when an Indian investor, Ashok Sancheti (himself a lawyer), filed a treaty claim against the U.K. government over rent arrears he owed on business premises he rented in New Bond Street, London (leased from the Corporation of London). The arbitration was under UNCITRAL rules. Sancheti nominated Umesh Chandra Bannerjee, a former judge of the Supreme Court of India, as arbitrator. He was represented by Morgan Walker, where he was employed at the time (Global Arbitration Review 2008). The second case arose when the Indian company Jindal Steel and Power, filed a claim against Bolivia at the ICC International Court of Arbitration. White & Case represented Jindal Steel & Power. After the Bolivian court set aside an arbitral award, it has been reported that Jindal is now in settlement talks with the Bolivian government (Thomson 2015b). Finally, there are instances in which Indian investors have demonstrated their willingness to use investment arbitration but bypass India's treaties and structure investments through the Netherlands, which has a numerous BITs. For example, in 2013, the ICSID registered an arbitration proceeding initiated by Spentex Netherlands BV, a subsidiary of the India-based Spentex Industrues against the Republic of Uzbekistan (ICSID case No. ARB/13/26).[14] In this case, Spentex Industries, a New Delhi-registered, Indian textile company, bypassed protections under the India–Uzbekistan BIT, thereby raising questions about the demand for Indian BITs when alternative ways of structuring investments are readily available (Kumar 2013).

Given the relative paucity of reported cases, it is difficult to reach a definitive conclusion as to the Indian government and private sector's support for outward investment through the use of investment arbitration. That said, in terms of the second proposition, it seems to fair to conclude that the government has displayed some signs of proactivity in protecting domestic investors, but there does not appear to be a coherent policy towards this, and in fact, some of the steps taken by the government have been effective disincentives for local law firms to develop an expertise in investment arbitration. The government's proactivity in using BITs as a tool for protecting Indian investors appears to have been further halted by India's reconsideration of its BIT negotiation program. Private investors continue to engage with the government in a limited way and primarily count on private sector protections.

V. FINDINGS AND IMPLICATIONS FOR FUTURE RESEARCH

The investment arbitration regime is both extraordinarily dynamic and currently, deeply contested. With its reasonably extensive network of BITs, India is at the center of the storm, reflecting many of the current debates in the field. One can spot traditional patterns: The large number of Indian BITs put in place to invite investment and the vivid struggle to respond to the first claim. This leads to the realization of the risks of the regime, capacity-building processes, and re-strategization. However, only a closer look at the politics of the legal field helps explain why Indian lawyers are not embracing the investment arbitration regime as India grows.

Investment arbitration is a high-stakes area of practice in India, but most important, it is a very small one in terms of scope of work or number of lawyers engaged. Investors use it as a last resort when other means have failed or in parallel to other international arbitration processes. The government itself has difficulty adopting a unified and consistent policy toward investment arbitration, and its support for developing domestic legal industry in this field of practice is limited. Entrepreneurial Indian law firms are the key drivers of socialization into the regime both as they position themselves to serve foreign investors with claims against the government and as they diffuse their investment arbitration expertise.

The Indian government appears to be becoming more responsive to investors and more engaged in public–private interactions, but investors seek to protect themselves through the private sector rather than counting on the government. Additionally, given the number of claims against it, the government is not shifting its focus toward protecting Indian investors at the expense of protecting its own autonomy and seems to be seeking a balance between these two competing interests. It appears that legal strategy, and in particular the combination of governmental strategy and commercial exigency, has constrained the socialization of lawyers in the investment arbitration regime. Indian investors' investment arbitration claims are almost nonexistent. There is also evidence of these investors bypassing Indian BITs, instead utilizing Dutch ones.

This research has been limited by the lack of transparency of investment arbitration practice and the common disadvantages of the methods employed. However, it offers insight into the complex dynamics of the legal field and offers clear directions for future inquiry. Three directions seem to be the most promising. First, there is little available information available on outbound investors' decision making related to investment protections and the extent of their efforts to "lobby" the government. Second, the relationship between international commercial arbitration and investment arbitration is intertwined in the evolution of the legal field, but how exactly does that relationship affect regime participation? For example, are there any differences in the drivers of the rapid evolution of Indian domestic legal capacity in commercial arbitration versus the relatively slow evolution of expertise in investment arbitration? Finally, there is a lot of emphasis on social relationships in the Indian legal field: A social network analysis of the investment arbitration area of practice would be able to capture how relationships impact regime participation.

Notes

1 Many investor-state disputes are decided in front of international arbitral tribunals, which are organized under the World Bank's International Centre for the Settlement of Investment Disputes (ICSID). Between 1967 and 1996, only 38 disputes were registered with ICSID, but in contrast, 459 disputes were registered between 1997 and the end of 2014. See. "The ICSID Caseload Statistics" issue (ICSID, 2015).

2 By the end of 2014, India had been notified as the respondent state in 16 known investor-state disputes. Since many investment dispute arbitrations are conducted under conditions of complete confidentiality, the real number may be higher (UNCTAD 2015, 115).

3 As of the end of 2013, seventy-two BIPAs had gone into effect and another eleven had been signed but had not yet gone into effect. A complete list of these is available at through India's Ministry of Finance.

4 For example, see a 2003 press release through the Ministry of Commerce and Industry, Government of India entitled "India cautions developing countries on multilateral framework on investment."

5 The expression 'egalization of world politics" was used by Kenneth Abbott and others to suggest that the increased legalization of international institutions, albeit uneven, is marked by three phenomena: obligation, precision, and delegation (Abbott 2000). Obligation refers to the binding nature of rules that subject state action to scrutiny, precision refers to the increasing precision in the content of these rules, and delegation refers to the enforcement and implementation of these rules by an ostensibly neutral third party. Building on this, the expression "judicialization of world politics" is used by C. Romano while providing a taxonomy of international adjudicatory bodies (Romano 2011).

6 For more, see Entry 14, List I of the Seventh Schedule, read with Article 253 of the Indian Constitution. Under Article 73 of the Constitution of India, the power of the executive arm of the Union of India extends to those matters on which Parliament has the power to make laws, subject to constitutional limitations.

7 The final award is dated 27 April 2005 and is available at www.italaw.com/documents/Dabhol_award_050305.pdf. Also, see the notice of arbitration filed by

OPIC, which had provided direct loans and political risk insurance to the private sponsor companies for this project, available at www.opic.gov/sites/default/files/docs/GOI110804.pdf.

8 For example, Fali Nariman was appointed chairman in the ICSID arbitration of *Chevron Bangladesh Block Twelve, Ltd. and Chevron Bangladesh Blocks Thirteen and Fourteen, Ltd. v. People's Republic of Bangladesh* (ICSID case ARB/06/10) and has acted as arbitrator in various other arbitrations under the ICSID system and under the UNCITRAL rules.

9 Kachwaha & Partners, for example, organizes "arb-excel," an India-wide writing competition on arbitration.

10 The appointments of Platinum Partners by Deutsche Telekom and Harish Salve by Cairn Energy and Vodafone appear to corroborate this.

11 The text of the model BIT is available from the Government of India available at www.mygov.in/group-issue/draft-indian-model-bilateral-investment-treaty-text/.

12 A list of existing Comprehensive Economic Cooperation Agreements and other "free trade agreements" as well as those being negotiated are available on the website of the Ministry of Commerce, Government of India.

13 For example, a FICCI sponsored conference entitled "Arbitration in an era of Globalization" was held in Delhi in December 2015 (www.blog.ficci.com/_events_/conference-arbitration) and "Master Classes" were organized by the CII on "International and Domestic Arbitration" in 2013.

14 This case is also referred to in the Audited Financial Results published by Spentex Industries available at www.spentex.net/Spintex%20March-2014.pdf.

References

2008. "Lawyer must fight parallel claims, court rules." *Global Arbitration Review*, December 1. www.globalarbitrationreview.com/news/article/14974/lawyer-fight-parallel-claims-court-rules/.

Financial Express. 2004. "UK's Evershed, Fox & Mandal New Solicitors In Dabhol Case." September 2. www.archive.financialexpress.com/news/uk-s-evershed-fox-mandal-new-solicitors-in-dabhol-case/113749.

Global Arbitration Review. 2014. "White Industries in the spotlight." July 7. www.globalarbitrationreview.com/journal/article/32783/delhi-white-industries-spotlight.

Abbott, K., R. Keohane, A. Moravesik, A. Slaughter, and D. Snidal. 2000. "The Concept of Legalization." *International Organization* 54 (3): 401–419.

Bajaj, V. 2012. "The Children's Investment Fund Wages Battle with Coal India." *The New York Times*, April 19. www.dealbook.nytimes.com/2012/04/19/coal-india-struggles-with-demands-of-the-childrens-investment-fund/?_r=0.

Bettauer, R. 2009. "India and International Arbitration: The Dabhol Experience." *The George Washington International Law Review* 41 (2): 381–387.

Blanshard, E., B. Young and J. Greenway. 2012. "India liable under BIT for extensive judicial delays." *Herbert Smith Freehills Dispute Resolution*, March 1. www.hsfnotes.com/arbitration/2012/03/01/india-liable-under-bit-for-extensive-judicial-delays/.

Bourdieu, P. 1977. "The Force of Law: Toward a Sociology of the Juridical Field." Translated by Richard Terdiman. *Hastings Law Journal* 38 (3): 805–853.

Brower, C.H. II. 2009. "Reflections on the Road Ahead: Living with Decentralization in Investment Treaty Arbitration." In *The Future of Investment Arbitration*. Edited by C.A. Rogers and R.P. Alford. Oxford: Oxford University Press.

Charney, J. 1999. "The Impact on the International Legal System of the Growth of International Courts and Tribunals." *NYU Journal of International Law and Politics* 31 (4): 697–708.

Chaturvedi, S. 2014. "U.K. Fund Exits Coal India." *The Wall Street Journal*, October 15. www.wsj.com/articles/childrens-investment-fund-management-sells-coal-india-stake-1413382522.

Crabtree, J. 2014. "Activist TCI Drops Coal India Campaign and Sells Stake." *The Financial Times*, October 14. www.ft.com/cms/s/0/604b0aae-53a8–11e4–929b-00144feab7de.html#axzz30q7afLiK.

Ministry of Commerce and Industry, Government of India. 2010. "Draft Press Note No. (2010)." Press Note. www.dipp.nic.in/English/policy/changes/pn9_2009.pdf.

Dezalay, Yyves and Bryanth Garth (eds). 2011. *Lawyers and the Rule of Law in an Era of Globalization*. New York: Routledge.

1998. *Dealing in Virtue: International Commercial Arbitration and the Construction or a Transnational Legal Order*. Chicago: The University of Chicago Press.

Francis, S. and M. Kallumal. 2013. "India's Comprehensive Trade Agreements: Implications for Development Trajectory." *Economic and Political Weekly* 47 (31): 109–122.

Goldstein, J., M. Kahler, R. Keohane, and A. Slaughter. 2000. "Introduction: Legalization and World Politics." *International Organization*, 54 (3): 385–399.

Gottwald, E. 2006. "Leveling the Playing Field: Is it Time for a Legal Assistance Center for Developing Nations in Investment Treaty Arbitration?" *American University International Law Review* 22 (2): 237–277.

Government of India, Ministry of Finance, Investment Division. 2011. "Bilateral Investment Promotion and Protection Agreements as of May 2011." www.finmin.nic.in/bipa/bipa_index.asp.

Government of India, Ministry of Commerce and Industry. 2013. "Bilateral Investment Treaties." May 6. www.pib.nic.in/newsite/erelease.aspx?relid=95593.

Gruber, L. 2000. *Ruling the World: Power Politics and the Rise of Supranational Institutions*. Princeton: Princeton University Press.

Guzman, A. 1998. "Why LDCs Sign Treaties That Hurt Them: Explaining the Popularity of Bilateral Investment Treaties." *Virginia Journal of International Law* 38 (3): 639–688.

Guzman, A. 2002. "A Compliance-Based Theory of International Law." *California Law Review* 90 (6): 1823–1888.

Hansen, K., R.C. O'Sullivan and W.G. Anderson. 2005. "The Dabhol Power Project Settlement: What Happened? And How?" December 22. www.chadbourne.com/files/Publication/a5aa1e52–4285–4bb5–87e672011238 95a0/Presentation/PublicationAttachment/352f8f09-ae96–40fc-a293720d0b8f0ca8/Dabhol_InfrastructureJournal12_2005.pdf.

Herbert Smith Freehills. 2012. "Supreme Court of India delivers landmark arbitration decision in Bharat Aluminium, overruling Bhatia International."

Herbert Smith Freehills Dispute Resolution, November 6. www.hsfnotes.com/arbitration/2012/11/06/supreme-court-of-india-delivers-landmark-arbitration-decision-in-bharat-aluminium-overruling-bhatia-international/.

Herbert Smith Freehills. 2014. “A BIT More Indian Investment Arbitration.” *Herbert Smith Freehills Dispute Resolution*, May 16. www.hsfnotes.com/arbitration/2014/05/16/a-bit-more-indian-investment-arbitration/.

Iyer, P.V. 2004. “Government in a Tizzy as Dabhol Defense Cracks.” *Indian Express*, September 15. www.bilaterals.org/?government-in-a-tizzy-as-dabhol&lang=fr.

Joseph, A. 2004. “UK Firm to Represent Govt in DPC Arbitration Case.” *Economic Times*, October 2. www.articles.economictimes.indiatimes.com/2004–10–02/news/27410323_1_fox-mandal-law-ministry-solicitor.

Karadelis, K. 2012a. “Counsel to India Rails Against “isuse” of BITs.” *Global Arbitration Review*, October 19. www.globalarbitrationreview.com/news/article/30910/counsel-india-rails-against-misuse-bits/.

Karadelis, K. 2012b. “Investment Treaty Claims Mount Against India.” *Global Arbitration Review*, April 2. www.globalarbitrationreview.com/news/article/30445/investment-treaty-claims-mount-against-india/.

Karadelis, K. 2014. “India Telecoms Claim Gets Underway in The Hague.” *Global Arbitration Review*, February 21. www.globalarbitrationreview.com/news/article/32442/india-telecoms-claim-gets-under-hague/.

Kaushal, A. 2009. “Revisiting History: How the Past Matters for the Present Backlash Against the Foreign Investment Regime.” *Harvard International Law Journal* 50 (2): 491–534.

Kumar, M. 2015. “India, EU Working to End Trade Huff Over Generic Drugs.” *Reuters*, August 17. www.in.reuters.com/article/2015/08/17/india-eu-trade-idINKCN0QM0DT20150817.

Kumar, S. 2013. “An Indian Company Goes Treaty Shopping.” *The International Law Curry* Blog, October 2. www.ilcurry.wordpress.com/2013/10/02/an-indian-company-goes-treaty-shopping/.

Kundra, P. 2008. “Looking Beyond the Dabhol Debacle: Examining its Causes and Understanding Its Lessons.” *Vanderbilt Journal of Transnational Law* 41 (3): 907–935.

The Lawyer. 2011. “Watson Farley Selected by Indian Govt for Dabhol Role.” March 3. www.search.proquest.com.ezproxy.library.tufts.edu/docview/218692742?accountid=14434. “Fox Mandal Little Launches a Book on Investing in India.”

Madanha, N. 2014. “Zim Loses Indian Investment,” *The Business Connect*, August 28. www.thebusinessconnect.co.zw/index.php/main-news/106-zim-loses-india-investment.

Madyam. 2013. “Whither India’s Bilateral Investment Treaty Framework?” *Madhyam Briefing bPaper No.* 15, December. www.madhyam.org.in/wp-content/uploads/2014/07/Whither-India-Bilateral-Investment-Treaty-Framework.pdf.

Mishra, A.R. 2011. “India Rejects Clause on Litigation.” *LiveMint*, July 4. www.livemint.com/Home-Page/T8uMUbH7Psx9sJawlwtzvN/India-rejects-clause-on-litigation.html.

Mishra, A.R. 2012. “India May Exclude Clause on Lawsuits From Trade Pacts.” *LiveMint* January 29. www.livemint.com/Home-Page/dTXmHaomYUyRrFk04HbiLP/India-may-exclude-clause-on-lawsuits-from-trade-pacts.html.

Narlikar, A. 2010. *New Powers: How to Become One and How to Manage Them*. New York: Columbia University Press.

Neumayer, E and L. Spess. 2005. "Do Bilateral Investment Treaties Increase Foreign Direct Investment to Developing Countries?" *World Development* 33 (10): 1567–1585.

Nishith Desai Associates. 2015. "Bite of the BIT – The Steady Rise of Bilateral Investment Treaties and a Pro-Investor Regime in the Global Economy." www.nishithdesai.com/fileadmin/user_upload/pdfs/Research%20Papers/Bite_of_the_BIT.pdf.

Papa, Mihaela. 2013. "Emerging Powers in International Dispute Settlement: From Legal Capacity Building to a Level Playing Field?" *Journal of International Dispute Settlement* 4 (1): 83–109.

Peacock, N. J. Hartzler, and J. MacKinnon. 2015. "Indian Government Seeks Comments on a Proposed Draft Model Text for the Indian Bilateral Investment Treaty." Herbert Smith Freehills Dispute Resolution, April 2. www.hsfnotes.com/publicinternationallaw/2015/04/02/indian-government-seeks-comments-on-a-proposed-draft-model-text-for-the-indian-bilateral-investment-treaty/.

Perry, Sebastian. 2012. "Logjam in Indian Courts Triggers BIT Breach." *Global Arbitration Review,* February 13. www.globalarbitrationreview.com/news/article/30167/logjam-indian-courts-triggers-bit-breach/.

2013. "Orrego Vicuña Disqualified From India Panel." *Global Arbitration Review,* October 11. www.globalarbitrationreview.com/news/article/31963/orrego-vicuna-disqualified-india-panel/.

Peterson, L.E. 2003. "Bechtel and GE Mount Billion Dollar Investment Treaty Claim Against India." *INVEST-SD News Bulletin,* September 23. www.iisd.org.

Peterson, L.E. 2004. "European Banks Move to BIT Arbitration Against India in Dabhol Dispute." *INVEST-SD News Bulletin,* December 17. www.iisd.org/pdf/2004/investment_investsd_dec17_2004.pdf.

Philip, Joji. 2012. "Loop Mauritius-Based Investors Invoke BIPA Under India–Mauritius." May 29. www.articles.economictimes.indiatimes.com/2012–05–29/news/31888116_1_loop-telecom-telecoms-licences-kaif-investment.

Poulsen, Lauge. 2014. "Bounded Rationality and the Diffusion of Modern Investment Treaties." *International Studies Quarterly* 58 (1): 1–14.

Pratyush. 2010. "India-EU Free Trade Agreement." *CIPRA*, December 31. www.bilaterals.org/spip.php?article19710.

Ranjan, P. 2010. Indian Investment Programme in Light of Global Experiences. *Economic and Political Weekly* 45 (7): 68–73.

Ranjan, P. 2014. "India and Bilateral Investment Treaties – A Changing Landscape." *ICSID Review* 29 (2): 419–450.

Ranjan, P. and D. Raju. 2014. "Bilateral Investment Treaties and the Indian Judiciary." *The George Washington International Law Review* 46 (4): 809–847.

2004. *The Politics of International Law*. Edited by C. Reus-Smit. Cambridge: Cambridge University Press.

Romano, C. 1999. "The Proliferation of International Judicial Bodies: The Pieces of the Puzzle." *NYU Journal of International Law and Politics* 31 (4): 709–751.

Romano, C. 2011. "A Taxonomy of International Rule of Law Institutions." *Journal of International Dispute Settlement* 2 (1): 241–277.

Rosert, D. 2014. "The Stakes are High: A Review of the Financial Costs of Investment Treaty Arbitration." *International Institute for Sustainable Development*, July 2014. www.iisd.org/sites/default/files/publications/stakes-are-high-review-financial-costs-investment-treaty-arbitration.pdf.

Ross, A. and C. Spalton. 2013. "India Appoints Curtis in 2G Spectrum Case." *Global Arbitration Review*, April 22. www.globalarbitrationreview.com/news/article/31511/india-appoints-curtis-2g-spectrum-case/.

Salacuse, J. 2009. "The Emerging Global Regime for Investment." *Harvard International Law Journal* 51 (2): 427–473.

Salacuse, J. and N. Sullivan. 2005. "Do BITs Really Work?: An Evaluation of Bilateral Investment Treaties and Their Grand Bargain." *Harvard International Law Journal* 46 (1): 67–130.

Sappideen, R and L.L. He. 2015. "Dispute Resolution in Investment Treaties: Balancing the Rights of Investors and Host States." *Journal of World Trade* 49 (1): 85–116.

Satish, B. and S. Jayasimha. 2015. "Indian Courts' First Brush with Investment Treaty Arbitration: Taking Some Lessons from the Calcutta High Court." *Kluwer Arbitration* blog, March 16. www.kluwerarbitrationblog.com/blog/2015/03/16/indian-courts-first-brush-with-investment-treaty-arbitration-taking-some-lessons-from-the-calcutta-high-court/.

Shaffer, G., M.R.S. Badin and B. Rosenberg. 2008. "The Trials of Winning at the WTO: What Lies Behind Brazil's Success." *Cornell International Law Journal* 41 (2): 8–49.

Singh, K. 2015. "India and Bilateral Treaties – Are They Worth It?" *Beyond BRICS* blog, *Financial Times*, January 21. www.blogs.ft.com/beyond-brics/2015/01/21/guest-post-india-and-bilateral-investment-treaties-are-they-worth-it/.

Sornarajah, M. 2009. "The Retreat of Neo-liberalism in Investment Treaty Arbitration." In *The Future of Investment Arbitration*. Edited by C.A. Rogers and R.P. Alford. Oxford: Oxford University Press.

Spalton, C. 2013a. "Satellite Arbitration Has Lift Off (For the Second Time)." *Global Arbitration Review*, May 13. www.globalarbitrationreview.com/news/article/31575/satellite-arbitration-lift-off-for-second-time/.

Spalton, C. 2013b. "Panel Formed in Billion Dollar BIT Claim Against India." *Global Arbitration Review*, April 24. www.globalarbitrationreview.com/news/article/31522/panel-formed-billion-dollar-bit-claim-against-india/.

Spalton, C. 2014. "Arbitrators Named in Vodafone–India." *Global Arbitration Review*, June 19. www.globalarbitrationreview.com/news/article/32741/arbitrators-named-vodafone-india/.

Subedi, S. 2013. "India's New Bilateral Investment Promotion and Protection Treaty with Nepal: A New Trend in State Practice." *ICSID Review* 28 (2): 384–404.

Thomson, Douglas. 2013. "Telecom Company Sues India As Talks Fail." *Global Arbitration Review*, October 3. www.globalarbitrationreview.com/news/article/31940/telecoms-company-sues-india-talks-fail/.

2013b. "New Satellite Claim Launches Against India." *Global Arbitration Review*, October 29. www.globalarbitrationreview.com/news/article/32004/new-satellite-claim-launches-against-india.

2014. "Vodafone Claim Still on After India Rules Out Tax Change." *Global Arbitration Review*, July 15. www.globalarbitrationreview.com/news/article/32818/vodafone-claim-india-rules-tax-law-change/.

2015a. "India Says No to Cairn Tax Arbitration." *Global Arbitration Review*, 29 June. www.globalarbitrationreview.com/news/article/33927/india-says-no-cairn-tax-arbitration.

2015b. "Mining Award Quashed as Bolivia and Jindal Talk," *Global Arbitration Review*, May 18. www.globalarbitrationreview.com/news/article/33808/mining-award-quashed-bolivia-jindal-talk/.

Times News Network. 2012a. "The Children's Investment Fund Sues Government, Coal India Directors Over Loss." October 13. www.timesofindia.indiatimes.com/business/india-business/The-Childrens-Investment-Fund-sues-government-Coal-India-directors-over-loss/articleshow/16790705.cms.

2012b. "Sistema Threatens Arbitration in 2G Case." February 28. www.timesofindia.indiatimes.com/business/india-business/Sistema-threatens-arbitration-in-2G-case/articleshow/12070637.cms.

Trubek, David., Yves Dezalay, Ruth Buchanan and John R. Davis. 1993. "Global Restructuring and the Law: Studies of the Internationalization of Legal Fields and the Creation of Transnational Arenas." *Case Western Reserve Law Review* 44 (2): 407–498.

United Nation Conference on Trade and Development. 2009. "The Role of International Investment Agreements in Attracting Foreign Direct Investment to Developing Countries." United Nations Conference on Trade and Development (UNCTAD) Series on International Investment Policies for Development. www.unctad.org/en/Docs/diaeia20095_en.pdf.

2014. "Reform of the IIA Regime: Four Paths of Action and a Way Forward." UNCTAD. *IIA Issues Note No. 3*. www.unctad.org/en/PublicationsLibrary/webdiaepcb2014d6_en.pdf.

2011. "Country-specific lists of BITs." Available at www.unctad.org/templates/Page.asp?intItemID=2344&lang=1. Accessed December 1, 2011.

2015. *World Investment Report 2015: Reforming International Investment Governance*. UNCTAD. www.unctad.org/en/PublicationsLibrary/wir2015_en.pdf.

Van Harten, Gus. 2011a. "Investment Treaties as a Constraining Framework." In *Towards NewDevelopmentalism: Market As Means Rather Than Master*. Edited by S.R. Khan and J. Christiansen, 154–175. London: Routledge.

Van Harten, Gus. 2011b. "Contributions and Limitations of Empirical Research on Independence and Impartiality in International Investment Arbitration." *Oñati Socio-Legal Series* 1 (4) 2–29.

Waibel, Michael. 2010. *The Backlash Against Investment Arbitration: Perceptions and Reality*. Alphen aan den Rijn: Kluwer Law International.

Wang, Guiguo. 2009. "China's Practice in International Investment Law: From Participation to Leadership in the World Economy." *Yale Journal of International Law* 34 (2): 575–587.

Wang, Guiguo. 2011. China's Practice in International Investment Law: From Participation to Leadership in the World Economy. In *Looking to the Future: Essays on International Law in Honor of W. Michael Reisman*. Edited by M.H. Arsanjani,

J.K. Cogan, R.D. Sloane, and S. Wiessner. 845–890. Leiden; Boston: Martinus Nijhoff Publishers.

Wei, Dan. 2012. "Bilateral Investment Treaties: An Empirical Analysis of the Practices of Brazil and China." *European Journal of Law and Economics* 33 (3): 663–690.

Woolley, Richard. 2014. "Indian Port Claim Leaves Dock." *Global Arbitration Review*, September 23. www.globalarbitrationreview.com/news/article/32988/indian-port-claim-leaves-dock/.

Yackee, Jason. 2012. "Controlling the International Investment Law Agency." *Harvard International Law Journal* 53 (2): 391–448.

Index